Visualization, Visual Analytics and Virtual Reality in Medicine

THE ELSEVIER AND MICCAI SOCIETY BOOK SERIES

Titles

Balocco, A., et al., Computing and Visualization for Intravascular Imaging and Computer Assisted Stenting, 9780128110188.

Dalca, A.V., et al., Imaging Genetics, 9780128139684.

Depeursinge, A., et al., Biomedical Texture Analysis, 9780128121337.

Munsell, B., et al., Connectomics, 9780128138380.

Pennec, X., et al., Riemannian Geometric Statistics in Medical Image Analysis, 9780128147252.

Trucco, E., et al., Computational Retinal Image Analysis, 9780081028162.

Wu, G., and Sabuncu, M., Machine Learning and Medical Imaging, 9780128040768.

Zhou S.K., Medical Image Recognition, Segmentation and Parsing, 9780128025819.

Zhou, S.K., et al., Deep Learning for Medical Image Analysis, 9780128104088.

Zhou, S.K., et al., Handbook of Medical Image Computing and Computer Assisted Intervention, 9780128161760.

MICCAI

Visualization, Visual Analytics and Virtual Reality in Medicine

State-of-the-art Techniques and Applications

Bernhard Preim
Computer Science Department
Otto-von-Guericke-University of Magdeburg
Magdeburg, Germany

Renata Raidou
Research Unit of Computer Graphics of the Institute of
Visual Computing & Human-Centered Technology
TU Wien
Vienna, Austria

Noeska Smit
Mohn Medical Imaging and Visualization (MMIV) center
Department of Radiology of the Haukeland University Hospital
Bergen, Norway

Kai Lawonn
University of Jena
Jena, Germany

ACADEMIC PRESS
An imprint of Elsevier

Academic Press is an imprint of Elsevier
125 London Wall, London EC2Y 5AS, United Kingdom
525 B Street, Suite 1650, San Diego, CA 92101, United States
50 Hampshire Street, 5th Floor, Cambridge, MA 02139, United States
The Boulevard, Langford Lane, Kidlington, Oxford OX5 1GB, United Kingdom

Notices

ISBN: 978-0-12-822962-0

For information on all Academic Press publications
visit our website at https://www.elsevier.com/books-and-journals

Publisher: Mara E. Conner
Acquisitions Editor: Tim Pitts
Editorial Project Manager: Emily Thomson
Production Project Manager: Erragounta Saibabu Rao
Cover Designer: Christian J. Bilbow

Typeset by VTeX

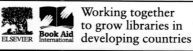

Working together
to grow libraries in
developing countries

www.elsevier.com • www.bookaid.org

Contents

PART 4 Virtual Reality in medicine

Preface

It is my great pleasure to write some accompanying words for this book. Bernhard Preim is one of the leading minds in medical visualization, which is actually still a young discipline in the medical world. I have followed his work with admiration for many years. When I began my work with computers in medicine in 1970, there was no computer at our university medical center, and therefore not a single bit of digital information. Pictorial information was only available in the form of analogue curves and photos, especially X-rays. When I retired from this area 23 years later, there were thousands of computers that mainly processed alphanumeric data, but to a large extent they supported clinical and research work by processing visual information in radiological diagnostics, surgery, radiation therapy, basic and advanced training. Bernhard Preim's first two books, from 2007 and 2013, cover the theory, algorithms, and applications in medical visualization in this era, an era linked to the blossoming of medical visualization. Numerous new methods were developed to obtain new pictorial information with a higher information value from genuine pictorial data. There was a lot of discussion on the value of methods developed for clinical, research, and educational applications.

Today the situation seems to have consolidated; visualization methods are standard tools in many medical disciplines. The new book, with the experience of another 10 years and with the expansion of the authorship, comprehensively describes the present state-of-the-art in medical visualization. The additional authors are without exception well identified by their own research. Noeska Smit is an expert in multimodal visualization and anatomy education. Renata Raidou is an expert in visual analytics and in particular in radiotherapy planning. Kai Lawonn is an expert in illustrative visualization, vessel visualization, and VR. The book thrives largely on the fact that they all, like the main author, have experience both in teaching and in the practical implementation in medicine.

New in the book are the topics visual analytics (i.e., combinations of information visualization and data analysis) and virtual reality. The importance of visual analytics for the lay public became obvious at the latest during the COVID pandemic. How do we, for example, present complex scientific findings to convince worried citizens? We can see many failed examples in the media. Serious understandable presentations play a decisive role in this. The chapter "Visual Analytics in Public Health" provides the methodology on how to make sense of large, high-dimensional data. Looking more to the future, the chapter "Visual Analytics in Clinical Medicine" discusses solutions to the problem of how the ever increasing amount of data relating to individual patients can be presented, sorted, or filtered in a way that supports therapy decisions.

The final part on virtual reality offers a glimpse into a previously distant future. Though the technique is not new in principle, for a long time it played no role in practical application because of its complexity and cost. This has changed since there has been affordable VR hardware that, far from medicine, is being promoted primarily by the gaming industry and rather dubious projects, such as the "Metaverse." The book here gives a serious algorithmic and application background to those who wish to advance in VR in medical treatment and education. In summary, this book is a treasure for anyone involved in visualization in medicine. I wish that as many software developers, researchers, doctors and also students as possible make use of it for the advancement of medicine.

Karl Heinz Hoehne
Hamburg, October, first 2022

Introduction

1

This book is motivated by a number of fascinating developments in recent years. Many new treatment methods reached the stage where they can be applied in clinical routine. As an example, for cancer patients considerably more treatment options are available, and these new treatment options can be combined and adjusted with respect to dosage and timing. Based on these developments, even cancer patients in the late stage 4 can benefit from these treatment options. However, the large variety of options and the often complex patient history make it increasingly difficult to decide about the best treatment for a particular patient. Visualization and visual analytics techniques were developed to handle this complexity, e.g., to present the patient history at a glance or to compare the current patient with a few very similar patients treated previously. While most discussions in the book aim at medical experts and their decision-making processes, medical visualization increasingly gets important for broader audiences, such as students, patients or the general public.

Relation to previous books

This book is strongly related to the books entitled "Visualization in Medicine: Theory, Algorithms, and Applications" (Preim and Bartz, 2007) and "Visual Computing for Medicine: Theory, Algorithms, and Applications" (Preim and Botha, 2013). However, it is meant as an addition to these earlier books, not as an update. The scope of the current book is much wider and the specific topics are chosen to complement the earlier books. If you are interested in a thorough introduction to medical image data, radiological practice, medical image analysis or surface and volume rendering, we refer to these older books. Also essential special topics, such as virtual endoscopy, visualization of fiber tracts, and intraoperative visualization, are discussed in the older books. The current book is self-contained; it does not *require* that the reader is familiar with basic medical visualization techniques.

To limit the book to a manageable size—despite the extended scope—the topics cannot be covered in a comprehensive manner. The book describes selected techniques and applications combining an understanding of actual user needs and technological possibilities. The discussion includes user research, e.g., task and requirement analysis, visualization design, and algorithmic ideas, but no implementation details. The target audience includes primarily students at the advanced bachelor and master level and also PhD students and medical researchers.

Visualization, Visual Analytics and Virtual Reality in Medicine. https://doi.org/10.1016/B978-0-12-822962-0.00007-9

Medical visualization techniques

The first part introduces selected medical visualization techniques. The selection is not comprehensive. In particular, there is no discussion of surface and volume rendering, topics that were discussed extensively by Preim and Botha (2013). Instead, we focus on areas where considerable new developments can be discussed, such as illustrative visualization, vessel visualization, medical animation, medical flow data, and multimodal visualization.

Illustrative visualization aims at emphasizing essential objects and supporting their shape perception. Silhouettes, more advanced feature lines, and hatching are essential for this purpose. Illustrative visualization enables to adapt the level of detail with which an object is depicted, a property that is essential for didactic purposes, and thus for reaching broader audiences.

Vessel visualization is a classic medical visualization topic and was also discussed in previous books. Here, we add recent developments in particular with respect to an improved shape and depth perception. Thus we introduce basic vessel visualization techniques and go on with discussions of refined variants, where, for example, colorscales or auxialiary geometries are employed to improve depth perception.

Multimodal medical image data is acquired more frequently in clinical practice. Whereas even the display of one high-resolution 3D dataset poses considerable (occlusion) problems, the simultaneous display of two (or even more datasets) requires to select the relevant information to be displayed. We focus on widely available data, such as PET/CT and SPECT/CT data, and discuss visualization options aiming at supporting the diagnosis and treatment planning of cancer patients.

Medical flow data may result from blood flow measurements, e.g., with ultrasound or a special type of magnetic resonance imaging. Image data, which represent a strong dynamics, suffer even more from artifacts and noise compared to static image data. On the other hand, the data is very complex: for every voxel in space and every point in time, a 3D vector represents the flow direction. Thus, in total, the datasets have seven dimensions and visual representations that need to be focused on relevant *flow features*, instead of presenting the raw data in its entirety. Though the measurement of blood flow is still restricted to large arterial structures, such as the aorta, flow in other vascular or air-filled structures may be simulated with computational hemodynamics. Simulated flow data, in contrast to measured data, is clean, smooth, and free of artifacts. However, simulations are based on many assumptions and parameter adjustments that often cannot be validated for a particular patient.

Animations in medicine may serve a variety of purposes. Animations may be created to explain a therapy to a patient, e.g., how a therapeutical intervention is carried out or how a biopsy is taken. Animations may involve a camera path, selected to provide smooth transitions of different viewpoints, or it may involve material transitions, where colors or transparency values are modified, e.g., to emphasize anatomical structures. Moreover, animations are a natural choice to convey dynamics in the data, e.g., how the blood flow changes over the cardiac cycle.

Selected applications

In all chapters related to medical visualization techniques, we extensively discuss medical applications in diagnosis, treatment planning, and education. In this part, we focus on two selected applications, namely anatomy education and radiation treatment planning.

Anatomy education benefits from interactive 3D visualizations. In addition to many research prototypes, also commercially successful solutions exist. Though early systems were used on desktop PCs using the native graphics hardware extensively, more recent systems are web-based, i.e., they can be used directly in the web browser without the need to install plugins. Also mobile solutions become more and more popular.

Radiation treatment as a major curative treatment for cancer patients experienced a rapid development and, as a consequence, the need for in-depth planning increased as well. The dose distribution related to the delivery of the radiation is simulated in advance and for different treatment options. The challenge for the physician is to carefully combine different plans with regard to the likelihood to control the tumor and the likelihood of severe damage of one of the surrounding structures. Moreover, this whole process involves considerable uncertainty, e.g., based on the delay between the planning CT and the actual treatment, based on motions, for example, due to breathing and muscle relaxation. We devote one chapter to the discussion of visual computing support for radiation treatment planning.

Visual analytics in healthcare

For a long time medical 3D visualization was focused on displaying and exploring data of one patient. Meanwhile, more often, patient groups are analyzed or compared with other patient groups, e.g., different age groups or patient groups with and without a certain health risk. The "IEEE Visual Analytics in Healthcare" workshop series, which started in 2010, is dedicated to discussing such developments.

In this book, we provide a part with three chapters on these topics. After an introduction to Visual Analytics, we discuss applications both in clinical medicine and in the public health sector. The focus in clinical medicine is on the treatment of patients who are actually ill or injured, and thus visual analytics solutions may contribute to a comparison of treatment options. In public health, the focus is on the prevention of diseases, and thus, the search for risk factors, the assessment of individual risk factors, and their interaction is essential.

Virtual Reality in medicine

Another essential development in the last decade is the rise of VR headsets that are affordable and provide a high-quality immersive experience. Current VR headsets have a wide field of view, similar to our visual perception of the real world, and also the spatial resolution is already good and likely to increase further. Modern VR glasses even perform the necessary computations in the glasses, instead of being connected (via a cable) to a computer. Thus users of VR glasses can really focus on the virtual world and are not forced to pay attention to a cable in the real world.

Such an immersive experience is particularly important for medical education, e.g., in anatomy, interventional radiology, and surgery, where medical students and physicians can better envision a complex patient anatomy and the interplay of medical devices and the target anatomy. We discuss technical aspects, such as the available VR headsets and interaction techniques, such as the navigation in a virtual environment, representing, for example, an operative room. After an introduction to virtual reality, we introduce applications in medical education and applications in clinical treatment.

VR-based medical education includes anatomy teaching but also surgery education. Though many VR systems in the past aimed at one user exploring a virtual world, we also consider more recent developments, where users cooperate in virtual reality, e.g., a surgeon and an anesthesiologist cooperate during surgery. These multi-user scenarios face a number of challenges, ranging from severe requirements with regard to network bandwidth and delay in relation to the awareness of other users and their activities, which is fundamental for cooperation in VR.

Clinical treatment includes the treatment of anxieties, the treatment of acute and chronic pain and the rehabilitation after a stroke. For all these treatments, there are solutions that are in clinical use after benefits for patients have been demonstrated.

Besides visual analytics and virtual reality, we discuss some more classical medical (3D) visualization techniques, such as the visual exploration of medical flow, the exploration of multimodal medical image and medical animations. Also in these areas, considerable developments occurred in recent years.

Acknowledgment

We want to thank our staff members, PhD, and master students for their research, for many fruitful discussions and for proofreading chapters of this book. We thank in particular Mareen Allgeier, Christian Hansen, Monique Meuschke, Stefanie Quade, Patrick Saalfeld, Vuthea Chheang, Sebastian Wagner (University of Magdeburg), Pepe Eulzer and Nils Lichtenberg (University of Jena), Rocco Gasteiger (exoCad GmbH Darmstadt), Matthias Schlachter and Katja Bühler (VRVis Research Center), Katarína Furmanová (Masaryk University Brno), Oliver Reiter, Nicolas Grossmann, and Marwin Schindler (TU Wien). Moreover, we want to thank Barbora Kozlíková (Masaryk University Brno, Czech Republic), Meister Eduard Gröller and Silvia Miksch (TU Vienna) for comments and fruitful discussions. Petra Schumann did a great job in handling all copyright-related issues. Emily Thompson, our Senior Editorial Project Manager from Elsevier, answered all our questions related to the editing process perfectly and helped us to stay on track.

Medical visualization techniques

In the first part, we discuss selected medical visualization techniques.

Illustrative medical visualization techniques, such as silhouette rendering and hatching, are introduced in Chapter 2. These techniques are primarily used to display segmented anatomical structures, such as organs. These structures are represented as polygonal meshes and illustrative techniques display features in such meshes, e.g., regions with high curvature or regions that separate visible from occluded parts.

Chapter 3 introduces vessel visualization techniques. A faithful and aesthetical pleasing visual representation of vessels is important for many medical treatment planning tasks. Moreover, these visual representations may incorporate additional information, such as wall thickness or simulated pressure on the walls. We consider broadly applicable techniques, as well as specialized systems, e.g., for the treatment of the coronary heart disease, cerebral aneurysms, or arterio-venous malformations.

A discussion of multimodal visualization is motivated by the increasing use of hybrid imaging, such as PET/CT and PET/SPECT. We consider 2D and 3D visualizations, which aim at integrating the essential information from two modalities (Chapter 4).

Chapter 5 is dedicated to the visual exploration of medical flow as it results, e.g., from hemodynamic simulations, simulation of airflow, or blood flow measurements. We discuss basic techniques and integrated systems designed for clinical use.

Finally, we discuss medical animations in Chapter 6. Such animations may be useful for treatment planning, medical education, and also in forensics. We emphasize generalizable methods to specify animations and to reuse existing animations for similar cases.

Illustrative medical visualization

2

2.1 Introduction

Modern graphics hardware allows computer-generated patient models to be displayed much more realistically than it was possible years ago. Nowadays, it is even possible to render a realistic scene in real time.

In medicine, doctors may use this realism to examine certain organs or diseases of a patient more closely and even plan treatment. However, before the doctors have the experience and routine to detect diseases or plan surgery, they need a lot of training and education. During their studies they therefore have to learn about anatomy and medical treatment options. This knowledge mostly comes from medical textbooks, especially medical atlases. One of the most famous medical books is Gray's Atlas of Anatomy (Drake, 2008). The first edition of Gray's Atlas of Anatomy was first published in 1858. It contains hand-drawn illustrations by the English anatomist and anatomy artist Henry Vandyke Carter. The book is still being developed today and now counts the 41st edition. These drawn pictures serve as inspiration for *illustrative medical visualization*.

Despite the development of photography, medical illustrations in medical textbooks remained drawn by hand. Even newer and more up-to-date anatomy atlases still offer medical illustrations drawn by hand or rendered with 3D computer graphics software. One reason for this may be that images offer the possibility to filter the information. Instead of showing the whole scene with all anatomical structures, drawn images can only provide the essential information. This becomes clear if you imagine a schematic sketch of an operation. Depending on the type of operation, it is quite conceivable that, for example, blood may obscure the essential processes of the operation, so that a hyper-realistic representation misses the point of the training and presentation. To filter unimportant details is one of the main ideas of illustrative visualization in the following short IllustraVis. This filtering is inspired by medical atlases and attempts to focus on essential information. IllustraVis techniques usually try to imitate an artist depicting medical structures with different styles of art.

Organization

This chapter is organized as follows: We will define illustrative visualization in Section 2.2. In Section 2.3, we discuss requirements for illustrative visualization. Furthermore, we provide the readers with some preliminaries for understanding the presented visualization techniques in Section 2.4. After mathematics is established and requirements are clear, various IllustraVis techniques are presented in Section 2.5. We will give an overview of IllustraVis. We will also show several works in which these techniques have been applied in the field of medicine.

2.2 Definition

When reading about IllustraVis, you will mostly encounter terms such as *abstraction* or *simplification*. Basically, that is the core idea of IllustraVis. It is the idea to turn away from the field of hyper photorealistic depiction. Some would also call IllustraVis as the opposite field. Instead of showing every detail, it is mostly considered as an abstraction or having the goal to depict an abstraction.

Definition 2.1. Illustrative visualization refers to a set of techniques that "employ established illustration principles such as abstraction and emphasis, layered organization, dedicated use of multiple visual variables, and support the perception of depth and shape—with the goal to create more effective, more understandable, and/or more communicative data representations than is possible with other visualization techniques (Lawonn et al., 2018b)."

The definition captures all aforementioned ideas in a single sentence. The expression *layered organization* means to employ IllustraVis techniques in a scene for, e.g., multiple objects. Having different stylizations on objects may improve the perception, and thus facilitates ordering the scene visually. In summary, the definition facilitates recognizing IllustraVis as an abstraction of physically correct depiction of objects.

2.3 Requirements

For all IllustraVis techniques, a few requirements should be fulfilled. Mainly, IllustraVis techniques are applied to 3D surfaces acquired by 3D scanners or generated from medical images data, e.g., CT, MRI. These surfaces may contain artifacts (erroneous local variations in shape) and noise.

Smooth surfaces

IllustraVis techniques benefit from surfaces with high smoothness, i.e., low curvature. Furthermore, discontinuities, i.e., deviations from a smooth behavior should represent true anatomical features or material transitions and not an artifact from imaging.

The reason for this is that most techniques calculate operations on the surface that are of higher-order derivatives. In case of non-smooth surfaces, this would result in detection of features that are actually noisy regions, and that would be misleading. Moreover, the additional (erroneous) features tend to make visualizations cluttered. Therefore before applying some IllustraVis techniques, surface models of the patient anatomy need to be preprocessed to ensure that the surface has a certain smoothness. Many techniques were developed for smoothing surface models reconstructed from binary surface models. As an example, the constrained elastic surface nets (Gibson, 1998) provides a good trade-off between smoothness and accuracy by restricting the modification of vertex positions. Bade et al. (2006) compared a number of mesh smoothing techniques w.r.t. different medical surface models, e.g., smaller and larger models, models of planar and compact structures. The comparison comprises accuracy, e.g., volume loss and smoothness that can be objectively assessed with curvature measures. Later, Mönch et al. (2010) enabled smoothing restricted to regions where artifacts actually occur. With this strategy, an even better trade-off between accuracy and smoothness can be achieved.

Even if the surface is smooth, the result should not vary that much if intrinsic properties of the surface are changed. Assume that a surface consists of millions of triangles (or other elements), and due to the memory consumption it would be necessary to reduce that surface to only a fraction of this portion. Even if the reduced surface is visually similar to the original surface, it may be that an IllustraVis technique gives a result that visually differs strongly. This is apparently not desirable, as the user should not be concerned about the number of triangles.

Interactive adjustment

A further requirement is an option to alter the result, in particular to control how many graphic primitives, e.g., lines are actually generated.

The simplest strategy towards this goal is to employ a threshold. If an illustrative measure, e.g., related to curvature or discontinuity, exceeds at a certain threshold the technique is applied, otherwise it is discarded. Since a surface may have locally different features, it may be useful to select a subregion, e.g., with a lasso selection, and apply a certain threshold locally.

Ensuring frame-coherence

The last requirement is called *frame-coherence*. If the user explores a 3D surface, meaning that typical navigation facilities are provided, e.g., translation, rotation, zooming, the visual result should be coherent during the exploration. Moving the object basically means that the output, i.e., the positions of the vertices on the screen, and therefore the pixels' color, change from one frame to the next frame. If the visual output would change drastically during the exploration, it would be irritating, and therefore distracting, such that the focus of attention may change a lot. This experience would be hindering. Therefore an IllustraVis technique should ensure that it is frame-coherent, i.e., the visual result does not drastically change during the exploration. In summary, the following requirements should be fulfilled:

- The surface to be illustrated should be sufficiently smooth.
- It should be possible to filter unwanted IllustraVis results.
- Frame-coherence during interaction needs to be achieved.

We also assume that the IllustraVis technique is computationally not so demanding that a real time interaction is no longer possible. Or in other words, even for larger medical surface models comprising several 10 K or even a few 100 K polygons, a frame-rate of at least 30 fps needs to be achieved. With today's powerful and flexible GPUs, the necessary calculations can be performed fast enough.

2.4 Preliminaries

This section provides an intuitive background of discrete differential geometry, which is necessary for the illustrative rendering of surface geometries. We will omit the technical details and refer to the following differential geometry books (do Carmo, 1976, 1992; Kühnel, 2006).

Curvature

The curvature measures how strongly the surface is bent at a certain point in a specific direction. Assume we are moving on a cylindrical surface in two directions (see Fig. 2.1). Starting from the red point, we may go along the azure (upper) path. The normals, which are colored in blue do not change during the walk, therefore the curvature along this direction is zero. On the other hand, when we follow the teal (lower) path, the normals change, resulting in a curvature value that is non-zero. The curvature values depend on the change of the normals along a direction. When speaking of curvature, we may think of a curvature value from a point along a direction as illustrated, or we mean two curvature values at a point. In the second case, we can think of all possible directions we may go from a starting point. For every direction, we determine the curvature value and keep the greatest and lowest possible curvature value. In this case, we speak about the principle curvatures. In case of the example of the cylinder, both paths lead to the greatest and lowest curvature value, taking a path between both results in a curvature value that is between both values.

Gradient and directional derivative

Previously, we saw that when we go from a starting point in different directions, the curvature may change. Now, we want to analyze local variations in certain directions and explain the *directional derivative*, precisely we answer the question what is the change of a scalar field φ in direction $\mathbf{v}$, i.e., $D_{\mathbf{v}}\varphi$. The directional derivative is a crucial part for certain IllustraVis techniques. Again, we only give an intuitive explanation. Assume, we have a triangle consisting of points, where every point has an assigned value (see Fig. 2.2 (left)). We want to determine the directional derivative of the triangle along the direction $\mathbf{v}$. For this, we have to linearize the scalar field φ. With linearization, we mean that we want to determine scalar values inside the triangle. Currently the scalar values are defined at the vertices of the triangle, but not inside the triangle. Linearization is the process of completing the triangle, and therefore to obtain scalar values at positions inside the triangle, where no values were defined before (see Fig. 2.2 (middle)). A closer look reveals that these scalar val-

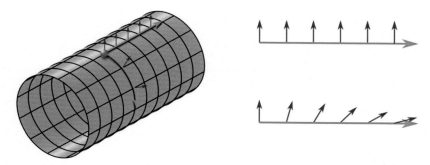

FIGURE 2.1

Walking on a cylinder from a point in two directions results in different variations of the normals. In the first case, the azure (upper) path, the normal does not change, which results in zero curvature, whereas the teal (lower) path has a change for the normals yielding a non-zero curvature.

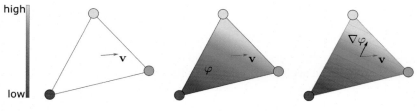

FIGURE 2.2

With a given triangle with a direction **v** and scalar values at the vertices (left), we can determine its directional derivative. For this, the scalar field inside the triangle is linearized (middle) to obtain φ. The direction of the scalar field along the highest increase is denoted with $\nabla\varphi$ (right). The dot product of both vectors yields the directional derivative.

ues change in a certain direction, which is denoted as the gradient $\nabla\varphi$ (see Fig. 2.2 (right)). With this information, the directional derivative is the dot product of **v** and $\nabla\varphi$:

$$D_{\mathbf{v}}\varphi = \langle \nabla\varphi, \mathbf{v} \rangle.$$

Note, that we denote the dot product $\mathbf{v} \cdot \mathbf{w}$ of two vectors $\mathbf{v}, \mathbf{w}$ with $\langle \mathbf{v}, \mathbf{w} \rangle$.

Isolines on surface meshes

The last section deals with the generation of isolines on a surface mesh. In the case where we have a given scalar field φ on the mesh and we want to generate lines with a certain value, most important are the so-called zero-crossing. Zero-crossing are the lines on the surface with a value of zero: the loci of points **p** with $\varphi(\mathbf{p}) = 0$. For every triangle, we check if the sign of the scalar values per vertex change or if all vertices have the same sign. If we have a changing sign, a zero-crossing inside the triangle

FIGURE 2.3

A brain model is illustrated with normal shading (left), with silhouettes (middle), and with contours (right).

occurs. Now, we determine the positions on the edges where the crossings occur and connect the lines afterwards. For this, we linearize the scalar values on both edges, determine the position where it is zero, and then connect them.

2.5 Illustrative visualization techniques

This section presents the most commonly used IllustraVis techniques. It presents several categories ordered according to the level of abstraction, starting with *silhouettes and contours*. Then, we will present *feature lines*, a family of line drawing techniques that aims to convey the most prominent features on the mesh. Afterwards, *hatching* methods are introduced. Hatching attempts to illustrate the mesh with a huge amount of lines that give a spatial impression for the mesh. The same goal is achieved by *stippling*, but instead of lines, points are used. Finally, we give an overview regarding *illustrative shading methods*.

2.5.1 Silhouettes and contours

The silhouette is defined as an illustration of the outline of an object, i.e., the border of the object to the background. With this definition, we refer to Étienne de Silhouette to whom this definition can be traced back. The occluding contour, on the other hand, is defined as the loci of points where the normal vector **n** and the view vector **v** are perpendicular:

$$\langle \mathbf{n}, \mathbf{v} \rangle = 0. \tag{2.1}$$

Fig. 2.3 presents for an overview of a brain model illustrated with normal shading, silhouettes, and contours. Detection and illustration of silhouettes and contours can be divided into three groups Hertzmann (1999); Isenberg et al. (2003):

- image-based,
- object-based, and
- hybrid techniques.

Image-based techniques operate on image information only, i.e., image coordinates and RGB values are used; object-based methods employ vertices and triangle information, and hybrid techniques use a combination of both. In the following, we show exemplary works of these categories.

Image-based techniques

Saito and Takahashi (1990) proposed a comprehensible rendering technique by using depth information. Not only could they depict contours, they also used this to enhance the shaded result and to generate a curved hatching to convey a spatial impression (see Fig. 2.4 (left)). Besides detecting silhouettes, detection of self-intersections is also of interest for visualization purposes. Thus Mitchell et al. (2002) provided a pixel shader technique to accelerate the image space silhouette detection, which comes also with detection of self-intersections.

Object-based techniques

Hajagos et al. (2012) introduced a technique that generates the geometry of the silhouette and crease strokes (see Section 2.5.2: Crease lines). This method can be applied in a single render pass and runs at real time. The contours are defined as the zero-crossing of the normal and the view vector, which are then interpolated at the triangle. Lawonn et al. (2015a) make use of the graphics pipeline on the graphic card to generate contours as a geometry object. For this, they detect triangles that should have a contour on the surface. Afterwards, a quad geometry is produced representing the contour. This idea was later improved and again applied on vascular models (Lawonn et al., 2017; Lichtenberg et al., 2017).

Hybrid techniques

One of the early approaches to illustrate the contour was presented by Rustagi (1989). For his approach, he had to render the surface mesh four times. For every render pass, the object is translated in the positive/negative x, y direction, which increases the stencil buffer if the object fills the viewport and, depending on the final value of the buffer, the stencil test passed or failed, resulting in a contour drawing. Later, Rossignac and van Emmerik (1992) introduced a contour depiction for hidden lines. Normally, contours were hidden by the front faces of the object or covered by other objects. Instead, they illustrated the hidden contours in a dashed style. For this, they employed the Z-buffer; they rendered the faces of the object with varying distances with first the faces, and then with a wireframe representation with wide lines (see Fig. 2.4 (middle)). A comprehensible technique that focuses on non-photorealistic image generation was presented by Gooch et al. (1999). They introduced cool and warm color choices for rendering, novel interactive silhouette detection methods, different shadow styles, line schemes for internal features and external outlines.

Aiming at high frame rates

With increased power of the hardware and better possibilities for GPU programming, research focused on methods that work at interactive frame-rates. Benichou and El-

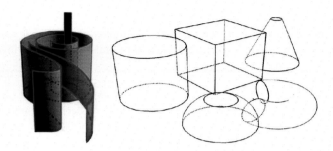

FIGURE 2.4

The illustration techniques by Rossignac and van Emmerik (1992) (left), and Dooley and Cohen (1990) (right) are shown. (Left image: ©1992 The Author(s) Eurographics Proceedings ©The Eurographics Association, right image: Used with permission of ACM from (Dooley and Cohen, 1990), permission conveyed through Copyright Clearance Center, Inc.)

ber (1999) and Northrup and Markosian (2000) introduced such algorithms to draw silhouettes. Pop et al. (2001) presented an efficient algorithm for the computation of silhouettes on surfaces meshes rendered with perspective projections.

Stylization of silhouettes and contours

An essential development relates to the stylization of the strokes, e.g., to use dashed lines or lines with varying thickness to improve shape perception (Markosian et al., 1997). Pioneering work was done by Dooley and Cohen (1990), who could depict the silhouettes and contours using various line styles to encode spatial relations, e.g., hidden lines were illustrated as dashed lines, see Fig. 2.4 (right).

Strothotte et al. (1994) enabled the user to manually adjust the rendering style, i.e., to add or remove detail locally. With their method, the user can set the parameters to obtain results that look like sketches and results that resemble hand-drawn images. Their SKETCHRENDERER is considered the first comprehensive sketch rendering system.

The lines can also exhibit a curved style such that the rendering appears more like a doodle. For dynamic scenes, where the surface changes, Raskar and Cohen (1999) presented a robust technique to render silhouettes using a polygonal rendering setup. Northrup and Markosian (2000) used a two step-algorithm that first detects the silhouette and second, renders it with stylized strokes. An approach that can be applied without connectivity information or pre-processing was presented by Raskar (2001), who introduced a one-pass technique to render prominent edges, such as ridges and valleys, as well as silhouettes.

Isenberg et al. (2002) provided an efficient algorithm to generate the contours with the use of the Z-buffer for the visibility test. After the contours are detected, stylized contour strokes are applied to illustrate the surface mesh.

Frame-coherence

Kalnins et al. (2003) paid special attention to display stylized contours in a frame-coherent manner when the surface is animated. It is also interesting to take the *stability* of contours into account, such that contours should not disappear when a small rotation is applied. Therefore Brosz et al. (2004) presented a stability measure to avoid this unwanted effect and allow to draw the result in various styles in a frame-coherent manner. Grabli et al. (2004) presented a user-controlled image creation tool. First, the extracted lines are presented, which can be interactively chained or split. Afterwards, various styles can be assigned, which allows flexible controls and results.

To increase the expressiveness of renderings, Isenberg and Brennecke (2006) presented G-strokes that store numerous attributes, e.g., line width, line style, color with a stroke during the rendering. The final drawing with the line stylization is then based on these attributes. The first energy-minimizing active contour method, was presented by Karsch and Hart (2011) to detect and stylize the contours. Their approach allows to detect the contours, even on animated surface meshes in a frame coherent manner. This is relevant when dealing with time-varying data, e.g., the animation of a heart during the cardiac cycle.

Cardona and Saito (2015) proposed a technique that combines object-space and image-space methods. Their technique allows to locally stylize extracted lines on the surface mesh. The stylization is carried out by the user, who can also draw new strokes. In particular, stylization is not only interesting for artists, but can also be interesting for surgical planning or training to highlight organ structures with different styles.

Another interesting approach to generate artistic contours was proposed by Chen et al. (2015). For this, the vertices of the back-faces are translated along its normal and, based on the curvature information, the amount of translation is determined, which builds the basis for the thickness of the contours. Lou et al. (2015) presented a method that enabled advanced stroke stylization and frame-coherent rendering. Whenever the surface mesh is rotated, the contour position change, and thus the triangles where the contours are drawn change as well. New contour triangles are searched nearby the contour triangle of the previous frame to ensure frame coherence. When lines are applied to the surface, they can also encode information, such as the uncertainty of physical processes. Then the question is how to properly stylize the lines. Sterzik et al. (2022) investigated and evaluated various stylizations of lines. The question here was, "What kind of lines are useful to distinguish, e.g., lines of different widths, dashed lines?"

For a comprehensive overview of silhouettes and contours, we refer to the course notes by Hertzmann (1999) and to the surveys by Isenberg et al. (2003); Lawonn et al. (2018b).

Current silhouettes and contour drawings

The contour comprises the edges, where the sign of the dot product of the view vector with the normals of the incident triangle normals changes. The contour can also

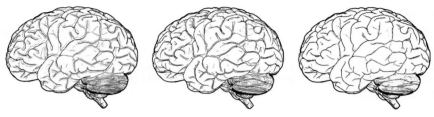

FIGURE 2.5

A brain model is illustrated with *ridges and valleys* (left), with *suggestive contours* (middle), and with *apparent ridges* (right).

be defined as a view-aligned quad, which, unlike simple line geometry, is a rectangular shaped object that can be drawn on, and therefore allows for more extensive stylization. The zero-crossing of the normal and the view vector can be determined along the edges, and this can be used to generate the quad. The quad can then be illustrated or it can be used to indicate the depth by varying the width (Lawonn et al., 2015a). A more sophisticated approach was presented by Lichtenberg and Lawonn (2019). They parametrized the surface mesh and illustrated the contours in various styles by using texture coordinates. In general, the contour gives a fast impression of the surface mesh, but it does not deliver an in-depth spatial impression.

2.5.2 Feature lines

Feature lines extend the idea of depicting the surface mesh with lines. In addition to drawing the silhouette and the contour, feature lines add lines to enable a better shape perception. Mostly these lines are placed at regions, where perceptual discontinuities occur. This may be a strong change of curvature information or a strong rise of the illumination values. Feature lines can be categorized in two groups:

- view-independent feature lines and
- view-dependent feature lines.

The first category, the view-independent feature lines, determine features that are based on surface information only. Thus calculated feature lines are displayed independent of the camera's position or the viewing angle (assumed the feature lines are not occluded). View-dependent feature lines on the other hand, take the camera information into account. Even if the algorithm depends on the lighting, the algorithm is considered a view-dependent technique, because mostly the headlight is used or the light position is relative to the camera's position. Depending on the application, view-dependent feature lines often seem to be more appropriate (Lawonn and Preim, 2016). Surface meshes with strong edges, e.g., typically CAD models yield better results if view-independent feature lines, such as ridge and valleys, were applied. Although most feature line techniques are defined on surface meshes, they can also be applied to volume data (Lawonn et al., 2015a). Fig. 2.5 presents examples of a brain model illustrated with *ridges and valleys*, *suggestive contours*, and *apparent ridges*.

2.5.3 View-independent feature lines

In the following, we focus on the most commonly used view-independent feature lines.

Crease lines

A simple extension of the contour definition is to vary the threshold for which a line is illustrated. For contours, we were looking at the loci of points where $\langle \mathbf{n}, \mathbf{v} \rangle = 0$ holds. *Crease lines* change this condition and look for the set of points where

$$\langle \mathbf{n}_t, \mathbf{n}_{t'} \rangle \geq \tau, \tag{2.2}$$

exceeds a user-defined threshold τ. Here $\mathbf{n}_t, \mathbf{n}_{t'}$ are the normals of neighbored triangles. *Crease lines* depend only on the surface normals, such that interactions, e.g., rotations of an object have no influence on the position of the highlighted lines. Therefore this approach is view-independent. A drawback of this method is that it can only detect strong features, i.e., where incident triangles enclose a high angle. In the case where there is a very smooth highly-tessellated feature, the *crease line* cannot depict this feature well as it only considers neighbored triangles. As crease lines employ a global threshold, they cannot depict small and strong features at the same time. This may be worse if the mesh has a lot of local noise.

Ridges and valleys

One of the first feature line techniques, the *ridges and valleys* for volume data, was presented by Interrante et al. (1995). It was later adapted to surface meshes by Ohtake et al. (2004). *Ridges and valleys* are based on the curvatures $|\kappa_1| \geq |\kappa_2|$ and the principal curvature direction (PCD) $\mathbf{k}_1$ corresponding to the greatest curvature. These feature lines are placed where the directional derivative of the curvature κ_1 in direction of the PCD $\mathbf{k}_1$ reaches an extremum:

$$D_{\mathbf{k}_1} \kappa_1 = 0. \tag{2.3}$$

Whether it is a ridge or a valley can be distinguished by

$$D_{\mathbf{k}_1} D_{\mathbf{k}_1} \kappa_1 \begin{cases} < 0, & \text{and } \kappa_1 > 0: \text{ridges} \\ > 0, & \text{and } \kappa_1 < 0: \text{valleys}. \end{cases} \tag{2.4}$$

At noisy regions, a lot of lines may be generated, which can be filtered out by a user-defined threshold. For this, connected line parts are traced to determine the curvature values along the path and if the user-defined threshold exceeds the accumulated curvatures, the line is discarded. Ridge and valley lines are view-independent and of 3rd order.

Demarcating curves

Kolomenkin et al. (2008) presented *demarcating curves* as the loci of points where the curvature derivative is maximal:

$$\langle \mathbf{w}, S\mathbf{w} \rangle = 0 \;\; \text{with} \;\; \mathbf{w} = \arg \max_{\|\mathbf{v}\|=1} D_{\mathbf{v}}\kappa. \tag{2.5}$$

Here, S denotes the shape operator and κ the maximal curvature. The *demarcating curves* looks for the strongest change of the derivative in the direction $\mathbf{v}$ of the curvature κ in this direction. The direction $\mathbf{w}$, which fulfills this property can be analytically determined as the roots of a 3rd-order polynomial. To filter noisy lines, the user has to define a threshold which discards lines if the curvature derivative in gradient direction is less than the given value. As the *demarcating curves* only employ curvature information, it is a view-independent approach. This method use 3rd-order derivatives, and thus is very susceptible to noise.

2.5.4 View-dependent feature lines

Suggestive contours

Suggestive contours is a view-dependent feature line method introduced by DeCarlo et al. (2003). The methods employs the surface normal $\mathbf{n}$, the view vector $\mathbf{v}$, and the projected view vector on the tangent space $\mathbf{w} = (\mathbf{Id} - \mathbf{nn}^T)\mathbf{v}$. Then the suggestive contours are defined as the set of points where the headlight shading $\langle \mathbf{n}, \mathbf{v} \rangle$ reaches a minimum in direction of $\mathbf{w}$:

$$D_{\mathbf{w}} \langle \mathbf{n}, \mathbf{v} \rangle = 0 \;\; \text{and} \;\; D_{\mathbf{w}} D_{\mathbf{w}} \langle \mathbf{n}, \mathbf{v} \rangle > 0. \tag{2.6}$$

The *suggestive contours* use 2nd-order derivatives, which is less susceptible to noise compared to 3rd-order derivatives. Later, Burns et al. (2005) adapted the suggestive contours to volume datasets, and Lawonn et al. (2014b) employed the suggestive contours for a novel shading technique. To investigate the effectiveness of the feature line method, various studies have been conducted (Lawonn et al., 2013b, 2014a). Here, the suggestive contours usually performed best.

Apparent ridges

An extension to ridges and valleys was presented by Judd et al. (2007) by introducing a view-dependent curvature term. *Apparent ridges* determine the set of points where the view-dependent principle curvature κ' assumes an extremum in the view-dependent principal direction $\mathbf{t}'$:

$$D_{\mathbf{t}'}\kappa' = 0 \;\; \text{and} \;\; D_{\mathbf{t}'} D_{\mathbf{t}'}\kappa' < 0. \tag{2.7}$$

Here, $\kappa' \geq 0$, thus the sign of the curvature yields whether it is a ridge or a valley. The filtering of undesired lines is achieved by a user-defined threshold. If it is higher than the view-dependent curvature, the lines are discarded. Apparent ridges use 3rd-order derivative, which are susceptible to noise.

Photic extremum lines

Photic extremum lines (PELs) by Xie et al. (2007) are based on significant changes in the illumination, and therefore rely on the shading of the surface. Formally, the lines are placed where the variation of the shading $f := \langle \mathbf{n}, \mathbf{v} \rangle$ reaches a maximum, i.e., with the light gradient $\mathbf{w} = \frac{\nabla f}{\|\nabla f\|}$; the PELs are placed at regions with

$$D_{\mathbf{w}} \|\nabla f\| = 0 \ \text{ and } \ D_{\mathbf{w}} D_{\mathbf{w}} \|\nabla f\| < 0. \tag{2.8}$$

Interestingly, PELs can be improved by adding additional light sources. To filter undesired lines at noisy regions, the integral along a line with respect to the magnitude of the light gradient is determined and compared with a user-defined threshold. Again, if the integral is less than the threshold, the line is discarded. The computation of the PELs uses 3rd-order derivatives.

Laplacian lines

Laplacian lines determine the Laplacian of the shading $f := \langle \mathbf{n}, \mathbf{v} \rangle$ and was presented by Zhang et al. (2011). The lines are the loci of points, where the conditions are fulfilled:

$$\Delta f = 0 \ \text{ and } \ \|\nabla f\| \geq \tau. \tag{2.9}$$

The filtering of noise can be achieved by a user-defined threshold that compares its value with the magnitude of the light gradient. Lines with less values than the threshold are discarded. *Laplacian lines* use 3rd-order derivatives, but it is only processed on the normal, thus it is a simplified preprocessing step that increases the performance during the exploration.

2.5.5 Hatching

In contrast to feature lines, where the line placement is strongly considered at certain regions, hatching uses a multitude of lines to convey a shading on the surface. Hatching approaches can be categorized in three groups:

- *image-based*,
- *texture-based*, and
- *object-based* hatching. (See Fig. 2.6.)

As suggested by Interrante et al. (1996), hatching lines are mostly placed along the principal curvature directions (PCDs). We will provide details of these categories in the following sections:

Image-based hatching

Image-based hatching approaches mostly use the view plane to hatch the surface mesh. Depending on the direction of the hatching strokes, the area of the surface mesh is filled with the overlaying hatching plane. This technique may lead to a shower door

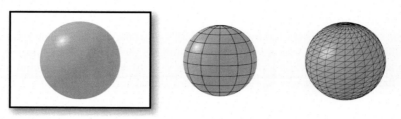

FIGURE 2.6

To illustrate an object with hatching, there are three categories: *image-based*, *texture-based*, and *object-based* hatching techniques. The first category uses mostly pixel coordinates with a color information, the second one uses texture-patches on the surface or a parametrization, and the last one employs the information of vertices and triangles of the underlying object.

effect. An effect where the lines slowly move across the surface, which may lead to a distracting perception.

Lake et al. (2000) presented a real-time algorithm for various IllustraVis techniques, including cartoon shading, pencil sketching, and silhouette edge detection and rendering. The hatching is obtained by constructing n two-dimensional textures. For this, different pencil strokes are generated, i.e., horizontal lines with differently curved appearance. These lines are randomly used to generate the two-dimensional textures. The shading of the surface mesh is determined with $f := \langle \mathbf{n}, \mathbf{v} \rangle$. For the front faces, f lies in $[0, 1]$, where the greater the lighting, the brighter the region. The interval $[0, 1]$ is then divided in n disjoint sets H_i such that $\bigcup_i^n H_i = [0, 1]$.

Every set H_i corresponds to a two-dimensional texture T_i, which is arranged by the strokes. If a set corresponds to darker regions, the lines are additionally vertically aligned, resulting in cross-hatches. Every texture is aligned with the view plane, such that textures T_i are projected onto the surface if the region corresponds to H_i.

Another hatching method was introduced by Rössl and Kobbelt (2000); their method is based on three phases:

- In the first phase, intrinsic geometrical attributes, such as normals and PCDs, are calculated. Afterwards, the surface mesh is rendered and stored in a frame buffer. Every pixel contains the normals, the PCDs, and the shading $[0, 1]$.
- In the second phase, the image is segmented in different regions with homogeneous principal direction fields.
- The third phase constructs the hatching lines in the image based on the shading, the PCD, and the segmented parts. In this phase, a so-called fishbone structure is generated. A line is traced along the PCD with the absolute minimal curvature.

A simple forward Euler is used to generate streamlines. Afterwards, the line is sampled and used to generate the hatching lines orthogonal to the fishbone. This corresponds to a tracing along the PCD with the maximal absolute curvature value.

Various stroke styles are used to enhance the surface mesh based on the shading value. Additional cross hatches support the visual effect of darker regions.

A simpler technique was presented by Lee et al. (2006) by using a novel blending approach to obtain appropriate hatching results. For every vertex, the incident triangles are projected on the view plane. The projected triangles are then covered by a hatching texture, which is aligned by the corresponding PCD. Thus every triangle is covered by three textures aligned by the PCD of their vertices. Blending the textures yields an appropriate result with less discontinuities at the edges. A substantial improvement to apply a hatching scheme on animated surfaces was presented by Kim et al. (2008). Their technique estimates the PCDs on the GPU. Afterwards, the PCD is represented as an angle in image in the range $[0, 180°)$. The directions are quantized and, based on the shading, a hatching texture is then used to illustrate the surface mesh.

Instead of projecting an image, Kwon et al. (2012) used line integral convolution in image space to generate hatching strokes. The direction is determined by calculating the PCD. Afterwards, the directions are smoothed to obtain visual pleasing and coherent results. The application of line integral convolution assumes a noise field. They produce three different noise fields, which are based on the shading, on the color, and on the feature. Afterwards line integral convolution is applied to the noise, here you can imagine that the noise is smeared along the PCD to get the hatching result. Lengyel et al. (2013) placed seeding point evenly in screen space to produce a reasonable distribution of hatching strokes on the resulting image. For the direction, the authors analyzed various methods and stated strength and weakness of each approach. The approaches include lighting values, screen space depth or normals, shading gradients, screen-projected normals, and the PCDs.

Later Lengyel et al. (2014) improved their method and provided an algorithm that combines light gradient and curvature-based line direction. Furthermore, due to camera movement, the seeding points are changed in relation to the surface mesh, which results in an unwanted shower door effect. Thus the method includes a screen space velocity map that ensures the coherence between the interaction of the surface mesh with the located seeding points.

Another approach was shown by Min (2013, 2015) by using three directions to compute the hatching illustration: the PCDs, the tangent directions of isocurves of view-dependent features, and the tangent directions of isophote curves. Afterwards, based on the strength of the feature, noise is applied on each triangle of the surface mesh. Finally, the directions are projected on the view plane and line integral convolution is applied. Another hatching method that works on animated surface in real-time was presented by Lawonn et al. (2014c). Instead of using the PCD, they employ the light gradient. The gradient was then projected on the view plane and, depending on features like ambient occlusion and view-dependent features, the hatching was generated by applying line integral convolution in the view plane. Their method illustrates the surface only at feature-determined regions, and it is more tessellation-independent. A similar idea was presented by Lichtenberg et al. (2016). Here, the user could set the visualization using a single parameter, which then displayed the object

FIGURE 2.7

A liver vessel tree (left) and a trachea (right) illustrated with the hatching method by Lichtenberg and Lawonn (2019) (©John Wiley & Sons Inc., 2019).

with a continuous transition of silhouettes, contours, suggestive contours, hatching, and shading.

As mentioned earlier, more sophisticated approaches can be used to parametrize the surface mesh (Lichtenberg et al., 2018; Lichtenberg and Lawonn, 2019). One advantage of a real-time parametrization is that it can also be used to apply a hatching illustration (see Fig. 2.7). Moreover, their technique is also independent of the underlying tessellation.

Texture-based hatching

Texture-based hatching approaches mostly use textures, which are projected onto the surface mesh. The textures illustrate different hatching styles, it may vary by the brightness where more or less strokes are used. For dark regions even cross-hatched textures are used. Depending on an underlying vector field, which is mostly based on the PCDs, the textures are projected on the surface. When the shading changes, the texture also changes to give the impression of an illuminated surface illustrated by hatching textures. Other approaches include the use of a parametrization, i.e., texture coordinates on the surface mesh. These coordinates can then be used to illustrate the surface.

Tonal art maps

Praun et al. (2001) presented an interactive rendering algorithms of 3D models based on hatching. Their technique is frame-coherent and can be applied to varying lighting conditions, which can be set interactively. This approach uses previously created hatching textures, which are called *tonal art maps*. *Tonal art maps* are a set of textures

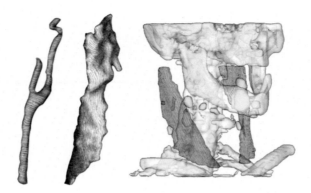

FIGURE 2.8

A vessel surface (left), a neck surface (middle), and two neck muscles illustrated with hatching lines in a scene with surrounding bone structures (Courtesy of Rocco Gasteiger, University of Magdeburg).

varying in tone and resolution. One property of these maps is that they include each other such that an image appears in all images with finer resolution, and all images with darker tone. The hatching is applied by projecting the textures on the surface mesh. To avoid discontinuities at the borders, a blending is used. The texture mapping in employed with the method by Praun et al. (2000). For this, image patches are placed at random regions on the surface such that the surface is covered. In the case of hatching strokes, the textures needs to be aligned with the PCD.

Later, Webb et al. (2002) introduced *volume tonal art maps*, which can be seen as an extension of the *tonal art maps*. The main difference is that they used volume textures instead of a set of textures. With this, a smoother transition for varying brightness is possible.

For vascular structures, Ritter et al. (2006) introduced a hatching method that employs the distance of the centerline and the surface. With further generated texture coordinates, hatching strokes can be generated in the fragment shader. Instead of encoding the brightness with the amount of hatching strokes, they used distances to encode the spatial impression by using the distance of the camera to the surface or to highlight the distance of a lesion to the surface.

An application of a hatching techniques to medical datasets was presented by Gasteiger et al. (2008). They first determined curvature information on the surface and combined it with a preferential direction. Afterwards, *tonal art maps* were applied along the determined direction to illustrate the surface with hatching lines (see Fig. 2.8).

Tonal art maps with image space strokes

A further extension to *tonal art maps* was presented by Szécsi et al. (2016). They provided *tonal art maps with image space strokes (TAMISS)* for a hybrid hatching approach. The idea is that an ID is assigned to every line, and in the fragment shader

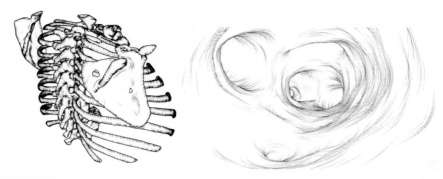

FIGURE 2.9

A hatching illustration of a rib cage and the inside of a pulmonary artery using the hatching method by Lawonn et al. (2013c) (©John Wiley & Sons Inc., 2013).

a curve is fit on each fragment sharing the same ID; this curve can then be extruded to textured triangle strips. The textured triangle strips are used to generate the hatching result. Before, there were only surfaces considered on which hatching strokes were applied to encode the brightness.

Suarez et al. (2017) extended this by presenting a hatching technique that can be used for surfaces with an associated texture. For this, tonal art maps were generated based on the associated texture of the surface mesh. This creates a hatching result, that also imitates the underlying texture, which can also be applied on animated surface meshes.

Object-based hatching

Object-based hatching approaches generate lines on surface meshes. The lines are seeded on the surface mesh, and then traced mostly along the PCD. This yields a hatching scheme without the use of a parametrization on the surface mesh, and can therefore directly be applied on medical surfaces, e.g., organs and vessels.

Elber (1999) used a hatching approach to freeform surfaces. First, a uniform point coverage technique was used to distribute points onto the surface. Afterwards, the parametric coordinates of the surface were used to generate lines along the initially created points. This technique was later improved (Elber and Cohen, 2006).

Instead of using randomly distributed points, Hertzmann and Zorin (2000) used regions with a high visual importance, e.g., silhouettes, boundaries, to illustrate the surface. On arbitrary surfaces, they used the PCDs to generate the hatching lines. Instead of directly using the curvature directions, they determined an optimized direction field by globally optimizing an energy functional, yielding a globally smooth result. The hatching strokes are then determined by tracing the streamlines along a certain direction. Their algorithm ensures that lines are separated by a user-defined threshold. Furthermore, their approach differs between various shaded regions. Here, regions which are closely folded appear darker by using cross-hatching. Brighter regions are illustrated by single lines.

Rössl et al. (2000) used streamlines to apply a hatching on a surface mesh. They fitted a second-order Taylor polynomial to a vertex and its neighbors. This polynomial is then used to approximate the PCDs on the surface mesh. Afterwards, seeding points are randomly distributed on the surface. These points are then located inside of randomly selected triangles. Then, for each seeding point, the PCD is interpolated inside the corresponding triangle by using barycentric coordinates. The hatching lines are determined by tracing the seed points along the PCD with the maximal absolute curvature by a simple forward Euler integrator.

Another approach to illustrate a surface with streamlines was shown by Zander et al. (2004). They also determined the PCD to generate streamlines on the surface mesh for hatching. Furthermore, they used cylinders around the streamlines to ensure a minimal distance from one hatching stroke to the next. Moreover, new line styles allow a large variety of hatching results. Varying the angle also allows to obtain cross-hatching strokes with arbitrary angles.

Medeiros et al. (2009) presented an interactive scheme to generate the hatching strokes. They assume that the hatching strokes are generated along a line. For a tubular surface, the user generates the centerline by defining points, which lie on the line. Afterwards, a B-spline is generated. The spline is equidistantly sampled and for every point the tangent is determined. The tangent is then used as a normal for a plane and the intersection of the plane with the surface mesh are used as the hatching strokes. Based on the shading of the surface mesh, the lines are faded out or drawn fully in black.

A distance-based approach was introduced by Singh and Schaefer (2010). They used a hierarchical approach to generate hatching strokes with specified distances. For a specific camera position, the view plane is rasterized in uniformly sized grids. The hierarchy consists of several grids with varying size. For a seed point in the view plane, a ray cast is applied to obtain the corresponding point on the surface mesh. Then, the stroke is computed by tracing the point on the surface mesh along the light gradient. Grid cells which are covered by the streamlines are not used for further seed points, ensuring a minimal distance from one stroke to the next. However, depending on the shading, the strokes can be closer, yielding the impression of a dark shaded region. The seeding strategy is based on regions where suggestive contours and contours would have been drawn. This approach yields remarkable results, but frame coherence cannot be guaranteed.

Gerl and Isenberg (2013) introduced an approach to hatch surface meshes based on hand drawn examples. Scanned-in hatching picture are used as an input and machine learning methods are applied to learn a model of the drawing style. Additionally, a user-interactive tool allows the placement and the variations of strokes on the surface. As shown by Lawonn et al. (2014d), this approach can also be applied on endoscopic views. Two possibilities to generate the hatching lines on the surface mesh were proposed by Lawonn et al. (2013c) (see Fig. 2.9). The first way is to trace the streamlines along the PCD with explicit methods, such as Runge-Kutta-4, and the other way is to solve an ordinary equation system to determine the streamline directly for each triangle. The calculation was computed on the GPU, making the generation of the lines much faster. Additionally, they hatched the surface only at selected regions to present a sparse hatching illustration.

2.6 Concluding remarks

Illustrative medical visualization has its origin in medical textbooks and is therefore more often used in the context of medical education. Nevertheless, it has great potential to be used in other application areas. We will see a variety of illustrative visualizations in the chapters on vessel visualization (Chapter 3) and medical flow visualization (Chapter 5). Also in the chapters on multi-modal visualization (Chapter 4) and anatomy education (Chapter 7), illustrative techniques are relevant and briefly discussed. One of the advantages is that it can be used to visualize a spatial impression with another visual channel to display additional information on the surface with a color map. Think, for example, of a physical scalar field distributed on the surface, shading techniques can no longer be applied using color coding. Thus IllustraVis techniques can be used not only as an alternative visualization technique, but also to provide an additional visual channel for more information.

Recommended reading

For more information on illustrative (medical) visualization, we recommend the following publications:

Andrea Brambilla, Robert Carnecky, Ronald Peikert, Ivan Viola, Helwig Hauser. "Illustrative Flow Visualization: State of the Art, Trends and Challenges," *Proc. of Eurographics, State of the Art Reports*: 75–94, 2012.

Hansen, Christian, Jan Wieferich, Felix Ritter, Christian Rieder, and Heinz-Otto Peitgen. "Illustrative visualization of 3D planning models for augmented reality in liver surgery," *International Journal of Computer Assisted Radiology and Surgery*, Vol. 5(2): 133–141, 2010.

Kai Lawonn, Ivan Viola, Bernhard Preim, Tobias Isenberg. "A Survey of Surface-Based Illustrative Rendering for Visualization," *Comput. Graph. Forum*, Vol. 37(6): 205–234, 2018.

Felix Ritter, Christian Hansen, Volker Dicken, Olaf Konrad-Verse, Bernhard Preim, and Heinz-Otto Peitgen. "Real-Time Illustration of Vascular Structures," *IEEE Trans. Vis. Comput. Graph.*, Vol. 12(5): 877–884, 2006.

Ivan Viola and Tobias Isenberg. "Pondering the Concept of Abstraction in (Illustrative) Visualization," *IEEE Trans. Vis. Comput. Graph.*, Vol. 24(9): 2573–2588, 2018.

Advanced vessel visualization

3

3.1 Introduction

The visualization of vessels is essential for the diagnosis of vascular diseases and for the treatment planning related to these diseases, e.g., the widening of a narrowed vessel with a catheter-based intervention or bypass surgery. Moreover, larger vascular structures are essential risk structures for basically any kind of surgery. Thus the surgeon must understand the spatial relations between pathologies and vascular structures to define a resection strategy that preserves the vascular supply and drainage in the target region. The specific requirements for vessel visualization vary depending on the diagnostic and treatment planning goals.

In this chapter, we discuss techniques to display vascular structures. All techniques assume that the vascular structures were segmented first, i.e., it is known which voxels of a medical image data set belong to a vascular structure. Some techniques also require the *vessel centerline*, for example, to fit graphics primitives along the centerline. We do not discuss the necessary image analysis techniques; we refer instead to an earlier version of this book (Preim and Botha, 2013).

In the case of liver vessels, for example, we are dealing with several intertwined vascular trees, i.e., hepatic arteries, portal vein, and hepatic vein. An essential requirement is to understand the branching pattern and to assess the vascular territories, i.e., the anatomical regions supplied or drained by a segment of a vascular tree.

Model-based and model-free visualization techniques

Due to the complexity of the vascular trees, overview visualizations are essential, where the specific shape of the vessels may be abstracted to convey the branching pattern. *Model-based visualizations* that enforce a circular cross-section of a vascular tree are examples for such abstracted visualizations. *Implicit* surface visualizations, such as convolution surfaces (Oeltze and Preim, 2005), provide particularly smooth easy-to-interpret vessel visualizations. *Explicit* surface visualizations, such as truncated cones fitted to the vessel centerline (Hahn et al., 2001), are an alternative that is computationally more efficient. These model-based techniques employ the vessel centerline and the local radius information for each point of centerline as input.

For displaying larger vessels, such as the aorta, visualizations should convey the morphology, i.e., the surface shape with local bulges, more faithfully. Also for diagnosing vascular diseases, accuracy is more important than a good overview. For these purposes, *model-free visualization techniques* are employed. These techniques display a vascular tree based on a vessel segmentation result as precisely as possible. A specific example, again from the family of implicit surface visualization techniques, are MPU Implicits, a technique where quadratic surfaces are fit locally to provide smooth changes of the surface orientation (Schumann et al., 2007). Model-free visualization techniques only require a segmentation result, which means that the necessary preprocessing is easier to carry out.

Perception-based vessel visualization

Since so many vessel visualization techniques were developed, the question arises how they could be compared with respect to their quality. One aspect of such comparisons is the perceptual quality of visualization techniques, i.e., how well do they support shape and depth perception. There are specific tasks and methods to carry out such a comparison in an objective manner. This is another topic to be discussed in this chapter.

Focus-and-context visualizations

The general concept of focus-and-context visualization is also useful for vessel visualization to emphasize critical regions, for example, those where a pathology occurs to provide sufficient anatomical context to interpret the position of that region.

Integrating vascular surfaces and blood flow

Whereas model-based and model-free vessel visualizations were discussed in detail in the previous book (Preim and Botha, 2013), the integrated display of vessel surfaces and internal blood flow is a more recent research topic that will be discussed in this chapter. The visualization challenge here is to display both the already complex vascular shape and the (time-dependent) internal flow, such that irregularities of the shape and flow patterns are clearly recognizable.

Such integrated visualizations are motivated by the mutual influence of the vessel shape and the flow. On the one hand, geometric configurations, such as a severe narrowing of a vessel, affect the flow in a characteristic manner, e.g., the flow is accelerated in the narrowing. On the other hand, certain flow patterns that prevail for a long time, affect the vascular surface in a characteristic way.

The basic motivation for an integrated visualization of morphology and flow are usually vascular diseases, such as *stenoses*, i.e., a narrowing of the vessel, and *aneurysms*, a pathological bulging of the vessel. An aneurysm harbors the danger of rupture, and thus the leakage of blood into surrounding tissues, which may have fatal consequences. The identification of an aneurysm leads to the question whether the patient should be operated or whether the risk is so low that a potentially dangerous operation is not worthwhile.

Organization

We provide an overview about perception-based vessel visualization in Section 3.2. The integration of vascular surfaces and blood flow is described in Section 3.3. We go on with a discussion of focus-and-context-based 3D vessel visualizations in

Section 3.4. Finally, we discuss selected applications related to the diagnosis and treatment of cerebral and cardiac vessel diseases in Section 3.5.

3.2 Perception-based vessel visualization

The visualization of vascular structures is challenging with regard to visual perception. Due to their elongated and branching character, occlusion problems occur frequently. This makes it difficult to estimate the relative position of individual branches, even when realistic lighting effects are used. Moreover, additional information associated with the vessel surface, such as derived blood flow parameters, e.g., pressure or wall shear stress, needs to be communicated. A well perceived presentation of this complex information is challenging. A basic requirement for the visualization of complex surface models is that spatial relationships and the distances between structures should be recognizable.

The basic idea of perception-based experiments is to provide a set of *stimuli*, e.g., given rendered images of vascular trees, the user is asked to perform some specific tasks. These tasks include to assess the local surface normal at predefined points, judging which of two points on the surface is closer to the viewer, or the estimation of a depth distance between given points on the surface. The true answers of these questions can be computed, and thus the users' answers can be compared with the truth. *Essential criteria* to assess the quality of a vessel visualization technique are:

- the accuracy of the users' answers (percentage of correct answers),
- the time to complete the tasks, and
- the confidence that users have in their assessment (Preim et al., 2016).

In the following, we give an overview about perception-based vessel visualization techniques.

3.2.1 Depth perception

The visual coding of depth determines how precisely and quickly complex 3D scenes can be perceived. There are *monoscopic* and *stereoscopic* depth cues. For the former, one eye is sufficient to perceive them. Shadows, perspective projection, partial occlusion, and shading are important monoscopic depth cues. Stereoscopic cues provide depth information via visual perception using the slightly different images that are perceived by both eyes.

Another discrimination is between *static* and *dynamic depth cues*. The monoscopic cues mentioned above are perceived in static and dynamic images. However, the motion of a 3D model, either as an animation or during interactive rotation, provides *motion parallax*, which is a quite important (dynamic) depth cue. While 3D vascular models are typically explored interactively, there are situations where static images are employed. Examples are print-outs, e.g., during a surgery. In these cases, additional depth cues are essential. Further subcategories of depth cues are motion-, surface-, and illumination-based cues. Common techniques are color scales, glyphs, or illustrative line drawings (Lawonn and Preim, 2016; Lawonn et al., 2018b).

Chromadepth color scale

A widely used encoding of depth information is *Chromadepth*, which uses the visible color spectrum often applied to vascular structures (Steenblik, 1987). In contrast, pseudo-chromadepth uses only a color palette from red to blue inspired by the scattering of light in the atmosphere (Ropinski et al., 2006). Red colors are perceived as closer than blue colors. A comparison of normal phong shading, chromadepth, and pseudo-chromadepth showed that the pseudo-chromadepth encoding lead to more accurate and faster responses regarding the perceived depth of branches (see Fig. 3.1). Similar to the chromadepth is the air perspective, where distant objects are perceived with less contrast (Gibson, 1950b). Kersten-Oertel et al. (2014) evaluated several depth cues for vascular visualizations, in which air perspective and pseudo-chromadepth improved depth perception the most.

FIGURE 3.1

Comparison of three visualization techniques to encode depth information of complex vascular structures (from left to right: Phong, chromadepth, and pseudo-chromadepth).

Applying chromadepth to a 3D surface makes it difficult to additionally encode attributes on the surface. Therefore illustrative techniques were used to improve depth perception. Ritter et al. (2006) introduced an illustrative technique, where hatch lines are drawn on the vessel surface to encode occlusions between the different vessel branches. Moreover, the distance to the viewer is encoded by varying the stroke width of a stroke texture. Joshi et al. (2008) combined different techniques to improve depth perception of vascular structures represented by a volume data set.

Another association was presented by Chu et al. (2008), who combined a chromadepth technique with hatching rendering and silhouettes (recall Section 2.5). Lawonn et al. (2015a) combined supporting lines, view-aligned quads, and illustrative shadows to improve depth assessment (see Fig. 3.2). In addition, a hatching scheme that uses different line styles is applied to encode vascular shape and the distance to tumors. Darker, strongly hatched vessel regions are close to the tumor. The resulting visualization can be displayed on monoscopic 2D monitors and on 2D printouts without the requirement to use color or intensity gradients.

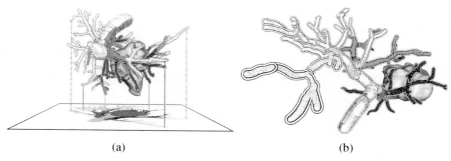

(a)   (b)

FIGURE 3.2

Illustrative visualization of liver vasculature with a tumor shown in perspective projection. In (a), illustrative shadows, supporting lines, and contours are used as depth cues. In (b), different hatching styles and a decent gray tone emphasize vessels at risk around the tumor (From: (Lawonn et al., 2015a), Reprinted by permission from Proceedings of MICCAI, Springer, ©2015).

Domain experts are often interested in visualizing additional properties on the surface, e.g., scalar properties of the flow, such as pressure. For this purpose, Behrendt et al. (2017) combined pseudo-chromadepth with another (discretized) color scale (see Fig. 3.3). Both color schemes are blended based on the Fresnel shading.

Supporting geometry

The 3D visualization of vascular trees may benefit from rendering additional supporting geometry, which is intended to ease the interpretation of the spatial relations. The following types of supporting geometry were employed for vessel visualization:

- supporting planes for shadow generation,
- supporting lines,
- supporting anchors,
- glyphs, and
- cutaways.

Supporting planes

A shadow plane, typically placed below the 3D vascular model, supports the perception of depth in a natural way (Lawonn et al., 2015a). Shadow is a quite powerful depth cue and provides a rendering as if the camera would be at the position of a light source, typically placed above the 3D model.

Support lines

Lawonn et al. (2015a) employed supporting planes to connect selected points in the 3D rendering with their projection in the plane (see Fig. 3.2). These *supporting lines*

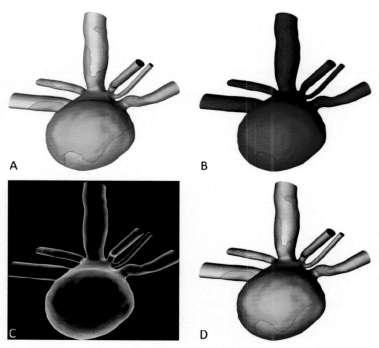

FIGURE 3.3

A discretized color scale (A) is combined with the pseudo-chromadepth color scheme (B) based on a Fresnel-inspired blending mask (C) to encode depth and an additional attribute (From: (Behrendt et al., 2017), ©2017 The Author(s), Eurographics Proceedings, ©The Eurographics Association).

represent a further hint to the spatial relations. It requires a careful selection of the respective positions in the vascular tree, a process that may also be done in a semi-automatic manner.

Supporting anchors

Moreover, supporting anchors are placed at the vessels that are connected with the rings on the cylinder to estimate depth relations of vessels (see Fig. 3.4).

Glyphs

Another possibility is to employ glyphs for depth encoding. Lichtenberg et al. (2017) used camera-oriented disc-shaped glyphs to represent depth relations at vessel end-points. The glyphs consist of multiple rings, where their number encodes depth. Besides, other properties such as the distance of vessel endpoints to a tumor can be encoded.

Cutaways

So far, we have discussed which geometry could be added to enhance the interpretation of vascular structures. Cutaways, in contrast remove a part of the geometry and typically serve to improve the visibility of important objects or regions, such as essential branchings of a vascular tree. Lawonn et al. (2017) combined a cylindrical cutaway view with supporting anchors to provide depth cues (see Fig. 3.4).

Virtual mirrors

In addition to the techniques discussed above, we also want to mention the *virtual mirror* introduced by Bichlmeier et al. (2009). This virtual mirror may be interactively placed, like the mirror used by dentists, or—like car mirrors—it may be fixed to the 3D object at a place defined by the developers. A virtual mirror adds a second perspective, and thus may solve problems with occluding geometry. The success of this technique is based on the familiarity of mirrors to a broad range of users; in other words, a *mirror* is an appropriate metaphor for a supporting geometry. Virtual mirrors were not intended for the exploration of vascular structures, but they are certainly useful also in this context.

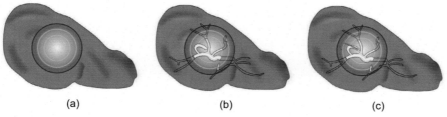

(a)　　　　　　　　(b)　　　　　　　　(c)

FIGURE 3.4

Overview of the cylindrical cutaway view. In a liver model, a cylinder is generated (a). Inside the cylinder, the vessels are drawn with hatching strokes (b). Finally, supporting anchors are automatically placed for improved depth assessment (c). The supporting anchors are connected to the cylinder, and rings on the cylinder indicate the depth of these anchors (From: (Lawonn et al., 2017), Reprinted from Computers & Graphics, Vol. 63, "Improving spatial perception of vascular models using supporting anchors and illustrative visualization," Page 39, ©Elsevier 2017).

These techniques have their strengths and weaknesses. Usually, methods that are able to convey the depth distribution of an entire model fail to detect subtle depth differences. For example, the pseudo-chromadepth easily covers an entire mesh, but small differences are hard to recognize due to the smooth color changes. Information at discrete surface points can be visualized using glyphs (Ropinski et al., 2011). The derivation of information about surface positions that are not covered by glyphs can require a high cognitive effort.

In addition to this mental comparison of different techniques, quantitative evaluations should be carried out to actually measure how effective these techniques are in terms of the criteria mentioned above, e.g., accuracy and completion times. The definition of specific depth judgment tasks should be carried out carefully. This involves to select pairs of points on the vessel surface that are relatively easy, moderately difficult or challenging to compare with respect to their depth values.

3.2.2 Shape perception

The assessment concerning shape perception is more challenging compared to the depth judgment tasks discussed above. Shape perception includes the overall impression of a geometric model as well as a local impression, e.g., whether a certain part on a surface is more roundish than others.

Usually, to evaluate shape perception, the user is asked to determine the surface normal at predefined positions on a model. Again, the selection of these predefined positions is a core task in the preparation of such an evaluation. In the case where the user can correctly estimate the surface normal based on a specific rendering technique, the valid hypothesis is that they have a good spatial impression for this visualization (Gibson, 1950a). Stevens (1983) introduced the task of placing gauge figures to assess the shape perception, which was used to improve or justify visualization techniques. A gauge figure is a small interactive asset placed on the surface, where the user has to estimate the surface normal at the corresponding position (see Fig. 3.5 for two examples).

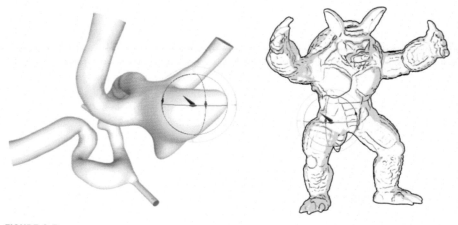

FIGURE 3.5

Two examples of gauge figures placed on two surfaces to estimate the surface normal at the corresponding position (From: (Meuschke et al., 2019b), Reprinted from Computers & Graphics, Vol. 82, "EvalViz-Surface Visualization Evaluation Wizard for Depth and Shape Perception Tasks", Page 259, ©Elsevier 2019).

Koenderink et al. (1992) employed gauge figures on photographs. The user mentally constructs a surface that matches the photographs, and is then asked to adjust a gauge that corresponds to the surface normal. Sweet and Ware (2004) evaluated parallel lines on surfaces. They extracted surfaces from height fields and applied Phong shading to them. The surfaces were additionally covered with different line textures, which are aligned in certain directions. The task was to orient a gauge such that it fits the mentally imagined surface normal. A notorious problem is the scale of gauge figures: since they occlude the surface exactly where its normal is estimated, they should be small. However, a small gauge is hardly recognizable. Sweet and Ware (2004) thus use an additional display to enlarge the gauge with the same orientation as the small gauge embedded in a corner of this figure (see Fig. 3.6). Finally, they analyzed for which line direction the angular deviation could be reduced.

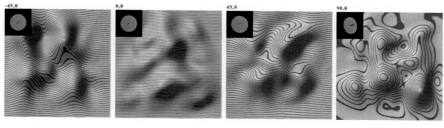

FIGURE 3.6

Examples of different line textures to encode shape information. In the upper left corner the focus is shown enlarged (From: (Sweet and Ware, 2004)).

O'Shea et al. (2008) evaluated the suitability of several light conditions to perceive shape correctly. For this purpose, they used different models and light positions. Again, users were asked to adjust the gauge concerning the surface normal. It was confirmed that shape perception works best if the light position is above the 3D model. Bernhard et al. (2016) compared monoscopic and stereoscopic displays with respect to shape perception by measuring the deviations of slant angles to a ground truth. For this purpose, the gauge figure task was applied to various well-defined objects.

Regarding illustrative techniques, Cole et al. (2009) performed a user study to explore how well line drawings communicate the shape of a surface. Different line renderings were applied to 3D surface representations. The general idea of such approaches is to convey the shape of a surface by just covering it by a small number of lines. However, the use of a few lines generally leads to an enormous loss of information, which raises the question whether certain techniques nevertheless enable shape perception. To investigate this, users were again asked to adjust a gauge corresponding to the surface normal. Šoltészová et al. (2011) presented a novel technique to enhance important structures by employing chromatic shadows. Similar to previous studies, accuracy of shape perception was evaluated with a gauge task.

Baer et al. (2011) evaluated a visualization technique to visualize blood flow data in the context of a surface depiction representing the morphology of an aneurysm. The visualization technique was designed to retain the perception of shape by simultaneously depicting hidden structures through additional transparency. The challenge was to adequately represent both the surface and the internal blood flow. Therefore they combined a view-dependent transparency rendering (Gasteiger et al., 2010) with shadows and atmospheric attenuation (see Fig. 3.7). Again, the shape impression was evaluated with gauge tasks.

FIGURE 3.7

Perception-based vessel visualization by combining a view-dependent transparency rendering with shadows and atmospheric attenuation applied to different aneurysm data sets (From: (Baer et al., 2011), ©John Wiley & Sons Inc., 2011).

3.3 Integrated visualization of vascular surfaces and embedded flow

In 3D visualization, we often have scenes with a few large 3D objects and other small objects that are fully embedded in these large objects. A visualization is needed that depicts the large object without fully occluding the internal objects. This problem is sometimes referred to as *layered surface visualization* problem (Bair and House, 2007).

As an example from medicine, let us assume that we have the model of an organ (such as the kidney), and internal objects, such as tumors or vascular structures. Another example is the rendering of vascular structures along with the internal flow. Such an integrated visualization is essential, since the flow over time modifies the shape of the surrounding vessel; the vessel shape also influences the flow. The blood flow can be, e.g., represented by streamlines color-coded to convey an attribute such as velocity or pressure. Strictly speaking, we do not have layered surfaces, since the flow is depicted by line-type primitives. However, the major techniques investigated for layered surface visualization apply as well.

A straightforward solution to the layered surface visualization problem is to render the outer surface transparent to make the inner structures visible (Gambaruto and João, 2012) (see Fig. 3.8a). The disadvantage of this simple technique is that the visibility of the outer surface, and thus the recognizability of shape details, is generally reduced, no matter whether internal structures are hidden or not. For blood vessels, it is desirable that the outer parts are not rendered strongly transparent so that the shape remains recognizable. Those parts of the vessel surface, however, that actually would hide the flow from the current camera perspective should be rendered strongly transparent to enable a clearly recognizable rendering of the internal flow.

An important application of the integrated visualization of vascular surface and embedded flow is the investigation of flow in the vicinity of vessel narrowings or close to the vessel wall. The flow close to vessel wall obviously has the strongest potential to influence the vessel wall.

We discuss three classes of advanced approaches to address the layered surface visualization problem:

- adapted/augmented transparency,
- front face removal, and
- front contour rendering.

Other approaches were explored as well, in particular, sparse grid-like textures of the outer surfaces, where the sparsity of the texture indicates the amount of opacity (Bair and House, 2007). However, these techniques were not applied to elongated outer objects, such as vascular surfaces, and probably they are not very useful in this context. In what follows, we discuss examples of techniques for displaying vascular structures and embedded flow.

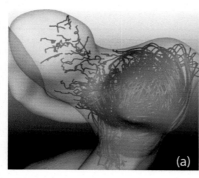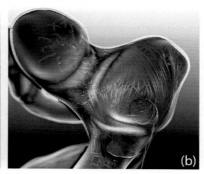

FIGURE 3.8

Near-context display: integral curve displays are frequently embedded in a semi-transparent rendering of the vessel wall *(a)*. An improved perception of surface depth and shape, while maintaining flow visibility, is achieved based on a view-dependent emphasis of feature lines *(b)* (From: (Lawonn et al., 2014b), ©John Wiley & Sons Inc., 2014).

Adapted transparency

Gasteiger et al. (2010) aimed at showing how the vascular shape and the inner blood flow mutually influence each other. To provide visual shape hints about the enclosing surface without occluding the inner streamlines, they employ a view angle-dependent transparency of the front faces. The depth perception is enhanced through local shadows and distance-dependent desaturation. van Pelt et al. (2012) coupled these techniques with a comic style rendering of the back faces.

Neugebauer et al. (2013) employed a framework that could analyze and visualize hemodynamic information near the vessel wall. The surface was represented by a constant transparency. Lawonn et al. (2013a) adapted the surface transparency of the front faces with respect to the suggestive contour measure (DeCarlo et al., 2003), enhanced by local curvature measures to visually differentiate valleys from ridges. They also use shadows to provide depth hints, but blur more distant sections of the vessel instead of desaturating them (Lawonn et al., 2014b).

Front face removal

If the local flow structures are of major interest, the embedding problem can be addressed by removing the front faces of the enclosing surface. de Hoon et al. (2014) visualized the improved signal-to-noise ratio for measured aortic flow. To provide anatomical context, they use a toon-shaded vessel representation with culled front faces. Thus the vessel anatomy acts as canvas and does not interfere with the high-fidelity streamline visualization. Behrendt et al. (2016) transferred the front-culling approach to vascular volume rendering. Though it is sufficient for polygonal surfaces to remove faces depending on their normal to show embedded structures, whole sections of the vessel volume must be removed to achieve a similar effect for direct volume rendering. This is achieved by tracking the points of entering and leaving the vascular structure along each casted ray.

Front contour rendering

Flow can be represented as volumetric structure, filling the complete vascular lumen. As this implicitly also represents the vascular shape, a silhouette-based depiction of the anatomical context is sufficient. As the complete vessel lumen is visually filled, only outer contours are used to emphasize the vascular shape (Schumann and Hennemuth, 2015). If additional shape hints are necessary, an advanced contour rendering can be applied. Lawonn et al. (2013c) complemented the outer contour with several types of curvature-based feature lines. Additionally, they start curvature-aligned streamlines from those lines to generate a local hatching.

3.4 Focus-and-context vessel visualization

In this book, we will see a variety of examples for so-called focus-and-context visualizations in different chapters. These visualizations are based on a classification of the geometric objects with respect to their importance for a given task, e.g., in diagnosis and therapy planning. Structures that are irrelevant, and thus would distract from more important objects, are not shown at all. Objects that are essential for the specific task are *focus objects* and are displayed in a prominent manner. Finally, objects that are needed to provide (anatomic) context are also displayed but alleviated to support the priority of the focus objects.

Anatomical context

Typical examples for anatomical context are large skeletal structures, such as the ribs or the spine, which serve as orientation when inner objects, such as organs, are displayed. These context objects may be displayed in a sparse manner with illustrative techniques, e.g., only silhouettes and some other feature lines are displayed. If context objects should be displayed with surface rendering, colors with low saturation should be employed and transparency may be used to avoid context objects occluding focus objects heavily.

Rendering focus objects

Focus objects, however, should be displayed such that they are clearly recognizable, i.e., with a strong contrast to surrounding objects. Saturated signaling colors, such as yellow or red, and a low level of transparency should be used such that the focus objects stand out and are highlighted.

Discriminating focus objects

The straightforward strategy of focus-and-context visualizations thus discriminates only two categories of visible objects. A more fine-grained discrimination may further distinguish in *near context* objects, being more important, and *far context* objects being less important. Thus near context objects are spatially close to a focus objects. Focus-and-context visualizations of medical surface models and their use for surgery planning were discussed by Tietjen et al. (2005). Though for near context visualizations there is often a direct functional relation between context and data presented as focus, this relation is less prominent when adding also far context. This is normally done to give a general hint of how the object of interest is oriented, positioned within the body, or attached to surrounding systems. Thus the depiction of far context facilitates presenting the overall shape and orientation instead of local surface features. As adding far context aggravates the layered visualization problem, cutting and filtering are typical approaches to avoid visual clutter and occlusion.

Applications to vessel visualization

This general strategy has been employed for vessel visualization with applications both in diagnosis and therapy planning. Vessel segments that contain a pathology, such as a stenosis or an aneurysm, representing focus objects and other vessel segments, depending on their diameter and distance to the focus objects, are context objects, or even irrelevant.

Hastreiter and Ertl (1998) presented a cerebral aneurysm together with the cerebral arterial system to allow for a fast localization and classification of the aneurysm.

To convey the location and orientation of an aneurysm, a volumetric skull rendering is added. As a complete rendering of the skull would eventually occlude the aneurysm, it is clipped axis-aligned, removing the skullcap and the skull base. van Pelt et al. (2011) employ an application-specific clipping of the volumetric vascular context. They visualize local flow with a virtual probe and cut the far context with respect to the flow orientation. Lichtenberg and Lawonn (2019) used an automatic approach to parametrize vessels, which can be used to texture the surface with additional information. Another approach to parametrize the carotid arteries was presented by Eulzer et al. (2021b). In this automatic approach, the surface was cut on the 2D domain, which allows to analyze the vessel at a glance, without exploring the surface in the 3D space. A survey about parametrization techniques applied on the cardiovascular system was provided by Eulzer et al. (2022).

Filtering

If volume data is used as far context, filtering is another essential tool to avoid visual clutter and occlusion. To be usable for an efficient generation of far context visualizations, the filtering should be mostly automatic. Neugebauer et al. (2009b) generated volumetric far context visualizations for cerebral aneurysms by automatically filtering larger cerebral arteries using general assumptions about their location within the skull. Additionally, smaller structures close to the aneurysm surface are shown through a distance-based filtering.

Transfer functions

Instead of filtering the data directly, the filtering can be applied during the volume rendering, using specific transfer functions. Higuera et al. (2003b) presented a 2D transfer function, that allows the inclusion of far context visualization, even if the aneurysm is located close to the skull base. Whereas contrast-enhanced vessels and bones exhibit a similar intensity, standard intensity-based transfer functions cannot be used to visually differentiate between them. However, this can be achieved by a transfer function that includes the gradient. In a follow-up work, Higuera et al. (2004) focused on automatically setting the 2D transfer function.

Surface rendering

The explicit definition of local surface directions allows for a broad range of rendering styles to depict far context. In most cases, the shading and color are reduced to avoid visual distraction from the central visualization. Hennemuth et al. (2011) employed a transparent, shaded surface rendering augmented with contour rendering to depict vessels close to the aortic arch. The arch itself is rendered with low contrast to allow for an undistracted view of the pathline within. van Pelt et al. (2010) presented a color-reduced style to provide information about the vessel location. They used a toon shading in combination with contours to differentiate between vessels and depict occluded vessel sections.

3.5 **Vessel visualization for diagnosis and treatment planning**

The diagnosis of vascular diseases, such as the coronary heart disease, cerebral, or abdominal aneurysms, and stenotic changes, is an important task in the clinical routine. For diagnostic purposes, overview and detail visualizations as well as quantitative information are essential.

Multiplanar reformatting

An important ingredient for a visualization system to diagnose and plan treatment of vascular diseases, is a multiplanar reformatting (MPR) view. Such a view presents the original data orthogonal to the local vessel centerline. This cross-sectional view, however, has to be mentally integrated in an overview of the vascular tree (see Fig. 3.9). The 3D visualization, in this context, serves to verify the image analysis results and to locate detailed information in the overall structure (Boskamp et al., 2004). Such techniques are meanwhile integrated in radiology workstations from large vendors, such as SIEMENS and PHILIPS.

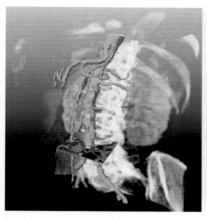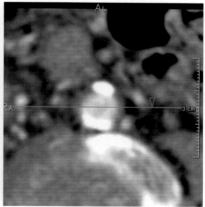

FIGURE 3.9

Left: direct volume rendering of bony structures combined with isosurface rendering of segmented vessels. **Right:** A small oblique MPR view is displayed. This view is centered at the skeleton and oriented perpendicular to the current direction of the skeleton. The position of the MPR view is displayed in the 3D visualization (left) to support the mental integration of both views (Courtesy of Tobias Boskamp, MEVIS Medical Solutions Bremen).

Transfer functions for diagnosis of vascular diseases

A lot of research in transfer function design is motivated by the diagnosis of vascular diseases. The separation between contrast-enhanced vascular structures and the display of a correct diameter of vascular structures are specific goals. Here, we describe more specialized methods aiming at supporting specific diagnostic procedures. These methods employ further information, in particular segmentation information, and are fine-tuned to highlight structures, such as atherosclerotic plaque in coronary arteries. A number of advanced transfer function design concepts, such as gradient-based transfer functions and size-based transfer functions, are largely motivated by diagnosing vascular diseases. Despite some promising results, none of these approaches considers two frequent problems in visualizing CT angiography data:

- The contrast agent is often not homogeneously distributed.
- In the case of severe pathologies, substantial calcifications occur in different regions of a vascular system.

Therefore a *global* transfer function, even a multidimensional transfer function carefully adjusted to the particular data set, is not able to cope with these *local* differences. Läthen et al. (2012) introduced a concept that employs filters to locally adapt transfer functions. In contrast to previous work, a novel *vesselness* value is computed and optimized for the visible portion of the data. The specific optimization is solely based on the intensity scale, and it is inspired by the way physicians adjust predefined transfer functions. They rigorously tested their methods with software phantoms and real clinical data, demonstrating a superior image quality with modest interaction effort. This superior image quality depicts connectivity better and also represents diameters more faithfully, thus it has the potential to improve the *diagnostic quality*.

3.5.1 Visualization of neurovascular diseases

In this section, we summarize visualization approaches to support the diagnosis and treatment of neurovascular diseases, focusing on arteriovenous malformations and carotis stenosis. The cerebral vascular anatomy of patients exhibits a high degree of variability. As an example, the circle of Willis is a complex network that provides vascular supply for a substantial portion of the brain. This essential structure is only in 40% of the patients complete and exhibits a normal topology. Thus patient-individual visualization of the vascular anatomy is essential for diagnosis and treatment. For the diagnosis, different modalities are used:

- *invasive angiography* is considered the gold standard, but implies a risk for the patient, since a catheter is moved in the intracerebral vasculature,
- *CT angiography (CTA)*,
- *MR time-of-flight (TOF)*,
- *MR angiography (MRA)* is increasingly used, and
- *rotation angiography*, a high-end imaging modality, is available at some university hospitals.

In the following, we focus on CT and MRI data due to their widespread use.

Diagnosis and treatment of arteriovenous malformations

Arteriovenous malformations (AVMs) are direct connections between arteries and veins. This short circuit is characterized by coils of vessel branches and needs treatment by either endovascular interventions or surgery. The prevalence of this disease is not quite clear, e.g., Weiler et al. (2012) state that 0.01–0.5% of the population are affected. With respect to the visualization challenges, AVMs in the brain are similar to cerebral aneurysms. Martin et al. (2000) discuss the treatment options and the related experiences in detail.

AVMs are treated by embolization with coils or surgically. The goal is to close the arteries. Typically, a nidus, the core of the AVM, has several feeders. The order in which these feeder arteries are embolized is highly relevant. For example, the occlusion of one artery can alter the blood flow in the other arteries such that a rupture may be induced.

Treatment planning for AVMs is based on MR-TOF or MRA and T1-weighted MRI. The vascular pathology needs to be located and the surrounding vascular structures, in particular the inflow vessels (*feeders*) and the draining veins, need to be understood. Moreover, there are frequently "en-passage" arteries passing the AVM that should not be ligated. The complete understanding of that complex vascular anatomy is further hampered by the fact that not a single image modality is able to capture all relevant information.

Bullitt et al. (2001) thus suggested to segment the feeding arteries and outgoing veins to selectively visualize essential components of the vascular architecture. Focus-and-context visualizations, where color and transparency are adjusted to emphasize the AVM and to display the essential context as well, are useful (see Fig. 3.10). Such visualizations, of course, require careful preprocessing. Weiler et al. (2011) employ, for example, the "vesselness" filter to enhance vascular structures. In an extension of that work, Weiler et al. (2012) presented a multimodal framework that is able to process and fuse DSA, CTA, and MRI data. The exploration of the multimodal data employs the strategies presented in Section 4.5.1, e.g., to employ different clipping planes for each modality.

Sprengel et al. (2021) described an application to support a patient-specific planning of AVM treatment focusing on embolization of the AVM's feeder arteries. They represented the different sequence of embolization steps, where the physician may get additional information about the best possible sequence. To enable the selection of the feeders, they simulated the blood flow behavior for all combinations of closed or unaltered feeders. Then, they provided a particle-based rendering of the blood flow data to investigate the different embolization sequences (see Fig. 3.11).

Diagnosis and treatment of carotis stenosis

Stroke is the second most frequent cause of death worldwide (GBD 2016 Stroke Collaborators, 2019). It often leads to permanent neurological disabilities. The increasing burden of stroke, which is partly attributed to the demographic shift towards an older population, calls for more effective prevention strategies (Gorelick, 2019).

The majority of strokes, about 87%, are caused by limited blood supply to the brain (Donnan et al., 2008). They typically arise from a localized narrowing of arteries (*stenosis*) caused, for example, by atherosclerosis. Stenoses occur most frequently in the carotids and their successive branches. The carotids are two large arteries, each

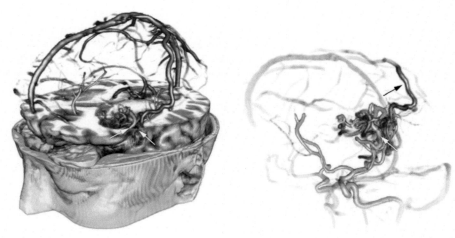

FIGURE 3.10

Visualization of the neurovascular anatomy for diagnosis and treatment of AVMs. **Left:** the complete context is displayed. **Right:** a focused visualization, where the AVM core is emphasized and shown along with the supplying vessels (the feeders). The right image provides the essential information for treatment planning (Courtesy of Florian Weiler, Fraunhofer MEVIS Bremen).

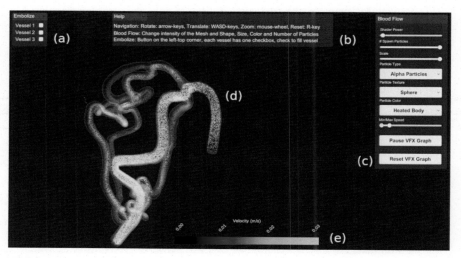

FIGURE 3.11

Virtual treatment of AVMs. Based on different blood flow simulations, the physician can explore different embolization sequences using a particle-based rendering of the blood flow (From: (Sprengel et al., 2021), Reprinted by permission from Proceedings of Bildverarbeitung fuer die Medizin, Springer, ©2021).

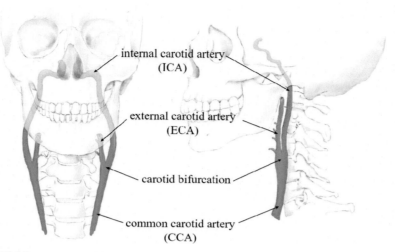

FIGURE 3.12

Anatomy of the carotids (From: (Eulzer et al., 2021a), ©John Wiley & Sons Inc., 2021).

consisting of two branches, the internal and external carotid artery, responsible for the majority of cranial blood supply, as shown in Fig. 3.12. They emerge from the common carotid artery (CCA). The point of separation is referred to as carotid bifurcation. It is a predilection site for the buildup of atherosclerotic plaque and stenosis formation.

A possible preventive option is an early treatment of developing stenoses through stent insertion or the surgical removal of plaque, thereby averting full closure (Halliday et al., 2010). This also alleviates the possibility of the separation of plaque particles, which can be carried upstream and often block smaller vessels. Carotid surgery, however, entails its own risks, which need to be carefully weighed against the probability of stroke (Halm et al., 2009).

Patients who have had a stroke or have symptoms that indicate possible stenosis are usually evaluated with carotid artery sonography. This ultrasound-based imaging is fast, cheap, and non-invasive. Multiple parameters are measured, which mostly relate to the hemodynamics of the blood flow. The stenosis generally lead to an increase in flow speed, which abruptly drops behind the stenosis. This sudden reduction in velocity leads to turbulence that also becomes visible.

In many cases, an angiography is also necessary, often in form of a CTA, to reveal the intracranial vessels and give a more accurate representation of the morphology, i.e., the 3D vascular shape. The injection of a contrast agent highlights the vessel lumen, i.e., the regions where blood actively flows. This allows to determine the position and size of a stenosis, based on which its severity can be derived. However, CTA and similar routinely used methods reveal no temporal information about the flow. Therefore computational fluid dynamics (CFD) simulations, which describe time-dependent properties of the blood flow over the cardiac cycle can complement the information gained through sonography and CTA.

Eulzer et al. (2021a) introduced a comprehensive visualization tool to identify, compare, and evaluate carotis stenoses. The goal is to facilitate clinical decision-making, and therefore advance stroke prevention. For this purpose, they defined relevant interaction and visualization tasks that the tool should support together with physicians. First, possible stenoses need to be identified. This is a substantial task, as patients often exhibit more than one critical region with a buildup of atherosclerotic plaque. Second, it should be possible to analyze morphological features with respect to questions like: *What is the diameter inside and after the stenosis? Over which length is the vessel constricted?* Third, the analysis of hemodynamic features is important, where physicians are mostly interested in the two timepoints of highest (systole) and lowest flow (diastole). *What is the peak velocity? Is turbulence visible?*

In addition, the location of a stenosis determines possible treatment and intervention strategies. Therefore the visualizations should keep this context information. Furthermore, the physicians should be able to assess the tissue around a stenosis. If plaque causes the stenosis, its type (e.g., soft or calcified) and configuration (e.g., even or fractured) can be used to judge pathophysiological factors. This answers questions like: *How fast did the stenosis develop? How likely is the rupture of plaque?* Last but not least, the left and right-side carotid are often contrasted for a full picture to inquire, for example, *Does one side compensate for a stenosis in the other?*

To support these tasks, the framework by Eulzer et al. (2021a) comprises several linked views for an integrated analysis of hemodynamic and morphological features (see Fig. 3.13). To gain an overview of the morphology and blood flow, a 3D vessel depiction with flow-representing lines is shown. Whereas the morphology is extracted from CTA data, computational fluid dynamics (CFD) is used to simulate the blood flow. Here, the user has the possibility to move a plane along the centerline to probe the spatio-temporal data. Cross-sections of the vessels at the probe location show the color-coded flow velocity. Moreover, a graph of the flow rate over the cardiac cycle and a map-based depiction of the vessel diameter allows a comparison of the left and right carotis branch. Volume rendering is provided to explore the tissue around the narrowed vessel segments (see Fig. 3.14). Depending on the set transfer function, other neighboring vessels or calcifications can be analyzed.

3.5.2 Visualization of cardiovascular diseases

Cardiovascular diseases (CVDs) are the leading cause of death worldwide. In this section, we summarize visualization approaches to support the diagnosis and treatment of CVDs, focusing on the coronary heart disease and aortic dissection.

3.5.2.1 Diagnosis of the coronary heart disease

Coronary heart disease (CHD) is the result of inflammatory modifications, leading to accumulations in the coronary artery wall, so-called plaques. Plaque deposits contain different accumulations and can be classified into soft, fibrous, and hard plaques. The

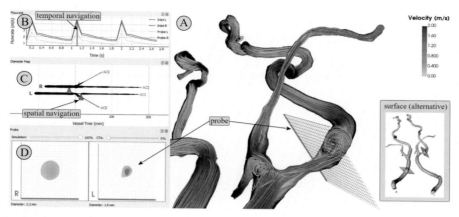

FIGURE 3.13

Visualization tool to analyze carotid stenoses. Four views are linked: a 3D depiction of the vessel wall and internal blood flow (A), a graph of the flow rate (B), a map-based depiction to analyze the carotid diameter (C), and cross-sections of the vessels at the probe location (D). The 3D view either displays a surface model or blood flow-representing lines (From: (Eulzer et al., 2021a), ©John Wiley & Sons Inc., 2021).

lipid-rich soft plaques are prone to rupture, and thus very dangerous. For individual soft plaque characterization, imaging modalities, such as intravascular ultrasound and optical coherent tomography, with a very high spatial resolution can be employed. However, this modality is still rare. Fibrous plaques and hard plaques consist of more dense accumulations and are more stable.

Hard plaque deposits contain calcium accumulations, and are thus also referred to as *calcified plaques*. The overall coronary calcium acts as an indicator for the patient's whole plaque burden. The early stages of atherosclerotic CHD do not necessarily lead to *significant stenoses*, since they can be compensated by a positive remodeling of the vessel wall (see Fig. 3.15). Therefore the evaluation of the coronary artery lumen is insufficient for the assessment of the patient's plaque burden, and the pathological change of the vessel wall has to be taken into account. Evaluation of the lumen and the vessel wall is carried out in 2D MPR and CPR views.

Thus the major goals in the diagnostic process are the following:

- assessment of the vessel morphology,
- assessment of the regional distribution of plaques, and
- assessment and quantification of the plaque decomposition.

CTA data

While the discrimination between different plaque types was limited with 64-slice CT technology, the most recent generation of CT scanners with 256 or 320 slices enables a discrimination of plaque types. With the short acquisition times, it is now possible

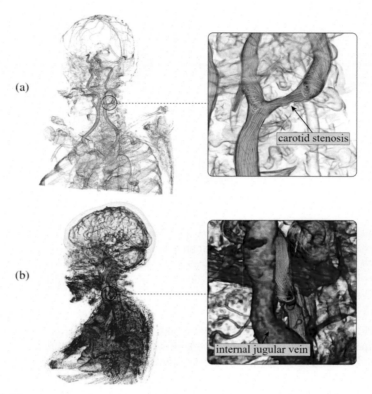

FIGURE 3.14

The volume rendering shows a stenosis in the upper neck area (a). Adjusting the thresholding and opacity (b) reveals that the internal jugular vein is in front of this stenosis, potentially complicating surgery (From: (Eulzer et al., 2021a), ©John Wiley & Sons Inc., 2021).

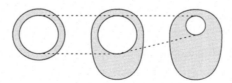

FIGURE 3.15

Illustration of remodeling in cross-sectional views. Left, a normal vessel wall (gray) is depicted. Early stages of CHD are compensated by positive remodeling—an increasing wall thickness (center). Negative remodeling, caused by progressive CHD, yields a stenosis (right) (Courtesy: Sylvia Saalfeld, University of Magdeburg).

to depict the coronary arteries in a sufficient quality, even for patients with accelerated heart beat or other abnormalities. With non-invasive contrast-enhanced CTA, the coronary heart disease may be reliably excluded. Especially for asymptomatic patients with a high risk (due to increased blood pressure, age, and body mass index), CTA is employed for non-invasive identification, characterization, and quantification of atherosclerotic CHD.

Quantification is carried out by applying *calcium scores* to the data, e.g., the AGATSTON SCORE, which defines a threshold for hard plaques as the sum of the mean plus twice the standard deviation of the non-enhanced blood intensity (Agatson et al., 1990). CT data is also used for monitoring of coronary stents (artificial support devices, e.g., stainless steel mesh tubes that are placed in a coronary artery to keep the vessel open).

Designing local transfer functions

The visual analysis of CT data has been investigated by Glaßer et al. (2010), where a prototypic solution is presented.

The specific visualization goal was to emphasize the vessel wall with its deposits. The 3D visualization employs an analysis of the vessel voxels' histogram and the vessel wall voxel's histogram (the segmentation of the coronary arteries can be accomplished semi-automatically, e.g., (Friman et al., 2010b) detects also small vascular structures in the periphery).

A Gaussian distribution of the intensity values in CT data is assumed. Its parameters μ and σ are determined by an optimal (least square) fit to the intensity distribution of the vessel voxels (actually the segmentation result needs to be postprocessed to account for boundary voxels partially belonging to other tissue). It turned out that μ_{blood}, σ_{blood} differ strongly, i.e., by more than 100 HU values, from data set to data set. These two data set-specific parameters are employed to determine the threshold for calcified plaques.

To selectively emphasize the vessel wall, a local histogram analysis for each coronary artery branch is performed (see Fig. 3.16). To identify these branches, the centerline of the segmented coronary artery tree is generated. The centerlines are transferred into a tree representation, where each branch consists of a list with the corresponding centerline voxels and is linked to adjacent branches. The local histograms for the vessel intensity approximation are generated by the intensity profile volume (IPV) extraction for each branch of the centerline.

The transfer function specification is carried out by determining supporting points, which depend on the mean intensity and standard deviation of the bloodpool (μ_{blood}, σ_{blood}) and the vessel wall (μ_{wall}, σ_{wall}).

The automatically generated transfer functions can be interactively changed by modifying two offsets. The first offset O_1 defines the relative position of the hard plaque separation, that is, S_6. The second offset, O_2, determines the average vessel wall intensity, and thus the control point S_3. Fig. 3.17 illustrates how the Gaussian parameters are estimated and used for generating control points for the opacity transfer function. Fig. 3.18 presents some examples of the renderings achieved with these transfer functions. In a similar way, parameters for a 2D transfer function (colors, brightness) are derived to emphasize wall abnormalities also in 2D.

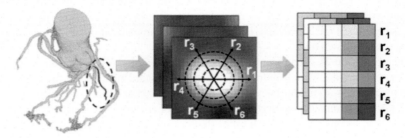

FIGURE 3.16

Extraction of the IPV. For each voxel of the local centerline of a coronary branch (left), a certain number (e.g., six) of rays perpendicular to the centerline is casted (middle). Along the rays, intensities are sampled and stored in a slice of the IPV (right). Repeating this procedure for each centerline voxel of the branch yields the complete IPV (From: (Glaßer et al., 2010), ©John Wiley & Sons Inc., 2010).

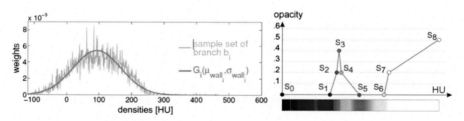

FIGURE 3.17

The transfer function specification is carried out by calculation of $\mu_{blood}, \sigma_{blood}$ and $\mu_{wall}, \sigma_{wall}$. Supporting points S_0 to S_8 are derived. Opacity values are linearly interpolated between the points. Since the HU values differ from data set to data set, the x-axis is not labeled (From: (Glaßer et al., 2010), ©John Wiley & Sons Inc., 2010).

3.5.2.2 Visualization of aortic dissection

The aorta is the largest artery in the human body. It carries the oxygen-rich blood coming from the left ventricle (heart chamber) into the body. Fig. 3.19a) shows the location and course of the aorta in the human body. The upper portion, known as the thoracic aorta, has a curved shape. The lower area, known as the abdominal aorta, shows a straight course down to the pelvic area. The aorta has a diameter of about 2.5 cm to 3.5 cm and a length of 30 cm to 40 cm.

Aortic dissection (AD) is a rare but life-threatening vascular disease (Wundram et al., 2020), it involves acute rupture of the middle layer of the vessel wall. This results in the formation of a new flow channel—the false lumen (FL)—within the thinned

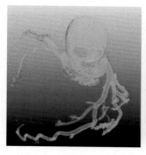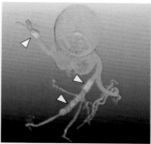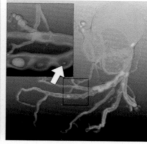

FIGURE 3.18

Direct volume rendering of three CTA data sets. The transfer function specification is based on an analysis of the segmented coronary arteries. On the left, the DVR view indicates a very low overall plaque burden. The data set in the middle exhibits three stents (arrowheads), whereas the visualization on the right shows many hard plaques. Even small hard plaques are recognizable (arrow) (From: (Glaßer et al., 2010), ©John Wiley & Sons Inc., 2010).

wall, separated from the original channel—the true lumen (TL)—by a membrane, the so-called *dissection flap*. The diagnosis of ADs is usually made with computed tomography angiography (CTA). CTA provides detailed anatomical information on therapeutically relevant features, such as TL and FL. Patients with dissection of the ascending aorta—type A—require urgent surgical correction (Chiu and Miller, 2016). When the descending aorta is involved—type B—the aorta can be repaired endovascularly. This treatment is mainly used when acute complications occur, such as a complete rupture of the aorta (aortic rupture) or occlusion of descending vessels (vascular perfusion). Patients without complications can be treated with medication. All survivors of acute AD are at high risk for late complications, primarily caused by improper degeneration of the lumen and aneurysm formation, and require lifelong monitoring and imaging.

Morphological features

Certain morphological features of aortic dissection appear to favor aneurysm formation and late complications. These features include the geometry and relative arrangement of the TL and FL, the connections between them across the dissection flap, and the specific arrangement of the aortic branch vessels in relation to both lumen. More branches arising from the false lumen improve drainage and presumably lower pressure in the false lumen. However, aortic dissections show high diversity in terms of their anatomical features. Moreover, the relationships between morphological features and early and late outcomes are not fully understood. Several features of the aorta that might indicate specific treatment strategies have been studied in isolation but not in their entirety. The problem is that, to date, the relationships cannot be discerned from the (qualitative) analysis of imaging data alone.

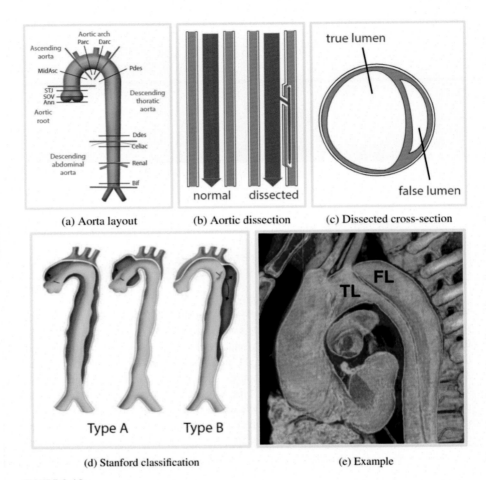

(a) Aorta layout   (b) Aortic dissection   (c) Dissected cross-section

(d) Stanford classification   (e) Example

FIGURE 3.19

Overview of aortic dissection. (a) shows the anatomical structure of the human aorta; (b) shows the expression of an AD. Due to a primary entry tear on the inner vessel wall, blood flows through an additional channel in the aortic wall called the false lumen. The main channel in which blood can still flow is called the true lumen (c). Depending on the location of the dissection, a distinction is made between type A and type B (d). An example of a type B dissection can be seen in (e) (From: (Mistelbauer et al., 2016), ©2016 The Author(s), Eurographics Proceedings, ©The Eurographics Association).

To improve risk analysis and treatment decisions of ADs, Mistelbauer developed a systematic 2D plot-based visualization of multiple features along the aorta, called *aortic dissection map* (ADM). With this, physicians are able to quantitatively evaluate the morphological features and derive the necessary therapeutic and prognostic implications. The ADM consists of four linked subplots: The diameter plot, the branching plot, the intervention plot, and the event plot (see Fig. 3.20). Each of these shows the arrangement of a single feature, but can be combined together to assess the risk on a higher level.

Diameter plot

The *diameter plot* gives a detailed overview of the aortic diameter at predefined landmarks. The diameter values can be determined automatically, which reduces the risk of manual measurement errors. Since ADs result in an enlargement of the aorta, it is important to investigate the diameter along the aorta. A large diameter indicates an advanced state of AD, and once the risk of rupture exceeds the risk of surgical morbidity and mortality, surgical repair is indicated.

Branching plot

The *branching plot* shows the volume of the blood outflow of all 21 arteries connected to the aorta. It is important that all outgoing vessels are well perfused to avoid serious complications. The color-coding shows the risk induced by the blood outflow volume. Red indicates high risk (zero outflow); yellow to green indicates low risk (high outflow). The risk values of each outgoing vessel are aggregated into an overall risk. The aggregate risk of the branching area is assumed to increase as the total volume of outgoing blood decreases.

Intervention plot

The *intervention plot* presents all surgical interventions over the course of an individual patient's AD disease. It is critical to track patients' intervention history to plan upcoming treatments or, in combination with the diameter diagram, to investigate the decrease in diameter following an intervention. The event diagram shows the probability of remaining free of an adverse event for one year, two years and five years. An adverse event is defined as a surgical intervention such as endografting or stent grafting. The visualization is based on five features as input parameters, and shows the adverse event-free probabilities below. The five features comprise the existence of genetic defects, the currently maximum aortic diameter, the size of the intimal tear, the FL thrombosis, and the length of the dissection. A risk is estimated for each plot, which in turn is used to determine an overall risk (see middle rectangle above).

Besides quantitative overview visualizations, such as the ADM, approaches to simulate blood flow behavior in an aortic dissection were able to distinguish between high-risk patients and other patients with uncomplicated type B AD (Sailer et al., 2017). However, the necessary morphological models of the vessel wall layers and lumen were extracted manually, which is very laborious. Detailed, semi-automatic modeling approaches are needed for patient-specific estimation of the pressure within the false lumen, which is ultimately the driving force for late complications. Therefore Mistelbauer et al. (2021) introduced an advanced reconstruction approach to generate surface representations of the AD and its multiple lumina (see Fig. 3.21). Their method is able to extract and reconstruct the inner contours of each flow channel and the outer vessel wall. The individual cross-sections are combined into

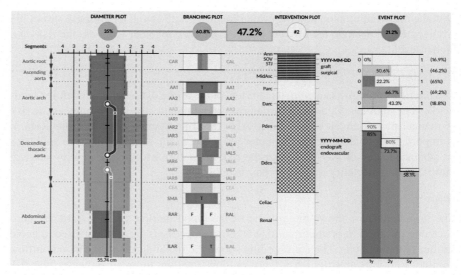

FIGURE 3.20

Aortic dissection map. From left to right: the ADM consists of a diameter plot, a branching plot, an intervention plot, and an event plot. The aortic segments are linked in the first three plots, as they are not included in the event plot. The ADM has three different levels of risk. At the top level, the aggregate total risk is shown in the box at the top center. The next finer level of risk is the aggregate risk values per plot, shown in circles above each plot. The finest level is the plots themselves, as you can see exactly which feature is contributing to the current risk value (From: (Mistelbauer et al., 2016), ©2016 The Author(s) Eurographics Proceedings ©The Eurographics Association).

branches and smoothly blended together to form the final lumen and wall surfaces. These high-quality surface representations can then be used as input for blood flow simulations.

Recently, Ostendorf et al. (2021) compared different shading techniques applied to ADs to identify appropriate combinations of shading styles and techniques (see Fig. 3.22) to visualize surface meshes of the inner and outer vessel wall together with the aortic dissection flap. For this reason, they used common and well-known physically-based and stylistic rendering approaches to highlight specific structures and focus the viewer's gaze on specific areas, while providing contextual information to maintain an overview of the surrounding anatomy. The outer vessel wall, the inner vessel wall, and the dissection flap can be rendered separately with different shading styles and techniques. The different combinations are rated by six experts comprising three radiologists, a clinical scientist, a computational fluid simulation expert, and a medical image processing expert, using a seven-point Likert scale.

All of them disagreed with the visualization of the dissection flap alone, which does not provide a complete visualization of dissection anatomy. Participants more

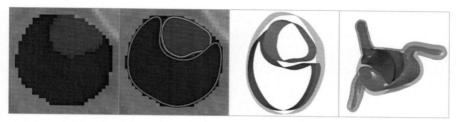

FIGURE 3.21

Extraction of high-quality surface representation of ADs. Based on segmentation results of the TL and FL (left), their corresponding contours are determined. Afterwards, surface representations of the contour regions and the lumina are reconstructed (right) (From: (Mistelbauer et al., 2021), ©John Wiley & Sons Inc., 2021).

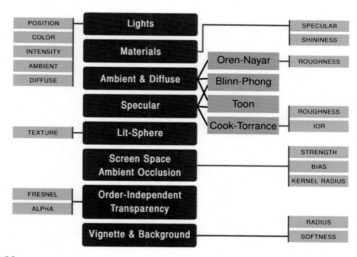

FIGURE 3.22

Overview of the main steps (black boxes) of the shading pipeline, consisting of various lighting shaders (green boxes) and parameters (red boxes). (From: (Ostendorf et al., 2021), ©2021 The Author(s), Eurographics Proceedings, ©The Eurographics Association).

or less agreed to display the true and false lumen surface (see Fig. 3.23, images 6–10). They preferred Oren–Nayar and Cook–Torrance (see Fig. 3.23, image 9) due to the more natural coloring and the true and false lumen contours. When combining the dissection flap, true and false lumen, and the outer vessel wall (see Fig. 3.23, images 19–30), participants were generally undecided to more or less disagree with the presented styles. However, they agreed with a transparent outer vessel wall and the flap rendered with Oren–Nayar and Cook–Torrance with Fresnel (see Fig. 3.23, image 19). In general, there was a lot of disagreement, especially between clinical and technical experts. Therefore more research is needed to explore how combinations of different diffuse and specular parts can be used to achieve focus and context visualizations sufficient for clinical practice and the visualization of CFDs.

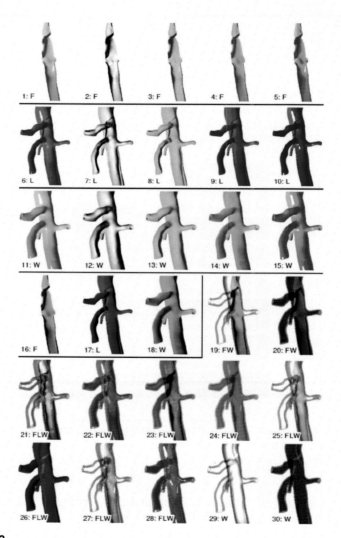

FIGURE 3.23

Analyzed rendering techniques for visualizing the aortic dissection flap (F), vessel lumen (L), and outer vessel wall (W). (From: (Ostendorf et al., 2021), ©2021 The Author(s), Eurographics Proceedings, ©The Eurographics Association).

3.6 **Concluding remarks**

In this chapter, we discussed the visualization of vascular structures with a focus on surface-based visualizations based on a previous segmentation. We discussed model-based and model-free visualizations that differ in the degree of smoothness and the accuracy, where model-based techniques enable a higher level of smoothness at the expense of a reduced accuracy.

An essential aspect discussed in this chapter was the ability for a vessel visualization technique to *support shape and depth perception*. Encoding depth values to color and the use of supportive geometries are examples for techniques aiming at improved visual perception.

We also discussed the situation when vascular structures should be displayed along with the internal blood flow. Focus+context visualizations are useful for vessel visualization, since they facilitate directing the user's attention, e.g., to pathologies or other areas that are particularly important.

Recommended reading

The following papers represent major developments in the visualization of vascular structures, covering surface, volume rendering, and illustrative techniques and their perceptual assessment.

Rocco Gasteiger, Mathias Neugebauer, Christoph Kubisch, and Bernhard Preim (2010). "Adapted Surface Visualization of Cerebral Aneurysms with Embedded Blood Flow Information," *Proc. of Eurographics Workshop on Visual Computing in Biology and Medicine*, pp. 25–32.

Peter Hastreiter, Christoph Rezk-Salama, Bernd Tomandl, Klaus Eberhardt, and Thomas Ertl (1998). "Fast analysis of intracranial aneurysms based on interactive direct volume rendering and CTA," *Proc. of Medical Image Computing and Computer-Assisted Intervention*, pp. 660–669.

Jan Kretschmer, Christian Godenschwager, Bernhard Preim, and Marc Stamminger (2013). "Interactive patient-specific vascular modeling with sweep surfaces," *IEEE Transactions on Visualization and Computer Graphics*, Vol. 19(12) (2013): 2828–2837.

Kai Lawonn, Maria Luz, Bernhard Preim, and Christian Hansen (2015). "Illustrative visualization of vascular models for static 2D representations", *Proc. of Medical Image Computing and Computer-Assisted Intervention*, pp. 399–406.

Gabriel Mistelbauer, Anca Morar, Andrej Varchola, Rüdiger Schernthaner, Ivan Baclija, Arnold Köchl, Armin Kanitsar, Stefan Bruckner, and Eduard Gröller (2013). "Vessel visualization using curvicircular feature aggregation," *Computer Graphics Forum*, Vol. 32(3pt2): 231–240.

Multimodal medical visualization

4

4.1 Introduction

Medical imaging data is becoming more and more complex. Not only are there advances in the types of medical imaging that can be acquired (modalities), for example, via magnetic resonance imaging (MRI) or computed tomography (CT) scanners, but also the amount of imaging data acquired per patient is steadily growing. In this chapter, we focus on visualization of multimodal medical imaging data, which is data that is acquired from multiple imaging sources. These different sources often provide complementary information. For example, CT scanners can provide a high-resolution view of anatomy of the human body (structural information), whereas positron emission tomography (PET) scanners are recording the uptake of radioactive tracer (functional information). Combining such modalities allows for inspection of healthy and pathological function and localization of this functional information based on structural imaging (see Fig. 4.1). Even from a single scanner, multiple types of imaging acquisition are possible, leading to what is often referred to as multiparametric data. An example of this is brain imaging via a single MRI scanner, where it is possible to acquire different image contrasts highlighting vascular structures, brain function (functional MRI), or brain connectivity (diffusion weighted imaging) using different image acquisition parameters. In addition, hybrid scanners, such as PET/CT or PET/MR scanners, are able to produce images of different modalities in a single hardware solution.

The main challenge in interpreting such multimodal or multiparametric imaging data is that it places higher demands on the person viewing these images. First, the sheer amount of imaging information increases, but also it can be challenging to form a complete mental model relating the different imaging sources to each other when viewed sequentially. Here, visualization can help to integrate the information from multiple sources for a more comprehensive *integrated view* on the data. However, visualization of such data is not trivial, since combining information from multiple sources that overlap spatially leads to a need to decide what is important to show, and the development of visualization techniques that allow for visualization of multiple volumes simultaneously.

Organization

In this chapter, which is based on a survey by Lawonn et al. (2018a), we provide an overview of multimodal medical visualization and why it is challenging. First, we

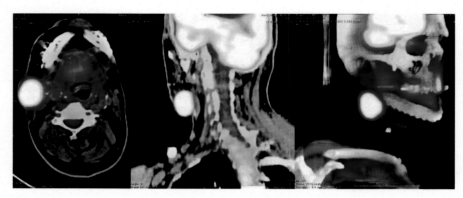

FIGURE 4.1

2D and 3D fused PET/CT images with superimposed CT and PET data rendered in the OsiriX software (From: (Rosset et al., 2006), ©2006 The Author(s), Radiographics, ©Radiological Society of North America).

discuss medical imaging techniques and hybrid acquisition solutions (Section 4.2). The clinical workflow related to multimodal imaging is discussed in Section 4.3. Afterwards, we look at interactive visualization approaches (Section 4.4). Finally, we conclude with an overview and summary.

4.2 Medical imaging modalities

In this section, we provide an overview of multimodal and hybrid imaging techniques. We discuss the individual modalities, their strengths and weaknesses, and associated visualization challenges.

4.2.1 Computed tomography (CT)

CT is an X-ray-based tomographic imaging technique, which results in stacks of 2D cross sectional images. Tissues such as bone, water, fat, and the air in the lungs are easy to distinguish on CT, due to the contrast they generate based on different levels of X-ray absorption. Through contrast agent injection, vascular structures can be highlighted. In 2019, over 90 million CT scans were made in the US alone, illustrating the relevance of this imaging method in clinical practice.

In addition to regular CT, hybrid CT scanners, such as dual source or dual energy CT (DECT) scanners, are now available, which fuse information from simultaneous high and low voltage image acquisition to provide even more tissue distinguishing capabilities. In CT scans, bone and contrast-enhanced blood vessels are hard to distinguish due to similar absorption rates, whereas in DECT these structures are easier to separate.

Typical CT scans feature a 512×512 pixels in-slice resolution and 0.3–2 mm slice thickness. Due to this relatively high resolution, high signal-to-noise ratio (SNR), and standardized intensity values (Hounsfield units, HU), CT is highly suitable for direct volume rendering and the use of reusable task-specific transfer functions.

4.2.2 Magnetic resonance imaging (MRI)

MRI scanners rely on a powerful magnetic field for image acquisition. Due to a wide range of configurable parameter settings, MRI provides a wide range of imaging sequences, which capture both structural and functional information. These sequences can be captured in a single acquisition session, which leads to mostly co-registered images. In 2019, over 42 million MRI scans were made in the US, which is less than half the amount of CT scans.

Unlike with CT, image intensities in MRI are not standardized, and the gray level distribution is inhomogeneous. This creates a need for careful data pre-processing, also varying intensity values across scanner vendors and clinics. In MRI, difficulties arise in applying transfer functions across datasets without adaptation and, in addition, inhomogeneity makes for more challenging volume rendering. MR images generally have a lower resolution and signal-to-noise ratio than CT images, but do not require the use of harmful radiation.

In addition to standard imaging protocols, more specialized sequences are available, such as magnetic resonance spectroscopy imaging (MRSI), dynamic contrast-enhanced (DCE-MRI), and diffusion tensor imaging (DTI). MRSI allows for measurement of spatially localized metabolites; DCE-MRI is able to measure tissue perfusion, and DTI detects the direction of white matter tracts in the brain representing connectivity. The latter is often visualized as a scalar field of fractional anisotropy (FA) values or by using glyphs or fiber tracking to represent diffusion tensors. Functional MRI (fMRI) detects subtle changes in blood flow in response to stimuli or actions and visualizes cortical activity. Blood oxygenation level dependent (BOLD) fMRI is the most frequently employed technique.

4.2.3 Ultrasound

Medical ultrasound employs high-frequency sound waves to measure tissue characteristics. It can be used both for diagnostic and for interventional procedure guidance. Since sound waves are employed, ultrasound is suitable for imaging soft tissue, but not able to visualize bone or air, or even structures that are occluded by such tissues. Through the use of the Doppler effect, ultrasound can be used to record functional information, for example, measuring blood flow in the heart or blood vessels. Contrast-enhanced ultrasound is possible through the use of microbubbles, an intravenous contrast agent with small gas bubbles surrounded by a shell, which gets metabolized by the liver. Compared to other imaging modalities, ultrasound is relatively cheap, safe, portable, and real-time. The low signal-to-noise ratio and limited field of view, however, make ultrasound more challenging to interpret and visualize.

4.2.4 Nuclear medicine modalities

Whereas CT and MRI scans provide detailed anatomical data, PET scanners are able to reveal functional information, such as metabolism. The technique relies on indirect detection of gamma rays emitted from the patient after administering a positron-emitting radionuclide, often referred to as a *tracer*. Common applications include the detection of cancer metastases with the tracer fluorodeoxyglucose (FDG). Since the metabolic activity of the metastases is elevated, they show up as high intensity regions on the PET scan. PET is also suitable for neurological and cardiological diagnostic purposes. In addition to FDG, other tracers are available, which may be better suited for a specific scenario.

Before visualizing, the PET data needs attenuation correction, which can be achieved by an additional PET transmission scan. In addition, 3D visualization of PET imaging data is challenging since healthy metabolic uptake is included and may occlude pathologic activity. Regions with the highest intensity are not always the most interesting.

Single-photon emission computed tomography (SPECT) also employs radioactive tracer material to detect gamma rays. However, unlike in PET, in SPECT gamma radiation is measured directly from the tracer. SPECT is employed for oncology applications, as well as for infection, thyroid, or bone imaging. SPECT can also provide localized function within organs for functional cardiac or brain imaging. Compared to PET, SPECT has a lower spatial resolution and contrast and is challenging to render in 3D for similar reasons as PET.

4.2.5 Hybrid scanners

In multimodal imaging, imaging modalities from different acquisition techniques are combined to have a synergetic effect, where the strengths of individual modalities are combined to form a more complete picture. A key opportunity here is to combine modalities that are good at structural imaging at high resolution, for example, CT or MRI, with modalities that can show metabolic function, such as PET or SPECT. This allows for exact localization of suspicious metabolic activity. When such images are acquired on separate scanners, image registration problems occur. The alignment of imaging volumes is easier to achieve in some areas, for example, the brain, than others, for example, the pelvis. However, to avoid the registration problem almost entirely, hybrid scanners have been developed. Such scanners integrate multiple acquisition techniques in a single device. Some combinations, such as PET/CT (see Fig. 4.2) or SPECT/CT, are already commonplace in clinical practice. Other combinations, such as PET/MRI or SPECT/MRI, are only more recently beginning to see pre-clinical and clinical use.

PET/CT

In this combination, CT data can be used to achieve noiseless attenuation correction for the PET data, which eliminates the need for the additional PET transmission scan, and reduce total scan time up to 40%. This combination also allows for detailed local-

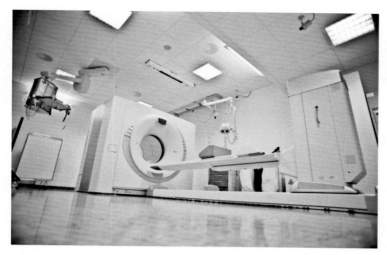

FIGURE 4.2

A PET/CT scanner developed by Siemens Healthcare. Photo courtesy of the Centre for Nuclear Medicine and PET, Dept. of Radiology, Haukeland University Hospital in Bergen, Norway.

ization based on the CT scan combined with metabolic activity from the PET scan. One disadvantage of a PET/CT hybrid scanner is that the acquisition is performed sequentially, which eliminates temporal correlation between modalities.

PET/CT is often employed clinically for oncological applications, such as diagnosis and staging of primary tumors or localization of metastases. In addition, it can be leveraged for surgical tumor operability assessment or treatment selection. PET/CT is able to assess recurrence and differentiate scar and active cancer tissue. PET is able to detect changes in tumors in an earlier stage than CT, as metabolic changes occur prior to anatomical size changes. Townsend et al. (2004) provide an extensive discussion of PET/CT acquisition. A recent method to display PET/CT data simultaneously, based on two thresholds adapted to the data, was presented by Liu et al. (2020).

SPECT/CT

Similarly to combining PET and CT in a hybrid scanner, a SPECT/CT hybrid acquisition also offers high-resolution structural anatomical details for localization combined with metabolic information. CT can also be used in attenuation correction for SPECT. As mentioned previously, SPECT suffers from lower spatial resolution and contrast, but is more cost effective than PET.

Buck et al. (2008) provide an overview of techniques and future direction for SPECT/CT. This is elaborated on by Mariani et al. (2010) in a more detailed review on clinical applications.

PET/MRI

PET/MRI scanners are a more recent introduction to clinically available hybrid scanners. Since 2014 the first devices are legally allowed and used in clinical practice. Initially, many applications focused on head and neck imaging, but integrated whole-body PET/MRI was also found feasible early on. In preliminary studies, PET/MRI imaging outperformed PET/CT and more frequently affected patient management decision, as shown by Catalano et al. (2013).

In general, hybrid scanners are able to provide complimentary information, which needs to be integrated and interpreted as whole, thus leading to a need for fused multimodal visualization.

4.3 Workflow and requirements

To design effective visualization solutions for multimodal medical image analysis, we must first understand the current workflow in clinical practice. With this workflow as a starting point, we outline visualization requirements, which should be considered when developing novel techniques.

4.3.1 Clinical workflow

Multimodal medical imaging data is in practice often interpreted by radiologists and/or nuclear medicine physicians. These disciplines each have their own skill-set and background, but an increasing number of physicians are now specializing in both areas working in joint departments. Though specific imaging protocols may vary per hospital, images are generally read on similar radiology workstations provided by major vendors, such as PHILIPS and SIEMENS. Multiple modalities can then be separately analyzed based on common views for individual modalities, for example, slice-based viewing in axial, coronal, and sagittal planes for CT-scans. For nuclear medicine modalities, maximum intensity projection (MIP) is commonly employed in a frontal or side view of the patient. If the clinical indication warrants it, more specialized visualization techniques can be employed, such as polar maps for cardiac SPECT data.

To visualize two modalities at once, a typical practice is to employ a slice-based approach with one modality in grayscale and the other modality superimposed with a colormap, which includes opacity settings. In this way, structural information is presented in gray-scale, whereas color showcases functional activity. This approach is highly effective as brightness and color hue are separate perceptual channels, which can be processed simultaneously. The choice of a color map is not standardized and subject to vendor-specific variation. The exact configuration of views may vary, but typically there is a central view combined with linked views or views of equal size that display different modalities and slice directions.

Combining two modalities with high spatial resolution, for example, CT and MRI, poses more visualization challenges. Therefore simultaneous exploration of CT and

MRI enriched with PET or SPECT information is currently not feasible in clinically available software. More advanced multimodal visualization techniques are currently not yet broadly available in clinical practice. In research software, however, multiplanar reformation (MPR), surface rendering, and direct volume rendering can be employed for fused multimodal datasets.

4.3.2 Requirement analysis

Medical imaging provides unique challenges that arise from measuring data from a living patient. Breathing, relaxing muscles, the beating of the heart, and movement all influence scanning results. Local differences arising from these processes during or between scans create a misalignment problem when acquiring multiple sequences, even in hybrid scanners. These misalignments can be remedied by a registration process, but no perfect matches are guaranteed. In visualization of multimodal data, special attention should be paid to providing opportunities for users to assess any registration error, for example, by superimposing registered data in a slice-based visualization.

General goals of multimodal medical image data visualization include the following:

- reducing complexity and thereby cognitive load
- improving the decision-making process
- providing custom visualizations for specific applications

For diagnostic purposes, examining a large amount of 2D slices individually to examine anatomy, pathology, and physiology can quickly become time-consuming and cumbersome as the number of slices and available modalities increase. In addition to such traditional 2D examination approaches, 3D techniques can give an overview visualization of full data sets at a glance, highlighting, for example, suspicious metabolic activity regions requiring closer inspection in anatomical context. Existing visualization techniques, such as the maximum intensity projection, which was first developed for nuclear medicine imaging, as discussed by Wallis et al. (1989), can provide an overview, but lack depth information.

General requirements for newly developed 3D visualization techniques that are suitable for multimodal medical imaging data are the following:

1. Visualization parameters should be easily *adjustable* to fit the needs of the user, such that the user is empowered to reveal what is important and de-emphasize or remove unimportant information.
2. For clinical applications, developed techniques should be *fast and interactive*, with *minimal or no pre-processing* required, given the time-constraints in clinical practice.

More specific requirements are strongly application-dependent and should be formulated together with domain experts based on their needs. In the following, we highlight some examples of specific application requirements. According to Lawonn et al. (2015b), for combined anatomical and functional imaging visualization for diagnostic purposes, the following additional requirements should be fulfilled:

1. The technique should show the combination of two or more modalities in a fused view, in which the functional activity of interest is always visible.
2. The technique should relate metabolic activity to nearby anatomical structures for accurate localization.

In addition to diagnostic purposes, 3D visualization is also beneficial for research and treatment planning applications. The general visualization requirements are the same for both diagnostic and research purposes, but a key difference is that researchers have more time available to spend on visualization and preprocessing than clinicians.

In surgical treatment planning, multimodal 3D patient-specific visualization can support tasks such as access planning. For example, in oncologic neurosurgery an access path to a brain tumor needs to be planned, which takes into account the structures at risk, e.g., arteries or functional brain regions. Beyer et al. (2007) stated that in such a neurosurgical context, a visualization application should:

- Provide high-quality, interactive, and flexible 3D visualization.
- Offer multimodal visualization for modalities, such as CT, MRI, fMRI, PET, or DSA.
- Provide interactive manipulation, such as simulated surgical procedures, endoscopic views, or virtual cutting planes.

In radiotherapy treatment planning, radiation targets should be visualized in the context of healthy structures at risk for radiation damage. Schlachter et al. (2014) outlined requirements for such an application, which include the following:

- Support for 4D PET and CT data and fusion of these modalities in a 3D view
- Visualization of segmented structures (i.e., tumor(s) and organs at risk around the tumor location)
- Visualization of dose distribution
- Clipping and/or masking parts of the volume

In general, multimodal medical visualization demands advanced visualization techniques to fulfill the presented requirements. Careful decisions need to be made on which parts of the rich multimodal imaging information are important to highlight, to show as context, or to de-emphasize. In the next section, we outline several visualization concepts that can be applied in multimodal medical applications.

4.4 Visualization techniques

A common issue when visualizing multimodal medical imaging data is that no clear view can be given on the features of each of the modalities simultaneously due to the overlapping spatial extent. Visualization techniques aim to remedy this problem by incorporating heuristics to assess information importance and by employing emphasis techniques to highlight information based on its importance. Smart visibility, Focus+Context, and other emphasis techniques are thus staples in visualizing multimodal medical imaging data. In this section, we summarize basic visualization techniques that seek to deal with occlusion, improve depth perception, and provide ways of presenting relevant information from multiple sources effectively.

4.4.1 Pre-processing

In multimodal visualization, registration or segmentation is often a pre-requisite step to prepare the data. Especially when data is acquired from multiple separate scanners, registration is needed for volume alignment. Whereas automatic alignment techniques are available for some modalities and application area, for example, brain MRI scans, many application areas require a semi-automatic registration. Examples of semi-automatic registration include performing a course manual alignment followed by an automatic process or placing corresponding landmark pairs.

Segmentation is not routinely performed in all clinical applications, but applications such as radiotherapy planning depend on it. In this case, segmentation can be used as a basis for further analysis, for example, volume measurements or visualization. As for registration, both manual, semi-automatic, and automatic segmentation techniques exist.

Direct volume rendering (DVR) and indirect volume rendering (IVR) are possible for multimodal data. For IVR, a triangulated surface mesh needs to be created based on a segmented structure of interest from the volumetric scan. The marching cubes algorithm is often employed to create such a mesh. Various shading techniques and visualization methods are available for mesh visualization. Illustrative visualization in particular, for example, hatching, is easier to do with surface meshes than volumetrically (recall Section 2.5.5).

Unlike IVR, DVR does not require a segmentation step, and in this way avoids potentially losing critical information. However, suitable transfer functions that assign color and opacity to intensity values still need to be designed.

4.4.2 Smart visibility

In most cases, users are interested in one or a group of specific structures, which may be surrounded by other objects that occlude or overlap. Smart visibility techniques, which require segmentation information, aim to resolve the occlusion problem, while still indicating surrounding structures. Simply hiding structures that occlude interesting structures is often not appropriate as they provide spatial context. Viola and Gröller (2005) define smart visibility as follows: "Expressive visualization techniques that smartly uncover the most important information in order to maximize the visual information in the resulting images." Smart visibility techniques encompass a variety of approaches, including cutaways and ghosted views.

Cutaway views

allow for an object of interest to be separated from surrounding context structures by, as the name suggests, cutting away structures that obstruct the view. This can be done, for example, by placing an object around the focus object aligned towards the camera and clipping away other structures within. The advantage of this approach is the clear view on the structure of interest, but a disadvantage is that all structures between the focus object and camera are lost. There are two main categories of cutaway techniques: predefined models and focus-oriented objects. Within predefined models, view-dependent and view-independent approaches can be distinguished. For both approaches, a predefined model, such as a cylinder, is used to test all non-focus structures to see which are inside and outside of this model. Only context structures that do not overlap with the pre-defined model are drawn. View-dependent techniques are more frequently used, combined with a conic model oriented along the view-vector. Pre-defined models are applicable if the focus object has a simple shape and does not vary over time, e.g., to visualize lymph nodes.

The second class of cutaway techniques is based on focus-oriented models. In this approach, a conic object is constructed based on focus object shape on the fly, as proposed by Viola et al. (2004). Later, Burns et al. (2007) applied these concepts to multimodal data. For real-time applications, calculation of this conic object needs to be efficient. Unlike pre-defined models, focus-oriented models allow for visualization of dynamic processes and complex shapes. An example of an application where focus-oriented models are employed is to visualize animated blood flow (Lawonn et al., 2014b). This technique then provides a way to guarantee a clear view on the blood flow within a vessel.

Cutaway views are also suitable for multimodal medical visualization. For example, one modality could be displayed outside the cutaway region, while the other is displayed within a cutaway. Hybrid PET/CT data could be visualized by using a cutaway view to reveal high-activity PET regions by clipping away occluding CT information. This allows for localization, whereas a maximum intensity projection does not offer depth cues. This approach may be beneficial for diagnostic purposes, treatment planning, or patient-doctor communication. Additionally, cutaways can be applied to both modalities for a clear view on a structure hidden by occluding structures.

Lawonn et al. (2015b) introduced an illustrative cutaway technique of PET/CT data. The functional information from the PET data is used as the focus. Thus the region that is automatically removed from the CT data set is large enough to reveal high-activity regions in PET data. With this strategy, these high-activity regions, suspected to contain a malignant tumor are visible in their anatomical context. Since the vascular supply of a tumor is essential, vascular structures around the high-activity regions are also shown (see Fig. 4.3). The specific appearance, e.g., the colors used to show the CT and PET data are controlled by means of transfer functions.

Since a typical PET data set contains several significant regions with high activity, multiple focus regions may arise (see Fig. 4.4). Fig. 4.5 compares the illustrative

FIGURE 4.3

PET/CT visualization with PET activity displayed as a focus area using cutaways and CT providing anatomical context for accurate localization. The border of the cutaway is emphasized (From: (Lawonn et al., 2015b), ©2015 The Author(s), Eurographics Proceedings, ©The Eurographics Association).

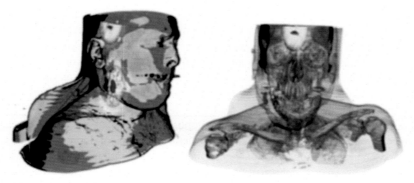

FIGURE 4.4

Visualization of a dataset from a patient with head and neck cancer and different TFs. The basic visualization method is the same as in Fig. 4.3 (From: (Lawonn et al., 2015b), ©2015 The Author(s), Eurographics Proceedings, ©The Eurographics Association).

rendering technique from Lawonn et al. (2015b) with more conventional multimodal visualization techniques.

Ghosted views

Transparency is a straightforward approach to illustrate a focus object and abstract surrounding context structures. However, multiple transparent objects can lead to

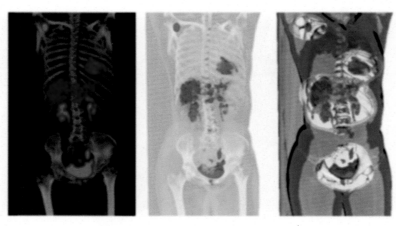

FIGURE 4.5

Comparison of rendering modes. MIP-based visualization, multi-volume rendering, lens-based focus+context visualization of PET/CT data (From: (Lawonn et al., 2015b), ©2015 The Author(s), Eurographics Proceedings, ©The Eurographics Association).

visual clutter and make depth and shape perception challenging. Ghosted view techniques attempt to remedy this limitation by varying the transparency according to object properties. Two main categories are smart transparency techniques and interactive approaches. Smart transparency (Carnecky et al., 2012) employs varying transparency based on surface curvature or normal vector information. For example, if the surface is nearly planar, it can be more transparent, and if curvature varies, it can be more opaque. This de-emphasizes similar regions and emphasizes regions where the shape changes.

For multimodal medical visualization, ghosted views can play a key role in removing emphasis from less important structures in one or more modalities. In combined anatomical and functional information visualization, ghosted views can be employed on anatomical structures, such that they do not occlude the view on functional information, while still providing spatial context. The main challenge is to develop a transparency management technique that is not disturbing, but still provides as much morphological context information as possible without occlusion.

Focus+Context

visualization, as the name implies, illustrates a focus object so that it is clearly perceivable, while simultaneously illustrating surrounding context structures, without distracting from the focus structure. This can be achieved by applying different shading techniques for focus and context structures. For such techniques, at least the focus object needs to be segmented. There is a wide range of possible techniques, varying from using unsaturated colors for context shading, to different shading methods per object class, to even varying entire rendering styles. Illustrative visualization techniques (recall Chapter 2) can play an essential role in emphasizing or de-emphasizing structures. Line drawing techniques in particular can be useful in the context of multimodal medical visualization.

There is no clear distinction between smart visibility and focus-and-context techniques. In our view, focus-and-context visualization techniques can be seen as a subcategory within the broader area of smart visibility approaches. The primary goal of all smart visibility techniques is to reveal interesting regions or objects, but this goal may also be achieved by enriching 3D visualization with 2D image planes. In such a case, there is no real focus object, though it is still a smart visibility technique. We conclude that focus-and-context techniques are part of this larger class of smart visibility techniques, which includes cutaways, ghosted views, exploded views, and techniques without focus objects.

One example of a such techniques applied to medical data is the work by Tietjen et al. (2006), who combined slice-based visualization with 3D illustrative techniques to reveal lymph nodes and vascular structures. This can be extended to a multimodal context by using different visualization techniques for each imaging modality. For example, a slice of CT or MRI data enhanced with segmentation contours can be integrated in a 3D SPECT or PET data. In general, different rendering techniques can be combined to show complementary information from multiple sources. As an example, Abellán et al. (2013) showcases different levels of multimodal information fusion combining anatomical and functional information from different imaging modalities. For a general overview of focus-and-context approaches, we refer to Bruckner et al. (2010).

Lens-based visualization

It is also possible to implement focus-and-context techniques as an interaction technique through the use of so-called *magic lenses*, which can be interactively placed to examine structures of interest. Here, the region within the lens is a focus area, whereas the area outside the lens serves as context. One example of such an application is to see through objects with the lens and reveal hidden structures within. There is a wide range of application areas for this technique, for example, showing the whole body outside the lens and revealing inner organs within the lens, or visualizing blood flow inside a lens. Multiple lenses may also be mirrored with linked interaction to compare the structures across its symmetry axes. In multimodal scenarios, lenses can be employed to control which modality is displayed, i.e., displaying one modality inside the lens and another modality outside.

Focus+Context techniques can be applied to multimodal data in two main ways:

- A spatial region of interest may be specified, which consists of all modalities as a focus area, whereas structures outside this area are rendered as context.
- One modality is assigned more importance to be the focus data set, whereas an additional modality is rendered as context.

For both approaches, suitable rendering techniques strongly depend on the application. We illustrate this with an example of tumor and vascular visualization. If a physician is interested in proximity of vascular structures to a tumor, an illustrative style only displaying the outline of the vascular extent could be sufficient. However, if a physician is interested in planning liver tumor surgery, it is very important to render in detail the spatial impression and shape of the liver.

4.4.3 Summary

Visual information is perceived based on different visual channels, such as for example color or orientation. Information can be perceived simultaneously if it is encoded in different channels. Multimodal visualization can benefit from this property by combining visualization techniques that can easily be perceived simultaneously, for instance displaying one modality in color and the other modality as a line drawing. This property is also leveraged in standard PET/CT visualization, where CT is displayed in a grayscale colormap, and PET is displayed as a color overlay.

To visualize multiple modalities in an integrated fashion, smart visibility techniques are crucial to avoid visual clutter and occlusion. The visualization designer needs to determine which of the modalities has priority, i.e., being the focus modality, and which serves as context. Potential indicators of importance for a data set are size and resolution, which can provide a hint as to which data set is best used for anatomical detail. Another decision needs to be made on what rendering styles are suitable to show focus, likely involving more detail, and context modalities. There may also be situations where both volumes have equal importance, for example, CT and MRI. Here, it may be more appropriate to emphasize regional areas as a focus region for both modalities. Visualization techniques that have been developed with a single modality in mind can be extended to multimodal scenarios, but require careful consideration of the application area requirements. Potentially, extensions of existing techniques are needed to fully support the multimodal visualization application.

4.5 Rendering and interaction techniques

In this section, we discuss rendering and interaction techniques for multiple or fused volumes. First, we discuss image fusion, which is a prerequisite for rendering multiple volumes together. After this, we discuss interaction techniques that are designed for use with multimodal medical data, including clipping and specialized transfer functions.

4.5.1 Fusion

Several techniques have been developed for medical image fusion in particular. Gupta et al. (2008) proposed a measure to evaluate PET/MRI data fusion. They proposed an entropy measure to determine which are the most interesting parts in PET and MRI data, and additionally applied this to a CT and MRI combination. Subsequently, Bramon et al. (2012) proposed a method for multimodal data fusion based on mutual information, and demonstrated their technique on CT, MRI, and PET data. This framework selects the most informative voxels from two volume and fuses the volumes in this way before rendering. Their evaluation with medical expert revealed that this approach could be useful for radiotherapy planning, treatment monitoring, and neurosurgical planning. Their method allowed for good differentiation between brain and bone tissue, as well as structural and functional information. Kim et al. (2016) proposed a slab-based intermixing method for fusion rendering of multiple medical objects. A more extensive discussion on medical image fusion can be found in the surveys by James and Dasarathy (2014) and Galande and Patil (2013).

4.5.2 Rendering techniques

Visualization of multimodal data does not only pose visualization design challenges, it also presents technical challenges in terms of efficient rendering of multiple volumes. Already in the 1980s, volume rendering for multimodal medical imaging data became technically possible. Though Drebin et al. (1988) and Levoy (1988) are often cited as the developers of the first volume rendering approach, Höhne and Bernstein (1986) were the first to perform volume rendering on a CT volume. Höhne et al. (1988) were also the first to develop a multiparametric rendering technique, which combined MRI with magnetic resonance angiography (MRA) to visualize vascular information (see Fig. 4.6).

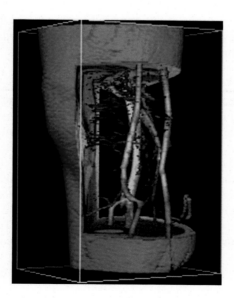

FIGURE 4.6

First multimodal volume rendering technique by Höhne et al. visualizing vascular MRA and anatomical MRI data simultaneously (From: (Höhne et al., 1988)).

There are multiple ways to mix volumes during rendering. Cai and Sakas (1999) presented seminal work on achieving a reasonable mix of opacity, color, and illumination during rendering of multiple volumes. They defined three levels of volume intermixing:

- Illumination model level intermixing
- Accumulation level intermixing
- Image level intermixing

Illumination model level intermixing

involves calculating opacity and intensity at each sample point directly from a multivolume illumination model. This avoids having to mix several opacity and intensity values. This is the most complex volume intermixing to achieve, and it leads to the most realistic results.

Accumulation level intermixing

relies on mixing opacities and intensities from different volumes during ray sample accumulation. This requires changes to the rendering pipeline, which can lead to time-consuming processes, but a benefit of this technique is that it provides correct depth cues.

Image level intermixing

The easiest way to achieve multiple volume rendering is *image level intermixing*. In this approach, two volumes are rendered independently and the image results are merged at the pixel level. This avoids having to change the rendering pipeline at the cost of incorrect depth cues.

Examples

In the following, we provide some examples of rendering techniques specifically aimed at multimodal data. Wilson et al. (2002) proposed a visualization approach to depict several image modalities simultaneously in different rendering styles at interactive framerates. One of the case studies in their paper presents the results of applying their technique on PET/MR small animal imaging. Ferre et al. (2004) proposed strategies for direct multimodal volume rendering (DMVR) and described at which steps of the rendering pipeline data fusion must take place for desired outcomes. They proposed a requirement analysis and outline five rendering methods: property-, property and gradient-, material-, shading-, and color fusion. They showcased their approach on SPECT/MR data and evaluated suitability of these five methods for this data.

Hong et al. (2005) proposed a technique to render multimodal volumes that solves depth cue issues in a time-efficient way. Their results demonstrated that depth of overlapping regions remains distinguishable based on *high-level shader language (HSLS)* for efficient volume fusion. They evaluated the performance of their method on PET and CT images.

Brecheisen et al. (2008) proposed a framework to render multiple volumes and used depth peeling combined with an arbitrary number of geometric shape intersections and demonstrated the capabilities of this framework on multimodal brain data.

Schubert and Scholl (2011) did a performance and perceptual comparison of multi-volume ray casting techniques, as well as provided an overview of visualization techniques, which employ data intermixing approaches and direct volume rendering methods, which employ raycasting. They added a fourth level to the three levels defined by Cai and Sakas (1999), which they describe as *classification level intermixing*. In such intermixing, volumes are mixed by a linear combination of sample values at the very start of the rendering pipeline. Sunden et al. (2015) introduced a volume illumination technique specifically designed for multimodal volume rendering. Their light-space-based algorithm employs illumination-importance metrics to compress multimodal data into an illumination-aware representation. They showcased their method on CT and MRI data and evaluated quality and performance. A more complete overview of large-scale volume visualization techniques can be found in the state-of-the-art report by Beyer et al. (2015).

4.5.3 Interaction techniques

In addition to techniques to render multimodal data, interaction techniques are also crucial to adjust which visible portions of the data set. For example, geometry-based clipping and cutting or attribute-based adjustment of transfer functions is possible, including intensity values, gradient magnitude, or curvature.

Clipping and cutting

Hastreiter and Ertl (1998) proposed to use clipping planes per volume to cut separate modalities in different ways. Their technique allowed to examine 2D slices and 3D visualization simultaneously and was demonstrated on the combination of CT and MR images. Using the same modalities, Fairfield et al. (2014) presented a so-called "curtaining" approach, which allows the user to define a clipping region in one modality, in which the other modality is revealed. Manssour et al. (2002) introduced a method to visualize inner structures in multimodal volume data by employing cutting and data intermixing. They demonstrated their approach on the skull, where cutting planes were employed to analyze the brain. Weiskopf et al. (2002) presented a more advanced clipping approach via per-fragment operations in texture-based volume visualization. Even though their approach was applied to a single modality, subsequently it was successfully used to do atlas-based clipping of a brain data set, which includes fMRI data by Rößler et al. (2006). Birkeland et al. (2012) proposed a *membrane clipping* approach that avoids cutting through data features. This technique features slab rendering as a trade-off between slice-based viewing and 3D rendering. Stoppel and Bruckner (2018) presented a technique to clip a volume based on smart surrogate widgets, which consists of linked spheres that are easy to specify and fit to anatomy. Though these techniques were not employed on multimodal data in particular, they have great potential to be used as such.

Transfer functions

When visualizing data from multiple volumes via direct volume rendering, occlusion issues likely occur. To remedy this, transfer functions (recall Section 3.4) can be employed to reduce the visibility of occluding elements. Transfer functions map data to optical properties, and the optical property that is essential to reduce occlusion problems is transparency. Thus the mapping is designed in such a way that essential information is either presented unoccluded or the occluding information is shown sufficiently transparent to enable the observation of the essential information.

Some transfer function designs are especially suitable for application in multimodal imaging data. Levoy (1988) introduced 2D transfer functions, which are essential in multimodal volume rendering as they allow for emphasis on boundaries. Kim et al. (2007c) focused on transfer function design for multimodal medical imaging data in particular by introducing a dual-lookup table for PET/CT data. This allows medical experts to set up separate transfer functions for every volume in a single view and allows for volume merging. Haidacher et al. (2008) proposed a more general information-based approach to transfer functions, which was successfully applied to PET/CT brain data. For a comprehensive survey on transfer functions for volumetric data, we refer to Ljung et al. (2016).

4.6 Selected applications

Though a detailed overview of multimodal medical visualization papers are presented in a previous survey by Lawonn et al. (2018a), we highlight selected examples here in a brief overview. Three main applications are

- medical research
- diagnosis
- treatment planning

Within those areas, diagnostic applications can be further subdivided into those aimed at the cardiovascular system and those aimed at oncology. Treatment planning and guidance is commonly found in neurosurgery and radiotherapy contexts. As radiotherapy is already covered in Chapter 8, we will omit this category from this overview.

Medical research

Multimodal medical visualization is often applied in a medical research context. In such a context, more often the images are acquired according to a consistent protocol, and there is more time to perform time-consuming tasks, such as image registration and/or segmentation than there is in clinical practice. An example of such research is the work by Rößler et al. (2006), which was previously mentioned. They described a GPU-based multi-volume rendering scheme that allows users to visualize an arbitrary number of volumes interactively for functional brain images. In particular, their tool was aimed at supporting cognitive neuroscientists in experimental studies and to communicate results to non-experts. To do this, they employ a template brain atlas to

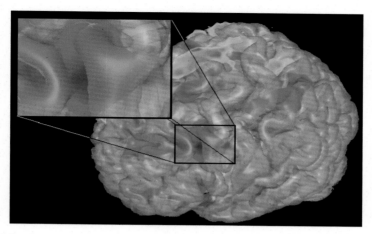

FIGURE 4.7

A non-polygonal isosurface revealing patient-specific functional information in anatomical context of a template brain (From: (Rößler et al., 2006).)

which patient-specific fMRI data is registered (see Fig. 4.7). Closely related to this application is the work by Nguyen et al. (2010). They proposed a technique to visualize and interact with real-time fMRI data in a neuroscience research context. Their key contribution is treating the fMRI signal as a light emission component and rendering it in the context of a patient-specific anatomical reference scan. The result is that the brain glows in active regions with only a 2-second delay from the measured fMRI signal.

Diagnosis

Not all multimodal medical imaging sequences are acquired for every patient in clinical practice, but some of the series are part of regular acquisition protocols. In some areas, however, such as oncology and cardiology, multimodal data is routinely acquired for the additional information it provides to aid diagnosis. In cardiology, essential diagnostic tasks include assessing plaque, heart infarction, heart valves, and congenital heart failure. Morphological information can be acquired through standard imaging modalities, but also functional information on wall motion and perfusion is important. The combination of perfusion data with other MR imaging modes is well explored in visualization research. The main challenge includes combining high-resolution anatomical imaging with potentially lower resolution perfusion data, which can be acquired through MRI or SPECT. As an example, Termeer et al. (2007) propose a visualization for the diagnosis of coronary artery disease based on cardiac perfusion MRI data. Their volume rendering version of a traditional bull's eye plot shows both how far scar tissue affects the wall, and s an anatomical perspective of the heart. This information is important to understand how infarction affects the heart and essential for prognosis and treatment. Hennemuth et al. (2008) developed an ap-

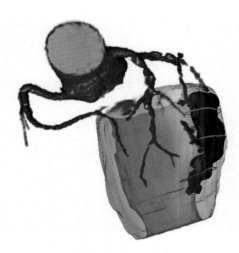

FIGURE 4.8

Integrated visualization revealing an infarcted area in dark blue, with hypo-perfused regions represented by contours. The myocardium is shown as a transparent colored surface that encodes the distance to the infarction (From: (Hennemuth, 2012)).

proach for the analysis of contrast-enhanced cardiac MR images. The approach (see Fig. 4.8) supports a full workflow to align different data sets, extract surfaces, and analyze the full multimodal information.

Treatment planning

In treatment planning, systems for neurosurgical interventions and radiotherapy (see Chapter 8) were a major focus of research. For neurosurgery, the identification of surgically relevant structures at risk for damage and the understanding of how these relate is the main focus. Such structures can be acquired from CT and various MRI protocols. For example, it is possible to identify functional areas in the gray matter and white matter fiber tracts in relation to a brain tumor or lesion. Neurosurgeons need to plan a safe access path to the lesion with the least amount of damage to vital functional areas and fiber tracts. Though often the focus is on brain tumor resection, applications aimed at deep brain stimulation (DBS) and arteriovenous malformations (AVM) surgery were also developed.

Another application for neurosurgery relates to brain tumor removal, (Rieder et al., 2008) presented a comprehensive approach to plan for the surgery based on fMRI and DTI data (see Fig. 4.9). The pathology is visualized using a distance-based transfer function to reveal functional data in close proximity to the lesion. For enhanced depth perception, they include a distance-ring to visualize how deep in the brain the lesion is from the current viewpoint. In addition, they provide an access path visualization and superficial landmarks that can be translated to the situation during the surgery.

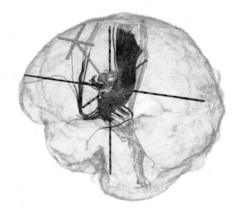

FIGURE 4.9

Path planning application for oncologic neurosurgery based on MRI, fMRI and DTI data (From: (Rieder et al., 2008), ©John Wiley & Sons Inc., 2008).

For most applications in multimodal imaging data visualization, qualitative evaluations with domain experts are presented, but quantitative evaluation and more elaborate clinical studies are often still needed before the techniques are ready for clinical practice.

4.7 **Concluding remarks**

Multimodal medical visualization is an active area of research. Initially, many technical contributions to *rendering techniques* paved the way for rendering multiple volumes interactively. By combining this with *smart visibility approaches*, such as focus-and-context techniques, ghosted views, and cutaways, it became possible to emphasize important information. This laid the important groundwork for medical applications building upon these techniques. Visualization research techniques and applications are rarely directly suitable for clinical translation, either due to time-consuming preprocessing steps, a steep learning curve, or lacking certification.

Multimodal visualization is not a solved research problem. With a further rise of data complexity, e.g., including time-varying, non-spatial, or cohort data, fully interactive visual techniques are no longer sufficient to address all analysis needs. For this, a combination of computational and visual approaches is needed, often referred to as visual data science. Furthermore, medical imaging data can be acquired at a large range of scales, from histopathology to full-body scans. Visualization of such multiscale data in a medical context poses an additional challenge. With the increase in the amount of data acquired and new modalities brought into clinical practice, multimodal medical visualization remains a promising research area for future developments.

If you are interested in contributing to research or learning more about this area, a wide variety of multimodal imaging data sets is openly available from the Cancer Imaging Archive.[1]

Recommended reading

The following selection comprises essential publications on multimodal medical visualization.

Johanna Beyer, Markus Hadwiger, Stefan Wolfsberger, and Katja Bühler. "High-quality multimodal volume rendering for preoperative planning of neurosurgical interventions," *IEEE Transactions on Visualization and Computer Graphics*, Vol. 13(6): 1696–1703, 2007.

Wenli Cai and Georgios Sakas. "Data intermixing and mulit-volume rendering," *Computer Graphics Forum*, Vol. 18(3), pp. 359–368, 1999.

Michael Burns, Martin Haidacher, Wolfgang Wein, Ivan Viola, and Eduard Gröller. "Feature emphasis and contextual cutaways for multimodal medical visualization," *Proc. of EuroVis*, pp. 275–282, 2007.

Martin Haidacher, Stefan Bruckner, Armin Kanitsar, and Eduard Gröller. "Information-based transfer functions for multimodal visualization," *Proc. of Eurographics Workshop on Visual Computing in Biology and Medicine*, pp. 101–108, 2008.

Kai Lawonn, Noeska N. Smit, Katja Bühler, and Bernhard Preim. "A survey on multimodal medical data visualization," *Computer Graphics Forum*, vol. 37(1): 413–438, 2018.

---

[1] https://www.cancerimagingarchive.net/.

Medical flow visualization

5

5.1 Introduction

Flow data describe the physical behavior of liquids or gases (medium) within a spatial environment (domain). Flow data appear in a variety of applications, for example, flows around vehicles, such as cars, airplanes, or ships, atmospheric flow for weather forecasting, or for describing dynamic systems. Accordingly, there are various goals to be achieved with the analysis of flow data, such as recognizing and understanding physical phenomena, modeling flow processes, optimizing technical designs, and searching for causes of damage.

Flow data are either measured with the help of specific equipment or simulated on the computer on the basis of mathematical models. Here, two categories of flow data are distinguished, which also influences the choice of visualization methods:

- static (time-independent)
- dynamic (time-dependent) flow data

Whereas static flow data describe only the spatial motion of the underlying medium within the domain, dynamic data contain a temporal component that encodes a spatio-temporally varying motion of the medium. A static example is flow of water in a pipe, where its velocity will change along the pipe toward the exit. An example of a dynamic flow is water that is pumped through a pipe by a pump, where the pump is switched off at a certain point in time. This leads to a temporal change of the flow behavior.

In medicine, there are two basic occurrences of flow data. First, flow data that describe the blood flow through the vessels, and second, flow data that are used to describe airflow inside the human respiratory system. In larger vessels, such as the aorta, blood flow can be measured, for example, with Doppler ultrasound or special MRI sequences. In smaller vessels, such as the cerebral arteries, or air-filled structures, such as the trachea, the spatial resolution would be insufficient for reliable flow measurements. Instead, flow is simulated, e.g., using computational fluid dynamics (CFD) due to the insufficient resolution of medical image modalities in such small structures. For both blood and air flows, steady and dynamic data can be generated describing the flow at a predefined time or over the entire cardiac/respiratory cycle. Though dynamic flow data are more realistic, steady data can be generated much faster; the results require much less memory, and are easier to study.

Visualization, Visual Analytics and Virtual Reality in Medicine. https://doi.org/10.1016/B978-0-12-822962-0.00012-2

The generation and analysis of medical flow data has considerable potential in personalized medicine for disease prevention, diagnosis, and treatment. The visual examination of blood flow data is motivated by research findings suggesting that the blood flow behavior changes in a characteristic way as a result of neurovascular diseases, such as aneurysms (Cebral et al., 2011b), or cardiovascular diseases, such as bicuspid aortic valves (Ebel et al., 2020). These diseases occur mainly in regions with complex (sometimes even turbulent) and unstable flow, which changes significantly over time. Similarly, flow characteristics change when the airways are blocked or deformed, e.g., by the presence of a tumor (Janović et al., 2020). Accordingly, on the basis of flow data, conclusions can be drawn regarding the initiation, progression, and severity of vascular and respiratory diseases.

Organization

We first provide necessary medical background information regarding hemo- and aerodynamics (Section 5.2). Then, we give an overview on how medical flow data are generated (Section 5.3). Here, we focus on measuring cardiac flow data and simulating cerebral and nasal flow data using CFD. We go on and describe general analysis tasks regarding the visual examination of flow data (Section 5.4). For each task, visualization methods are summarized to investigate cardiac blood flow related to diagnosis of cardiac diseases, simulated blood flow for treatment planning in cerebral aneurysms, and simulated nasal aerodynamics to understand the interplay between air flow changes and occurrence of nasal diseases. After discussing methods and techniques, we introduce selected medical flow analysis and visualization systems (Section 5.5). Finally, we summarize the main aspects of this chapter and provide further literature (Section 5.6).

5.2 Medical background of flow data generation

The investigation of hemodynamic and aerodynamic properties is important to improve the diagnosis and treatment of cerebro- and cardiovascular pathologies and diseases of the respiratory system. This chapter describes relationships between flow information and the occurrence of various vascular diseases that are important for understanding the following chapters.

5.2.1 Cerebral hemodynamics

Cerebrovascular diseases are pathological changes in the vessels of the brain. *Cerebral aneurysms* (also called intracranial or brain aneurysms) are local dilatations of the vessel wall and belong to the most common brain vessel diseases. The danger associated with cerebral aneurysms is a progressive weakening of the arterial wall until rupture of the aneurysm. This leads to an internal bleeding (*subarachnoid hemorrhage* (SAH)), which is associated with a high mortality and morbidity rate.

Frequently, aneurysms are discovered by chance due to the increased use of imaging procedures for assessing the patient's state in the case of widespread symptoms, e.g., persistent headaches. Most aneurysms are asymptomatic and will never rupture (Wermer et al., 2007). However, the detection of a cerebral aneurysm represents a severe dilemma; it has to be communicated to the patient and may induce anxiety. Treatment is often possible, but with a considerable risk of severe complications, which can exceed the risk of a natural rupture (Cebral et al., 2015).

A typical treatment is *stenting*, where a metal implant (stent) is inserted into the supporting vessel (parent vessel) of an aneurysm to stabilize the vessel wall. Often, additionally coils are inserted in the aneurysm to reduce the flow in the aneurysm, and thus the pressure on the wall. Cerebral aneurysms are difficult to treat due to the long and convoluted path the doctor has to navigate to place the stent into the parent vessel. Thus it is highly desirable to restrict treatment to high-risk patients.

Besides genetics, vessel morphology, and inflammation, hemodynamic changes cause aneurysm initiation, evolution, and rupture (Krings et al., 2011). Since, neither the hemodynamics nor the wall can directly be measured at a sufficiently high resolution, CFD simulations are carried out to model the aneurysm hemodynamics. For this purpose, geometrical models of the patient-specific vasculature are used as input for the simulation. Derived hemodynamic characteristics, comprising quantitative features, such as *wall shear stress* (WSS) or *pressure* and qualitative features, e.g., vortices seem to influence the aneurysm wall stability. In addition, the influence of different therapeutic options can be simulated and visually compared (Oeltze et al., 2014; van Pelt et al., 2014b).

5.2.2 Cardiac hemodynamics

Medical studies emphasize the essential role of patient-specific hemodynamics in the assessment of the cardiovascular system (Hope et al., 2012; Mahadevia et al., 2015). These studies aim to better understand the causes and progression of cardiovascular diseases (CVDs). There seems to be a strong correlation between the development and the severity of CVDs and characteristic blood flow patterns, such as vortices, where the flow rotates around a line (Hope et al., 2010). Much work focuses on pathological changes in the aorta, which is the largest vessel in the human body. Using 4D phase-contrast MRI (4D PC-MRI), patient-specific aortic hemodynamics can be measured non-invasively over the cardiac cycle (Dyverfeldt et al., 2015).

To better understand the interplay of morphological and hemodynamic aspects with respect to the development and progression of CVDs, medical studies are performed with homogeneous groups of patients. Depending on the pathology, occurring vortices are counted and classified according to certain characteristics, such as size, shape, phase of the cardiac cycle (systole/diastole), vascular segment of occurrence, and direction of rotation. Accordingly, e.g., patients with aortic aneurysm were frequently found to have distinct helical vortices in the ascending aorta, which are not found in healthy individuals, where the flow is basically laminar, i.e., without any vortices (Hope et al., 2007; Frydrychowicz et al., 2007). However, a particular vortex shape does not exclusively indicate a single pathology. Therefore current research is more interested in the *existence of vortices* in patient data and the correlation between pathologies and specific vortex shapes. Analysis of blood flow in terms of irregular flow patterns is important to understand their influence on the development and worsening of CVDs.

5.2.3 Nasal aerodynamics

Normal nasal breathing can only occur when the nasal airways are unobstructed, allowing air to flow freely. Common causes of restricted nasal airflow are diseases such as sinusitis or nasal polyps. Depending on the severity of the restriction, surgery may be required to restore normal airflow (Pallanch et al., 1985; Bui, 1997). Despite steady medical advances in the treatment of ear, nose, and throat (ENT) disorders, it is difficult for physicians to make a patient-specific prediction regarding the chance of success in establishing normal nasal airflow.

To analyze flow phenomena in the nose before and after surgery, several research groups have used CFD simulations of nasal airflow (Lindemann et al., 2006; Zachow et al., 2006). Complex flow information, such as pressure, velocity, the occurrence of turbulence, or the distribution of aerosols, can thus be modeled and studied at high spatio-temporal resolution. Such flow simulations are computed on patient-specific anatomy to reveal typical airflow patterns for healthy and pathologically altered airways and to determine the optimal functional shape of the entire nasal airway. By providing important flow information prior to surgery, CFD simulations can support decision-making for functional surgical rhinoplasty. In addition, CFD helps explore new approaches to drug delivery, such as nasal spray applicators.

5.3 Generation of medical flow data

The generation of medical flow data regarding cerebral aneurysm hemodynamics, aortic hemodynamics, and nasal aerodynamics consist of multiple steps, illustrated in Fig. 5.1. For a space-saving representation of all steps, the order of the applications has been swapped here. Each row represents an application, whereas each column shows an individual step of the pipeline. At the beginning, medical image data is acquired within each application. For the cardiac data, a reduction of artifacts follows that are a typical problem with 4D PC-MRI. Then, the relevant morphology is segmented based on the acquired image data, where a 3D surface of the anatomy is reconstructed from the segmentation mask. In addition, geometric features, such as the vessel centerline, are extracted in the case of cerebral and cardiac hemodynamics. Then, another simulation-specific step follows, where the enhanced surface mesh is transformed into a volume mesh as input for the subsequent CFD simulation. In the last step of all applications, aerodynamic or hemodynamic attributes are computed. In the following subsections, these steps are described in more detail, bearing on the commonalities and differences between the application areas.

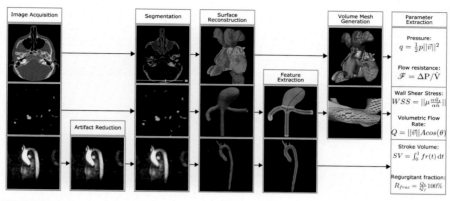

FIGURE 5.1

Flow data generation pipelines of nasal aerodynamics (top row), cerebral aneurysm hemo-dynamics (middle), and aortic hemodynamics (bottom). The surface enhancement and the CFD simulation are not depicted (From: (Oeltze-Jafra et al., 2019), ©John Wiley & Sons Inc., 2019).

5.3.1 Medical image acquisition

Patient-specific simulations of blood and air flow require as input a high-quality 3D geometry of the associated anatomy. The basis for reconstructing this geometry is medical image data representing the target structure in high resolution. As a basis for blood flow simulations, angiography data is often used, where vessels can be clearly separated from surrounding tissue. For nasal simulations, CT data are used, because air and bone can be separated well. In contrast, cardiac hemodynamics can be measured directly with an imaging technique, which also allows extraction of the 3D vessel geometry to represent the data.

Cerebral aneurysm hemodynamics

Cerebral vessels and associated pathologies can be assessed with MRI, CT, 3D rotational angiography (3DRA), and 2D digital subtraction angiography (DSA). In CT and MR, a contrast agent is administered to the patient to visualize the vessels resulting in CT angiography (CTA) and MR angiography (MRA). Another option is to use time-of-flight (ToF) MR sequences, resulting in non-contrast bright blood imaging of vessels and cerebral aneurysms. CTA has a short acquisition time but requires a lot of contrast agent, which is often not applicable in patients with decreased renal function. In contrast, MRA takes a comparatively long time, which is problematic in emergency patients. Whereas MRA and CTA are non-invasive, 3DRA and DSA images require invasive catheter-based delivery of contrast agent. The basis for 3DRA is CT, so a 3D model of the vessel geometry can be reconstructed directly from the images. DSA—the gold standard for cerebral aneurysm imaging—is a 2D X-ray-based technique that produces images with high spatial and temporal resolution. Only the vessel lumen is imaged in these modalities. Information about the nature of the vessel wall, such as inflammation, as well as specific properties, such as wall thickness cannot be acquired (see Fig. 5.2).

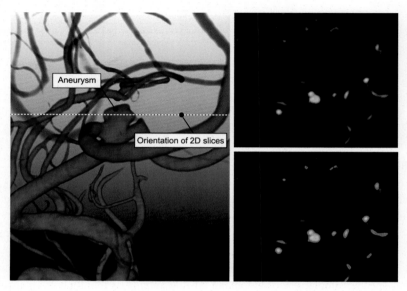

FIGURE 5.2

3D view of a cerebral aneurysm and the surrounding vascular tree based on 3DRA (left). Contrast-enhanced vessels (top right) allow the vascular tree to be extracted with threshold-based segmentation (bottom right) (From: (Oeltze-Jafra et al., 2019), ©John Wiley & Sons Inc., 2019).

Cardiac hemodynamics

In larger vessels, such as the aorta, patient-specific blood flow can be measured using PC-MRI. Basically, in this method, the activation of a main magnetic field leads to the alignment of all protons in the hydrogen atoms of the vessels and in the surrounding tissue. Additional bipolar magnetic field gradients cause a position-dependent phase shift of the protons, which is more pronounced in vessels with flowing blood than in surrounding tissue, providing a signal-rich representation of blood flow. The measured phase differences correlate with the flow velocity and lead to a high signal intensity of the blood flow. In clinical routine, 2D PC-MRI measurements are mostly performed with parameters such as flow rates, flow velocities, or blood pumped per heartbeat, which can be analyzed in a 2D plane. Compared to 4D PC-MRI, these 2D measurements are much faster, but also highly dependent on the inclination of the selected plane.

A 4D PC-MRI data set consists of three-phase and magnitude images, one each for the x-, y-, and z-dimension. The phase images contain the flow directions and flow magnitudes and are calculated from the phase differences. The magnitude images are reconstructed from the signal intensities and contain only the flow strengths. A measurement consists of multiple time points and spans a complete cardiac cycle with systole and diastole. A typical resolution of a 4D PC-MRI data set is 150×200 voxels in each slice, with 1.5–2.5 mm spacing between two data points for about 20–50 slices. Between 15–40 time steps are acquired, with 20–50 ms spacing each. Unlike 2D measurements, 4D PC-MRI allows for the detection of suspicious flow patterns, such as eddy currents and monitoring them over the cardiac cycle, thus offering the potential to significantly improve the diagnosis and assessment of cardiovascular disease.

Nasal aerodynamics

In clinical practice, anatomical changes in the airways are usually assessed with the aid of endoscopic imaging procedures. However, this examination method is quite time-consuming and smaller cavities are difficult to view with an endoscope. In addition, factors such as varying illumination, reflections, and close distance between the camera and the anatomy result in poor quality 3D reconstructions of the airway from these image data. In contrast, 3D models with high spatial resolution can be reconstructed from CT images of the airways. However, the disadvantage of using CT is the ionizing radiation. In comparison, MRI does not involve radiation exposure. However, structures such as bones and air-filled spaces can be poorly distinguished in MRI data, which negatively affects the reconstruction of 3D models. Therefore CT is the method of choice to create patient-specific 3D models of the airway for CFD simulation.

5.3.2 **Correction of imaging artifacts**

PC-MRI data can contain various image artifacts (Köhler et al., 2017).

Eddy currents

in the electromagnetic field create a slowly changing spatial and temporal gradient that is added to the phase images. This is also known as velocity offset and can be automatically corrected in the image data (Lorenz et al., 2014).

Phase wraps

are other artifacts in 4D PC-MRI data. When measuring flow velocities, the velocity encoding (VENC) specifies the maximum measurable velocity per direction. The higher the VENC selected, the greater the loss of contrast in the data. Ideally, the VENC is chosen such that areas with high flow velocities are still correctly captured, but the data still contain as much contrast as possible. A typical value for measurements of the aorta is 1.5 m/s (Markl et al., 2012). If the VENC is exceeded, *phase wraps* occur. In this case, the measured value is mapped to the other end of the value range. Phase unwrapping algorithms attempt to find and correct for such regions (Díaz and Robles, 2004). An important assumption for a successful phase unwrapping is that pixels adjacent to the artifact do not differ in their value more than the adjusted VENC. This is necessary, because phase unwrapping algorithms work similarly to a median filter, and otherwise no correct filtering of the damaged pixels would be possible.

Uncorrelated noise

is a third type of artifact that is caused by air outside the human body or directly adjacent to the aorta in the lungs. Noise masking techniques use a threshold to select and remove air-filled regions (Bock, 2012). The threshold can be set either interactively or by a heuristic. The resulting mask is multiplied by the flow field to remove air-filled regions.

Divergence

in the flow data results from the measurement errors described. Since blood is an incompressible fluid, it should be divergence-free. Therefore there are various techniques for filtering divergence components (Sereno et al., 2018). The basic idea is to regulate the flow field by taking into account physical properties, such as its curvature, divergence, or the rotational behavior.

5.3.3 Image segmentation

The use of contrast agents in imaging often allows intensity-based methods to be used to segment vessels. The greater motion of cardiac vessels induced by the heartbeat complicates their segmentation and requires individual segmentation per time step of the cardiac cycle. Problems with segmentation of the nasal cavities arise from small, closely spaced structures that are not adequately imaged due to insufficient resolution of the imaging modalities. Advanced approaches are needed to correctly segment the anatomical structures.

Cerebral hemodynamics

Numerous methods exist for the segmentation of cerebral vessels (Kandil et al., 2018). Simple approaches, such as thresholding and region growing, rely on the intensity values of the image data and generate a binary voxel mask. However, they are prone to image artifacts, such as inhomogeneous signal intensity distributions or blending, due to the partial volume effect. More advanced approaches, such as active contours or level-set segmentations, deform a 2D contour or 3D surface as a result of various forces derived from the image data, such as gradient information and curvature. These methods are more robust against image artifacts and generate a subvoxel segmentation, which makes a subsequent surface extraction obsolete. However, they are more computationally intensive and difficult to parameterize.

Cardiac hemodynamics

For cardiac vessel segmentation intensity-based methods, such as region growing or watershed transforms on a PC-MRA image, or graph-based methods, such as graph cut on temporal maximum intensity projection images (MIP) can be used. A temporal

MIP is a 3D volume, where every voxel represents the highest intensity over all time steps. Thus in a temporal MIP, vessels are emphasized, and thus easier to segment. Also model-based methods, such as deformable surfaces on temporal maximum intensity projection images were employed. Unlike in the cerebral region, vessels near the heart deform a lot. Therefore segmentation approaches must segment vessels not only during a single time step, but over the entire cardiac cycle. One way to do this is to use interactive segmentation methods, such as the modified graph-cut algorithm of Köhler et al. (2016a) to segment the vessel surface over time.

Nasal aerodynamics

Similar to cerebral vessels, intensity-based methods can be used to segment the air-filled structures in the head region. At best, a contiguous region representing the nasal airways from the nostrils to the trachea can be detected. However, even here, image artifacts and partial volume effects negatively affect segmentation results and entail costly manual post-processing. Amira supports segmentation of nasal cavities by using deformable models (Stalling et al., 2005). The segmentation results in labeled image data, where each voxel is associated with a specific structure of the nasal airway, such as trachea and pharynx.

5.3.4 Surface reconstruction and enhancement

For the reconstruction of a surface model based on the generated segmentation mask, similar approaches can be used for cerebral and cardiac vessels. For the nasal airways, special methods are needed to reconstruct the closely spaced structures. Basically, the goal is to generate a high-quality surface model for the simulation in cerebral vessels and nasal airways, which is especially important for the simulation in cerebral vessels and nasal airways. Usually, in a post-processing step, methods are used to improve the surface triangles to keep the number of triangles as low as possible, although the triangles should be equilateral.

Cerebral and cardiac hemodynamics

Basically, methods for reconstructing the vessel surface from a segmentation mask can be divided into *model-based* and *model-free* approaches [PO08]. Model-based approaches usually assume simplifications of the vessel shape, such as a circular cross-section. In contrast, model-free approaches usually map the data more accurately. One of the simplest approaches is to directly apply the marching cubes algorithm (Lorensen and Cline, 1987) to the binary segmentation mask. However, staircase artifacts on the surface are problematic. To reduce these artifacts, geometric filters can be applied with the goal of preserving the features of the surface. More sophisticated model-free approaches derive an implicit surface description based on local properties of the segmentation mask. Implicitly defined cross-sectional contours along the vessel centerline are used to generate a smooth surface description of vessels (Kretschmer et al., 2013).

Nasal aerodynamics

The reconstruction of the separating boundaries of the nasal airways requires non-binary segmentation masks to represent the fine internal structures. Based on such a segmentation mask, generalizations of the marching cubes algorithm may be employed for the surface reconstruction. Generalized marching cubes is quite complex since many different configurations exist when three different materials share a voxel instead of only two (Hege et al., 1997).

The resulting polygonal surfaces typically consist of several millions of triangles. Therefore remeshing algorithms are subsequently applied to reduce the number of triangles, while maintaining topological properties (Zilske et al., 2008).

5.3.5 Feature extraction

Geometric features, such as the vessel centerline are primarily determined to focus visual exploration and analysis of flow data on specific anatomical regions. Antiga et al. (2003) introduced a widely used approach to extract the vessel centerline. They serve as initial geometry for seeding integral curves in the flow field (van Pelt et al., 2011), or for generating sectional planes perpendicular to the flow direction (Lawonn et al., 2016). Though geometric features, apart from the centerline, have so far played a minor role in the exploration of cardiac and nasal flows, much research has focused on the extraction of geometric and hemodynamic features of cerebral aneurysms to better understand their growth and rupture. A brief summary of important features follows.

To automatically determine these parameters, the aneurysm must first be detected and separated from the healthy parent vessel. In recent years, numerous semi-automatic approaches have been developed to find the interface between the aneurysm and the parent vessel, the so-called *ostium*. Since the results of these methods are highly dependent on user input, automatic methods have recently been developed that, based on machine learning, can reliably detect the ostium, and thus any aneurysms present (Lawonn et al., 2019).

Based on the ostium, other morphological features can be determined automatically that provide information about the aneurysm anatomy and the anatomical relationship to the parent vessel (Meuschke et al., 2018b; Mittenentzwei et al., 2021). Typical features include the height, width, diameter of the aneurysm, and the relationship between aneurysm diameter and the diameter of the parent vessel. The ANEULYSIS system supports the whole workflow of extracting morphological descriptors and provides support for an analysis of a cohort of aneurysm datasets (Meuschke et al., 2021a).

5.3.6 Generation of volume mesh

For numerical simulations, such as CFD, the entire surface model must be transformed into a volumetric mesh. To obtain valid simulation results, the generated volume mesh must meet several requirements. A volume grid must be continuous and must not overlap.

- The volume elements should not be highly distorted.
- The volume elements should have rather equal angles.
- Very low angles are associated with sliver-shaped grid cells that may lead to very high numerical errors.

Within the mesh, the sizes of the elements should be able to vary to adapt to local details, while the size of adjacent elements should be similar. Often, unstructured tetrahedral meshes are used to fulfill these requirements (see Fig. 5.3). They are particularly well suited for complex geometries and can be generated efficiently and robustly. Moreover, they can be adaptively refined by using a user- or algorithmically defined size field (Lamecker et al., 2009).

The choice of a suitable mesh resolution depends on various criteria. Usually, a trade-off between computational effort and accuracy is required. The size of the smallest mesh elements is determined by the smallest considered features of the geometry and the flow, e.g., the smallest vortices. However, the finite resolution leads to a discretization error during the simulation. To keep this as small as possible, several simulations with different resolutions can be calculated to achieve a so-called *grid-independent* solution.

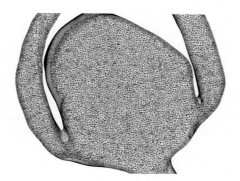

FIGURE 5.3

Volume mesh generation of an cerebral aneurysm. Within the aneurysm, tetrahedral volume cells are used, where the aneurysm wall is modeled by multiple prism layers.

Cerebral hemodynamics

In addition to discretizing the vessel section to be simulated, in the case of cerebral aneurysms, additional unstructured grids can be integrated to represent medical implants (coils, stents), which may be inserted into the aneurysm or parent vessel to stop blood flow into the aneurysm. Since the resolution of the entire mesh is determined by the finest geometric detail, grids for the simulation of treatment options are finer resolved than untreated cases.

Nasal aerodynamics

Due to the complexity of the nasal airway, creating a high-quality volumetric mesh that represents the involved anatomical structures faithfully, is challenging. A suitable approach for this is the advancing front algorithm, which can deal with complicated edges and internal interfaces (Löhner, 1996). Here, it is also possible to vary the size of the elements.

In addition to the tetrahedral meshes for the enclosed flow regions, dense layers of prism elements are generated at the interfaces between air and mucosa and air and skin. This allows physical changes at the interfaces, such as changes in air velocity at the mucosal walls, to be simulated. Subsequently, the mesh is optimized with respect to dihedral angles and tetrahedral aspect ratios (Zachow et al., 2009). The former smoothes the mesh (reducing strong differences in the surface orientation of adjacent elements). The latter avoids the low angles and associated slivers already discussed.

5.3.7 CFD simulation

In the following, we provide a short introduction into CFD (for more information, please refer to the textbooks (Kleinstreuer, 2016; Zikanov, 2019)).

The motion of viscous, heat conducting fluids in a volume is described by three equations:

- the continuity equation (conservation of mass)
- the Navier–Stokes equations (NSEs) (conservation of momentum; three equations)
- the energy equation (conservation of energy)

The NSEs establish a relationship between the velocity, pressure, density, and dynamic viscosity of the fluid. Add to these five equations a thermodynamic relationship for conservation of energy and the equation of state for conservation of mass, and you have seven equations with seven unknowns. For solving these coupled non-linear partial differential equations (PDE), boundary conditions must be specified for the boundaries of the domain, such as inlets, outlets, and walls. Once these conditions are established, the equations can be solved numerically. For this purpose, the equations are discretized to find a solution for each cell of the generated volume mesh. Thus the desired physical quantities, such as the time-dependent flow velocity and pressure, can be predicted.

Cerebral hemodynamics

CFD simulations usually model blood as a fluid with constant density and viscosity, a so-called *incompressible Newtonian fluid*. Although this does not correspond to the physical properties of blood, this simplification has no relevant impact on accuracy and significantly speeds up computation (Sforza et al., 2009).

Boundary conditions include pressure profiles at incoming and outgoing vessels, a velocity profile over the cardiac cycle, and a slip-free boundary, i.e., zero velocity at the boundary (e.g., the vessel wall). For blood flow simulations in smaller vessels remote from the heart (such as vessels in the head), the vessel wall is typically assumed to be rigid. A cardiac cycle is typically simulated with a temporal resolution of 0.0025–0.005 s, resulting in a 3D velocity vector field in each of the 200–400 time steps (Gasteiger, 2014).

Nasal aerodynamics

Typically, CFD simulations of the nasal airway assume incompressible flow. In addition, a transport equation for water vapor is integrated to model the humidification of the nasal airflow (Menter, 1994). Diffusion and convection are considered within the entire domain, including the mucosal walls, to represent both the moisture loading of the nasal mucosa and its moisture transfer to the breathing air.

Basis for the definition of patient-specific boundary conditions for the CFD simulation are measurements of air resistance during breathing through the nose (Zachow et al., 2009). In addition, approximate values for ambient pressure, density and dynamic viscosity of air, ambient air temperature, skin and body temperature, ambient relative humidity, and mucosal wall humidity are assumed as boundary conditions.

5.3.8 Parameter extraction

Various characteristics can be derived from CFD simulation results and the measured 4D PC MRI data. These can be divided into hemodynamic/aerodynamic properties, describing the flow field and wall properties, e.g., vessel/mucous wall. In what follows, we describe the most common characteristics used in CFD or flow imaging to investigate medical flow data.

Cerebral flow simulation

In cerebral aneurysms, hemodynamic and wall characteristics are analyzed to better understand the patient-specific rupture risk and to derive an optimal treatment strategy.

Hemodynamic parameters

Derived hemodynamic characteristics can be divided into *quantitative* parameters, defined per vertex or volume element of the domain, and *qualitative* structures, such as vortex flow derived using flow visualization techniques, or directly computed using feature extraction techniques. Both, quantitative and qualitative parameters play an important role in the analysis of ruptured and unruptured cerebral aneurysms (Cebral et al., 2011a,b).

Quantitative parameters are numeric values directly derived from the underlying flow field. The most common parameters are the following:

- **Velocity** encodes flow direction and speed per grid point and time step by a vector $\vec{v}$.
- **Fluid pressure** q is the scalar kinetic energy per unit volume of a fluid particle. It is calculated per grid point and time step.

- **Wall shear stress (WSS)** encodes the force tangential to the vessel wall exerted by the blood flowing past. It is computed for each time step at grid points along the wall as the scalar magnitude of the corresponding WSS vector $\vec{\tau}_{WSS}$.
- **Oscillatory shear index (OSI)** indicates flow disruption by the time average strength of temporal deflection of $\vec{\tau}_{WSS}$ from the time-averaged WSS vector.
- **Turnover time** ToT encodes the average elapsed time of a blood flow particle from entering to leaving a particular vascular region. A high ToT value for the aneurysm region indicates slow flow, which promotes thrombus formation.

Qualitative hemodynamic parameters describe structures and properties of the blood flow pattern. They are often derived by means of standard flow visualizations techniques, such as integral curves, colored cut planes, and line integral convolution (LIC) (Cabral and Leedom, 1993):

- **Vortices** represent regions of flow swirling around a straight or curved axis, which is also referred to as *vortex core line*. They are very frequently observed in cerebral aneurysms (Oeltze-Jafra et al., 2016).
- **Recirculation** occurs when a forward blood flow reverses and flows backward. The links with aneurysm growth and rupture have been studied but are still incompletely understood (Shojima et al., 2004; Tanoue et al., 2011).
- **Inflow jet and impingement zone** refer to the structure of the high-speed, parallel inflow into an aneurysm and the associated wall area of first impingement. In a large study, ruptured aneurysms showed a more concentrated inflow jet and a rather small impact zone compared with non-ruptured aneurysms (Cebral et al., 2011b).
- **Flow type** can be *laminar* or *turbulent*. In laminar flow, particles move mostly parallel or in a swirling motion along a common axis (vortices), whereas in turbulent flow, chaotic property changes are observed.
- **Flow complexity and stability** describe the number of vortices in an aneurysm and their persistence over the cardiac cycle. If only one vortex exists, the flow is characterized as *simple*. If this vortex neither moves nor collapses and reappears over time, the flow is described as *stable*. Simple and stable flow patterns occurred more frequently in unruptured aneurysms, whereas complex and unstable patterns were mostly observed in ruptured aneurysms (Cebral et al., 2011b; Byrne et al., 2014).

Cardiac flow measurement

Similar to cerebral blood flow analysis, wall and hemodynamic properties play an important role to examine the heart function and to investigate the emergence and progress of cardiovascular diseases.

Hemodynamic parameters

Köhler et al. (2017) provide an extensive overview of hemodynamic parameters relevant for assessing aortic blood flow. Most of the parameters extracted from cerebral simulations are also relevant in the cardiac domain, e.g., vortices (Köhler et al., 2013) or blood flow jets (Köhler et al., 2018). However, OSI and impingement zone seem to receive little attention. Other parameters are specific to the cardiac domain:

- **Regurgitation fraction (RF)** refers to the abnormal return of blood, e.g., from the aorta through the aortic valve into the left ventricle. It is measured in a cross-section directly above the pulmonary or aortic valve.
- **Stroke volume (SV)** indicates the amount of blood pumped per heartbeat by one of the heart's two chambers. It is also measured in a cross-section directly above the pulmonary or aortic valve.

Wall properties

The in-vivo investigation of aortic wall properties is currently very limited due to lack of a non-invasive imaging technique that is capable of depicting the aortic wall. The aortic deformation as a result of the heartbeat can be derived from 4D PC-MRI data (Lantz et al., 2014; Köhler et al., 2016b). For this purpose, the aorta has to be segmented in 4D PC-MRI data over time. Also, a surface correspondence must be established across time steps to derive the displacement vectors that describe the direction and magnitude of the deformation.

Nasal flow simulation

From nasal simulations, properties regarding the aerodynamic and mucous wall are derived to investigate differences between normal breathing and changes due to pathological processes.

Aerodynamic parameters

The simulation of several breathing cycles yields a set of aerodynamic parameters being exported (Zachow et al., 2009). Though most of the parameters extracted from cerebral simulations are also relevant in the nasal domain OSI, inflow jet and impingement zone do not receive special attention. Other parameters are specific to studying nasal airflow phenomena:

- **Air temperature (T/t)** is a measure of heat or cold, per grid point and time step.
- **Humidity (H)** describes the relative amount of water vapor in the air for each grid point computed per time step.

Wall properties

Besides nasal resistance, the mucous walls and the nasal secretion play an important role in physiological nasal airflow (Hildebrandt et al., 2013a). Wall shear stresses appear to induce an important interaction between airflow and the epithelial lining fluid of the nose. This leads to a mechanical and biological fluid-structure interaction (Hildebrandt et al., 2013b). While wall shear stresses on mucous walls seem to be important for nasal diagnostics, the in-vivo investigation of mucous wall properties is still very limited due to a lack of a non-invasive imaging techniques.

5.4 Task-based visual analysis of medical flow data

Numerous visualization techniques exist to support visual exploration and analysis of flow data. Oeltze-Jafra et al. (2019) have analyzed such techniques and derived tasks that are fundamental to the analysis of flow data and influence the design of visualization techniques:

- Spatial overview
- Interactive probing
- Feature filtering
- Temporal analysis
- Comparison
- Validation
- Uncertainty analysis

Moreover, they distinguish three spatial areas in which the respective techniques are specialized. Visualization techniques can support the visual analysis of flow features:

- in the vessel lumen or nasal cavity
- on vessel wall or mucous wall
- simultaneously in the vessel lumen+vessel wall or nasal cavity+mucous wall

The first two spatial areas require quite different visualization approaches, as a lumen-based analysis is based on a volume grid, and the vessel wall or mucous wall is defined by a surface mesh. More advanced methods are still required for simultaneous exploration of both structures.

Spatial overview

Due to the complexity of medical flow data, their exploration usually begins with an overview of hemodynamics and wall properties over the entire domain. This gives the user initial insight into the overall flow structure, which is critical for a subsequent detailed assessment of regions with prominent flow and wall properties, as well as of correlation between different flow attributes and wall properties. Basic challenges for overview visualizations are a clear representation of multiple data attributes and the reduction of occlusion problems in 3D.

Interactive probing

Once an overview is obtained, the analysis often focuses on specific spatial regions, such as the arch in the aorta. Flow characteristics in these regions may be more relevant to answering a particular research question than flow in the rest of the domain. Therefore interactive methods must be provided for the user to visually explore flow selectively in specific regions.

Feature filtering

In addition to the targeted exploration of specific regions, the extraction of physically significant patterns is a frequently used method of flow analysis. Here, the visualization is limited to these so-called features. Features can be extracted either on the basis of an explicit mathematical description or by filtering uninteresting parts of the flow. Filtering can be used to identify flow features, such as turbulence, which provides information about the complexity of flows, as well as suspicious vessel wall regions, such as regions with low wall thickness and high pressure. To do this, reliable descriptions of the desired features must be defined as input to the filtering process, and visualizations of the filtering result must be provided.

Temporal analysis

A temporal analysis of flow data over the cardiac respiratory cycle is important to assess the stability of the flow. Presumably, unstable flow, i.e., collapse and recurrence of vortices, favors the progression of vascular disease and the development of consequential diseases, such as aneurysms and stenosis. Approaches to visually examine blood flow data should present features of interest and their evolution over time to allow detailed examination of these features.

Comparison

Comparison of multiple instances of medical flow data is essential in many scenarios, e.g., to evaluate the effects of different virtual treatment procedures, to investigate anatomical variability between patients, or to validate CFD simulations with measurements. Visual exploration approaches need to provide an *integrated representation* of multiple data instances to enable comparison by highlighting differences between instances and providing interaction capabilities to explore these differences.

Validation

Medical flow simulations are based on non-patient-specific assumptions and have limited spatial and temporal resolution. Therefore it is important to validate methods for generating medical flow data to increase their acceptance among physicians, and thus their use in clinical practice. The requirements for visual exploration approaches overlap with those of the comparison task. In addition to comparison with a ground truth, validation is used to check whether the data are correct and meaningful.

Uncertainty analysis

The generation of medical flow data involves several steps in which there are multiple sources of uncertainty, e.g., noise in the data, partial volume effects due to insufficient resolution, or manual parameter adjustments during grid generation. Simplifying assumptions during simulation and numerical inaccuracies contribute to the aggregate uncertainty. It is important to investigate the influence of these sources on the validity and interpretation of the flow data. Visual exploration approaches should show uncertain data regions to the user and help understand the variability in flow characteristics and wall properties.

In the subsections that follow, we provide an overview of visualization techniques that play an important role in the analysis of medical flow data. In each case, we distinguish between the three spatial areas.

5.4.1 Gaining a spatial overview

Numerous methods have been developed to generate overview representations for medical flow data. Typical methods in works focused on fluid mechanics comprise integral curves integrated in the computed or measured vector fields (Cebral et al., 2015; Tan et al., 2012), arrow glyphs (Buonocore, 1998) or particles (Xi et al., 2014). Often, a dense sampling of curves is used to cover the entire domain, which quickly leads to highly cluttered visualizations. Hemodynamic attributes defined on the vessel or the mucous wall are often color-coded on a corresponding surface representation (Cebral et al., 2015). However, this way only one attribute can be analyzed in the currently visible section of the surface. Therefore advanced visualization approaches were developed to generate an occlusion-free overview of flow patterns and multiple wall-related attributes.

Vessel lumen or nasal cavity

A common way to simplify flow representation inside the aneurysm or aortic lumen is to apply clustering methods (Oeltze et al., 2014; Meuschke et al., 2016b) that decompose the flow into similar regions. For the subdivision of the flow, it is usually represented by integral curves, where similar curves are grouped into clusters. Realizing this strategy requires a *similarity measure* that defines how similar two curves are. The distances between pair-wise points, global features, such as line length and overall curvature, need to be taken into account. Each factor is associated with a weight such that a specific understanding of similarity can be realized. With unsteady data, it gets a bit more complex, because the similarity of lines in space and time needs to be defined and weighted appropriately. A graphical representative can be calculated for each cluster, which together give a visual overview of the flow. The cluster representatives can be visualized in different ways using path arrows (van Pelt et al., 2012), stream tubes (Oeltze et al., 2014), or illustrative ribbon-like structures (Born et al., 2013a).

Another way to generate overview depictions of flow fields are plot-based visualizations. Zachow et al. (2009) used a combination of different linked diagrams, such as histograms, scatter plots, and parallel coordinates to give an overview of the aerodynamic domain. Regarding aortic flow fields, the vessel geometry may be straightened (Angelelli and Hauser, 2011), where a flow attribute, such as the flow velocity, is color-coded inside the stretched vessel to provide an occlusion-free overview. Several of these illustrations are arranged side-by-side to show multiple time steps of the cardiac cycle or flow attributes simultaneously.

Vessel wall or mucous wall

Visual overview plots to represent wall-related attributes play an important role in simulated blood flow data in cerebral aneurysms due to their 3D geometric complexity and the large number of attributes derived from simulation results. Various parameterization techniques from cartography can be used to create a 2D representation (Neugebauer et al., 2009a; Meuschke et al., 2017b) of the vessel wall. On the resulting 2D map, an attribute such as the WSS can be color-coded

(Goubergrits et al., 2012). However, the disadvantage of parameterization techniques is, the distortion of angles or area, which cannot be avoided due to the complex surface of aneurysms. In contrast, Glaßer et al. (2014) linked a scatter plot opposing wall thickness and WSS to a 3D aneurysm surface presentation to provide an overview of these attributes. Behrendt et al. (2017) combined *Fresnel shading* and a *pseudo chromadepth* color scale applied to a 3D surface representation to provide an overview about a scalar attribute by visually encoding depth information.

Lumen+wall or cavity+wall

Similar to wall-related overview visualizations, the generation of visual summaries of wall and flow-related attributes was mainly researched for cerebral aneurysms. One important aspect is the visual inspection of hemodynamic characteristics near the vessel wall. Neugebauer et al. (2013) introduced multiple 2D widgets to show near-wall flow at wall regions with high curvature that potentially represent rupture sites. In each widget, the near-wall flow is visualized by unrolled, and thus occlusion-free, streamlines. In contrast, multiple embedded 3D wall representations can be used to show the wall thickness, where the near-wall flow is displayed with arrowhead glyphs (Lawonn et al., 2016). Illustrative rendering styles and cutaway views reduce occlusions of the 3D representations. In addition, the previously described 2D aneurysm maps can be extended by illustrative rendering styles and bar charts to generate visual overviews of more than one attribute (Meuschke et al., 2017a, see Fig. 5.4).

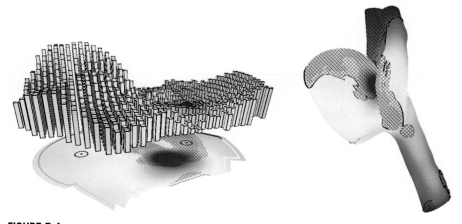

FIGURE 5.4

Left: 2.5D overview visualization of wall deformation magnitude (color), WSS (hatching), and wall thickness (bar chart) based on a flattening of the aneurysm surface. **Right:** A 3D visualization is linked to the overview for maintaining spatial orientation (©2017 IEEE, Reprinted with permission from: (Meuschke et al., 2017b)).

5.4.2 Probe

Probing means to inquire data values at selected positions or regions. When a mouse cursor is moved over a CT slice in a radiology viewer, the system displays the Hounsfield value at the selected position. When a region is encircled, it displays the average Hounsfield value, the standard deviation, and the range of values in the corresponding region. In a similar manner, flow data may be probed to get accurate values of attributes, such as flow speed and pressure. Probing, typically, is applied after the user got an overview of the data.

Standard probing techniques used in fluid mechanics comprise cut planes colored according to an attribute (Bates et al., 2015), isosurfaces of an attribute (Cebral et al., 2011a), and integral curves seeded in a specific region within the domain (Wigström et al., 1999). To get detailed insights into complex flow field, derived flow attributes, and wall-related attributes at interesting surface regions, advanced interactive probing methods were developed. There are also methods that allow a combined analysis of flow and wall-related attributes to identify correlations between them. Whereas there are several approaches for blood flow data, less work was done to probe nasal flow data.

Vessel lumen or nasal cavity

Advanced probing methods can be classified into techniques that generate a probing geometry for seeding integral curves and techniques that do not employ a probing geometry. Though there are many geometry-based approaches, methods without a probing geometry seed either integral curves in user-defined regions, such as high vorticity areas (Broos et al., 2016), or let the user inject virtual particles into the flow field (Saalfeld et al., 2015).

A main concept of geometry-based approaches is to add an interactive component to the cut plane definition. In cerebral aneurysms, the ostium surface has been used as probing geometry to study the inflowing and outflowing blood stream (Neugebauer et al., 2011). Additional cut planes can be defined and moved in the parent vessel and within the aneurysm. These serve as seeding geometries for integral curves and show hemodynamic attributes by combining different rendering styles, such as color-coding and illustrative techniques.

To probe aortic blood flow data, either segmentation-based or segmentation-free approaches can be employed. Segmentation-based methods (Hennemuth et al., 2011; Köhler et al., 2016a) first generate a 3D surface representation of the aorta and calculate the centerline. Along the centerline, perpendicular cut planes can be defined and moved by simple click interactions. In segmentation-free approaches, the cut plane is defined based on characteristics regarding the vessel orientation and diameter encoded in the image data (van Pelt et al., 2010, 2011). Instead of using just a 2D cut plane, also 3D objects, such as a truncated cone oriented along the flow field, were used as seeding geometry for illustrative particles, integral lines, and integral surfaces (van Pelt et al., 2011).

Another concept is to combine the probing in 3D with 2D representations of the probed region to support the interpretation of the obliquely oriented probe and to display additional information (Oeltze-Jafra et al., 2019). Close-ups of color-coded cut planes besides the cut plane position (van Pelt et al., 2010), additional views of corresponding image data overlaid with hemodynamic attributes (Hennemuth et al., 2011), as well as statistical diagrams and line graphs (Angelelli and Hauser, 2011) to display, e.g., the flow magnitude through the cut plane over time, are employed. Furthermore, probing can be combined with clustering approaches (Englund et al., 2016). Within the probed region, integral curves are seeded, which are combined to bundles, and a representative for each bundle is displayed (see Fig. 5.5).

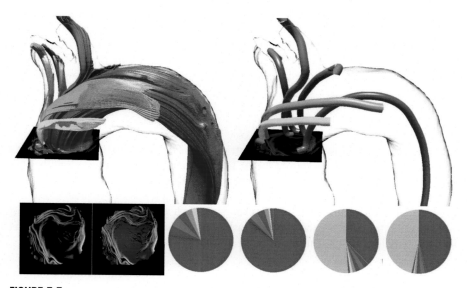

FIGURE 5.5

Flow field in the aorta is probed by means of a plane widget. Pathlines are seeded on the widget, clustered, and cluster representatives are displayed. Map views below support adding and removing clusters. Pie charts encode cluster size in terms of pathline count (From: (Englund et al., 2016), ©2016 The Author(s), Eurographics Proceedings, ©The Eurographics Association).

Vessel wall or mucous wall

Similar to probing flow fields, cut plane-based approaches are used to probe wall-related attributes. For cerebral aneurysm, a slice widget linked to a 2D contour plot of the vessel walls was developed, which can be dragged along the centerline to investigate the wall thickness and WSS (Glaßer et al., 2014). For probing the nasal cavity, the concept of combining 3D probing with 2D representations is used (Doorly et al., 2008). On the 3D surface, the WSS is color-coded, where a 2D line chart shows the WSS distribution along a selected surface perimeter.

Lumen+wall or cavity+wall

For the simultaneous probing of flow- and wall-related characteristics, different probing geometries and visualization techniques can be combined. One option is to use *interactive lenses* that are either overlaid on the 3D surface (Gasteiger et al., 2011) or mapped directly onto the 3D surface following its geometry (Rocha et al., 2017). The lens can be dragged across the domain, where different attributes can be visualized inside and outside the lens area to investigate possible correlations. Applied to simulated cerebral data, for example, WSS can be related to the underlying flow. Outside, the vessel surface is rendered opaque, and WSS is mapped to color, while inside, a transparent surface rendering is used to show colored isocontours of conspicuous WSS values embedded in a streamline visualization of the underlying flow field. Another possibility is to use multiple cut planes to probe, for example, different flow attributes at specific locations inside the aorta along the centerline (Markl et al., 2010). The cut planes are linked to a diagram view, where the specific flow attributes are color-coded.

5.4.3 Filter

Filtering of medical flow data aims to restrict the visualization to regions or features of interest or to visually highlight them. The remaining flow structures can then be explored separately to get a better understanding of the flow behavior. Whereas the "Features" task aims at similar goals, advanced filtering refers to a manual definition of target structures using different mechanisms, such as dynamic queries or linking and brushing. In contrast, the Features task is based on (semi-)automatic detections and computations of the features of interest, such as an automatic vortex extraction.

Vessel lumen or nasal cavity

In many works the filtering is based on integral curves that represent the flow field. To select curves that fulfill one or more predefined properties, line predicates (Salzbrunn and Scheuermann, 2006; Salzbrunn et al., 2008) can be applied to the integral curves. Several scalar measures are computed for an integral line, such as curvature, which are used as filtering criteria. In cerebral aneurysms, this concept was used to separate aneurysm inflow and outflow, as well as slow and fast flow based on flow directions and flow velocities (Neugebauer et al., 2011). Similarly, line predicates were used to filter features such as vortices (Köhler et al., 2013), jets, and blood with high residence times (Born et al., 2013b) in measured blood flow data. Besides line-based selection techniques, filtering can also be applied to quantitative flow attributes, such as the λ_2 criterion, where negative values represent vortical regions (Köhler et al., 2015).

Whereas line predicates restrict the visualization to specific flow characteristics, there are techniques to highlight integral curves that represent user-defined features, e.g., vortices, by decreasing the opacity of the remaining curves (Kanzler et al., 2016). The adjustment of the opacity can happen either on the basis of a calculated importance value, or on the basis of the current viewing direction of the viewer. In the first, an importance measure must be calculated that assigns a high value to integral lines of the target structure and a low value to all others. These importance values are then mapped to the opacity values of the rendered curves. Different importance measures exist, such as curvature-based (Günther et al., 2013) or perception-based measures (DeCarlo et al., 2003; Lawonn, 2014), where their application depends on the target structure. In the second case, interesting structures, such as vortices that lie in the viewer's line of sight, can be emphasized, while other vortices outside are attenuated (Oeltze-Jafra et al., 2016).

In contrast to dynamic queries, the brushing and linking concept can be applied to filter interesting regions. Zachow et al. (2009) used information visualization techniques, such as time series, scatter plots, and parallel coordinates to visualize the parameter domain of simulated nasal airflow. The user can brush regions in these plots to filter flow regions that fulfill the brushed ranges, where the selected flow regions are also highlighted in a 3D view (see Fig. 5.6).

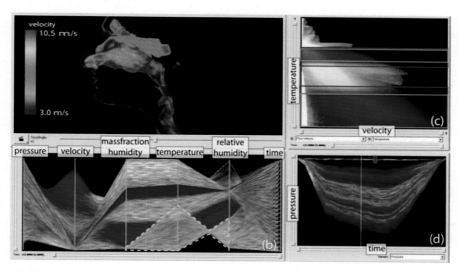

FIGURE 5.6

Coordinated multiple views for the interactive visual analysis of nasal airflow. A parallel co-ordinates view *(b)*, a scatterplot view *(c)*, and a time curve view *(d)* are linked to each other, and brushing is applied to the scatterplot (turquoise rectangles) to filter out less interesting data items. The filtering result is visualized in a linked 3D focus+context view *(a)* (©2009 IEEE, Reprinted with permission from: (Zachow et al., 2009).)

Vessel wall or mucous wall

The brushing and linking concept can be efficiently used to highlight wall regions with interesting values regarding defined attributes. Glaßer et al. (2014) provided a scatter plot that opposes wall thickness and WSS in cerebral aneurysms. The user can brush regions in the scatter plot, which are highlighted on the aneurysm wall.

Similarly, a scatter plot matrix can be used to highlight surface regions with respect to multiple attributes of simulated blood flow data (Meuschke et al., 2018a).

Lumen+wall or cavity+wall

For the simultaneous exploration of vessel lumen and wall, again the interactive lens approach can be used (Gasteiger et al., 2011). Adapting parameter ranges of the corresponding attributes restricts the visualization inside the lens to structures that fulfill these ranges. Similarly, Meuschke et al. (2017b) employed a user-driven definition of attribute ranges to restrict the visualization to aneurysm wall regions, where suspicious attribute combinations occur. To filter two attributes, the first one is color-coded on the aneurysm surface and the second one is visualized using an image-based hatching scheme. Regarding the hatching, a threshold has to be adjusted, such that either lower or higher attribute values are emphasized by a higher number of cross-hatches. Furthermore, dynamic queries can be defined to filter more than two attribute value ranges. Later, Meuschke et al. (2021a) extended their approach by a web-based component to support the collaborative analysis of aneurysm data. Behrendt et al. (2018a) introduced an approach where the user selects suspicious wall regions based on a discretized color-coding of an attribute, e.g., WSS. The selected region is then used to filter pathlines, representing the internal flow, which are close to the selected surface region.

5.4.4 Features

Whereas medically (Markl et al., 2012) or flow imaging focused literature (Byrne and Cebral, 2013; Byrne et al., 2014) mainly relies on manual filtering techniques to focus the visualization to specific flow characteristics, such as vortices, this section describes advanced approaches to automatically or semi-automatically extract flow features. The visualization is focused on flow features, e.g., vortices, features of the wall, e.g., critical points of the WSS field, or features of both.

Vessel lumen or nasal cavity

Besides simplified flow visualizations, clustering techniques are used to extract specific flow features. Different state-of-the-art clustering techniques, such as k-means, agglomerative hierarchical, spectral, and density-based methods, were applied to simulated (Oeltze et al., 2014) and measured blood flow data (Englund et al., 2016) to group flow-representing integral lines. Based on cluster validity measures, an evaluation study focused on simulated cerebral aneurysm flow suggests that spectral and agglomerative hierarchical clustering are the most suitable. Using clustering, also special shapes of vortices can be detected, so called *embedded vortices*, i.e., a small vortex enveloped by a larger one swirling in the opposite direction (Oeltze-Jafra et al., 2016). For nasal airflow, in addition to vortex flow, the calculation of aerosol deposition zones are essential in understanding the development of respiratory diseases and developing effective treatments. For this purpose, Xi et al. (2014) performed a particle simulation inside an airway model to compute the inhaled particle deposition that are visualized with circular glyphs.

In the case of time-dependent flow data, clustering techniques have to be applied that integrate the temporal component of the flow field. This makes it possible to track unstable vortices that decay and re-emerge during the cardiac cycle, which, e.g., seem to play an important role in aneurysm rupture risk assessment (Meuschke et al., 2018c). To avoid seeding of integral curves, Kuhn et al. (2011) present a hierarchical clustering method, which can be directly applied to time-independent vector fields. The principal idea is to derive a scalar field from the vector field, whose minima separate the individual clusters. With this, laminar, swirling, and turbulent flow regions could be distinguished in simulated aneurysm flow data.

Since vortical flow is essential for the assessment of cerebral aneurysms and cardiac vessel diseases, clinical research tries to better understand their influence on the development and progression of such diseases. Therefore medical studies manually classify vortices according to specific properties, such as their size, location, orientation, or shape. A vortex may be classified as small, near-wall, and peak-systolic, which means that it is fully visible only at the peak systole. A manual classification is a time-consuming and subjective process. Automatic vortex classification methods were developed that calculate several vortex characteristics, either based on predefined templates (van Pelt et al., 2014a) or on geometrical properties of the vortex-representing lines (Meuschke et al., 2016a, 2019a). Whereas for the template approach, the flow field serves as input, clustered integral lines are used as input for the geometry-based classification. In the case of aortic blood flow, classified vortices are presented by a 2D and 3D visualization (see Fig. 5.7). A 2D circular plot shows at which position within the vessel and at what time in the cardiac cycle each vortex appears, where the 3D representation displays its size and orientation by using a color-coding and arrow glyphs.

Vessel wall or mucous wall

For the patient-specific rupture risk assessment of cerebral aneurysm, a combined investigation of different wall properties is important. The goal is to find suspicious correlations of these properties that influence the aneurysm progression and rupture risk. Again clustering techniques are used to find regions in the vessel flow that show suspicious wall properties. Initial approaches limited the clustering procedure used to a combination of two properties, wall thickness, and WSS (Glaßer et al., 2014). The resulting clusters are visualized by applying a yellow to orange color scale to the vessel surface. A more advanced clustering approach allows a combination of multiple attributes to detect more complex attribute correlations (Meuschke et al., 2018a). For each cluster, a risk factor is computed based on the considered attributes that is color-coded on the vessel surface.

Lumen+wall or cavity+wall

To better understand physiological processes in healthy and diseased vessels, a combined analysis of hemodynamic and morphological features is important. Gambaruto

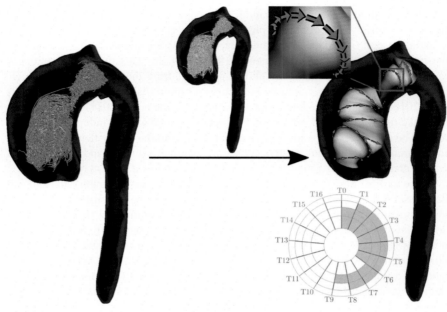

FIGURE 5.7

Semi-automatic classification of aortic vortical flow of a patient with an aortic dilation. Starting from the pathlines, two clusters are generated that are visualized by a 2D plot and a 3D glyph-based depiction (From: (Meuschke et al., 2016a), ©John Wiley & Sons Inc., 2016).

and João (2012) extracted flow and wall features, such as WSS critical points, vortices, and surface shear lines, which are related to rupture of cerebral aneurysms. The results are visualized by spherical glyphs, vortex-isosurfaces, surface lines with arrowheads, and streamlines. Besides these features, the shape of the inflowing main blood stream (*inflow jet*), the size of its impact area on the vessel wall (*impingement zone*), and near-wall flow patterns play a major role in the aneurysm investigation. Methods were developed to automatically detect these features in simulated flow data (Gasteiger et al., 2012; Neugebauer et al., 2013), where a combination of arrow glyphs and surface contours was used to depict the inflow jet and impingement zone. Detected flow patterns near the vessel wall at interesting positions are visualized by integral curves projected to a 2D plane (Neugebauer et al., 2013).

5.4.5 Observe

This section presents advanced visualization approaches to investigate the temporal behavior of medical flow data. In medicine or CFD, side-by-side views of different time steps along the cardiac or respiratory cycle are used to analyze data dynamics (Feliciani et al., 2015; Bates et al., 2015; Wong et al., 2009). However, for interpretation, the user has to mentally combine multiple images, which is time-consuming and tedious. Advanced approaches are either based on animations or static visualizations, where interesting spatio-temporal features are automatically highlighted.

Vessel lumen or nasal cavity

Typically, time-dependent flow data are represented by animated pathlines or particles. Media player functions, such as pause and resume, are provided to control the animation (Lawonn, 2014). To compensate the animation length, (Köhler et al., 2016c) introduced a feature visibility function that is evaluated in each frame. Based on the function values, the animation speed is decelerated if interesting characteristics, such as vortical flow, are visible. Otherwise the speed is increased to quickly pass less interesting temporal regions.

In the case of pathlines, just a short part of the integral line is usually shown to convey the dynamic flow behavior. To improve the perception of flow characteristics using these techniques, several visual enhancements were applied. Instead of shortening and animating pathlines, (van Pelt et al., 2010) draw pathlines in their full length, where the temporal dynamic of cardiac blood flow is illustrated by a time-depended highlighting of pathlines. This helps to better perceive the flow direction. Moreover, the particle-based flow visualization was improved by using ellipsoid-shaped particles with attached speed lines to display the flow direction over a limited amount of time (van Pelt et al., 2011).

Besides geometry-based approaches, more abstract circular plots are used to depict time-dependent aortic blood flow (Köhler et al., 2015; Meuschke et al., 2016a). They are inspired by clinically used plot visualizations, called bull's eye plot, where each segment of the plot represents an anatomical region within the heart. Along the plot's angle the time steps are encoded, while spatial locations inside the vessel are mapped to the radius. Köhler et al. (2015) designed such a 2D plot to show the spatio-temporal behavior of aortic vortex flow by color-coding the λ_2 criterion. Meuschke et al. (2016a) extended this plot to depict the spatio-temporal behavior of vortex clusters. Therefore the plot is discretized into sections along its radius and angle. For each cluster, the corresponding plot segments are determined and dyed according to the cluster color.

Vessel wall or mucous wall

Time-dependent attributes defined on the vessel or mucous wall can also be investigated using animations, where the corresponding attribute is color-coded on the surface. Moreover, statistical visualizations to depict, e.g., time-varying WSS values (Glaßer et al., 2016b). Meuschke et al. (2018a) extended the 2D plot approach to investigate the temporal behavior of multiple attributes defined on aneurysm walls. For this purpose, the aneurysm surface is divided into different regions, where an individual color is assigned to each region. Along the plot radius, the different attributes are encoded. Within a plot segment the regions are color-coded, where the corresponding attribute values fulfill a user-defined threshold. Thus the user can see at which points in time and in which regions on the aneurysm the attributes fulfill specific thresholds.

Later, they extended their approach and used 3D bar charts placed on a 2D map-based representation of the aneurysm surface, called *skyline visualization*, to show the temporal behavior of multiple attributes (Meuschke et al., 2021b). By using bar charts, the resolution of spatial regions on the aneurysm can be increased.

Lumen+wall or cavity+wall

A simultaneous analysis of interesting wall and flow features during the cardiac cycle is challenging due to the visual complexity. One possibility is to apply *smart visibility* techniques, such as dynamic cutaway views (Lawonn et al., 2016) to reduce occlusion problems between the vessel surface and internal blood flow represented by pathlines, see Fig. 5.8. Another possibility is a smart camera control, including an adequate viewpoint selection. Based on the selected viewpoints, a camera path can be automatically computed around user-selected flow patterns (Neugebauer et al., 2013) or around the whole vessel surface (Meuschke et al., 2017b; Apilla et al., 2021). For the whole vessel animation, optimal viewpoints showing interesting surface regions have to be computed and connected, e.g., via splines. The computation is based on a target function that includes flow and wall attributes, as well as possible occlusions between adjacent vessels, where the local maxima of this function represent the optimal viewpoints.

FIGURE 5.8

Animated pathline segments represented by arrow glyphs illustrate the flow inside an aneurysm and its parent vessel at three subsequent time steps. Dynamic cutaways reveal the passing inner flow. Wall thickness is color-coded on the outer wall using a discretized scale (bright regions indicate a thin wall). The inner vessel wall is superimposed using illuminated contours (©2016 IEEE, Reprinted with permission from: (Lawonn et al., 2016)).

Besides a fully automatic computation of a camera path, the expert knowledge of the user can be integrated, resulting in a semi-automatic animation computation (Meuschke et al., 2017a). During the interactive planning of a camera path, the user selects attributes they are most interested in, where for each attribute a threshold needs to be defined. This limits the animation to regions with suspicious attribute values. After the path computation, the camera moves from one point in time to the next in a smooth way. By default, one view per time step is considered in the animation. However, the user can start a local camera animation to explore interesting regions within a time step.

5.4.6 **Compare**

The comparison of medical flow data plays an important role in different scenarios, e.g., before and after a virtual treatment, among different treatments, across patients, or to compare simulated and measured flow data. Whereas in medicine and CFD, side-by-side views are typically used (Larrabide et al., 2012; Garcia et al., 2007; Andersson et al., 2015), advanced approaches provide integrated comparative visualizations or more abstract representations, which are easier to compare.

Vessel lumen or nasal cavity

Since medical and CFD experts are familiar with side-by-side views, different extensions of this concept simplify the comparison task. Oeltze et al. (2014) linked side-by-side views of flow clustering results generated before and after virtual treatment of a cerebral aneurysm and for different treatment options. Linking is achieved by coupling the camera parameters of the different views. Another option is to simplify the depiction within the side-by-side views by showing a standardized straightened representation of the vasculature (Angelelli and Hauser, 2011). This especially supports the comparison of different patients.

In addition to using side-by-side views, two-dimensional color scales applied to integral curves can be employed to compare, e.g., different treatment options and their effects on the blood flow (Goubergrits et al., 2010). Similarly, combinations of color and glyphs are suitable to compare simulated and measured blood flow data, see Fig. 5.10 (de Hoon et al., 2014). Measured information are encoded by gray vector glyphs, whereas simulated data is depicted by vector glyphs color-coded to differences in orientation angle compared to the measured values. Similarly, pathlines of measured data are shown in gray, whereas those traced in the simulated data are color-coded according to the Hausdorff distance. Behrendt et al. (2018b) used the more abstract bull's eye plot to compare aortic flow features between patients and healthy volunteers.

Vessel wall or mucous wall

Similar to the comparison of flow attributes, side-by-side visualizations with simplified geometric representation can be used to compare wall-related data. Goubergrits et al. (2012) generated disc-shaped representations of aneurysms, which can be arranged side-by-side to compare WSS distributions in ruptured and unruptured aneurysms. Also a side-by-side arrangement of the 2D abstract circular plots can be used to compare vortex flow across patients (Köhler et al., 2015). To compare multiple attributes defined on the surface for different configurations, scatter plot matrices can be used. Here, the upper triangular matrix is used to show attribute combinations, e.g., before treatment, and the lower triangular matrix shows attribute combinations after treatment (Meuschke et al., 2018a). In addition, glyphs are a powerful option to compare flow attributes mapped to the vessel wall. Meuschke et al. (2017c) introduced several glyph-based techniques to compare stress values between the inner and outer vessel wall of cerebral aneurysms.

Lumen+wall or cavity+wall

Glyphs are well suited for the comparative analysis of wall and flow features. van Pelt et al. (2014b) designed a comparative visualization of *inflow jet, impingement zone* (Gasteiger et al., 2012), and WSS for simultaneous exploration of an untreated aneurysm and up to four virtual treatment configurations (see Fig. 5.9). The *inflow jet* and the *impingement zone* are visualized by arrow glyphs and surface contours, respectively, and their color encodes the corresponding treatment configuration. In addition, glyphs are designed and placed on the surface that encode the WSS value and its temporal evolution over the cardiac cycle. Recently, Meuschke et al. (2022c) introduced the framework COMFIS that allows a comparative analysis of two configurations for all three components of a simulated flow data set, including vessel surface, flow volume, and pathlines. Side-by-side views and integrated visualizations are provided to compare quantitative and qualitative flow information, e.g., before and after stenting of a cerebral aneurysm.

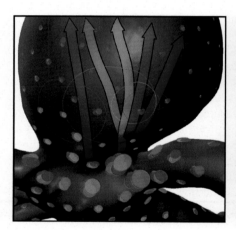

FIGURE 5.9

Left: visualization of four virtual stenting scenarios and the untreated case. *Inflow jets* (arrow glyphs), *impingement zones* (surface contours), and WSS (surface glyphs) can be compared. **Right:** With an increasing zoom level, the glyphs' density and level of detail are increased (adapted from (van Pelt et al., 2014b), ©John Wiley & Sons Inc., 2014).

5.4.7 Validation

Medical flow simulations requires several assumptions to reduce the computational effort, which often do not reflect patient-specific conditions. Results have been shown to vary (Scheid-Rehder et al., 2019), depending on the methods used for segmentation, mesh generation, and flow simulation. In contrast, measured blood flow data have a limited spatial and temporal resolution. Thus integrating measured and simulated blood flow data is a promising approach. However, to increase the acceptance of such integrated flow data in clinical routine, validation is required.

There are multiple studies that statistically quantified differences between simulated and measured flow data for cerebral, cardiac, and nasal structures (Cebral et al., 2016; Goubergrits et al., 2015; Chung and Kim, 2008). Occurring differences depend on the quality of the underlying image data used for model reconstruction. Simulation results based on high-quality surface models showed in general good agreement with measurement results. The glyph-based approach by de Hoon et al. (2014) is a smart visualization approach supporting the validate task (see Fig. 5.10).

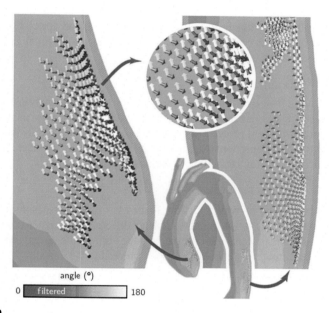

FIGURE 5.10

Comparative visualization for an aortic dissection case. The visualization comprises information from measured 4D PC-MRI data (gray arrows) and simulated blood flow (color-coded vectors). The color-coding maps angles > 90° between the vectors. The example indicates acquisition artifacts near the vessel wall due to the strong differences between measured and simulated data, conveyed by the white-colored arrow glyphs close to the boundary (From: (de Hoon et al., 2014), ©John Wiley & Sons Inc., 2014).

5.4.8 Uncertainty

During the generation and processing of medical flow data, different sources of uncertainty exist. This section summarizes visualization approaches to convey the uncertainty of medical flow data.

Vessel lumen or nasal cavity

Image artifacts lead to uncertainties in flow measurements, which may be represented by wrong courses of integral lines. Based on a probabilistic sampling, integral curves are traced, where flow maps can be used to visualize regions that are often passed with different sampling configurations (Friman et al., 2010a; Schwenke et al., 2011). Regions passed less often indicate artifacts.

Besides uncertainties of qualitative features, also quantitative uncertainties, e.g., regarding the net flow volume (NFV), i.e., the volume of pumped blood per heartbeat, arise in measured blood flow data. The NFV is computed by measuring the flow that orthogonally passes through a placed plane in the aorta. Köhler et al. (2016a) investigated uncertainties in NFV measurements using a box plot-based graph and found high deviations due to slightly different plane angles and vortex flow. Actually, this leads to the recommendation of not quantifying flow in a vortex region since this cannot be precise.

Vessel wall or mucous wall

Similar to measured flow data, applied reconstruction kernels in the image acquisition of cerebral vessels lead to uncertainties in the extracted vessel surfaces. Glaßer et al. (2016a) compared different reconstruction kernels and used semi-transparent surface meshes and statistical depictions to depict the reconstructed surfaces. They found strong differences regarding branching vessels and vessel diameters.

Lumen+wall or cavity+wall

To analyze uncertainties of wall and flow features, simulation ensembles are used comprising different simulation runs, each with different parameter configurations. From these ensembles, probabilities for the presence of local features, such as critical points in WSS and flow vector fields, can be computed (Petz et al., 2012; Pöthkow and Hege, 2013). Based on color-coded probability values, uncertain features can be detected (see Fig. 5.11).

5.5 Medical flow analysis systems

In clinical practice, it is essential that the whole workflow, including image analysis, simulation, feature extraction, visualization, and quantification, is provided within *integrated systems*. Thus instead of using a variety of tools, to export results, import them in other tools, the whole processing needs to be available under one unified and consistent user interface. There are a few systems supporting such an integrated analysis for simulated cerebral blood flow, such as ANKYRAS from GALGOMEDICAL and measured cardiac flow, such as BLOODLINE from the university of Magdeburg (Köhler et al., 2019).

ANKYRAS serves for planning stent treatment and provides image analysis (segmentation, skeletonization) of intracranial vessels and suggests where to place a stent. The user may select a special stent and may adapt the stent length and position. They

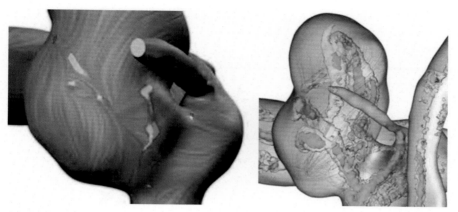

FIGURE 5.11

Uncertain flow features of a cerebral aneurysm obtained from an ensemble simulation.
Left: Critical point probabilities of the uncertain WSS vector field. **Right:** Swirling motion core probabilities over a full cardiac cycle (From: (Petz et al., 2012), ©John Wiley & Sons Inc., 2012).

get a couple of diagrams, including a quantification of the diameter within the relevant section of the vessel, the cross-sectional area, and the porosity of the stents (see Fig. 5.12). A couple of publications describes the underlying technology. As an example, Fernandez et al. (2015) describe how the stent length changes when it is deployed in a cerebral artery. This system is used in clinical practice and clinical research (Joshi et al., 2018).

BLOODLINE supports the whole pipeline of processing and analyzing measured cardiac blood flow in the aorta. Segmentation of the time-dependent data is provided with a variant of graph-cut, a semi-automatic method. Six measurement planes are automatically placed at standardized positions derived from anatomical landmarks. Forward and backward flow is analyzed and quantified. A number of features is automatically determined and used for quantification (see Fig. 5.13). BLOODLINE is open source software, available at GitHub and was also used for medical research, e.g., for studying the effect of different imaging protocols (Ebel et al., 2020). A recent paper defines gender- and age-specific ranges of normal values of flow parameters, such as helical flow, flow jets, and wall shear stress (Ebel et al., 2022). The latter serves to better discriminate healthy aging from pathologies.

An essential topic in medical research and clinical practice is to support the generation of reports that summarize the results related to a case, including screenshots, labels, and quantifications. The report generation process for simulated medical flow data is discussed by Meuschke et al. (2018b) and for measured cardiac flow data by Meuschke et al. (2022b).

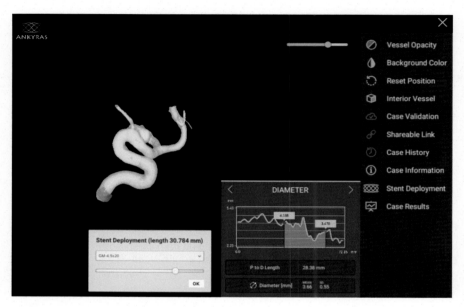

FIGURE 5.12

The inflow region related to a cerebral aneurysm is shown. In the highlighted area, a stent with a certain type should be applied. One of five diagrams is shown that presents quantitative information related to the selected stent configuration (Image courtesy of Mentice - Ankyras personalized simulation - Intracranial aneurysms).

5.6 Concluding remarks

In this chapter, we provide an overview how medical flow data are generated from medical image data or directly measured. Whereas the simulation data is clean but relies on assumptions that are uncertain, measured data is noisy and contains artifacts, making advanced image analysis necessary. Our focus was on visualization techniques to explore medical flow. We classified them regarding the underlying domain: vessel lumen/nasal cavity, vessel wall/mucous wall, and the combination of both. Furthermore, the discussed visualization techniques are grouped according to analysis tasks, which are important to understand the complex information and to gain new insights regarding pathological processes. The best supported task is the feature filtering task, independently of the application domain. A likely reason is that medical and CFD research results are linking features such as vortices to initiation, progression, and severity of a pathology. The interactive probing and temporal analysis tasks are equally often supported. The spatial overview and comparison task have received a little less overall attention. The spatial overview task was more often addressed in the context of cerebral aneurysm hemodynamics. Most of the corresponding approaches incorporate WSS and properties of the wall, both of which are harder or impossible to

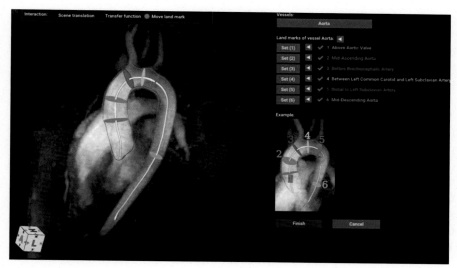

FIGURE 5.13

After the whole image analysis is performed, BLOODLINE provides suggestions for six measurement planes, oriented perpendicular to the local vessel centerline as the basis for flow quantification (From: (Köhler et al., 2019), Reprinted from Computers & Graphics, Vol. 82, "Bloodline: A system for the guided analysis of cardiac 4D PC-MRI data", Page 37, ©Elsevier 2019).

derive from measured 4D PC-MRI data. In the cerebral domain, the comparison task is mostly accomplished to determine the optimal outcome of a virtual intervention, while in the cardiac domain, measured and experimental simulated data, patients, or time steps are compared. The validation and uncertainty analysis task are the least supported.

In the future, guidelines are needed as to when which method should be used to perform a particular task. This requires a more detailed comparison of the methods regarding perceptual aspects and cognition. The increasing use of medical flow data in clinical practice motivates the development of visualization techniques appropriate for broad audiences, including patients and their relatives. In a recent study, Kleinau et al. (2022) designed a slide show entitled "Is there a tornado in Alex' bloodflow?," using the metaphor of a tornado for a dangerous situation in the flow.

Recommended reading

The following papers represent a selection of essential papers on medical flow exploration, comprising measured and simulated blood flow and nasal airflow.

Silvia Born, Matthias Pfeifle, Michael Markl, Matthias Gutberlet, and Gerik Scheuermann (2012). "Visual analysis of cardiac 4D MRI blood flow using line predicates," *IEEE Transactions on Visualization and Computer Graphics*, Vol. 19(6): 900–912.

Rocco Gasteiger, Mathias Neugebauer, Oliver Beuing, and Bernhard Preim (2011). "The FLOWLENS: A focus-and-context visualization approach for exploration of blood flow in cerebral aneurysms," *IEEE Transactions on Visualization and Computer Graphics*, Vol. 17(12): 2183–2192.

Benjamin Köhler, Rocco Gasteiger, Uta Preim, Holger Theisel, Matthias Gutberlet, and Bernhard Preim (2013). "Semi-automatic vortex extraction in 4D PC-MRI cardiac blood flow data using line predicates," *IEEE Transactions on Visualization and Computer Graphics*, Vol. 19(12), 2773–2782.

Roy Van Pelt, Javier Olivan Bescos, Marcel Breeuwer, Rachel E. Clough, Eduard Gröller, Bart ter Haar Romenij, and Anna Vilanova (2010). "Exploration of 4D MRI blood flow using stylistic visualization," *IEEE Transactions on Visualization and Computer Graphics*, Vol. 16(6): 1339–1347.

Stefan Zachow, Philipp Muigg, Thomas Hildebrandt, Helmut Doleisch, and Hans-Christian Hege (2009). "Visual exploration of nasal airflow," *IEEE Transactions on Visualization and Computer Graphics*, Vol. 15(6): 1407–1414.

Medical animations

6.1 Introduction

Computer-generated animations have a long tradition. Powerful animation tools were developed already in the 1980s, primarily motivated by the needs of the film industry. Computer-generated animations are created based on metaphors from traditional films, such a *story board* and *key frames*, which are interpolated to achieve smooth transitions (Kahn, 1979). Animation provides enormous flexibility, which is potentially very useful for medical applications. A virtual camera may be rotated in a fixed distance around a pathology to assess its morphology (*orbiting*). The virtual camera may display a region around a pathology, zooming in particularly interesting regions, e.g., to assess a pathology, or it may zoom out and move to another interesting viewpoint.

Animated displays provide *motion parallax*, an essential depth cue that supports the interpretation of volume-rendered images, which are otherwise difficult to interpret (Sakas et al., 1995). Motion parallax relates to the understanding of depth relations caused by changing the viewpoint typically in a continuous movement.

Animation may also be used to smoothly change parameters of a transfer function, and thus to display or hide structures, to change colors or textures for emphasis of focus objects, and to adjust clipping planes or more complex resection geometries. Virtually every parameter of a static display may be smoothly changed to a different state. These transitions are carried out by means of interpolation, i.e., a set of intermediate states is interpolated.

Animated visualizations may be completely predefined with no or only basic interaction. At the other end of the spectrum, highly customized animations may be created on demand, where the author has full control over all parameters. Thus the purpose ranges from *communication of known facts* with predefined animations to *exploratory data analysis* (DiBiase et al., 1992).

Re-use of animations

Like static medical visualizations benefit from carefully chosen default values, the parameters that guide an animation may be re-used in similar cases, e.g., to report cases with a similar pathology in a reproducible manner (Iserhardt-Bauer et al., 2002). In addition to these animations where no dynamic process is visualized, animation is a natural choice to display dynamic medical image data, such as simulated or mea-

Visualization, Visual Analytics and Virtual Reality in Medicine. https://doi.org/10.1016/B978-0-12-822962-0.00013-4

sured blood flow, or motion of the heart wall. "Animation let us observe how an object changes its shape, size, and position . . . over time" (Akiba et al., 2010).

Animating surface and volume renderings

Medical visualization comprises both direct volume rendering controlled by a transfer function and (polygonal) surface rendering. These two families of visualization techniques also occur in medical animation. However, surface-based rendering is prevailing due to the large flexibility to adjust polygonal models, e.g., by smoothing or simplifying them. Moreover, medical animations often contain additional elements, such as surgical instruments, which are represented as surface models.

Applications

Animations may be used for surgical planning and training, for anatomy education, and for patient education. Whereas forensic use cases require a high degree of realism (referred to as *scientific animations*), patient education benefits from plausible, abstracted visualizations, where also aesthetic aspects are considered. In contrast, animations for medical education are driven more by learning-theoretic considerations, e.g., motivational aspects and cognitive load theory (Khalil et al., 2005).

The camera may also be moved inside anatomical structures similar to the movement of an endoscope as a diagnostic procedure, e.g., to assess the state of the colon. This *virtual endoscopy* is particularly important to assess the bronchial tree (virtual bronchoscopy) and the colon (virtual) colonoscopy (Lorensen et al., 1995).

Organization

This chapter, which is based on Preim and Meuschke (2020), is organized as follows: We discuss fundamentals of animation design (Section 6.2). Animation of static data, with a focus on surface representations of anatomical structures, is discussed in Section 6.3. Animations, based on volume data, as the second major representation of the patient anatomy are introduced in Section 6.4. In Section 6.5, we discuss medical animations based on dynamic data, e.g., perfusion data, functional MRI, and blood flow data. Whereas these three sections focus on methods, concepts, and algorithms, we discuss major applications in Section 6.6. A crucial issue is the interaction to steer animated displays, which is described in Section 6.7. Patient-specific animations for diagnosis and treatment planning must be generated effectively in clinical medicine. Therefore we discuss animation tools and strategies to re-use animations in Section 6.8.

6.2 Fundamentals

In this section, we provide a high-level discussion of perceptual and cognitive issues involved in the interpretation of animations, including motion perception, change blindness, and cognitive load (Section 6.2.1). Since medical animations often aim at educational purposes, we also briefly discuss learning theories (Section 6.2.2). As a further ingredient in animation design, we discuss principles from film making that were applied to computer-generated animations (Section 6.2.3).

Other areas of visual perception, such as color and contrast perception, shape, depth perception, and flow perception are also relevant for animation design. For the sake of brevity, we do not discuss these other areas.

6.2.1 Fundamentals from perception and cognition

The design of animations has to consider a number of aspects related to perception, cognition, motivation, and learning theory. The effectiveness of animations may depend on (Ruiz et al., 2009):

- the actual content to be displayed
- the specific processes that are shown
- learner characteristics, such as domain knowledge and spatial abilities
- the context in which the display of animations is embedded, e.g., verbal instructions

Research in this area in medicine is not comprehensive. As a consequence, our discussion also considers non-medical animations.

Motion perception

is the rather low-level process of identifying and assessing movements. Humans are very sensitive to motion, i.e., motion attracts attention. This attention-guiding character is largely influenced by the speed of movements: fast movements are perceived as urgent and are noticed without any cognitive effort (Bartram et al., 2001).

An essential aspect is the ability to detect all changes. In a series of experiments, it was demonstrated that viewers may miss even movements of larger characters (*change blindness*) (Simons and Levin, 1997). This has a number of reasons, including saccadic eye movements that occur when a new region in an image is fixated. For a period of up to 200 ms, humans are blind during these eye movements (Gregory, 2015). In addition to the unreliable detection of changes, humans are also not aware that they have not fully understood a video sequence. Thus even viewers who miss essential changes report to be certain in their assessment, a phenomenon called *change blindness blindness* (Levin et al., 2000). For animation design, emphasis techniques, such as arrows and the use of colors that grab attention, may avoid change blindness. Change blindness also depends on the speed of presentation. Neither very slow nor fast movements are beneficial to support the detection of changes.

Correct interpretation of an animation not only requires that viewers detect changes, they also should interpret the character of a change. Therefore perception researchers use change detection (CD) levels, where

- CD 1 relates to the detection of a change
- CD 2 to the direction of change
- CD 3 to the amount of change (Goldsberry and Battersby, 2009).

Evaluations reveal that viewers may notice changes despite having not enough time to figure out what exactly changed. Perceptual research indicates that the problems are more severe when it is necessary to pay attention to different regions in an image. This *split screen attention* situation reduces the human change detection ability (Alexander and Wickens, 2005).

Cognitive load theory

considers the limited resources of the human brain to process information. Working memory is limited, and as a consequence information overload may interfere with learning (Sweller, 2004). Researchers investigating cartographic animation therefore suggest to restrict both the complexity and the duration of animations (Harrower, 2007). Animations should be rather short, typically below one minute.

Ruiz et al. (2009) discussed evidence that breaking an animation into smaller chunks reduces cognitive load and is beneficial for learning. They recommend that the information should remain available at the end. Cognitive load is further distinguished in *intrinsic* cognitive load, which comprises the information that need to be processed, and *extrinsic* cognitive load comprises other information that consumes cognitive resources without any effect on learning. Obviously, extrinsic cognitive load, e.g., anything that may distract, should be minimized (Sweller, 2004). Whether information is considered distracting depends on learner characteristics, in particular experience (Khalil et al., 2005). Khalil et al. (2005) suggest *learner-controlled* animations, where the amount of information to be displayed may be adapted.

Due to the transient nature of animations and the limited working memory, content displayed in an animation may be easily forgotten, even if initially perceived correctly. When the displayed information is subsequently used, e.g., to answer questions, failures of learning may be reduced (Khalil et al., 2005).

6.2.2 Fundamentals from education

A considerable number of medical animations serve educational purposes. The use of animation in educational settings is driven by the attempt to "increase student interest in the subject material" (Fisk, 2008). Since the current student generation is so familiar with videos, animations are a natural choice for them. Though there is consensus about this motivational aspect, the evidence that animations improve learning is controversial. Animations may be distracting, and thus should be consequently designed with specific educational goals in mind, where the dynamic character is likely beneficial.

Fisk (2008) also discusses the importance of an *adequate preparation*. Basic introductory information should be given to students prior to observing an animation. Also during the animation, "narration should be used to explain the events occurring in the animation," e.g., by audio recordings or embedded text (Fisk, 2008). Whereas audio recordings have the advantage that spoken text can be better perceived concurrently to an animation, displayed text requires visual attention to be split between observing the animation and reading text.

Ruiz et al. (2009) summarize research on animations for effective learning. They conclude that movements similar to those a learner is expected to perform later are highly effective. As a consequence, the actual handling of instruments and the conduct of steps in surgery can be learned based on animations. Less effective— according to this theory—are animations that explain, for example, how a machine or the heart works. Ruiz et al. (2009) argue that even the best animations may not ideally serve their (learning) purpose if they are not carefully embedded in an overall learning strategy, comprising more *active* types of learning.

6.2.3 Fundamentals from animation design

At the beginning of animation design, careful discussion about the major goal, the *intent* of an animation is required. "What story are we going to tell" (Okemow, 2020) is the major question in this stage. The answer could be the reason why a medical product or a drug was developed. Before some physiological facts for example are illustrated, the viewer must be prepared, by providing relevant and interesting context information, a process known as *framing*. As a consequence, typically an *establishing shot* is created, e.g., an appropriate view of an operating room.

As a general planning document, a storyboard is also frequently employed in the design of medical animations. It includes a series of thumbnail images representing different states of an animation (Okemow, 2020), often with associated text to explain these states. These images are assigned to shots and scenes according to the structure of an animation. There are specific tools to support the storyboarding process, which provide many design elements and means to connect and structure them. Okemow (2020) mention STORYBOARD PRO as a viable example.

The design of medical animation often involves a geometric model with fine details appropriate for exploration, but when moved with moderate or even high speed, the details may be unnoticed. Okemow (2020) emphasizes the important role of pan and zoom operations that are extensively used to focus on different sections of a 3D (patient) model. Details, such as the surrounding of a pathology, the position of a biopsy needle, or branching patterns of a vascular tree require close-up views, whereas bird's eye views are employed to introduce a scene. Okemow (2020) discuss many more aspects of animation design, e.g., how to provide a sense of continuity of the objects, using depth cueing techniques and spotlights to support focusing on certain structures.

Since the viewing directions are determined by an animation author, parts of a geometric model may always be hidden or appear too dark, based on the lighting specification, which the viewer typically also cannot influence (Habbal and Harris, 1995). In addition to a main 3D view, insets, labels, and leader lines need to be considered.

Temporal coherence

is an issue: Visualization techniques that involve stochastic sampling or slight inaccuracies may lead to distracting flicker if tiny elements show up and disappear suddenly.

As a consequence, animations must be iteratively developed and refined to reduce the risk of unwanted effects. Hand-drawn character animation provides an essential basis for animation design. Lasseter (1987) mentioned eleven design principles. Though some of them apply primarily to facial expressions and other peculiarities of character animation, the following principles are also relevant for medical animations of static data.

Plausibility

Animations should be plausible with respect to mechanical laws, which means that animated objects should be guided by gravity and inertia. Viewers will use such knowledge to interpret an animation, e.g., an object that can be accelerated very fast must be light, whereas heavy objects make slower movements. Objects are stretched and squeezed during motion, at least if they are not completely rigid.

Anticipation

The principles described by Lasseter (1987) further explain that the actual movement shown in an animation requires preparation. In the language of film, this is referred to as *anticipation*. Lasseter gives the example of a boy kicking a ball: The foot must be pulled back before the ball can be kicked. In a similar way, also a step of a surgical intervention can be prepared. Otherwise, viewers tend to miss the essence of a movement. "Anticipation is a device to catch the audience's eye, to prepare them for the next movement and lead them to expect it. … Anticipation is also used to direct the attention … to the right part of the screen at the right moment." (Lasseter, 1987).

Staging

After the anticipation, the core of a movement takes place. Just one movement at a time should be shown to support focused attention. If an animation should convey different movements, these should be serialized (Fisk, 2008; Lasseter, 1987). In a "busy" animation with many moving objects, the eye tends to focus on relatively still regions, missing the dynamics completely (Lasseter, 1987). According to the staging principle, the moving object should further be emphasized. In essence, with careful anticipation and staging, the author of an animation can effectively guide the viewer to certain objects in a certain sequence, exactly what is desirable to realize a communicative intent, e.g., for an educational purpose.

Arcs

Another principle, briefly referred to as *arcs*, relates to camera movements: Cameras typically move along arcs and only rarely along straight lines. The camera orientation changes only slightly. To realize camera movements along arcs, animation systems employ spline-based interpolation techniques.

Slow in and out

This principle applies to the interpolation between keyframes. According to this principle, the movement starts slowly, is then accelerated and slowed down before it comes to an end. It is relevant, e.g., when a camera movement is carried out to change the viewpoint. Lasseter (1987) mentions splines as means to accomplish such movements. Catmull (1972) presented a scripting language, the *motion picture language*. It supports accelerated and decelerated movements as well as concurrent or overlapping processes.

Though we emphasized the pioneering work of Lasseter (1987), we want to point out that the use and adaptation of film-theoretic knowledge to animation design remained an essential topic later as well. For example, the camera control techniques presented by Drucker and Zeltzer (1994), as well as concepts on virtual story telling (Wu et al., 2018), employ metaphors and concepts from film theory. The concept of a metaphor will be employed several times in this book, primarily in the context of virtual reality, where we explain it in Section 12.6.1.

Animations have a number of essential characteristics:

- *Duration.* Typically, animations for educational purposes are rather short, mostly below a minute.
- *Speed.* The speed determines how much time is available to detect and interpret changes. The preferred speed may vary considerably and should be adjustable.
- *Temporal scale.* When dynamic data is displayed, a certain *world time* interval is mapped to a *display time* interval. A temporal scale of 1:1 is often natural, e.g., to show the changes in anatomy during the cardiac cycle.
- *Interpolation.* The specific interpolation method used for the transition between states or positions, e.g., linear or cubic. The interpolation determines the smoothness of camera movements.

There are three types of motion in an animation (Zettl, 2013; Stollfuß, 2017):

- *Primary motion.* Movements of the actors, e.g., a car, or a cat escaping from a dog. In medical applications, growth processes or changes due to a contrast agent that diffuses over time are examples of primary motions.
- *Secondary motion.* Movements of the camera, e.g., pan and tilt, and movements of the lens elements, e.g., zooming, are examples. Also adaptations of illumination settings belong to secondary motions. In medical animations, also transfer function parameters may be animated.
- *Tertiary motion.* Switches from one shot to another, i.e., transitions, such as fade, dissolve, and wipe.

Primary motions are the core of animations of dynamic data, whereas secondary motions occur primarily in animations of static data. Tertiary motions are relevant, e.g., for longer animations of static data to provide smooth transitions between different shots. As a final classification, based on Parent (2012) and Stollfuß (2017), we distinguish among the following:

- *Artistic animation* "in which the animator has the prime responsibility for crafting the motion" (Parent, 2012).

- *Data-driven animation*, "where live motion is digitized and then mapped onto graphic objects" (Parent, 2012).
- *Procedural animation*, "in which there is a computational model . . . used to control the motion. Usually, this is in the form of setting conditions for some type of physical . . . simulation" (Parent, 2012).

We will see examples of each of these categories.

Scientific and non-scientific animations

Medical animations can be used to convey physiological properties, e.g., the pulsatile blood flow and the resulting vessel wall movement. Also biomechanical properties, e.g., the range of motion of the shoulder, can be effectively communicated. This leads to a further useful discrimination of animations (Fisk, 2008).

- *Scientific animations* are based on the laws of physics, such as energy conservation and kinematic laws. They aim for a high degree of realism and correctness. Typical areas of application are medical research and selected diagnostic processes.
- *Non-scientific animations*, in contrast, aim at a plausible depiction of movements without any guarantee that the behavior is correctly shown. They may be used for patient education or narrative visualization for broad audiences, e.g., in a science museum.

6.3 Medical animations of static data

A wide variety of animation techniques have been developed to convey the complex spatial relations within the human anatomy. These animations are primarily *artistic*. In this section, we discuss algorithms and concepts that are essential without details about specific applications. We start with the computation of good viewpoints (Section 6.3.1) and continue with camera path planning (Section 6.3.2), which comes in two flavors: the computation of a path to show a patient model from outside and the computation of a path for a flythrough, e.g., inside the bronchial tree. We discuss strategies to annotate (medical) animations (Section 6.3.3) and scripting languages developed to translate high-level instructions in the low-level commands for a graphics library (Section 6.3.4). Finally, we discuss *hybrid animations* that combine aspects of animations using both static and dynamic data (Section 6.3.5). The discussion in this section is focused on *surface data*, e.g., surfaces representing anatomical or pathological structures, medical instruments, or symbols, such as arrows.

6.3.1 Viewpoint selection

For animating static data a camera path is valuable to show a complex anatomy from different perspectives. The definition of a camera path can be supported by algorithmic components. The overall task breaks down in the selection of good viewpoints and the combination of these viewpoints to a smooth movement. The selection of good viewpoints can be guided by geometric considerations. Some target structures should be visible at least to a large extent and their projection should not be too small. *Viewpoint entropy*, a measure from information theory, turned out to be a good quality criterion for selecting viewpoints (Vázquez et al., 2001). In essence, a minimum set of viewpoints is selected that conveys the maximum amount of information.

Viola et al. (2006) and Mühler et al. (2007) sampled a sphere around the scene of the relevant anatomy to determine good viewpoints. Viola et al. (2006) determine one characteristic viewpoint for each object in a pre-processing step. Mühler et al. (2007) also integrated preferences of surgeons, e.g., familiar views. Furthermore, a *stability* criterion was incorporated: A viewpoint is only selected if viewpoints in the neighborhood are also appropriate. Therefore the camera stays for a while in a beneficial region, e.g., to see a tumor and its surrounding. This stability criterion also supports the interactive exploration, i.e., if the animation is interrupted for exploration, the target structures remain visible. Viewpoint selection algorithms are also available for volume-rendered images.

Once viewpoint candidates are determined, a selection can be computed taking into account that the resulting set should be as diverse as possible. Thus it is ensured that a target structure is seen from significantly different perspectives. Viewpoints are also characterized by the distance to the interesting structures.

6.3.2 Camera path planning

The selected viewpoints need to be ordered to establish a meaningful sequence, a process called *camera path planning* or *camera composition*. This sequence of viewpoints is connected following the *arc* principle (recall Section 6.2.3). Also the *slow-in, slow-out* principle is essential for a camera path (Lasseter, 1987). There are many ways to combine viewpoints into a camera path. The following criteria are essential:

- The path should be as short as possible.
- A path should be chosen where relevant information is displayed during the whole camera movement.
- Unfamiliar or uncomfortable views should be avoided.

Obviously, trade-offs are necessary. The shortest geodesic path between a set of points on the surrounding sphere does not necessarily reveal relevant information. It may also contain unfamiliar viewpoints. Therefore a weighted combination of the criteria may serve as objective function for an optimization process. Camera path planning may be combined with adjustments of transparency to ensure the visibility of essential anatomical structures. As an example, if a pathology should be shown, occluding objects are rendered semi-transparently, as long as they actually occlude the target object. Viola et al. (2006) discuss primarily how two viewpoints v_1 and v_2—each serving to emphasize one structure—may be connected, also restricting movements to the surrounding sphere. Their major idea is to determine a *contextual viewpoint* v_c that is traversed along the path, i.e., the geodesic movement between v_1, v_c, and v_2 is used for an animated transition to a new focus object.

Virtual endoscopy

The definition of a camera path is also an essential part of flythrough animations inside anatomical structures. However, the requirements and solutions are fundamentally different, since the virtual camera in these applications always remains inside the target structure. Thus we postpone a discussion of virtual endoscopy to Section 6.6.3.

6.3.3 Annotating animated visualizations

Labeling is essential in medical education and surgical planning. Textual annotations, measures, arrows, and other metagraphical symbols may be used to emphasize structures. Though labeling static medical visualizations was extensively analyzed (Oeltze-Jafra and Preim, 2014), the problems and possible solutions related to labeling animated objects are rarely discussed.

Labeling animated objects requires real-time capable layout algorithms (Götzelmann et al., 2007). Moreover, *temporal stability* of label positions and, if present, connection lines needs to be ensured. An internal label that is embedded within the related graphical object is moved with that object, which is perceived as natural (Maass and Döllner, 2008). However, strong changes of the viewing direction may hide the label and strong zooming operations lead to very large or very small labels. External labels that are connected via a reference line to the related graphical object may stay at a constant position. Therefore only the connection line needs to be updated. The drawback of this strategy is that the place occupied by labels may be subject to relevant changes in the data. Thus, though labels may be placed at regions where they initially do not occlude important parts of the data, they may later occupy salient regions. Götzelmann et al. (2007) suggest the use of video processing techniques to identify *calm regions* with little changes that may serve for label placement. They employ examples from engineering, e.g., labeled animations that explain complex engines. The strategies can be translated to 3D models of a patient anatomy.

6.3.4 Scripting languages

Modern visualization toolkits, such as *Amira* (Stalling et al., 2005), contain simple and general scripting facilities to generate camera movements and object transformations. These, however, are not sufficient, e.g., to effectively explain the anatomy in a particular region or to support a tumor board discussion on the tumor resectability. In the following, we describe more powerful mechanisms for animation generation, including scripting languages.

Early general scripting languages

The generation of animations based on a scripting language was first described by Catmull (1972). Zeltzer (1991) refers to the level on which an animation is specified as *the task level*, where *visualization goals* are described. An example of a task may be "show object NAME." As a prerequisite for using such scripts, a 3D model with an object structure is needed, and each object should be assigned a meaningful name, e.g., the name of an anatomical structure.

To bridge the gap between such high-level task specifications and the low-level commands of a graphics library, where precise coordinates for cameras, light sources, and other objects are needed, *decomposition rules* are used. These rules represent knowledge how to achieve a communicative intent with a video sequence. Several authors describe decomposition rules inspired by traditional film-making. An early example is ESPLANADE (expert system for planning animation, design and editing) (Karp and Feiner, 1993). They employ a 4-level-hierarchy with tasks on the top level, and sequences, scenes, and shots at lower levels. ESPLANADE supports primary, secondary, and tertiary motion (recall Section 6.2.1). The sequence level contains tertiary motions, such as dissolve and wipe.

ESPLANADE was employed to illustrate technical models. The animations also include exploded views and cutaways that ensure the visibility of essential objects. It is straightforward to apply the same principles to medical surface models with pathologies and their local surrounding.

Scripting anatomical animations

Preim et al. (1996) adapted the aforementioned strategies to generate animations for anatomy education. In addition to the objects of the scene, also meta-graphical symbols, such as arrows, were provided to explain anatomical structures as in instructional videos in medicine. Moreover, textual labels and multi-line explanation could be integrated in a smooth animation. For this purpose, continuous zooming techniques were employed to provide the space to include the textual components. At the task level, authors could specify which objects or groups of objects should be explained. Their ILLUSTRATORCONTROL language provides commands to further specify how objects should be explained, e.g., whether an arrow should be used to show an object (see Fig. 6.1). The goal of this language was to generate expressive animations, even with very short descriptions, but to enable more fine-grained control optionally. In particular, authors can specify with how much detail an object is explained. The author does not need to specify timings; the inbuilt rules compute how much time is needed for certain changes based on observations of what can be interpreted. However, this prevents authors from deviating from the default animation speed. The ILLUSTRATORCONTROL language supports primary motions, e.g., motions of arrows and other pointing devices and secondary motions.

An OPEN INVENTOR program controls the interpretation of the script controls, where primarily interpolator nodes were employed. Similar support for animation generation was available in more recent (web-based) graphics libraries, such as VRML and X3D. Dev (1999) describes applications for medical education. He also

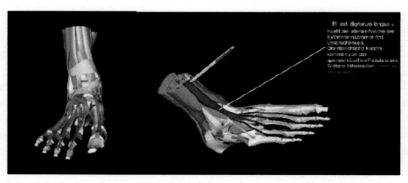

FIGURE 6.1

Two screenshots from an animation for anatomy education: The initial view of the foot anatomy is rotated to improve the visibility of the muscle; a pen points at the origin of a muscle, and a ligament that partially occluded the muscle was made transparent. The use of a pen was inspired by medical teaching videos. A textual explanation is displayed. In the further course, arrows follow the different branches of the muscles guided by the muscle's centerline (From: (Preim et al., 1996), Reprinted by permission from Proceedings of Visualization in Biomedical Computing (VBC), Springer, ©1996).

employed animated adjustments of the transparency to fade out an outer object, e.g., an organ, to make an internal object visible.

Scripting surgical animations

Mühler et al. (2006) also provide a scripting language with a focus on surgery planning. They also incorporate movements of clipping planes, the presentation of slice-based visualizations and simple animated volume renderings based on changes of 1D transfer functions. Clipping planes may be selective, e.g., they may be applied to a subset of all anatomical structures. Camera positions are specified relative to objects instead of using absolute coordinates. The time in this scripting language is explicitly specified as an interval, i.e., an instruction starts and ends at an absolute time (in seconds). Thus the execution of instructions may overlap, e.g., a second instruction specifies a movement that starts two seconds later and ends at the same time as the first instruction. Fig. 6.2 gives an example of an instruction and screenshots from the generated animation. The terms used in the scripting language are related to therapeutic questions. Also this scripting language supports primary and secondary motions.

Discussion

Although individual scripting languages provide considerable support specialized on a number of medically relevant tasks, they are not comprehensive. As an example, no medical animation system provides support for tertiary movements, e.g., typical transitions between scenes.

```
[0,5] 'Scene' sceneIntroduction
[6,9] 'Tumor' viewDistance 'Vessels'
```

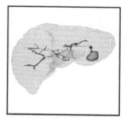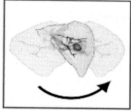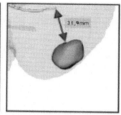

FIGURE 6.2

The two instructions specify an animation. The numbers specify the temporal interval. The "sceneIntroduction" creates a horizontal rotation. The "viewDistance" statement creates an animation that zooms to the two specified objects and integrates the display of their minimum distance (From: Mühler et al. (2006), Reprinted by permission from Proceedings of MICCAI, Springer, ©2006).

6.3.5 **Hybrid animations**

The animated display of 4D data may benefit from a hybrid combination of techniques from animating static and dynamic data, i.e., if different viewpoints are beneficial to display relevant changes in different periods. In such cases, the camera may be zoomed out, moved, and zoomed to another region (techniques from animating static data). Also the presentation may be adapted such that different regions are emphasized (animated emphasis) while the dynamic data, e.g., blood flow is displayed. It even may be useful to *follow* a moving flow feature, i.e., there is a constant movement of the camera during the dynamic data presentation.

There is, of course, a higher risk that the viewer misses essential information when both the camera and the data change simultaneously. Thus it may be considered to generate animations as sequences of presenting dynamic data from a fixed viewpoint and with fixed parameters and viewpoint changes.

6.4 **Animated volume rendering**

Volume rendering is essential for medical diagnosis and treatment. Animations of volume-rendered images have to consider three main challenges:

- getting an overview of important structures and their relationships within a dataset
- a detailed inspection of specific focus structures, where the context should be visible to support the navigation and orientation of the user within the data
- the dependency of the resulting visualization on the applied transfer function (TF), which leads to a high degree of uncertainty that should be conveyed to the user

Different approaches may tackle these challenges, which we will summarize in what follow.

6.4.1 Camera paths for volume data

In general, camera paths for volume data should fulfill the same requirements as paths for static data animations (recall Section 6.3.2). Thus the computation of appropriate paths for volume data is influenced by similar criteria, such as the visibility of targets, path length, and smoothness. Unlike animations for surface objects, animations for volume data require careful consideration of blending between different TFs to create a good transition between different focus objects.

During the exploration of a volume data set, many different images may be produced by changing parameters of TFs or lighting conditions. Wu et al. (2007) provide a framework to present these intermediate results in an understandable manner. For this purpose, they used the *color wheel metaphor* to arrange preselected TFs and lighting conditions on a wheel. Based on these functions, intermediate images can be generated, which are integrated in the wheel representation. This supports the orientation of the user during the whole exploration process. By defining some keyframes, an animation can be generated that shows a transition and blending of the affected TFs applied to the loaded data set, where the user gets an overview of existing structures. Their technique allows the authors to generate overview animations efficiently.

Hsu et al. (2013) presented an animation framework to design camera motion and to generate optimal paths for volumetric models with a focus on the exploration of the data. In the first step, the user has to select points of interest. Moreover, a roadmap is built, which describes the space where the camera is allowed to move. This free space results from an applied opacity value. Based on the roadmap, a global optimization is applied considering the multiple camera and path criteria to find smooth corridors connecting the user-selected points of interest. The user may interactively change the criteria weighting, where the resulting camera path is updated and displayed in real time. To visually support the tuning of criteria weighting, they visualized their influence using colored line segments along the path.

Hsu et al. (2013) applied their camera model to three volume data sets, including an MRI scan of a human brain with a tumor. Their technique is suitable to find appropriate and short paths in transparent regions. An expert confirmed that the animations support the exploration and navigation of complex volume models, e.g., it helps to analyze the shape of tumors and their relationships to adjacent risk structures.

6.4.2 Animation for focus+context visualization

The simultaneous visualization of different focus structures, e.g., a tumor or vessels near the tumor, while maintaining context structures, e.g., skeletal structures, is one of main difficulties of volume rendering. Focus+context visualizations for volumetric data often require manual adaptation of TFs to highlight interesting structures. Therefore different methods were developed to improve the generation of focus+context volume renderings by applying animation techniques.

Animation transfer functions

Woodring and Shen (2007) presented *animation transfer functions* (ATF) to render focus data and the context information at a similar level of detail. An ATF comprises a set of animation frame indices, where each index data is mapped to changing visual properties, such as color, texture, opacity and lighting. To generate animations, the user selects regions and chooses the types of animations that should be applied to them. Each region can receive an individual local TF. During animation, for example, the position and/or color of selected areas change over time so that interesting structures are highlighted. Motion turned out to be best suited to draw the user's attention towards regions of interest.

Dynamic focus+context

The previously described approaches change properties of the focus object continuously during animation. This can lead to complex scenes that make it difficult for the user to focus attention on important areas. Therefore Sikachev et al. (2010) introduced the *dynamic focus+context* method, which employs animation only during and shortly after interaction. They assume that interaction is a critical aspect of the exploration process, which should be *guided*.

Their system comprises three main components: an interaction type, a style function, and a visualization style. They investigated three basic interaction types, i.e., rotation, zooming, and panning. The style function controls the animation speed and the adaption of the visual representation, where three visualization styles can be applied, i.e., DVR-MIP interpolation, radial opacity change, and focus translation. The representation adapts at the beginning of the interaction and at the end the representation returns to its original rendering style.

The dynamic focus+context technique was applied to different medical data sets, e.g., to highlight denser structures, such as bones during panning, and actually allows a controlled use of animations to explore complex volume data. However, in contrast to the previously described approaches, these visualizations are highly dependent on user interaction.

Temporal focus+context

Radeva et al. (2014) described a temporal focus+context framework that allows an extensive exploration of multiple focus regions with defined context regions. With the help of a *magic lens* to select focus regions, various visualization styles can be applied to different parts of the data. This supports the data exploration by different medical experts, where, e.g., radiologists prefer other rendering styles to diagnose specific diseases than surgeons to plan operations. If different slices of a focus object are explored, the system stores the first and last seen slice and creates an animation afterwards, similar to the concept by Sikachev et al. (2010). To further facilitate the collaborative data analysis, a second lens can be activated. Thus animations can be generated, where both experts can interact with their focus region with a visualization technique of their choice.

These examples demonstrate how interactive exploration and animation complement each other and may be tightly integrated.

6.4.3 Animated display of uncertainty for diagnosis

Medical volume data involves considerable uncertainty (noise, artifacts) due to the acquisition process. Thus a volume rendering with a specific TF leads to one possible interpretation of the anatomical situation. Slightly modified TFs lead to a different, but also possible interpretation. Small changes in the TF parameters may lead to similar small changes in the visualization, which indicates stability. However, small changes may also lead to diagnostically relevant changes, in particular for the assessment of vascular structures. Radiology textbooks inform physicians that the diagnosis of a stenosis should not be based on *one* transfer function.

Lundström et al. (2007) use animations to convey different TF settings. The border of a vascular structure is considered as an instance of a probability density distribution. Based on an appropriate sampling of the probability density distribution, different instances are created, sorted according to similarity, and combined in a smooth animation. A stenosis—based on this animation—is only diagnosed if it appears in *all* frames of the animation. A *sensitivity lens* is used to restrict the animation to a (small) region, e.g., the region where a static display suggests a stenosis (see Fig. 6.3). This way, the foveated vision is focused on this area and reliably detects major changes if they would occur.

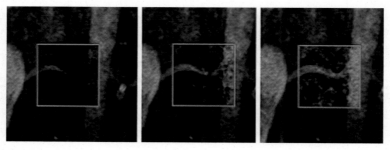

FIGURE 6.3

Slightly different transfer functions strongly affect the appearance of a vessel. In a short animation, the possible visualizations are integrated and support an effective interpretation (©2007 IEEE, Reprinted with permission from: Lundström et al. (2007)).

6.5 Medical animations of dynamic data

In this section, we consider dynamic medical image data, including *simulated* and *measured* dynamic data. Measured data includes MR perfusion, 4D PC-MRI data, and 4D angiography data. Animations of measured data are *data-driven*

Table 6.1 Major animation techniques of dynamic data (ordered chronologically).

Data	Application and Major Technique	Key Publications
2D Echocardiography	Diagnosis of heart motion, interpolation	Jilin et al. (1987)
Video-captured data	Reconstruction of heart anatomy and function	Habbal and Harris (1995)
2D Echocardiography	Diagnosis of heart motion, motion estimation	Suhling et al. (2003)
Simulated blood flow	Surgery education, particle visualization	Müller et al. (2004)
Functional image data	Quality control	Choyke et al. (2003)
Spatial health statistics	Spatial epidemiology, map animation	Chen et al. (2008)
Modeling with H-Anim	Forensic investigation, level of articulation	Ma et al. (2010)
Measured blood flow	Cardiac diagnosis, particles	van Pelt et al. (2011)
Simulated blood flow	Diagnosis of aneurysms, animated pathlines	Lawonn et al. (2014b)
Measured blood flow	Cardiac diagnosis, adaptive temporal scale	Köhler et al. (2016c)

(Parent, 2012), representing *primary motion* captured in dynamic medical image data. We also consider *procedural animations*, e.g., animations resulting from biomedical simulation, e.g., computational hemodynamics, airflow dynamics, or biomechanics. In these situations, there is a physically-based world time. Animations employ a certain temporal scale, i.e., a mapping from world time to display time. Whereas data-driven animations have to cope with the limited accuracy and noise of measured data, simulation data can be used for an animation directly, i.e., without preprocessing.

We start this section with a short discussion on preprocessing measured dynamic data (Section 6.5.1), continue with animations based on measured dynamic data (Section 6.5.2), and discuss 3D animations based on unsteady simulations in Section 6.5.4. Table 6.1 summarizes animation systems related to dynamic data.

6.5.1 Preprocessing measured dynamic medical image data

Dynamic medical image data represents a series of measurements over time. The time between two measurements is usually constant. As a consequence, dynamic data is characterized by a certain temporal resolution, e.g., about 0.40 seconds for 4D PC-MRI data. Dynamic data contains both *interesting patterns*, e.g., locally different distributed contrast agent, the emergence of flow features or the activation of brain regions, and *unwanted patterns*, e.g., due to breathing, muscle relaxation or pulsatile behavior of vessels. Moreover, medical image data is noisy and may contain artifacts. This holds in particular for dynamic data, where a living patient is imaged.

Thus spatio-temporal smoothing and motion compensation are essential steps to be performed before the actual visualization. We cannot go into detail here, but dedicated spatio-temporal smoothing algorithms, e.g., Lysaker et al. (2003), are available to increase the coherence between frames.

Motion correction

As an example of unwanted patterns, if the contrast enhancement in the female breast is analyzed to characterize a tumor suspicious to be a malignant cancer, the tumor is moved primarily due to breathing, and therefore a voxel with coordinates x, y, z at time t_i often does not correspond to a voxel with the same spatial coordinates at time t_{i+1}. Similar problems occur in measured medical flow data, where a physician may be interested in the flow near the wall of the aorta that, however, moves significantly over the cardiac cycle, and thus a vortex at the same spatial location varies strongly in its distance to the vessel wall. In this example, not the movement of the target structure (the flow), but of the reference structure (the wall) needs to be considered.

Motion correction, actually a type of image registration, is therefore necessary as a preprocessing step. Motion correction is a trade-off between the goal to preserve the relevant patterns, the accuracy of the data, and the removal of temporal artifacts.

Temporal interpolation

The temporal resolution of measured or simulated data may be insufficient for a smooth display. In a biomedical simulation, the temporal resolution directly influences the computational effort. Therefore a lower resolution may be chosen to limit the computation time. Measured data may have a rather low temporal resolution since often a trade-off between spatial and temporal resolution is necessary. Temporal interpolation techniques may enhance data acquired with 4D medical imaging (Lee and Lin, 2000).

6.5.2 Medical animations of measured dynamic image data

In what follow, we discuss medical animations related to dynamic image data. We emphasize topics that are frequently discussed either in the computer science or medical literature. Our discussion is structured according to the data type. We consider the following topics:

- blood flow data (vector + time)
- perfusion data (scalar + time)
- heart motion data (scalar + time)
- functional MRI data (scalar + time)

Animated display of blood flow data

Blood flow is increasingly investigated to understand the course and development of vascular diseases, such as atherosclerosis, thrombus formation, and aneurysms (Davies, 1995). It is also employed for risk prediction and treatment decisions to restrict risky interventions to patients who likely benefit. Blood flow in the aorta and the pulmonary artery is measured primarily with 4D PC-MRI data, a variant of MRI, which employs the phase contrast to depict temporal changes (Markl et al., 2012). In smaller vascular structures, such as the cerebral arteries, the flow cannot be directly measured, but is simulated based on the extracted vascular geometry and further boundary conditions.

A standard method for visualizing time-dependent flow is to compute pathlines. Pathlines are favorable compared to the computation of streamlines in every time step, since they represent dynamic changes and lead to a frame-coherent display of the dynamics.

Animations of dynamic data are typically characterized by a constant temporal scale, i.e., a factor that translates world time to display time. This is usually beneficial, in particular if viewers are accustomed to such animations, e.g., physicians who routinely analyze dynamic medical image data. However, a constant temporal scale implies that some parts of an animation are less interesting, e.g., because the rate of change is low or the changes are not essential for the diagnostic task. On the other hand, other parts of the same animation may be considered too fast to recognize and interpret changes. When analyzing cardiac blood flow data, for example, physicians look carefully when vortical behavior is visible and wait when no such behavior occurs. Vortex flow is essential for diagnosis and prognosis (Kheradvar et al., 2019).

Adaptive temporal scales

Based on these observations, Köhler et al. (2016c) described the choice of an *adaptive temporal scale* based on an "interestingness" measure. The system is applied to 4D PC-MRI data and the interestingness measure is based on vorticity, e.g., more time is spent on temporal intervals with strong vortical behavior, whereas intervals where the flow is laminar are displayed faster. The underlying algorithm is inspired by histogram equalization, i.e., it aims at a constant amount of feature visibility over the whole animation.

The feedback from physicians was positive in general (Köhler et al., 2016c). The physicians emphasized that it is necessary to have an option to disable this behavior. Thus the adaptive temporal scale may not replace the constant scale, but it gives a valuable additional perspective. Another aspect of the physician's feedback was that the adaptive character needs to be communicated by an appropriate legend. Because constant scale animations are so widespread, viewers need to be made aware if a different scale is employed. This strategy may be applied to a wide range of dynamic image data and interestingness measures that may be interactively adjusted.

Perfusion data

Perfusion data represent contrast enhancement over time. They are acquired, e.g., to analyze the perfusion of the brain after an ischemic stroke or to analyze the perfusion of the heart muscle after an infarction. In these examples, the temporal resolution is rather high (approximately one second), and therefore an animation can be generated that represents sufficient temporal continuity. Since one frame per second is inconvenient for viewing, the data is typically presented faster than it was measured. The animations cycle through the time frames are valuable "to assess image noise and artifacts, but especially for the assessment of enhancement patterns" (Preim et al., 2009). The temporal continuity may be enhanced by applying pharmacokinetic models, such as the Tofts model. These models have parameters to fit the resulting curve as close as possible to the time-intensity curve. Instead of a discrete temporal signal, a polynomial function describes the dynamic nature, which can be sampled at any resolution. The use of animated functional image data for quality control was also emphasized by Choyke et al. (2003).

Perfusion data is also acquired for the diagnosis of tumors, e.g., in the breast, kidney or prostate, to discriminate between benign and malignant tumors (Preim et al., 2009). Due to strong neovascularization, the contrast enhancement of a malignant tumor is often stronger and faster than for a benign tumor. Tumor perfusion data exhibit a low temporal resolution of about one minute. Thus only with a model fitting the data can the same be presented in an animation. Therefore static and interactive temporal visualizations dominate for the assessment of tumors.

Heart motion

Animation is essential for the education of medical students and heart surgeons, as well as for diagnostic purposes. The heart has a complex morphology with many substructures contributing to a coordinated pumping behavior. Animation may show the physiology of the heart and pathologic changes (Dayan et al., 2004).

In the diagnosis of the coronary heart disease, animation is also used to study the ventricular wall motion. Transthoracic ultrasound or special MR sequences are used to represent the regional wall motion (Jiang and Yu, 2014).

Typically, the most abnormal behavior is represented by *akinetic regions* that do not contribute to the wall motion, since this tissue is ischemic after an infarction. Heart motion is usually assessed with 2D echocardiography, where physicians analyze the wall motion in a few selected slices and mentally combine their impressions to a model of the complex movement and its pathological variations. Already Jilin et al. (1987) described how the information extracted from individual slices may be combined in a smooth 3D animation. They suggested to manually contour four slices, representing two longitudinal and two cross-sectional slices (both at end-systolic and end-diastolic state), and to interpolate between them.

The visual inspection may be enhanced by a quantitative analysis of the velocity magnitude and direction. Suhling et al. (2003) introduced optical flow methods to fit velocity distributions to echocardiography data and superimposed either velocity magnitude (color-coded) or velocity direction (using arrows) on the animated display. Since then, substantial research was carried out to improve motion estimation. However, no recent publication discusses visualization techniques to display the results in animations.

Dayan et al. (2004) describe the generation of animations for explaining the functioning of the mitral valve. They combine anatomical information derived in high quality from the histological sections of the VISIBLE HUMAN dataset with motion-captured data from a cadaver, where fiducial markers were tracked. The anatomical information comprises 28 anatomical structures, including the mitral annulus, the leaflets, and the subvalvular apparatus. The models were textured to increase the realism. Dayan et al. (2004) prepared animations from the *surgeon's perspective*, e.g., the learner can observe the movement from a perspective that resembles the view a surgeon in the operating room typically has.

Functional MRI data

Functional MRI data (fMRI) is widely used to study functional regions in the brain, e.g., the motor cortex and the visual cortex, as well as their interactions when performing tasks that require eye-hand coordination. These data are acquired primarily when a healthy volunteer or a patient carries out cognitive or motor tasks, such as performing finger tapping.

Functional MRI data represent changes in the blood oxygenation level that is surrogate for neuronal activity. "The temporal information, provided by the fMRI acquisition, is usually ignored" (Aguerre et al., 2003). Aguerre et al. (2003) argue that fMRI data needs to be carefully rescaled in time to display the activation patterns in a perceivable speed. Moreover, they fit models to the time-course of the measured data, e.g., assuming that each activation follows a Gaussian distribution, and thus the data is a accumulation of various individual Gaussian functions. This use of a model is similar to the pharmokinetic models employed in the advanced analysis of perfusion data (recall Section 6.5.2).

The use of these models has a smoothing effect on the data and leads to a better interpretation of an animation. Potentially, these models even reduce the effect of measurement noise, i.e., the smoothed data *may* be even more accurate than the raw data. The feedback from neuroscience researchers is that they are primarily interested in the sequence of activated regions.

6.5.3　Animations of dynamic map-based medical data

In medical visualization, projection-based (or map-based) techniques are often used to reveal the distribution of parameters at a glance, i.e., without occlusion problems inherent to 3D visualizations (Kreiser et al., 2018). For dynamic data value changes, e.g., pressure or blood flow velocity, are typically color-coded leading to dynamic heat maps.

Spatial epidemiology

is an area at the intersection between medicine and geosciences. The incidence of diseases, and potential risks, is depicted on maps (typically with data aggregated over administrative units). Since the underlying data is time-dependent, temporal visualizations, such as change maps or animations, are generated. MacEachren et al. (1998) show medical examples of map animations. These are generated on the fly after the user specified a temporal interval. Moreover, attributes, such as the incidence of heart diseases among men and the unemployment rate, may be chosen. We discuss spatial epidemiology, including more examples of animated visualizations in the chapter on visual analytics in public health (Chapter 10).

Temporal re-expression

An idea from cartographic animation that is potentially useful for medical animation is to change the presentation order to convey relations and trends not easily recognizable in the original sequence of data. Kraak et al. (1997) suggest to display periodic data aggregated over the months of the year, such that firstly all January measurements are shown, then all February measurements, and so on. For epidemiology data, such animations would reveal the variability of the incidence of influenza within a season, whereas a conventional display would emphasize the seasonal differences. Data that is dependent on the heart beat may be re-expressed such that all peak systolic data are displayed sequentially and all peak diastolic data as well.

6.5.4 Animating medical simulations

Many processes in medicine are simulated, often because they cannot be directly measured. Another reason to simulate medical processes is to *predict* treatment response, e.g., the blood flow after inserting certain vascular implants, or the temperature distribution after a thermal tumor ablation is performed with certain needles and certain voltage applied for some time.

Animating hemodynamics simulations

Animation techniques, developed to convey measured blood flow (recall Section 6.5.2), are in general useful for simulated blood flow as well. The major difference is the need for preprocessing, where measured blood flow suffers from various artifacts and noise (see Köhler et al. (2017) for a discussion of this preprocessing). Simulated blood flow data is clean and does not exhibit noise, thus the data can be displayed more directly. Though most of the research to explore hemodynamics simulations is focused on interactive exploration, e.g., zoomable user interfaces, map-based overviews, and dynamic filtering (see (Oeltze-Jafra et al., 2019)), a few authors also discussed animated displays.

Particle animations for blood flow

Particle animations are widely used to show natural phenomena. They are also a natural choice for displaying blood flow, e.g., as part of a surgical training system. Müller et al. (2004) introduced a particle-based system "to realistically animate blood of water." They apply smoothed particle hydrodynamics to simulate the flow. The visualization of the particles may be color-coded to convey the speed of the particles. Use cases discussed by Mueller et al. include the simulation of injuries of vascular structures during surgery. Later, also van Pelt et al. (2011) employed particle animations to convey blood flow. Their animations are embedded in an interactive system, i.e., the user may probe the flow, and thus insert particles at a particular region. A short

FIGURE 6.4

Animated pathlines represent simulated blood flow over time. In the scheme, one pathline enters the aneurysm, whereas the second one remains in the parent vessel. The part of the pathline that corresponds to the current time is emphasized by color. A Gaussian was used to modify the color saturation with a peak at the current time point (From: Lawonn et al. (2014b), ©John Wiley & Sons Inc., 2014).

animation reveals the movement of the measured flow, starting from this seed region by means of particles.

Pathlines for unsteady blood flow results

Lawonn et al. (2014b) animated pathlines, representing simulated blood flow in cerebral aneurysms. Like in most flow simulations, computational fluid dynamics (CFD) is employed and the vascular anatomy, representing the inflow and outflow area along with the aneurysm, is extracted from clinical data and represented as a surface mesh. The animation conveys differences in speed, which is essential for risk analysis. High-speed flow that enters the aneurysm and hits the wall is related to an increased risk. The display of the pathlines is adjusted such that portions of the pathline close to the vessel wall are emphasized (see Fig. 6.4). This is valuable since the spatial relation between the pathline and the wall of curved vessels may be difficult to perceive, e.g., due to occlusion. The wall movement is not severe in cerebral vessels, and thus ignored. Whether these animations correctly convey all relevant information or are too difficult and cause change blindness was not tested.

Coppin et al. (2014) aimed to create "illustration-inspired" flow visualizations based on CFD simulations of flow in cerebral aneurysms and the surrounding vascular geometry. The major motivation of their work is to replace "dense engineering representations" that contain "both relevant and irrelevant details." They compute vortex core regions over the cardiac cycle, i.e., regions where the flow swirls, which is not physiologic and thus hints to a pathology. The resulting images are imported into Adobe Photoshop and enhanced frame by frame by a digital artist to better convey transitional and turbulent flow characterized by the vortex core regions. It is not clear whether the quality of such visualizations can be created with a semi-automatic approach.

Animation in functional anatomy

Functional anatomy comprises an understanding of the relation between anatomical structures and their function. This includes the movement of joints (biomechanics), the pumping of the heart muscle and the pumping of the Eustachian tube (Habbal and Harris, 1995). Animations to convey these functions are typically based on an explicit modeling of these movements. The basis for modeling the dynamics is often a (static) medical data set of a patient or a healthy person. CT data are used to create models of the relevant skeletal anatomy, whereas MRI data are a suitable basis for extracting the relevant soft tissue structures.

Various groups developed functional animations to convey biomechanical properties. As an example, Chao et al. (1993) described a knee model comprising "muscles, tendons, ligaments, bone, and joint anatomy" for interactive use and animation. Thus users explore the model interactively and can trigger short animations. The roles of an *author* and a *viewer* in this context merge. Besides, Davies and deSilva (2000) presented a simpler knee model containing only the bones. With this model, they created animations of rotational movements in the sagittal and transverse plane and demonstrate that only very small movements in the axial plane are possible. Students see how the femur glides on the tibia in these animations. Again, the animations are generated by the user in an interactive system. Unfortunately, the actual animations, e.g., speed and duration, as well as the interpretation of the animations by the target group are not discussed.

H-Anim standard

The H-Anim ISO/IEC standard (https://www.web3d.org/standards/h-anim) is an essential basis for the animation of biomechanical movements. It comprises a model of the human anatomy consisting of joints and segments (H-Anim is an abbreviation for humanoid anatomy) (Jung and Behr, 2008). The movements resulting from using H-Anim are based on Newtonian's laws of motion (*scientific animations*). They are employed, e.g., for forensic investigations (Ma et al., 2010). Based on H-Anim, CT, or MRI data can be used to extract a skeleton and match it with the abstract data incorporated in the standard. Then, the model may be animated displaying correct movements. The H-Anim standard incorporates a hierarchy of joints, e.g., when the arm is moved, the hand is moved as well. The joints are modeled at four "levels of articulation" (Ma et al., 2010). The coarsest model consists of an 18-joint skeleton; more detailed levels comprise 71, 94, and 144 joints, respectively. H-Anim also provides a Web3D-capable motion viewer that may export animated films. H-Anim is used in particular to move the whole human body, not just the skeleton. This way, skin vertices, for example, are also moved in a realistic manner when associated joints are moved.

6.6 Applications of animations based on static data

In this section, we give an overview of applications, where static data was employed to support medical education, diagnosis, treatment planning, and also forensic use cases. We comment, if possible, on the specific animation design and evaluations that assess the value of animation, typically by comparing with other modes of information presentation.

6.6.1 **Medical education**

Animations were developed and evaluated for anatomy education, embryology (neonatal development), surgery training, histology, cellular processes, and regional anesthesia teaching. Dev (1999) emphasizes the essential role of visual information in all stages of medical education, ranging from students to recertification of experienced practitioners. Videos and computer-generated 3D animations were considered as *engaging modes* of visual communication. Embryology education, for example, benefits from animations that show the complex development of human organs, such as the development of the strongly twisted gut from a straight line (Dev, 1999). Animations for educational purposes should be designed with the findings of learning theory on the reception of animation in mind (recall Section 6.2.1). We postpone a discussion of animations for anatomy education since this topic better fits Chapter 7 "3D Visualization for Anatomy Education".

Surgical training

Dynamic presentations play an essential role in surgery training, as they can convey the deformability of organs and tissue as a result of the use of surgical instruments. However, intraoperative video is the prevailing presentation mode. As an example, WebSurg (https://www.websurg.com) provides thousands of videos for explaining a large variety of surgeries. The videos are structured according to major steps of the surgery and contain textual explanations. In addition, computer animations often show slice-based visualizations and related annotations that make the user familiar with the pathology and the surrounding anatomy.

Cutting et al. (2002) provide evidence that 3D animations are valuable for surgery training. They address cleft lip and palate surgery and developed an animation based on polygonal models of skin, bone, cartilage, and muscles. The models were smoothed, simplified, and imported in MAYA (ALIAS/WAVEFRONT, Toronto, Canada). We discuss this paper in more detail since it is a pioneering work for using high-quality 3D animations for surgery education.

The animations show the action of a scalpel. The major problem is that the use of a scalpel changes the geometry radically: incisions alter the topology of the underlying geometric models. Commercial animation systems do not provide support for adequately treating such topology changes. As a consequence, Cutting et al. (2002) prepared many small animations (without topology changes) and combined them in a final step. Since the anatomical model contains different layers, transparency is used to display the skin and inner layers, e.g., the nasal cartilage complex, simultaneously. Movements of the skin are propagated to the (linked) inner layer representing cartilage and muscles. The animation is a hybrid between animations of dynamic and static data. The dynamic component is a simulation of the pump mechanism of the Eustachian tubes, whereas camera movements and zooming operations represent the techniques from animating static data.

Qualter et al. (2004) also discussed the use of 3D animations for surgery education. They emphasize the necessity to control the size of the polygonal meshes to achieve a sufficient frame rate. Based on the photographic data of the

VISIBLE HUMAN data set and related segmentation information, they used MAYA to re-color the organs according to didactic principles and applied textures that resemble living tissue more than the textures captured in the cadaver data set. So-called *deformers* are used to control tissue deformation, and thus convey the dynamic changes occurring during surgery. As showcase example, they use colon surgery. The authors do not discuss how the deformation is actually realized.

Endoscopic ultrasonography

Endoscopic ultrasonography requires considerable experience to be used effectively. Burmester et al. (2004) developed a training system to support the understanding of ultrasound data. The system was based on the VOXELMAN, a comprehensive anatomy education system that employs the Visible Human data set (Schiemann et al., 2000). Ultrasonography images were simulated to create appropriate animations.

Regional anesthesia teaching

Regional anesthesia involves inserting a needle to initiate anesthesia that only affects a local area. Physicians have to know the target anatomy well to avoid complications, and they must be skilled to manipulate the needles properly. Lim et al. (2004) observed that training opportunities largely depend on suitable patients and decreased over time. In their specific example, they aim at a training of regional anesthesia for arm and shoulder operations.

Lim et al. (2004) prepared short animations, lasting between 2 s and 8 s, showing individual steps of the procedure. TrueSpace from Caligary was used (the system is no longer available). A neck model was used for selecting good viewpoints to demonstrate surface landmarks and the needle movement. Similar to Cutting et al., Lim et al. (2004) emphasize the importance of transparency to convey spatial relations. They also emphasize the role of incorrect handling of the needle and their consequences as part of the generated animations.

The evaluation was carried out with 24 physicians. The large majority (21 physicians) stated that the animations enhanced their anatomical and technical understanding. The physicians also had to set surface markers for needle placement. Those with little to moderate experience improved their performance significantly after watching the integrated animations, leading Lim et al. (2004) to the conjecture that "less advanced trainees would probably benefit more from didactic teaching. Therefore, we chose a less interactive approach."

Discussion

3D animations are very useful for training procedures to explain individual steps or the composition of a procedure based on these steps. Carefully designed animations use several viewpoints that provide an unobstructed view to the relevant anatomical structure and instruments, including viewpoints that are impossible to realize when preparing a real video. "Intraoperative video is only slightly more useful than 2D views because it is usually filmed with a stationary camera" (Cutting et al., 2002). Transparency is another powerful mechanism in a 3D animation to convey spatial relations, e.g., within a transparently rendered organ. Moreover, the visual display in an educational 3D animation is easier to interpret compared to an intraoperative video. For interventions, such as anesthesia teaching, a video could not show interesting internal details. Cutting et al. (2002) argue that animation supports an *early stage* of learning, whereas more experienced learners benefit more from active learning, e.g., solving tasks in a virtual reality system.

6.6.2 Patient education

Complex spatial information needs to be conveyed in the process of patient education before surgery or interventions. The information comprises major steps of the intervention and the risk of associated complications. In what follow, we describe three animation systems for patient education.

Hermann (2002) compared the quality of patient education with 3D animation with a conventional approach based on textual information. The regional anatomy around the thyroid gland and basic steps of surgery are shown in an animation created with CINEMA4D. The specific complications that may arise related to anatomical structures, e.g., nerves, in close proximity are also displayed. The control group had 10 minutes time to read a textual explanation carefully adapted to patients. The animation group (both groups comprise 40 patients each) reported significantly better subjective understanding and more trust. However, no details about the design of the animation, e.g., duration, speed, camera paths, are given. The screenshots indicate that the visualizations are rather simple and clear with high contrast. The anatomical structures are strongly smoothed, and thus easy to perceive. The animated anatomy is not patient-specific. It was prepared once and re-used often to justify the expense of around 20, 000 euro.

The SINUSENDOSCOPY system was also used for patient education (Krüger et al., 2008). The surgeon explained the surgery and associated risks based on patient-specific data. The virtual camera moved along a precomputed path, leading to animations that last about 40 seconds. The animations were presented by the operating surgeon on a large 40-inch monitor to explain the surgical strategy to the patient. The evaluation revealed that the large majority of 127 patients found these animations helpful. Additional comments reveal that patients gained trust in the procedure. The implications are described by Strauss et al. (2009).

McGhee (2010) describes an approach to generate animations that emphasize aesthetics, appeal, and artistic proficiency to engage learners or patients. As an example, material properties and shaders are carefully tweaked to achieve highly reflective vessel visualizations (derived from clinical MR angiography). They contain blood cells and indicate blood flow during the cardiac cycle (see Fig. 6.5). McGhee also emphasizes the "narrative," the story that is conveyed by means of dynamic images to "engage students and improve their understanding of disease … and treatment" (McGhee, 2010). McGhee also provides a discussion of further evidence that pictorial content is beneficial for patient education.

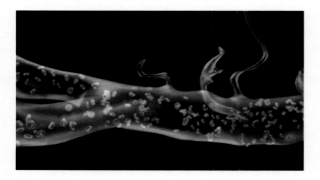

FIGURE 6.5

The human aorta and some of its side branches extracted from MRI data and combined with a particle simulation with blood flow (From: (McGhee, 2010), ©John Wiley & Sons Inc., 2010).

6.6.3 Virtual endoscopy

Virtual endoscopy, where a camera is moved inside the human body, is probably the most important area for generating animations in medicine. Virtual endoscopy is essential for diagnostic tasks, e.g., as a screening examination, but also for therapy planning. Virtual endoscopy is an umbrella term for different diagnostic procedures:

- virtual bronchoscopy relates to the inspection of the bronchial tree
- virtual colonoscopy addresses the search for polyps in the colon
- virtual angioscopy relates to inspection of arteries

An animated "flythrough" is generated to inspect the walls of tubular structures. Due to the complex shape of tubular structures, such as the colon, a keyframe animation based on user-selected key viewpoints is tedious (Jolesz et al., 1997). Instead, the generation of a flythrough requires little user input, i.e., the user selects a start point and an endpoint in the target structure, e.g., the colon.

Camera path planning

We discussed camera path planning before, with the goal to create view sequences that display the relevant anatomy from *outside*. The fundamental difference in virtual endoscopy is that the camera is restricted to the interior of anatomical cavities. Based on a segmentation and centerline determination, a path is created that connects the start and endpoint. All points along this path are inside the target structure, approximately in the middle. For strongly curved self-intersecting structures, this is not easy to achieve. A focus of path computation is to *avoid collision* with the wall of the target structure. The centerline may be post-processed to better serve as a camera path. It is often smoothed to avoid sudden changes of the camera direction. However, collision avoidance always has higher priority. The centerline may contain many branches caused by bulges. It is questionable whether the camera should actually traverse all these bulges. Simple heuristics may be used to prune such structures and reduce them to a main path with a few relevant side branches.

These processes may be performed with default parameters in a predefined manner and result in a path that smoothly connects the start and endpoint. The sensitivity in the detection of polyps along the wall may be improved considerably if the physician watches a second animation that displays the path from the end to the start point. Some folds are better visible if the camera looks at them from the opposite direction.

Lorensen et al. (1995) adapted concepts from robot motion planning to derive a path where the camera does not collide with anatomical structures. Camera path planning can be treated as an optimization problem with different criteria, such as path length and smoothness and constraints related to obstacles. Hong et al. (1997) described the first comprehensive virtual colonoscopy system, including a careful discussion of useful interactions. The user is guided from the start to the target point and *glides* in the colon center, a navigation inspired by the *submarine metaphor*. Bartz (2005) gives a survey on the first decade of virtual endoscopy developments.

Synchronized animation

A virtual camera that moves inside a complex structure, such as the bronchial tree, reveals the *local* detail of the bronchial wall surface, but does not convey where the camera is in relation to anatomical landmarks, i.e., the *global* context is missing. Virtual endoscopy systems therefore typically generate *synchronized* animations that display the endoscopic view and a 3D view from outside indicating the current camera position and orientation. An alternative is the display of 2D slices along with the endoscopic view, where the currently displayed slice contains a cross-hair cursor to indicate the current camera position. A split screen display, where external 3D views and 2D slice views are synchronized with the virtual endoscopy view, was suggested by Jolesz et al. (1997). Even the three orthogonal slicing directions (axial, sagittal, coronal) are often displayed simultaneously with the endoscopic view to support the interpretation of the current camera position and orientation in context (see Fig. 6.6). On the other hand, this split-screen situation raises split-attention problems, i.e., the cognitive load is increased (recall Section 6.2). Thus the animations need to be viewed several times to extract all relevant information in the different displays and understand their relation.

Surgery planning

Virtual endoscopy is also useful for planning endoscopic surgery (Çakmak and Kühnapfel, 2000; Krüger et al., 2008). The different target user groups lead to slightly different requirements related to the interactive data exploration. Surgeons may use an animated flythrough to define a cutting position in the tissue. Thus they do not only want to interrupt an animation, but also to mark a position or draw a line. Radiologists, on the other hand, may also annotate an endoscopic view when they see a suspicious region.

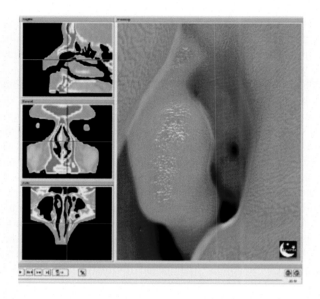

FIGURE 6.6

SINUSENDOSCOPY: A flythrough the nasal cavities for surgery preparation. The current camera position is indicated in three orthogonal slices (left), whereas the right view shows the endoscopic view (©2008 IEEE, Reprinted with permission from: Krüger et al. (2008)).

Çakmak and Kühnapfel (2000) created textured geometric models from the VIS-IBLE HUMAN data set and assigned mechanical properties to realistically deform medical tissue when forces, such as instruments, are applied. Mass spring models are employed for modeling the dynamic changes. Such functional animations may convey complications, such as bleedings, and the smoke when tissue is ablated (Baur et al., 1998).

Krüger et al. (2008) developed the SINUSENDOSCOPY system for surgery planning in the nasal cavity and patient education (recall Fig. 6.6). The risk is highly patient-specific, e.g., only in some cases surgery involves areas close to the optic nerve. Since there are no tubular structures that guide the virtual camera, the camera path is manually defined by selecting points in the slices. The surgeon used the generated animations for rehearsal. However, the effort to prepare such animations is large, and thus the system is no longer used.

Discussion

Stollfuß (2017) discusses animated flythroughs, including the influence of parameters that control illumination, texture, and other aspects, related to the perceived realism. From a didactic perspective, he emphasizes that animated endoscopy is based on data and many decisions of an author. We discussed McGhee's work to characterize the potential of aesthetically pleasing and informative animations for patient education (recall McGhee (2010)). Their focus was on *enhanced virtual endoscopy* applied to the vascular system. Animated flythroughs may benefit from the use of CAD (computer-aided detection) findings, e.g., suspicious regions in the colon that likely represent polyps (Zhao et al., 2006). In an animated transition, these findings may be emphasized and shown from different directions.

Whereas most animations are restricted to one viewport, multiple synchronized animations may provide different perspectives, similar to multiple coordinated views for interactive data exploration. Synchronized animations of internal and external 3D views are typical for virtual endoscopy (Jolesz et al., 1997).

6.6.4 Animation for the diagnosis of medical blood flow data

The visual exploration of patient-specific blood flow data is important for the diagnosis and treatment planning of vascular diseases. To assess the severity of a disease and find appropriate treatment, morphological and hemodynamic aspects have to be analyzed simultaneously. This is a challenging task due to the complexity of the time-dependent data.

We already discussed cerebral aneurysms in Section 6.5.4, based on techniques to display simulated flow data as an example for animating dynamic medical data. However, the dynamic 3D data also involves problems of finding good viewpoints to observe essential characteristics. Therefore we discuss the topic here again as an example of medical animations that benefit from techniques developed for animating static data.

For this purpose, Meuschke et al. (2017a) developed an automatic selection of optimal viewpoints that are connected to an animation for the visual exploration of time-dependent blood flow data in cerebral aneurysms. With this system, suspicious surface regions can be analyzed according to flow attributes without a time-consuming manual exploration.

The selection of viewpoints is modeled as an optimization problem. It consists of three major steps:

1. A target function is formulated that should be optimized.
2. Start points for searching appropriate views are chosen that serve as input for the optimization problem.
3. The resulting viewpoints are connected to a camera path.

The target function considers visibility of the aneurysm surface part and an interestingness measure derived by two user-selected attributes, e.g., low wall thickness and high wall shear stress. For start point selection, an ellipsoid around the whole vessel surface is sampled discretely. To reduce the number of necessary runs of the optimization procedure, only the top 10% of viewpoints are further processed. Moreover, a clustering algorithm is employed to group the remaining start points, and a representative per cluster is used to determine an optimal viewpoint. Thus views from different perspectives are generated around an aneurysm showing possible rupture-prone areas. Finally, a camera path gliding around the target structure (orbiting) is used to create an animation. The evaluation indicates that the generated animation is useful for the assessment of the rupture risk. Manually selected views from medical experts were quite similar to the automatically selected views with respect to camera position and view direction. However, additional manual exploration is required, e.g., to explore small structures, such as additional bulges on the surface, called blebs.

6.6.5 Forensics

Animated visualizations in forensics are generated in the case of shootings or other severe crimes. They may integrate different viewpoints, representing, e.g., the position of witnesses. Animations integrate *raw data*, representing the patient anatomy, gun or knifes, other aspects of the crime scene and *reconstructed data*, e.g., the bullet path (Ma et al., 2010). The major use cases for such animations are to discuss possible reconstructions with respect to plausibility and likelihood, and to demonstrate the results to the judges in the court room. Ma et al. (2010) report that computer-generated animations are admitted in the courtroom in the UK if correctness is carefully analyzed. "Physically accurate forensic animation may shed light on investigating what exactly happened at a specific crime scene, causes and effects that embrace the issue who is at fault or guilty." (Ma et al., 2010).

This development is largely based on the increasing use of *virtual autopsy*, i.e., post-mortem CT and MRI data (Thali et al., 2005). The data acquisition may be carried out as a whole body scan or as a scan of different body parts, which are later combined (Villa et al., 2017). Due to the large size of the data, efficient rendering is challenging (Ljung et al., 2006). Fig. 6.7 shows an example of a reconstructed crime based on post-mortem data.

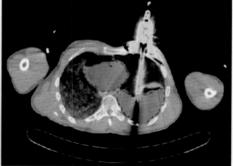

FIGURE 6.7

Reconstruction of a crime scene. The cadaver data set was imaged with CT; the puncture of the lung with a knife is visible (From: Preim et al. (2005), Reprinted by permission from Proceedings of Bildverarbeitung fuer die Medizin, Springer, ©2005).

Table 6.2 Major animation systems related to static data in medicine (ordered chronologically).

Data	Application and Major Technique	Key Publications
Geometric models	Anatomy education, scripting language	Preim et al. (1996)
MR head data	Anatomy education, neuroscience, morphing	Thompson and Toga (1997)
Abdominal CT	Virtual colonoscopy, path planning	Hong et al. (1997)
Abdominal CT	Virtual colonoscopy, combined 2D and 3D views	Jolesz et al. (1997)
Abdominal CT	Endoscopic surgical training tool, bleeding	Baur et al. (1998)
Visible Human	Virtual endoscopy, surgery training	Çakmak and Kühnapfel (2000)
Abdominal CT	Surgery training, palate surgery, transparency	Cutting et al. (2002)
Abdominal CT	Pelvic and liver anatomy, morphing	Lamecker et al. (2004)
Geometric models	Anesthesia training, transparency adaptation	Lim et al. (2004)
Neck CT	Surgery planning and education, scripting language	Mühler et al. (2006)
CT angiography	Vascular pathologies, uncertainty lenses	Lundström et al. (2007)
Head CT	Virtual endoscopy, patient education	Krüger et al. (2008)

In Section 6.2.3, we briefly discussed the term *scientific animation*. Animations in forensics fall into this category. The whole animation generation process aims at faithfulness and credibility. Aesthetic considerations are not essential. Biomechanical animations are employed to discuss possible postures of a victim during a crime. Ma et al. (2010) employed the H-Anim standard with a moderate level of detail (Level 2 with 71 joints) for this purpose.

Table 6.2 summarizes animation systems using static data.

6.6.6 Summary

A common factor in animations of static medical image data is that the 3D patient anatomy needs to be visualized. Moreover, the visual focus needs to be directed towards essential structures, e.g., the region where a pathology is supposed or was found. Thus animations often serve to convey the spatial relations in this focus region and to embed them in a broader anatomical context. Changes of the camera position and emphasis techniques, such as modifications of color and transparency, are frequently used. Whereas forensic animations and animations for diagnosis aim at high accuracy, animations for medical education in anatomy and surgery may stronger deviate from reality in favor of a good understanding of spatial relations.

6.7 Interactive animations

Interaction is essential to control animations independent of the field of application. We employ cartography to discuss interactive animation, since it is widely used. In cartography, it is well-known that viewers are frustrated if they cannot control the animation (Monmonier and Gluck, 1994). Ogao and Kraak (2002) define the following interaction tasks for temporal cartographic animations:

- Adjust spatial and temporal resolution
- Adjust spatial and temporal scale
- Enable multiple linked (dynamic) views
- Query temporal data
- Use mouse-over, e.g., show labels, measures

Whereas these interaction tasks are relevant for map-based (2D) animations, additional interaction tasks are essential for 3D animations. The user may stop a 3D animation, and then interactively explore the data by zooming and rotation. Once the user is finished, a short animation may be generated to return to the initial state before the animation is continued. The animations generated for anatomy education (recall Preim et al. (1996)) can be interrupted in this manner. Such a feature is even more importance for virtual endoscopy. The automatically generated animation leads the physician to a particular point along the centerline where they may notice a suspicious lesion. Then they should be able to explore this lesion, measure its extent, annotate it for a report, and then "ask" the system to continue the flythrough.

The discussion of interactive control also comprises input devices. The joystick is a natural choice to control presentation speed (Stollfuß, 2017), but also to steer the camera, e.g., in virtual endoscopy. We found no research comparing input devices for steering medical animations, in particular in endoscopy.

6.8 The process of animation generation

Since a large number of medical animations has been created with general purpose software, instead of dedicated systems for medical use, we mention major tools in Section 6.8.1. One essential aspect for many applications is the re-use of carefully generated animations for similar cases. We discuss re-use strategies and specific examples in Section 6.8.2.

6.8.1 Tools for animation design

Animations are often created with professional general purpose animation software. In the articles discussed in this chapter, 3D studio max (Ma et al., 2010), Cinema4D (Hermann, 2002), Maya (Cutting et al., 2002; Qualter et al., 2004; Dayan et al., 2004), and Caligari TrueSpace (Lim et al., 2004) are mentioned. These animation tools are intended for digital artists and animators. They provide support for geometric modeling, including the transformation of traced contours to splines, the transformation of these splines to surface models, and mesh decimation. Thus a geometric model can be created based on medical image data.

Animation software also supports enhancing these models with textures, e.g., photos from anatomical structures taken intraoperatively. Moreover, keyframe animations are supported, where the author defines a set of keyframes and may choose among different strategies to create smooth animations based on an interpolation scheme. These interpolation-based techniques are often referred to as "Tweening" (Sakchaicharoenkul, 2006). The complex tools aim at efficient support for professional authors, instead of an easy-to-use lean interface for casual users. We use the term *author* to refer to the person that creates an animation and the term *viewer* to refer to the recipient.

More recently, authoring tools were developed that support animation generation based on principles from traditional cinematography, i.e., the generated animations should be particularly engaging. An example is DATACLIPS, a system introduced by Amini et al. (2016) to generate animations based on data sets and selected (film-based) techniques. Such tools are very useful for generating animations, or data videos, based on statistical data. They do not provide techniques to create 3D animations.

6.8.2 Re-use of medical animations

Medical animations may be unique, i.e., exactly *one* animation is generated and frequently used (as it is). They are often based on data of a healthy and "normal" person, e.g., the VISIBLE HUMAN data set, abstracting from any anatomical and pathological variations of a patient. However, in routine diagnosis and therapy planning, only patient-specific animations are meaningful. It is essential that they can be created in a cost-effective manner, i.e., without a large amount of user input. Thus re-use in the sense of adapting the animation to a similar patient is essential. The idea of re-using an animation is conceptually similar to *example-based animations* (Wang and Lee, 2008); a concept that was used, for example, for clothing animation (Wang et al., 2010). Although similar, the concepts are not identical. Wang and Lee (2008) use different animations to compose a new animation. We consider re-use, as defined by Mühler and Preim (2010), as the transfer of a single animation to similar data sets.

In addition to effectiveness, standardized approaches to animation generation also ensure *reproducibility*, e.g., animations are less dependent on the actual author. There are considerable efforts in all areas of radiology to standardize documentation, e.g., with respect to protocols, sequences, and terminology. The incorporation of 3D visualization and animation in documentation obviously requires also to standardize the use of algorithms and parameters (Higuera et al., 2003a). This standardization includes transfer function specifications, viewing directions, and clipping planes. Ideally, the expert knowledge of a physician is only necessary to create a first or very few animations, and further animations are automatically *adapted* based on these examples.

We start with simple animations based on MIP and go on with attempts to create animations that are adapted to other cases as automatically as possible. We discuss an example from neuroradiology, the diagnosis of cerebral aneurysms. Finally, we discuss surgery planning.

Orbiting with maximum-intensity projections

Maximum-intensity projection (MIP) is a simple method to display contrast-enhanced vascular structures without preprocessing and the need to adjust parameters. It is based on the assumption that regions in the data with the highest values are particularly interesting, which is often the case with vascular structures. However, no depth cues are provided, i.e., the maximum along each viewing ray is depicted, no matter where in the data it actually occurs. To compensate for this drawback, a series of images is precomputed offline and shown in an animation that provides a horizontal loop around the data set. Most vascular structures appear unoccluded in one of these views. Thus a simple reusable animation is required that employs the bounding box' extent and center to incrementally change the viewing direction, resulting in an orbiting around the data set. Orbiting around a reference object with a fixed distance is a widely used *guided* technique that contributes to a mental understanding of complex spatial structures (Tan et al., 2001). The continuous movement follows the arc-principle (recall Section 6.2.3).

Such animated visualizations of the vascular anatomy were first mentioned by Pavone et al. (1992). Later research aimed at a fast generation of the animations, exploiting preprocessing, graphics hardware, and memory-efficient schemes (Mroz et al., 2000; Kiefer et al., 2006). This way, real-time performance could be achieved with high-quality renderings that involve trilinear interpolation, instead of the poor quality achieved with nearest neighbor interpolation (Mroz et al., 2000).

With similar approaches, also local MIP visualizations are animated (Sato et al., 1998). A local MIP is a modification, where instead of the global maximum along a ray, the first local maximum beyond a threshold is considered. This modification enables a better display of smaller vascular structures in front of larger (and thus brighter) vessels. However, this advantage is only achieved if the threshold is carefully chosen.

Re-use of animations for aneurysm diagnostics

For diagnosis, it is essential that a pathology is detected, that its shape can be recognized in detail, and be quantitatively assessed, e.g., its size or volume is determined. Based on such information, radiologists report on the existence of a pathology and the stage or severity of a disease. 3D visualizations and animations may be beneficial in case of pathologies with a complex shape that are partially occluded or otherwise difficult to assess, e.g., vascular pathologies. Vascular pathologies include plaques, stenoses, aneurysms, and arterio-venous malformations (AVMs). We describe the (re)use of animations for the diagnosis aneurysms that may occur in the whole arterial system, e.g., abdominal aortic or cerebral aneurysms.

Cerebral aneurysms are dilations of a cerebral artery that carry the risk of rupture. Iserhardt-Bauer et al. (2002) created standardized animations to support a systematic search for such aneurysms based on the locations where they occur most frequently. CT angiography data are used, and subvolumes are extracted in a standardized way. Clipping planes are inserted at specific landmarks, and the transfer functions are adapted to a new case in a clearly defined manner. The basic strategy for this adaptation is a histogram analysis involving also derived data, such as gradient magnitude. Instead of one large video sequence, five smaller sequences are generated. Each consists of circular 360° flights around a subvolume.

The approach was refined by Rößler et al. (2007) who provide a GPU-based solution. Thus the computation of transfer function parameters, the direct volume rendering, and video encoding are distributed to achieve optimal load balancing.

Re-use of animations for surgery planning

We previously discussed simple animations of MIP images to provide a spatial impression without the need to interact with the data. The same principle can be applied to more complex 3D surface models as they occur, e.g., in liver surgery planning. Here, the liver anatomy is segmented to provide selective visualizations, e.g., of vessels and tumors, or tumors and vascular supply areas (Newe et al., 2014). Newe et al. (2014) embed such animations in 3D PDFs, and thus provide a portable user-friendly solution evaluated by 138 physicians who used the 3D PDF for more than 1000 cases. They report that animations from a restricted set of viewpoints do not convey the full spatial information, but may serve as a good starting point. The use of 3D PDFs for patient education is also discussed, since about one third of the physicians mentioned this use case. However, the short discussion does not reveal whether automatically generated videos or interactive exploration was used for patient education.

A precise understanding of the pathology and the spatial relationships is also essential for surgery planning. Additional requirements relate to the discussion of different surgical strategies, e.g., the selection of an implant, or the choice of a more or less radical intervention.

Access planning and assessment of infiltrations

Mühler and Preim (2010) designed and evaluated animations for oncologic neck and liver surgery planning to summarize a longer individual planning process for collaborative discussions, e.g., in a tumor board. This requires an easy generation of animations and the re-use of one animation for similar cases. For tumor surgery planning, access planning and the assessment of infiltrations are typical examples. Access planning can be supported by an animation that moves the camera gradually from the outside closer to the tumor, eventually combined with fading out occluding structures. The assessment of potential infiltrations requires to study the tumor and nearby structures, such as vascular structures. A careful investigation from many dif-

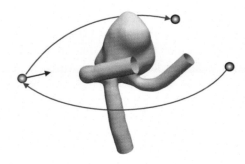

FIGURE 6.8

Animation generation: The spheres indicate the camera path. Their size, the number of steps, and the temporal resolution can be adjusted (Courtesy of Monique Meuschke, University of Magdeburg).

ferent viewpoints is necessary, i.e., an animation where the infiltration of all potential risk structures is displayed sequentially. Mühler and Preim (2010) provide automatically generated and manually selected viewpoints to define a smooth camera path. So-called *key states* can be defined and stored for later re-use with a different data set.

Slice-based animations

Mühler and Preim (2010) also animated slice-based visualizations, where important pre-segmented structures are emphasized with either colored contours or a certain fill style. The slice-based animations may be structured in meaningful parts, e.g., assessment of lymph nodes of a particular region. All methods for animation support were integrated in the medical exploration toolkit (METK) along with other medical visualization techniques to support the rapid development of surgical planning and training systems (Mühler et al., 2010).

Planning neurovascular compression syndrome surgery

The neurovascular compression syndrome is characterized by vascular structures that touch the intracranial nerve, which may lead to considerable pain that requires neurosurgical treatment. Higuera et al. (2003a) use the techniques developed in the same group (recall (Iserhardt-Bauer et al., 2002)) to create standardized animations for surgery planning. The animations were used for rehearsal in the operating room, where they could be watched via a laptop. The animation generation could be controlled by parameters, such as the temporal resolution, the number of steps, and the size of the ellipsoid on which the virtual camera rotates (Higuera et al., 2003a) (see Fig. 6.8). In the terminology of DiBiase et al. (1992), this represents an *on-demand computation* of an animation to explore the data.

6.9 **Concluding remarks**

Animation design has to consider perceptual and cognitive limitations related to motion perception, change blindness, and cognitive load theory. According to these theories, animations should be rather short and exhibit a low or moderate complexity. Simplifications or smoothing of medical surface models may contribute to a lower complexity. Of course, there is trade-off between scientific credibility and extensive simplification that must be carefully considered. Film theory is another area that provides essential experiences useful for the design of animations of static data. Few studies were carried out that consequently compare the knowledge transfer based on animations and static visualizations of the same data. Hoyek et al. (2014) presented the largest study related to a comparison between animations and static 2D visualizations.

Dynamic processes

Animation in medicine is primarily motivated by complex dynamical processes, such as movements of heart valves, ventricles, and vascular structures. Such complex and related movements cannot be fully understood by means of static images that only depict a "frozen concept" (Habbal and Harris, 1995). The dynamics involved in animation may naturally display growth processes, e.g., in embryology, the beating heart, joint movements, pulsatile blood flow, and enable a deeper understanding compared to a sequence of static displays.

Animating static data

Animation is regularly used in virtual endoscopy and in the diagnosis of vascular diseases by means of MIP-based animations. Radiology workstations provide a cine-mode to loop through the slices and to the time-points in the case of dynamic image data. In these examples, however, the data is static. Animations of static data typically employ different camera positions. The computation of candidates for a good camera position and the computation of a path that combines the selected candidates is essential for creating animations. Computer scientists developed animation systems for a wide range of visualization tasks. Often, they are based on scripting languages that enable modifications of presentation parameters, such as per-object transparency and transfer functions. Facilities to adjust transparency, and thus visibility of essential structures, were often reported to be particularly useful. Widespread use of animations requires a streamlined generation process, including re-usable components, such as templates (Akiba et al., 2010).

Animations as part of educational and therapy planning systems

Animations may be carefully integrated in overall workflows related to medical education and therapy planning. In educational settings, animations are particularly useful at early stages to make the learner familiar with certain processes. In therapy planning, animations may provide an efficient overview of the relevant patient anatomy, whereas the in-depth exploration of 3D and 2D slice-based visualizations support the actual decision process. Animations are not restricted to a passive mode of presentation: Animations may be generated on demand, they may be interrupted, and even a sequence of observing a video and interactively exploring a region is possible.

Animation as narrative genre

Animation (or film) is one of seven *narrative genres* identified as suitable for reaching broad audiences in narrative visualization (Segel and Heer, 2010). Animations may be combined with other genres, e.g., short animations are embedded in interactive poster presentations, where they introduce the relevant patient anatomy or handling of a surgical instrument. For broad audiences, e.g., in a science center, the complexity of animations need to be further reduced. On the other hand, the aesthetic appeal is even more important to engage users. An early example of narrative medical visualization is a YouTube-video entitled "Prof. Roentgen Meets the Virtual Body - VOXEL-MAN and X-ray history." Recently, the first papers that describe narrative medical visualization appeared (Meuschke et al., 2022a) and explain a case study related to cardiac blood flow (Kleinau et al., 2022).

Recommended reading

For more information on methods and applications related to medical animation we recommend the following publications:

Dirk Bartz. "Virtual endoscopy in research and clinical practice," *Computer Graphics Forum*, vol. 24(1): 111–126 2005.

Xavier Bonaventura, Miquel Feixas, Mateu Sbert, Lewis Chuang, and Christian Wallraven. "A survey of viewpoint selection methods for polygonal models," *Entropy*, Vol. 20(5): 370, 2018.

Rick Parent. *Computer animation: algorithms and techniques*, Newnes, 2012.

Bernhard Preim and Monique Meuschke. "A survey of medical animations", *Computers & Graphics*, Vol. 90: 145–168, 2020.

Selected applications

In the second part, we discuss selected applications of visual computing in medicine. We want to present how the techniques described in the first part are actually applied for medical education, diagnosis, and treatment. In practice, a number of techniques need to be carefully combined to solve real-world problems in medicine.

We start this part with a discussion of anatomy education since anatomy is the basis for all clinical disciplines in medicine (Chapter 7). This discussion includes a classification of different aspects of anatomy as well as techniques and systems to support anatomy education. The systems provide 3D visualization and interaction techniques and enable the exploration of carefully segmented 3D models with associated semantics, e.g., textual labels of anatomic structures.

We continue in Chapter 8, where we discuss how image analysis and visualization is used to visualize the relevant patient anatomy for tumor treatment along with the results of the simulated radiation treatment. In this chapter, we will see applications of multimodal visualization techniques to present the patient anatomy along with the simulation results.

3D visualization for anatomy education

7.1 Introduction

The study of human anatomy deals with understanding the shape, position, and relations of structures in the human body. Anatomy education serves to provide students with a deep understanding of these aspects, for example, how organs are positioned and which nerves and vessels connect to these organs. This knowledge is essential for a variety of medical practitioners, such as surgeons, radiographers, and nurses. There is quite some variation in shape, location, and even topology between individuals, which is not considered to be pathological. For example, these variations can lead to different branching patterns for blood vessels, which are also important to understand. Traditionally, anatomy education is based on lectures, text books and anatomical atlases, and cadaver dissection. The latter plays a key role in training manual dexterity and communication skills (Brenton et al., 2007). Disadvantages to specimen dissection are that the color and texture in specimens is quite different from living patients, high costs, supply difficulties, degradation, and scalability. Dissection involves cutting in superficial structures to expose deeper structures. Since this process is irreversible, the cadaver degrades over time. Scalability means that cadaver dissection involves a limited number of students only. Cadaver dissection is not available for all students who follow anatomy education. For example, sport science and dentistry students do not always have access to these resources.

Interactive 3D visualization combined with specific learning tasks have great potential to complement to traditional anatomy education methods, perhaps even replacing some of them in the future. This would address shortage issues in the amount of donated bodies and available teaching time (Brenton et al., 2007). Moreover, interactive 3D visualizations do not suffer from degradation and scalability problems. Studies indicate that students find interactive systems valuable learning resources, and that they lead to substantial progress in understanding spatial relations (Azer and Azer, 2016; Nicholson et al., 2006).

Novel medical visualization techniques

Anatomy education is an inspiring application area. Thus many novel medical visualization techniques were developed for this area, e.g., high-quality rendering for segmented volume data techniques (Tiede et al., 1998) or efficient clipping and cutting techniques (Pflesser et al., 1998) through the use of a virtual scalpel, aimed at anatomy education. *Labeling*, consisting of sophisticated algorithms for efficient and aesthetically pleasing label placement, was also motivated by anatomy education (Preim et al., 1995). Though in later years there was a lot of emphasis on medical visualization for diagnosis, treatment planning, and intraoperative support, anatomy education remained an area in which considerable progress was made. With the advent of novel web-techniques, such as WebGL, and progress in affordable VR glasses (see Chapter 13), the field further developed both in a research context and in commercial settings.

Motivational design

In addition to the technically motivated developments, motivational design, partially inspired by serious games, is essential. The goal is to find the proper balance between self-directed learning and guidance. Essential questions relate to how the learning is affected and which students benefit from virtual anatomy systems.

Teacher's and learner's perspective

Virtual anatomy education can be discussed from the teacher's perspective and from a learner's perspective. The teacher's perspective focuses on authoring interactive 3D visualizations and relating them to concepts, such as anatomical terms, categories, and relations. In this chapter, we focus on the learner's perspective, i.e., the character and quality of the available information and techniques to explore and acquire knowledge. We do not focus on how the information resources were created and restrict ourselves to anatomy education for medical students. Learning goals include to know where certain anatomical structures are located, how they are named, how they are supplied with blood, and to which functional system they belong.

Virtual anatomy systems

There are a lot of systems that support anatomy education. Some include 2D images and associated text, video, or audio. They could be seen as multimedia versions of traditional anatomy atlases. In this chapter, we instead discuss systems that support exploration of anatomy in 3D, and refer to such systems as *virtual anatomy* systems. Some of these systems integrate both 2D slice-based visualizations and 3D models such that the relation between the views can be understood. Virtual anatomy systems can display anatomical structures from any viewpoint and are not restricted to selected viewpoints in the way that traditional text books are. They can be desktop solutions, web-based, semi-immersive, or virtual reality systems. In this chapter, we focus primarily on non-immersive VA systems, while VR for medical education is discussed in Chapter 13. We refer readers interested in augmented reality in medicine to the survey by Chen et al. (2017). Other recent developments not discussed here include the creation of physical models with 3D printing and surgery simulation for training.

Organization

In this chapter, primarily based on the survey by Preim and Saalfeld (2018), we provide an overview visualization and interaction techniques for anatomy education.

This topic was also touched upon in previous books, with a focus on surgical training, in particular by Preim and Botha (2013). Here, we focus more on recent developments and take a look at how techniques are integrated into virtual anatomy systems and how they are evaluated. We summarize educational background (Section 7.2), underlying data (Section 7.3), visualization techniques (Section 7.4). We go on with knowledge representation and labeling techniques (Section 7.5), and discuss interaction techniques that are essential to explore anatomical models and the related semantic information (Section 7.6). We study established virtual anatomy systems (Section 7.7) and more recent web-based systems (Section 7.8). Finally, we study the learning effectiveness of virtual anatomy systems by describing relevant evaluation strategies (Section 7.9).

7.2 Educational background

E-learning, or electronic learning, is a trend in many disciplines. Key characteristics are that students can use e-learning resources at any time and adapt the system to their learning goals. Typically, they include self-assessment facilities, such as multiple choice questions, careful guidance, and motivational strategies. There are also communication features that allow for learners and teachers to share thoughts and questions to further enhance learning. E-learning systems can be tailored to individual users by managing their learning progress and adapting the tasks and materials presented. It works best with highly motivated and self-disciplined users, as medical students tend to be. The survey by Jastrow and Hollinderbäumer (2004) reveals that students consider online anatomy resources as motivating and appreciate high-quality visualizations, keyword searches, and up-to-date information.

General principles of e-learning, for example, instruction design and use of media, apply to anatomy education as well. A unique characteristic of anatomy in particular is the complex structure of the human body, with multiple systems closely related to each other. This requires an extraordinarily high level of *spatial understanding*, requiring learners to recognize different perspectives, relations, and integration into regions and systems (Stull et al., 2009). Interactive 3D visualizations allow for learners to actively explore anatomical structures and their interrelations in a direct way (Chittaro and Ranon, 2007).

7.2.1 Learning theories

Learning theories are important to justify design decisions for virtual anatomy systems. The theories go beyond learning facts, as was common in early drill-and-practice e-learning programs. Dev (1999) describe further pedagogical background and the history of e-learning in medicine since the 1960s.

Constructivism and embodied cognition

Constructivism theory states that active learning leads to spontaneous knowledge construction and reduces cognitive load compared to traditional learning experiences. In virtual anatomy systems, handling anatomical structures through interactive rotation resembles rotating real objects, such as bones in their hands. This similarity benefits learning through *embodied cognition*, which considers the perceptual and motor systems as essential ingredients of cognitive processes (Chittaro and Ranon, 2007).

Kosslyn et al. (2001) found that physical rotation leads to stronger motor cortex activation in a subsequent mental rotation task. The similarity between movements in the real world and the virtual world will be higher with a 3D input device or head tracking in VR compared to 2D mouse interaction. A 3D input device has a so-called good *stimulus-response compatibility*, meaning that there is a close correspondence between movements and resulting changes in the visualization. According to Jang et al. (2017), there is an additional learning effect from interactive manipulation of 3D content compared to passive video sequence viewing. High quality didactic anatomy learning environments require more than passive viewing to provide the best learning experiences. Examples of combining constructivism with anatomy education include using physical models of anatomical structures and having learners perform tasks with these models. This could also be achieved with virtual systems. Ma et al. (2012) propose a way to learn anatomy by having students develop a serious game. This requires powerful and easy-to-use authoring systems.

Problem-based learning

Instead of learning isolated facts, in *problem-based learning* (PBL), groups of students cooperate and solve problems together. In anatomy education, an example could be that students have to locate a deep anatomical structure and describe the regional surroundings and relations. A tutor should facilitate this problem solving by making necessary resources available (Brenton et al., 2007). In virtual anatomy systems, carefully chosen tasks could also fit a problem-based curriculum. Chittaro and Ranon (2007) discuss this educational background in more detail in the context of interactive online 3D virtual learning environments.

Blended learning

Virtual anatomy systems are more efficient if they are linked to other forms of learning, for example, when supported by anatomy educators explaining when and how to use them. Combining different styles of learning, such as online educational materials and interaction with physical classroom methods, is referred to as *blended learning*. Purely virtual systems are not a replacement for other types of anatomy education. Brenton et al. (2007) discuss the benefits of dissection in the presence of a virtual anatomy system. Lectures also remain indispensable. Some virtual systems are not primarily intended for self-study, but meant to be used in the classroom or during dissection. As an example, Phillips et al. (2013), demonstrate how a virtual system displaying medical imaging (radiographic) data of a specimen supports learning in the dissection room by explaining the relation between the two.

7.2.2 Aspects of anatomy education

There are many disciplines that benefit from anatomical knowledge, and for this reason anatomy education is a part of the curriculum for a wide range of students. For example, prevention of surgical complications requires a good understanding of the anatomy in the region of interest. A distinction can be made between non-spatial and spatial anatomical knowledge. Non-spatial knowledge covers terminology, taxonomy, and function, whereas spatial knowledge includes position, orientation, extent, and shape (Nguyen et al., 2012). In this chapter, we focus on spatial knowledge in particular. Anatomy can be understood according to various aspects:

- *clinical anatomy*: the study of anatomy most relevant to medical practice
- *comparative anatomy*: the study of anatomy across organisms or topological variations in branching structures
- *cross-sectional anatomy*: anatomy viewed in the transverse planes of the body (imaginary slices perpendicular to structures of interest)
- *radiographic anatomy*: the study of anatomy through imaging techniques, such as X-ray, MRI, and CT
- *regional anatomy*: the study of anatomy by parts of the body. All biological systems are studied with an emphasis on system interrelation and regional function, often supported by dissection.
- *systemic anatomy*: the study of anatomy by biological system across all body regions. Dissection is less relevant here.
- *macroscopic anatomy*: the study of anatomy through direct visual observation, often through dissection
- *microscopic anatomy*: the study of anatomy through light or electron microscopes. Microscopic anatomy is based on very high resolution images and provides insight at a level that is neither possible with tomographic image data nor by dissecting cadavers.
- *surgical anatomy*: the application and study of anatomy relevant for surgical procedures, e.g., relevance in avoiding complications or for surgical guidance

These aspects represent different views on anatomy. As an example, the kidney is part of the abdomen in *regional anatomy* and part of the urogenital system in *systemic anatomy* (Pommert et al., 2001). Ideally, virtual anatomical education systems integrate all aspects by blending in data at different scales. However, current systems do not support this due to the need for data acquisition and visualization techniques at all of these scales. Few systems integrate microscopic anatomy. An example is the VIRTUAL SURGICAL PELVIS, which integrates cryosection data to visualize surgical anatomy at a higher resolution than radiological images can provide (Kraima et al., 2013; Smit, 2016).

An early example combining different anatomy aspects is the DIGITALANATO-MIST, which provides 3D overviews with marked slab positions, where CT slices and photographic data are available (Brinkley and Rosse, 1997). Visualizing comparative anatomy requires a variety of data sets that represent typical anatomical variations and is not supported by most systems. Instead, many virtual anatomy systems focus on regional anatomy and represent the relation between labels and segmentation results. An early example combining different anatomy aspects is the DIGITALANATOMIST, which provides 3D overviews with marked slab positions, where CT slices and photographic data are available (Brinkley and Rosse, 1997). Visualizing comparative anatomy requires a variety of data sets that represent typical anatomical variations and is not supported by most systems. Instead, many virtual anatomy systems focus on regional anatomy and represent the relation between labels and segmentation results.

7.3 Datasets

Radiological imaging is very important in anatomy education, as the relation between such data and patients is important to understand for many physicians. Virtual anatomy systems often combine imaging data with segmentations to highlight anatomical structures. With such data, it is possible to allow for interactive exploration using direct volume rendering and surface rendering techniques. Whereas for clinical applications segmentation speed and accuracy is paramount, in an education setting, high quality results are more important and can be achieved through careful image analysis and modeling. Visualization accuracy plays less of a role as the models are not used for patient-specific surgical planning. Instead, smooth surfaces without distracting features are preferred.

Commercial 3D model catalogs can be used as a source for anatomy education. Many commercial anatomy systems, such as ZYGOTE BODY (Kelc, 2012) and the BIODIGITAL HUMAN 3D (Qualter et al., 2012) rely on artistically created 3D models.

7.3.1 Anatomical specimens

For diagnostic purposes, radiological image quality is only as good as clinically necessary to cut down on scan time and potential radiation dose. However, when working with deceased human bodies (cadavers) or anatomical specimens, it is possible to focus more on high resolution and low noise level acquisition. Acquisition speed, radiation dose, and patient movement are not a concern in these cases. For this reason, virtual anatomy systems are often based on anatomical specimen imaging data. A special type of imaging data that is only possible with anatomical specimens and not living patients is cryosectional data. This data is acquired by placing the specimen in an embedding medium, freezing it, cutting off a small part, and taking high-resolution photographs of the remaining block after every slice.

The most widely used data sets based on anatomical specimen data are the VIS-IBLE HUMAN (VH) data sets from the National Library of Medicine. They consist of anatomical images (photographic cryosectional images) combined with fresh and frozen CT data, and an MRI of the head and neck. The VISIBLE HUMAN MALE has 1871 anatomical images at 1 mm slice distance, whereas the VISIBLE HUMAN FE-MALE has 5189 anatomical images at .33 mm slice distance. Though the quality of both the anatomical images and CT data were unprecedented at that time, the body was cut into blocks, which leaves some gaps in the data. Many virtual anatomy systems are based on the VH data sets. Notable examples include VOXEL-MAN (Höhne et al., 2000), the "Internet Atlas of Human Gross Anatomy" (Jastrow and Hollinder-bäumer, 2004), and the "Anatomic VisualizeR" (Hoffman et al., 2001a). The VH project website[1] lists over 25 products based on the VH data sets; the review by Juanes et al. (2003) highlights early applications of the VH for anatomy education.

In addition to the VISIBLE HUMAN project, others started producing their own data sets in a similar fashion. The VISIBLE KOREAN HUMAN Park et al. (2006) and CHINESE VISIBLE HUMAN Zhang et al. (2006), for example, avoided some of the problems with the original VH data sets by not cutting the bodies into blocks before image acquisition. The ONLINE ANATOMICAL HUMAN virtual anatomy platform is based on the Visible Korean data set, considered to be qualitatively one of the best VISIBLE HUMAN data sets available with cross-sectional intervals of 0.2 mm at 4368×2912 pixels resolution (Smit et al., 2016a) (see Fig. 7.1).

An alternative approach to working with cryosection of anatomical specimens to digitize anatomical information is to perform surface scanning or photogrammetry. In this way, it is possible to directly construct virtual models, for example, after dis-section. Vandenbossche et al. (2022) outline how high-fidelity anatomical models can be produced with 3D scanning techniques such that they can be digitally preserved, archived, and subsequently rendered through various media. They propose a novel methodology, digital body preservation, for combining and matching scan geometry with radiographic imaging. In addition, they explore the influence of mesh simplifica-tion in combination with texture mapping on the quality of the 3D models in terms of physical fidelity with respect to anatomical features. Depending on the model, mesh sizes ranging from 3% to 10% of the original size were feasible and as such usable in learning applications. Mesh size plays a key role in particular for web-based virtual anatomy systems.

7.3.2 Clinical imaging

The image quality when acquiring radiographic clinical data is lower than that which can be achieved with anatomical specimens, as outlined above. This typically leads to a lower signal-to-noise ratio. One reason is keeping the radiation burden for patients "as low as reasonably achievable" (ALARA) in X-ray-based modalities. In addition,

---

[1] https://www.nlm.nih.gov/research/visible/products.html.

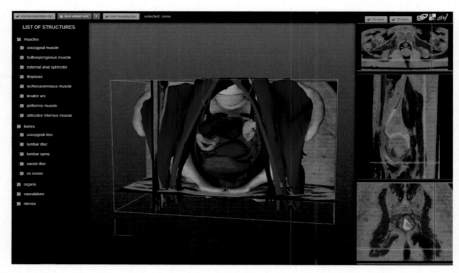

FIGURE 7.1

The online anatomical human virtual anatomy system is based on high-resolution cryosectional imaging data of the visible Korean human data set combined with 3D models based on segmentation (From: (Smit et al., 2016a), ©2016 The Author(s), Eurographics Proceedings, ©The Eurographics Association).

patient movement (voluntary and involuntary) can create imaging artifacts. However, some imaging techniques are only possible with live patients, for example, functional imaging of the brain via MRI. For this reason, clinical imaging data can still be a useful basis for virtual anatomy systems. In this case, the imaging data used should not depict pathology or specific anatomical variations. An example of a virtual anatomy system based on clinical imaging is the first version of VOXEL-MAN, featuring a cerebral MRI data set (Höhne et al., 1992a).

7.3.3 Segmentation

Segmentation is one of the paths to reconstructing 3D virtual models from imaging data sets by annotating structure of interest and performing mesh construction based on the label volumes. This can be accomplished by manual annotation, or using general segmentation techniques familiar from computer vision literature, such as thresholding, region-growing, live wires, or watershed segmentation. These days, deep learning also plays a big role in radiological image segmentation. When working with cryosectional data, such as the VISIBLE HUMAN data sets, special care is needed to take into account that the data consists of colored voxels, for example, 24 bits representing red, green, and blue components. For segmentation of this type of data, regions in RGB-space have to be separated (Schiemann et al., 1997).

In anatomy education, all anatomical structures that can be derived from the imaging data are relevant. For this reason, more objects are typically segmented than in cases where segmentation is needed for clinical purposes, such as radiation therapy. The VOXEL-MAN is based on the segmentation of 650 objects, for example. It is challenging to delineate functional areas, as these are not recognizable as visible objects in the imaging data. Segmentation of such areas requires expert knowledge. However, in particular for the brain, many atlas standards already exist (Smit and Bruckner, 2019).

7.4 Visualization techniques

In this section, we briefly summarize visualization techniques that are typically used in virtual anatomy systems, such as surface visualization, volume visualization, illustrative visualization, viewpoint selection, and animation.

7.4.1 Surface visualization

Most virtual anatomy systems are based on surface rendering. According to Azkue (2013), the surface representations resemble real anatomical structures with their solid appearance. To construct such surfaces, there are three main approaches:

- Segmented objects from volumetric data can be converted into polygonal meshes.
- The meshes can be constructed with modeling software.
- Anatomical models can be made by surface scanning real anatomical specimens.

It is also possible to combine these approaches, for example, creating a mesh based on partial segmentation in imaging data and using this as input for a modeling process. An example of this would be to segment major blood vessels from an imaging data set and completing the model with smaller vessels by fitting splines to cross-sections as Pommert et al. (2001) did with their "tube editor".

To go from image segmentation to a surface mesh, an algorithm, such as Marching Cubes, can be used, but this leads to terracing artifacts due to the limited spatial resolution and the anisotropic character of medical image data. Often, it is necessary to do mesh smoothing to reduce these artifacts. We briefly discussed this issue in Section 2.3 and mentioned that a trade-off between accuracy and smoothness is required (recall (Bade et al., 2006)). Mesh simplification is carried out afterwards to remove unnatural edges and reduce the number of polygons. A considerable reduction is often possible, taking into account that regions with low curvature can be faithfully represented with a low number of polygons, i.e., only high curvature regions, such as the nose and the ear in a human face, require a large amounts of polygon. Mesh simplification is essential to reduce mesh size such that transferring and rendering the models becomes faster, which is particularly important in web-based applications.

Anatomical features of interest need to be preserved with such mesh processing steps (Vandenbossche et al., 2022). For elongated branching structures, such as blood vessels or nerves, special mesh reconstruction methods are available based on splines, convolution surfaces, or other implicit surfaces (see Chapter 3).

To add to the realism of surface models, it is possible to texture them. Models resulting from surface scanning typically include a texture already. Texturing can also be done manually in 3D modeling applications by artists, leading to high-quality results. The pelvis model in Fig. 7.1 was textured manually by a company. In some cases, it is also possible to automate the texturing process using, for example, procedural terrain modeling techniques. Saalfeld et al. (2017) use an automatic approach to texture vascular models based on the surface normals. This works well when texture orientation does not matter, but in some cases, such as for muscles and tendons, texture orientation is very important. Gasteiger et al. (2008) proposed a technique for such cases based on principal curvature to determine the direction of a hatching texture.

7.4.2 Volume visualization

Whereas surface models are typically hollow inside, volume data allows for interactions, such as clipping and cutting, to reveal inner structure information (virtual dissection). It is also possible to combine volume rendering with surface mesh visualization (see Fig. 7.2). The additional information comes at a cost, as volume data typically requires more memory than mesh representations do, and can cause bandwidth-issues in web-based systems. In addition to regular volume rendering techniques assigning a color and opacity to voxel intensity, techniques that can work with segmented structures are essential for virtual anatomy systems. High-quality rendering of such *tagged volumes* is essential. Tiede et al. (1998) introduced a technique where object boundaries are displayed at subvoxel resolution to avoid terracing artifacts. Further opportunities provided by working with volume rendering techniques for anatomy education are to simulate what the X-ray of a region would look like. This can be achieved by simulating X-ray attenuation on the GPU (Vidal et al., 2009).

Due to advances in GPU performance and computer graphics techniques, it is possible to do photorealistic rendering in real-time. Advanced techniques, such as Monte-Carlo path tracing (Kajiya, 1986), allow for simulating complex interactions of photons with human anatomy, leading to photorealistic results with effects such as soft shadows and volumetric scattering. The random character of Monte-Carlo techniques, however, introduces some noise, which may be reduced with appropriate smoothing (Zwicker et al., 2015). Such photorealistic renderings of complex anatomical models were too time-consuming until recently. Meanwhile dedicate hardware enables to render quite realistic models in real time (Deng et al., 2017).

Advances in the camera model allow for simulation of depth-of-field and motion blur. Examples of systems using these approaches are EXPOSURE RENDER (Kroes et al., 2012) and the CINEMATICRENDERER (Fellner, 2016; Fellner et al., 2017) developed by SIEMENS. The additional opportunities come with a need for additional rendering parameter settings, which can be addressed through providing templates

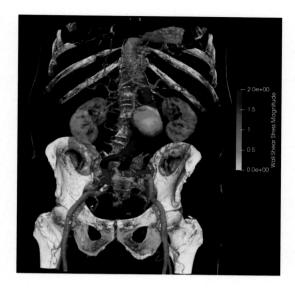

FIGURE 7.2

Direct volume rendering of CT scan data is combined with surface volume rendering to reveal wall shear stress simulation data on an aneurysm. Rendering in Paraview Ahrens et al. (2005) by Noeska Smit, data provided courtesy of Jelmer Wolterink (UT Twente) and Kakkhee Yeung (Amsterdam UMC).

for anatomical structures, such as bones and muscles (Fellner, 2016). Shape perception seems to benefit from increased realism (Lindemann and Ropinski, 2011), but the differences in knowledge gains in an anatomy education context have not been evaluated so far.

7.4.3 Illustrative visualization

Though illustrative visualization was already covered in detail in Chapter 2, we briefly comment on the potential for illustrative visualization in anatomy education here. For centuries, illustration has played a key role in knowledge dissemination. Before photography, there was no other chance to convey shapes and structural relations. Even after photography became widely available, illustrations remained the primary resource to convey anatomical information via text books and atlases. Colors, abstraction levels, and viewing angles are carefully chosen to optimally convey relations with sufficient contrast and aligned with educational goals. Ghosh (2015) summarize the historical development of such illustrations up until modern times.

Anatomical illustrations require expertise both in anatomy and art. Historically, human anatomy was shown alongside plants and animals, but later illustrators, such as Henry Gray and Frank Netter focused exclusively on human anatomy. In modern

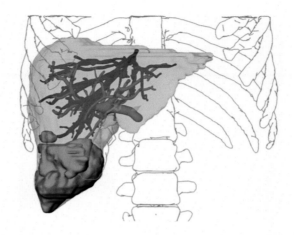

FIGURE 7.3

Surface rendering of the liver anatomy embedded in a silhouette rendering of the skeletal structures to provide anatomic context (From: Tietjen et al. (2005), ©2005 The Author(s), Eurographics Proceedings, ©The Eurographics Association).

times, a medical illustrator receives specialized training and education in medicine, science, art, design, visual technology, communication, and learning theories.

Since the 1960s, radiological image data also became a part of anatomy education materials (Phillips et al., 2013). This was later expanded on with computer-generated 3D models displayed in illustrative styles. Corl et al. (2000) have done pioneering work in this field, focusing on specific medical scenarios, for example, the position of the kidney in the abdomen. Research in computer graphics and visualization focused more on general methods that generate feature lines and hatching for polygonal surfaces (see Chapter 2). At this point, it is unclear whether anatomy education systems benefit from such illustrative approaches, as they were not evaluated for this application. Pure line-based renderings without shading are unlikely to convey enough shape information (Cole et al., 2009), but there is potential for using such techniques to display anatomical structures at varying levels of detail. Tietjen et al. (2005) have successfully combined silhouettes, surface, and volume rendering in a surgical education context (see Fig. 7.3). Here, the rendering style can display structures as focus objects in more detail or anatomical context in less detail using line-based rendering.

7.4.4 Viewpoint selection

As medical illustrators carefully consider the best viewing angle when drawing anatomy, similar considerations should be made for the best camera angle for viewing 3D models of human anatomy. Though it is possible to change the camera position through interaction or animation, a sensible default view should be chosen. Here, Stull et al. (2009) argue that *canonical* orientation should be used, for example, a frontal or lateral view. By picking a recognizable viewpoint initially, the mental load on the learner is reduced. Another situation, in which a sensible viewpoint needs to be chosen, is when a structure is selected and should be emphasized. This requires good structure visibility. Vázquez et al. (2001) developed methods to automatically selected good viewpoints for polygonal model objects using *viewpoint entropy* (recall Section 6.3.1). This was later incorporated into an anatomy education framework (Vázquez et al., 2008). An extensive survey on viewpoint selection has been conducted by Bonaventura et al. (2018).

7.4.5 Animation in anatomy education

Though medical animation is discussed at length in Chapter 6, we briefly summarize the impact of animation in anatomy education here, partly based on the survey by Preim and Meuschke (2020).

Video sequences are an established resource in anatomy education (Jaffar, 2012). In the last decade, such videos also became available in digital form, for example, on YouTube. The effectiveness of videos to assist anatomy students was also evaluated (Mahmud et al., 2011; DiLullo et al., 2006). Videos are perceived as useful learning resources, but do not always improve examination scores (Mahmud et al., 2011). The successful use of videos inspired researchers to develop computer-generated animations using geometric models combined with a knowledge base. These animations rely on motion parallax as an essential depth cue, but are not superior to static images in all circumstances. As the information provided is transient, it may lead to information overload for complex cases. In addition, it can lead to the *illusion of understanding* (Hoyek et al., 2014; Tversky et al., 2002).

Jastrow and Hollinderbäumer (2004) created animations of cross-sectional data and show adjacent slices of the VISIBLE HUMAN data set of a region. From discussions with radiologists, we know that they infer additional information from such animations compared to the analysis of static images. For this reason, radiology workstations provide a *cine mode*, animating through slice stacks. Müller-Stich et al. (2013) used such animations in a virtual liver anatomy education system.

Animations that introduce an anatomical region, for example, by slowly zooming in on it, removing outer layers of information, and rotating around a canonical axis may be very effective to give a first impression of the region. Animated emphasis, where gradually reducing opacity or saturation of nearby objects, helps to focus on a target object and can be a useful component of such animations. Passive viewing of predefined animations is less effective than active exploration (Jang et al., 2017), but can help prepare learners for such an active stage.

Vernon and Peckham (2002) discuss teaching aids, including 3D models and animation, for medical teaching. They provide recommendations, largely focused on commercial tools and their use. Keyframe animation and motion capture to support biomechanical animations are emphasized. Compared to the large number of systems that provide interactive exploration of 3D models for anatomy teaching, the use of animation in this area is limited.

Fisk (2008) discusses the value of animations for various medical disciplines. With respect to anatomy education, he emphasizes the possibility to display objects from unusual viewpoints that are hardly possible, e.g., when dissecting a cadaver. Only few virtual anatomy systems offer animations or explicitly discuss their use in anatomy education. Pioneering work was carried out by Habbal and Harris (1995). They argue that the potential of animation is particularly high for displaying functional anatomy. They employed drawings of the human heart, imported them in a professional tool (3D STUDIO MAX) and used keyframing to create animations that depict the complex relation between the valves and the ventricles. They included movements of incompetent valves to illustrate this pathological process. The whole animation design fulfills their philosophy: "A successful animation requires three mutually dependent components: good artistic modeling, high-quality images and a story to tell" (Habbal and Harris, 1995).

Animation generation with scripting languages

Manually creating animations with 3D modeling software is expensive and strongly tailored to specific learning scenarios. To remedy this, researchers developed systems to generate animations based on high-level textual descriptions (recall Section 6.3.4). Inspired by computer-generated animations for technical illustrations and anatomy teaching videos, Preim et al. (1996) introduced a scripting language for object emphasis and technique selection for medical education. They discuss the generation of animations to convey the spatial relations between bones, muscles, and ligaments. The animations contain rotations to show particular structures, the display of instructional text, e.g., the innervation and origin of a muscle, and emphasis by changing colors. Inspired by the way lecturers explain elongated structures, such as muscles, pointing devices are used to illustrate the course of such structures. The underlying geometric models consisting of a few dozens of labeled anatomical structures were created by digital artists and acquired from a commercial vendor.

Mühler et al. (2006) expanded on this work to include clipping planes, distance and angle annotations, and optimized viewpoints. This allows for object emphasis using a camera position with optimal structure visibility. Computer-generated animations need to consider motion perception. Thus the camera path should be smooth, and the position should change gradually. Sudden speed changes should be avoided. It is possible to perceive only few movements simultaneously, otherwise, change blindness occurs.

Effectiveness of animations depending on spatial ability

The effectiveness of animations depends on the spatial ability of learners (Hoyek et al., 2014). Only learners with at least a minimum spatial ability benefit from 3D animations. Spatial ability is assessed with mental rotation tests, such as the test by Vandenberg and Kuse (1978). For learners with lower spatial ability, static and interactive visualizations are beneficial. In addition, when animations are used, viewers should be able to slow down, stop, and repeat segments of the animation as needed. Hoyek et al. (2014) created 3D animations of the upper limb and provided these to

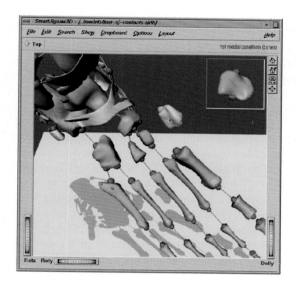

FIGURE 7.4

Exploded views of the foot skeletal anatomy were created in an animation and embedded in an anatomy education system (From: Ritter et al. (2000)).

students through a video player that allowed them to slow down and repeat animation segments. Students with low scores in the mental rotation test (recall Vandenberg and Kuse (1978)) were not included since previous research indicates that they would not benefit from 3D animation. Compared to a control group, where students looked at Powerpoint slides with static images, those using the animations were able to answer spatial questions slightly better. Hoyek et al. (2014) recommend a mix of teaching methods, including 3D animations, since some learners benefit from them. They do, however, not conclude that 3D animations are "the best instructional tools to teach musculoskeletal anatomy." Instead they conjecture the "selective usefulness of 3D animations".

Animated exploded views are often used in technical illustrations and the same principles were employed in an anatomy education to reveal spatial relations (Ritter et al., 2000), see Fig. 7.4. Exploded views can be achieved by slightly scaling down anatomical structures, thereby increasing the gap between them. Animating the transition between the original state and the exploded view reduces the mental effort to understand the relation between both.

Most evaluations related to medical animations indicate that medical students *perceive* an enhanced anatomical and technical understanding (Lim et al., 2004). However, they do not involve a control group. Thus it is not clear whether animations are more effective in knowledge transfer compared to other modes of presentation.

7.4.6 Modeling and visualization for functional anatomy

Examples of functional anatomy are the range of motion of joints, the tension of muscles and tendons, and the physiology of anatomical systems, such as the respiratory tract. Virtual anatomy systems aiming at functional anatomy require modeling underlying movements. Modeling human limb movement can be done by motion tracking based on markers attached to limbs or marker-less using depth cameras, such as the KINECT. Albrecht et al. (2003) outlined how they created a dynamic model of limb movements based on motions captured from ten people, selected to be "average" in weight and height. Models also consider constraints, such as non-compressibility and collision constraints (Bauer et al., 2014). Skin and soft tissue movement typically follows from modifying parameters such as muscle contraction. In biomechanics and computer graphics, there are a number of detailed anatomically plausible models that can be used in functional anatomy education, as shown by Bauer et al. (2014), for example. Such models can be used to generate animations. Functional anatomy benefits from animations that display the dynamic character of the processes, for example, breathing and heart beats. In addition, animation can show the range of motion for limbs.

7.5 Knowledge representation and labeling

To support the learning process, interactive visualizations need to be combined with related symbolic knowledge for mental integration. Symbolic knowledge relates to concepts, names, and functions of anatomical objects and the relations between them.

7.5.1 Knowledge representation

When virtual anatomy systems are based on segmentation information, it becomes possible to represent knowledge and add relations between individual objects based on what structure the segmentation label represents. For example, it is possible to model an object to be *part of* a specific system. It is also possible to add additional information on clinical relevance, e.g., complications that would arise if this particular structure is damaged. A sophisticated representation of symbolic anatomical knowledge builds an *ontology*, a set of concepts and categories that shows their properties and the relations between them. The first advanced digital knowledge representation was developed by Schubert et al. (1993) as a *semantic net* that forms the basis for interactive querying. Among others, *part of*, *is a*, and *supplied by* relations could be described. The relation between labeled volumes and symbolic knowledge is referred to as *intelligent voxels*. Systems such as the DIGITAL ANATOMIST (Brinkley and Rosse, 1997) and the OPEN ANATOMY BROWSER (Kikinis et al., 1996) relied on similar concepts.

Researchers at the University of Washington subsequently developed the foundational model of anatomy ontology (FMA), an evolving open source virtual knowledge source for biomedical informatics (Rosse and Mejino, 2008). The FMA is a domain ontology that represents a coherent body of explicit declarative knowledge about human anatomy that is both human understandable and navigable, parsable, and interpretable by machine-based systems. It currently features 75,000 classes and over 120,000 terms, with over 2.1 million relationship instances from over 168 types of relations. The connection of virtual anatomy systems to a standardized ontology is currently a standard approach Halle et al. (2017). This has been used, for example, in databases for anatomical concepts, such as BODYPARTS3D/ANATOMOGRAPHY.[2]

7.5.2 Labeling anatomical models

Labels are used to establish a bidirectional link between the visual representation of anatomical structures and their textual names. Important learning goals in anatomy education include knowing what anatomical structures are called, where they are, and their shape features. Most labeling techniques presented here were inspired by traditional anatomical illustrations and integrated in research prototypes (Vázquez et al., 2008; Preim and Raab, 1998). Interestingly, none of them were integrated in wide-spread virtual anatomy systems.

Interactive labeling

The simplest approach to labeling is to leave the task to the user. They might select a position, initiate a label command, and interactively place the label. The label name then corresponds to the object visible at the indicated position. A line can then be generated to connect the textual label with the specified position. When many labels are needed, the user needs to avoid label overlap. This does not work so well in interactive scenarios where objects can be rotated and zoomed in on. Labels might be occluded by other structures or labels or even disappear out of the view. In addition to predefined labels, users can place textual descriptions, such as personal notes and flexibly move and save these labels. The BIODIGITAL HUMAN 3D Qualter et al. (2012) provides such advanced interactive labeling.

Automatic labeling

Automatic labeling strategies can be classified as *internal* and *external* (Götzelmann et al., 2005). Internal labels overlap with the objects to which they refer, whereas external labels are arranged outside of the structures of interest and connect to the visual representation of their reference object with a leader. Oeltze-Jafra and Preim (2014) provide a survey of labeling techniques in medical visualization, whereas Bekos et al. (2019) subsequently provided a comprehensive survey and taxonomy of external labeling techniques.

The use of external labels requires *anchor points* and *connection lines*. Selection of good anchor points is crucial for clear labeling. Though external labels are more challenging to associate to reference structures, they have better legibility as they are

---

[2] https://lifesciencedb.jp/bp3d/.

placed on top of a uniformly colored background. They also do not interfere with shape perception for complex shapes.

7.5.3 External label placement

Based on the work by various authors in labeling (Bruckner and Gröller, 2005; Preim and Raab, 1998; Hartmann et al., 2005), we can distill the following labeling requirements (LR):

- **LR1**: Anchor points should be visible.
- **LR2**: Labels should not hide any visual representation.
- **LR3**: Labels should be placed as close as possible to their reference points.
- **LR4**: Labels should not overlap.
- **LR5**: Connection lines should not cross.
- **LR6**: Label placement should be coherent in dynamic and interactive illustrations (strong and sudden changes in anchor points and label positions should be avoided).

Assuming that there is one anchor point per label, reasonable defaults might be the closest visible vertex to the center of gravity for the reference structure. To find visible vertices (LR1), the projection of an object in screen space should be checked for visible segments. If there are several such segments, the largest could be chosen (Hartmann et al., 2005).

To fulfill LR2–LR5, some general layout strategy is necessary that takes these requirements into account. There are two typical strategies in medical illustration both fulfilling LR2: labels can be arranged in vertical columns to the left and right of the illustration or they are placed closely to the reference structure outline. As it is difficult to place labels in concave notches, Hartmann et al. (2004) and Bruckner and Gröller (2005) both suggest to use the projection of the convex hull of objects to guide label placement (see Fig. 7.5). Proximity of labels and objects (LR3) is known to be essential for cognition (Moreno and Mayer, 1999). This makes convex hull placement a better choice than vertical column arrangement, according to LR3.

LR4 and LR5 concern the distribution of labels in the area reserved for labels. Based on a defined region where labels can be placed, a layout algorithm is necessary that manages occupied space and ensures there is no overlap and that connection lines do not cross. For example, the approaches by Hartmann et al. (2004) and Bruckner and Gröller (2005) suggest to start with initial labels close to the model silhouette. Afterwards, labels are exchanged or translated to prevent label overlap and crossing lines. A maximum number of iterations is set so that it is certain that the algorithm terminates at some point.

Interacting with a 3D scene changes the area occluded by the model. This means that label positions need to be updated to take this into account. Considering the 3D bounding box of the model can help to consider label position updates that are needed, but it is important that the label positions are not updated for every small rotation. Updating could be initiated on user request or after the rotation stops instead.

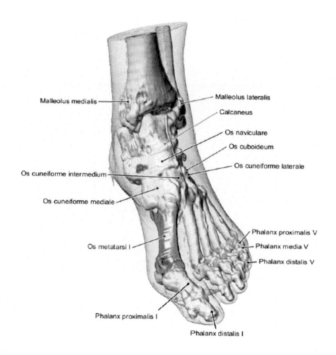

Malleolus medialis

Malleolus lateralis

Calcaneus

Os naviculare

Os cuboideum

Os cuneiforme laterale

Os cuneiforme intermedium

Os cuneiforme mediale

Phalanx proximalis V

Phalanx media V

Os metatarsi I

Phalanx distalis V

Phalanx proximalis I

Phalanx distalis I

FIGURE 7.5

External labeling of a foot model. Labels are arranged close to the convex hull of the model. They do not overlap each other, and connection lines do not cross (©2017 IEEE, Reprinted with permission from: Bruckner and Gröller (2005)).

Preim et al. (1995) outline an approach for external label placement with respect to a balanced layout.

Anchor point determination

Simple strategies work well enough for compact and visible object labeling, but can fail for branching objects or objects that are only partially visible. In these cases, more potential anchor points are needed. This requires an analysis of the shape of graphical objects, for example, through skeletonization. As an object, skeleton represents the median axis; points on the skeleton are good anchor point candidates. Still, the visibility has to be considered in addition (Hartmann et al., 2004).

Using potential fields for label placement

A more advanced labeling algorithm is based on potential fields and their applications in robot motion planning (Hartmann et al., 2005). Here, label placement requirements are translated to defining attracting forces between label and associated anchor point and repulsive forces between different labels and other anchor points. Starting from

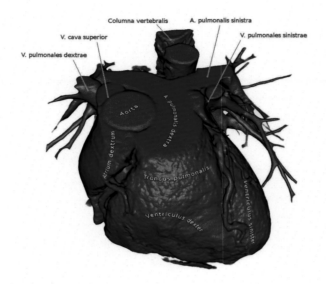

FIGURE 7.6

Internal and external labels were placed automatically. The placement of internal labels is guided by the skeleton (From: Ropinski et al. (2007)).

an initial layout, labels are then moved according to the forces influencing them, similar to a force-directed graph layout.

7.5.4 Internal label placement

Internal labels are placed directly overlapping the objects they refer to. This is only feasible when the objects have large enough visible surface area to accommodate such labels (Ropinski et al., 2007). For legibility, it is best to place labels horizontally. If this is not possible, Götzelmann et al. (2005) propose to place a label along the object centerline, for example, on a smoothed skeleton path (see Fig. 7.6) illustrates this approach. The readability of internal labels has been improved by imposing limits on allowable path curvature. Internal labels play a role also when an object is zoomed in on in interactive scenarios. Alternatively, it is possible to place numbers instead of textual labels with a legend linking the numbers to associated names (Azkue, 2013). Though number placement is easier due to limited space requirements, the use of a legend increases cognitive load.

7.5.5 Labeling interactive illustrations

Labeling interactive 3D illustrations poses several challenges. When zooming in, the visibility of objects and relative positions do not change, unless the zooming causes parts of the object to be projected outside of the visible window. Otherwise, only connection lines need to be updated in an external labeling strategy. If labels start to occlude the object, switching to an internal labeling strategy might make sense.

In 3D rotation, object visibility and relative position in screen space will change. To take this into account, several strategies are possible. Labels for objects no longer visible could be hidden or made more transparent to indicate that the associated structure is currently not visible. Labels can also be rearranged vertically or horizontally to reflect the new screen space position of the anchor points. This may lead to longer or even crossing connection lines. It can also be distracting when labels fly around a 3D model while the user tries to focus on anatomical structure details instead. It is better to update the labels only after the rotation is finished or to trigger a command that recomputes the labels (Preim et al., 1995). Mühler and Preim (2009) discuss even more options, such as changing the rendering style of the connection line when the anchor point becomes hidden.

The survey on labeling techniques in medical visualization by Oeltze-Jafra and Preim (2014) discusses more labeling strategy details, such as line width and fonts, as well as the implementation of labeling algorithms. This survey also outlines labeling of 2D images for radiographic and cross-sectional anatomy.

7.5.6 Other annotations

In addition to textual labels, it is also possible to use other annotation types for educational purposes. Fairén González et al. (2017), for example, use red and blue arrows to indicate arterial and venous blood flow, respectively. It is also possible to place circles or arrows to highlight specific anatomical aspects or relations. If such annotations are to be placed automatically, they require an appropriate layout strategy, where the annotations are clearly visible and do not hamper the recognition of other structures.

In addition to connecting textual labels with anchor points for describing anatomical landmarks or entire structures, sometimes the anatomical labels describe anatomical regions or lines. In these cases, annotations such as colored areas or lines drawn onto a surface could be considered (Smit et al., 2016a; Vandenbossche et al., 2022).

7.6 Interaction techniques

Berney et al. (2015) outline a cognitive task analysis learning functional anatomy with 3D anatomical models. Based on this and other publications, it is possible to outline basic requirements that interaction possibilities in virtual anatomy systems should support.

7.6.1 Basic interaction techniques

Some basic interaction functionality is available in almost all virtual anatomy systems. A hierarchical list is often available to show or hide individual anatomical structures or whole categories, such as muscles or bones (recall Fig. 7.1). Some systems support layer-based exploration, where outer structures can be removed, followed by inner structures. Such layer-based exploration works well with volume-rendering systems in combination with clipping.

Object selection is typically possible by picking, often resulting in structure emphasis and potentially revealing a label. Some systems allow for probing tools that can list all anatomical structures along a ray or inside a selection sphere (Smit et al., 2012). These need to be efficiently implemented to support a responsive system without interaction lag. Hierarchical data structures, such as octrees, can accelerate computation of polygons hit by a selection ray. As an alternative requiring less pre-processing, Smit et al. (2016a) suggested to use an off-screen renderer with a unique color code per face. This allows the render buffer color to reveal which object is visible at the selected pixel.

Rotation is a core function in any virtual anatomy system. Typically it is unrestricted and implemented as a virtual trackball metaphor, where anatomical surface models can be rotated along any axis. Panning and zooming are also essential features. Mouse-based rotation of 3D models is typically not very intuitive, in particular to users who have no experience navigating in 3D scenes on a 2D screen in this manner. Adding handles to structures to indicate an object-specific reference frame may be helpful. Vision research indicates that mental rotation benefits from a clear reference frame. An orientation widget, for example, a cube or mannequin, can convey the current viewing direction and allow for resetting the camera to the initial position to improve the navigation experience.

7.6.2 Advanced interaction techniques

There are more advanced interaction techniques that are not supported by all virtual anatomy systems, but still worth mentioning, as they are justified by the education goals. For example, some systems provide measurements features that allow students to understand absolute and relative size of anatomical structures using a virtual ruler (Hoffman et al., 2001a). Another advanced feature is to let users duplicate an object to inspect it in a separate view. Such a ghost copy allows for detailed inspection (Tan et al., 2001).

Clipping and cutting operations are typically exclusive to systems based on direct volume rendering. In addition to standard cutting planes, cuts using virtual scalpels (Pflesser et al., 1998), deformable cutting planes (Konrad-Verse et al., 2004), or illustrative membrane clipping (Birkeland et al., 2012) are possible. The virtual scalpel and deformable cutting planes draw inspiration from surgery and have a good link to clinical medicine. Illustrative membrane clipping avoids structures being cut if their border is close to the clipping plane, and is often more in line with user intent. Peel-away visualizations (Birkeland and Viola, 2009) provide templates that can separate anatomical regions rendered with different transfer functions. This is a focus-and-context technique that is view-dependent. Magic lenses (Viega et al., 1996) are another potentially useful interaction technique for exploring virtual anatomy. For example, a virtual lens can be moved over a model and reveal different information layers, such as the nerves. Of these techniques, mainly the virtual scalpel was actually used for anatomy education.

Facilities to enable drawing on surfaces to mark regions, place comments, or share with others are also useful. Self-assessment exercises and real-time feedback are essential components in virtual anatomy systems (Brenton et al., 2007). Surface annotations can be used in a quiz context, for example, asking learners to specify the name of a highlighted region on a structure.

Haptic interaction

Haptics can greatly enhance the experience of learners interacting with virtual anatomy. Actions, such as cutting, in particular would benefit from tactile feedback to convey tissue stiffness and elasticity. Basic strategies to incorporate haptics in anatomical model exploration were developed by Petersik et al. (2002). Tactile feedback requires a higher frame rate than visual information. This can be challenging with complex geometry, but is feasible. At the time of writing, we are not aware of virtual anatomy education systems integrating haptic feedback, though it is employed in a variety of surgical simulation and training systems.

Gesture and touch input

With the advent of the iPhone's multi-touch interaction, many students are familiar with this type of input. The MEDICAL VISUALIZATION TABLE by SECTRA provides a great user experience based on touch gestures to support panning, zooming, and rotation (Ynnerman et al., 2015). Later improvements to the system allow for collaborative medical education, where team-based learning is supported by split-screen possibilities, allowing four people to interact with and edit images simultaneously.

Gesture-based input could improve user experience and contribute to learner motivation as a natural interaction style. Both Hochman et al. (2014) and Smit et al. (2016a) allow for gesture input for 3D interaction via the MICROSOFT KINECT and LEAP MOTION controller, respectively. However, both systems were not evaluated with respect to the long-term experience for learners. It is currently not clear how beneficial incorporating gesture-based interaction is for anatomy learning.

Sketching

Free-hand sketching could be another interesting interacting mechanism for education, though this has not been carefully evaluated yet. Pihuit et al. (2010) developed the first system inspired by chalkboard illustrations made by anatomy educators. Anatomy educators draw, explain, and refine such illustrations and explain how they relate to the overall system or organ. Students can reproduce such sketches and memorize the spatial relations in this way. This approach was limited to 2D illustrations. Saalfeld et al. (2016) followed up this work with a similar technique using the semi-immersive zSpace and pen-based input. It is possible to sketch entire 3D models, or to enhance existing models by drawing additional detailed structures (see Fig. 7.7).

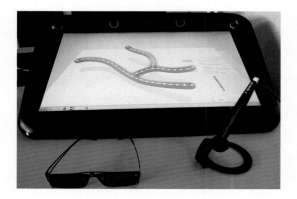

FIGURE 7.7

The stereoscopic display zSpace 100 with head-tracked glasses and 6DoF stylus for input allows for sketching vascular centerlines in (From: Saalfeld et al. (2016), ©2016 The Author(s), Eurographics Proceedings, ©The Eurographics Association).

Guidance

Users can be further supported by guidance, rather than a highly flexible system that lets them do everything at once without support for efficient learning. An example of this is to define predetermined learning paths that are available as optional orientation. Halle et al. (2017) suggest defining an *anatomic tour* that consists of bookmarks created by groups of learners. Similar to how a guided tour works for tourists, such a tour could be a good starting point for navigation and exploration.

7.7 Virtual anatomy systems

In this section and the next, we describe selected virtual anatomy systems, focusing on non-commercial developments. For a more complete overview, we refer to the survey by (Preim and Saalfeld, 2018). We emphasize the new concepts introduced by these systems and their main features and underlying data. Most systems do not refer to specific educational concepts or learning theories, but rather explore the space of possible solutions to virtual anatomy and textual information visualization. Most systems were described as a *digital atlas*, a fitting metaphor, as medical students are rather familiar with the function of an anatomy atlas. However, the term atlas does not encourage 3D interaction particularly and brings up expectations of static content. We begin our discussion with a brief outline of general system requirements, followed by a summary of several early anatomy systems. In the next section, we look into more recent systems leveraging web technology. For a discussion of virtual reality-based medical education systems, we refer to Chapter 13.

The basic system requirements (SR) for virtual anatomy systems are the following:

- **SR1**: It should provide a data set where the target anatomy is represented at a sufficient level of detail to recognize essential structures.
- **SR2**: It should provide facilities to flexibly explore 3D data from arbitrary perspectives and at a user-selected scale.
- **SR3**: It should provide techniques to explore related semantic information.
- **SR4**: It should provide direct support for repetition, for example, quizzing functionality.
- **SR5**: It should provide clipping and cutting tools to enable users to expose inner structures to study relations to outer structures.

SR1 is not fulfilled by all systems, in particular, nerves and the lymphatic system are often not visualized due to difficulties acquiring imaging data that can highlight these efficiently. Kraima et al. (2013) discuss the creation of anatomically complete models that include all necessary details by incorporating information from multiple imaging modalities based on immunohistochemical staining and radiographic imaging. Smit et al. (2012) outline the data structures needed for a unified model with a joint coordinate system for multimodal heterogeneous data. SR2–SR4 are typically fulfilled to some extent, whereas SR5 is only fulfilled when systems are based on direct volume rendering.

VOXEL-MAN

The VOXEL-MAN is a pioneering project that inspired many later developments (Höhne et al., 1992b, 1995). The first version was based on clinical data, whereas later versions were based on the VISIBLE HUMAN data sets. Two key developments led to its success. First, substantial visualization research was carried out, e.g., to achieve high-quality and efficient rendering of tagged volume data and cut surfaces (Tiede et al., 1998; Pflesser et al., 1998). In addition, imaging-based data was combined with a sophisticated knowledge based prepared by an anatomist (Schubert et al., 1993). The knowledge base was designed to be extendable. The system supports cross-sectional, regional, and systematic anatomy education (see Fig. 7.8). Later developments added X-ray correlation, and correlation of ultrasound images with 3D anatomy (Pommert et al., 2006). A special feature of the system was that it is was possible to do a virtual endoscopy, flying through air-filled or fluid-filled structures, such as the bronchial tree and the lungs.

Digital anatomist

The DIGITAL ANATOMIST was also an early and influential system with a deep and comprehensive focus on the knowledge representation (Brinkley and Rosse, 1997; Rosse et al., 1998). In 1999, the system already incorporated 26,000 anatomical concepts connected with 28,000 links. The system combined 3D rendering with predefined movies, some of which showed exploded views to help clarify spatial relations. The system is based on specimen scans and clinical MRI data. It supports regional and cross-sectional anatomy in the brain, including fiber tracts and functional areas. To support educational goals, it includes a tutorial and question-and-answer mode.

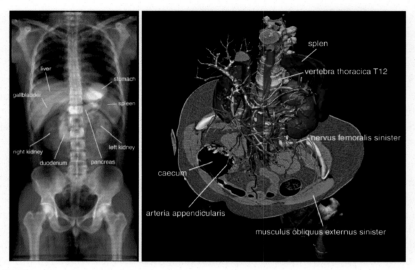

FIGURE 7.8

The VOXEL-MAN combines different rendering and presentation modes, such as simulated X-ray, surface and volume rendering, and display of cross-sectional data (From: Pommert et al. (2001)).

A limitation is that pre-rendered images of 3D anatomy are used, but interactive exploration is not possible. In later developments, a knee and thorax atlas were added.

Anatomy browser

The ANATOMYBROWSER also focuses on neuroanatomy and is based on multimodal brain MRI data, supporting comparative, regional, and cross-sectional anatomy (Kikinis et al., 1996; Golland et al., 1998). The cases also include patient data, providing a direct link to clinical medicine. A comprehensive knowledge base is combined with interactive labeling. This labeling is flexible and allows users to adjust color, line style, font, and font size.

Anatomic VisualizeR

The ANATOMIC VISUALIZER focuses more on virtual dissection and puts the emphasis on clipping tools (Hoffman et al., 2001a). It was developed to be flexible and extensible and can be linked to images, textual information, video, and animation. There are detailed renderings based on the VISIBLE HUMAN data set, but also schematic 3D renderings are available for an introduction and to compare the two views. In contrast to the previously mentioned systems, the ANATOMIC VISUALIZER provides guidance. A *study guide* provides an organized overview of key concepts, exercises, and recommended actions for each learning module.

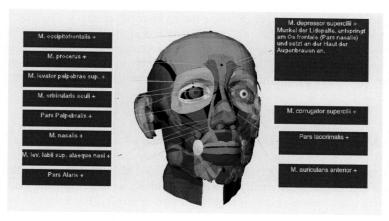

FIGURE 7.9

Integration of labels and textual explanations with the 3D model in the ZOOMILLUSTRATOR. The face muscle that is textually explained is emphasized in the 3D model.

ZoomIllustrator

The ZOOMILLUSTRATOR focuses on interactive exploration of the information space consisting of 3D models, labels, brief explanations, extended explanations, and figure captions (Preim et al., 1997, 1998). It consists of a zoomable user interface that flexibly allocates space for the required textual explanations (see Fig. 7.9). The models were bought from a commercial vendor that created the models manually. In this system, the figure captions are generated automatically to reflect visible objects and the viewing direction, as well as structure colors. It is possible to display views side by side and have shared labels rendered in-between both views. The labeling is automated and animations can be created based on a scripting language (Preim et al., 1996). The evaluation of the system focused primarily on acceptance and usability (Pitt et al., 1999) and demonstrated that students rarely used the available 3D interaction facilities.

3D puzzle

The 3D PUZZLE was developed at the same institution and using the same data as the ZOOMILLUSTRATOR, partially as a consequence of its evaluation. The main goal was to encourage 3D interaction using a puzzle metaphor. A 3D model could be composed of many individual objects based on grabbing, rotating, and zooming. A snapping mechanism to predefined docking positions supports finding the correct position. Learners have to consider the order of docking actions, as internal structures should be placed before outer ones. This thinking about tissue layers corresponds well to relevant anatomical knowledge. The system incorporates depth cues, such as shadows, stereo rendering, and collision detection to ease structure placement. Interaction is handled as 3D input via a SpaceBall with bimanual support. Object selection triggers an animation that shows and emphasizes the anatomical structure. The 3D PUZZLE is designed to provide *implicit guidance* by task design (Ritter et al., 2000). Dev (1999) mention enabling learners to compose or decompose anatomical structures as an anatomy learning strategy associated to *constructivism*. In a way, the 3D PUZZLE could be considered a serious game, though it did not incorporate the motivational potential of reward strategies as such.

VarVis

The VARVIS system aims at comparative anatomy education (Smit et al., 2016b; Smit, 2016). It is focused on visualizing healthy anatomical variation in the topology of branching structures. For example, arteries can have additional or missing branches or can be connected up differently between individuals without this being pathological. Which exact variant occurs is highly relevant in surgery. For example, knowing which anatomical variant a patient has before colorectal surgery through a preoperative 3D reconstruction of the vascular anatomy reduces variability of operating time and estimated blood loss (Willard et al., 2019).

Major learning goals when teaching variational anatomy are knowing which variants can occur, how frequently they occur, and their similarities and differences. VARVIS is based on a textbook illustrations of variants combined with CT imaging data and patient-specific models (see Fig. 7.10). A global view indicates the similarity between variants, whereas a local view enables in-depth analysis of differences between a pair of variants. Branching structures are modeled as graphs with nodes representing branching points and end points and graph matching is used to calculate similarity.

Despite the importance of anatomical variation in clinical practice, educational scenarios rarely focus on these aspects. In addition to VARVIS and the LIVERANATOMYEXPLORER (Birr et al., 2013) (see Section 7.8) focusing on topological variation of the liver vasculature, Hacker and Handels (2009) focus on conveying shape variation in organs such as the kidney.

Summary

There is a wide variety of virtual anatomy systems that differ in the underlying data and viewing tools available to the learners. As pointed out by Halle et al. (2017), a large drawback of most developments is that atlas data and viewing tools are not standardized and cannot be interchanged freely. Furthermore, another limitation is that none of the major VA systems discussed here support cooperation.

7.8 3D web-based anatomy education

E-learning is meant to make resources for learning available at any time and place. The need for such solutions became especially pressing as the global COVID-19 pandemic and subsequent lockdowns created an urgent need for virtual anatomy education possibilities with dissection rooms no longer available. A notable development

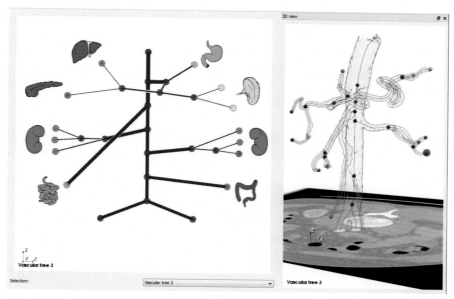

FIGURE 7.10

The VarVis anatomy system links graph-based representations to CT imaging data, patient-specific models, and anatomical variation illustrations to teach variational anatomy in branching structures, such as blood vessels (Courtesy of Noeska Smit, University of Bergen).

in this regard is the VanVR App (Virtual Reality Anatomy and Pathology Project),[3] which provides an immersive virtual learning environment, where medical students can interact with scans of real anatomical and pathological specimens. Web-based virtual anatomy systems can support remote learning by reaching a large number of learners and supporting collaborative learning. The design of such systems should consider general experiences and recommendations for web-based learning environments, as discussed by Cook and Dupras (2004). A special challenge in anatomy education is to handle large geometric models.

7.8.1 Open web-based standards

Since 3D visualizations are a cornerstone for virtual anatomy systems, 3D standards for the web are essential. The first web-based anatomy education systems, for example, (Warrick and Funnell, 1998) and (Lu et al., 2005), were built on top of the virtual reality markup language (VRML) standards developed by the Web3D consortium. This standard enables complex 3D model representation as a hierarchy, using

---

[3] https://hive.med.ubc.ca/projects/vanvr-app/.

anatomical categories as group nodes. Transformations, material properties, animations, and predefined viewpoints can be specified for individual objects and groups. Behr and Alexa (2001) integrated volume rendering in VRML, which was essential for virtual anatomy systems. VRML did require plugins to be installed, something which was often not possible in hospitals. This problem persisted with the X3D standard (Behr et al., 2009), where the X stands for extensible. This standard supports programmable shaders, multi-texturing, and clipping planes in an XLM-like structure. The Web3D consortium's medical working group continues to develop X3D and related technologies for medical use, in particular to integrate the technology with the DICOM standard.

WebGL, a Javascript graphics API based on OpenGL ES 2.0 finally enabled 3D graphics displayed in web browsers and on mobile phones without plugins required. The current version, WebGL 2.0 further extended the capabilities with 3D texture mapping, which allows for volume rendering. As WebGL relies on client-side rendering, it scales to a large amount of learners without performance issues.

Based on WebGL, recently VTK.js was released, a rendering library made for scientific visualization on the web based on the popular visualization toolkit (VTK). It brings high-performance rendering into the browser and has great potential for volume rendering of medical imaging data. To bring surface models to the web, the Three.js library is a popular choice, also built on top of WebGL.

7.8.2 Selected examples

Brenton et al. (2007) discuss general concepts and considerations around web-based virtual anatomy systems. As a specific example, they showcase how the nervous system of the brachial plexus, a complex nerve network extending from the neck to the arm, can be modeled as diagrammatic representations with labels, measurements, and visible branchings. They show the vertebrae as anatomical context and argue that high-quality surface models are needed without distracting details. They show how this can be achieved with subdivision modeling.

Educational virtual anatomy

A prominent example for web-based anatomy learning was EVA (educational virtual anatomy) presented by (Petersson et al., 2009). The system focused on arteries extracted from clinical CT angiography data in nine body regions. They used the proprietary QuickTime VR standard in combination with the medical image viewer OSIRIX. They provided 3D visualizations at three levels of detail, resulting in more or less finer branches present with color-coding to separate major branches. The arteries were shown in the context of skeletal structures. Text from Gray's Anatomy was displayed alongside the area of interest with matching color-coded terms highlighted and hyperlinks to other arteries.

Google and zygote body

The first virtual anatomy system based on WebGL was GOOGLE BODY introduced in 2010. It is based on surface models with realistic textures created by artists and provided an easy-to-use zoomable interface, inspired by other Google applications, such as GOOGLE MAPS. It was possible to freely explore, search, hide, and reveal different anatomical layers. On selection, all other anatomical structures were rendered transparently to emphasize the focus object. ZYGOTE subsequently took over the project and maintains the work as the ZYGOTE BODY project with a licensing system (Kelc, 2012). The system design is linked to constructivist theory.

BioDigital human 3D

The development of the BIODIGITAL HUMAN 3D started at the School of Medicine's Division of Educational Informatics at the New York University and turned into a commercial product of BIODIGITAL in 2013 (Qualter et al., 2012). It is a comprehensive web-based system that incorporates anatomy and health conditions, featuring over a 1000 high-quality textured models created by artists. They offer a highly flexible authoring tool that allows for the models to be personalized for both teachers and users. At the time of writing, over 4 million students, teachers, clinicians, and professionals use BIODIGITAL.

LiverAnatomyExplorer

Another early virtual anatomy system built on top of WebGL is the LIVERANATO-MYEXPLORER (Birr et al., 2013) (see Fig. 7.11). It features surface models based on anonymized clinical data to teach surgical vascular anatomy. A large variety of cases derived from clinical CT data are available to represent the variability of the arterial supply and venous drainage in this area. Liver pathologies, such as metastases, were also visualized. In addition, the system supports visualization of 2D slice images as SVG, which can be integrated with the 3D scene.

Online anatomical human

The ONLINE ANATOMICAL HUMAN (Smit et al., 2016a) also combines slice-based and 3D visualization (recall Fig. 7.1). In this case, the cross-sectional images are from the VISIBLE KOREAN FEMALE data set and linked to the Virtual Surgical Pelvis atlas model (Smit, 2016). The system provides advanced functions to annotate the surface models, including support for placing anatomical landmarks, lines, and regions. The functionality can be used by educators to provide information or in a quiz context, where learners should draw on the structures. The system also supports gesture-based input via the Leap Motion controller. It was used in a Massive Open Online (MOOC) by over 50,000 learners.

Open anatomy browser

Halle et al. (2017) published the OPEN ANATOMY BROWSER based on long-term experience at the Surgical Planning Lab in Boston to create digital atlas data and viewers (Kikinis et al., 1996; Golland et al., 1998). It is based on WebGL and em-

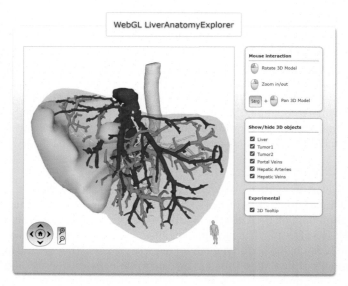

FIGURE 7.11

The LIVERANATOMYEXPLORER (Birr et al., 2013) shows hepatic anatomy in the browser. The model is based on anonymized clinical data. On mouse-over, labels are revealed. Screenshot taken from http://liveranatomyexplorer.steven-birr.com/.

ploys clinical MRI data. In this system, the cooperation between users is directly supported by sharing bookmarks and dynamic views. In addition, there is an architecture in place that decouples atlas data and viewing tools. Both the atlas information and viewing tools are available open source. When atlas data is represented based on official and widely used standards, this opens up for others to create viewing tools. This also allows for the atlas data to be subject to interpretation and revision. The project is inspired by Wikipedia and a team effort to maintain the knowledge source based on mechanisms to check for consistency and support versioning. (Azkue, 2013) also argued that surface meshes should be reviewed for anatomic accuracy and educational relevance before widespread adoption.

Mobile anatomy education

is potentially useful, but the small display is a disadvantage to display complex anatomy in great detail. Lewis et al. (2014) mention VISIBLE BODY, 3D4MEDICAL, and POCKETANATOMY as leading examples. All are commercial applications, where no scientific publications describe their design and evaluation. From their websites and video demonstrations, it appears all use convenient touch-based interaction combined with detailed surface models.

The availability of virtual anatomy systems in the browser, in particular without the need for plugins to be installed, can help increase the uptake of virtual anatomy systems worldwide. Performance aspects, such as providing a high frame-rate and ensuring that surface models are sufficiently compact and simplified, are particularly important for such systems. Being web-based also allows for cooperative educating and learning, though these features are currently not used to their full potential in most systems.

7.9 Evaluation of virtual anatomy systems

In this section, we discuss general principles in virtual anatomy system evaluation and highlight selected examples. Yammine and Violato (2015) provide a structured overview of evaluation studies for virtual anatomy systems. They identified 36 high-quality evaluations that consist of peer-reviewed full papers with a convincing study design and high number of participants. Most studies were randomized, meaning neither educators nor learners influenced the decision on whether a virtual anatomy system or alternative approach was used. This avoids selection bias. It is likely that students volunteering to evaluate a virtual anatomy system differ in their capabilities from other students. Almost all evaluated systems focus on a limited regional anatomy aspect, such as neuroanatomy, vascular anatomy, pelvic, or abdominal anatomy.

There are four typical categories in the evaluation of medical educational software (Dev, 1999):

- **Preference**: Do learners prefer the e-learning system compared to other learning resources?
- **Knowledge gain**: Do learners acquire new knowledge from the e-learning system?
- **Usability**: Is this e-learning system easy to learn and efficient to use?
- **Behavioral change**: Does the use of the e-learning system change the way learners practice medicine?

Although the last category is the most important, evaluations of virtual anatomy system typically focus on knowledge gain. The reason for this is that behavioral change is too difficult to assess in anatomy education. Typically, by the time students are learning anatomy, they are still far from practicing medicine. The knowledge gain is often compared to a conventional learning approach. We will use the term *intervention group* for the group of learners using the new technique and the term *control group* for the other group. Some studies report on the time learners take to complete a test in addition. However, we consider knowledge gain more important than time differences. A high degree of usability is typically a prerequisite for acceptability and knowledge acquisition. Still, a virtual anatomy system scoring high on usability but low on knowledge gain is not very meaningful. In most evaluations, usability is not discussed explicitly.

In addition to measurable knowledge gain, the subjective assessment of the learners can also be considered. Questions, such as whether they trust a virtual anatomy system to provide an efficient way to learn anatomy, are also essential.

Systematic and in-depth evaluations of virtual anatomy systems have mainly been conducted recently. Nicholson et al. (2006) found only four randomized controlled studies before 2005 in a systematic search, but Azer and Azer (2016) already reported on 30 in 2016. This increase is likely due to the availability of comprehensive commercial systems that allow anatomy education researchers to carry out such studies without having to build models and systems themselves.

7.9.1 Evaluation strategies

We briefly discuss selected evaluation studies emphasizing evaluation criteria and strategies. This should enable the reader to design similar evaluations themselves.

Assessment of knowledge gain

All evaluations described here use a pre-test to assess the knowledge level of the learners before using a virtual anatomy system or alternative approach. Multiple choice questions are a popular choice for this. An alternative to this are video-recorded open interviews with subsequent assessment by instructors. A post-test is ideally performed in the same way after using the system. The difference between the two test results then constitutes the knowledge gain. The questions in both tests should focus on spatial aspects of anatomy, and various questionnaires were designed for this purpose. Verbal questions about the shape and position of objects can be complemented with drawings. Nguyen et al. (2012), for example, show a horizontal line for several 3D models and ask learners to select a matching cross-sectional image from a stack of images.

Spatial ability

As not all learners are likely to benefit in the same way from virtual anatomy education systems, their spatial ability is typically assessed based on the mental rotation test (MRT) according to Vandenberg and Kuse (1978). This can be used to correlate knowledge gain to MRT results or to classify learners in low and high spatial ability groups to analyze separately. Nguyen et al. (2012) show that high spatial ability learners using animated rotations are able to solve spatial anatomical tasks significantly faster and more correctly than low spatial ability learners.

In addition to spatial ability, there are other learner-related factors that can influence results (Azer and Azer, 2016; Yammine and Violato, 2015):

- Experience with 3D applications such as video games
- Experience with graphics modeling
- Familiarity with computers
- Active experience with painting and sculpting

Evaluations of virtual anatomy systems should analyze individual difference and relate them to learner performance.

Integration in the curriculum

An essential aspect of any virtual anatomy system evaluation is whether and how it is integrated in the curriculum (*blended learning*). This influences what we can assume students know already. It is also important to know whether the use of the system is guided by an instructor and whether this instructor provides feedback or answers questions about the system when they arise. Azer and Azer (2016) suggest that evaluations should be explicit about these matters.

7.9.2 Selected examples

All evaluations mentioned here are designed as comparisons between virtual anatomy systems and a more classical form of teaching, either conventional learning or a virtual anatomy system with reduced functionality. We highlight in particular how the evaluations differ in their approaches, although many aspects are similar.

Carpal bone anatomy

Garg et al. presented a series of evaluations based on teaching carpal bone anatomy, a group of wrist bones (Garg et al., 1999, 2001). The first study revealed that there was no advantage to presenting carpal bone anatomy in multiple views (15 degree steps) over presenting three key viewpoints only Garg et al. (1999). The second experiment allowed the intervention group to control multiple views of the carpal bone, whereas the control group saw only key views Garg et al. (2001). Questions were then divided into two groups: one half where key viewpoints should be sufficient to answer and one half where unfamiliar views are needed that strongly differ from these. High spatial ability learners in the intervention group improved their spatial understanding in both types of questions. Low spatial ability learners could not benefit. These findings were later explained by the connection between mental rotation tasks and manual rotation. Low spatial ability learners are less effective in manually rotating a virtual object. The study authors state that key viewpoints are important, but that the active control of the viewing direction close to the key viewpoints adds a sense of the third dimension. In the evaluation, it also turned out that the learners spent much more time close to the key viewpoints. The authors conjecture that anatomy education benefits from 3D models, but probably more from physical models than virtual ones.

3D puzzle

The 3D PUZZLE (Ritter et al., 2000) (recall Section 7.7) was evaluated with 16 physiotherapy students with previously acquired basic anatomy skills divided into two groups (Ritter et al., 2002). To understand the effect on knowledge gain, two systems were used for learning, both using the same foot anatomy models and textual information, only differing in 3D puzzle support. The pre-test anatomy knowledge was on average 52% for all questions, increasing by 11% for the intervention group, and

8% for the control group. The difference was observed for all questions relating to spatial knowledge. The participants also took part in a test focusing on mental rotation, figurative classification, and recognition. The differences in post-test knowledge could not be explained by spatial ability differences. Furthermore, students in the intervention group were more confident in their abilities. They liked to use the 3D space mouse for model rotation, even though it took some time to become familiar with it.

Use of supportive handles

We previously briefly described the idea of providing *supportive handles* to support rotation interaction for anatomical structures in Section 7.6. The handles represent a local coordinate system for a selected object and can be based on anatomical knowledge or a shape analysis to identify principal components. To test the effectiveness of such handles, Stull et al. (2009) assembled a number of difficult rotation tasks until the view matches a provided target view. The tasks are designed to test whether students can recognize anatomical structures from different viewing angles. Seventy-five (75) participants were divided into two groups: an intervention group (17 and 21 students with high and low spatial ability, respectively) and a control group (19 and 18 students with high and low spatial ability, respectively). Learners could use a 3D input device to ease 3D rotation tasks compared to mouse input or touch gestures. The results of the study revealed that both low and high spatial ability learners benefited from the supportive handles, but that the low spatial ability learners benefited more strongly. This reduces the difference between both learner groups, where the cognitive load for low spatial ability learners gets reduced. In addition, the intervention group learners had faster task completion times enabled by more goal-directed object rotation.

EVA evaluation

The EVA system (Petersson et al., 2009) (recall Section 7.8) was also carefully evaluated. The questions were chosen such that unusual views not present in traditional anatomical atlas illustrations are needed. In the knowledge assessment part of the study, groups of 89 second semester learners (41 using EVA, 48 using alternative resources) and 77 fifth semester learners (51 using EVA, 26 using alternatives) were compared. The mean score for the second semester students was significantly higher in the EVA group, whereas for the fifth semester group the results were almost the same, without any significant difference in knowledge gain. In addition to this quantitative assessment, preferences were analyzed comparing EVA to anatomy text books, lectures, and dissections. On average, EVA was considered to be similar. It was rated to be slightly better than text books (16/37 considered them equal and 12/37 considered EVA better) and similar to lectures. EVA was considered worse than dissection by most students (19 students said EVA was worse, whereas 7 said it was better). Individual differences were quite striking, some students do not prefer the interactive visualization and may also perform worse with EVA, whereas others consider it the best teaching resource. Limitations of this study include that EVA was not integrated into the curriculum, that the QuickTime plugin was not easily available for some students. It was also unclear whether the case studied was relevant for the examinations.

7.9.3 Discussion

Most recent studies noted a positive impact of virtual anatomy education. This could be due to the fact that underlying models are more realistic and that the interactivity increased more than in early days of virtual anatomy education. To summarize the findings, it is likely that for complex spatial regions and systems, interactive virtual anatomy systems based on detailed models favor learning and deep understanding. However, not all students will benefit in the same manner, as shown by the studies separating students into high and low spatial ability learners. We would like to summarize the study findings with a quote from Estai and Bunt (2016): "evidence shows that learning anatomy using computer-based learning can enhance learning by *supplementing rather than replacing* the traditional teaching methods".

Though there are a number of studies evaluating the general effects of interactive 3D visualization, the value of specific techniques such as clipping, virtual dissection, endoscopic views, and focus-and-context views have not been assessed so far. In addition, the knowledge gain assessed is typically a surrogate for the actual situation. Further studies are needed that analyze the *external validity* of such results, e.g., by analyzing the resulting competence in cadaver dissection tasks. More research is necessary to better understand how to optimally integrate virtual anatomy systems in overall anatomy education and its wide variety in implementation, which likely impacts optimal use.

7.10 Concluding remarks

Many resources are available for students in medicine and related disciplines to learn anatomy. Virtual anatomy systems with their emphasis on exploring shapes and spatial relations play a key role. Powerful visualization techniques that support shape and depth perception, labeling, and interaction techniques are the essential technical ingredients. In addition, the learning scenarios and motivational strategies to be supported are the educational foundations. A large variety of software libraries was used to develop virtual anatomy systems. In recent years, game engines became more popular approaches with their potential for a wide range of input devices and interaction techniques. Due to advances in web technology, virtual anatomy systems also moved online in recent years, making educational content available any place and any time, without the need to install software.

Most virtual anatomy systems are not carefully integrated into an existing curriculum with optional use, giving rise to unclear relevance. The wide availability and commercial success of some systems indicates that there is at least a sizable portion of the student population using them.

Outlook

The knowledge provided in virtual anatomy systems is often limited to 3D models and related text. Diagrams, dissection photos, and video clips might further enrich the experience with careful integration. Typically, systems support open exploration with limited guidance. Based on experience in e-learning, powerful search and retrieval functionality needs to be added. Virtual anatomy systems might have a long lifetime, and thus need to be easy to maintain, extend, and update in terms of contents. This requires a clean separation between software and content.

We have seen that only few systems support variational and functional anatomy education. As such, there is a strong demand for future research in these areas. The usefulness of current virtual anatomy systems largely depends on the learner and their spatial ability. Further research could also focus on how systems could adapt to cater to learner differences.

Another recent development is the use of data physicalization in anatomy education.[4] For example, Stoppel and Bruckner (2017) allow for paper-printed volume visualization with some interactivity, whereas Pahr et al. (2021) are able to create printed holograms of anatomical structures. Turning virtual anatomy back into physical objects, for example through 3D printing (Ang et al., 2019) or through papercrafts (Schindler et al., 2020, 2022), that can be manipulated by learners directly, is an interesting avenue of further exploration with potential benefits for patient education in addition.

Finally, integration of realistic haptic feedback that conveys mechanical properties of different tissue types would be a highly useful addition. Several studies indicated that dissection is still perceived as more important than virtual anatomy-based learning. It could be that haptic interaction plays a role here. It is already successfully employed in surgical training, but virtual anatomy systems need to be cost-effective due to their larger audience. Recent developments in creating detailed anatomical models by surface scanning specimens could also bring virtual anatomy education closer to the dissection experience (Vandenbossche et al., 2022).

Recommended reading

The following selection of influential papers on anatomy education based on interactive 3D visualization is recommended:

Claes Lundstrom, Thomas Rydell, Camilla Forsell, Anders Persson, and Anders Ynnerman (2011). "Multi-touch table system for medical visualization: Application to orthopedic surgery planning," *IEEE Transactions on Visualization and Computer Graphics*, 17(12): 1775–1784.

Helge Petersson, David Sinkvist, Chunliang Wang, and Örjan Smedby (2009). "Web-based interactive 3D visualization as a tool for improved anatomy learning," *Anatomical Sciences Education*, Vol. 2(2): 61–68.

---

[4] http://dataphys.org/list/.

Andreas Pommert, Karl Heinz Höhne, Eike Burmester, Sebastian Gehrmann, Rudolf Leuwer, Andreas Petersik, Bernhard Pflesser, and Ulf Tiede (2006). "Computer-Based anatomy: A prerequisite for Computer-Assisted radiology and surgery," *Academic Radiology*, Vol. 13(1) (2006): 104–112.

Victor M. Spitzer and Ann L. Scherzinger (2006). "Virtual anatomy: An anatomist's playground," *Clinical Anatomy*, Vol. 19(3): 192–203.

Kaissar Yammine and Claudio Violato (2015). "A meta-analysis of the educational effectiveness of three-dimensional visualization technologies in teaching anatomy," *Anatomical Sciences Education*, Vol. 8(6): 525–538.

Visual computing for radiation treatment planning

8

8.1 Introduction

Radiation therapy (RT) is one of the major curative approaches for cancer. To destroy malignant cells, RT makes use of ionizing rays, such as photon or proton radiation. Though tumors need to receive high radiation doses to be treated, adjacent healthy organ tissues must receive as low doses as possible to minimize the side-effects of radiation for the patient. As RT involves a much higher dose of radiation than diagnostic modalities, such as CT and X-ray, this generates a high risk of tissue damage, therefore planning prior to treatment is very crucial.

Visual computing is a fundamental component of RT planning, providing solutions in all parts of the process: from the acquisition of the image data of the patient to the actual delivery of the therapy. The complex data, the compound processes, and the multitude of user groups involved in RT make it interesting for several fields of research, e.g., image processing, visualization, visual analytics, and machine learning. Given the increasing demand for more personalized therapy, RT is expected to become even more tightly coupled with visual computing, in an effort to provide more targeted patient treatment comprising additional patient- and tumor-specific information (Tanderup et al., 2006). Developing novel methods to support RT planning requires interdisciplinary strategies, that is, integrating the whole visual computing portfolio from data, image, and information fusion (Schlachter et al., 2017), to interaction (Aselmaa et al., 2017), exploration and visual analytics (Raidou et al., 2017). The topic is also manifold, involving different sources of data and uncertainty, several specialist users and a variety of applications and challenges. This chapter provides an overview of the compound planning process of RT and of the ways that visualization has supported treatment planning in all its facets.

Organization

This chapter is organized as follows: We start by providing a basic and necessary (historical) background on cancer and its treatment (Section 8.2). We proceed with the basics of RT, including its workflow, as well as the data and users involved in it (Section 8.3). The main part of the chapter discusses popular visual computing approaches for the distinct steps of the RT workflow, namely the definition of target volumes and surrounding organs at risk (Section 8.4), the design of the treatment plan and the dose calculation as performed in dedicated treatment planning software (Section 8.5), the plan review and treatment evaluation (Section 8.6), and finally image-guided adaptive RT (IGART), which tries to optimize dose delivery by taking into account changes during dose plan delivery (Section 8.7). The chapter finishes with concluding remarks that summarize the main trends encountered in literature (Section 8.8).

8.2 Background on cancer

The term *cancer* is credited to Hippocrates (c. 460–370 BC), due to the resemblance of tumor shapes to a crab (Pelengaris and Khan, 2013). It was not until the early 18th century that the French physician Claude Gendron (1663–1750) described cancer as a locally hard-growing mass, which needs to be removed (Pelengaris and Khan, 2013). In the same century, Astruc and Peyrilhe conducted experiments, seeking a better diagnosis, new treatments and deeper understanding of the causes of the disease (Pelengaris and Khan, 2013). With the development of microscopes, in the late 19th century, the examination of cancer tissues and tumors demonstrated that cancer cells differ in appearance and behavior from normal cells (Olson, 1989).

By examining the genetic information of cells, scientists have obtained a better understanding of the processes that initiate cancer in an organism. Current theories support that genetic mutations in otherwise non-reproductive cells, stimulate abnormal cellular growth (Washington and Leaver, 2015). Cells start proliferating and dividing in an unregulated way, which results in tumor growth.

Tumors can originate from any cell and are, in general, divided into two categories: *benign* and *malignant* (Washington and Leaver, 2015). The former are well differentiated and do not invade surrounding normal tissues, but can compress it, causing damage. The latter tend to spread to other body parts through the bloodstream or the lymphatic system, in a process called *metastasis*; they can also divide and grow by creating new blood vessels to sustain themselves, in a process called *angiogenesis* (Folkman, 2002). A schematic depiction of the abnormal processes taking place before and during the multiplication of cancer cells is presented in Fig. 8.1.

Cancer is a leading cause of death worldwide, accounting for nearly 10 million deaths in 2020 (Ferlay et al., 2021). Early detection and diagnosis is an important factor in tumor treatment, as chances of metastasis are lower. However, not all cancer types are accompanied with clear symptoms, making detection and diagnosis difficult in the early stages. Advances in medical imaging have increased the capabilities of physicians to detect tumors through screenings, such as mammography for breast cancer, or colonoscopy for colorectal cancer. Additionally, medical imaging has facilitated also patient treatment, and currently, cancer can be treated through a vast selection of techniques.

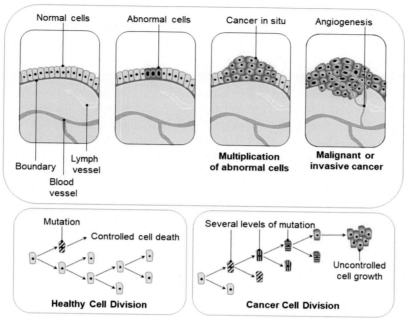

FIGURE 8.1

Schematic depiction of a malignant tumor and the processes occurring during the uncontrolled division and growth of cancer cells.

8.3 Radiation therapy (RT)

For most cancer types, treatment is nowadays pursued through radiation therapy (RT; or radiotherapy) and/or surgery. The role of RT can be *therapeutic* to cure the disease, or *adjuvant* to prevent tumor recurrence, or *palliative* to relieve symptoms. Often, RT complements surgery, chemotherapy, hormonotherapy and/or immunotherapy (Washington and Leaver, 2015), as more than 60% of patients receive RT at some point during their treatment.

Historical development

RT has been treating cancer patients for more than a century (Slater, 2012), dating as far back as to 1896. With the discoveries of Marie Curie, a new era in medical research and treatment began, although the hazards of radiation exposure were back then unknown (Thariat et al., 2013). Initially, the only source of radiation was radium, but after WWII, additional artificial radioisotopes have been introduced (Kerst, 1941). The 1950s brought linear particle accelerators (Bryant, 1994), and in the 1970–80s, new imaging technologies allowed for 3D radiation delivery (Leibel et al., 2002). These advancements enabled better treatment outcomes and less side-effects for healthy tissues (Thariat et al., 2013).

Basic concept

The basic concept of RT is that ionizing radiation, such as photon or proton radiation, damages the genetic information of cancerous tissues (Washington and Leaver, 2015). Tumors are treated with higher radiation doses, whereas adjacent healthy organ tissues must receive lower doses to minimize the side-effects of radiation for the patients. The administered radiation dose used in RT is measured in Grays (Gy), and varies depending on the type and stage of cancer, as well as the intent of the treatment. The response of tumor tissues to radiation is determined by their size and radiosensitivity (Thariat et al., 2013): More radiosensitive cancers, such as leukemia or epithelial tumors, can be treated by moderate doses, whereas more resistant ones, such as renal cancer, require much higher doses.

Since RT involves very high doses of radiation than diagnostic modalities, there is a high risk of tissue damage, leading eventually to secondary cancer (Hall and Wuu, 2003) and other severe side-effects. Due to the risky nature of RT, pre-treatment planning is more important than in any other type of medical treatment. Careful delineation of the target tumor and all adjacent organs at risk (OARs) is necessary; dose simulations are carried out for each patient to assess whether a sufficient dose to destroy the tumor is achieved, while maintaining tolerable doses to the OARs.

Internal and external radiation treatment

The RT treatment process can be *internal* or *external* (e.g., external beam RT or EBRT) (Washington and Leaver, 2015). An essential internal treatment method is brachytherapy, where radioactive sources (seeds) are positioned precisely within the area to be treated, affecting only a very localized area (Gerbaulet et al., 2002). The small seeds consist of radioactive materials, such as Palladium 103 or Iodine 125 and are implanted precisely into the treatment area, while being guided by a template attached to an ultrasound probe. The number of seeds varies, depending on the size of the area to be treated. A schematic depiction of radioactive seeds placement during prostate brachytherapy is presented in Fig. 8.2.

Variants of external radiation treatment

In EBRT, the radiation source is a linear accelerator (LINAC) and is located outside of the patient. The LINAC accelerates electrons, allowing them to collide with a heavy metal target to produce high-energy X-rays, structured to conform to the shape of the target volume covering the tumor. To reduce the toxicity to the normal tissues, radiation beams need to be shaped and aimed from several angles of exposure, to cumulatively target the tumor (Washington and Leaver, 2015). The beam is shaped by a multileaf collimator and is directed to the tumor by a gantry rotating around the patient, who lies on a movable treatment couch. Common examples of EBRT are intensity-modulated RT (IMRT) and volumetric arc therapy (VMAT), which can precisely address concave tumors, such as tumors enclosing the spinal cord or major blood vessels. This is achieved by modulating the intensity of the radiation beam near the tumor volume, while decreasing or avoiding the radiation among the surrounding healthy tissues (Webb, 2001).

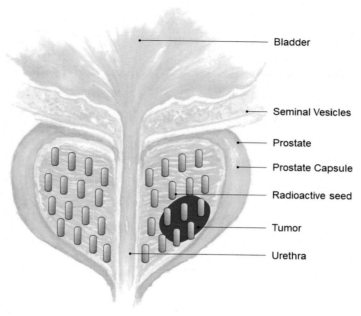

Bladder

Seminal Vesicles

Prostate

Prostate Capsule

Radioactive seed

Tumor

Urethra

FIGURE 8.2

Schematic depiction of positioning of internal radioactive seeds (in gray) used in brachytherapy for a prostate tumor (in dark red).

8.3.1 Basic RT workflow

RT planning follows a general workflow (see Fig. 8.3). The time required for the planning procedure differs for each individual patient and is specific to the characteristics of the case and tumor. An in-depth workflow analysis has been presented by Aselmaa et al. (2013) and by Schlachter et al. (2019). In this section, we summarize the basics of the RT workflow, and in the upcoming sections we discuss visual computing in all steps, after the imaging acquisition.

Image acquisition

After diagnosis and referral, patient images are acquired. As discussed in Chapter 4 of this book, the combination of multiple imaging modalities can improve detection, diagnosis, and staging. Clinical imaging techniques may capture anatomical features (e.g., with the use of computed tomography; or CT), or functional characteristics (e.g., metabolism captured with positron emission tomography; or PET) (Evans, 2008). Multi-modal imaging can additionally include different magnetic resonance imaging (MRI) sequences, diffusion-weighted imaging (DWI), dynamic-contrast enhanced (DCE) CT, or MR imaging and MR spectroscopy imaging (MRSI).

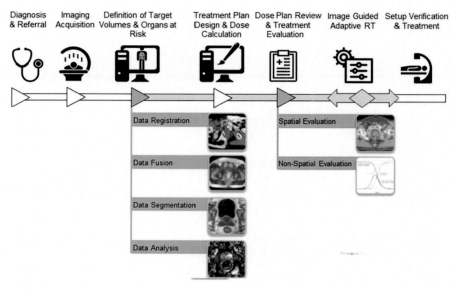

FIGURE 8.3

The basic steps of the RT planning workflow.

Definition of target volumes and organs at risk

A crucial step of treatment planning is the definition of target volumes (i.e., the tumor tissue) and *organs at risk* (OAR) (i.e., volumes representing whole organs or parts thereof, which are healthy and need to be spared) (Njeh, 2008). Target volumes and OAR definition comprises the segmentation (often by manual delineation) of the structures, employing more than one imaging source to improve specificity and sensitivity (Lee et al., 2012). This is done in registered images (Zitova and Flusser, 2003) that are transformed into the same coordinate system as the planning CT (i.e., a high-quality CT scan that serves as the basis for all planning). Through data fusion, various information channels are integrated and combined; interactive approaches for the exploration and analysis of the data are also employed.

Treatment plan design and dose calculation

After the localization of the tumor and adjacent healthy organs, one (or more) initial treatment plan(s) is (are) designed, using treatment planning software. Two well-known manufacturers of RT-related software and solutions are MIRADA MEDICAL and VARIAN MEDICAL SYSTEMS. Complex constraints and guidelines are employed to determine the geometric, biological, and dosimetric aspects of the treatment, taking into account the OAR, and optimizing for tumor treatment and healthy tissue preservation. For target volumes, a required minimum dose is prescribed, according to guidelines, whereas OARs should receive doses as low as possible (Barentsz et al., 2012). The final prescribed radiation dose is not administered all at once. Fractionation is a common practice, where the total dose is spread out over time, to allow the recovery of normal cells and to prevent the repair of tumor cells between fractions (Thariat et al., 2013). For example, in some cases of prostate cancer treatment, 8–13 fractions might be considered, depending on the radiosensitivity, i.e., the sensitivity of the tissues to radiation

Dose plan review and treatment evaluation

The calculated treatment plan(s) will undergo further review and approval. The common practice in RT includes using dose volume histograms (DVH) (Drzymala et al., 1991) to summarize the distribution of doses to the target and OARs. To assess the selected RT strategy, tumor control probability (TCP) modeling (Webb and Nahum, 1993) and normal tissue complication probability (NTCP) modeling (Marks et al., 2010) are used as part of radiobiological modeling. Radiobiological models aim at determining the biological effects of a selected treatment plans or modality, and they typically relate a physical quantity (e.g., absorbed dose) to a biological quantity (e.g., cell survival fraction). In practice, they are statistical models that quantify the probability that, given a specific radiation dose, a tumor is effectively controlled (i.e., treated), and that normal tissue is not affected, respectively.

Image-guided adaptive RT (IGART)

Sometimes, changes in the tumor location and shape, or anatomical changes of the patient (e.g., due to weight loss, or due to rectal and urinary filling) require further plan modifications between treatment fractions. This is done through IGART, which verifies whether the initial plan is still applicable; this applies also during treatment. At the point of treatment delivery, a prior verification step ensures that the patient is correctly positioned.

8.3.2 Data involved in the RT workflow

The entire workflow of RT planning is based on the imaging acquisitions of the anatomy and pathology of the patient (input). The outcome (output) of the workflow is a dose plan, which incorporates 2D or 3D radiation dose information to be administered to the patient. During this entire planning process, several imaging and non-imaging data of the patient are taken into account (Putora et al., 2015).

Imaging data

In the image acquisition step, the necessary images needed for RT planning are acquired from a multitude of sources (Hricak et al., 2007). As discussed in the previous section, these can be CT and MRI data, as well as data derived from these, depending on the target anatomy. For example, DWI, DCE, MRSI are used for prostate and cervical tumor treatment planning (Barentsz et al., 2012). For lung tumors, the use of functional imaging, such as (4D) PET/CT, can be advantageous for tumor definition (Schinagl et al., 2006). Brain tumors may additionally require diffusion tensor imaging (DTI) (Mabray et al., 2015). Details on each modality can be found in Chapter 4 of this book. During this step, a high-quality CT, which plays an important role in the planning, and provides the reference coordinate system (the basis) for target definitions is acquired. This is called the planning CT. Registration, for example, is also performed according to the CT planning (i.e., fixed image).

Target volumes and organs at risk

An important concept within RT is the use of *target volumes* (Berthelsen, 2007). These follow the standards of the International Commission on Radiation Units & Measurements (ICRU), and they indicate regions of (or around) the volume that need to be targeted by the ionizing radiation. A schematic overview can be found in Fig. 8.4.

- The volume that contains the visible, macroscopic part of the tumor (within the limits of the employed imaging technique), is called the *gross tumor volume (GTV)*.
- The *clinical target volume (CTV)* contains the GTV, with additional microscopic extensions into healthy tissues that may not be visible in the acquired images (Berthelsen, 2007).
- The *internal target volume (ITV)* compensates for uncertainties, introduced by organ motion (Jaffray et al., 1999). This is the CTV, expanded by margins for setup errors (Stroom and Heijmen, 2002). The ITV is not always required, except for lung cancer, where it is used to compensate for breathing motion (Jang et al., 2015).
- The *planning target volume (PTV)* is the volume that accounts for anatomical variations in position, shape, and size during the fractions of the system. It accounts also for uncertainties, such as patient setup errors (Stroom and Heijmen, 2002), to ensure that the CTV will receive the prescribed and planned dose. It is calculated by adding specific margins to the CTV (or ITV) (Bentzen, 2008). Based on the PTV, appropriate beam sizes and beam arrangements will be calculated (Berthelsen, 2007).
- Finally, the *treated volume (TV)* is the volume that receives a minimum dose. For example, if the prescribed dose is 40 Gy, and the minimum dose was 5% below, the TV is then enclosed by a 38 Gy isodose surface.

Organs at risk (OAR) are normal tissues, whose radiation sensitivity may significantly limit the treatment. These can be the spinal cord in lung tumor treatment, or pelvic organs in prostate tumor treatment, or the eyes in brain tumor treatment. In analogy to the PTV, safety margins can be added around the delineated OAR volumes (McKenzie et al., 2002) (*planning organ at risk volume, or PRV*). Target volumes and OARs may overlap, or even include each other. Some overlaps are more critical than others. Determining the margins is not straightforward, and depends on a multitude of factors (van Herk, 2004). Overlaps of target volumes and OARs present a challenge in RT, as the distribution of the prescribed dose might not be enough for tumor coverage, or OARs might receive higher doses, as shown in Fig. 8.4.

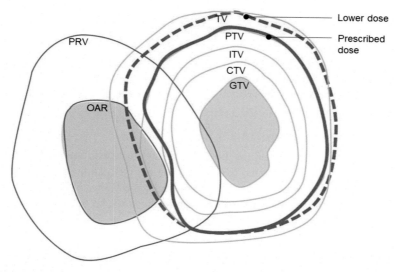

FIGURE 8.4

Volume concepts used in RT planning for a target close to an OAR. The gross tumor volume (GTV), clinical target volume (CTV), internal target volume (ITV), and planning target volume (PTV), as well as the organ at risk (OAR) are denoted. The treated volume (TV) is implicitly defined (by a dose value) after dose calculation. The PTV and ITV account for patient setup errors and other sources of inaccuracy during the administration of the radiation dose. Planning organ at risk volume (PRV) and internal target volume (ITV) are not always defined. Overlapping volumes can have an impact on the dose calculation and might lead to insufficient PTV coverage or high dose levels for the OAR.

Uncertainty

RT planning is—among all therapy planning processes—the one where uncertainty, validation, and verification are considered most essential by the involved physicians. A useful definition of uncertainty is given by Griethe and Schumann (2006), as *a composition of different concepts, such as error (outlier or deviation from a true value), imprecision (resolution of a value compared to the needed resolution), subjectivity (degree of subjective influence in the data), and non-specificity (lack of distinction for objects)*. In RT planning, we define uncertainty as any source that may cause variations in the workflow and in the treatment outcome.

Concerning imaging modalities, both DWI and DCE imaging have highly varying sensitivity and specificity for tumor detection (Turkbey et al., 2010), depending on patient characteristics, on the tissue zone, and on the scanning procedure itself. DWI is additionally dominated by poor spatial imaging resolution and image distortions, due to magnetic field inhomogeneities at the interfaces between different tissues (Bonekamp et al., 2011). Often, to minimize uncertainty, different imaging modalities are combined (Hricak et al., 2007), whereas the previously discussed targets and OARs have been introduced to deal with uncertainties due to patient motion or due to changes in anatomy and pathology of the patient. Uncertainties are also present in segmentation, most commonly in the form of errors (Reiter et al., 2018) or inter-observer variability (Watadani et al., 2013); as well as in radiobiological modeling, mainly due to parameterizations (e.g., choice of parameters in the employed model) or parameter sensitivity (i.e., fine-tuning of a parameter impacts the behavior of the model) (Raidou et al., 2018).

Dose plans and dose distributions

Dose plans convey information on the 2D (or 3D) dose distribution, as generated from treatment planning systems, based on a 3D reconstruction of a planning CT scan. Dose distributions are scalar data maps, where the values indicate (in Gy) the radiation dose administered to the patient within the space of the planning CT. An example of a dose plan is shown in Fig. 8.5.

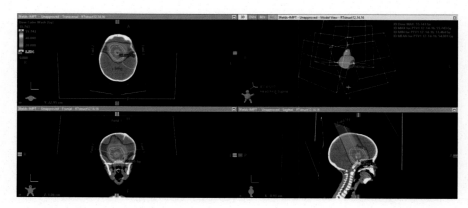

FIGURE 8.5

The axial, sagittal and coronal slices together with a 3D overview to evaluate the simulated dose distribution used to treat brain cancer. The 3D overview (upper right) shows the previously segmented anatomical structures. The slice views employ isolines and colored regions to display the target along with the dose distribution, respectively. Images courtesy of Laura Toussaint and Ludvig P. Muren from the Danish Centre for Particle Therapy (DCPT) at Aarhus University Hospital, and Daniel J. Indelicato from the Department of Radiation Oncology at the University of Florida Health Proton Therapy Institute.

Often, dose plans are regarded together with *dose volume histograms (DVH)* (Drzymala et al., 1991). A DVH, as shown in Fig. 8.6(a), summarizes the 3D dose in a 2D plot, relating radiation dose (horizontal axis) to tissue volume (vertical axis). This may concern a tumor target or a healthy organ, and the plot can have a differential or cumulative form. A DVH often includes all targets and OAR involved in the RT plan, where each structure is represented by a color-encoded line. Additionally, TCP and

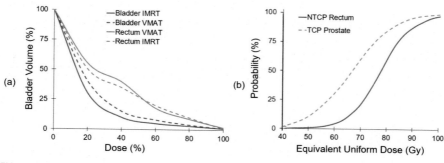

FIGURE 8.6

(a) DVH relating radiation dose (horizontal axis) to tissue volume (vertical axis) for two organs (bladder and rectum) for two strategies (intensity-modulated RT: IMRT and volumetric arc therapy: VMAT). (b) TCP/NTCP models quantifying, respectively, the probability that a tumor is effectively controlled and the probability that normal tissue around the tumor is affected, given a specific radiation dose.

NTCP models are also carefully examined. TCP models quantify the probability that a tumor is effectively controlled (i.e., tumor will not recur), given a specific radiation dose distribution in a specific treatment strategy, and the sensitivity of the tumor cells. NTCP models quantify the probability of complications for normal tissues (e.g., in healthy surrounding organs), given a specific radiation dose distribution. A plot of TCP and NTCP models is shown in Fig. 8.6(b).

8.3.3 Users involved in RT

An important aspect of RT is the variety of specialists involved in the different steps of the RT workflow. Therefore the needs of different users have to be addressed, increasing the complexity of the visual design (Dinka et al., 2009). The most relevant specialist groups are the following:

1. radiation oncologists (responsible for the prescription, approval, and supervision of the treatment);
2. medical physicists (scientists who advise on the best treatment strategy);
3. radiologists (doctors who specialize in medical imaging acquisition and interpretation);
4. radiotherapists (or therapy radiographers, specialists who operate the treatment machines);
5. dosimetrists (responsible for the careful calculation of the dose in the specialized equipment).

For more details on the expertise and tasks, we refer to Aselmaa et al. (2013).

8.4 Definition of target volumes and organs at risk

After all images are acquired, the tumor with its respective volume definitions and the adjacent OARs are delineated. With regard to the approaches related to target and OAR definition, visual computing has focused mainly on segmentation and multi-parametric data exploration. However, also data registration—especially concerning patient motion and fusion—is relevant.

8.4.1 Data registration

Data registration for RT revolves around three major topics:

- *motion correction*
- *multimodal registration*
- *accuracy assessment*

Motion correction

Tumor motion is a particularly persistent problem in lung tumor treatment, where deformable image registration (DIR) plays an important role (Rietzel et al., 2005). The amount of data generated with 4D imaging significantly increases the time needed for image review and target volume delineation. However, 4D imaging provides valuable information that cannot be captured in any other way. For example, in lung cancer treatment, 4D imaging is able to capture the breathing patterns and also the heart motion, and to support the generation of a treatment plan that is robust enough to account for these motions, without affecting important organs, such as the heart or the spine. DIR can be used for contour propagation (Orban de Xivry et al., 2007) to reduce the workload of manual delineations (Wolthaus et al., 2008). In other approaches, DIR has been used to model breathing motion (Ehrhardt et al., 2008) by generating a mean model of the lung that predicts the breathing motion of a patient.

Multimodal registration

Interactive rigid image registration of multiple imaging modalities using a volume-view-guided system has been developed by Li et al. (2005). To distinguish each volume in the registration process, mono-color visual representations are used for each imaging modality, such as red, green, or blue. The color distribution on the voxel volume or a sub-volume can be used as the registration criterion, where the homogeneity of the color distribution is used as an indicator for an optimal match. Interactive DIR using landmarks to steer the algorithm has been presented by Cheung and Krishnan (2009). Landmarks can be added, removed, and adjusted between repeated registrations. In their approach, landmark pairs are based on visual correspondences, identified by the user on the images to be registered. The visualization methods used for showing the quality include a checkerboard display of the fixed and moving images, a 3D visualization of the deformation field using glyphs overlaid on a slice of the target image, and a warped grid to show the transformation warping.

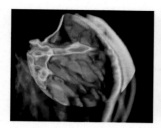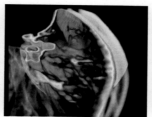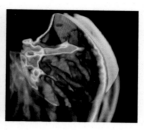

FIGURE 8.7

Assessment of deformable image registration quality, measured by local image dissimilarity and visualized together with the original images. The three subimages indicate different rendering modes. This approach allows for a detailed inspection in areas where dissimilarity indicates errors due to the underlying registration algorithm (©2016 IEEE, Reprinted with permission from (Schlachter et al., 2016)).

Accuracy assessment

For the visual assessment of the registration accuracy, Hamdan et al. (2017) use checkerboard visualizations to verify the alignment of the registration of MRI and CT images for prostate images together with contours. Visualization of DIR quality using local image dissimilarity has been proposed by Schlachter et al. (2016), where the verification is based on voxel-wise calculated dissimilarity values to indicate the match or mismatch. Furthermore, it includes different interaction and visualization features for exploration of candidate regions to simplify the process of visual assessment (see Fig. 8.7).

8.4.2 Data fusion

Image fusion is the combination of various images into a single image (James and Dasarathy, 2014). It is required for an integrated interpretation of the complementary information in the underlying imaged structures, such as PET/CR or PET/MRI data (recall Chapter 4). Often, the different modalities are overlaid and presented with a color coding scheme. An approach that goes beyond the mere color-encoded, overlaid representation of fusion is proposed by Kim et al. (2007b), for the interactive multi-volume visualization and fusion of PET/CT images, applied to lung and brain cases. The tumor target is initially segmented, and the resulting segmentation map, together with the initial PET and CT data are rendered, fused, and interchanged.

Chavan and Talbar (2014) support visualization, accurate diagnosis, and appropriate treatment planning through different fusion rules. These are employed and evaluated against each other for uncertainty minimization. Illustrative rendering of PET/CT data was presented by Merten et al. (2016), providing an excellent spatial perception and evaluation of tumor position, metabolic and therapeutic agent activity. Additional information has been incorporated with the inclusion of MRSI data in the fusion process (Nunes et al., 2014).

8.4.3 Data segmentation

For the definition of the tumor target and the surrounding organs at risk, conventional approaches involve *manual segmentation* through expert delineation and *(semi-)automatic segmentation* methods. An overview of medical image segmentation can be found in the book of Birkfellner (2014), and—with a focus on interaction—in (Olabarriaga and Smeulders, 2001). A review of deep learning in medical imaging segmentation, focusing on MRI data, was given by Lundervold and Lundervold (2018). Yet, recent deep learning solutions are not the particular focus of this chapter. In general, automated segmentation algorithms—even well-established ones, such as statistical shape modeling—can greatly reduce the delineation time and the efforts of a human expert. However, when automatic segmentation is employed, the resulting segmentation needs to be verified before being used as an input to dose calculation.

Three main sub-topics can be regarded within this category: approaches *aiding* the segmentation of relevant structures, approaches *enhancing* the segmentation outcome by post-processing, and approaches *assessing* the outcome of the segmentation.

Aiding segmentations

An approach for the detection, modeling, and visual stylization of structures of interest from CT images was proposed by de Geus and Watt (1996). Stylization, within the work of de Geus, is defined as a combination of segmentation and 3D visualization, where the resulting segmentation of the critical structures conforms to the bounding volume of the real shape. Here, assisted contouring can be employed to reduce some of the manual workloads or to adjust the result of automatic segmentations. Assisted contouring based on interpolation methods has been proposed by Zindy et al. (2000), where the user is able to add few scattered data points on the CT slices and interpolation methods are used to iteratively define the contours.

Enhancing segmentations

Smoothing algorithms allow to reduce artifacts from mesh generation, but often degrade accuracy. Li et al. (2010) present fast 3D-reconstruction and visualization of tumor target and organs at risk from a series of cross-sectioned contour points. In this approach, after the pre-processing of the contour points data set, an iso-surface is extracted and simplified. Then, the surface model undergoes a linear transformation and smoothing. The proposed approach, despite being simple, is accurate and fast, and the visualization part consists of simple iso-surface renderings of the involved organ structures. Mönch et al. (2010) present a modification to common mesh smoothing algorithms to preserve non-artifact features by focusing on previously identified staircase artifacts.

Assessing segmentations

Raidou et al. (2016a) propose a visual tool to facilitate the exploration and analysis of the outcomes and errors of automatic segmentation methods. In this way, they support cohort and individual patient investigation for the detailed assessment of their pelvic organ segmentations. This work has been extended by Reiter et al. (2018)

into a web-based visual analytics approach to facilitate understanding how the shape and size of pelvic organs affect the accuracy of automatic segmentation methods, and to enable a quick identification of segmentation errors and their correlation to anatomical features (see Fig. 8.8).

Schlachter et al. (2017) introduced a visualization framework for quality assessment of temporal segmentations. The framework allows for fusion of 4D multi-modal data sets and joint visualization of segmentation data. The focus of the framework was to allow the exploration of the full 4D imaging information and to offer interaction and navigation features for the simplification of this process.

8.5 Treatment plan design and dose calculation

The design of the treatment plan and the dose calculation are performed in dedicated treatment planning software. This software optimizes for an accurate assessment of the dose distribution, often based on Monte Carlo simulations. The input to these simulations is patient-specific information, such as CT images of the patient, and structure definitions (targets and OARs), as well as beam geometry properties. The output of such simulations is the dose plan. Treatment plan design and dose calculation approaches have not been intensively investigated within visual computing. The only approach that has been integrated into clinical practice is MINERVA (Wemple et al., 2004), which incorporates a simple—yet, robust—2D-based strategy.

Other automatized approaches exist, involving neural networks for tissue density calibration (Liu et al., 2006). A combined Monte Carlo-based dose calculation and visualization system was developed by Kimura et al. (2010) to make a validation or a comparison of results between a Monte Carlo simulation and an analytical simulation, such as the one employed in the RT treatment planning system. The visualization system deals with displaying detector geometry, particle trajectories to simultaneously display the patient data and dose distributions calculated by the simulation. Other interactive systems for real-time dose calculation and visualization that allow treatment plan assessment have been proposed (Schlaefer et al., 2013), but none of them is currently employed in clinical routine.

8.6 Dose plan review and treatment evaluation

RT is heavily concerned with security aspects throughout the pipeline, and the verification and evaluation of the plan prior to administration. Therefore there is a lot of research in visual computing regarding this step of the workflow. The evaluation of dose plans is conducted in two ways:

- the *spatial evaluation*, which implies the assessment of the planned dose distribution for eventual changes
- the *non-spatial evaluation*, which involves DVH and TCP/NTCP analysis

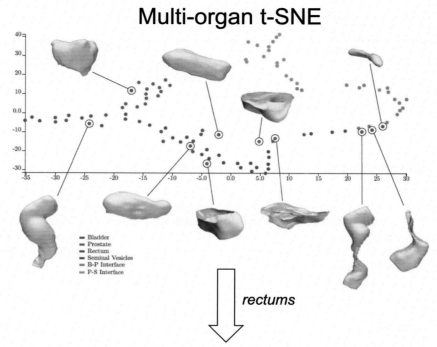

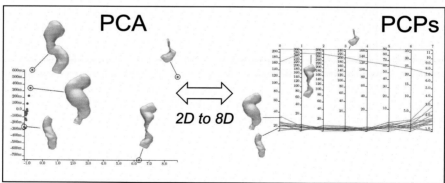

FIGURE 8.8

A web-based visual analytics approach, proposed by Reiter et al. (2018), to understand how the shape and size of pelvic organs affect the accuracy of automatic segmentation methods, and to enable quick identification of segmentation errors and their correlation to anatomical features (©2018 The Author(s) Eurographics Proceedings ©The Eurographics Association).

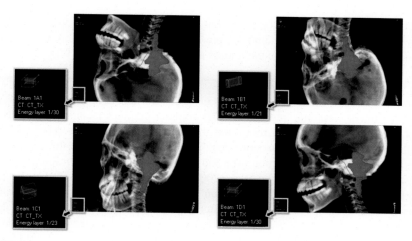

FIGURE 8.9

Four beam's eye views for a posterior fossa ependymoma treated with four pencil beams (each subimage represents one beam's view and the zoomed-in figure indicates the beam's configuration). The brainstem is indicated with the brown line, the spinal cord with blue and the gross tumor volume (GTV) is indicated with the filled red surface. Images courtesy of Laura Toussaint and Ludvig P. Muren from the Danish Centre for Particle Therapy (DCPT) at Aarhus University Hospital, and Daniel J. Indelicato from the Department of Radiation Oncology at the University of Florida Health Proton Therapy Institute.

The spatial assessment of a treatment plan includes approaches that revolve around the *2D visual representation* of the planned dose distributions, *3D volume renderings* thereof, and potentially more immersive *VR/AR and holographic approaches*. Here, we will also discuss *simulation approaches* of the delivery step, to complement the plan evaluation.

2D/3D spatial assessment

Initial approaches on volume rendering in radiation treatment planning have been proposed already in the 1990s (Interrante et al., 1997). The authors tackled perception problems of multi-modal visualization, by looking into ridge and valley lines for better shape and depth perception of structures, or texturing of layered surfaces. A big revolution has been considered to be the so-called *beam's light view* (Alakuijala et al., 1997), which presents a texture mapping method to be used together with traditional 3D RT renderings from the beam's eye view (i.e., what the RT beam "sees") and room's eye view (i.e., a view of the entire room), as shown in Fig. 8.9. The utility of volume rendering as an alternative visualization technique to surface rendering for head and neck RT planning has also been discussed by Lee et al. (1999).

Several toolkits for 3D rendering of isodoses were introduced (Gambarini et al., 2000). Fonseca and Campos (2016) propose SOFT-RT, a software for IMRT simulations, which produces a 3D rendering of a set of patient images, including the tumor target definitions and the OARs, as well as the features and orientation of the radiation beams. The rendered outcomes represent the tissues exposed to radiation, and the amount of absorbed dose in the tumors and the healthy tissues.

VR/AR in RT

Virtual reality (VR) in RT includes Su et al. (2005), which proposes the use of VR in RT treatment planning, integrated with computer graphics techniques for the reconstruction of the treatment room and the collimator, and image reconstruction techniques from CT for the patient body. The authors discuss how the system can be expected to reduce preparation time and can be employed in RT training, paving the way for others, such as Patel et al. (2007) and Boejen and Grau (2011). Patel et al. present a VR solution for the evaluation of RT plans, with a focus on understanding spatial relationships in the patient anatomy and on illustrating the calculated dose distribution. Similarly, Boejen et al. propose an immersive visualization for planning and delivery of external RT, targeting in particular the understanding of spatial relationships in the patient anatomy. Boejen et al. focus on the training purposes of such a VR system.

Also, Ward et al. (2011) presented an immersive virtual environment (VERT) that simulates an RT treatment room to provide staff and students with training aids for the treatment of virtual patients. VERT is one of the very few immersive approaches used in clinical environments for training, and in some cases also for patient information.

Augmented reality (AR) approaches in RT include applications for the evaluation of the plans and also for patient education (Wang et al., 2009a; Chu et al., 2009). On the other hand, Cosentino et al. (2017) propose an AR tool for RT to present the real RT world scene and to demonstrate the RT procedure to patients. For an introduction to virtual reality, see Chapter 12 of this book.

Dose delivery simulation

Integrating the simulation, planning, treatment, and verification phases has been proposed by Moore et al. (1997), to give clinicians access to a common, virtual environment, designed to objectively model the complex 3D irradiation of cancer patients. Cai et al. (2000) propose a similar system with an additional collaborative component so that physicians at different locations can work together via a network to plan or to validate the plan. A 3D simulator for EBRT has been developed by Karangelis et al. (2001) with volume visualization of patient images, beam geometry visualization and room view, where the model of the simulator room is reconstructed using surface rendering techniques. A real-time simulation and visualization framework that models a deformable surface lung model with a tumor has been presented by Santhanam et al. (2008). They simulate the tumor motion and predict the amount of radiation doses that would be deposited in the moving lung tumor during delivery.

The current limitations of the optimizers do not allow for a thorough exploration of the solution space of the treatment plan. Usually, only one or very few plans are computed (e.g., 2 nominal plans with a few offsets) and assessed to pick the most robust plan. Although a more broad assessment would be able to yield more accurate results, this is not practical given the extremely long computation times (e.g., one plan takes approx. 8 hrs or more to compute). Therefore the most reliable plan is picked, i.e., the plan with the least uncertainties or the most conservative plan that ensures the least risks.

Assessment with DVHs

DVHs are widely used in clinical practice for the non-spatial evaluation of treatment plans. Trofimov et al. (2012) discuss the integration of uncertainty coming from setup errors to the DVH calculation and the DVH representation. When delivery uncertainties are present, the DVH may not accurately describe the dose distribution actually delivered to the patient. Therefore on top of the traditional plots depicted in Fig. 8.6(a), the authors employ the intensity of the shading in the bands as a visual cue that reflects the relative probability of the outcome, and they conduct a thorough clinical study that proves that better-informed clinical decisions can be achieved with DVH bands that represent additional information about possible dosimetric variability.

Assessment with anatomical features

Analyzing anatomical features and shapes was first performed by Oh et al. (2014) with GLOBE (geometric relocation for analyzing anatomical objects evolution), a technique to quantify and compare anatomical shapes, with a proof-of-concept application on cervical cancer. Here, the contour surface is triangulated to form a mesh, which is subsequently deformed to a sphere using parametric active contours. Then, the magnitude of the deformation is sampled on the geodesic dome and, finally, it is unfolded to a plane. These unfolded planes can be subsequently color-coded to show various parameters, such as the magnitude of the surface normal vector from planning CTV to PTV, systematic, and random variations, or other distributions. In this way, they allow for easy juxtaposed comparison, either across time or across patients.

Visual analytics approaches have also been presented for the exploration of the anatomical variability of OARs. Raidou et al. (2018) use the example of bladder toxicity in prostate cancer analysis to present a novel tool for the detailed visual analysis of the impact of bladder shape variation on the accuracy of dose delivery. The BLADDER RUNNER enables the investigation of individual patients and cohorts through the entire treatment process. It can give indications of RT-induced complications, allowing clinical researchers to correlate bladder shape variations to dose deviations and toxicity risk through cohort studies. This work has been extended to include the variability of all pelvic organs, even more complex ones, such as the rectum (Grossmann et al., 2019; Furmanová et al., 2020). An example of VAPOR (Furmanová et al., 2020) as the multi-organ extension of BLADDER RUNNER, is shown in Fig. 8.10.

TCP/NTCP assessment

With regard to TCP analysis, Raidou et al. (2016b) propose a visual tool that enables clinical researchers to explore image-based TCP models, by supporting uncertainty

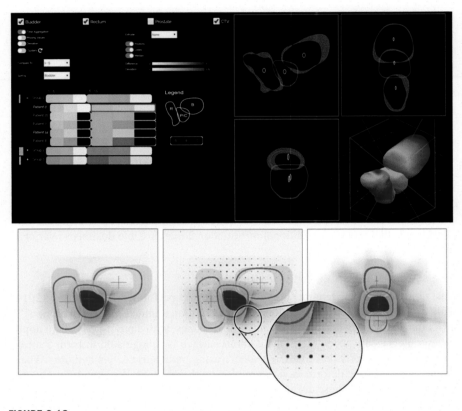

FIGURE 8.10

The interface of VAPOR (Grossmann et al., 2019; Furmanová et al., 2020) as the multi-organ extension of BLADDER RUNNER. This visual analytics approach supports the exploration of the anatomical variability of a multi-organ case. VAPOR enables the users to see whether there are "main modes of variation" in the cohort's anatomy throughout the duration of treatment and to correlate anatomical variability to dose distribution and potential side-effects for the patient. Image courtesy of Katarína Furmanová, Masaryk University.

and parameter sensitivity exploration, while enabling an inter-patient response variability analysis. This visual analysis tool has been used in a clinical study to quantify dose and TCP uncertainty bands, where initial cell density is estimated from MRI-based apparent diffusion coefficient maps of the patients (Casares-Magaz et al., 2018). NTCP models are also analyzed with curve diagrams or through renderings of the affected organs, in a similar way as TCP models. Other approaches include the work of El Naqa et al. (2008) on methods for the visualization of the high-dimensional space composed of the interaction between toxicities and treatment, anatomical, and patient-related variables of NTCP in head and neck patients.

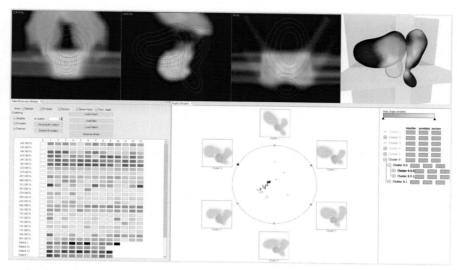

FIGURE 8.11

PREVIS (Furmanová et al., 2021) employs records of during-treatment changes from a retrospective cohort to build a generative model that predicts how an incoming patient's anatomy will evolve during treatment. The generative model is interactively linked to treatment plan evaluation through DVH and TCP/NTCP, and supports domain experts to decide on which RT strategy to follow. Image courtesy of Katarína Furmanová, Masaryk University.

To this end, they employ an approach based on PCA and support vector machines (SVM), where prediction can be performed based on resampling within logistic regression to find the balance between dosimetric indicators and other patient variables. The visualization consists of a combination of static plots, such as surface plots and histograms, to aid decision-making.

Predictive assessment

Visual steering to support understanding and predicting RT outcomes in head and neck cancer treatment, based on previously treated similar patients, has also been proposed by (Wentzel et al., 2019). The link between DVHs, NTCP analysis, and anatomical variability is made in PREVIS (Furmanová et al., 2021). PREVIS employs records of during-treatment changes from a retrospective cohort, and matches these to new incoming RT patients to infer their expected anatomical changes, using a generative model. The generative model is interactively linked to treatment plan evaluation through DVH and TCP/NTCP, supporting the decision-making with regard to the selection of the optimal treatment strategy. An example of PREVIS is shown in Fig. 8.11.

8.7 Image-guided adaptive RT

Here, we introduce adaptive approaches, which try to optimize the treatment either by re-planning or by modification during the delivery. During the course of RT, both the tumor and healthy surrounding organs are variable in size and position. This can be attributed to anatomical changes between fractions (inter-fraction) or to changes during beam delivery within one treatment fraction (intra-fraction). The former can happen in patients with a tumor in the pelvic area, where the position is dependent on bladder and bowel filling, but changes can also occur due to weight loss and tumor shrinkage (Kong et al., 2013). The latter can happen, e.g., in patients with lung cancer, where the tumor moves with breathing (recall Section 8.4.1).

One way to compensate for these uncertainties is by including them into the PTV (or ITV) with appropriate safety margins as explained in the previous sections. Otherwise, image-guided adaptive RT (IGART) aims to optimize dose delivery by taking into account intra- and inter-fractional image data. Image-guided adaptive RT is a relatively new concept that has not yet been established in clinical practice.

To change the plan or to re-plan according to the recent state of anatomy every time would be too time-consuming. An alternative is to keep the original plan, but recompute the accumulated dose based on the current state of the anatomy. If this deviates too much compared to the planned dose, re-planning might be a better option. The calculation of the true dose distribution for a patient requires accurate DIR to reduce dose warping uncertainties due to the registration algorithm (Veiga et al., 2015). Registration for IGART has different problems as there are regions within the images to be registered, where explicit correspondences cannot be established (Khamene et al., 2009).

Song et al. (2005) evaluate the efficacy of image-guided adaptive RT techniques to deliver and escalate dose to the prostate. Furthermore, the normal tissue sparing potential of adaptive strategies in RT of bladder cancer has been shown by Wright et al. (2008). Open-source software suites, such as DIRART (Yang et al., 2011) or SlicerRT (Pinter et al., 2012) targeting multiple aspects of IGART, including registration and visualization, are freely available. A multi-modality image registration and visualization framework, which addresses the transfer of structures of RT plans onto follow-up images for re-planning, has been presented by Wang et al. (2009b).

8.8 Concluding remarks

Visual computing is a significant factor in keeping the balance between tumor treatment and avoidance of healthy tissue damage in radiotherapy. Advances of the field of visual computing are supporting the entire pipeline of radiotherapy, with a particular focus on the assessment of radiotherapy plans prior to patient treatment. Slice-based 2D representations are still one of the most common (and preferred) ways to visualize data involved in clinical practice, also in clinical systems. In 3D volume visualizations for RT, illustrative approaches are supporting depth and structure perception to convey organ and tumor contours and iso-dose surfaces. VR/AR approaches are not so widespread in the domain of RT, with the exception of solutions targeting clinical training. While traditional slice-based and volume representations keep evolving, at the same time, the dimensionality of medical data is exploding. Patient cohort acquisitions are often employed in retrospective studies, and population studies are becoming widespread. The data of these studies are complex and heterogeneous, but they offer valuable information for clinical research. For this kind of data, visual analytics (and supporting machine or deep learning approaches) can be particularly suitable and can provide new ways of support for RT specialists.

Recommended reading

For a deeper understanding of radiation treatment planning, it is recommended to read one of the following books or essential articles:

C.M. Washington and D.T. Leaver. "Principles and Practice of Radiation Therapy" (4th Ed.) Elsevier Health Sciences, 2016.

M. Schlachter, R.G. Raidou, L.P. Muren, B. Preim, P.M. Putora, K. Bühler. "State-of-the-Art Report: Visual Computing in Radiation Therapy Planning," *Computer Graphics Forum*, Vol. 38(3), pp. 753–779, 2019.

R.G. Raidou, K. Furmanova, N. Grossmann, O. Casares-Magaz, V. Moiseenko, J.P. Einck, E. Gröller, L.P. Muren. "Lessons Learnt from Developing Visual Analytics Applications for Adaptive Prostate Cancer Radiotherapy." In *The Gap between Visualization Research and Visualization Software (VisGap)*, pp. 51–58, 2020.

Visual analytics in healthcare

3

In the third part, we discuss visual analytics methods to make sense of large medical data as they arise in the treatment of patients or in health surveys. Visual analytics comprises data analysis techniques, such as clustering, decision tree computation, and association rule mining as well as interactive information visualization techniques, such as scatterplot-based representations, parallel coordinates, and graph-based techniques, e.g., for displaying decision trees. Instead of carefully analyzing the data of one patient, we now consider cohorts of patients or healthy volunteers. The underlying data is no longer restricted to image data and derived features, but also contains other diagnostic features, features related to drug consumption, socio-demographic features. This wealth of heterogeneous, time-dependent data is analyzed, e.g., to identify risk factors for diseases or for an early outbreak of a disease. Lifestyle-related risk factors are particularly important, because they are to some extent avoidable. Other risk factors, such as genetic predisposition, are essential to trigger screening measures for early detection and better cure of diseases. We start this part with an introduction of visual analytics, where we want to provide an intuition about the kind of problems that can be solved with the integration of information visualization and data analysis (Chapter 9). Visual analytics techniques have scalability limits, i.e., they are no longer effective if data sets are very large and complex. We pay attention to these scalability problems. The applications in health care are subdivided in public health and clinical medicine. Public health (Chapter 10) is focused on prevention, and thus analyzes health trends in populations to identify protecting factors and risk factors with respect to essential diseases. Clinical medicine (Chapter 11) aims at an improvement treatment of patients. Thus techniques to visually summarize the state of individual patients, to compare different patients, and even to compare groups of patients are essential. These techniques enable to display event-based time-oriented data, where events represent changes in the treatment or a diagnostic result.

An introduction to visual analytics

9

9.1 Introduction

Visual analytics is a field that emerged around 2005 (Thomas and Cook, 2006) motivated by the need to analyze increasingly large and complex data. Data is also often time-dependent, has some quality problems, such as noise, outliers, duplicate entries, and missing values. An appropriate analysis of such data requires more than a straightforward visualization. Also, hypothesis-based statistical analysis or data mining in isolation are not promising. Visual analytics is an *interdisciplinary* process, where data visualization, statistics, and data mining is combined and steered by an analyst by means of appropriate visual interfaces. This integration is motivated by the attempt to combine human strengths, such as judgment and recognition of patterns, with the strengths of automatic data processing. In a more formal definition, Thomas and Cook state that visual analytics is "the science of analytical reasoning facilitated by interactive visual interfaces" (Thomas and Cook, 2005).

Difference from visualization

Visual analytics serves as an interface between humans and computers, providing (interactive) data representations to the user on demand. Such approaches can be used to understand data, to confirm or reject hypotheses, and to discover new knowledge. Therefore visual analytics and visualization primarily differ by the aim: the former supports analytical tasks or advances knowledge through interactive visual methods that make use of other interdisciplinary approaches (such as machine learning), whereas the latter represents data graphically. Additionally, the two fields differ in terms of employed strategies: visual analytics heavily supports the interplay between human and machine and provides a junction between automated analysis techniques, visualization, and human-computer interaction. Here, the user–analyst is the most significant component, as they steer the entire process.

User in the loop

There is an increased understanding that a user-steered process involving visualizations of the underlying data also leads to more trust in the results compared to the application of a black-box type machine learning model, such as a neural net. Moreover, being *actively* involved in the analysis of data leads to a deeper understanding and increased memorability of the results compared to situations where the user is passive. Visual analytics serves primarily for an undirected search for trends and structures, i.e., the analyst could not precisely describe what they are searching for. This is in contrast to hypothesis-based statistics, where the analyst has a clear idea what they want to investigate.

Fig. 9.1 presents the major components of a visual analytics system at a high level. The arrows indicate the transitions and the reasoning process. "Data" refers to the input data, e.g., questionnaire results related to the lifestyle and symptoms of patients. An essential observation in real-world application is the limited quality of the available data, i.e., data is often partially incomplete and not perfectly reliable. As an example, the number of *reported cases* of a certain type of crimes or diseases is lower than the actual number of these cases. And even the portion of reported cases over time may change significantly as a consequence of increased or decreased awareness or test procedures. "Knowledge" involves elementary observations, e.g., some outliers or strong correlations of a certain type, but also a more general and mature type of knowledge acquired after many iterations, including the acquisition of new data. "Models" comprises all results from data mining or machine learning or statistics, e.g., the description of clusters or a decision tree that enables a classification of the input data. "Visualization" comprises not only techniques to show and explore the data, but also the display of model results. For example, the raw data may be visualized by means of a scatterplot, and the results of clustering are overlaid with different colors for each cluster. An important component here is "interaction," which could be considered a way of accomplishing parameter refinement and is facilitated by the use of interactive visualizations.

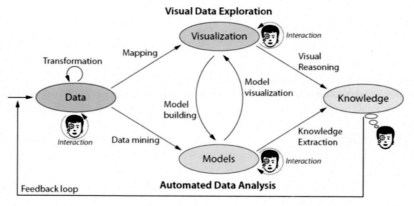

FIGURE 9.1

Concept for a visual analytics system. Data is mapped to visual representations and analyzed with data mining techniques, leading to a model. The analyst may interact with the visualization and with the model. Both serve to extract knowledge (Courtesy of Steffen Oeltze-Jafra, University of Magdeburg, adapted from (Keim et al., 2008a)).

Visual analytics serves to support analysts in their problem-solving and decision-making processes. As a consequence, an understanding of these processes is essential for creating powerful tools. Often, it is necessary to support analysts in a structured analysis of complex data. *Guidance* may be provided at various stages and in different detail (Ceneda et al., 2017). Guidance may be lightweight and unobtrusive, such as the display of tooltips but also quite strict, e.g., by enforcing a certain sequence of actions.

Visual data mining and visual analytics

The need for combining data mining and information visualization was considered before the advent of visual analytics (Keim et al., 2002). However, *visual data mining* was typically restricted to the use of data mining in a pre-process, i.e., data mining produced results, such as clusters, to be employed in interactive visualization. Visual analytics, in contrast, aims at a close loop of data mining and interactive visualization, where the interactive facilities may be used to refine the data mining results and derive "findings" and other components of knowledge (recall Fig. 9.1). Because of this close loop with the user in a central role, visual analytics research involves human-computer interaction, e.g., means how analysts can effectively tune parameters or adapt visual representations.

Applications

Visual analytics has proven to be useful in many applications, such as crime analysis, network security, and business analytics. Powerful tools were developed to support data scientists with interactive visualizations. Often, web-based tools are employed to support sharing results, and thus easy collaboration. The potential of visual analytics is also essential for medical applications. Visual analytics may be employed to find patterns in the complex data represented in hospital information systems or electronic health records. As an example, patients who were treated in the intensive care unit (ICU), dismissed from ICU, and sent to ICU soon again, represent a pattern that deserves special attention. In addition to the health-related data directly collected for medical treatment and billing purposes, there are increasingly large data collected within health surveys to better understand the health situation in the general population, to identify risk factors, and assess their severity. The ultimate goal of these activities is to predict the further development and reduce negative effects, e.g., an increased burden due to certain diseases. Medical data and the tasks in their analysis have a number of special aspects related to the needs of physicians, clinical workflows, and legal requirements to the processing of sensitive patient data. Thus in 2010 the IEEE *Visual Analytics in Healthcare* workshop series[1] was founded, where these aspects are regularly discussed.

Organization

In this chapter, we introduce visual analytics components that are frequently used in medical applications. We first present the basics of visual analytics and information visualization techniques that are frequently used to display medical data and

---

[1] https://www.visualanalyticshealthcare.org/.

data mining results (Sections 9.2–9.3). Here, we sometimes provide basic examples abstracted from the medical field, for the sake of simplicity. We go on with statistical methods employed in visual analytics (Section 9.4) and with automated analysis techniques (Sections 9.5–9.7), such as dimension reduction techniques that map high-dimensional to low-dimensional data, or clustering methods. Such techniques are essential since medical data are complex and are rich data that cannot be immediately visualized. Here, we also discuss approaches that aim at revealing specific relations in the data, i.e., association rule mining approaches (Section 9.8) and correlation-based methods (Section 9.9). Finally, we discuss basic interaction approaches often employed in visual analytics approaches (Section 9.10).

9.2 The data–users–tasks design triangle

Miksch and Aigner (2014) propose a design triangle, which considers three main aspects to ease the design of visual analytics applications concerning time-varying data. In this section, we adopt the same design triangle to discuss the characteristics of the data involved in clinical applications, the users and their tasks, abstracted from the inherent characteristics of the data.

Data

In biomedical visual analytics applications, the most prominent characteristic of the data is their diversity and heterogeneity. Visual analytics researchers often look at a very wide spectrum of data, imaging, and non-imaging, spanning from genome to cellular and tissue data; multimodal images revealing structural and functional information, simulations, models of physiological processes, signals, data from trackers, information from population studies or from translational medicine. All these might be investigated simultaneously, i.e., we might have data sets and data of different types to address in the same application (recall Chapter 4 where multimodal visualizations were discussed). Except for the usual scalar (or field) data coming from various imaging acquisitions (e.g., computed tomography or magnetic resonance imaging), *data set types* can also be tabular (e.g., data from electronic health records), network data (e.g., global health network data or decision data in clinical boards), or geospatial (e.g., data from patient cases across the world). All these data set types can also be time-varying (e.g., longitudinal data showing the progress of a treatment). *Data types* can be both numerical and categorical. For more information on data set and data types, we refer to the book of Tamara Munzner (Munzner, 2014). Time-varying data are covered in the book of Aigner et al. (2011).

Users

The users are also quite diverse in such applications. They might have different *expertise* depending on the application or a different *working focus*. For example, a radiation oncologist and a radiologist are interested in different subsets of information when looking at cancer patient data. Additionally, analyzing prostate cancer data differs from analyzing lung cancer data. Finally, a clinical researcher and a clinical practitioner might also have a different scope, which is often dictated by the amount of time available for data analysis, i.e., a clinical researcher has enough time to interact freely with the data and explore their different aspects offline, whereas a clinician needs to make a decision within a few minutes. This diversity of focus can be also extended to physicians, nurses, healthcare providers, insurance, and policy makers, as well as patients: each of these target groups have totally different focus of interest or need. *Experience* is another significant factor, as well as other *user-specific characteristics*, such as age, cultural influences, visualization, and computer literacy, or vision.

Tasks

Depending on the application, the tasks that the user wants to accomplish through the use of visual analytics can be quite diverse. In general, the following *high-level tasks* are often encountered in visual analytics frameworks: data exploration, discovery of new knowledge, hypothesis confirmation or rejection, and clinical decision-making. Brehmer and Munzner (2013) discuss a multi-level typology of *mid-level tasks*, distinguishing why and how a task is performed, and the task inputs and outputs. This is a non-domain-specific typology and can also be applicable to biomedical applications to support the translation of domain-specific problems into tasks (and subsequently to help design their evaluation). We refer to Brehmer and Munzner (2013) for more information on mid-level tasks. *Low-level tasks* are often application-specific, therefore we do not discuss them further here.

Developing and designing effective visual analytics solutions demands that the designer or developer has a very detailed understanding of the tasks that the user needs to conduct. Tasks are often designed in a collaborative approach together with the intended users and require an in-depth understanding of the information that the users need and the analytical processes that they follow to acquire it. Some of these tasks may not be known a priori and may be exploratory, whereas others can be better defined. As discussed by Rind et al., there is no formal definition of a "task" in visualization and visual analytics (Rind et al., 2016), but many taxonomies agree that the space of a task comprises a *"why"* and a *"how"* part. Additionally, these tasks may be concrete (e.g., *what is the value of the blood pressure of the patient*), or may be abstract. Often, tasks are further broken down into smaller subtasks, where smaller steps towards obtaining insights are taken.

For more details on task abstractions, we refer the reader to the work of Rind et al. (Rind et al., 2016). Andrienko and Andrienko have provided a systematic review specifically on spatial and temporal data. Andrienko and Andrienko (2006) and Schultz et al. discuss a five-dimensional design space, where different user roles (developers, authors, and end users) with different levels of expertise are considered (Schulz et al., 2013).

9.3 Information visualization

Information visualization comprises techniques that serve to display abstract data, i.e., the data have no inherent spatial coordinates. This is in contrast to medical image data, such as a CT data set, where volume or surface rendering are used to display anatomical structures. When data is abstract, the spatial layout can be computed flexibly. Often the proximity of visual elements in an information visualization represents similarity with respect to the underlying data. Information visualization (InfoVis) techniques are often characterized with respect to their *scalability* properties. When only a few dozen or a few hundred of data sets with a small number of dimensions need to be displayed, most InfoVis techniques lead to clear and easy-to-interpret visualizations. However, with large amounts of data, heavily cluttered visualizations may arise, which may not be interpreted at all. Therefore for all techniques described in this section, we also briefly discuss scalability.

9.3.1 Visualizing distributions

The first step in the analysis of a high-dimensional data set is often to look at the individual dimensions, i.e., the attributes of the data set. The analyst may be interested in assessing the type of distribution, e.g., whether the distribution is symmetric or skewed, whether it follows a normal (Gaussian) distribution or not. The typical visualization of the distribution is a histogram that is based on binning scalar data with a certain resolution. For each bin, the frequency is mapped, typically to the height of a bar. A histogram may reveal that there are several distinctive peaks in the data, or that some values are far away from others (outliers), or that there are gaps where certain values do not occur at all.

A histogram consumes considerable space. Thus if histograms for all dimensions should be displayed simultaneously, visual clutter may arise. Alternative visualizations, such as a *boxplot*, aggregate the data and show instead some key characteristics, such as the median, the 10%, 25%, 75%, and 90% quantiles (see Fig. 9.2). Outliers are often indicated as additional glyphs, e.g., circles, above the 90% quantile, or below the 10% quantile. The boxplot reveals whether the distribution is symmetric or screwed. In between boxplots (quite abstract) and histograms (very detailed), there are some intermediate representations with tradeoffs between accuracy and the required space. Notable examples are *bean plots* (Kampstra, 2008) and *violin plots* (Hintze and Nelson, 1998).

9.3.2 Scatterplot-based representations

As a second step of an analysis of high-dimensional data, i.e., after analyzing individual dimensions, pairs of dimensions are often analyzed with respect to correlations. For this purpose, scatterplots are widely used. In the healthcare system, we may be interested in a dependency between income and health and choose the life expectancy as a measure for health. We may represent each person with a dot indicating their position on the two scales "income" and "life expectancy." We would find a weak

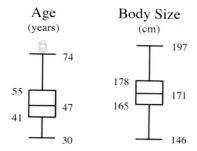

FIGURE 9.2

Two boxplots convey the distribution of age and body size of the participants of a health survey. The age distribution is slightly screwed, whereas the body size dimension follows a rather symmetric distribution (the median is in the middle of the 10% and 90% quantiles) (Courtesy of Paul Klemm, University of Magdeburg).

correlation, e.g., life expectancy for people with a higher income is slightly higher than for people with an income below the median. Such a correlation would give rise to further analysis, e.g., whether people with a higher income have better access to the health care system or have a healthier lifestyle.

Overplotting

A scatterplot reveals patterns, such as clusters and correlations, only if all data is mapped to distinct points. With large data sets, e.g., representing all customers of a health insurance company, overplotting may be frequently expected. Thus when the data of a new customer is mapped to screen space, the same screen area is required that was already used for another customer. Larger amounts of overplotting, e.g., when pixels are re-used several times on average, severely affect the interpretation. With a conventional scatterplot, the user would not be aware of overplotting. Therefore the display would be just misleading. Because of the severity of this problem, different refinements were introduced to alleviate this problem.

The following measures against overplotting are frequently employed:

- color scales
- jittering
- interaction
- binning

Color scales. Instead of rendering dots in the foreground color for every data set, a color scale may be used to indicate *how often* the dot was plotted. When heavy overplotting occurs, a larger contrast may be created, e.g., black on a light background, whereas a pixel used only once is displayed in light gray with little contrast.

Jittering means that the position of a dot is slightly transformed when the related pixels are already set in the foreground color. Thus the rendering algorithm computes

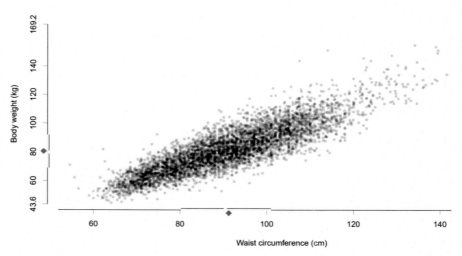

FIGURE 9.3

A scatterplot displays the relation between body weight and waist circumference for some 4000 participants of a health survey. The scatterplot is scaled according to the range of values that actually occur. Color coding is used to reveal overplotting. Small red dots (attached to the two axes) indicate the median for both variables and the slightly displayed lines indicate the interquartile range, e.g., half of the participants exhibit a waist circumference between 80 and 101 cm and a weight between 68 and 92 kilogram (Courtesy of Paul Klemm, University of Magdeburg).

a position in screen space to place a dot. When this position is *occupied*, the algorithm searches for adjacent positions that are not occupied. Jittering is a remedy for a moderate amount of overplotting. If, however, in certain high-density areas positions would be overplotted ten times on average, the algorithm would only find occupied positions in the near neighborhood.

Interaction is widely used in visual analytics to cope with scalability issues. For scatterplots, zooming is particularly important. With the adapted scale, different data sets may now be mapped to different coordinates, reducing overplotting. However, strong zooming also comes at a price, it may be difficult to understand the whole data when the currently visible portion is only a small subset of it.

Further useful interactions may relate to the data transform. Typically, a linear scale is used for both axes (see Fig. 9.3). If the user can switch to alternative scales, e.g., a logarithmic scale, areas of the scatterplot with a very high density may be stretched. Often scatterplots are scaled such that the range of actual values is considered, i.e., if the x values are in the interval $[x_{min}, x_{max}]$, the horizontal extent of the scatterplot represents this interval typically with a slight margin added. An outlier, e.g., a data set with an x value that is twice as large as the largest x value of other data sets aggravates overplotting, because most of the space of the scatterplot will remain empty. As a useful interaction, users may exclude outliers. Color-coding, jittering, and interaction may also be combined and push the scalability limits of a scatterplot display considerably.

The fourth strategy, **binning**, is independent from the other measures. Instead of displaying individual data sets, they are aggregated based on a grid with a certain spatial resolution. For each cell of the grid, the number of data sets that fall in this cell is represented, typically by color coding. This technique avoids cluttering very effectively and actually has no scalability limit at all. The interpretation, however, crucially depends on the resolution of the grid.

Adding information

The analysis of a scatterplot may benefit from adding some information, e.g., the correlation coefficient, the regression line that represents the optimal fit for a linear function. Also the median and interquartile range for both variables may be useful. It may turn out that a linear regression does not capture the data well. There could be, for example, a quadratic relation, which is actually quite common in medicine. If the influence of the sleeping duration or the body weight on some health indicators is analyzed, it turns out that there is an interval representing "normal" values, where the health indicators are typically good, whereas deviations from this normal range, e.g., strong over- or underweight are related to low values for health indicators. In such situations, a quadratic function captures the variability well.

Other results from data analysis may be overlaid to a scatterplot. For example, if the data is decomposed in clusters, i.e., groups of data objects with similar characteristics. The membership of data sets to one cluster may be revealed by a joint symbol type or a joint color. Also, *outliers*, i.e., data points that differ significantly from others, may be detected by an algorithm and emphasized.

A scatterplot-based representation may also be enhanced by labeling some data points, e.g., data points that are far away from others. Such data points are referred to as *outliers*. Labeling makes sense only when the data points have meaningful labels. In a health survey, the persons have an anonymized "ID," which carries no meaning but in a comparison of the health situation in different countries; the country names carry meaning.

Multi-class scatterplots

A scatterplot may comprise data sets that are categorized, for example, with respect to gender or age groups. Thus different visual representations may be employed to reveal to which category a data set belongs. Most frequently, distinctively different color hues are employed to distinguish the category at a glance. We briefly mentioned the combination of clustering and scatterplots. The membership of a data set to a cluster is another instance of a multi-class scatterplot. A multi-class scatterplot may reveal that certain correlations only exist for one class or cluster (see Fig. 9.4).

Vector plots

This scatterplot-based representation indicates the difference between two scatterplots, e.g., scatterplots that display the dependency between x and y at different

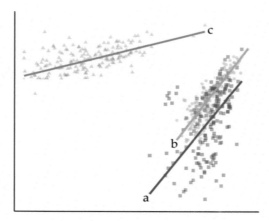

FIGURE 9.4

A scatterplot display considering three clusters. The correlation between the two variables is noticeably different within the three clusters, as the fitted regression lines indicate (Courtesy of Uli Niemann, University of Magdeburg).

points in time. This way, trends may be highlighted. In addition, the differences may be quantitatively analyzed, e.g., with respect to the average length of the vectors or the average direction.

Scatterplot matrices

Any reasonable clinical study or health survey contains more than two dimensions. Therefore the display of a single scatterplot is not sufficient. A scatterplot matrix is a matrix-based visual representation, where every cell with indices i, j is a scatterplot displaying the dependency between the dimensions represented by i and j (see Fig. 9.5). If i equals j, e.g., the cells representing the main diagonal may show the distribution for this dimension. Typically, the label of this dimension is added to the histogram to enhance the interpretation.

Scalability

The number of available pixels per scatterplot reduces strongly with an increased number of dimensions, and thus overplotting becomes more and more severe. Instead of rendering very small scatterplots, scrolling may be used to select an interesting region in the scatterplot. However, even with this interaction support, a scatterplot matrix representing more than 20 dimensions is very hard to analyze.

9.3.3 Mosaic plots for visualizing categorical data

Though scatterplots reveal dependencies between *scalar variables*, such as body weight, blood pressure, and some laboratory values, they are not useful for *categorical variables*. In medical data, categorical variables may represent whether the patient

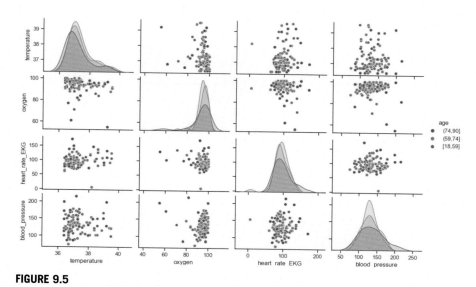

FIGURE 9.5

A scatterplot matrix displays pairwise correlations between 4 × 4 variables of patient data.

regularly takes certain drugs, whether they experience certain symptoms, whether they are married or have children. The default visualization technique for such data is the *mosaic plot*. A mosaic plot reveals how frequently a categorical value occurs. Thus the scales are labeled with the dimension and the categorical values and every combination of categorical values is mapped to a rectangle. The size of the rectangle represents the frequency of this particular combination. If all categorical values for both dimensions occur with the same frequency, the width and height of all rectangles would be the same.

The interpretation of a mosaic plot may be enhanced by color-coding the cells. The mosaic plot in Fig. 9.6 reveals that persons with an increased need for sleep report back pain more frequently. It is evident from this figure that mosaic plots are often used for a limited number of dimensions, therefore when larger data sets need to be represented, other solutions, e.g., contingency matrices, may be preferred.

9.3.4 Parallel coordinates

Parallel coordinate (PC) views display multi-dimensional data by mapping the values for each dimension on a vertical line and connecting the resulting points with straight lines. Since the vertical lines are parallel, this visualization technique is referred to as *parallel coordinates*. Thus every data set is represented by a polyline (Inselberg and Dimsdale, 1990). Fig. 9.7 shows an example. A PC view is an alternative to a scatter-plot matrix. Whereas the space required for a scatterplot matrix grows quadratically with the number of dimensions, the space for a PC view grows only linearly.

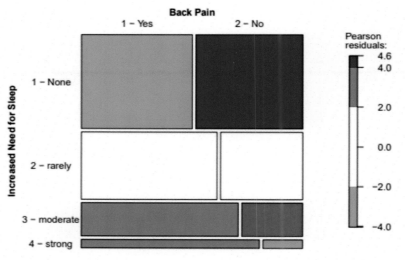

FIGURE 9.6

Example for a mosaic plot of two variables with 2 × 4 values. Subjects with increased need for sleep exhibit back pain more frequently. The colors represent the residual level of each combination (0 is the expected level). Red/blue means that there are less/more observations in a cell than expected (Courtesy of Paul Klemm, University of Magdeburg).

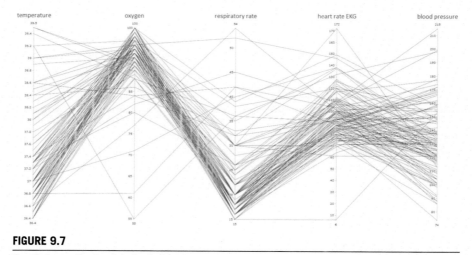

FIGURE 9.7

Parallel coordinates for displaying the multi-dimensional data of Fig. 9.5 as polylines.

Scale

The vertical lines representing each dimension are typically scaled such that the lowest value represents the minimum in this variable and the highest value represents the maximum in this variable. Thus even if the ranges and measurement units are quite different, as in the data set represented in Fig. 9.8, they can be displayed and correlations can be identified. In some situations, e.g., when the same measurement units occur, another scale may be more useful. Thus it can be beneficial if the same value for different dimensions is mapped to the same vertical position. In some situations, it is even useful to flip the scales so that the highest values are mapped to low y-coordinates. This way, it could be achieved that across all dimensions values perceived as "good" or as "strength" are displayed with high y-coordinates (Heinrich and Weiskopf, 2013). This is a typical case, where the composition or design of the representation is influenced by the type of task that needs to be conducted.

Ordering

Analysts examine PC views, for example, scatterplots, to identify patterns, such as correlations, clusters, and outliers. The interpretation of a PC view depends on the order in which the dimensions are mapped to vertical lines. If two dimensions are arranged immediately next to each other, correlations are easy to recognize. However, if they are mapped far away from each other, it is extremely difficult to perceive a correlation. As a consequence, interactive re-ordering of an axis is often provided, i.e., the analyst may drag and drop vertical lines. Moreover, algorithmic support is possible. As an example, for all pairs of dimensions, a correlation coefficient can be computed and a layout algorithm uses these coefficients as input to place dimensions next to each other if they are strongly correlated (Peng et al., 2004; Johansson and Johansson, 2009).

Scalability

PC views have scalability limits in terms of the number of data points and dimensions. When the number of dimensions exceeds 20 (horizontal), scrolling should be enabled. For more than about 60 dimensions, however, even with scrolling, it is very cumbersome to analyze the data with PC views. The scalability in terms of the number of data sets can be strongly improved compared to the basic variant. An essential concept is *edge bundling*, where polylines with a similar course are visually summarized reducing intersections of lines and increasing separability between the data sets (Holten, 2006). Similar to the use of colors in scatterplots, they may be used in PC views and improve the separability as well. Frequently, color and/or opacity are used to emphasize certain data sets, e.g., all patients of a certain age group (Johansson and Forsell, 2016).

There are different approaches for data information enhancement and readability improvement in PCPs. Most of the cases aim at showing clustering in the data or at improving a cluttered display and the ability to identify patterns; there are also cases that employ animation or interaction. Some approaches require the manipulation of the axes of the representation, using reordering (Ankerst et al., 1998). These approaches are able to reveal hidden data patterns and facilitate the interpretation of the data. However, when a large number of data points needs to be visualized, the expressiveness of the visualization cannot be enhanced by solely reordering.

Other approaches visually enhance the PCP representation by rendering them as curves instead of lines (Theisel, 2000). Such an approach is especially effective at reducing clutter at the crossings of PCP lines. Though these techniques enhance certain patterns, such as correlations, they might suppress others, such as outliers, or make them less discernible. Although they enable mental clustering of the data, they might obscure information about data patterns or relations.

Another commonly encountered group of techniques requires clustering, combined with different kinds of visual enhancements:

- manipulating PCPs by averaging polylines and visualizing correlation coefficients between polyline subsets (Siirtola, 2000),
- filtering PCPs based on frequency or density of the data (Artero, 2004),
- combining polyline splattering for cluster detection and segment splattering for clutter reduction (Zhou et al., 2009),
- using cluster-based hierarchical enhancements and proximity-based coloring schemes to provide a multiresolution view to the data (Fua et al., 1999),
- enabling context visualization at several levels of abstraction, both for the representation of outliers and trends (Novotny and Hauser, 2006)
- using several transfer functions to reveal specific clusters and patterns in the data (Johansson et al., 2005).

Interaction is another commonly employed approach for local and dynamic data representation enhancement. This can be performed either with the use of lenses (Ellis and Dix, 2006) or with brushing (Hauser et al., 2002). Fig. 9.8 gives an example how the scalability of PC views can be improved with interaction.

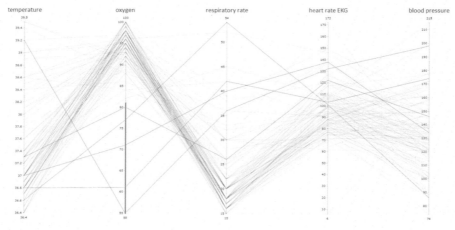

FIGURE 9.8

The user selects a range for one dimension (low oxygen values) and the corresponding datapoints are emphasized. The other datapoints are shown as context in an attenuated manner.

9.3.5 **Glyph-based visualization**

Glyphs represent another option to display multidimensional data. Glyphs are symbols that may depict different variables, e.g., by mapping them to a certain shape, size, or color. Glyphs are often used in combination with map displays, e.g., to convey local differences in some health-related attributes. Thus glyphs may indicate for a region the following: how many patients suffer from a disease, how many of them are hospitalized, and how many of them need intensive care treatment. Moreover, glyphs are used along with 3D surface visualizations to reveal how certain values differ over the brain or heart surface. A *glyph legend* is necessary to explain the mappings of variables to attributes of a glyph. A very simple glyph design and its use along with cerebral data is shown in Fig. 9.9.

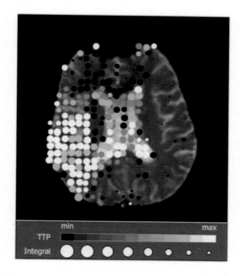

FIGURE 9.9

Simple circular glyphs represent two attributes with their size and color. The glyphs are only displayed when the values are relevant based on an interestingness measure. As a consequence, the underlying MRI data of the brain is partially visible (Courtesy of Steffen Oeltze-Jafra, University of Magdeburg).

Glyph mapping

When using glyphs to represent information, an essential decision relates to the specific mapping of data to glyph properties. Imagine in a public health scenario, you want to convey the number of hospital beds, the portion of occupied hospital beds, the number of beds in intensive care units (ICU), and again the portion of occupied beds in the ICU. A good strategy is to map the number of beds in the two categories to the length of bars. The occupied beds and the available beds (in both categories) are related. Thus bars with the same starting point are useful to enable a comparison.

Colors may be used to further improve the interpretation of the data. As an example, the available beds could be displayed with green bars and the occupied beds with red bars (or gray, if we want to use a colorblind-safe colorcoding). This whole information can be summarized in one glyph per hospital, which can be displayed in a map-based view. This special use of glyphs in maps is called a *dot plot*, and we will see examples in Section 10.4.4.

Glyph placement

In the example briefly discussed above, we would display one glyph for each hospital. The placement, in this case, is trivial. Imagine the map is shown in a large scale and we see a portion with a high density of hospitals. In this case, we run into an overplotting problem, as discussed for scatterplots. As a remedy, we could slightly distort the position where we place a glyph, i.e., we would use a *jittered placement*. In other situations, we are even more flexible in presenting glyphs. Imagine, that we have simulated some properties in a 3D mesh of anatomical structures, e.g., strain and stress on the hip as a prediction of the post-operative situation. Such a simulation may help to select the right implant, that not only fits anatomically, but is also reasonable from a biomechanical point of view (Dick et al., 2009).

Data for a few hundred thousand of cells in the simulation grid is generated by far too many to be displayed at once. Thus we may choose a density of glyphs that is appropriate to the current scale with more glyphs being shown when the user zooms in. We could also think about an adaptive strategy: When there are strong local changes in one of the simulated data, we display glyphs in a higher density. In contrast, in homogeneous regions, a lower number of glyphs is sufficient to reveal the distribution of the values. An adaptive glyph placement may also be used to focus on regions where critical values occur, e.g., there would be too much load after surgery with a selected implant.

Thus *glyph mapping* and *glyph placement* are at the heart of using glyphs for showing abstract data in a spatial context. A survey article on glyph-based medical visualization describes many examples (Ropinski et al., 2011). In this survey, the scalability issue of glyphs is also discussed: the use of glyphs is often prone to clutter due to overdrawing, where mechanisms such as grouping or use of different levels of details (i.e., parts where values change drastically use a representation with a finer resolution) are employed.

9.3.6 Visualizations of relational data

Relational data are fundamentally different from scalar data, as the information is not a single data value, but an actual relation (i.e., association) between two or more items. Relational data could refer to hierarchical or to network data, which can be addressed with graphs and tree visualizations. In this subsection, we review these two types of visualization within the context of medical applications.

Graph visualizations

Graphs are general types of relational data. Graphs with ordered edges are called directed, and graphs without ordered edges are called undirected. Depending on the type and size of graphs, different visualization methods are most applicable. Common representations of graph data include node-link diagrams and orthogonal layouts. Force-directed layouts are also common. Force-directed layouts are based on an energy function that measures the quality of the layout and on optimization algorithms to minimize this function by considering that adjacent nodes, i.e., nodes connected via an edge, should be attracted and adjacent nodes should be repelled.

An important component of graph visualization is *edge routing*: often orthogonal edge routing or edge bundling are used to declutter the view. The former makes use of vertical and horizontal line segments, which do no cut through nodes and do not overlap with any other edges. The latter method is often employed to reduce visual complexity when displaying large hierarchical graphs by visually grouping (or bundling) edges that are visually closing to each other. Bundling, similar to edge bundling in parallel coordinate plots, is depicted in Fig. 9.10. Other approaches to reduce clutter in graphs include graph-splatting techniques, where the graphs resemble density plots.

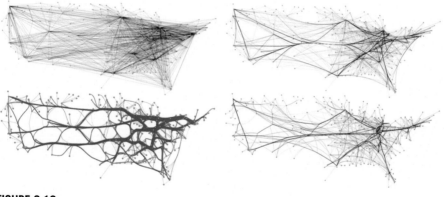

FIGURE 9.10

The effect of three edge bundling techniques applied to a large graph. The top left image shows the unbundled graph and the other three different configurations of edge bundling (From: (Holten and Van Wijk, 2009), ©John Wiley & Sons Inc., 2009).

Tree visualizations

A tree is a particular type of relational data, consisting of a set of nodes (also called vertices) and a set of edges, where each edge represents a connection of a pair of nodes. In a tree, we can define a unique path (i.e., a set of nodes connected by edges) between any two nodes in the tree without any loops. Nodes are ordered for semantic reasons and trees follow a hierarchical structure of a parent with child nodes. Here, a parent can have many children, but a child can only have one parent. A node without a parent is called a *root* and a node without children is called a *leaf*. As depth of a tree, we define the length of the longest path that connects a leaf to the root. Usual representations include node-link visualizations, ball-and-stick visualizations, rooted tree layouts, radial tree layouts, and treemaps (Schulz, 2011).

Treemaps (Van Wijk and Van de Wetering, 1999) have been designed to sparingly use the drawing canvas of the representation by using semantic rectangular partitions of the canvas to represent subtrees, instead of the usual node-link representation, which leaves big parts of the canvas blank. Squarified or cushioned versions of treemaps have also been designed to improve the use of space and the visibility of the inner levels. An example of a node-link diagram and its respective treemap is shown in Fig. 9.11. Such representations are often encountered within the context of medical applications in connection to clustering algorithms (see Section 9.6). In terms of scalability, treemaps scale well with a high-number of datapoints, as additional strategies can support it (such as cushion treemaps, or cut-off values).

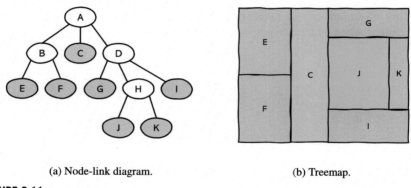

(a) Node-link diagram.   (b) Treemap.

FIGURE 9.11

A node-link diagram and its respective treemap. The hierarchy is explicit, and thus easier to recognize in the node-link diagram.

9.3.7 Geospatial visualizations

In several cases, we are interested in obtaining insight on the relationship between data and its location. For example, during the COVID-19 pandemic, people were interested in identifying—at a glance—which countries or regions within countries were mostly affected. To support the localization of phenomena, geospatial visualization is concerned with overlaying data directly on maps. This is interesting also beyond the domain of medical visualization, for example, in weather forecasting. The primary focus of geospatial visualization revolves around maps, and how they can be used as the basis for encoding data. Spatial information are directly encoded on the position (latitude and longitude) of the involved elements, which can vary from very localized information within a city to global information of the entire planet. On top of this, shapes and color can be employed for encoding the additional variables. The most common representations employed for geospatial visualization within the context of medical applications are proportional symbol maps, choropleth maps, point distribution maps, heat or density maps, and isopleth maps.

- **Proportional symbol maps:** These maps show quantitative data for individual coordinates using size. This is similar to the glyph representations shown in Section 9.3.5, with the difference that the coordinates reveal actual geolocations.
- **Choropleth maps:** These maps often show ratio and rate data in pre-determined areas. For example, countries or regions are colored to encode statistical variables (e.g., proportions of a population).
- **Point distribution maps:** These maps are employed to highlight visual clusters in data by showing the precise locations of events.
- **Heat or density maps:** These maps show the frequency of occurrences and are often employed to highlight trends in the data.
- **Isopleth maps:** These maps are very similar in use to isolines or isocontours, and they show a range of quantitative data.

Examples of each of these maps are shown in Fig. 9.12. When designing geospatial visualizations, two factors are of particular importance:

- the scale of the map (i.e., small-scale vs large-scale, to indicate the total geographic area for the visualization). The decision for the scale takes the proportion between distances/sizes on a map and their actual distances/sizes on earth into account. Here, scalability plays a very important role, especially with regard to the granularity, which can be displayed or the number of variables.
- the projection employed (i.e., the process of visualizing the 3D globe on a 2D picture, which will result in distortions of areas of angles).

9.3.8 Visualization of time-varying data

A *time series* is a collection of data observations obtained through time. Timeseries data can be obtained, for example, during an electrocardiogram (ECG), i.e., a test that monitors in real-time the signal produced by the electrical activity of the heart, or by measuring a patient's blood pressure in regular intervals, or by acquiring multiple CT scans from a patient through the course of a treatment. Time series can be *continuous*, when observations are made continuously through time. They are *discrete* when observations are taken only at specific times. Discrete data are either the result of sampling (when readings are obtained at specific, equal intervals, i.e., the blood sugar levels of a patient as measured every morning), or the result of aggregation (when readings are aggregated over equal intervals, i.e., average blood sugar values of a patient in a week). We refer to Aigner et al. (2007) for a complete taxonomy of time-varying data.

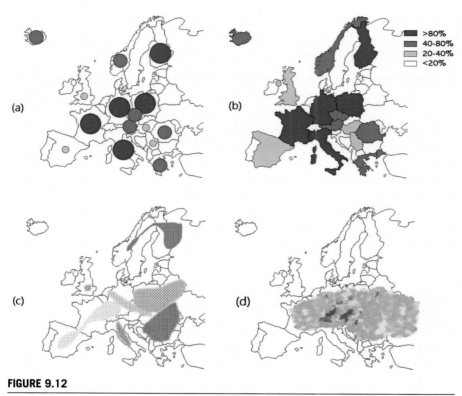

FIGURE 9.12

From top to bottom and from left to right: Examples of (a) a proportional symbol map, (b) a choropleth map, (c) a point distribution map, and (d) a density map.

In medical applications, when visualizing time-varying data, we are mainly interested in giving emphasis to changing trends. These can be, as mentioned above, intra-day or day-to-day variations, but they can also be extended series traversing weeks or months. The most commonly employed representation of time-varying data are the following:

- **Line plots** are the standard way to show time-varying data. They display information as a series of data points connected by straight lines. The line is often drawn chronologically, and usually linear axes are employed. When few data points are available, or when the data are irregular, data points can be used as a simplification (similar to a scatterplot, where the horizontal axis represents the time, and vertical axis represents the data value). Sometimes, if future projections need to be shown (as a result of a prediction), fan representations are used to show uncertainties in forward events.
- **Timelines** display a list of events in chronological order. In this representation, bars that represent events are drawn along an axis that indicates time. This plot

is often employed to show contemporaneous events or evolutions in events. Examples of special types of timelines are Gantt charts and stock-price charts. Thus timelines could be considered a special case of bar charts.

- **Calendar heatmaps** are used to show temporal patterns or activities (daily, weekly, monthly). Such representations allow users to plot and analyze events that run through a long period of time. However, this kind of representation is often too abstract, at the expense of showing precision in quantity.

Fig. 9.13 showcases the above discussed representations.

Note

Often, when working with time-varying data, we need to deal with comparing two or more non-equal length vectors. This is important if we are measuring similarity between two temporal sequences, which may vary in speed, such as motion activities by two people who are moving at different speeds. An important method used to simplify the representation of time series data is dynamic time warping (DTW) (Müller, 2007). This method is instrumental in calculating the distance between the vectors of time-varying data at hand.

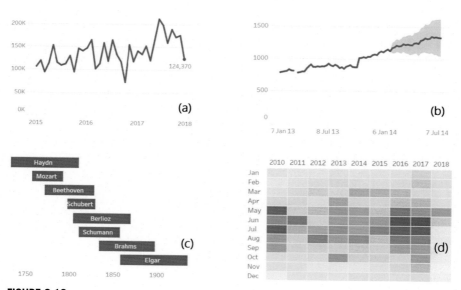

FIGURE 9.13

From top to bottom and from left to right: Examples of (a) a line plot, (b) a line plot with missing data (see gap on the line) and a fan to denote uncertainty of future prediction, (c) a timeline plot, and (d) a calendar heatmap. Images created with Tableau software (https://www.tableau.com/).

9.3.9 Multiple coordinated views

We saw that multidimensional data can be visualized with different techniques. Some of them are useful for categorical data, such as mosaic plots, some of them are used to display scalar data, such as scatterplots. Glyphs, map-based, or time-line-based visualizations may also be relevant.

For the comprehensive visualization of (medical) data, we need systems that *integrate* different visualization techniques. *Integration* means that not only different views are available, but that they are somehow synchronized or *coordinated* with each other. An example for such a coordination relates to the selection of data sets in one view (brushing). As a consequence, other views should be updated and emphasize the selected data sets as well (linking).

Brushing and linking is a core mechanism in *multiple coordinated views* (MCVs) (Wang Baldonado et al., 2000). When designing MCVs, it is also essential to consider the specific layout, i.e., how much space is available for each view and how they are arranged. A matrix-based view, e.g., with two rows and three columns could be an option. Fig. 9.14 provides an example of the *ComVis* system, which was used primarily for analyzing multidimensional data in engineering applications, but due to its general design would be applicable also in other areas (Matkovic et al., 2008).

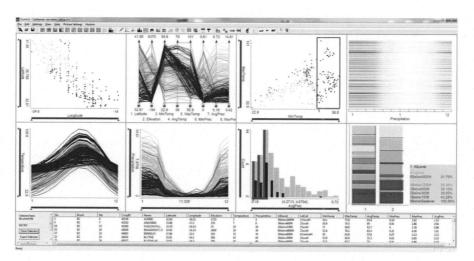

FIGURE 9.14

The *ComVis* system provides support for a wide range of analysis tasks. In this layout scatterplots, parallel coordinates and bar charts are combined. In one view in the upper row, a rectangular selection is made. The corresponding data sets are shown in blue in all other views. An earlier selection led to the emphasis of data sets in red (©2008 IEEE, Reprinted with permission from: (Matkovic et al., 2008)).

9.4 Statistical methods employed in visual analytics

Statistics is a form of mathematical analysis that concerns the collection, organization, analysis, interpretation, and presentation of a given set of experimental data or real-life studies. We already discussed methods for visualizing the distribution of the data in Section 9.3.1. This section aims at reviewing other essential statistical concepts in visual analytics frameworks.

- **Central tendency.** The term is used to describe a central or typical value for a distribution (see Fig. 9.15). Measures of central tendency provide a descriptive summary of the data set using a single value to reflect the center of the distribution. The most common measures are the *mean*, i.e., the average of the data set, the *mode*, i.e., the most frequent value in a data set, and the *median*, i.e., the middle value of an ordered data set. Often, the *skewness* is also used as a measure of symmetry and the *kurtosis* to show whether the data is heavy-tailed or light-tailed relative to a normal distribution.

- **Variability.** The term is used to describe the divergence of data from its mean value. The most common measures related to it are the *range*, i.e., the difference between the lowest and highest value in the data set; the *percentiles*, i.e., the value below which a given percentage of observations in a group of observations falls; the *quantiles*, i.e., the values that divide the number of data points into four more or less equal parts, and the *interquartile range*, i.e., a measure which is based on the quartiles (see Fig. 9.2). The *variance* is a measure to show how spread out the data is relative to mean, and its square root is called a *standard deviation*.

- **Relationship between variables:** The most important relationships between variables are *causality*, i.e., a relationship between two events, where one event is affected by the other *covariance*, i.e., a quantitative measure of the joint variability between two or more variables, and *correlation*, i.e., a measure that shows the (linear) dependency of two variables. A high correlation *may* indicate a causal relation, but often it is not.

- **Hypothesis testing and statistical significance.** A statistical hypothesis test is a method for statistical inference, where a hypothesis is tested for acceptance or rejection. A *null hypothesis* is a general statement that there is no relationship between two measured phenomena or no association among groups, and its contrary is called an *alternative hypothesis*. As part of testing, a *significance level or critical value* (α) needs to be selected as a probability threshold, below which the null hypothesis will be rejected. Common values are 0.05 and 0.01. The *p-value* indicates the probability of the test statistic being at least as extreme as the one observed given that the null hypothesis is true. When $p > \alpha$, we fail to reject the null hypothesis; otherwise, we reject the null hypothesis, and we can conclude that we have a significant result. There are several tests that can be used for statistical significance, e.g., z-test, t-test, χ-square test, ANOVA. The choice of test depends on the assumptions made about the data set or on its characteristics.

- **Regression.** Linear regression is an approach that helps us model the relationship between two variables: an independent, i.e., the variable that is controlled in an experiment to test the effects on the dependent variable, and a dependent, i.e., the variable being measured in an experiment. There is also a multiple linear regression version, which deals with two or more independent variables.

Statistical methods are employed in medical visualization as a means for calculating errors and uncertainty and also for depicting them (among other applications). This is often the case with margins, for example, in radiotherapy planning to increase robustness with regard to potential errors in the acquisition and in segmentation of tumors and surrounding organs. Also, uncertainty is most commonly described as a boundary around a measurement, i.e., an interval or as a distribution of measurements, depending on what is the focus of the application at hand. If we are interested in a confidence margin around the measurement, then usually the former is used. The latter is used if we are looking into the occurrence of a set of measurements. In this second case, boxplot, bean, or violin plot representations are often employed. In this book, we do not look further into statistics for uncertainty, and we refer the reader to a recent survey written by Gillmann et al. (2021).

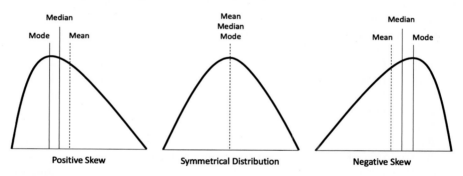

FIGURE 9.15

Examples of typical distributions.

9.5 Dimension reduction

We discussed a number of techniques to visualize multidimensional data, such as PCs and scatterplot matrices. We also discussed scalability limits, i.e., these techniques are not efficient to explore truly high-dimensional data, as they often occur in public health and clinical medicine. Dimension reduction summarizes techniques that project data from a high-dimensional (HD) space to a low-dimensional (LD) space. The LD space is chosen such that it can be displayed and explored efficiently and is often 2D or 3D.

The transformation from HD space to LD space aims at reducing the information, while preserving major features. Often, dimensions correlate strongly, and thus values for one dimension can be predicted quite well from a combination of other dimensions. Another reason for removing a dimension could be a low *entropy*, e.g., when the values of this dimension differ only slightly. Despite dimensions with low entropy and with high correlation, a transformation to a 2D space, in general, cannot be realized without any loss of information.

This raises the question which features in the data are essential and should be preserved. If data sets, e.g., information related to a patient, are very similar in HD space, they should also be similar in LD space. On the other hand, if data sets are dissimilar in HD space, they should also remain dissimilar. Outliers in HD space should be preserved in LD space. And again, no "new" outliers should be introduced as an artifact of the reduction. The similarity is then employed for a layout, where similar data sets are mapped close to each other, i.e., similarity is mapped to proximity.

For the analyst employing a visualization based on a dimension reduction, it is essential to understand *how* well the properties of the HD data could be preserved. This may include a global quality value, but also local quality assessments. A projection may preserve distances in some areas, but stretch or expand distances in other areas.

For the sake of brevity, we cannot fully explain all frequently used dimension reduction techniques, but we shall mention and briefly characterize selected techniques, and we categorize them in linear and non-linear techniques. We refer the interested reader to the recent survey of Huang et al. (2019).

9.5.1 Linear dimension reduction

Linear dimension reduction techniques map a set of dimensions H to a low-dimensional space L such that every dimension D_{li} of LD is a linear combination of the dimensions D_{hj} from HD. In other words, every dimension from HD contributes to the D_i from LD with a certain weight. The most important linear dimension reduction technique is the *principal component analysis* (PCA) (Hotelling, 1933). The PCA works as follows: Each data set is represented by a vector. After some preprocessing, the PCA computes the covariance matrix (COV), where each N-dimensional vector is multiplied with its transposed vector, resulting in an $N \times N$ matrix. An eigenanalysis is applied to the COV, and the resulting eigenvectors are the principal components of a new coordinate system, which is aligned with actual distribution of the data (see Fig. 9.16).

With a PCA, N-dimensional data is mapped to N-dimensional data, thus the number of dimensions is initially not reduced. With every principal component, there is a *loading* computed that specifies how much of the variability of the data can be explained with that dimension. Loadings are values between 0 and 1, and the sum of all loadings equals 1. As a consequence, when the sum of the first three or four loadings is >0.9 or even >0.95, we may reduce the number of dimensions accordingly to three or four. With a PCA, for every LD subspace of the transformed data, the projection error compared to the original data is minimized. Despite this desirable property, it cannot be guaranteed that clusters and outliers are preserved.

Standardization

An essential prerequisite for applying a PCA (and many other dimension reduction techniques) is to normalize the ranges of the data. This normalization has two aspects: the data should be centralized such that the average value is zero, and the range should be the interval [-1,1].

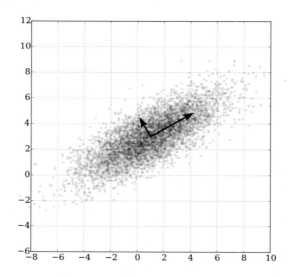

FIGURE 9.16

Normally distributed data in 2D, and the result of a PCA indicated by the two orthogonal arrows. The longer arrow represents the first principal component that explains the largest part of the variability (From Wikipedia, https://creativecommons.org/licenses/by/4.0/deed. en).

Interpretation

A problem inherent to PCA, but also to other dimension reduction techniques is that the new dimensions are very hard to interpret. A new dimension may be a linear combination of "body weight," "alcohol consumption," and "blood pressure" with certain weighting factors. Considerable research was carried out to aid analysts in interpreting results of a PCA (Jeong et al., 2009), but in general, this remains difficult and cannot be automatized. The interested reader may have a look at a tutorial on PCA (Smith, 2002).

9.5.2 Non-linear dimension reduction

Non-linear dimension reduction techniques offer more freedom in the transformation, and actually they are used more frequently in visual analytics compared to linear methods. The most frequently used techniques are:

- Multidimensional scaling (MDS)
- t-Stochastic neighborhood embedding (t-SNE)
- Uniform manifold approximation and projection (UMAP) since recently

Multidimensional scaling (MDS)

is a non-linear iterative optimization method, where the distance of points in HD space is preserved optimally when transforming to LD space (Cox and Cox, 2008). With MDS, dimension reduction is considered as an optimization problem based on a *stress function* that maximizes the preservation of distances. It is solved with a non-linear optimization method, e.g., gradient descent. At the core of MDS is a distance metric that defines distances between any pair of data sets. A typical choice would be the Euclidean distance. However, it may be necessary to normalize the dimensions before applying the metric or to assign individual weights to the dimensions.

MDS introduces an error that is quantified by the stress value. The more dimensions are preserved, the lower the stress value and the higher the accuracy. Stress values are in the range of [0,1]. They are often interpreted as follows: When the stress is larger than 0.2, the projection is poor, when it is between 0.1 and 0.2, it is fair, when it is between 0.05 and 0.1, it is good, and stress values below 0.05 indicate an excellent projection. We discussed the interpretation of PCA results in the last subsection. With MDS, the axis of the visualization has no meaning at all. What matters is only the spatial configuration, i.e., which data sets are mapped close to each other or far away from each other (see Fig. 9.17).

Stochastic neighborhood embedding (SNE)

and its most popular variant (t-SNE) are in contrast to the previously described *non-deterministic* approaches, i.e., when you apply the algorithm several times to the same data, the results will differ. The basic idea of SNE is to maximize the likelihood that the closest neighbors of a point p in HD space are also the closest in LD space. Thus the method does not explicitly aims at preserving distances, instead it preserves neighborhoods. t-SNE models the data in HD space as a student t-distribution (with one degree of freedom) and aims at a similar student t-distribution in LD space (Van der Maaten and Hinton, 2008). The optimization requires a measure for the difference between two distributions (HD and LD space). The *Kullback–Leibler divergence* is particularly useful for this. The choice of the t-distribution turned out to be favorable, compared, e.g., to a Gaussian distribution, because the projected data is not too strongly focused on the center of the projection space.

The essential parameter of t-SNE is the *perplexity*. It specifies the number of close neighbors to be considered. Typical values range from 5 to 50. The perplexity value should be considerably smaller than the number of data sets. It is useful to compare the results for different values of the perplexity parameter, as Wattenberg et al. (2016) emphasize: "Getting the most from t-SNE may mean analyzing multiple plots with different perplexities." All dimension reduction techniques described in this section are widely available in software libraries, such as R.

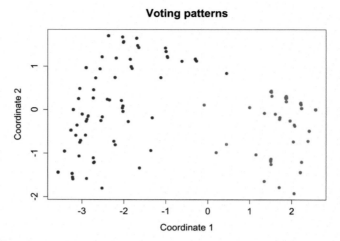

FIGURE 9.17

Example for the use of MDS. The voting behavior of the members of the US States House of Representatives is depicted. Red and blue dots represent members of the Democratic and Republican Party. The expected similar voting behavior of members of one party becomes obvious, but also considerable differences between some members of the same party (From Wikipedia, https://creativecommons.org/licenses/by/3.0/).

Uniform manifold approximation and projection (UMAP)

is a recently developed technique by McInnes et al. (McInnes et al., 2018) to offer a number of advantages over t-SNE. UMAP and t-SNE have similarities in their basic concept, as they both rely on graph layout algorithms to create a low-dimensional (2D or 3D) representation of the high-dimensional data set. UMAP constructs a high-dimensional graph representation of the data, using a so-called *fuzzy simplicial complex*, which is a weighted graph with edge weights representing the likelihood that two points are connected. Subsequently, a radius is extended from each point, and two points are connected if their radii overlap. The choice of the radius value is significant. If this value is too small, this will result in small isolated datapoints; otherwise, everything will be connected together. In UMAP, this is solved by a local choice of the radius value for each point, based on its distance to the n-th nearest neighbor. As the radius grows, the likelihood that two points are connected decreases, generating the fuzzy graph. In this way, UMAP ensures that the preservation of the local structure is well-balanced to the preservation of the global structure of the data set. Then, the algorithm optimizes a low-dimensional graph to be as structurally similar as possible to the high-dimensional one. This is done in the same way as in the t-SNE implementation, but much faster.

Overall, the advantage of UMAP over t-SNE is that it manages to better preserve the global structure of a high-dimensional data set and scales well both for data set size and dimensionality, while having a much better time performance. The two most important parameters in UMAP are

- the number n of approximate nearest neighbors in constructing the fuzzy high-dimensional graph, which controls the balance between local (low n) and global (high n) structure
- the minimum distance between points in low-dimensional space, which controls how tightly points are packed together in the embedding (i.e., low value results in a tight packing)

By conducting a hyperparameter search, i.e., by running UMAP multiple times with a variety of hyperparameters, the impact of the parameters on the projection can be investigated.

9.6 Clustering

Clustering is a method of unsupervised learning, which is used in many fields as part of exploratory and statistical data analysis (Saxena et al., 2017). The main task behind clustering is to group data points into specific groups. In theory, data points belonging to the same group should have similar properties and/or features, and data points belonging to different groups should have highly dissimilar properties and/or features. It is used in many applications, including medical applications. The task of clustering is similar to that of classification, but the difference is that classification learns in a supervised manner, a method for predicting the class (i.e., the group) based on pre-labeled (i.e., classified) instances, whereas clustering finds a natural way of grouping instances based on patterns within unlabeled data. Practically, classification tries to attribute each data point to one class from a given number of classes, whereas clustering finds subgroups of similar data points within a dataset.

There are different motivations for performing clustering on a data set. Clustering can be employed for

- grouping data (e.g., we could be interested in finding data classes)
- data reduction (e.g., we could be interested in finding representatives of groups within the data)

Let us assume that we have data from a large population that has been vaccinated against COVID-19. We aim to study the characteristics of the vaccinated population to understand which people can benefit most from it. A clustering algorithm will create subgroups of the population that reveal similarities within each group and dissimilarities across groups (e.g., one feature could be age). The formed clusters might reflect different kinds of responses to vaccines or different degrees of immunity. However, at the same time, the clustering might reveal outliers, i.e., people who deviate from the other observations in the data set. In other domains, such as marketing, these cases might be considered noise or erroneous, but in clinical applications they should be taken into account for developing more robust treatments.

Clustering should satisfy a number of requirements, such as scalability, ability to deal with different types of attributes, ability to deal with clusters of arbitrary shape, minimum domain knowledge requirements to identify adequate parameterizations for the selected algorithm, and robustness to noise. At the same time, clustering often faces issues such as being able to deal with a large number of dimensions and/or data items within reasonable computational times, sensitivity to the distance metrics (i.e., how we determine which data points are similar), and interpretability of the outcome of clustering algorithms.

The choice of distance measures is a critical decision in clustering, as it determines how the similarity of two data points is calculated. The classical methods for distance measures are Euclidean and Manhattan distance, but correlation-based distances have also been employed, e.g., for the analysis of gene expression (Kriegel et al., 2009). Minkowski distance is a popular metric for high-dimensional data, which is considered the generalization of both Manhattan and Euclidean distances (Irani et al., 2016). Below, we review a number of commonly employed algorithms and discuss their suitability for medical applications (Saxena et al., 2017):

- *k*-means clustering separates data points in a pre-determined number *k* of clusters of equal variance, by minimizing their inertia or within-cluster sum-of-squares. The algorithm scales well to a large number of samples and has been used for many applications, but it suffers from three main drawbacks. First, it requires that *k* is specified, i.e., that it is "known." In exploratory analytical processes, this value will not be known a priori, but there are methods (such as the elbow method) that can be employed to find the most suitable value. Second, it assumes that the clusters are convex, which means that it cannot deal with irregularly shaped manifolds. Finally, the employed metric of inertia is not a normalized metric, which—based on our experiences—requires a dimensionality reduction measure to be conducted prior to clustering.
- **Mean-shift clustering** is a mode-seeking algorithm that aims to discover the maxima of a density function. Although the algorithm does not assume any predefined shape of data clusters and can deal with arbitrary feature spaces, the whole procedure relies on a bandwidth parameter, which dictates the size of the region to search through for the maxima. This is not trivial; an inadequate selection of the parameter leads to sub-optimal results. To address this, adaptive approaches have been developed.
- **Density-based spatial clustering of applications with noise (DBSCAN).** The DBSCAN algorithm defines clusters as high-density areas separated by low-density areas. Therefore DBSCAN has been preferred in the past due to its characteristic of not assuming a specific shape for the clusters. To define formally "high density" areas that form a cluster, two parameters are employed, which need to be adequately tuned. These control the sensitivity of the algorithm to noise and

to merging local neighborhoods. The main disadvantage of the algorithm is that DBSCAN does not work well when we are dealing with clusters of varying densities or with very high-dimensional data.

- **Hierarchical clustering** refers to a general family of algorithms that act upon merging or splitting groups of data points iteratively. Often, a tree representation is used to represent the outcome of the algorithm, which can be done in two ways: agglomerative or divisive. Agglomerative hierarchical clustering refers to a "bottom-up" approach, where each data point starts as a cluster, and moves up the hierarchy being merged with similar clusters. Divisive hierarchical clustering refers to a "top-down" approach, where all data points start in one cluster, and are iteratively split into sub-clusters as we move down the hierarchy. Agglomerative approaches are more common, and a linkage criterion determines how the merge is performed (e.g., Ward, maximum, average, single linkage). The main advantage of hierarchical clustering is that it can use any valid distance metric, but the linkage criterion is crucial. Such algorithms are often criticized for their time performance.

- **Gaussian mixtures.** A Gaussian mixture model is a probabilistic model that assumes all data points are generated from a mixture of a finite number of Gaussian distributions with unknown parameters. The model comes with different options to constrain the covariance of the estimated classes: spherical, diagonal, tied, or full covariance. The main advantages of the algorithm are its speed and that it is structure-agnostic (as opposed to k-means, for example); the main disadvantage is that estimating covariance matrices from few data points can be problematic.

Choosing an appropriate clustering method is not trivial. In R and `python`, there are packages that help to compare simultaneously multiple clustering algorithms and support the identification of the best clustering approach and the optimal number of clusters. Each of them has specific advantages and disadvantages, as well as suitability for a given data set and its structure. Knowledge about the data set characteristics helps making an informed selection.

Visualizations for clustering

The most common ways of visualizing clustering results are with the use of *scatterplots* (where belonging to a specific cluster is color-encoded additionally on the scatterplot points) or *density maps* (see Fig. 9.18). *Trees* are often employed to show the outcome of hierarchical algorithms (see Fig. 9.19). Often, these representations are additionally employed to provide an interface for cluster selection. For example, visual clusters or actual clusters can be selected in a scatterplot, and then, their characteristics can be further explored in other linked views. Density maps often support this selection, as they provide a better view on significant (e.g., large) clusters. A second example includes the usage of trees as a means for selecting the clustering level in a data set, i.e., when a hierarchical approach is used.

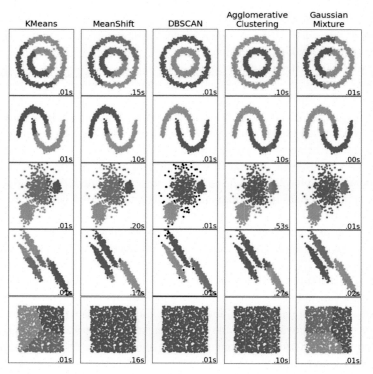

FIGURE 9.18

Example for the use of different clustering algorithms (columns: k-means, mean shift, DBSCAN, hierarchical algorithm, and Gaussian mixtures) on different data sets (rows; depicting different kinds of manifolds). The time required for each algorithm and data set pair is also depicted in the figure. Results obtained with scikit-learn (https://scikit-learn.org/stable/modules/clustering.html).

9.7 Subspace clustering

Subspace clustering is useful for analyzing high-dimensional data (> 20 dimensions), where global clustering is not promising due to the *curse of dimensionality*. The curse of dimensionality basically means that in a truly high-dimensional space, there are no dense regions, even adjacent points are rather far away. For health-related data, subspace clustering is beneficial, since persons are likely to be similar in some dimensions but not in all. Subspace clustering is typically a two-stage process: *clusterable subspaces*, where some regions have a very high density are identified in the first stage, and a clustering method, such as DBSCAN (Ester et al., 1996) or OPTICS (Ankerst et al., 1999), is applied to these clusterable subspaces in the second stage. As an example, for the first stage Kailing et al. (2003) provide a ranking of subspaces and enable the analyst to choose, for example, the top N subspaces for clustering.

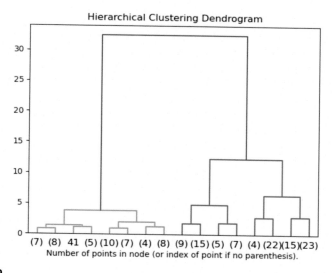

Hierarchical Clustering Dendrogram

Number of points in node (or index of point if no parenthesis).

FIGURE 9.19

Dendrogram representing the outcome of a hierarchical clustering using agglomerative clustering. Figure obtained with scikit-learn (https://scikit-learn.org/) and scipy (https://scipy.org/).

Subspace clustering involves several parameters that influence the search and ranking of subspaces and the clustering within the selected subspaces. In the work of Assent et al. (2007), dimensionality unbiased subspace clustering and a novel distance function for subspace clusters are proposed. To explore and analyze the outcomes, visualization techniques allow users to browse the entire subspace clustering, to zoom into individual objects, and to analyze subspace cluster characteristics in-depth. Parameter sensitivity analysis, i.e., an investigation of the effect of parameters on the data, is also possible, allowing to choose the best clustering result for further analysis. Another example towards the direction of visual assessment is the work of Hund et al. (2016). This work also provides visual support for comparing quality criteria of subspace clusterings at three granularity levels: a global view of cluster similarity and estimated redundancy in cluster memberships, a view with a pre-selection of multiple clusters for an in-depth analysis of distributions and overlaps, and a detailed view about each individual cluster.

Tatu et al. (2012) presented an integrated data analysis and visualization tool for mining patterns in multidimensional data using user-steerable subspace clustering algorithms. This work supports the characterization of subspace cluster analysis tasks and their resulting design space, which is visually analyzed through novel visualization approaches. More recently, Xia et al. (2017) focused on dimensional overlapping between subspaces and data overlapping between clusters through a hyper-graph visualization, which enables the dynamic analysis of dimension relevance.

More specifically to the medical domain, Niemann et al. (2014b) considered the application to cohort study data as not feasible, since the results are too sensitive to a number of parameters. A cohort study relates to a group of humans who are analyzed over time to detect trends. Cohorts of patients, students, and clients are interesting in the respective domains.

As a consequence of the problems with subspace clustering, the same group developed a constraint-based technique, where the clustering is guided by a small set of constraints, given by an expert (Hielscher et al., 2018). As an example, for a few pairs of participants diagnosed with fatty liver, the expert specifies that these participants must be in the same clusters, whereas some other pairs of participants are forced to be in different clusters, since one in each pair is diagnosed with the disorder and the other is not. This semi-supervised subspace clustering turned out to yield relevant results for epidemiologists (Hielscher et al., 2018).

Visualization of subspace clustering results

For the visualization of subspace clustering results, the most common representations are two-dimensional heatmap matrices or multiple scatterplots. In the former, one dimension represents belonging to a cluster and the second dimension represents the dimensions involved in the specific setup (see Fig. 9.20). In the latter, small multiple scatterplots are employed to show all possible outcomes. As an alternative, or even as addition to the scatterplots, parallel coordinates can also be employed (see Fig. 9.21). In addition to these representations, *glyphs* are employed to encode clusters in a scatterplot (i.e., instead of individual data points, a circular glyph of varying areas is used to indicate the size of clusters). Graphs are often employed to convey dimensional overlapping through subspace alternatives and data overlapping through clusters.

9.8 Association rule mining

Association rule mining helps to identify rules that describe interesting relations between variables in large databases. For example, in medical diagnosis, association rule mining helps to identify the probability that an illness occurs depending on patient factors and symptoms. Like clustering, association rule mining is a kind of *unsupervised learning*, and thus appropriate for the exploration of data.

In practice, association rules are "if–then" statements that help to discover *correlations* (i.e., the degree to which a pair of variables are linearly dependent) or *co-occurrences* (i.e., two or more variables occurring together) between variables. Hence, association rule mining is particularly suitable for non-numeric, categorical data. For numerical data, a split value or cutoff value is required, i.e., data sets where the variable is below or above the cutoff value are discriminated by a rule.

There are basically two goals in association rule mining:

- efficiently extract all relevant rules from large transaction data sets
- visualize and drill-down to the most interesting rules

Dimension

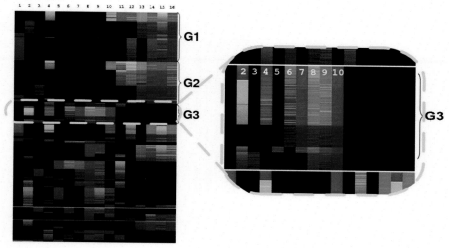

FIGURE 9.20

Matrix of subspace cluster groups (Assent et al., 2007). Rows represent the cluster and columns the dimensions; groups are separated by white lines (see right part). Color map HSV: Hues represent the value in each dimension of the subspace cluster; saturation and value represent a special interestingness measure (Courtesy of Ira Assent, Aarhus University).

The most important components (or characteristics) of association rules are summarized below:

- An association rule has two parts: an *antecedent* (an "if," i.e., an item that is found within the data) and a *consequent* (a "then," i.e., an item that is in combination with the antecedent). The antecedent may consist of different variables, e.g., age and body mass index (BMI). The consequent is often an outcome, e.g., a health risk or a diagnosed disease.
- Association rules are created by searching databases for frequent "if–then" patterns using *interesting measures*.
- The following interesting measures are most common in determining the efficacy of the rules: *support* (i.e., how frequently the items in the antecedent appear in the data), *confidence* (i.e., the number of times the association rule is found true), and *lift* (i.e., the ratio of confidence to support). Greater lift values (» 1) indicate stronger associations.

Let us assume a database of m patients $P = \{p_1, p_2, \ldots, p_m\}$ and a set of n items, i.e., binary attributes, which represent symptoms $S = \{s_1, s_2, \ldots, s_n\}$. Each patient in P contains a subset of items in S. A rule will be defined as $X \Rightarrow Y$, where $X, Y \subseteq S$. Here, X is the antecedent, and Y is the consequent. An example of a rule for the

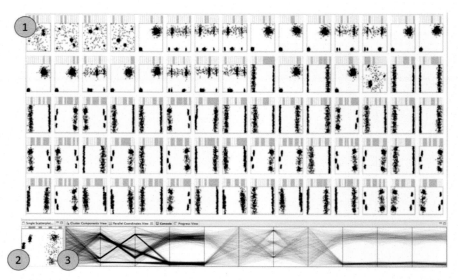

FIGURE 9.21

(1) Linearly sorted view of a subset of 75 out of the initially computed 296 subspaces for a given data set. The selected subspace in this view is shown in a (2) single subspace view to enable interaction, and in (3) a parallel coordinates view with the subspace dimensions as the first axes (highlighted) (©2012 IEEE, Reprinted with permission from (Tatu et al., 2012)).

symptoms could be $\{lack\,of\,sleep, tiredness\} \Rightarrow \{headache\}$. This rule would indicate that the combination of a lack of sleep and tiredness is associated with a high risk for headaches. In practical applications, a rule needs a support of several hundred patients before being considered statistically significant.

When we have numerical data, a search for association rules may yield a rule $AR_1 : age > 52 \,\&\, BMI > 30 \,\&\, Daily\,Alcohol > 50\,ml \rightarrow Fatty\,Liver$. Thus this rule indicates that the combination of certain variables increases the risk for the fatty liver disorder. The *lift* value would tell us how much the risk is actually increased.

9.8.1 Searching for association rules

When we have hundreds of variables in our database, an exhaustive search for association rules would lead to an overwhelming amount of rules. Thus the rule search is guided by the *interesting measures* mentioned above, i.e., primarily by the support, confidence, and lift values.

A rule should exceed a user-defined threshold ($min_{support}$). One percent (1%) may be a good value for this threshold. The $min_{support}$ can also be stated as an absolute value, e.g., we may require at least 100 patients to avoid that the resulting rules are affected too strongly by statistic uncertainty.

A $min_{confidence}$ threshold may further restrict the display. The selection of this value is not straightforward. Imagine, we have 100 patients where the rule is true and another 200 patients where the antecedent is fulfilled, but the consequent is not. This leads to a confidence of $(100/(100+200)) = 0.333$ (or 33.3%), e.g., in most cases our rule is wrong. Imagine that in the whole database only 3.33% exhibit a fatty liver. Then, our rule specifies a condition where the risk for fatty liver is ten times increased. This makes the rule interesting, even if most patients exhibiting the condition do not suffer from a fatty liver. Therefore also a minimum value for the *lift* parameter is useful to restrict the search.

Finally, the $maximum_{length}$ is often employed. The longer a rule, the lower the support will be, since *all* conditions need to be fulfilled. Thus very long rules are very unlikely. On the other hand, adding a variable to the antecedent makes it more specific, increasing the confidence. Even rules with more than three or four variables in the antecedent may be infeasible, since every variable relates to a measure that needs to be acquired from the patient. Moreover, as a very general thought in machine learning, the risk of overfitting a classification model to the actual data is increased with a complex model, e.g., long rules.

An association rule mining algorithm, such as APRIORI (Agrawal and Srikant, 1994) receives the parameters described above as input. We do not want to discuss algorithms and their efficiency here; just assume that we yield a comprehensive set of rules in a reasonable time.

9.8.2 Visualization of association rules

Searching for association rules, even when the search is restricted according to the described measures, may yield a large rule set. For the analyst, an overview of these rules and a detailed inspection is necessary. Thus we are interested in appropriate interactive visualizations. These visualizations should be fast to generate so that they can be updated immediately, if the rule search is repeated with different parameters.

In the following, we present three widely used techniques for the visualization of association rules, primarily for an initial overview:

- Scatterplots
- Two-key plots
- Graph-based views

These three visualization techniques are available in the ARULES package of R (Hahsler, 2017). In a real-world scenario, the rule sets are large, and thus interaction may be necessary to understand the rule collection. Panning, zooming, selection of subsets for further exploration in a separate view are useful interaction techniques.

Scatterplot

A scatterplot groups association rules with respect to two interestingness measures, typically support and confidence. A third interestingness measure, such as lift, could be mapped to the color of the dots in the scatterplot (see Fig. 9.22). The length of

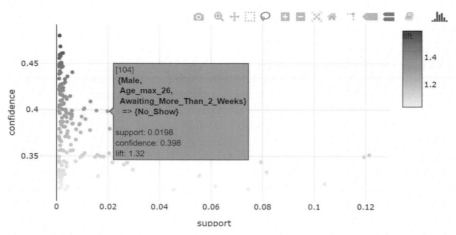

FIGURE 9.22

Scatterplot representation of association rules created with ARulesVis. The icons on top represent interaction options, e.g., various selections. The rule closest to the cursor is presented textually (Courtesy of Uli Niemann, University of Magdeburg).

the association rules, can be mapped to the size of the dots. This way, the quality of rules presented close to each other is similar. However, what the scatterplot does not reveal, is which variables are actually involved in the association rules. Thus two rules, where the antecedent has common variables and the consequent is the same, may be placed far away from each other.

Two-key plot

The other two visualizations convey the relation between the variables in the antecedent and the consequent. The *two-key plot* (Unwin et al., 2001) is a matrix-based view, where the dashed lines ensure that the relation of the rule to the involved items is clearly recognizable (see Fig. 9.23).

Graph-based views also convey items (variables) that contribute to several rules. In a graph-based view, there are two types of nodes, namely rules and items. Edges represent which items are involved in a rule. Since graph-based views of rule sets may get overwhelming, interaction may be necessary to understand the rule collection. Panning, zooming, selection of subsets for further exploration in a separate view are useful interaction techniques. The graph-based views in the R package, ARULESVIZ, enable the emphasis of the currently selected node (see Fig. 9.24).

Visualization for detailed inspection

Also for a detailed inspection of one association rule, scatterplots may be employed if two numerical variables are involved (see Fig. 9.25). Moreover, tooltips may be employed, which present the rule in a textual form on demand. A further ingredient of a rule exploration system is a *rule browser*, which may present the rules in a

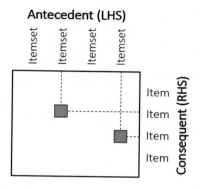

FIGURE 9.23

A two-key plot is a matrix visualization developed for representing association rules (From: (Hahsler, 2017)).

FIGURE 9.24

A graph represents an overview of association rules (left). In the right view, the selected rule is annotated and the visualization focused on this rule (Courtesy of Uli Niemann, University of Magdeburg).

table-like fashion. The rule browser should be linked to the overview visualizations. Thus a rule selected in the rule browser should lead to the emphasis of this rule in an overview visualization. For an efficient exploration of a larger rule set, sorting is crucial, e.g., the presentation of the rules can be sorted according to the different interestingness measures, such as support, confidence, and lift.

Also for a detailed inspection of one association rule, scatterplots may be employed if two numerical variables are involved (see Fig. 9.25). Moreover, tooltips that present the rule in a textual form on demand may be employed.

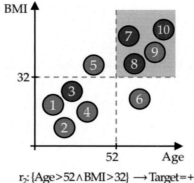

$$r_2: \{Age > 52 \wedge BMI > 32\} \longrightarrow Target = +$$

FIGURE 9.25

A scatterplot indicates how many data sets are actually affected by one classification rule with two elements (age and body mass index), and how many data sets are correctly or wrongly classified with respect to the fatty liver disease (Courtesy of Uli Niemann, University of Magdeburg).

Clustering

If the rules resulting from a rule search are sorted according to some interestingness measures, the first rules are often very similar, e.g., they overlap in the variables in the antecedent or the consequent. Waist circumference, hip circumference, and BMI are examples for strongly correlated variables. The analyst may be interested in rules that are good (in terms of interestingness measures) and representative for the data, i.e., they are as diverse as possible. To support such an analysis, rules may be clustered, and the exploration is focused on *representatives* of each cluster.

9.9 Correlation-based visual analytics

Regression is a core part of statistics (recall Section 9.4) and regression analysis is a valuable part of visual analytics systems. Regression models may *explain* the data, e.g., why a subgroup of the population is at higher risk to get diabetes and to *predict* future developments, e.g., the need for electric energy within the next week based on the current weather forecast.

Let us discuss a medical example: The life expectancy in some regions of a country may be much lower than in others (Latzitis et al., 2010). Public health researchers would like to understand

- *why* these differences occur
- whether there are factors involved that may be changed
- what effect can be expected from counter measures

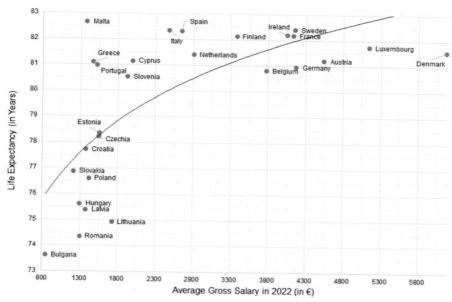

FIGURE 9.26

European countries differ in income and life expectancy. A trendline (best fit of a logarithmic function) is overlaid to support the perception of a correlation. Image created with Microsoft Excel based on data from the World Bank Group, 2022 Review.

The researchers employ socio-demographic data, e.g., on income levels, educational status, unemployment rates on a per-district basis. Also climate-related data, e.g., air pollution, and results of interviews with selected inhabitants regarding their lifestyle may be available. In traditional statistics, analysts would start with a hypothesis, typically related to one variable, such as income, and investigate the strength of a correlation (see Fig. 9.26). With nowadays big data, this is not efficient to detect *all* potentially interesting correlations. Even for a moderate number of 100 variables and the restriction to one type of correlation, there are already 10,000 pairs of variables where interesting correlations may occur. And often, the interplay of two or three variables is essential to predict a target variable. Thus the space to be considered grows exponentially.

9.9.1 Types of correlations

The simplest regression model is a *linear model*, i.e., we optimize the two parameters of a linear function to yield a line that provides an optimal fit to the data (recall Fig. 9.26). The *correlation coefficient* represents the strength of a correlation. This value is in the range [-1,1], where 1 represents the strongest possible positive correlation, and -1 the strongest possible negative correlation, i.e., when the values of x

increase, the values of y decrease. Optimality is typically defined in a least square sense, where there is a large penalty for strong deviations from the line. Therefore the result of a search for strong correlations may be severely affected by outliers.

There are indeed many examples of linear correlations in medicine, e.g., substances that represent a health risk (ionizing radiation, alcohol, and tobacco) increase the risk for many diseases, and the higher the dose of the damaging substance, the higher is the risk.

Non-linear regression models

Many correlations within and outside of medicine are non-linear. In medicine, there are many U-shaped characteristics. This means that the risk for a disease is low when a health-related parameter is in a certain *normal range*. The risk increases for values below or above that normal range. The body mass index or the sleeping duration are examples for such health-related parameters. The influence of such parameters can be captured with a quadratic regression model, where the three parameters of a quadratic function need to be determined. Of course, even higher-order polynomial functions are possible and may fit even better to the data. However, care is necessary to avoid overfitting to the data.

Multiple regression models

Regression models may involve a single variable (regressor) and assess its influence on a target variable, or it may involve several regressors. The latter regression models are referred to as *multiple regression models*. Using more than two regressors, in particular if the number of data sets is rather low, also increases the risk of overfitting to the data.

Logistic regression models

Medical data is often categorical or even binary, e.g., whether patients received a drug or not. *Logistic regression* is the type of regression where categorical variables are involved (Hosmer and Lemesbow, 1980).

Partial regression models

A final distinction is between global and partial regression models. If we analyze whether values of y can be predicted as a linear combination of $x_1, \ldots, x_n$, it may turn out that this works only for certain intervals of these variables. A global fit of a regression line would be quite inaccurate, but for the relevant interval, there may be an excellent fit. A seminal paper for detecting and validating partial regression models was published by Mühlbacher and Piringer (2013).

Preprocessing

Since regression models are sensitive to outliers, it may be useful to remove them. Outlier removal may be guided by algorithms that suggest candidates for removal, but should be interactively controlled. Regression modeling is also sensitive to missing data. Therefore strategies for removing incomplete data or imputation of missing values are relevant. Finally, in a preprocessing step, subsets of the data may be identified to restrict the regression modeling to them. Also regression modeling may benefit form scaling of the variables, such that their ranges and standard deviations are comparable.

9.9.2 Rank-by-feature framework

The rank-by-feature framework is a powerful means to efficiently identify strong correlations of a particular type (Seo and Shneiderman, 2005). The system is typically used in the following way:

As a first step, the individual variables are analyzed. For an efficient search for interesting variables, a feature is selected, e.g., the deviation from a normal distribution. Then the variables are ordered according to the selected feature, and the analyst may explore the top N variables in more detail, e.g., by inspecting their histogram, which reveals more insights into the distribution.

As a second step, analysts may search for pairs of variables with a strong correlation. Again, a feature, e.g., Pearsson correlation or quadratic correlation, is selected and the corresponding value is computed for all pairs of variables. Thus a sorted ranking of these pairs can be presented. Moreover, a matrix view is created where each cell represents the measure of correlation between a pair of variables. Color is used to convey whether the correlation is positive or negative and whether the absolute value is low or high. Again, a detailed inspection of a selected entry, i.e., a pair is enabled (see Fig. 9.27). For this purpose, a scatterplot is displayed to reveal the raw data. The rank-by-feature framework was widely used for challenging analysis tasks, e.g., to analyze gene expression data to understand which genes behave similarly under a wide range of environmental conditions.

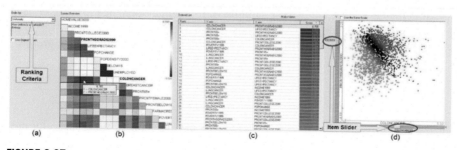

FIGURE 9.27

The rank-by-feature framework enables the selection of a ranking criterion (left), generates a matrix-based overview and a sorted list according to the selected criterion, and enables the detailed inspection of a selected pair of variables. The diverging color scale emphasizes both strong positive and strong negative correlations (J. Seo and B. Shneiderman, Information Visualization, Vol. 4(2), pp. 96–113, ©by SAGE, Reprinted by permission of SAGE publications (Seo and Shneiderman, 2005)).

The rank-by-feature framework is convincing by its careful combination of analytical components and interactive exploration. The fully automatic determination of regression models is not promising, but a semi-automatic approach with the user being in control enables many applications (Mühlbacher and Piringer, 2013).

On the practical side, it is challenging to perform the analysis sufficiently fast for an interactive exploration. Even for moderately-sized data with thousands of data sets and hundreds of variables, the computation of all pairwise correlation coefficients is time-consuming. The use of GPU computing and parallel computing may reduce the computation times considerably (Klemm et al., 2016).

9.9.3 Correlation and causality

Analysts typically want to understand whether a *causal effect* exists, e.g., in the sense that an increase of x directly implies and causes an increase of y. A simple search for correlations cannot reliably establish a causal relation. Strong correlations more likely imply causality than weaker correlations, but even verified and strong correlations may be misleading. In particular, it is not clear whether x implies y or y implies x. As a medical example: Homeless people are in bad health. The underlying causality may be that people in bad health are at a higher risk of getting homeless, but also that once being homeless, people's health deteriorates. In reality, it is a mixture of both, which cannot be inferred by data collected at one point in time only. If event A happens *before* event B, this increases the likelihood that A causes B. However, many events in life occur before a patient suffers a heart attack, and typically most of them are not the cause of the bad clinical condition. Thus even the sequence of events cannot reliably predict a causal effect.

A typical problem in the interpretation of a correlation between x and y is a *confounding variable z*. If both x and y are strongly correlated to z, a strong correlation between x and y can be misleading. z may even be causally related to x and y, which is then a *hidden factor* (see Fig. 9.28). In medical data, age is often either a confounder or a hidden factor. As a consequence, the influence of age needs to be controlled, for example, by performing a separate analysis for different age groups.

9.10 Interaction

Two mantras summarize the essential elements of interacting with graphically presented information in visualization and visual analytics. The visual information seeking mantra is *"Overview first, zoom and filter, then details-on-demand"* (Shneiderman, 1996). According to this, users should first have an overview on the data, which can give a global impression about the information within the data. Then, users should be able to zoom in and filter the data to obtain more detailed information. At the end, all detailed information should be shown on demand. This process should be enabled through interaction. The visual analytics seeking mantra (Keim et al., 2008b) is an adaptation of the visual information seeking mantra, adapted to

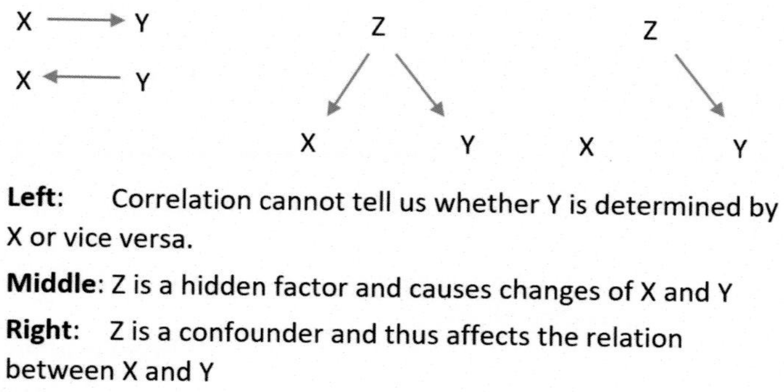

Left: Correlation cannot tell us whether Y is determined by X or vice versa.

Middle: Z is a hidden factor and causes changes of X and Y

Right: Z is a confounder and thus affects the relation between X and Y

FIGURE 9.28

Strong correlations do not always imply a causal effect.

fit within the field of visual analytics. It states *"Analyze first, show the important, zoom/filter, analyze further, details on demand."* In contrast to the original mantra, the data need to be initially analyzed to show the most interesting or relevant aspects, and will then be further investigated.

Basic interaction approaches

As already mentioned in the previous subsections, interaction is a significant component of visual analytics, helping to *clean up the view* on the data, to *provide a different view* of the data, or to *link distinct views* on the data. In many of the approaches discussed in Section 9.3, e.g., in scatterplots, or in parallel coordinates, interaction is used to alleviate clutter in the display. Specific subsets of the data can be selected to be brought forward in otherwise cluttered views. Additionally, they can be selected for further exploration within the same view or in multiple coordinated views. We hereby discuss the most significant terms related to interaction:

- *Navigation* is the directed movement in discrete or continuous information space. This can often be accompanied by *zooming*, *panning*, or other manipulations of the space.
- *Zooming* is one of the basic interaction techniques, often employed to overcome the limited display of information due to resolution and color depth of a display. There are three main zooming techniques:

  1. *geometric zooming*, i.e., the user can specify the scale of magnification and increasing or decreasing the view by that scale,
  2. *fisheye lenses*, i.e., a zoom where the outside information is not lost from view, but only distorted to keep only the zoomed part in focus (Furnas, 1986), and
  3. *semantic zooming*, which changes the shape or context in which the information is presented (e.g., zooming followed by display of additional information) (Perlin and Fox, 1993).

- A *magic lens* is an arbitrarily shaped user interface element, which can be placed over a part of objects to locally change their appearance or behavior. Usually a magic lens is used as a metaphor for a magnifying glass over the graphical representation to provide more (detailed) information on the data (Bier et al., 1993).
- *Brushing and linking (B/L)* (Becker and Cleveland, 1987) is a concept that involves selecting one or several interesting items in one view, and highlighting corresponding items in another. As stated by Keim, this method is meant to *overcome the shortcomings of single techniques*, and provides more information than the exploration of individual views.
- The idea behind *Focus+Context (F+C)* (Rao and Card, 1994) is to present items at different levels of detail. More interesting or relevant items are presented with more detail, whereas less important items are presented with less detail, but are retained in the view to provide context for a better understanding and insight.
- The notion of the *Overview+Detail* technique (Cockburn et al., 2009) is related to the combined use of Multiple Views and Focus + Context. Here, at least two views are presented to the users: one with a rough overview on the entire visualization space, and one with a detailed view of a smaller portion of the space.
- *Dynamic queries* filter the data as taken from a database, update them continuously, and visualize them (Ahlberg and Shneiderman, 1994). This happens in real-time (instantly), as users filter the data, i.e., adjust sliders or select buttons. This term is related to the *direct manipulation of the data*.

9.11 Challenges in visual analytics for clinical applications

In biomedical research, data has to be anonymized to prevent the identification of the involved individuals. This always happens for the metadata of the patient images or the electronic health records, where the tags are removed in dedicated software. For the electronic health records, anonymization is relatively easy, as an ID is assigned to the patient and personal information can be hidden. However, medical images are more complicated. With the new advances of medical imaging and visualization techniques, such as high-quality volume rendering, the high resolution of the acquired patient images can reveal the identity of the depicted person. The *data privacy and protection* of collected non-imaging data is also another big topic of discussion, especially with respect to the new laws about General Data Protection Regulation (EU GDPR).

Given the multitude of data involved in visual analytics applications, *data integration*, i.e., the combination and representation of multisourced data, and *data standardization*, i.e., reaching consensus and developing standards to maximize compatibility, interoperability, safety, and repeatability, are significant (and competing) challenges. Often, the former comes at a cost of the latter, while the latter also competes against the design and development of scalable approaches.

Though the involved data is steadily increasing in *complexity*, and we are more and more often dealing with big and "rich" data, we are still restricted by our limited knowledge about the data. Often, even experienced domain experts do not know a priori they are looking for, making automated data analysis approaches not suitable, and semi-automated analysis is sometimes still considered tedious. In this case, user-in-the-loop approaches can be of significant help, but additional notions of *guidance* can support a more structured data analysis.

Clinical adoption and integration of visual analytics approaches is still slow and rare, due to three main reasons. First, visual analytics tools are often quite complex to use and require a lot of interaction with the data, introducing a significant time overhead for clinicians. Second, they heavily rely on automated analysis approaches, which are rarely understandable, explainable, and thus not trusted by clinical users. Finally, the results of the interactive, visual analysis are not necessarily reproducible, making clinical adoption a difficult task.

Trustworthiness, explainability, and transparency are significant concerns stemming from the use of automated analysis approaches that hamper clinical adoption, mainly due to the *lack of legal frameworks* that determine liabilities for potential diagnosis and treatment mistakes. In addition to this, in clinical and medical practice, strenuous certification processes are required to adopt prototypes in the diagnosis and treatment routine, and visual analytics approaches are not yet accommodated within these frames.

The large variety of potential users, as discussed in the previous sections, generates also severe challenges in the design of visual analytics approaches that can be adopted by many different institutions and that can be *reused, extended, or generalized* for different contexts. For example, suitability of an approach for clinical research does not necessarily guarantee suitability for the clinical workflow. To support a more robust design of approaches, bridging the gap between the visualization and the domain experts, including both clinical researchers and industrial partners, would be required. This becomes even more challenging when applications are developed for broader audiences.

A final challenge is related to *achieved level of integration* of automated data analysis approaches into visual analytics solutions. Automated approaches from machine learning can be used in different ways. First, they can be used agnostically, as toolboxes, where the outcome is obtained and used as input to visualizations. Second, they can be used with limited manipulation of fine-tuning functionality, where the user can actually "play" with some of the parameterizations of the automated algorithms in real-time. This can be done for visual parameter space analysis, i.e., thorough exploration and analysis of the entire spectrum of suitable input parameters with respect to the generated outputs, or for parameter sensitivity analysis purposes, i.e., to investigate the impact of (slight) parameter changes on possible outcomes of the simulations and experiments. Finally, they can be used in-line in a progressive manner: the user cannot only monitor the progression of the algorithms, but ideally also actively steer it towards data subspaces of interest on which to focus computational resources.

9.12 **Concluding remarks**

In this chapter, we introduced the general field of visual analytics. We gave particular emphasis on how the goals of visual analytics go beyond those of visualization. In visual analytics, we often deal with large, complex, multi-variate data, which need both automated approaches (e.g., from machine learning) and a human-in-the-loop strategy to be analyzed. Therefore we could say that what makes visual analytics approaches unique is their interdisciplinary nature and the interdependency of their components, whether these are the computer, the human, or the interactive interface between them. Visual analytics is a vast field; in this chapter we only touch upon several of its components. In the upcoming sections, we will discuss more specific fields of application of visual analytics to the medical domain.

Recommended reading

For a deeper understanding, we refer to the following books or essential articles:

Laurens Van Der Maaten, Eric Postma, and Jaap van den Herik, "Dimensionality reduction: a comparative review," *Journal of Machine Learning Research*, Vol. 10(66–71), p. 13, 2009.

Cristopher M. Bishop. Pattern recognition and machine learning, *Information Science and Statistics*, Springer, 2007.

Wolfgang Aigner, Silvia Miksch, Heidrun Schumann, and Christian Tominski. *Visualization of time-oriented data*, Springer Science & Business Media, 2011.

Min Chen, Helwig Hauser, Penny Rheingans, and Gerik Scheuermann. *Foundations of Data Visualization*. Springer International Publishing, 2020.

Christian Tominski, and Heidrun Schumann. *Interactive Visual Data Analysis*, CRC Press, 2020.

Visual analytics in public health

10

10.1 Introduction

Public health has a strong focus on *prevention*, and thus aims at advocating behavior and policy changes for maintaining or improving human health. This includes measures to improve the air quality, the quality of food, to limit the outbreak of acute diseases, and the reduction of chronic diseases and injuries. Though acute waves of infectious diseases and accidents causing a higher number of injuries attract a lot of attention, the major driver for health care costs are chronic diseases, such as asthma, arthritis, diabetes, and kidney failure. Raghupathi and Raghupathi (2018) mention that 45% of all Americans suffer from at least one chronic disease, and this high number is even further increasing. This is strong motivation to collect and analyze relevant data to reduce the prevalence and severity of chronic diseases. The aforementioned authors discuss a number of essential questions to be answered in this context, such as: Which of the chronic diseases are more prevalent in different regions? Which patients suffer from a certain combination of chronic diseases? What are the costs related to the prevention of chronic diseases in relation to the costs for disease management? Which attributes of the lifestyle are associated with health disorders?

For this purpose, data is collected to identify trends in human health, to derive hypotheses, e.g., related to risk factors, and to get insights in the data and the underlying phenomena. Most public health data have a *temporal character*. Moreover, the *spatial character*, e.g., spatial clustering of diseases, needs to be considered.

Visual analytics has a great potential to support the public health (PH) care sector. Interactive visual interfaces enable filtering, i.e., to restrict the amount of information to be displayed, flexible combinations of different aspects or layers of information, and an adaptation of the visual representation, e.g., to switch between various levels of aggregation. Visual analytics techniques involve pattern mining, (subspace) clustering, imputation of missing values, visual queries, as well as visualization and interaction techniques for spatio-temporal data. We describe requirements, tasks and visual analytics techniques that are widely used in PH before discussing applications. These include outbreak surveillance and epidemiology research, e.g., cancer epidemiology. We classify the solutions based on the visual analytics techniques employed.

This book chapter is based on a survey article (Preim and Lawonn, 2020). Though the article covered the subject in a comprehensive manner, the description here is shorter, focused on particularly important aspects. Moreover, it is carefully updated in particular with respect to developments around the pandemic COVID-19, which highlight the essential role of PH.

The classical definition from Winslow (1920) characterized PH as follows:

Definition 10.1. "*Public health* is the science and art of preventing disease, prolonging life and promoting human health through organized efforts and informed choices of society, organizations, public and private, communities and individuals".

Despite changes in the history of PH (Rosen, 2015), including a stronger focus on environmental health, this definition is still widely accepted.

PH activities aim at concrete measures, e.g., with vaccination campaigns, screening programs to detect severe diseases early, or measures to improve the safety in traffic or at work. PH academics acknowledge the "immense capacity" of visualization tools "to examine various dimensions of PH data including spatial, temporal and other attributes ... beyond the capacity of statistical analysis" (Joshi et al., 2017). PH experts consider visual analytics also as a means to improve the "ability to communicate findings and key messages" (Martinez et al., 2016). However, PH academics also raise concerns, e.g., that "visualization is misleading users due to misinterpretation" (Carroll et al., 2014).

As a basis for disease understanding, epidemiological research employs clinical data and population-based studies, where a representative set of volunteers in a region is involved. The identification of risk factors, the analysis of the relative risk of single factors and their combined influence, the so-called *interaction*, are primary research goals in preventive health care. We also consider urgent problems, related to the increased frequency of a health problem, e.g., in case of a food-borne or infectious disease that spread stronger than expected based on seasonal patterns.

Organization

In Section 10.2, we describe the scope of PH activities, the essential stakeholders, high-level tasks, and requirements for visual analytics support. In Section 10.3, we describe data that is frequently used in PH. In Section 10.4, we discuss visualization and interaction techniques, e.g., geospatial views and time-oriented visualizations.

We describe specific applications in different branches of PH in the sections that follow. The detection of disease outbreaks and response management is discussed in Section 10.5. In Section 10.6, we analyze a wide range of epidemiology research questions, e.g., related to cancer epidemiology, and air quality. In Section 10.7, we discuss the analysis of cohort study data aiming at the assessment of risk factors for frequent health disorders. In these studies, largely healthy volunteers (the cohort) are followed over time to characterize health risks and their influence on diseases. In Section 10.8, we discuss evaluation strategies and selected results.

10.2 Public health

PH activities typically start with gathering information about a potential health problem, e.g., after an alert, including the exploration of the available data, e.g., recent cases of a reportable disease, and go on with statistical analysis and presentation of results, e.g., a set of diagrams. We focus on health problems in a narrower sense and PH activities dealing with long-term developments of *incidence* and *prevalence*. Since these terms will be frequently used, we define them in the following:

Definition 10.2. The *incidence* is the proportion of a population that *newly* acquires a disease in a certain period.

The incidence is often stated with respect to 100,000 persons, e.g., the incidence of lung cancer in western populations is about 66 for 100,000 persons per year. Also in the COVID-19 pandemic, the incidence was often reported per country and region. For infectious diseases, however, it is often given per week.

Definition 10.3. The *prevalence* is the proportion of a population *currently affected* by a disease.

The prevalence is primarily used for assessing the burden related to chronic diseases. For a chronic disease, such as diabetes, the incidence is rather low, but since most persons live for decades with the disease, the prevalence is high.

A focus of preventive health care is a better understanding of *avoidable* lifestyle-related risk factors, e.g., obesity, low level of physical exercises, or poor nutrition and environmental factors, such as air quality. A related aspect is the analysis of disease networks, i.e., if a certain disease frequently co-occurs with another one, or whether the outbreak of a disease involves a higher risk for the outbreak of another, often more severe disease. Health care data often exhibits quality problems, such as noisy, unreliable, or missing data. Thus visual analytics solutions should consider potential quality problems and provide remedies.

PH institutions exist at various levels: from community authorities to the World Health Organization (WHO). These institutions are engaged in the comprehensive surveillance of major issues related to the health of populations. In the US, the CENTER FOR DISEASE CONTROL AND PREVENTION (https://www.cdc.gov/) also provide up-to-date information for the general public and PH experts. The NATIONAL HEALTH SERVICE plays a similar role in the UK (Tong et al., 2017).

Interventions to improve health need to be justified by an in-depth analysis of data, which are to a large extent collected for the purpose of informing health policy. Therefore there is a growing demand for *evidence-based health measures* (Ola and Sedig, 2014), which includes the need for re-evaluation whether certain measures are as effective as supposed when they were established. Whereas the effect on human health is the dominant criterion, other issues, in particular cost-effectiveness, are also considered and re-evaluated. Despite the trend towards evidence-based PH, policy development is also based on media attention for a health problem (Zakkar and Sedig, 2017).

10.2.1 Epidemiology

Epidemiology originally dealt with the outbreak of infectious diseases (Winslow, 1920). JOHN SNOW's detection of the source of a cholera outbreak in London in the 1850s was a landmark event. SNOW found a contaminated water pump as source of the outbreak. To communicate this finding, he depicted the home of the patients on a map, and thus the high frequency of patients in close proximity to the pump became obvious. Today, epidemiology, as an essential part of PH, aims at evidence-based knowledge related to the distribution of diseases. The *demographics*, e.g., the characterization of the patients in terms of age, gender, race, income levels, and family status, the spatial distribution of patients and temporal developments are core aspects. Epidemiology also investigates *exposures*, i.e., risks that may influence the health status. Environmental conditions, poisoned air or water, or a genetic variant are factors to which a part of the population is exposed. Epidemiology research aims at identifying relations between exposures and diseases in a *defined population*, i.e., the population of a specific region, eventually further restricted to an age group. A *representative* sample of this population is defined in a randomized manner and invited to participate in a study.

Correlations and causality

If a disease is correlated with an exposure, research follows to assess whether correlations imply a causal effect. Often, this is not the case, e.g., because a confounding variable is responsible for the observed effect. A famous example is a strong association of shoe size with life expectancy: people with larger shoe size die earlier. The confounding variable here is the gender: people with large shoe size are typically men and men die earlier than women (Fletcher and Fletcher, 2011).

Hypothesis-based analysis

Epidemiology research is often triggered by observations from clinical medicine, which lead to the generation of hypotheses. Hypothesis-based testing, the use of confidence intervals, the statistical significance of correlations, and the computation of effect sizes are specific examples for this statistical basis. As a further ingredient, epidemiologists employ *biological and medical knowledge* to derive hypotheses and to assess the plausibility of findings.

Subfields

Epidemiology is specialized according to organ systems and related health indicators and diseases, i.e., an epidemiologist is often an expert for a subdiscipline such as

- *Neuroepidemiology*, the field that aims, for example, at the prevention of neurodegenerative diseases, such as Morbus Alzheimer and Morbus Parkinson, analyzing the influence of nutrition, physical exercises, social relations, cardiovascular risk factors, and genetic variants on disease outbreak.

- *Pharmacoepidemiology*, the field that analyzes the use of drugs and their effects on human health, including adverse effects.
- *Cancer epidemiology*, the field that deals with tumor diseases and the influence of lifestyle-related variables and genetic variants. An important observation is that some risk factors affect a variety of tumor diseases, whereas others, e.g., some virus types, are associated with the specific risk for one type of cancer.

The specialization of epidemiologists is necessary, since the interpretation of any statistical finding requires background knowledge related to the biological and physiological processes that may explain such phenomena. At the same time, strong specialization may restrict epidemiology research. Modern large-scale epidemiology is interdisciplinary, involving experts from different disciplines, to identify and further study more complex relations, e.g., between mental illness and nutrition (Firth et al., 2018). In Section 10.6, we present visual analytics solutions for the three subfields mentioned above.

10.2.2 Study types

The selection of a *study type* is based on the research questions that should be answered and on available resources. According to Pearce (2012) study types include

- *case series*
- *case-control studies*
- *cross-sectional studies*
- *cohort studies*

Case series

comprise patients who suffer from a disease or persons exposed to a risk. These persons are monitored over time to study patterns of the development of their health status.

Case-control study

comprise a case group and a control group. The control group is as similar as possible to the case group in terms of major demographic factors, such as age, gender, and health status. However, the members of the control group are not exposed to the risk.

The British doctor's study is a famous example. This study indicated that tobacco smoking (case group) significantly increases the risk of getting lung cancer (Doll and Hill, 1956). The major result of case-control studies is the *odds ratio*, which characterizes how the chance of getting a disease is affected by an exposure. An odds ratio significantly above 1 reveals a risk factor. A special type of a case-control study is the *interventional study*, where one group is treated with an intervention, and the control group is not treated. This study type was used, for example, to assess the effects of vaccination against COVID-19 with respect to getting infected or being hospitalized.

Cross-sectional studies

have only one point in time where data related to the health status of a group of patients or healthy volunteers is gathered. Cross-sectional studies often serve to analyze the prevalence of diseases, and are therefore often called *prevalence studies*. As an example, in the COVID-19 pandemic, various antibody studies were carried out to assess how many persons in a region actually had the disease, even if they were never tested positive. An estimation of this prevalence is relevant for predicting the further development and for judging about the necessity of preventive measures.

Cohort studies

serve to understand how the prevalence and incidence of diseases develop in a group of volunteers. Since the volunteers are followed for a period of time, the term *longitudinal study* is used as a synonym (Pearce, 2012). A cohort study can be seen as a series of linked cross-sectional studies. Cohort studies are appropriate for a wider range of research questions. The analysis of the temporal development of the health status of volunteers may give hints to causal relations. If persons were exposed to a risk before getting a disease, the likelihood for a causal relation is larger compared to the pure coincidence.

Visual analytics solutions

are particularly useful for population-based cross-sectional and cohort studies since they typically involve many variables, and thus may reveal surprising associations. These study types enable a broad analysis of risk factors, whereas case studies, case-control, and interventional studies are restricted to a specific disease (and a specific treatment). These disease-specific studies are assessed with statistical methods.

Cross-sectional and cohort studies may be based on data of one or more hospitals, or it may involve data from volunteers that are representative for a *defined population*. The latter are referred to as *population-based* studies. Population-based studies involve primarily healthy volunteers, i.e., the prevalence of most diseases is low.

10.2.3 Task analysis and requirements

In the following, we discuss the target user groups, tasks, and requirements relevant to them. According to Revere et al. (2007), we distinguish between *PH experts* and *PH academics*. PH experts have to solve routine tasks, sometimes also urgent tasks related to an unusual situation, e.g., a pandemic. PH academics, on the other hand, are able to focus on exploratory investigations and more complex data analysis. The major result of their activities are scientific publications related to new insights, e.g., about risk factors. A more fine-grained analysis of stakeholders reveals among others (Ola and Sedig, 2014; Revere et al., 2007; Maciejewski et al., 2008) the following:

- *Epidemiologists* analyze data with an in-depth understanding of statistics, often to identify and assess potential risk factors.

- *Communicable disease specialists* are involved if an infectious disease spreads and contribute with their experience related to possible interventions to limit the effects of an outbreak.
- *Specialists for nutrition* provide their knowledge of food and diseases potentially related to food.
- *Environmental health scientists* analyze the air or collect samples from the ground to investigate contaminations.
- *Health policy makers* aim at changing health policy, e.g., with respect to new screening procedures.

Task analysis involves interviews with the stakeholders, observations during their activities ("look over the shoulder"), written questionnaires, and studies of publications in their area. Various authors performed a task analysis in PH being a good starting point for new developments (Ola and Sedig, 2014; Revere et al., 2007; Thew et al., 2009). Major results include information needs, sources of information, and descriptions of the decision-making process based on the available information.

Tasks

On an abstract level, PH experts face typical analytical tasks, such as identifying relations, testing assumptions, generating hypotheses, and supporting conclusions with sufficient evidence. On a more concrete level, the tasks of PH experts involved include (Ola and Sedig, 2014; Thew et al., 2009):

T1 *Exploration.* Gathering information about a health problem, exploring available data, e.g., recent cases of reportable disease, aggregating and displaying these data.

T2 *Assessment and pattern identification.* Analyzing a health problem, e.g., drill down to vulnerable subpopulations, such as children. This includes an analysis of the distribution of a disease in a population with respect to gender and comorbidities.

T3 *Associations.* Finding and analyzing associations between lifestyle-related factors, environmental factors, health risks, and diseases. Considering different strengths of associations and emphasizing stronger associations.

T4 *Verification.* The *verification* of an assessment, pattern or association relates to the quality of the data and the significance of results. A strong type of verification is the transfer of derived knowledge to another cohort to assess whether it can be replicated there.

T5 *Comparisons.* Support comparisons between populations, e.g., case and control group. Comparisons may be part of the verification process, e.g., when current data are compared with historic data to assess plausibility and decision-making.

T6 *Policy development.* Design of interventions to prevent health problems or limit their effect, including priority setting and assessment of involved costs.

T7 *Dissemination.* Informing and educating the public about health problems and strategies to avoid them; ensure awareness for potentially severe health problems.

These tasks may involve *cooperative* situations where, multidisciplinary teams jointly analyze the data.

Syndromic surveillance comprises the collection and analysis of health data for outbreak detection and response management (Ali et al., 2016). For syndromic surveillance, e.g., related to infectious diseases, the following tasks need to be supported (Maciejewski et al., 2011):

T8 *Preparedness*. Regional authorities should be trained how to respond to a major outbreak, and the health care system should provide sufficient resources, e.g., hospital beds.

T9 *Outbreak detection*. Based on the monitoring of available data and assumptions, related to seasonal patterns and disease types, an outbreak should be detected as early as possible and assessed regarding its severity.

T10 *Spatio-temporal assessment*. An outbreak needs to be monitored in space and time to understand paths of disease spreading. An analysis in different spatial scales and for selected temporal intervals is essential.

T11 *Prediction*. Based on the available data, the progress is simulated under different assumptions, e.g., with or without certain interventions established. Predictions involve uncertainty that needs to be conveyed.

Ola and Sedig (2014) discuss PH problems based on a food poisoning scenario, which occurs in an unseasonable period of the year: PH experts analyzed confirmed cases, and displayed these data on a map along with sources of water that may serve mosquitos to breed. As a consequence, map-based visualizations are essential for a wide range of PH tasks (T10).

Livnat et al. (2012) make general statements about visual analytics support for syndromic surveillance. It should support *convergent* and *divergent* thinking, i.e., on the one hand, some tasks may be supported with guidance, but on the other hand, a visual analytics system should encourage users to consider alternative decisions and assess potential consequences. Thus a system could counteract cognitive biases that lead to a narrow decision space.

Among the means to support epidemiologists, Thew et al. (2009) discuss query mechanisms and a statistics wizard, which *guide* users to statistical tests, suggests appropriate tests for the specific data, and issues warnings when problems occur that may prevent a reliable result. Furthermore, Thew et al. revealed the interest in complex analysis questions, where the combined influence of variables is analyzed.

Requirements

As general requirement, PH systems should be designed in a user-centric way to enable users to transform the heterogeneous health data to *actionable information* (Gesteland et al., 2012). The following requirements are essential:

R1 *Provide an overview of the data.*
R2 *Enable analysts to integrate expert knowledge.*
R3 *Provide familiar visualizations.*
R4 *Provide integrated information.*
R5 *Provide visual support for association analysis.*
R6 *Provide visual support for comparisons.*

The techniques discussed to fulfill R1 to R4 are primarily related to T1 (exploration).

In the following, we discuss the specific meaning of these general requirements for visual analytics in PH. This set of requirements needs to be extended for any specific application. Additional requirements may arise, for example, with respect to analytical components, spatial and temporal visualizations.

R1: provide an overview of the data

Users benefit from an overview of the available dimensions and the distribution of values for *exploratory analysis*. For a small number of dimensions, histograms may serve as an overview. For spatial data, frequency should be presented along with a map. Time-line-based visualizations, e.g., box plots over time, display a temporal development. For large numbers of dimensions or huge number of patients, more abstract visualizations are necessary, e.g., a diagram that shows for each dimension the interquartile range. An overview that emphasizes pairs of variables with strong correlations is also desirable.

R2: enable analysts to integrate expert knowledge

In particular for hypothesis-based analysis, it is essential that analysts can specify which data sets and dimensions they are interested in. This may include the specification of demographic features and the selection of volunteers based on lifestyle or variables characterizing their medical history. Moreover, analysts should be enabled to exclude volunteers they consider as outliers.

R3: provide familiar visualizations

Some visualizations, e.g., certain map-based visualizations, time-line-based visualizations, Kaplan-Meier curves, and Mosaic plots are widely used in PH. Kaplan–Meier curves display the portion of patients who survive after diagnosis for a certain amount of time. They may also be used to compare the survival between subpopulations, e.g., with different health status or to compare the survival for different kinds of treatment, e.g., to report on a case-control study. Familiar visualization techniques should be preferred over techniques primarily known to visual analytics experts. Visualization techniques also should be given names that are familiar in PH, e.g., a time-line-based visualization that indicates how the frequency of a disease changes over time is called an *epicurve* (see Section 10.4.5).

Visualization techniques based on age pyramids are widely used to show which age groups are affected and whether there is a gender effect. An age pyramid consists of two vertical histograms that indicate the number of women and men in this age group in a certain region. The number of people is shown for age groups of five years, or for age groups of one year. They can also be used to display the incidence or prevalence of a disease in this age group (see Fig. 10.1), which is referred to as *outcome pyramid* (Chui et al., 2011).

R4: provide integrated information

This requirement (R5) is related to T3 (finding associations). The complexity of PH tasks and the underlying data requires the design of a set of coordinated views.

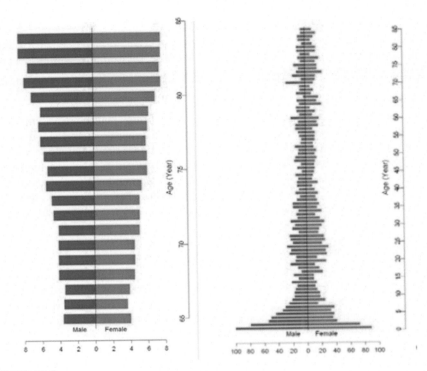

FIGURE 10.1

Age pyramid-inspired visualizations of disease frequency. **Left:** Salmonellosis in the whole United States elderly population (aged 65 to 85). **Right:** Salmonellosis cases in Massachusetts with strongly increased frequency for small children and a smaller second peak among young adults (From: (Chui et al., 2011), ©Chui et al.)

A careful selection of individual views, an appropriate spatial layout that supports the user in assessing relations and synchronization techniques, e.g., synchronized emphasis of information in different views, may support complex surveillance tasks. Overview types of visualization, in-depth display of selected data sets or dimensions, displays of relations between dimensions and map-based visualizations are typical components of visual analytics systems for PH.

R5: provide visual support for association analysis

Association analysis (T3) requires dedicated support. A visual analytics system may compute correlations for all pairwise attributes or a user-specified subset. Matrix views may color-code correlation coefficients to direct the user to strong (positive or negative) correlations. Different correlation measures may be incorporated (Klemm et al., 2016).

R6: provide visual support for comparisons

Since comparisons are essential in PH activities (T5), specific support needs to be provided. We already discussed age pyramids as a tool for gender and age comparison. Comparison support is often also needed for temporal developments, e.g., data from a current outbreak should be compared to historic data. Temporal alignment and synchronization are essential issues. Many techniques are available to support comparisons in side-by-side overviews or in an integrated manner, where different data sets are overlaid.

The requirements and tasks discussed in this section are quite general for PH. For a specific PH problem, e.g., injury or cancer prevention, further, more specific requirements arise.

10.3 **Data for public health**

We now describe the data that is acquired or already available for PH activities. The large amount of data, related to patients' symptoms, diagnoses, and treatment in hospitals and insurance companies can be used for disease understanding and for preventing diseases or further complications of an already diagnosed disease. PH-related data has unique properties that make the analysis difficult.

- The *high number of dimensions*, e.g., in population-based cohort study data, often several thousand dimensions hamper a comprehensive analysis.
- Data is *heterogeneous*, including scalar, ordinal, categorical, and binary variables. Measures derived from blood or urine samples are scalar data. The stage or severity of disease is an example for ordinal data, e.g., non-hypertensive, mild, moderate, and severe hypertension. Diagnosis, previous treatments, and prescribed drugs are examples for categorical data. There are even hierarchies of categories, e.g., respiratory diseases and cardiovascular diseases as high-level categories. Exposure to a risk is a kind of binary data, e.g., being a smoker.
- Data often have a *temporal* and a *spatial dimension*, e.g., data related to the outbreak of infectious or food-borne diseases that start from a certain place, and then distribute over time often in surprising patterns.
- Despite measures to ensure data quality, it is often far from perfect. The amount of *missing data*, e.g., patients dropping out of follow-ups in cohort studies, typically is too high to restrict the analysis to complete cases.
- Data is not perfectly *reliable*, in particular self-reported data, e.g., on nutrition behavior, alcohol and tobacco consumption is biased towards social expectations, i.e., people pretend to follow a healthier lifestyle than they actually do.

A wide variety of data is systematically collected to study *PH indicators* (Zakkar and Sedig, 2017), including:

- *public health status*, e.g., prevalence of diseases, such as diabetes
- *health risks*, e.g., high blood pressure or obesity

- *outcomes of healthcare programs*, such as cancer screening
- *health equity indicators* that indicate how similar the health status is for population groups defined by social, economic, or regional factors. Health equity is an essential goal of PH activities.
- *performance indicators*, e.g., waiting times for certain diagnostic procedures or surgical intervention

Severe diseases, such as all types of cancer, are *reportable*, and all cases are collected in specialized registers to enable continuous monitoring. The same applies to severe infectious diseases, heart diseases, and neurodegenerative diseases. Also severe injuries are recorded in *trauma registries*.

For the analysis of temporal changes, it is essential to relate the data to regulations and legislative issues, e.g., the introduction of a screening program or the prohibition of smoking in restaurants (Revere et al., 2007). The reported cases may strongly differ from the actual cases. Thus when the (reported) numbers change over time, analysts need to understand whether the likelihood has changed that a disease is actually reported, e.g., based on media attention or a different test strategy, to avoid wrong conclusions. Prescription data and over-the-counter sales of drugs are timely data, and therefore useful to analyze short- and long-term trends.

10.3.1 Population-based cohort study data

Population-based cohort studies are used to answer research questions related to the "combined effects of lifestyle, occupation, and environment, social and psychological factors and genetic predisposition on disease development" (GNC Consortium, 2014). General goals of population-based studies include:

- understanding the differences between healthy aging and beginning pathologies
- identification of pathways from risk factors to chronic diseases
- evaluation of markers for diseases in a preclinical stage to foster specific prevention measures
- assessment of geographic and socio-economic differences in health status

Population-based studies involve a representative sample of the population in the target region (recall Section 10.2.1). Strict quality insurance policies apply to all types of data acquisition. As an example, all enrolled physicians and study nurses are instructed *how* to perform a measurement, e.g., of blood pressure, to achieve the highest possible degree of reproducibility. For the same reason, the hard- and software of MR scanners employed in a cohort study needs to be kept constant in the whole four-year period of a cycle. Publications on cohort studies in epidemiology journals therefore dedicate a large portion to "Quality control" (John et al., 2001). The strong emphasis on data quality and the unbiased selection of participants are major differences to the retrospective analysis of data acquired in the clinical routine. Not all examinations that are desirable from a research point of view are actually integrated in cohort studies. Ethics, data protection, and cost-effectiveness lead to constraints for the design of cohort studies.

Whereas most of the goals can be achieved with regional and mid-sized studies (several thousand volunteers), in particular the last goal requires large, nation-wide or international studies. Cohort studies are carefully planned, including an in-depth discussion of the instruments to be used, i.e., the specific choice of examinations, questions to be answered by the volunteers, laboratory tests, and imaging.

Related to the privacy issues, data need to be consequently anonymized, which means that personally identifiable information, such as the volunteers' names are encrypted or deleted. Also the exact birth date is removed. Only the year of birth is typically registered to categorize volunteers with respect to age groups.

Image data

In modern cohort studies, imaging is regularly used to detect early subclinical signs of diseases or precursors thereof. Hepatic steatosis (fatty liver) and left-ventricular function are examples for such subclinical signs. In population-based studies, primarily MRI and ultrasound data are used. X-ray or CT involve ionizing radiation, and are thus potentially harmful, representing an ethical problem in the case of healthy volunteers. For the same reason, MRI is used without a contrast agent (Bamberg et al., 2015). In what follow, we describe two examples of cohort studies.

Rotterdam study

This study was started in 1989 with a cohort of 7983 persons aged over 55 years (Heeringa et al., 2006; Ikram et al., 2017). This cohort was repeatedly examined to understand age-related effects of health with a focus on diseases with high prevalence in the elderly. This includes the coronary heart disease, neurodegenerative diseases, and eye diseases, such as glaucoma. To enable comparability, the set of investigations was rather stable over time. Only few new tests were included in later cycles, e.g., because of wider availability or increased interest in certain diseases. The initial cohort was examined in six cycles until 2015 when the cohort was reduced to 1153 persons. New cohorts with younger participants were established in 2001, 2006, and 2014 (Ikram et al., 2017).

Key objectives of the study include the prevention of the first cardiovascular event, e.g., cardiac infarction, secondary prevention following a first event, and the prevention of chronic diseases. Gender-specific differences were considered, e.g., the concept of a *healthy menopause* was developed for characterizing women's health.

A large variety of age- and gender-specific effects was reported based on the Rotterdam study (Ikram et al., 2017). To give a few examples, it was observed that men are at a higher risk to develop coronary heart disease as first cardiovascular event, whereas women are at a higher risk to develop cerebrovascular disease with the risk of getting an ischemic stroke. The study also enabled the analysis of the combined influence of endocrine, inflammatory, and other factors on disease initiation. Thus risk markers for disease monitoring and early detection could be identified.

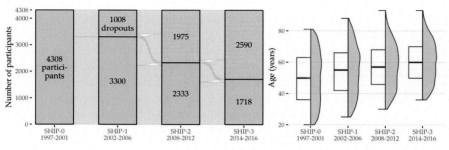

FIGURE 10.2

The number of volunteers of the SHiP study decreases considerably and the age increases over time (Courtesy of Uli Niemann, University of Magdeburg).

Study of Health in Pomerania (SHiP)

This study is carried out in the northeastern part of Germany. It was initiated in the 1990s when this region suffered from a high unemployment rate and below-average health and life expectancy after the German re-unification. It was known that differences between the East and West German population existed in terms of health indicators, such as allergies. The SHiP aimed at extending this knowledge with comprehensive data acquisition. In contrast to the Rotterdam study, a large age range of adults (20 to 79 years) was considered (Völzke et al., 2011). The SHiP aims at a broad range of diseases. As an example, complex dental and medical examinations were carried out and new hypotheses for relations between the dental status and a range of diseases were derived. In-depth interviews were carried out covering many aspects of the volunteers' social life, family history of health-related events, and working conditions (John et al., 2001). The SHiP started with 4308 volunteers in 1997 (SHiP-0) with follow-up investigations every five years (see Fig. 10.2).

Joint analysis of cohort study data

Although the above-mentioned cohort studies enable statistically significant results for frequent health disorders and moderate effect sizes, they are often not sufficiently large to study subtler effects or less frequent diseases. Moreover, it is scientifically more convincing if the effect that was observed in one study can be replicated in another one. This kind of confirmation could largely exclude specific local effects, e.g., due to nutrition patterns. The joint analysis of cohort study data is challenging, because the examinations are not completely standardized.

Summary

Comprehensive cohort study data is acquired for medical research. Most data are available for all examination cycles, however, some were added or removed based on changing research priorities and availability of instruments. The data from the Rotterdam study was widely used for image analysis research. The SHiP data was used for visual analytics research (see Section 10.7).

10.3.2 **Clinical data**

Clinical data are not the focus of most PH activities, but they add valuable information in the case of urgent health problems. *Electronic medical records* contain all information related to the hospital stay of each patient, e.g., all diagnostic results and treatments. They primarily serve for billing purposes. Thus information that would be interesting for research may not be available or is tedious to extract since no filtering of cohorts or statistical analysis of relations is supported (Bernard et al., 2015). Recently, tools were developed that support research based on medical data, e.g., the Observational health data sciences and informatics (OHDSI) system (Hripcsak et al., 2015). The OHDSI system was used by an international team with eleven partners summarizing data from 250 million patients mapped to a joint standard (Hripcsak et al., 2016). Such tools have a great potential, but the large majority of medical researchers is faced with hospital information systems optimized for billing purposes, without support for research tasks. Hospital admission and emergency department data, including basic demographics and major symptoms, are further sources of information used for the analysis of outbreaks (Gesteland et al., 2012).

10.3.3 **Other data for public health**

A wide variety of sources is employed for solving PH tasks. These include national census data and health surveys. Moreover, the temporal development of web queries related to symptoms and diseases, prescription data, and results of laboratory tests, including microbiological testing for respiratory and gastrointestinal pathogens, are useful for analyzing an acute epidemic (Gesteland et al., 2012). Ali et al. (2016) mention emergency calls, school absentees and ambulatory data as further sources for infectious disease outbreak detection. Mortality data, involving a precise classification of the cause of death, is essential for monitoring long-term trends, related, e.g., to cause of injuries or cancer epidemiology.

A *cancer registry* is an information system where comprehensive data on cancer patients is in a standardized manner to support statistical analysis and answer questions related to trends in particular types of cancer, e.g., changes in the incidence or survival rates (Bieh-Zimmert et al., 2013). Cancer registry data is available in most countries and includes gender- and age-specific incidence and mortality rates (the rate of people dying from a disease), which is spatially referenced, e.g., with zip codes (Chen et al., 2008). These registries are population-based, i.e., *all* cancer cases in the respective region are considered avoiding a selection bias. Whereas some cancer registries only represent diagnostic information (type of cancer, stage of the disease, tumor grading), others also represent the treatments and their timing supporting an analysis of the effectiveness of treatments.

A cancer registry is a special instance of a *patient disease registry* that track the incidence of a particular disease in a population. Other examples are stroke, heart diseases, and infectious diseases in different countries. Such registries provide an essential basis for establishing and updating guidelines for the diagnosis and treatment.

10.3.4 Data preparation and data management

The data from different sources needs to be loaded, validated, cleaned, and integrated. This is often a time-consuming process, which is not fully automated since the variety of formats is large (Martinez et al., 2016). A subsequent step is the storage of the data in an appropriate way that enables fast and convenient access. A classic relational database is not ideal for storing the complex and heterogeneous data of cohort studies, since it is not sufficiently flexible and leads to performance problems in the case of queries that require table joins (Angelelli et al., 2014).

A data dictionary is typically provided along with a cohort study. The SHiP, for example, contains a data dictionary with specific information about each variable, data type, admissible range, and consistency rules that define admissible combinations between variables.

10.4 Commonly used visual analytics techniques

In this section, we describe rather general techniques. Later, we describe specific problems and systems that use such general techniques, but may add some special techniques or combine the general techniques in a special way.

10.4.1 Dashboards and multiple coordinated views

In most PH applications, several views are combined and coordinated to give an overview on heterogeneous data (recall Section 9.3.9 and Fig. 10.3). General strategies for multiple coordinated views (Roberts, 2007) also apply for PH care applications. Chui et al. (2011) present a variant of multiple coordinated views, which is useful for a wide range of PH tasks. They combine three views to enable mental integration:

- an *age* or *outcome pyramid*, where age is depicted on the vertical axis
- an *age-time image plot*, where age is depicted on the vertical axis and the horizontal axis represents time
- a *timeline*, where the horizontal axis represents time and the vertical axis represents the incidence of a disease (recall Section 9.3.8)

The image plot is a 2D histogram, where the joint frequency of a disease and an age group is counted and mapped to brightness, or another 1D color scale. Such image plots may have characteristic patterns, e.g., oblique regions with increased values representing a subpopulation that suffered from a disease early and carries the disease along as they age. The three plots are aligned such that the correlation between them is easily perceived (see Fig. 10.4).

Though multiple coordinated views (MCV) is the established term in the visual analytics field (recall Section 9.3.9), PH experts frequently use the term *dashboard*

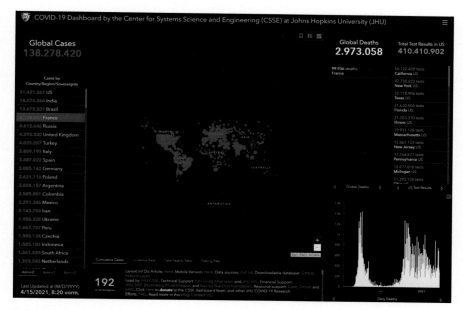

FIGURE 10.3

COVID-19 Dashboard downloaded at 4/15/2021. Map-based visualizations and time curves add to the presentation of the raw numbers (From Wikipedia, This file is licensed under the Creative Commons Attribution-Share Alike 4.0 International license.)

(recall Fig. 10.3). A dashboard presents all relevant information of a specific process or for a particular task in an integrated manner, often to support monitoring tasks, e.g., in a health office. The information typically presented in a car is a well-known example: Drivers recognize their current speed, the outside temperature, whether they are low on fuel, whether a problem occurs, such as low oil. Gauges and symbols are employed for displaying this information.

Dashboard design should consider visual perception. Gestalt laws are useful for generating layouts that are perceived well, i.e., it is easily recognizable which information belongs together. Individual views are carefully aligned and lead to an aesthetically pleasing layout (Few, 2006). Creating a great dashboard requires iterative design, e.g., prototypes are sketched and refined after careful discussions about layout, use of colors, symbols, and individual visualization techniques.

Many dashboards are created with frameworks, such as TABLEAU https://www.tableau.com/. A difference relates to the coordination between the views. Though such a coordination is mandatory for MCVs, the individual views in a dashboard are often not coordinated. PH publications include dashboards that are designed for simplicity, i.e., rather simple charts or map-based visualizations are used (Joshi et al., 2017).

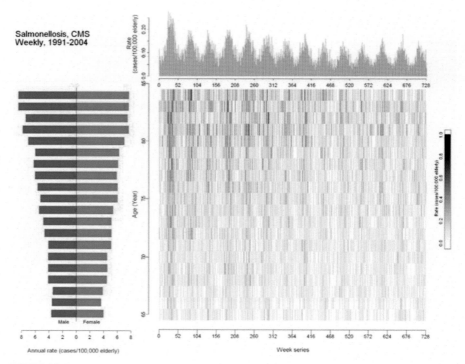

FIGURE 10.4

An outcome pyramid (left), an image plot (lower right), and a time-line-based view (upper right) are combined. Please note the common axis and the alignment of the views (From: (Chui et al., 2011), ©Chui et al.)

Dashboards and MCVs often comprise scatterplots, partially enhanced with regression lines (Angelelli et al., 2014; Steenwijk et al., 2010). Scatterplots and scatterplot matrices often display two classes, e.g., volunteers with a health risk and those without (see Fig. 10.5, left), or woman and man. The number of patients or volunteers is typically not huge. Therefore overplotting is not considered. Whereas scatterplots represent scalar values, mosaic plots are used for nominal or binary data (see Fig. 10.5, right). Graph and network visualizations are employed to study associations (T3), e.g., between different diseases, or between diseases and exposures (Bhavnani et al., 2014). Histograms and other summary views may also be incorporated (Livnat et al., 2012).

In the EPINOME system, Livnat et al. (2012) also enable to add or remove views. They discuss, however, that the typical approach to update *all* views affected by a selection for example, is often not desirable and advocate *loosely coordinated views*, where only summary views are adapted. Web-based solutions are frequently used to support easy access of various stakeholders.

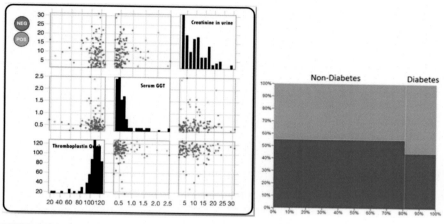

FIGURE 10.5

A subpopulation of the SHiP data is analyzed with respect to hepatic steatosis (fatty liver). The scatterplot matrix (left) displays laboratory values for volunteers with and without fatty liver. The mosaic plot (right) indicates that volunteers with a diabetes diagnosis are at higher risk for fatty liver. In both images, orange represents volunteers with fatty liver (Courtesy of Shiva Alemzadeh, University of Magdeburg).

10.4.2 Interactive subpopulation definition

Traditionally, health data are separately analyzed for women and men, and often also for different age groups to understand if certain populations are particularly affected by a disease. In an interactive system, this is supported by *demographic filtering*. Often, analysts are interested in *subpopulations* that share some risk factors or other health attributes and investigate the prevalence of diseases for them. Subpopulations may be defined in an interactive manner or by means of analytic techniques, such as pattern mining, clustering, or decision trees. Basic interactive selection techniques include range sliders for numerical values, checkboxes, or radio buttons for nominal data, such as gender. Since often several hundred variables are available, some user guidance is essential.

The challenge is to present the essential interactive facilities in an easily accessible manner. The analysis of subpopulations with statistical methods requires a minimum size. Therefore this information should be easily recognizable whenever the filter changes. When subpopulations in a cohort study or case-control study are selected, this is referred to as *cohort construction* (Krause et al., 2015).

More complex specifications may be useful, e.g., to select patients who experienced adverse drug effects within a certain interval after taking a drug. Thus certain *events*, e.g., begin/end of symptoms, begin/end of treatments, admission/readmission in the hospital, may be used to filter the data.

This way, epidemiologists may drill down further, e.g., with respect to co-occurring drugs, or the indication or severity of medical problems. Whereas the initial event-type analytics was focused on single patients, later smaller and even larger groups of patients could be analyzed by a combination of query methods and event simplification strategies. Advanced visual query methods (Gotz et al., 2014; Zhang et al., 2015) have been developed for such temporal event data based on temporal logic (Allen and Ferguson, 1994). These methods address the specification of an initial query, the presentation of the results, and the refinement of a query in a convenient manner. Though temporal event specification is essential in clinical health care and some branches of PH, it is less important for cohort study data with a few points in time only.

10.4.3 Analytical methods for subpopulation definition

Vulnerable subpopulations with a strongly increased risk for a disease are interesting. Thus when the risk of a subpopulation differs strongly from the global mean, epidemiologists want to understand the features that characterize such subpopulations. We got to know subspace clustering (recall Section 9.7) and association rule mining (recall Section 9.8) as analytical methods for identifying subpopulations in an unsupervised manner. These methods are steered by some input parameters and yield quite complex results. Interactive visualization is required to support the adjustment of the input parameters and to inspect the results.

Association rules

may characterize subpopulations and were therefore used for PH data (Hrovat et al., 2014; Niemann et al., 2014a). Typically, PH academics are interested in rather short rules, avoiding a complex description of a subpopulation. For time-dependent data, *temporal association rule mining* may represent how subpopulations change over time. Temporal association rule mining was employed by Hrovat et al. (2014) to analyze about seven million hospital discharge data, including up to 15 diagnoses along with demographic data. Niemann et al. (2014a) present the INTERACTIVEMEDICALMINER, which combines decision tree classification with association rules, and presents the results graphically to support the adjustment of parameters for decision tree and association rule computation. Their system was applied to a subset of the SHiP data (recall Section 10.3.1).

Subspace clustering

Alemzadeh et al. (2017a) used semi-supervised subspace clustering for high-dimensional PH data. They described the visual exploration of subspace clustering results for the SHiP data. As an overview, subspace clusters are displayed in a 2D view, where multidimensional scaling was applied to map the similarity between the clusters to spatial proximity (see Fig. 10.6, left). Similarity for subspace clusters relates to the overlap between the dimensions and the instances of subspaces (Assent et al., 2007). As an example, age is a dimension that contributes to different subspace clusters.

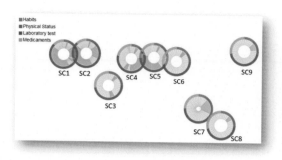

FIGURE 10.6

Overview of the subspace clusters of cohort study data (left). Each subspace cluster is shown as a donut, where donuts with a larger inner circle (hole) represent clusters with few members. Gray values represent dimensions that do not contribute to this subspace cluster. Colors represent dimensions of different categories, e.g., medication and laboratory values. The detail view (right) reveals information on the volunteers. Darker colors represent greater values (From: (Alemzadeh et al., 2017a), ©2017 The Author(s) Eurographics Proceedings ©The Eurographics Association).

For selected subspace clusters, details are presented in additional views (see Fig. 10.6, right). The colors represent different categories of the data, e.g., laboratory values, medication, physical status, and habits. To explore a selected subspace cluster in detail, scatterplot matrices are provided (recall Fig. 10.5, left). For supporting an overview, also scaled bar charts were employed. They reveal for a health risk, such as high blood pressure, the portion in the different clusters. Thus it becomes obvious when a cluster (representing a subpopulation) exhibits a risk that is strongly increased compared to the global mean (see Fig. 10.7).

Subspace clusters may have arbitrary shapes. Epidemiologists, however, prefer hyperrectangular clusters, such that a subpopulation may be described by a set of intervals, related e.g., to some laboratory values, the body mass index, and alcohol consumption. A hyperrectangle is the generalization of a rectangle to N dimensions. Alemzadeh et al. (2017a) therefore support the transformation from arbitrary shapes to hyperrectangular clusters.

10.4.4 Spatial epidemiology

The *spatial context* of health data, e.g., regional differences in demographics, social status, health risks, or prevalence of diseases is essential to understand spatial correlations. Spatial epidemiology aims at an understanding of the link between environmental factors and human health, pathways of spatial distribution, and resulting health risks (Beale et al., 2008). Spatial epidemiology has its roots also in cartography. Map data is needed to relate information to geographic destinations accurately. As a consequence, geographic information systems (GIS) may be enhanced

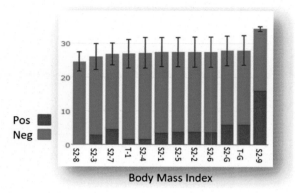

FIGURE 10.7

For all subspace clusters, red indicates the portion of volunteers with a positive outcome, e.g., fatty liver, and green represents the healthy volunteers. The *y*-axis indicates the average (and variance) of the body mass index (BMI) in these subpopulations. Members of subspace cluster S2-9 (most right) with a BMI index of about 30 have an increased risk for fatty liver. Such visualizations are provided for all dimensions that contribute to several subspace clusters (From: (Alemzadeh et al., 2017a), ©2017 The Author(s) Eurographics Proceedings ©The Eurographics Association).

to provide support for PH tasks that involve spatial information. The consequences of atmospheric pollution and climate change are examples for topics addressed in spatial epidemiology (Jerrett et al., 2010).

Disease mapping

Map-based views of disease frequency are useful if there is a rather constant background risk for getting a disease and a peak frequency is likely attributed to a source of contamination. Disease mapping is also used to detect *disease clusters*, i.e., frequent co-occurrences of diseases. Elliott and Wartenberg (2004) mention as an example that the spatially increased occurrence of infectious diseases, such as Hepatitis B and some types of cancer, lead to the hypothesis that these infections increase the risk of cancer.

Layer-based visualization

Map-based data is often represented in different *layers*, e.g., a background layer with major cities, rivers, and administrative borders and various layers, which may be combined with the background layer, e.g., locations of hospitals, diseased persons, or water reservoirs as possible sources for infectious diseases. An overlay of different layers is typically superior to side-by-side displays of the individual map layers, as already discussed by Bertin (1966). Luz and Masoodian (2014) discuss the use of a semi-transparent foreground layer to improve the interpretability of the map-based data. They use examples from epidemiology to discuss the appropriateness of three transparency levels, depending on the background complexity. Colors are widely used in spatial epidemiology. The ColorBrewer (Harrower and Brewer, 2003) provides guidance for a careful selection of colors for map displays.

Malaria Atlas project

As an example for a global activity, the Malaria Atlas project aims at integrating and communicating information on parasite rates, parasite types, and epidemiological data, e.g., population at risk, malaria morbidity, and mortality (Guerra et al., 2007). The density of information sources is quite diverse and a map-based visualization conveys this essential information. Furthermore, various charts are potentially useful, e.g., related to land coverage, such as portions of forests, rivers, and cities. Spatial queries, e.g., the search for the *k* nearest neighbors, often are supported (Ali et al., 2016).

In this subsection, we discuss general aspects of spatial epidemiology. In Sections 10.5 and 10.6, we shall discuss specific examples, e.g., those related to infectious disease outbreak and air quality surveillance.

10.4.4.1 Data

Spatial epidemiology relies on detailed geo-referenced health data along with precise population data. Only if these two sources of information are accurate, summary measures per area, such as standardized mortality rates (SMR), are meaningful. SMRs, the number of deaths divided by population size, is an essential characteristics for the burden related to different types of cancer. The underlying spatial data, e.g., various health indicators, environmental factors, and population data, are rarely independent. Thus spatial autocorrelation has to be taken into account (Beale et al., 2008).

10.4.4.2 Small area epidemiology

Elliott and Wartenberg (2004) discriminate *small area statistics* and more global statistics. Small area statistics, e.g., local indicators of spatial association, are employed to understand the effect of socio-economic differences or pollution on health. Small area statistics identify and summarize regions with an unusual incidence of diseases. Bayesian models and generalized mixed linear models are frequently applied to study spatial effects, taking into account confounding variables, e.g., the effect of air pollution on respiratory diseases, with smoking behavior as confounder (Jerrett et al., 2010).

10.4.4.3 Visualization techniques

The discussion that follow extends the short introduction to geospatial visualization in Section 9.3.7 and explains how the techniques mentioned there are used and adapted for PH.

Choropleth maps

are used to visualize *area-based geographic information* along with associated data, such as influenza cases per region (see Fig. 10.8). The data underlying a choropleth

FIGURE 10.8

A choropleth map indicates the mortality due to pancreatic cancer on a county level. The maps can be generated for a certain year and for different age groups. Users may see details, including uncertainty for the selected county as tooltip (Screenshot generated from http://www.healthdata.org/data-visualization/us-health-map at 14/4/2022).

map is an aggregation within an administrative unit, such as a county. However, administrative units are often not ideal for such aggregation, since they may strongly differ in size and do not necessarily represent physical boundaries (Beale et al., 2008). Choropleth maps are sensitive to misinterpretation in the case of incomplete or sparse data (Carroll et al., 2014). For example, they may be misleading in the case of smaller regions with a low absolute number of diseases. In such cases, Castronovo et al. (2009) suggest to re-aggregate the data, i.e., to merge adjacent districts until a significant number of cases is achieved. However, aggregation bears the risk to aggregate low- and high-risk regions, and thus ignore this information by averaging. Elliott and Wartenberg (2004) discuss *smoothing* methods that create *interpretable risk surfaces* to avoid wrong conclusions based on small numbers.

Heatmaps

are also used to display area-based geographic information. In contrast to choropleth maps, they assume continuous data over a surface and provide more precise informa-

FIGURE 10.9

A heatmap (left) shows the cases of hemorrhagic fever in Pakistan with a hotspot in the northeast. The right view contains markers for the most recent cases (From: (Ali et al., 2016), Reprinted from Public Health, Vol. 134 (Supplement C), Id-viewer: a visual analytics architecture for infectious diseases surveillance and response management in Pakistan, Page 81, ©Elsevier 2016).

tion (see Fig. 10.9). Discrete or continuous color scales are used to map nominal or quantitative data. Since data is typically not available for every unit of the map, e.g., in sparsely populated areas, missing values are often interpolated. Jerrett et al. (2010) discuss various interpolation methods for spatial data. Maciejewski et al. (2008) employ interpolation based on kernel density estimation, in particular a variable-sized kernel that adapts to the population density.

Isopleth maps

represent scalar values measured over continuous 2D data using isolines or discrete colors. Like heatmaps they differ from choropleth maps such that there are no discrete changes at administrative units. In contrast to heatmaps, where also the dependent variable is represented over a continuous range, here the range is binned, leading to a few isolines or a few different colors, instead of a continuous color scale. In spatial epidemiology, they are used frequently (Jerrett et al., 2010).

Dotplots

represent point-based health data, e.g., positions of health care institutions or cases of a severe disease (Carroll et al., 2014) (see Fig. 10.10). In contrast to choropleth and heatmaps, dotplots and isopleth maps are sparse representations, which leave room to display the underlying geographic data. Like a scatterplot, a dotplot may suffer from overplotting. Additive opacity may reduce this effect (Maciejewski et al., 2008). The exact depiction of patient data in a dotplot at a map with street level scale involves privacy issues. Therefore aggregating, e.g., at zip code level is recommended (Maciejewski et al., 2008). Table 10.1 summarizes essential properties of these mapping techniques.

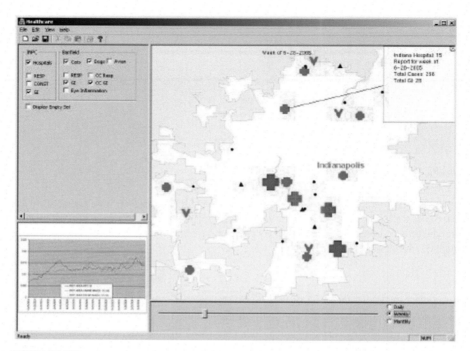

FIGURE 10.10

A screenshot of the LAHVA system. The spatial distribution of emergency departments (red crosses) and veterinary hospitals (green crosses) is shown in a dotplot. The size of the glyphs represents the number of cases. In the lower left, the temporal changes of cases are shown (©2007 IEEE, Reprinted with permission from (Maciejewski et al., 2007)).

Table 10.1 Mapping techniques and their properties.

Technique	Sparse	Dense	Continuous	Discrete
Choropleth maps		x		x
Heatmaps		x	x	
Isopleth maps	x		x	
Dotplots	x			x

Multivariate maps

Spatial epidemiology comprises several aspects, such as susceptibility of persons, exposures to risk, and actual diseases. Stacked multivariate maps, where each layer represents one of these aspects integrate different types of information (Lindley et al., 2007). To avoid visual clutter, layers of information can be displayed or hidden. The simplest multivariate maps represent for two variables the binary state whether or not a threshold is exceeded. Thus an exposure and disease frequency may be mapped with appropriate colors. MacEachren et al. (2004) use such visualizations, e.g., to compare regions with respect to the income level (low/high) and the frequency of diseases, such as AIDS (normal/elevated frequency). DiBiase et al. (1994) give an overview of multivariate map displays.

Focus-and-context visualization

Chen et al. (2008) present maps where only a circular region contains sharp high-contrast information, whereas the remaining map is shown blurred and with low contrast. Such a focus-and-context visualization may enable the focused analysis of regions of interest. *Focusing* in the context of health maps typically means that only regions where a variable exceeds a threshold are mapped to color, whereas other regions are shown in gray (MacEachren et al., 2004).

10.4.4.4 Uncertainty quantification and visualization

Uncertainty quantification and visualization is widely discussed in cartography and geo-visualization (Zhang and Goodchild, 2002). Uncertainty is due to sampling variability, biased information, or low absolute numbers, e.g., in case of rare diseases. Map-based visualizations often include interpolation, simplification, or binning of data, transformations that may reduce precision and affect interpretation. Uncertainty in map-based data also occurs with respect to positions (*location uncertainty*), values, completeness, and time (MacEachren et al., 2005). The combined influence of these uncertainty types may considerably affect trends detected in spatio-temporal analysis. Appropriate uncertainty visualization may increase trust in the data and may influence decisions, e.g., in health policy.

Uncertainty quantification

Most spatial analysis in PH is related to population data, e.g., the prevalence of diseases (recall Section 10.2). This requires up-to-date and reliable population data, a requirement that is often only partially fulfilled in developing countries or in the case of stronger recent migration (Zhang and Goodchild, 2002).

Confidence intervals should be computed, in particular for all area-level statistics (Beale et al., 2008). This information must be conveyed at least as temporarily available information, e.g., via tooltips. Confidence intervals assume approximate normality of the data. This assumption is typically not fulfilled for sparse data. In this case, a boxplot with interquartile ranges may better capture the uncertainty. Fuzzy set theory and probability theory are also used to model and quantify uncertainty in spatial data (MacEachren et al., 2005).

Uncertainty visualization

Various methods may display uncertainty, and thus reveal local differences. Most of them depict the most likely interpretation of the data along with its uncertainty. As an alternative, also different interpretations of the data may be displayed in sequential frames or combined in an animation (Fisher, 1993). User-adjustable uncertainty thresholds are also used to restrict the display of map-based data to regions where the certainty exceeds the threshold (Howard and MacEachren, 1996). Uncertainty visualizations (in maps) may be *intrinsic* such that the presentation of the data is adapted or *extrinsic*, where additional symbols, e.g., uncertainty glyphs, are added to the display (MacEachren et al., 2005).

Beale et al. recommend to analyze map displays with and without smoothing to understand the effects of statistical smoothing. Monmonier (2006) suggest to consider uncertainty as a second dimension and encode it with bivariate choropleth maps (an intrinsic visualization). Uncertainty in maps is often mapped to the saturation of a color, the transparency, or blur (MacEachren et al., 2005).

The interpretation of map-based views depends on the chosen color scale and on the spatial resolution, e.g., how spatial districts are summarized. By changing these parameters, different valid interpretations may arise (Elliott and Wartenberg, 2004). Also, Chen et al. (2008) argue for analyzing and displaying health data at different scales to derive valid conclusions. They introduced *reliability maps* that indicate the certainty of the statistical measures. They employed spatial clustering with slightly different parameters to identify *hot spots*, regions with an elevated risk for some type of cancer. Whereas some clusters are determined reliably with widely varying parameters, others are sensitive to small parameter changes.

Evaluation

The effect of uncertainty visualization on the map users' perception, interpretation, and actual decision-making needs to be analyzed in evaluations. Intuitiveness and trust in decisions are criteria in such evaluations (MacEachren et al., 2012).

10.4.5 Temporal visualizations

Temporal visualizations are an essential component of many visual analytics systems (recall Section 9.3.8, where timelines and calendar-based views were introduced). Temporal health care data is often displayed with timelines. In contrast to discrete event-based clinical data, PH data is aggregated for populations and primarily continuous, e.g., the number of cases for reportable diseases is continuously monitored. Timelines are typical components of dashboards for PH experts. Several time-dependent data may be shown simultaneously to enable a comparison, e.g., the number of cases for different diseases, or the number of influenza cases along with the number of hospitalized influenza cases. Temporal visualizations may be guided by the restriction to certain regions in a spatial context.

Epidemic curves

Timeline-based visualizations of disease-related data are often referred to as *epidemic curves* or in short, *epicurves* (Livnat et al., 2012). They have a characteristic shape, depending on the reason for an outbreak. One peak is typical for poisoned food that is consumed at one point in time, whereas for a continuous contamination, such as a water pump, the number of new cases decreases slowly. Epicurves, representing infectious diseases, typically show an increase for a longer period. The scaling of such curves is important. To display temporal intervals with low and very high values simultaneously, e.g., influenza cases, logarithmic scaling is recommended. The temporal axis should be properly labeled. Since most surveillance data are collected on a weekly basis, labeling based on weeks is favorable (Chui et al., 2011). Even if data is collected on a daily basis, there may be distortions due to a lower reporting activity on the weekend. Thus the data is often averaged over a week before being displayed. For the exploration of longer time series, temporal zoom and stronger aggregated values are possible.

Static visualizations of temporal data

Calendar-based views may be employed to display the incidence of diseases on a daily basis. A clock metaphor may be used to display the disease frequency for the 12 months of a year in different regions of a map display. In static visualizations, scalar values are mapped to color, typically with green denoting low frequency of a disease and yellow, orange, red denoting higher frequency. Typically, time is considered along a linear 1D scale. However, the incidence of diseases may follow seasonal patterns, and thus visualizations that consider the *periodic character* of time are useful (Maciejewski et al., 2007).

Animation

The second major type of time-based visualizations is animation, where one or a few variables are displayed on a map, and an animation indicates changes over time (recall Chapter 6). Spatio-temporal patterns may be directly observed in such *dynamic maps*. Castronovo et al. (2009) applied principles from cartography animation (Harrower, 2003) to generate dynamic maps that do not overwhelm the analyst. Fabrikant and Goldsberry (2005) emphasize the necessity to quantify the magnitude of change between different frames to adjust speed and duration of an animation.

Dynamic maps may be used to compare developments, e.g., the rate of Salmonella infections with the temperature development or the concurrent development of morbidity and mortality related to a disease. Dynamic maps may reveal relationships that are not recognizable in static visualizations. However, such animations need to be observed several times to enable an appropriate interpretation (Castronovo et al., 2009). Dynamic maps are appropriate for data with a high temporal frequency and require a careful selection of the temporal scale. Users may scroll in the temporal domain, and thus select a single point in time. They may also advance time incrementally with a certain step size, e.g., a week, and restrict the dynamic map generation to a temporal interval (Maciejewski et al., 2008). Harrower (2003) discuss principles for dynamic map generation and its application for environmental health data. This includes a discussion of the complexity, comprehensibility, and confidence in the observations gained from viewing such animations.

10.5 Analysis and control of epidemics

This is the first from three sections to discuss a particular class of PH problems. The outbreak of infectious diseases is a severe problem leading to rigorous surveillance activities in PH institutions. Worldwide infectious diseases are the second most frequent cause of death (25%), only exceeded by cardiovascular diseases (Gonna, 2000). An epidemic is defined as an excess of a severe infectious illness far beyond normal expectancy (Marathe and Vullikanti, 2013). Epidemics relate to *communicable diseases*. Whereas air-borne infections dominate in the Western world, water-borne and vector-borne infections, such as Malaria, are most frequent in developing countries.

Infectious diseases may have devastating effects, such as the influenza epidemic in 1918 that killed more people than World War I. The 1918 epidemic indicates the importance of PH authorities to prepare for worst case scenarios (Maciejewski et al., 2011). Due to technical developments and the increased mobility of people as well as demographic changes (urbanization), the potential for a rapid spread of infectious diseases has strongly increased (Gesteland et al., 2012). The COVID-19 pandemic has a strong effect on health, economics, and well-being of societies. In contrast to previous pandemic, strong measures have been taken to limit the outbreak. However, the side-effects of these measures are enormous. Future epidemiologists will likely analyze the spread of COVID-19 to deal with the effects of measures.

To assess an outbreak of a tropical disease, such as dengue fever, a multitude of information needs to be combined. Masoodian et al. (2016) mention the geographic distribution of human populations, patterns of land use, location of forests and water reservoirs, weather information, along with disease case reports.

Often, streaming data from various sources is analyzed in real-time to identify an outbreak early (Ali et al., 2016). Maciejewski et al. (2008) mention symptoms reported by patients in emergency departments as essential to detect outbreaks before a large number of confirmed diagnoses is available. Diseases may not only spread locally, but connections between cities and the flow of people between them may be relevant. Therefore any forecast needs to be compared regularly to currently available data. The likelihood for the outbreak of infectious, air-borne and water-borne, diseases depends on seasonal patterns and weather conditions (Ali et al., 2016). Thus syndromic surveillance requires to monitor multiple streams of heterogeneous information. *Outbreak alert* algorithms are used, but produce many false positive alarms, since at an early state an outbreak is hard to discriminate from natural variations of disease frequency. Visual analytics solutions have the potential to effectively analyze such alerts, including hypotheses generation and testing (Maciejewski et al., 2008).

The simulation of epidemics primarily serves the support of decisions about interventions. Interventions include

- *pharmaceutical measures*, such as vaccination
- *non-pharmaceutical measures*, such as information campaigns, school closures, travel restriction policies, or cancellation of events that attract a lot of persons (Guo, 2007)

These interventions are carried out to minimize the negative effects, e.g., travel between distant regions is restricted to avoid that the disease spreads in a so far unaffected region, whereas the more frequent traffic within a spatial cluster may remain unaffected (Guo, 2007).

Descriptive and generative models

Whereas the analysis of cohort study data leads to *descriptive models*, the control of an epidemic requires *generative simulation models* for predicting the further development (Marathe and Vullikanti, 2013). Simulation results include the number of persons that are expected to get ill, to get hospitalized, or to die. Moreover, simulation results indicate the demand for healthcare resources, such as hospital beds, and thus whether the healthcare system is at risk to be overloaded by critically ill patients. A testbed for experiments enables simulations under different scenarios to understand the effect of various interventions. The temporal aspect is crucial, i.e., the question of how much time is available for a certain measure to be effective. For example, even if vaccination is possible, the question is whether a sufficient amount of vaccine may be supplied fast enough.

10.5.1 **Interactive visualization**

The most straightforward support for the analysis of epidemics is an interactive visualization of all relevant information, with support for overview and detail visualization along with filtering mechanisms according to Shneiderman's mantra (Shneiderman, 2003).

Cooperative visual analysis

Masoodian et al. (2016) described interactive visualizations with a focus on tropical diseases. Geo-referenced disease data is displayed on cartographic and satellite maps. The maps are annotated with comprehensive case reports, including information on patient demographics and housing conditions. The specialty of their NU-VIEW system is the support for synchronized co-located collaborative analysis, i.e., several users analyze the data together at the same place. Based on a careful task analysis, they designed the integration of a shared display and private displays, where parts of the private display may be shared.

Mapping travel route information

A system, introduced by Dunne et al. (2015), provides visualization support focused on travel routes at different scales, since these routes are potentially important to understand diffusion patterns. The authors combine different visualizations: global flight connections are displayed as arcs, but also travel routes at lower scale, in particular daily commuting patterns, are displayed. Borders between communities that belong to frequent community pathways are emphasized and (automatic) labeling of the resulting visualizations is also discussed. A special feature, motivated by the goal to better recognize detail, is the transformation of a map with community borders to a Voronoi tessellation, which provides sufficient space to embed symbols for each community, e.g., to encode the population size.

10.5.2 Simulation of spreading

The simulation of outbreaks is a large research area (Marathe and Vullikanti, 2013). We only touch this area to understand the interface of such simulation engines, namely the input and output space. Simulations are based on assumptions and input parameters. As an example, communicable diseases are characterized by:

- a *transmission rate*, i.e., the likelihood that the disease spreads to healthy persons
- an *incubation time*, i.e., the time after infection until the disease leads to symptoms
- an *infection time*, i.e., the time after an infection when the patient may spread the disease
- the *duration of the disease* until the patient is cured or died

The transmission rate is affected by the duration of the disease and the basic reproduction number R_0. The latter was widely reported in the COVID-19 pandemic. It reflects how many persons get on average affected by a single patient. If R_0 exceeds 1.0, in the long run the majority of the population would be affected without any counter measures. COVID-19 is an example where the infection time starts before the patient develops symptoms, e.g., within the incubation time. The incubation and infection times are modeled as a probability distribution. For mosquito-borne diseases, for example, the local differences in mosquito count are essential, but can only be guessed based on land coverage data (parks have a higher count than office buildings) (Bryan et al., 2015). For infectious diseases, differences in the local population density affect the development. Such parameters are not precisely known, and thus need to be estimated, e.g., based on earlier outbreaks.

Modeling mobility and transmission

The mobility of people and the contact between individuals in geographic space determine the spread of a communicable disease. As an example for a simulation model, Eubank (2002) modeled the course of an epidemic by a *contact graph* that represents people (as nodes) and whether they had contact (as edges). This results in a graph representation of the social network of persons.

Activity graphs represent locations that are connected when people (frequently) move between them. This information is integrated in a *diffusion* model that represents how the disease spreads over time. Such a diffusion-based simulation can be applied to a wide range of diseases. Simulations aim at identifying specific locations, e.g., restaurants, or age groups that are part of a *critical transmission path*. Though such a simulation allows for accurate modeling, it requires a lot of information that is typically not available. Guo (2007) employed the simulation model from Eubank et al. for a large-scale simulation involving 1.6 million people. Based on data from the Bureau of Transportation statistics, they achieve a reliable estimate of traffic, e.g., how many persons move between certain locations.

Visualization

The simulation of spreading with detailed transportation statistics and *contact graphs* yields huge data, which needs aggregation to be displayed. Flow maps are a useful technique for displaying the movements of people. For scalability, locations may be spatially clustered or only considered if the number of people moving between them exceeds a threshold (Guo, 2007). The visualization aims at identifying spatial disease clusters to consider interventions to limit this influence.

10.5.3 Predictive analytics for the simulation of outbreaks

Simulation results depend on the choice of input parameters, such as the transmission rate. Since these parameters are estimated, they carry some uncertainty. Instead of simulating the outbreak only once, multiple simulations runs with slightly changed input parameters reveal the space of possible developments (Bryan et al., 2015). The resulting ensemble data reflect the temporal and spatial development. Bryan et al. (2015) discuss how the large variety of results that arise from varying several input parameters can be explored for assessing the resulting predictions. Due to performance reasons, not every configuration of input parameters is actually used for a full simulation. Instead, interpolations are employed to *emulate* simulation results. Bryan et al. extended an epidemic simulation system (EpiSims) with predictive views that enable an exploration and comparison of different simulation runs. As a case study, they present the simulation of a mosquito-borne disease in the Washington DC area with about 500,000 persons involved.

The EpiCanvas

The EpiCanvas (Gesteland et al., 2012) provides comprehensive information related to the development of regional infectious diseases. The focus is on an integrated display of the various streams of information. Their design is largely inspired by weather maps. The central idea is to design a tag cloud visualization that connects relevant concepts (see Fig. 10.11). The tag cloud in the concept view can be steered by selecting tag groups and specific tags relevant for the current task. The concept view supports T3, namely to show associations (recall Section 10.2.3). For the layout, various graph drawing algorithms are provided.

The size of a tag intuitively shows its frequency, e.g., of gastrointestinal pathogens in a certain temporal interval. The EpiCanvas also contains time-series graphs to display how diseases developed over time. The system is based on emergency department visit data from a children's hospital in Utah (Gesteland et al., 2012). Data for a one-year period was available, representing different outbreaks of respiratory and gastrointestinal infectious diseases. Demographic data, including location and age group, were available in addition to symptoms and microbiological test results.

Infectious disease viewer (idViewer)

This system is used to process real-time streaming data from emergency departments visits, emergency calls, and drug sales to detect outbreaks of epidemics in Pakistan

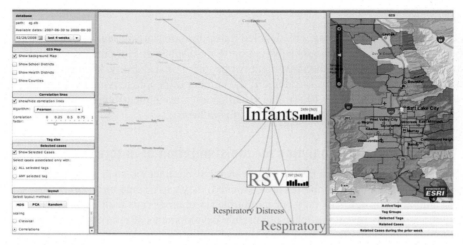

FIGURE 10.11

The EPICANVAS can be configured with respect to a temporal interval and map display options. The central part contains a tag cloud with "infant" and "respiratory syncytial virus" selected. The choropleth map displays the local incidence of the disease (Per Hans Gesteland, Yarden Livnat, Nathan Galli, Matthew H Samore, and Adi V Gundlapalli, "The EpiCanvas infectious disease weather map: an interactive visual exploration of temporal and spatial correlations," Journal of the American Medical Informatics Association, 2012, by permission of Oxford University Press).

(Ali et al., 2016). An essential component is the classification of symptoms and complaints with respect to the most likely disease. Since the likelihood for diseases depends on seasonal patterns, the seasonal character (rainfall and temperature curves) is taken into account along with the symptoms for the classification of a disease. This input is processed by a neuronal net. Taking into account the weather information increased the overall sensitivity for outbreak detection from 89% to 94% for nine major diseases. As an example, a set of symptoms that may relate to dengue fever in summer is much more likely to indicate a respiratory disease in winter. The frequency of diseases is color-coded in heatmaps (recall Fig. 10.9). A prediction component is incorporated to support response management.

10.5.4 Modeling COVID-19

Since the beginning of the COVID-19 pandemic, considerable research effort was spent on analyzing the available data and predicting the further course of the pandemic under different assumptions, with respect to political measures and human behavior. Since COVID-19 is an infectious disease, the modeling of the spread and the tasks in the analysis are very similar to a severe outbreak of influenza. However, the devastating effect of COVID-19 triggered substantially more research. As an example, Mueller and Papenhausen (2021) presented a system that analyzed the pandemic in the US based on comprehensive data at county level. This data contains demographic information, but also substantial information about the socio-economic situation, e.g., the job market and the educational level of the inhabitants. They performed their visual analysis in May 2020 when some counties were already hit hard by the pandemic, whereas others were not affected yet. Their major idea was that a county with similar characteristics like a county with a high mortality, is likely to be affected from a high mortality as well. Thus they predicted a very difficult pandemic situation in several counties for June and July 2020. Such a prediction helps to prepare the healthcare system in these counties.

   The major analytical component of their system was a pattern mining engine, i.e., they identified several patterns consisting of typically three attributes that explain why the death rate is strongly above the US mean. The age distribution is not surprisingly one of these attributes, but also a low portion of Asian people and a high portion of other migrants explain a high number of severe cases. Asian people are very likely to wear face masks and to be aware of other measures to limit the spread of an infectious disease. As a consequence, a high portion of these inhabitants is protective. Also attributes, related to the job market in a county turned to be of high explanatory power. People who have several low-paid jobs that cannot be performed at home and involve a lot of contacts carry a high risk for infection. The major visualization components include scatterplot-based views that convey the distribution of the values for the identified attributes, such as the portion of Asian population and the mortality rate. Thus the plausibility of a pattern may be visually assessed. A map view indicates where the counties with a high risk are located. Though some clusters could be noticed, it was also shown that counties with a similar risk may be far away from each other.

10.5.5 Training of outbreak response

PH experts cannot rely solely on their personal experience with previous outbreaks. Severe outbreaks are rare and do not represent a learning opportunity. Similar to the education of pilots and surgeons, training environments are essential to learn how to respond in the case of critical situations, complications, or failures of devices. Robinson et al. (2011) described a user needs study among PH experts. The need for the training of specific workflows was emphasized. For outbreak control, comprehensive training tools are essential. Such tools should provide realistic data, e.g., based on historical outbreaks and allow to simulate the unfolding of an outbreak. They should also include various decision points, where PH experts can enable interventions, such as contact tracing and vaccination of close contacts in the case of new infections. Storing these decisions and "replaying" the simulation eventually with alternative decisions is a powerful means to train appropriate response. A visual analytics framework is required to steer the simulation and to observe and analyze the effects of interventions. In the following, we describe two training systems developed to improve *preparedness* of PH authorities (recall T8, Section 10.2.3).

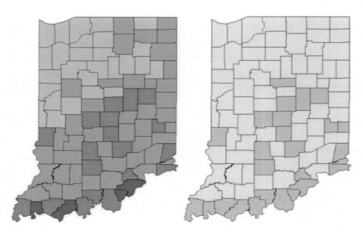

FIGURE 10.12

The course of an influenza outbreak near Chicago is simulated on a national level. The number of diseased persons in various parts of Indiana is displayed as choropleth maps. The situation without any intervention (left) and the situation after media alerts (right) are compared (From: (Maciejewski et al., 2011), Reprinted from Journal of Visual Language Computing, Vol. 22, "A Pandemic Influenza Modeling and Visualization Tool," Page 273, ©Elsevier 2011).

PanViz

The PANVIZ system (Maciejewski et al., 2011) supports state and local communities to be prepared for a severe outbreak of influenza. This visual analytics toolkit analyzes the effects of measures implemented during a simulated pandemic influenza scenario. Age distribution and population density are taken into account when simulating a pandemic starting at a certain origin. PH experts can explore the effects of the pandemic on the population. Major traffic routes are considered, e.g., the traffic between the 15 most important airports. Based on this information, the spread of an outbreak on a national level may be predicted. Once the disease reaches the nearest airport, it spreads on the following day along the airway connections. The core component is an interactive spatio-temporal view, where users can move through time and insert decision points. Thus the impact of decisions can be displayed and compared to a situation without any intervention (see Fig. 10.12). Major quantitative results of the simulation are linked to the visualization, allowing users to flexibly adjust parameters and enable intervention measures.

Epinome

Livnat et al. (2012) present the EPINOME training system. They incorporated the simulation of a pertussis outbreak using detailed representations of social networks and contact patterns. The underlying simulation is stochastic, i.e., multiple runs of the simulation lead to different results, thus representing uncertainty in the prediction.

The visual analytics system combines a large number of views along with considerable flexibility to adjust the layout, i.e., add or remove views depending on the current task. In addition to map-based views, epicurves, and a list with the latest new cases is displayed for an in-depth analysis. An elaborate filtering mechanism was included to enable a focus on geographic regions or demographic groups. The authors discussed the value and challenges of coordination between views. The views are *loosely* coordinated, i.e., only summary views are adapted when the user brushes a region. Too many adjustments after filtering were found to be confusing.

10.5.6 Zoonotic diseases

Animal diseases may be important to human health if the companion pets of a human are effected, e.g., by influenza. Respiratory symptoms occur in dogs approximately ten days earlier than in accompanying humans. Therefore data related to diseases of pets may be analyzed to create warnings for a human outbreak. The LAHVA system (linked animal-human health visual analytics) was a pioneering work with respect to the joint analysis of human and animal health data (Maciejewski et al., 2009, 2007). They employed ED visit data, data of pet owners, and data from veterinary hospitals, e.g., related to respiratory diseases of dogs. The LAHVA system (recall Fig. 10.10) combines a statistics component and a visualization component. The number of cases over time is presented as timeline, to which data transformation, i.e., logarithmic transform, was applied. Diseases are categorized as respiratory, gastrointestinal, and eye inflammation. Seasonal trends were detected with seasonal trend decomposition. A spatial view shows the positions of emergency departments and veterinary hospitals with glyphs scaled according to the number of cases in the selected temporal interval.

Table 10.2 summarizes essential visual analytics systems for outbreak detection and training.

10.6 Visual analytics for epidemiological research

In this section, we give an overview of visual analytics solutions for epidemiological research, a second category of important PH problems. The target user group for the solutions described in the following are *PH academics* doing exploratory analysis to generate new hypotheses in selected applications. In contrast, the solutions described in the past section address PH experts performing routine tasks or, in the case of an outbreak, urgent problem-solving. Since these situations are fundamentally different, we dedicate special sections to both.

10.6.1 Pharmacoepidemiology

Drugs may control symptoms, but they are often related to adverse effects. These effects have a high impact on the healthcare system, and therefore pharmacoepi-

Table 10.2 Major visual analytics systems for outbreak detection.

System	Key Features	Key Publications
id viewer	Combined analysis of diseases and weather conditions	Ali et al. (2016)
Epinome	Ensemble simulation, map-based views, loosely coordinated views, and epicurves	Livnat et al. (2012)
Outbreak training	Data of historic outbreaks used for decision support	Robinson et al. (2011)
PanViz	Use of transportation statistics, predict consequences of interventions, choropleth maps	Maciejewski et al. (2011)
LAHVA	Combined analysis of human and animal health, dotplots	Gesteland et al. (2012)
EpiCanvas	Tag cloud visualization of concepts to study associations, graph drawing	Maciejewski et al. (2007, 2009)
nu-view	Analysis of tropical diseases, collaborative visualization	Masoodian et al. (2016)

demiology, as discussed in Section 10.2.1, is an important branch of epidemiology research. This applies primarily if several drugs are taken together, if drugs are taken for a longer time, and if patients are elderly with a reduced kidney function that is less capable of segregating drug components. Despite rigorous testing before drugs are admitted to regular use, rare but severe unwanted effects may arise and registration of such *adverse drug effects* is mandatory.

Adverse effects reporting

The adverse effects reporting system of the Food and Drug Administration in the US registered about 1.8 million adverse drug effects (ADE) in 2017, from which about 164,000 lead to death of the patient. The system serves for detecting anomalies as a prerequisite for a detailed analysis of the cases and explanations of the ADEs. An ADE is stored with the following properties (Mittelstädt et al., 2014):

- indication, i.e., the reason why the drug was prescribed
- co-occurring drugs
- adverse reaction
- laboratory results
- outcome, i.e., the severity ranging from reactions that require intervention to life-threatening situations and death

The entries are categorized into effects that are mentioned in the product documentation (expedited) and non-expedited ADEs, to which approximately half of the entries belong. This data is stored along with basic demographic information.

Data mining

Classic approaches for identifying adverse drug effects rely on data mining, primarily the search for association rules, with a minimum support and lift (recall Section 10.4.3) and Bayesian classifiers. As an example, Chazard et al. (2011) identified 236 ADE detection rules related to about 115,000 hospital stays in France. However, rare events with a frequency only minimally above the expected frequency are hardly detected. Moreover, confounders often are not identified.

Visual queries

Monroe et al. (2013a) discuss a visual query approach to identify temporal events in a drug-related database to study interactions between drugs. They support the visual specification of interval-based events, e.g., the search for overlapping intervals representing drugs that were given partially at the same time and the search for point and interval-based events, e.g., whether a symptom (point event) occurred during an interval, where a drug was given. Also the absence of an event can be searched for.

Visualization support

Mittelstädt et al. (2014) introduce visual analytics-based hypotheses generation with an overview of drugs and adverse effects as well as interactive features to drill down, e.g., to search for co-occurring drugs for the same indication. Moreover, they support hypothesis-driven testing by an advanced query interface that enables the selection of drugs, adverse effects, and temporal intervals that characterize when the adverse effect happened in relation to treatment time.

For the overview, the frequency of ADE is mapped to the size of circular glyphs, directing attention to more frequent ADE. The ADEs are color-coded with respect to the severity. Concentric circles are generated to represent how often a drug leads to ADEs that require hospitalization, to life-threatening situations, or death. A temperature metaphor was used for the color scale with "hot" values (red, orange) representing the most severe events.

The automatic component also employs a significance analysis based on the odds ratio (recall Section 10.2.2). Thus the n most significant ADEs are emphasized. Temporal overviews are provided to indicate seasonal patterns of ADEs.

10.6.2 Surveillance of air quality

"With the rapid development of industrial society, air pollution has become a major issue in the modern world that has attracted increasing attention from the public and governments because of its impact on human health and societal development" (Zhou et al., 2017). Numerous studies investigated *how* air pollution actually affects human health (Devalia et al., 1997; Peden, 1997), and thus demonstrate causal effects. Air pollution is considered responsible for 3.2 million deaths in 2010 worldwide (Lim et al., 2012). Moreover, many respiratory diseases are considered to be caused at least partially by air pollution. As a consequence, monitoring air pollution, e.g., levels of respirable dust and NO_2, is regularly performed to identify changes in air pollution patterns and the influence of vehicular traffic, factories, terrain attributes, and meteorological aspects on air pollution. This allows analysts to detect sources of excessive air pollution and supports decision-making about measures to improve air quality. Since air quality problems were especially severe in fast-growing Asian cities, major efforts were carried out there first (Qu et al., 2007; Zhou et al., 2017).

Data

Data is available in high quality and high spatial resolution. Air quality monitoring stations provides streams of data. However, the analysis is carried out at a certain temporal granularity. Often hourly measurements are employed (Du et al., 2016). Preprocessing is required to remove obviously wrong sensor values (Du et al., 2016). Air quality data typically relates to six scalar values representing fine dust ($PO_{2.5}$, PO_{10}) and (CO, NO_2, O_3, SO_2). The surveillance of air quality requires the visualization and analysis of spatio-temporal air quality data sets (Qu et al., 2007; Zhou et al., 2017).

Requirements and tasks

The spatial character of air quality data requires map-based visualizations. The temporal character also needs to be displayed. In addition to the linear time component, the periodic character of air quality data is also essential, e.g., daily, weekly, and seasonal periods. Air quality data is moderately high-dimensional. Thus techniques such as parallel coordinates, may be used to show the data of selected stations. Analytical components may help to identify strong correlations, or to group stations with similar air quality or to analyze timeseries data to select and emphasize important intervals. Emissions due to vehicular traffic and industry should be integrated to support the identification of the *causes* of elevated pollution (Du et al., 2016).

Multiscale visual analysis of air pollution data

A first system for monitoring air quality (in Hong Kong) was presented by Qu et al. (2007). The indicators of air quality data were displayed with parallel coordinates and in a separate view, weather data was presented. Whereas air quality is often analyzed on a local or regional level, it is also interesting to analyze large-scale patterns, e.g., on a country or even international level. Zoomable user interfaces, focus-and-context visualizations, and displays that automatically adapt to the amount of data to be displayed, are viable solutions. Du et al. (2016) introduced the AIRVIS system that enables in-depth analysis at the country level. Calendar-based views are employed to show temporal data. For a station selected in the map, these views are presented as tooltips (see Fig. 10.13).

Visual analytics of air quality data

The system presented by Zhou et al. (2017) was motivated by a project in Chinese cities. The underlying data represent six typical pollutants recorded at 946 stations in

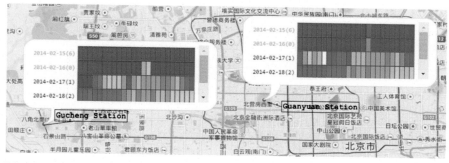

FIGURE 10.13

A map-based view with tooltips for two selected stations. The tooltips contain a scrollable view that initially color codes air pollution for four successive days on an hourly basis (From: (Du et al., 2016)).

190 cities covering a temporal range from July 2014 to May 2015. The data representing the amount of pollutants was averaged for both 8 and 24 hours. Their visual analytics system comprised multiple coordinated views:

- a map view with the monitoring stations
- a view where the air quality is clustered
- a *story line* that depicts changes of the air quality indicators per monitoring station over time

A hierarchical clustering enables the analyst to inspect clusters at different levels. To explore the hierarchy, a treemap view is provided. The air pollution data is categorized in lower, moderate, and higher values of a pollutant. The temporal course of the information is aggregated to daily, weekly, monthly, and yearly patterns. The visualization component supports a wide range of analysis tasks, including an overview of temporal developments and a fine-grained analysis.

Discussion

Typically, the risk of individuals is computed based on their home address. Pollution, however, may be quite different at their working place or other essential places of their activity space. This limits the expressiveness of small neighborhood statistics (Jerrett et al., 2010). Predictions of air quality are typically related to pollutant concentrations, land use, and traffic. Since the quality of such data is often limited, satellite imaging as a remote sensing technique is discussed as an alternative (Jerrett et al., 2010). From a PH point of view, it is important to correlate measures of air pollution with the incidence of respiratory diseases to provide orientation for political measures.

10.6.3 Cancer epidemiology

Cancer epidemiology is an essential field due to the high incidence and mortality of cancer (recall Section 10.2.1). Cancer epidemiology deals primarily with the identification and assessment of risk factors. An essential aspect is the spatio-temporal analysis, e.g., whether a certain type of cancer is uniformly distributed in space, time, and space-time or whether there are certain hot spots. A more fine-grained analysis also investigates the stages at which the tumor disease is diagnosed, i.e., whether there is a higher frequency for late-stage colorectal cancer in a certain region (DeChello and Sheehan, 2007). Such an analysis could give rise to campaigns for early detection measures.

Bieh-Zimmert et al. (2013) discuss scalable visualizations to support the exploratory analysis of cancer registry data. Such data is typically analyzed with hypothesis-driven statistics. Simple diagrams, such as histograms, bar charts, and pie charts are used to convey major facts. Bieh-Zimmert et al. (2013) provide an initial prototype for cancer registry data that employs parallel sets to reveal relations, e.g., between different age groups and frequent locations of tumors.

Spatio-temporal analysis

The commercial software Biomedware (https://www.biomedware.com/) provides support for analyzing cancer registry data. Space-time clustering may be performed and the results are visualized along with various map types to identify regions and temporal intervals with significantly increased incidence of a certain cancer type. As an example, Nordsborg et al. (2014) provides a visual analysis of breast cancer data from the Danish cancer registry. SATSCAN (https://www.satscan.org/tutorials.html) is another commercial software for analyzing disease clusters. The SATSCAN website lists numerous publications, where the software was used for analyzing georeferenced health statistics, e.g., for colorectal cancer (DeChello and Sheehan, 2007).

Iqbal et al. (2016) analyzed a large volume of patient visit data to better understand diseases associated with cancer. Data from the National Health Insurance Claims database was employed for this research. The data relates to 782 million patient visits, representing 20 million unique patients. Compared to epidemiological studies, however, fewer dimensions were available. In addition to age and gender, the procedural codes for diseases were stored. For each patient, a disease-disease association was assumed if the patient had both diseases within a 36 month period.

Animated display

For nine types of cancer, Iqbal et al. (2016) found that some chronic diseases, such as diabetes, are associated with a moderately increased risk, e.g., for breast and colon cancer. They displayed these associations for the entire population and for persons of certain age groups. Whereas most time-varying PH data is visualized with timeline-based techniques, Iqbal et al. employ animation and refer to their system as CAMA (cancer association map animation). The animation conveys how the prevalence of diseases changes depending on age. Animated glyphs represent the co-morbidities of chronic diseases and cancer.

Table 10.3 Major visual analytics systems for epidemiological research.

Application area	Key Features	Key Publications
Cognitive aging	Advanced data management, display of fiber tracts and related statistics	Angelelli et al. (2014)
Food-borne diseases	Analysis of arsenic in different food categories	Johnson et al. (2010); Sims et al. (2011)
Adverse drug effects	Overview of indication, frequency, and outcome	Mittelstädt et al. (2014)
Air quality	Spatio-temporal analysis of pollutants along with weather data	Qu et al. (2007); Zhou et al. (2017)
Asthma research	Relation between cytokine levels and asthma, bipartite graphs	Bhavnani et al. (2014); Jerrett et al. (2010)
Cancer epidemiology	Animated bubble charts, colored circular glyphs	Iqbal et al. (2016); Bieh-Zimmert et al. (2013); Nordsborg et al. (2014)
Prostate cancer	Cohort definition, display of cohort at four levels	Bernard et al. (2015)

Table 10.3 summarizes major applications in medical research, for which visual analytics solutions were developed.

10.6.4 Investigation of frequent chronic diseases

As an essential example for the use of visual analytics in PH, Raghupathi and Raghupathi (2018) investigate the burden related to the most frequent chronic diseases with respect to regional differences, gender differences, and other demographic variables, such as race and gender. The analysis is focused on the United States and based on data from the Center for Disease Control. In addition to the mere prevalence of diseases, such as diabetes, chronic heart disease, and kidney failure, the severity (hospitalizations, deaths) is also considered. Moreover, health risks are represented in the data, such as obesity, smoking, and drinking behavior or low physical activity.

Without advanced computations, e.g., for prediction, the authors focus on descriptive statistics. The statistics reveal significant gender- and race-specific differences that enable to focus prevention on regions and subpopulations that are particularly vulnerable. The major findings are communicated with a series of rather simple visualizations. Choropleth maps (recall Section 10.4.4) are employed to convey the local differences in the prevalence of diseases and health risks. Bar charts indicate per region the chronic diseases with the largest prevalence. Scatterplots and regression coefficients indicate relations between health risks and diseases. Also the relation between different diseases are analyzed and visualized by means of scatterplots and regression lines. Such an analysis may produce a number of interesting details that can lead to actionable consequences. As an example, also the relation between an acute disease, such as influenza, and a chronic disease, such as Asthma, may indicate whether patients with a chronic disease should be vaccinated with a high priority.

Also the interaction between mental health problems and chronic diseases is a relevant research topic to improve health at a population level.

10.7 Visual analytics of population-based cohort study data

We now discuss a special problem in more depth, namely the analysis of population-based studies (recall Section 10.3). Population-based studies involve healthy volunteers, no patients, as the research described in Section 10.6. The available data is much more comprehensive compared to clinical data, since the volunteers get a wide range of examinations and interviews lasting for one or two full days.

The design, conductance, and analysis of such studies is a major task for PH academics. These specialized epidemiologists should be enabled to reveal also subtle effects of lifestyle and environmental factors on human health. The wealth of data acquired in such studies enables a range of retrospective research goals that may not be completely anticipated when the cohort study was designed.

Since population-based data contain randomly selected participants, many diseases and injuries are rare. Therefore the focus is on the following:

* frequent disorders, such as adipositas or fatty liver, known to be risk factors for a number of diseases
* frequent diseases, such as diabetes and coronary heart disease

Population-based studies aim at an understanding of complex interactions between lifestyle, genetics, and the outbreak of diseases.

10.7.1 Visual analytics and radiomics

Modern cohort studies involve medical image data, such as ultrasound or MRI (recall Section 10.3.1) to characterize the presence or absence of pathological abnormalities. As an example, the SHiP data contains the diagnosis of fatty liver based on ultrasound data. Despite efforts to standardize the process, manual diagnosis is to some extent subjective. Thus automatic solutions are also considered to provide more reliable information.

Based on a segmentation of organs or other relevant structures, *imaging biomarkers* may be derived to characterize the morphology, e.g., the size, volume, circumference, compactness, or non-sphericity of anatomical structures. A whole branch of research in radiology relates to the diagnostic value of features derived from image data. Inspired by genomics data, this branch is referred to as *radiomics*. Radiomics features are particularly interesting if they serve to identify diseases at a preclinical stage. Most applications aim at the characterization of tumor diseases but, of course, a broader range of research questions is possible, e.g., related to neurodegenerative diseases or back pain. The combination of radiomics and visual analytics has a great potential (Bannach et al., 2017; Meuschke et al., 2018b). Radiomics features can be used for content-based image retrieval and cohort construction (recall Section 10.4.2).

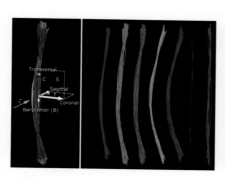 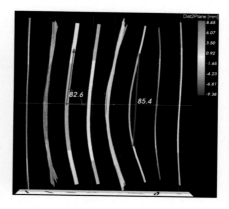

FIGURE 10.14

Visualizing the spinal canal variability in a cohort of patients. The side-by-side visualization serves to explore the different modes and to detect outliers (From: (Klemm et al., 2013), ©2013 The Author(s), Eurographics Proceedings, ©The Eurographics Association).

Image analysis

Most radiomics-related research is carried out by radiologists and relies on manual segmentation. This involves a limited accuracy and reproducibility. For large or mid-sized cohort study data, it is also not feasible, since too many data sets need to be processed in a tedious manner. Thus there is a need for (semi)automatic processes to derive radiomics features.

Automatic segmentation is challenging due to the large variety of anatomical and pathological variants. MRI and ultrasound data, the prevailing modalities in cohort studies, exhibit more artifacts than CT data. The choice of image acquisition parameters is a trade-off between patient comfort, image quality, and costs (for scanning thousands of volunteers). As a consequence, the image quality might not be ideal. On the other hand, epidemiology data comes with a lot of demographic data, e.g., gender, weight, height, and age, which may be employed to decrease learning costs for a machine learning image analysis (Tönnies et al., 2015).

Applications

Klemm et al. (2013) used the SHiP data to analyze the shape of the lumbar spinal canal to investigate whether it is associated with lower back pain, based on a hypothesis of the epidemiologists. After the lumbar spine was extracted and transformed to a 3D surface model, its centerline was generated as a representative for the lumbar spine shape. This kind of abstraction turned out to be useful to characterize such elongated shapes. Afterwards, these centerlines are clustered using a similarity measure that takes the curvature values along the spine into account. To visualize these clusters, a ribbon-based visualization was designed (see Fig. 10.14).

In their subsequent work (Klemm et al., 2014), spine shape variation is additionally put in relation to a multitude of other patient variables, such as gender and

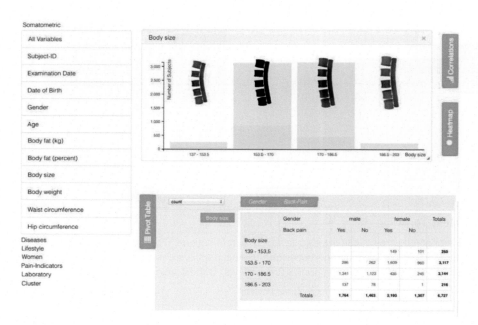

FIGURE 10.15

Visual analytics for heterogeneous cohort data, where spine shape is correlated with other patient variables, e.g., gender, height, and pain (©2014 IEEE, Reprinted with permission from: (Klemm et al., 2014)).

height, to support a more general population-based analysis. The data is aggregated using pivot tables, and histograms are used to show the distribution of a certain parameter. Based on an analysis workflow, they developed a web-based framework that supports the generation of hypotheses and their statistical analysis. All variables in the cohort are listed, the expert can drag and drop certain variables onto the main canvas, which leads to a representation of the mean lumbar spine model of the patients in the selected group (see Fig. 10.15). Additional refinement or selection of new variables results in a visualization showing correlations. With this framework, epidemiologists were able to explore shape information of the lumbar spine and its influence on diseases.

10.7.2 Identification of strong correlations with disorders

Due to a large number of variables, epidemiologists benefit from an automatic analysis related to potential associations between lifestyle-related variables and disorders, such as increased breast density, which is a known risk factor for breast cancer. Klemm et al. (2016) presented the 3D regression heatmap to analyze correlations between variables. Their idea is to let the experts input simple regression formulas, e.g., *Cancer* $\sim X + Y$, to explore the correlations. This calculates all combinations of pairwise variables for a correlation of cancer by using the R^2 metric. For the visualization, a heatmap was employed. When an expert typed $Z \sim X + Y$, a regression cube was generated showing for every slice a 2D heatmap of correlations. The downside of their approach was the computation time: a data set of 100 features needs roughly 14 h to compute $Z \sim X + Y$.

10.7.3 Data quality

Visual analytics may help to identify and characterize quality problems in cohort study data, such as outliers, missing values, and double counts (Johnson et al., 2010). Severe outliers, for example, are preattentively identified in an appropriate visualization and as a consequence, outlier removal may be considered. Johnson et al. argue that visual analytics applications should "clean up the data or make the analyst aware of the shortcomings in the data" (Johnson et al., 2010). Few attempts were made to assess and improve the quality of PH data. Shneiderman and Plaisant (2019) recently provided a discussion of visual event analytics with a number of examples from health care, including their use for detecting data quality problems. As a specific example, an appropriate visualization clearly revealed that some patients were recorded to be admitted to the hospital much more often than being dismissed, a typical example where data relevant for billing is correctly registered and less relevant data contains errors. There are general strategies to clean data using visual analytics (Gschwandtner et al., 2014), but no specific solutions for PH. The exception is related to missingness, which we discuss in what follows.

Missingness

is an essential quality problem that occurs widely. In the evaluation of a visual analytics solution for cohort study data, PH academics encouraged "techniques for detection and handling of missing data," e.g., the presence of incomplete data needs to be clearly communicated (Steenwijk et al., 2010). Missingness may occur in one cycle of a longitudinal study, i.e., the values for one participant are not complete, or between cycles, where participants do not show up in a later stage (*drop out*). *Missingness maps* (Honaker et al., 2011) may serve to identify patterns, i.e., situations where missingness is not completely at random (see Fig. 10.16). There are various strategies to cope with missingness (Sterne et al., 2009):

- *Complete case analysis*, where only complete datasets are analyzed
- *Single imputation*, where missing values are replaced with a median or average value
- *Multiple imputations*, where dependencies between variables are considered and multiple replacements are computed

The first two strategies are straightforward to realize but not appropriate for typical PH data. If only complete cases are considered, the number of cases often shrinks

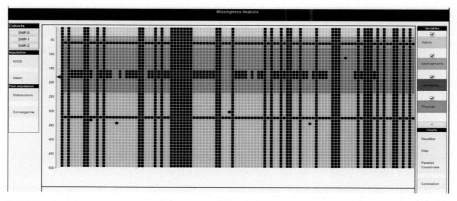

FIGURE 10.16

Overview of missing data from an epidemiologic study: Rows represent variables and columns show volunteers. Missing values are indicated in black. Completely black columns represent drop-out volunteers (From: (Alemzadeh et al., 2017b), ©2017 The Author(s), Eurographics Proceedings, ©The Eurographics Association).

drastically. The resulting subset may be no longer representative, if the missingness is not completely at random, i.e., the likelihood of a missing value for one variable depends on the value of another variable. Single imputation preserves all data sets, and thus also the representative character. However, the median or average is often not a good guess for the missing value. If all missing values are replaced with the (same) average value, the variability of the distribution gets reduced.

Multiple imputations are based on a regression analysis: for a variable v_1 that is affected by missingness, the (linear) correlation to all other variables is computed. To save computational effort, only variables with a high correlation (e.g., one of the N highest values or above a threshold) are used for the *prediction matrix*, which is employed for imputing the missing value. Imputation is performed several times, leading also to an estimate of the uncertainty involved. In addition to the size of the predictor matrix, the number of iterations influences the computational effort. The default value for this number is often five (Alemzadeh et al., 2017b).

10.8 Evaluation

Even if the development of a visual analytics system is based on an extensive requirements analysis, the prototype needs to be evaluated before any valid claims can be made regarding the benefit for the target users. Systems should be evaluated with respect to their ability to prevent errors, i.e., misleading information display, and with respect to their ability to support evidence-based explanations.

Evaluations of PH activities require the actual use of the systems by PH experts doing "real" work with representative data (Zakkar and Sedig, 2017). A typical lab experiment with a short timeframe is not sufficient. Informal evaluations with a few experts and different instruments, such as thinking aloud, video analysis, and interviews are more promising. Insight-based evaluations may be carried out to understand the potential of a VA solution for knowledge discovery (Saraiya et al., 2005).

Other publications gather feedback based on a presentation of the prototype or a video that illustrates how the prototype is intended to work. Such a video presentation was used, e.g., by Masoodian et al. (2016) and the discussion with four physicians, including two epidemiologists who revealed some insights and ideas for extensions, e.g., related to a better support of cooperations.

Klemm et al. (2014, 2016) were inspired by the seven evaluation scenarios discussed by Lam et al. (2011) and chose the *visual data analysis and reasoning* scenario to evaluate their systems. Klemm et al. (2014) for example discussed how two epidemiologists employed a system for analyzing cohort study data for hypothesis generation and testing with an in-depth discussion of understanding associations, use of clustering, and detailed inspection of clustering results. Gesteland et al. (2012) employed a *technology acceptance model* (Venkatesh et al., 2003) in their evaluation of the EPICANVAS. According to this model, they questioned the *intent to use*.

The EPINOME system was extensively evaluated (recall Section 10.5.5 and (Livnat et al., 2012)). Ten outbreak scenarios from which the 27 participants got a random selection of four and were enabled to use the system, including the assignment of interventions, such as prophylaxis of high-risk contacts. The participants were selected to be as representative as possible for the target user group in terms of age, responsibility, experience, and gender. The underlying data is realistic: it discriminates the reported cases and the actual (higher) number of cases. The simulation considers also paradox effects, i.e., systematic contact tracing increases the number of reported cases, but reduces the actual number of cases since some cases can be avoided by warning or vaccinating contact persons. The users appreciated that they can analyze what-if scenarios in detail.

Zakkar and Sedig (2017) performed an informal evaluation with a demonstration part, an exploration part, and a feedback interview. Seven PH experts with different background and experience were recruited from health research centers. Although the used visualizations, prepared with TABLEAU, appear rather simple, users said that information overload and clutter needs to be avoided. They prefer simple charts, and some were even skeptical that a choropleth map may be interpreted wrongly.

In summary, different evaluation methods are used to assess the benefit of visual analytics systems in PH, including gathering informal feedback, the use of questionnaires, the analysis of the reasoning processes, distributed cognition, and technology acceptance models. The evaluations focus on the overall impression and usefulness of systems.

10.9 Concluding remarks

Public health employs large, heterogeneous, partially incomplete data that is often geo-referenced and time-dependent. This complex data is extremely challenging for our cognitive abilities. Visual analytics solutions may support knowledge discovery and problem-solving if the needs of the different stakeholders, such as epidemiologists and environmental health specialists are adequately addressed. A wide variety of visual analytics techniques and strategies are incorporated in PH applications, including graph-based visualization, (subspace) clustering, dimension reduction, coordinated views, regression-based visualizations, and various time-based visualizations. Most systems contain multiple views, histograms, scatterplots, and timelines for temporal data. Different variants of clustering are widely used to analyze subpopulations. Clustering results are displayed along with a variety of visualization techniques, typically by color-coding the membership of items. The limited completeness and reliability of the underlying data is rarely considered. Most systems take the loaded data for granted and apply analytic and visualization techniques directly. Whereas incompleteness is obvious and may give rise to the use of imputation strategies, unreliability is more difficult to quantify, which would be a prerequisite for an uncertainty-aware visual analytics process.

Many systems support the spatio-temporal analysis of disease-related data. They are designed to afford comparisons at different temporal and spatial scales and are typically realized as multiple coordinated view frameworks. Outbreak surveillance systems often incorporate simulation to enable predictions, and thus to directly support decision-making with respect to possible interventions.

Despite the strong potential and in-depth research activities from both visual analytics and PH experts, simple and often static visualizations dominate in routine practice (Zakkar and Sedig, 2017). A tight coupling of visual analytics and statistics is of utmost importance. Though visual analytics solutions often help to detect patterns and correlations, ultimately they are supposed to favor an *understanding* of the underlying mechanisms, e.g., biological and physiological processes that *explain* the findings.

Recommended reading

The following articles are particularly useful for an in-depth understanding of visual analytics solutions in public health.

Shehzad Afzal, Ross Maciejewski, and David S. Ebert. "Visual analytics decision support environment for epidemic modeling and response evaluation," *Proc. of IEEE Symposium on Visual Analytics Science and Technology*, pp. 191–200, 2011.

Ross Maciejewski, Stephen Rudolph, Ryan Hafen et al. "Understanding syndromic hotspots-a visual analytics approach," *Proc. of IEEE Symposium on Visual Analytics Science and Technology*, pp. 35–42, 2008.

Oluwakemi Ola and Kamran Sedig. "The challenge of big data in public health: an opportunity for visual analytics," *Online Journal of Public Health Informatics* Vol. 5(3): 223, 2014.

Bernhard Preim and Kai Lawonn. "A survey of visual analytics for public health," *Computer Graphics Forum*, vol. 39(1), pp. 543–580, 2020.

Wullianallur Raghupathi and Viju Raghupathi. "An empirical study of chronic diseases in the United States: a visual analytics approach to public health," *International Journal of Environmental Research and Public Health*, Vol. 15(3), 431, 2018.

Visual analytics in clinical medicine

11.1 Introduction

Clinical medicine involves the diagnosis, prognosis, treatment, and follow-up of individual patients. Whereas the major goal of public health is to establish and monitor preventive measures, clinical medicine is not interested in the development of largely healthy participants, but in patients who exhibit symptoms and seek treatment. Symptoms, clinical observations, blood and urine samples, signals over time, such as EKG data and medical image data are taken into account to determine the underlying disease, its sub-type and severity. In treatment planning previous treatment attempts with their side-effects and outcome are considered. As an example, imagine a late-stage tumor patient with several co-morbidities, a variety of symptoms and a long history of previous treatments. Because of the large variety of the information required for treatment planning, an integrated visual summary is often needed. Our discussion in this chapter is quite broad in terms of the diagnostic and treatment procedures that are supported. However, a focus in clinical medicine is on the treatment of cancer diseases, which unfortunately occur frequently, are severe, and lead to particularly rich patient histories, often involving many treatment steps.

When even data for a group of patients needs to be analyzed, also analytical components are needed. Thus visual analytics solutions are beneficial. For single patients and patient groups, *time-dependent* visualizations are required to reflect the sequence of symptom onsets, treatments, results, and eventually recurrence of symptoms, hospital stays, and so on. Obviously, only symptoms that begin *after* a drug therapy *may* be unwanted side-effects of that therapy. In contrast to the health surveys that are carried out in public health, the history of a patient with a long-term or chronic disease contains many *events*, i.e., points in time where something essential happens. Thus these discrete events need to be displayed at a glance.

The comparison of patients involves an integrated visualization of their patient histories. For this integration, a *temporal alignment* is crucial, i.e., one joint event in the histories is chosen that is displayed at the same point on the (horizontal) time-scale, and other events are *relative* to that key event. As an example, the history of patients suffering from a stroke typically would be aligned according to the date of the stroke, making it easy to see what happens before and after the stroke, e.g., how long patients stayed in hospitals or took part in neuro-rehabilitation. The analysis of a patient database for treatment planning may be further enhanced by the search for the most similar cases and a presentation of the cases sorted according to the similarity.

Visualization, Visual Analytics and Virtual Reality in Medicine. https://doi.org/10.1016/B978-0-12-822962-0.00020-1

The discharge from the intensive care unit or hospital could also be an alignment event. Thus interaction is needed to control the display of events, the time span that is analyzed, and the alignment. In this chapter, we discuss methods to visualize, explore, and compare patient data.

Organization

This chapter is organized as follows: We start with an overview of the data involved in clinical medicine (Section 11.2), and continue with a thorough discussion of visual analytics for event-typed data motivated by the importance of such data in clinical medicine (Section 11.3). On this basis, we address the visualization of single patient data (Section 11.4), and then move on to cohort data (Section 11.5). The chapter continues with a discussion on predictive visual analytics (Section 11.6) and visual analytics solutions for clinical decision support (Section 11.7), and finally we review also three selected applications in clinical medicine (Section 11.8).

11.2 Data in clinical medicine

Healthcare clinical data includes several sources of data, among which are

- electronic health records (EHR)
- administrative data
- claims data
- health surveys
- clinical trial data

Electronic health records (EHR) or electronic medical records (EMR) comprise any type of medical data that are recorded during a patient's visit. EHRs were created to store all available patient information in a secure location that protects patient confidentiality. Examples of data that can be accessed in an EHR include a patient's name, date of birth, address, any vital signs, lab values, test results, head-to-toe assessments, healthcare provider notes, and billing information, such as diagnoses according to the ICD (*International Classification of Diseases*). Although EHR data were created to save time and resources, as it supports the easy and quick management of all available patient information, this type of data is rarely cross-checked or improved, due to time constraints in hospitals. Thus the data quality is not ideal.

Administrative data is collected and stored to help portray an accurate understanding of a patient's visit. This can include, for example, admission information and discharge data, and is supposed to facilitate sharing information across facilities.

Claims data refers to insurance claims and financial costs of diagnostic or treatment procedures.

Health surveys are filled out by patients and serve to evaluate, e.g., the satisfaction of a patient with regard to the health services they received, or to self-assessment surveys, e.g., to track vaccination rates along other demographic information. Thus this type of data—despite being affordable and easy to obtain—is not considered a reliable source of information due to the potential of false self-reporting.

Clinical trial data (rather databases) are collected in clinical trials that help clinical experts to understand the effects, efficacy, and safety of (new) treatments. Manufacturers are required to carry out such trials to demonstrate the quality of their products, e.g., drugs or instruments, under real-world conditions. The trials are needed to get formal admission to use a new product in healthcare.

Furthermore, clinical data often include additional information from *sensors or monitors*, which may comprise

- monitoring the cardiac functions through electrocardiography (ECG)
- monitoring blood properties, such as hemodynamics (blood pressure or blood flow) or blood glucose
- monitoring respiration through pulse oximeters
- neurological monitoring through electroencephalography (EEG)
- monitoring neuromuscular activity through electromyography (EMG)
- monitoring temperature

11.3 Visual analytics of event-type data

Event-type data plays an essential role in many areas, such as business analytics, (where they represent customer behavior) and social media analysis, where tweets, posts, and likes represent the events to be displayed and analyzed. Events change the state of a system or person suddenly. Often a decision, e.g., the customer buys an article, is represented as an event. Events are associated with time stamps, i.e., they occur at discrete points in time. Event-typed data is a special instance of time-dependent data, but differs strongly from continuously monitored data, which typically exhibit a constant and high temporal resolution, e.g., values recorded by a sensor (Aigner et al., 2011). With appropriate interactive visualizations, analysts may identify typical patterns of event sequences and strong deviations from "normal" patterns.

Event-typed data in medicine

Event-typed data in medicine typically represents the state of single patients, one group of patients, or several groups of patients who should be compared, e.g., with respect to the effectiveness of treatment. Event-type visualizations in medicine may provide insight regarding which sequences of diagnostic or treatment steps are associated with a positive outcome, i.e., the patient recovered fully. Thus a comparison of all event sequences with a positive outcome with all sequences related to negative outcomes is useful.

Event-type visualizations may also be used for quality control of the underlying data, in particular for plausibility checks. When an event that represents the death of a patient occurs before a diagnostic or treatment step, obviously an error occurred.

Thus the above-mentioned low quality of EHRs may be monitored and improved by such checks.

For medical decision-making not only the current state of the patient, but also the patient history has to be taken into account. To get an overview of the patients' state, the events are typically marked on a *timeline visualization*. To interpret such a timeline, the marks need to be labeled. Moreover, it is useful to *segment* the timeline, e.g., in calendar years, or three-months periods. This segmentation is added to the timeline with an appropriate labeling.

Since there are potentially many different event types, a categorization is useful. Categories in medical data include

- the onset of symptoms
- diagnostic procedures
- the prescription of drugs

A categorization enables a visualization where events of the same category are visualized equally and at the same time differ distinctively from events of another category. Subcategories are frequently used, e.g., the drug category may be refined in drugs against hypertension and drugs against depression. In most cases, colors (different hues) are employed to visually distinguish categories. Subcategories can be displayed with variations of a base color, e.g., by modifying saturation or brightness.

It is also possible to employ glyphs, e.g., different shapes, such as triangles, circles, arrows pointing in a certain direction. When color and glyph shape are employed, color may represent a categorization at a higher level and glyph shape a categorization at a lower level. In the case of a rich data set with many events (recall the example of a late-stage tumor patient), it may be useful to filter the displayed events based on the categories.

Point and interval events

Events may be fully represented by one point in time. A medical example is a severe health event, such as an ischemic stroke, or a surgery. Point events are visually represented by one mark on a timeline. Interval events, in contrast, are characterized by a start and an end event. Examples include the interval in which the patient takes a drug or the period that the patient has to stay in a hospital.

It is essential to consider start and end of an interval event not just as two independent point events. Instead, it must be conveyed that they belong together. Thus for a certain point in time t, it can be analyzed whether it is inside an interval I. Moreover, it may be interesting whether two interval events I_1 and I_2 overlap. Imagine the first event I_1 represents the interval of a drug treatment, and I_2 represents the interval in which severe symptoms occur. If both intervals overlap and the drug treatment started earlier, the symptoms may be side-effects of the drug treatment.

Visual analysis of single event sequences

Early systems were restricted to displaying the data of a single patient. The LIFE-LINES system represents the pioneering work in this area (Plaisant et al., 2003). With

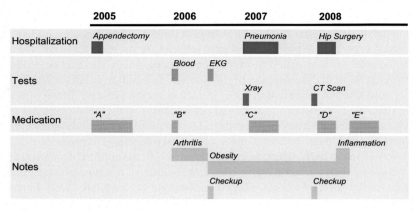

FIGURE 11.1

LifeLines: The patient history over several years is summarized based on events, categorized, e.g., in tests and hospitalization. Clearly different colors are used for the presentation
of each category (Inspired by Plaisant et al. (2003)).

LifeLines, the visualization can be restricted to a certain temporal interval, and the
display of events could be filtered according to event types (see Fig. 11.1). Other
patient data, e.g., the image data of an ultrasound examination, were linked with the
event-typed data, and thus could be integrated in the visualization.

Even for a single patient, the display may get cluttered. As an alternative to a
linear presentation of time, intervals with a high density of events may be stretched,
and intervals where no events occurred may be compressed. The timescale needs to
be labeled accordingly to make the analyst aware of this modification.

11.3.1 Filtering and simplifying event-type data

A straightforward visualization of complex event-type data easily gets cluttered.
Event-data visualizations are challenging when the number of data sets, the number
of events, or the number of unique event sequences gets very large. Thus techniques
were developed to restrict the visual analysis on the instance and feature level (filtering). The event-type character enables specific filtering options, e.g., based on

- the occurrence of a certain event category, e.g., a specific diagnosis
- the frequency of an event category, e.g., the number of prescriptions of a drug
- the duration of interval events
- the gap between events

In addition to filtering, there are techniques to simplify and aggregate the data that
are often applied after filtering.

Filtering event-type data

Often, a database, e.g., the EHRs of a hospital, contains a large number of data sets, from which only a small portion is actually relevant for an analytical task. Du et al. (2016) mention studies related to asthma or epilepsy, where the data were filtered according to the actual occurrence of the disease. In addition to this *instance level* filtering, also filtering of the features, i.e., the actual events, is useful. Elderly patients, for example, have frequent eye and dental examinations. If these, however, are not in the focus of the current analysis, they should be removed from the visualization.

When filtering data, one may think of a query language representing logical expressions, such as SQL, which is frequently used for conventional databases. However, the use of such a general query language is clumsy for temporal data. A query language for temporal event data is based on temporal logic (Allen, 1983). In temporal logic, 13 unique relations between point events and interval events occur. As an example, both point events and interval events may be within an interval event. Two interval events may also overlap or be disjoint.

Filtering of event-type data may also consider the *duration* of interval events, e.g., we may be interested in patients with a particularly long stay in the hospital. Moreover, an unusual sequence of events may be used for filtering, e.g., when a patient was admitted to the intensive care unit (ICU), dismissed from the ICU, and re-admitted to the ICU within a certain interval. Such an event sequence may indicate a problem with decision-making. But, of course, in case of a newly diagnosed disease, it may also be a natural development. The event filtering enables to take a closer look at such situations.

Instead of the whole medical history of a patient, we may be interested in a certain *temporal window* (Du et al., 2016). As an example for a cancer patient, the five or ten years after the diagnosis may be the relevant temporal window. To study the effects of a vaccination, a short temporal window may be used to identify potential side-effects of the vaccination, and a longer temporal window to assess whether the vaccination effectively avoided infections. As "a last resort," if the volume of the data is still too large, random sampling may be applied to restrict the data to a manageable size (Du et al., 2016).

Matching and non-matching events

So far, we discussed filtering primarily with the goal to restrict the visualization to a feasible number of data sets. Another essential use of filtering is to *compare* patients who match a filtering criterion with those that does not match it. In the simplest case, this comparison relates to a positive or negative outcome. But filtering is powerful and enables a more fine-grained specification of patients to be compared. Fig. 11.2 gives an example.

Simplifying event-type data

Even after filtering, the remaining data may still be too large and complex to be directly visualized. The following list describes strategies for simplifying event-type data (based on Du et al. (2016)):

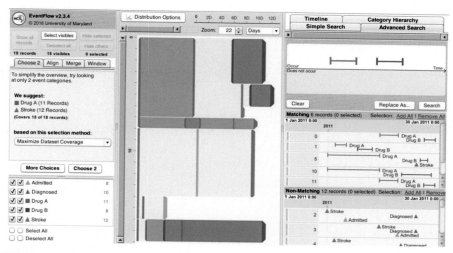

FIGURE 11.2

A control panel on the left enables filtering and alignment. An overview of the 18 patients is displayed in the middle. On the right, the matching and non-matching records are displayed. A stroke occurred rarely when two drugs were given (From: Monroe et al. (2013b)).

- *Grouping event categories.* In medicine, a huge number of categories exist, e.g., there are thousands of drugs and thousands of diagnostic codes. There are widely used and even standardized taxonomies that enable a summary, e.g., vascular diseases is an umbrella term for diseases of the arterial and the venous system, and the diagnostic codes further discriminate between, e.g., diseases of the cerebral, coronary, or peripheral vessels.
- *Identifying features linked to outcomes.* An outcome is the result of a treatment, e.g., patients died or survived; they may be healthy or get a relapse of the disease. Event-type data may be simplified by restricting the analysis to a certain outcome, e.g., tumor-free survival.
- *Employ milestone events.* Some events, such as the diagnosis of a chronic disease, may occur often in a data set. However, only the first occurrence is actually relevant, and thus the data may be further simplified.
- *Coalescing repeating events into one.* Patient data may contain many events of the same time that may be summarized. Du et al. (2016) mention a series of blood pressure measurements yielding values in a normal range. Not only such point events may be summarized; also interval events, such as sequential prescriptions of the same type of drug.
- *Merging events.* When a patient is admitted to the hospital and gets surgery, many events are registered in an EHR data set, relating to diagnostic procedures, drugs, e.g., to avoid thrombosis after surgery. These events may be merged to one essential event, in our example, the type of surgery.

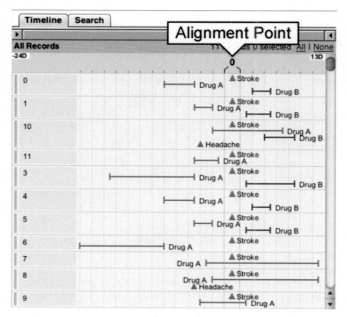

FIGURE 11.3

Event-type data representing patients filtered according to one symptom (headache), two drugs, and a severe diagnosis (a stroke). The first occurrence of a stroke is defined as alignment event. Thus the situation before and after the stroke can be compared (©2013 IEEE, Reprinted with permission from: (Monroe et al., 2013b)).

Summarizing event-type data

In many areas, inside and outside of medicine, it is interesting to compare event-type data sets and give an overview that may elicit recurring patterns. The behavior of customers, the investment decisions of clients of a bank, and the disease-related data of a patient are examples. To enable an overview, individual event-type data typically needs to be aggregated, and thus abstracted as previously discussed. For comparison of a small set of event-type data, the question arises how to *align* these data sets. Instead of using the same overall temporal scale, certain *sentinel events* may be used for alignment (see Fig. 11.3). A reasonable strategy, implemented in popular systems, such as EVENTFLOW (Monroe et al., 2013a), is to provide an overview and a detailed inspection of selected data sets.

11.4 Visualization of single patient data

After describing the display of event-type data, we here focus on patient data and consider the following aspects:

- Visualize patient state, highlight critical values
- Visualize treatment plans
- Decision-making based on patient status, symptoms, medical history, past and ongoing treatments

Very early work on the visualization of personal clinical histories has been conducted by Plaisant et al. (1996). Their LIFELINES (recall Fig. 11.1) is a general visualization for personal histories, which can be applied to medical data, but also to any other biographical, time-oriented data. The interface includes an overview with multiple facets of the records using individual time lines as a basis. Various encodings (such as color or thickness) are employed to enrich the view, and filtering is used to provide information on demand. LIFELINES was later extended to LIFELINES2, also to display multiple records. This approach has been put in practice and integrated into the NIH's clinical repository, the Biomedical Translational Research Information System (BTRIS).

To facilitate disease management in the clinical environment, clinical guidelines and protocols are employed. These are often captured using natural language or—in a more schematic form—through flow diagrams and flowcharts, which support the execution of a plan. Miksch et al. (1997) developed a time-oriented, plan specification language, called ASBRU, which serves as the basis for ASBRUVIEW, a viewer that supports the visualization of the plan in an easy-to-understand way. The approach has been evaluated on a scenario of mechanically ventilated newborn infants, where the authors analyzed expressiveness of ASBRUVIEW with collaborating physicians.

To address the representation of complex high-dimensional, time-oriented EHR data and to provide adequate interactive support in their exploration and navigation, Bade et al. (2004) conducted a detailed study, where they present and assess different interactive visualization techniques, which enable the users to reveal insights in the data at several levels of detail and abstraction. They showcase their designed approaches on a case of patients with pulmonary embolism.

CAREVIS by Aigner and Miksch (2006) is another interactive visualization approach, which provides multiple linked views to cover different aspects of treatment plans and patient data. CAREVIS builds upon both LIFELINES and ASBRU; it additionally supports the management of temporal uncertainty in the data. By temporal uncertainty, the authors denote variability or unreliability with regard to the exact start or end of planning events, i.e., if it is not known when a specific treatment procedure started or ended. Gschwandtner et al. (2011) later introduced CARECRUISER to provide visual and interactive means for assessing effects of applied treatment plans on patients and to compare multiple patients at the same time. An example of the interface of CARECRUISER is shown in Fig. 11.4.

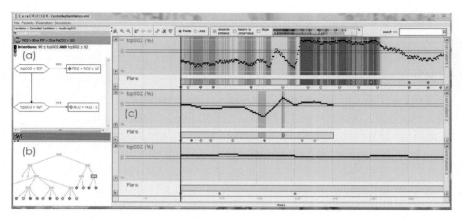

FIGURE 11.4

The interface of CARECRUISER, where the logical structure of a treatment plan is shown with a flowchart (a) and a tree to emphasize hierarchies (b). The time-oriented view (c) focuses on the temporal-qualities of applied treatment plans, clinical actions, and patient parameters (©2011 IEEE, Reprinted with permission from: (Gschwandtner et al., 2011)).

11.5 Visualization of patient cohort data

Patient cohort data is partially different from a population cohort (recall Chapter 10), as a patient cohort is assumed to have some homogeneity in their health characteristics (e.g., a group of patients, in which all have the same disease or risk, or even the same stage of a diseases). A population cohort is a more diverse group of people, i.e., a subsample from the general population that share only the geographical area where they live.

The visualization of patient cohorts is not part of the daily clinical routine, but essential for clinical research in contexts, such as

- In treatment decisions, where it may be helpful to compare one patient to a group of patients.
- In retrospective studies, e.g., for predictive purposes, where a past cohort is used as the basis for understanding a new patient or preemptively acting for their benefit.
- To discover a correlation between (a set of) variables and a specific disease/disorder.
- To identify specific sub-populations that are at particular risk.
- For survival analysis.

As an example, for a clinical guideline, it is essential to know early when a patient, e.g., with COVID-19 or another lung inflammation, is likely to develop severe symptoms requiring intensive treatment. Thus understanding features of the patient that put them on a high risk is required.

Steenwijk et al. (2010) introduced a framework for the visual analysis of patient cohort data based on the simple concepts of features, mappers, and studies to analyze difficult diseases. Features in their work can be any information regarding the state of the patient, be it simple yes-or-no blood test results or more complex 3D data sets. These features can then be transformed using mappers to extract additional information. By combining multiple features of a patient's state, a study for a disease is created. To support these analytical tasks, a wide range of visualizations is offered, including parallel coordinate plots to show high-dimensional features, scatter plots with linked points to provide information about how certain feature points change over time, and ellipsoid plots to visualize the variability inside a set of points in a scatter plot.

Angelelli et al. (2014) presented a visual analysis method for the analysis of higher-dimensional and heterogeneous data encountered in cohorts of patients. Their system works on the basis of multiple linked views, which support the seamless integration and exploration of the heterogeneous data, as well as linking spatial and non-spatial views on these data. The approach is showcased on a scenario for the explorative visualization and analysis of data that was acquired as part of a longitudinal study on cognitive aging.

Later, Basole et al. (2015) discussed the development of a system with multiple, coordinated views that supports the analysis of care processes on the basis of 5784 pediatric emergency department visits over a 13 month period, for which asthma was the primary diagnosis. They provide a summary of the available data of the patient cohort, an interactive specification of a sub-cohort, where querying and filtering based on clinical and demographic characteristics is enabled, and different views on the data, which also enable comparisons between sub-cohorts.

Federico et al. (2015) introduced GNAEUS, a system that takes the domain knowledge acquired by clinical experts and formalizes it into computer-interpretable guidelines (CIGs) to improve the automated analysis, the visualization, and the interactive exploration of EHRs. Their solution enables the simultaneous exploration of both individual patients and cohort data, the integrated analysis of patient conditions and treatment data, and supports the analysis of time-oriented EHR data.

More recently, Bernard et al. (2018) presented an interactive system that supports the visual analysis of a cohort of prostate cancer patients with a large set of attributes. The system includes several visualization techniques, which allow the user to generate hypotheses and test them statistically on the basis of different cohorts. An example of this work is depicted in Fig. 11.5.

In the central part of Fig. 11.5, the patient histories are presented in a list-based visualization to provide an *overview* of their status. A traffic-light color coding (green, yellow, or red) allows a quick overview of their status in three phases. From this view, the user can drill down *by filtering* to relevant sub-cohorts, which can at any point during the analytical process be recalled. The accompanying views to the left and right provide *details-on-demand* regarding the distributions of user-selected measures, and dynamic querying further supports this direction. Additional red and blue color coding in these views guide the user to look for interesting relations in the cohort. The

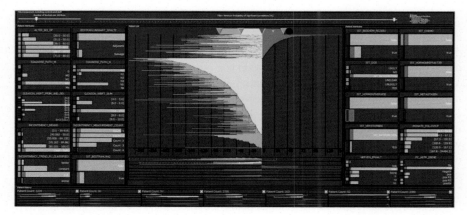

FIGURE 11.5

The interface of PROSTATE VIS to support the analysis of prostate patient cohort data with multiple attributes (©2018 IEEE, Reprinted with permission from: (Bernard et al., 2015)).

system has been demonstrated on cohorts comprising about 16,000 prostate cancer patient histories.

The combined exploration of imaging and EHR data has been discussed in the work of Jönsson et al. (2020) and Mörth et al. (2020). Jönsson et al. (2020) introduce an integrated visual analytics environment for hypothesis formation and reasoning in studies with fMRI and multivariate clinical data, combined. The users are enabled to conduct an interactive correlation analysis between spatial regions in the brain and clinical measurements. An example of this work is depicted in Fig. 11.6. Mörth et al. (2020) present a visual analytics tool that enables radiomic tumor profiling in combination with clinical markers. Their approach supports the analysis of multiparametric medical imaging data in combination with multivariate clinical parameters in an environment that facilitates hypothesis formation and validation.

11.6 Visual analytics for prediction

Scope of predictive visual analytics

The examples discussed in the previous section either target descriptive purposes, which had already occurred, or diagnostic analysis with the purpose of understanding a phenomenon and its cause. Yet, the field of visualization has also provided visual analytics solutions for predictive purposes, where past trends in the patient data serve to answer questions and hypotheses about the future. This could be useful, for example, in the following cases:

- Information from retrospective patients are used to predict treatment outcomes in a new incoming patient.

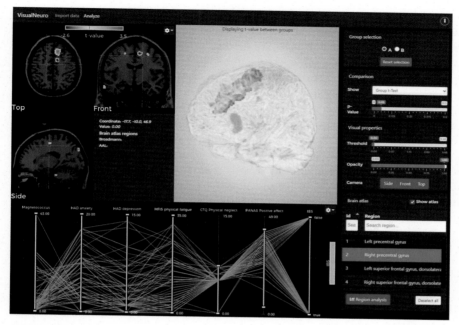

FIGURE 11.6

Overview of a visual environment for the combined exploration of fMRI and multivariate clinical data. Parallel coordinates support the selection of subject groups, whereas spatial views support the representation of group differences. Image courtesy of Daniel Jönsson, Linköping University.

- Information can be used to analyze outbreaks.
- Information from a patient can be used to determine their risk for developing specific conditions in the future.

In clinical medicine, *outbreaks* relates primarily to an outbreak within a hospital that needs to be urgently controlled given the vulnerable state of patients in a hospital. Predictive analytics can also be used as the basis for prescriptive scenarios, where the predicted information can be used to implement specific preventive measures against the potential risk. We, however, do not go into the prescriptive aspect of such scenarios, and we hereby revise a few recent examples for predictive visual analytics.

Predicting the impact of anatomical variations on treatment

As discussed in Chapter 8, radiotherapy requires meticulous planning prior to treatment, where the plan is optimized with organ delineations on a pre-treatment CT scan of the patient. However, the delivered dose distribution may often deviate from the planned one, due to changes in the anatomy of the patient (e.g., due to weight loss or organ filling). Furmanová et al. (2021) recently introduced PREVIS, a visual analytics tool that supports medical physicists to predict changes in patient anatomy for an upcoming treatment, and to assess which options are best for the patient, with respect to the anticipated changes. To do this, records of during-treatment changes from a retrospective imaging cohort with complete data are employed to infer expected anatomical changes of new incoming patients with incomplete data using a generative model. Using dimensionality reduction and clustering, PREVIS reveals the main modes of organ variability and evolution in the retrospective cohort of patients, so that when a new patient with few initial measurements for the first days of treatment comes in, they are matched to one or several of the existing modes of organ variability. Subsequently, a principal component analysis (PCA)-based generative model, which reaches at least 95% accuracy, describes the predicted spatial probability distributions of the incoming patient's organs in the upcoming weeks of treatment, based on observations of past patients. This information can also be used to predict which treatment might provide less side-effects and better tumor treatment for the given patient.

Predicting radiation dose distributions

Also in the context of radiotherapy, Wentzel et al. (2019) presented a visual computing approach to support planning, based on spatial similarity within a patient cohort. The authors proposed a novel spatial measure, T-SSIM, which summarizes tumor-to-organs distance and organ volume, and then use this measure to generate a predictive algorithm for dose distribution. Their application is supported by visual steering to provide better spatial context. Visual steering indicates interaction mechanisms that allow the user to adjust parameterizations of the dose plan on the interface and dynamically see simulated changes induced by the alterations in the parameter space. This allows them also to leverage domain-specific knowledge and to easily discover patterns in the data, by allowing users to analyze the spatial and dosimetric information of cohort clusters along with a patient's data, while comparing them to other similar patients. An interesting component of this work is the use of stylization for the 3D radiation plan, i.e., the use of a specific style with pre-determined visual properties that aim at simplifying the view on the dose plan instead of using the typical encodings, as shown in Chapter 8. This is depicted in Fig. 11.7.

Predicting disease and symptom progression

Floricel et al. (2021) presented THALIS, an interactive data mining environment that supports exploration and analysis of longitudinal symptoms in a cohort of cancer patients. This tool targets oncologists who work on symptom research and determine symptoms that may worsen over time. Practically, THALIS is designed and implemented in such a way that allows them to predict the evolution of the symptoms—as the authors call it, the *symptom trajectory*—also in the context of a larger group of patients. To this end, they employ association rule and factor analysis together with visual analytics and statistics to estimate how a symptom evolves through time in the context of cancer therapy and taking into account other, similar patients. This approach has also supported users to explain a longitudinal symptom trajectory in

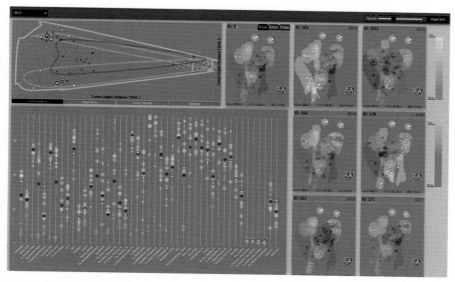

FIGURE 11.7

Cohort-based radiation therapy prediction using T-SSIM, where a stylized 3D view of the predicted radiation plan of the current patient is used (left). Additional RT views show the most similar patients who contribute to the prediction. Image courtesy of Elisabeta G. Marai, University of Illinois at Chicago.

an actionable manner, while linking it to other demographic and diagnostic data. An example of THALIS is shown in Fig. 11.8.

Predicting disease progression has also been studied by Kwon et al. (2020). Their DPVIS system provides interpretable and interactive visualizations for several chronic disease pathways (e.g., Parkinson's or Huntington's disease). Given a set of patients over time and a disease state, DPVIS allows its users to drill down into the characteristics of disease states, to understand state transition patterns when patients are transitioning through different paths, to explore the relationship between states and other patient variables, such as health outcomes, and finally to obtain details about subgroups of patients and individual patients.

Predicting impact of treatment on rehabilitation

Moving on to a different domain of application, precision medicine is a promising paradigm aiming to improve a patient's treatment by taking individual characteristics into account. Means to analyze and predict the impact of varying treatment strategies to sub-cohorts of patients are required to successfully deal with large and complex data sets, which are the necessary foundation for this kind of analysis.

Bernold et al. (2019) developed PREHA, a precision rehabilitation visual analytics dashboard that allows clinical domain experts and engineers to fulfill data analytics

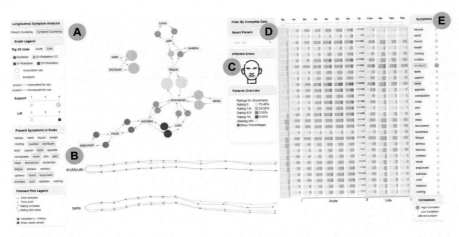

FIGURE 11.8

THALIS analysis of longitudinal symptom data. An association rule diagram panel shows the most frequent late-stage symptoms (A), and a symptom trajectory panel shows frequent observations in the acute stage (left side) towards the late stage (right side) (B). Additionally, an illustration is used to depict selected symptoms (C), while a cohort symptom panel (D) and a correlation matrix (E) allow the exploration of the cohort data. Image courtesy of Elisabeta G. Marai, University of Illinois at Chicago.

tasks in a rehabilitation context. For the data analysis, they use a data set of 46,000 EHRs. Flexible interactive dashboards, including a variety of visualizations, are used as the front end, while a set of interconnected modules is running in the background: The preprocessing module collects the data from various sources (e.g., database tables) and fuses the data to a single data structure. Then, the storage module is the primary persistence unit for PREHA. Once the preprocessing module stores data in it, the data are not modified further. The dashboard editor module is the user interface of the application, where the analytical tasks are answered. It features dashboards with rich sets of visualizations that are used for data analysis by the data analysts. The predictive analytics module is responsible for advanced data analytic tasks, such as machine learning and predictions based on random forest regression. The last three modules (dashboards editor, predictive analytics, and data storage) may interact in an iterative process. An example of a dashboard generated for PREHA is shown in Fig. 11.9.

11.7 Clinical decision support

Clinical decision support comprises a variety of tools to support and enhance decision-making in the clinical workflow. Examples for such tools

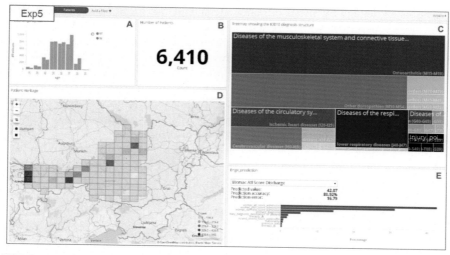

FIGURE 11.9

Dashboards of the PREHA system for precision rehabilitation. It consists of a bar chart (A) that displays the number of patients per facility and the total number of patients (B), a treemap view on the entire cohort (C) and a choropleth map showing their geolocation (D). The predictive analytics panel (E) is added to the visualization, providing assessment information (From: (Bernold et al., 2019), ©2019 The Author(s), Eurographics Proceedings, ©The Eurographics Association).

- may provide information relevant to particular patients
- reminders for preventive care
- alerts about potentially dangerous situations

In this section, we primarily discuss cancer treatment, as the majority of visual analytics systems developed for clinical decision support is in this area. However, the principles and concepts discussed below could also be applicable to other diseases.

In clinical decision support, simple interfaces for a clean knowledge presentation without complex interactions and explanatory (or transparency) support are required. Therefore visual analytics, which often come with a multitude of linked views and heavily rely on interaction, might be too complex for use in the clinical routine. We hereby discuss three representative examples of visual analytics for clinical decision support, focusing mainly on the aspects of simplicity in terms of visualization and interaction and of transparency support.

Tumor staging and grading

The treatment of cancer patients requires an accurate diagnosis, which involves *tumor staging* and *tumor grading*, as well as precise localization, including statements about possible infiltrations of adjacent structures. Tumor staging (also referred to as TNM staging) is carried out by means of radiologic and nuclear medicine image data. The tumor stage is described with respect to the primary tumor (T), the existence of local lymph node metastasis (N), and of remote metastasis (M). The T component may be 1, 2, 3, or 4 for some tumors further discriminated in 2a and 2b or 3a and 3b. The T component primarily reflects the size of the primary tumor (the longest diameter) and in some tumors also infiltration. N and M are binary attributes for most tumors: The type of metastasis exists ($N = 1$) or not ($N = 0$). For some tumors, there is a further discrimination with respect to the location of lymph node metastasis, thus we may have $N = 2$ when they are further away from the primary tumor.

Tumor grading is carried out by means of tissue samples gained from a biopsy. The tissue samples are analyzed by pathologists with a microscope. Tumor grading involves an analysis on the cellular and subcellular level, e.g., with respect to the mitosis rate (how often tumor cells replicate). This grading typically results in number 1, 2, or 3, representing more or less aggressive tumor subtypes.

Staging verification

A first approach to automated TNM staging verification on the basis of visualization was proposed by Rossling et al. (2011), applied to the domain of ENT (i.e., ear, nose, and throat) surgery. This approach provides automatic measurement of the largest diameter of a tumor and, subsequently, visualizations support a collaborative process of discussing about possible infiltrations and deciding on the type of surgery that should be preferred. In this work, 3D visualizations of patient imaging data (tailored to specific treatment questions) are proposed with the purpose of improving perception of spatial relationships, and complementing other diagnostic sources. An additional contribution of this work is the possibility to provide a documentation of diagnostic information, treatment decisions, and patient consultation in the form of an electronic report.

Cypko et al. (2017) addressed visual analytics within the context of cancer staging verification support. Each cancer patient undergoes an evaluation at a tumor board, where the best therapy option is discussed and agreed among physicians from different disciplines, including surgery, oncology, radiation treatment, and radiology. In cases where multiple physicians are involved in the TNM staging of a patient, this might be inconsistent. Therefore the physicians go back to the patient's records and discover all the necessary information to verify the staging of the patient. Cypko et al. (2017) use Bayesian networks to support this tedious process. Using information from the patient records and Bayesian inference, the network computes the TNM staging; the underlying information are then represented in a graph.

Interaction is used in an uncomplicated way, while the employed representations do not clutter the view, despite providing lots of information, such as the TNM-related knowledge, but also probabilities (encoded in tailor-made glyphs) and comparisons between TNMs. In the initial display of the graph, the nodes of the T, N, and M states are displayed in the center and strung along a ring representing the circular focus region (the first ring in the graph of Fig. 11.10). Their adjacent nodes are arranged circularly in the proximity and connected via dashed spline curves to denote staging

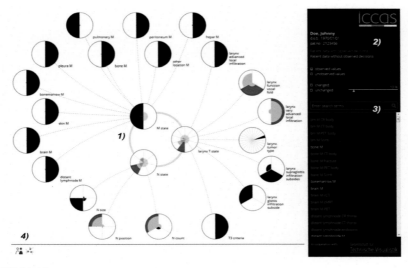

FIGURE 11.10

The interface of a visual analysis system to support staging verification through Bayesian networks. The interface includes (1) a graph view, (2) a view for patient information summary, (3) a variable selector, and (4) a tool set (From: (Cypko et al., 2017), ©John Wiley & Sons Inc., 2017).

of different structures adjacent to the tumor. For example, the upper part of the graph indicates M staging for different structures, such as the bones, the brain, or the bone marrow. All nodes of the graph are represented by circular glyphs of equal size. Each glyph is partitioned into equally-sized slices that contain three decision nodes corresponding to the T, N, and M states. The sliced display can be interpreted as a circular bar chart showing the probability distribution of the corresponding variable adding up to an overall of 100% (see Fig. 11.10).

Transparency

Although the work of Cypko et al. indirectly supported the explanation of decision-making processes, they did not specifically address *transparency*, i.e., the ability to track down, explain, and communicate the flow of reasoning that led to a specific decision. This is a particularly important aspect in clinical decision support, as transparency can lead to higher trust and higher acceptance rates for inclusion into clinical workflows. For physicians, it is important to know all the key aspects that have brought a specific recommendation and its potential alternatives, as well as their degree of certainty.

Transparency has been addressed by Müller et al. (2020) in an approach similar to Cypko et al. (2017). In both cases, the authors use a glyph-based solution comprising multiple views that provide a visual summary of all evidence together with linked

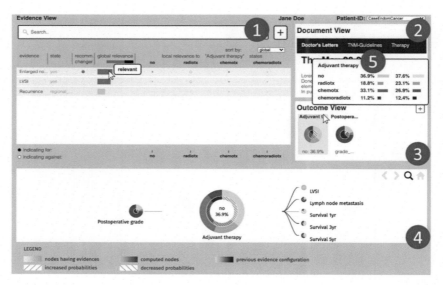

FIGURE 11.11

Interactive multiple views approach to explainable computerized clinical decision support: (1) The evidence view showing the observed evidence items sorted with regard to their relevance; (2) the document view to show clinical guidelines and doctor letters; (3) the outcome view to show the recommendation outcome of the model, and (4) a view to support a structured exploration of the underlying Bayesian model. (5) Additional information can be displayed on demand (From: (Müller et al., 2020), Reprinted from Computers & Graphics, Vol. 91, "A visual approach to explainable computerized clinical decision support," Page 5, ©Elsevier 2020).

textual information, and also views for the certainty and for the investigation of the reasoning behind recommendations. Despite the similarity in the provided views, the scope is different. The work of Müller et al. targets the unraveling of patient-specific data and clinical guidelines together with Bayesian network-based reasoning models, but it particularly allows the users to understand the underlying reasoning process to improve the acceptance and trustworthiness of a recommendation. To do so, they enable a view on the (un)certainty of the computed recommendation, where guidance in the form of highlighting and emphasis is used to convey the importance of evidence, and whether one or more alternatives could perform better. An example of the work of Müller et al. is shown in Fig. 11.11.

11.8 Selected applications

In this sections, we discuss three selected applications: digital pathology, gait analysis, and sleep monitoring.

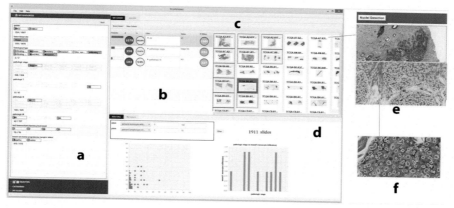

FIGURE 11.12

The interface of PATHONE, which includes views for (a) cohort selection by filtering, (b) querying information, (c) viewing the slides gallery, (d) patient distribution viewing, (e) biological filtering of slides, and (f) nuclei detection (From: (Corvó et al., 2016), ©2016 The Author(s), Eurographics Proceedings, ©The Eurographics Association).

11.8.1 Digital pathology

Digital pathology comprises the acquisition, management, sharing, and interpretation of tissue information in an image-based environment. Whole slide images of tissues are generated and pathologists are called to analyze and diagnose them digitally on a screen. However, the most common problem is that whole slide images have a very high resolution, as they are often represented in a pyramid structure consisting of multiple images at different resolutions, reaching even 100,000 × 100,000 pixels. To "read" and analyze these high-resolution slides, pathologists are often required to zoom in up to 40×, which makes it hard to find the most interesting locations to look at and characterize. Visual analytics can prove to be useful Corvó et al. (2019b).

Initially, Corvó et al. (2016) introduced PATHONE, a tool that integrates cohort specification, slide exploration, and selection of whole-slide images (Fig. 11.12). In a subsequent work, they introduced PATHOVA (Corvó et al., 2017), a visual analytics system for computer-aided pathology diagnosis (Fig. 11.13). PATHOVA supports the recording of the reading of the pathologist in a digital tissue slide viewer, from which a diagnostic trace is constructed automatically. Practically, as the pathologist characterizes cells and histological sections of tissues, the system traces this, and this trace is visualized and further enhanced with quantitative data about the tissue obtained by image analysis. Using this visualization, the pathologist is supported in filling up the required report. SURVIVIS, which was published a few years later builds upon the previous efforts to enrich standard survival plots, also known as Kaplan–Meier (KM) curves, by juxtaposing interactive views for quick data understanding and analysis of patient survivals Corvó et al. (2019a).

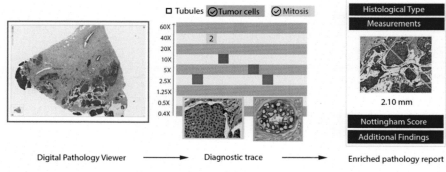

FIGURE 11.13

PATHOVA is a computer-aided diagnosis tool for pathologists, which integrates a digital tissue slide viewer (left), a visualization of the diagnostic trace (middle), and reporting (right). Here, the pathologist is characterizing three different types of cells: tubules (i.e., the most common kidney cells), tumor cells, and cells undergoing mitosis (i.e., preparing for division) (©2017 IEEE, Reprinted with permission from: (Corvó et al., 2017)).

FACETTO (Krueger et al., 2019) is a scalable visual analytics system for identifying single-cell phenotypes in multi-channel microscopy images of human tumors and tissues, which is the state-of-the-art in digital histology. FACETTO integrates unsupervised and supervised learning to support the analysis of the images and the exploration of their features for new insights into cancer biology. This system was developed using a user-centered design process with pathologists, oncologists, and computational biologists. Clustering is deployed to discover and isolate new cell types, and then feed the results to train classifiers, which are then used to assign labels to new image data. In Fig. 11.14, we show an example of the interface of FACETTO.

FACETTO has been a source of inspiration for many other works, linking additionally to the analysis of effectiveness of cancer drugs on individual cell lines based on microscopy data, as demonstrated in the work of Lange et al. (2021). Recently, Focus+Context approaches have also been discussed for pathology data, where the employed resolution poses significant challenges. SCOPE2SCREEN Jessup et al. (2021) is a system for Focus+Context exploration and annotation of whole-slide, multi-channel tissue images, using a lens metaphor that works both at multiple levels of details, i.e., both at single-cell and tissue level. This approach allows to leverage multi-channel and multivariate information and to explore and analyze the available data at different scales, while at the same time annotating images and linking exploration to the actual clinical needs of pathologists.

11.8.2 Gait analysis

Walking is an essential function for most activities in daily life. Motion disruptions can have severe health implications. Therefore gait rehabilitation is an important is-

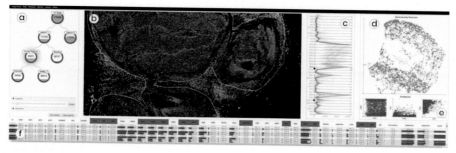

FIGURE 11.14

The interface of FACETTO: Multiple coordinated views in FACETTO for interactive and hierarchical phenotype analysis of 36-channel image data. (a) Phenotype tree resulting from hierarchical data filtering and cell calling. (b) Multi-channel visualization of high-resolution CyCIF image data showing the current clustering and classification results. (c) Ridge-plot of high-dimensional feature data to steer visual analysis and data filtering. (d) UMAP projection of the sampled feature space of cells, colored by cluster ID. (e) Scatterplots showing feature value correlations. (f) Table view of all cells and their features (©2019 IEEE, Reprinted with permission from: (Krueger et al., 2019)).

sue for clinical medicine. Gait analysis allows clinicians to explore and analyze the gait of a patient (and its improvement or worsening) and supports decision-making related to treatment. This, however, requires the simultaneous analysis of multivariate and heterogeneous data sources, such as kinematics, external forces, and other time-varying data, which are often acquired in real-time while the patient is performing a walking exercise. The complexity and inter-linking of the involved data requires sophisticated data analysis methods, which can be found in visual analytics.

Wagner et al. (2018) introduced KAVAGAIT, a system that allows the user to store and inspect complex, time-varying patient data obtained during clinical gait analysis. It supports two main clinical scenarios: the assessment of newly acquired patient data, and the exploration and adjustment of available stored data. The latter practically supports the externalization and storage of implicit knowledge from clinicians, making it available also to others and supporting clinical decision-making. The interface of KAVAGAIT is shown in Fig. 11.15.

As an extension to KAVAGAIT, Rind et al. (2022) presented GAITXPLORER, an explainability-enriched visual analytics approach for the classification of gait patterns. The authors combine modern predictive machine learning approaches with time-series visualizations to make the underlying machine learning models transparent. The interface of GAITXPLORER is shown in Fig. 11.16.

11.8.3 Sleep monitoring

Sleep disorders affect the overall health and quality of life of the patient. Therefore individuals with (suspected) sleep disorders are subject to polysomnography tests,

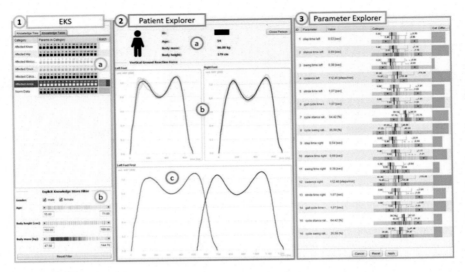

FIGURE 11.15

User interface of KAVAGAIT with its three main areas for gait analysis. 1) The table structure in (1a) shows an overview of the stored gait patterns along with the controls in (1b).
2) The patient explorer, including the (2a) Person Information, the (2b) visualization of the
vertical ground reaction force for each individual foot, and the (2c) visualization of the combined force from both feet. 3) Shows the parameter explorer (©2018 IEEE, Reprinted with
permission from: (Wagner et al., 2018)).

which provide brain signal measured by electroencephalography (EEG). These tests,
together with additional EHR data of the patient, need to be explored and analyzed
by clinical experts. Yet, this process is still done manually by annotating (or tagging)
pieces of the signals as sleep stages. This manual approach is tedious and cannot be
applied at a large scale.

To solve this scalability issue, recent work focuses on applying deep learning
models to sleep data, but understanding whether the model actually performs correctly remains a challenge. Recent work of Garcia Caballero et al. (2019) deals with
a real-life scenario, in which the deep learning model is not perfect and no ground
truth is available, but still the users need to discover if there are potential misclassi-
fications and their causes. To this end, they introduce V-AWAKE, a visual analytics
approach that aids users to find, store, analyze, and correct faulty deep learning sleep
staging outcomes, in the absence of ground truth. The interface of V-AWAKE is presented in Fig. 11.17.

Subsequent work of the same authors supports further explainability of deep
learning models (Caballero et al., 2021), focusing on understanding the performance
of the models that experts employ for the classification of sleep staging. Therefore
they presented PERSLEEP, which was the first visual analytics approach that supports the comparative assessment of two models in sleep staging along with patient

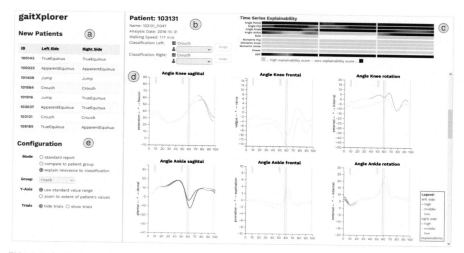

FIGURE 11.16

Visual interface showing a patient's data in explainability mode: (a) list of new patients that need to be classified; (b) master data of the current patient including controls to select a gait classification; (c) compact overview of the patient's time series with color encoding that indicates the relevance (grounding) for the automated prediction; (d) time series details as line plots with color intensity according to their relevance (discretized into three levels, i.e., high, middle and low); (e) controls to switch between modes and change settings (From: (Rind et al., 2022)).

data. The novelty of this work is the assessment of multiple, complex models, which can be applied on time series data of individual patients, selected groups of interests, and the entire population. PERSLEEP enables the exploration of distributions of patient attributes to detect odd model behaviors, identification of correlations between data attributes, performance analysis for the employed model, and the comparison of patient hypnograms. Such explainable AI methods are promising enhancements of visual computing solutions in other medical applications.

11.9 Concluding remarks

In this last chapter of the part "Visual Analytics in Medicine" we discussed clinical medicine, i.e., our focus was on exploiting visualization and analytical components for the diagnosis and treatment of patients. Event-type data that capture changes in the state of a patient as well as in diagnosis and treatment play a key role in clinical medicine. Therefore we discussed how to structure such data, how to visualize it, how to focus the visualization of the patient state to temporal windows or interesting aspects. This brought us to the visual analysis of groups of patients, where a proper

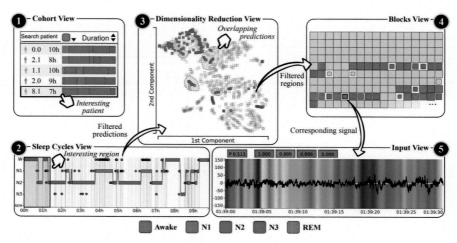

FIGURE 11.17

User interface of V-AWAKE. First, a patient is selected (1) and the predictions from the deep learning model are displayed in 2, 3 and 4. Next, some of the predictions are selected (2) and the data in the dimensionality reduction plot is highlighted (3). Some regions in the scatter plot are selected and the corresponding predictions are marked in the blocks view (4). Finally, selecting a prediction block makes the input view display the corresponding input (5), which can be analyzed to determine if the prediction is correct (From: (Garcia Caballero et al., 2019), ©John Wiley & Sons Inc., 2019).

alignment of individual histories is essential. To cope with the even larger amount of data, we discussed its simplification.

Visual analytics is useful to predict the further course of diseases, and in the case of severe diseases also the patient survival. This involves experiences with previous patients and some model assumptions. In addition to the raw patient data, data from prediction is employed in clinical decision-making. Potentially, the methods discussed in this chapter can be applied to a large variety of medical conditions and their treatment, e.g., with regard to COVID-19 data (Stritzel and Raidou, 2022). Our discussion of applications is by no means comprehensive, as we put a focus on the diagnosis and treatment of cancer patients. This is motivated by the large number of cancer patients, the severity of the diseases and the long-term character of cancer treatment in many cases. Thus in hospital settings a large amount of resources is devoted to these patients. We would like to emphasize the difference between decision-making support approaches and the solutions discussed in Chapter 8.

Finally, we should mention that clinical treatment makes considerable progress. Genetic examinations, again primarily in tumor patients and degenerative diseases, play an increasing role in identifying mutations and in supporting the selection of a treatment strategy that takes the occurrence of mutations into account Somarakis et al. (2021). There are already examples of dedicate visual analytics systems that process this kind of data, but these have not been integrated into this chapter.

Recommended reading

For more insights in this topic, we refer the readers to the publications below and in general to the proceedings of the IEEE Visual Analytics in Healthcare (VAHC) workshop series. The workshop started in 2010 and predominantly focuses on clinical applications of visual analytics techniques.

David Gotz, Fei Wang, and Adam Perer. "A methodology for interactive mining and visual analysis of clinical event patterns using electronic health record data," *Journal of Biomedical Informatics*, Vol. 48 (2014): 148–159.

Yi Guo, Shunan Guo, Zhuochen Jin, Smiti Kaul, David Gotz, and Nan Cao (2021). "A survey on visual analysis of event sequence data," *IEEE Transactions on Visualization and Computer Graphics*.

A. Rind, T.D. Wang, W. Aigner, S. Miksch, K. Wongsuphasawat, C. Plaisant, and B. Shneiderman. "Interactive information visualization to explore and query electronic health records," *Foundations and Trends in Human-Computer Interaction*, Vol. 5, 3(2013), 207–298.

V.L. West, D. Borland, and W.E. Hammond. "Innovative information visualization of electronic health record data: a systematic review", *Journal of the American Medical Informatics Association*, Vol. 22.2 (2015): 330–339.

Virtual Reality in medicine

The last part of this book is motivated by the strong improvements in afford-able VR technology and the potential of VR in medicine. Research prototypes for VR-based surgical planning, surgical simulators and neurorehabilitation were already developed in the 1990s; currently there are mature systems, including commercially available systems.

We start with an introduction into virtual reality, including hardware, major interaction tasks, and avatars that represent the user in a virtual environment (Chapter 12). We go on with discussions of two broad application areas. First, we discuss applications in medical education, where the strong immersion and the high degree of realism enables to virtually "grasp" and understand anatomy, to train surgery, including handling of complications and teamwork (Chapter 13). Finally, we discuss the use of virtual reality for medical treat-ment. These clinical VR systems were developed to support the treatment of phobias, such as fear of height and fear of flying, to treat patients with acute and chronic pain, as well as for the rehabilitation treatment of brain damage, e.g., as a result of strokes (Chapter 14).

Introduction to Virtual Reality

12

12.1 Introduction

Virtual reality (VR) aims at providing an environment where the user is *immersed* in a 3D environment. The user may move their head and the displayed information is adapted to this new viewing direction immediately. The image content is shown in high spatial resolution and high quality to generate the impression of *being there*. The image content is provided for both eyes, considering the slightly different positions of the eyes, thus creating a stereo effect. The user is *part of* a virtual environment and perceives it from an *egocentric perspective* in contrast to a visitor who looks through a window in a virtual world. Multiple senses are stimulated in VR, enabling a deep imagination and engaging experiences, such as listening to classic music of an orchestra based on high-quality audio rendering, the excitement when walking through a beautiful landscape, the fear when approaching a cliff and also the excitement and physical effort related to doing sports. Immersive VR may provide an extraordinary emotional depth that is beneficial among others for learning, e.g., in surgery or interventional radiology. Moreover, it has applications in medical treatment, e.g., to overcome anxieties and pain.

The term "virtual reality" was coined by JARON LANIER in 1987. LANIER, a company founder, tried to bring VR to the public. Different definitions characterize virtual reality. We mention some of them to set the stage for the further discussion.

- "Primary defining characteristic is inclusion; being surrounded by an environment" (Bricken, 1991).
- "Virtual reality refers to immersive, interactive, multi-sensory, viewer-centered, 3D computer-generated environments and the technologies to build them" (Cruz-Neira, 1993).
- "Virtual reality is defined to be a computer-generated digital environment that can be experimented with and interacted with as if that environment were real" (Jerald, 2015).

VR may overcome restrictions of the real world, e.g., users may walk through very small phenomena, such as molecules or the inner ear. The laws of physics do not necessarily apply. Objects may be floating in the air, instead of falling down due to gravity. However, if VR systems deviate from our real-world experience, users may get confused, as Marks et al. (2017) indicate: "We observed a larger hesitance in students for whom this was their first experience, specifically when having to move through seemingly solid surfaces."

Some historical remarks

For many years, the technical challenges of developing VR hardware, computing hardware, and efficient rendering algorithms hampered the widespread use of VR technology. The hardware was rare and expensive and the setup was tedious, limiting VR to a few research centers and design departments of large companies. This has changed significantly in the last decade. With more affordable VR headsets, the focus shifted towards designing attractive rewarding *experiences* for professional applications as well as entertainment. Thus the considerable knowledge acquired by usability, professionals aiming at a high *user experience* becomes relevant. Also the achievements of the gaming industry, such as powerful and realistic rendering, are essential.

Medicine always was an essential area for VR with applications ranging from surgical training, medical team training, to rehabilitation. Visionary inventors, such as RICHARD SATAVA, expressed early how VR may contribute to medical training and treatment (Satava, 1993). A specific conference series "Medicine Meets Virtual Reality" was already started in 1993. Meanwhile, medical VR is discussed in many different journals and at different venues.

Components of VR systems

A VR system has the following components and aspects (Sherman and Craig, 2018):

- *A virtual world.* A geometric model representing a certain use case, e.g., a model of a city or a part thereof.
- *Immersion.* The illusion of being "really there."
- *Sensory feedback.* Feedback provided by visual, auditory, or haptic stimuli. Even olfactory or gustatory interfaces are developed.
- *Interactivity.* Options to navigate through the virtual environment (VE) and to change it, e.g., to select and parameterize objects.

According to these components Sherman and Craig (2018) define virtual reality as follows:

Definition 12.1. "Virtual reality is a medium composed of interactive computer simulations that sense the participants' position and actions and replace or augment the feedback to one or more senses, giving the feeling of being mentally immersed or present in the simulation."

In the following paragraphs we describe the components in more detail.

Virtual world

A geometric model representing all components of a virtual world, e.g., a factory, a city model, or in medicine a model of an operating room or the patient anatomy.

These models may contain fine details and more abstract representations. It may include textures and lighting specifications to ensure a proper level of realism. The virtual world also represents relations and constraints, e.g., the range in which a joint may be moved. Also the reaction to collisions between elements of the virtual world may be specified. *Avatars* as representations of the user(s) position and orientation are often parts of a virtual world. They may represent a part of the human body, e.g., the hands only up to full body representations.

Immersion

The sense of immersion is largely determined by display characteristics and the performance of the VR system. Too abstract renditions that look artificial may break the sense of immersion. The same holds for noticeable delays in the presentation, e.g., after head movements. There are many other aspects that may distract and break the immersion, e.g., when textual labels are displayed on 2D planes, instead of being fully embedded in 3D (Maass and Döllner, 2008). Any distractions from the real world hamper the sense of immersion. Therefore we focus on situations that are fully immersive, e.g., where the user is completely surrounded by the display of a virtual environment.

Sensory feedback

Visual perception is the most essential communication channel for humans given the high bandwidth of information conveyed visually. However, our real-world orientation also benefits from acoustic signals: We hear a car approaching and we perceive the sound of an ambulance as urgent. We perceive audio feedback independent from our current viewing direction, and we can estimate our distance and direction towards the source of the sound. Thus a convincing VR system provides also audio feedback. When objects in the virtual environment are associated with tactile properties, such as stiffness, roughness, and temperature, haptic feedback may be provided. This touching sensation is important for surgery education, since the tactile impression is essential in real surgery.

Interactivity

VR also comprises interaction as an essential aspect. Basic interaction relates to the navigation, e.g., the change of the orientation and position to explore the virtual world. Typically, users may rotate their head and walk around while the view is adapted (head tracking). In a VR system, e.g., for training, participants are enabled to perform tasks, e.g., to simulate the maintenance of a machine. Moreover, the hands or hand-held controllers are tracked, enabling interactions, such as grabbing objects. When the limited space where tracking is provided is too small, *locomotion techniques* enable to exceed these limits. Such a task requires that the user may select and grasp objects, move them away, or put them together. Controllers for VR enable the selection of objects and options as well as to invoke commands, e.g., to display a menu. A particularly useful interaction for medical applications is to employ hand-held cutting planes to slice a medical volume data set in an arbitrary direction

(Sutherland et al., 2019). Controllers are characterized by the *degrees of freedom* (DOF) they support. Most controllers provide 6 DOF, meaning that the position and orientation in space are tracked (3+3 DOF).

The design of a VR system is characterized by an enormous flexibility. Developers have to consider effects of interactions in the virtual environment, e.g., when an object is moved in the free air it may be exposed to gravitation. If the user grasps a flexible object, it may get squeezed as in reality. Also the movement of one object into another, a *collision*, may be realized such that the colliding objects experience forces, e.g., leading to deformation or movement. The highest amount of realism is not always desirable and useful. Some tasks may be facilitated if they are not realized in a realistic manner, e.g., if an object *snaps* to another one if it is close enough to support a *docking task*. Finally, VR design affects emotional aspects, which are crucial issues for any educational application. The selection of colors, materials, interactions, and user feedback influences the mood of users, their engagement, and motivation. Game-inspired elements may be used to further strengthen the motivation of the users, e.g., by involving them in a kind of competition with other learners.

VR programming

Powerful toolkits were developed that enable a VR developer to think at a higher level of abstraction. As an example, developers often do not have to specify transformation matrices and process them. Lightsources, cameras, and selection rays are among the abstractions provided.

Game engines, such as UNITY and UNREAL ENGINE, are also frequently used in the medical domain (Sutherland et al., 2019). They are not only powerful but also well-documented and realized in a user-friendly manner. Moreover, the modeling effort involved in designing characters as avatars and in building a virtual environment was reduced considerably. On the one hand, modeling tools get more and more powerful; on the other hand, an enormous variability of virtual environments is already available for often low prices, e.g., in the UNITY AssetStore. The virtual reality toolkit (VRTK) provides many basic interaction techniques in VR and can be accessed conveniently inside a UNITY application.

Limitations

Though the potential of VR is large and many prototypes have been developed and refined after feedback from pilot studies, VR systems have limitations as well. Despite all progress in technology and modeling tools, the development of a VR solution often involves a larger budget compared to a similar solution for desktop use. Thus cost justification is an issue. Not only the development of a VR system is expensive, but also the user has to invest in VR headsets and in the setup of a room for example. This additional effort needs to be justified. Users may encounter headaches, vomiting, and nausea, symptoms of *cybersickness* or VR sickness. The design of a VR system should take this problem into account and prevent movements that involve a high likelihood for discomfort.

Semi-immersive and immersive VR

Due to the limitations of immersive VR, it is worth to consider *semi-immersive VR*. Systems of this category provide more immersion than a mere desktop solution but no full immersion. Semi-immersive VR systems (also called *Fishtank VR*) (Ware et al., 1993) employ stereo displays with head tracking. A modern example is the zSpace (https://zspace.com/), which was also frequently used for anatomy education. Semi-immersive VR is useful when a system requires users to notice also the real world and when usage over a longer time is envisioned. Fully immersive VR still is not convenient enough to be used regularly for several hours.

Organization

The remainder of this chapter is organized as follows: We refine the discussion of *presence* and *immersion*, which are fundamental for VR systems (Section 12.2). After the discussion of the potential of VR, we also think about one of its problems, namely VR sickness (Section 12.3). We go on with the introduction of VR headsets and other frequently used hardware components (Section 12.4). We discuss the design of avatars, the representations of user in virtual environment (Section 12.5). Basic interaction techniques for immersive VR are explained in Section 12.6. Locomotion techniques for navigating, e.g., in a digital operating room (OR), are described in (Section 12.7). Finally, we consider how the immersion and the degree of realism can be further improved by adding haptics (Section 12.8) and audio feedback (Section 12.9).

12.2 Immersion and presence

3D User interfaces, and in particular VR applications, aim at a high level of immersion since this is the major potential advantage of VR.

Immersion

is a broadly used term. Two meanings are essential for VR:

- *Mental immersion* characterizes a deep engagement and involvement in a task, e.g., controlling a bleeding in a surgery training application.
- *Physical immersion* is the feeling of physical deep involvement, by stimulating various senses in a plausible manner, e.g., walking around in a virtual environment that provides also realistic visual and auditory sensations.

High mental immersion may already be possible with a good book or a computer game. Mental immersion is more subjective than physical immersion.

Suspension of disbelief

This widely used term is related to the presence and immersion in VR. The term *suspension of disbelief* was coined in the 19th century to characterize human perception of fantasy, fairy tales, magic actions, e.g., in a circus, where humans are cut in pieces and transformed into animals. Although spectators are aware that such a transformation is not possible, they tend to believe it to a certain extent.

Presence

is a crucial term in VR but actually was introduced earlier in robotics, where the feeling of an operator to control a remote robot was characterized (Minsky, 1980). Presence in VR basically means that users (willingly) suspend disbelief.

Presence in VR involves the followings aspects (Slater and Wilbur, 1997; Sanchez-Vives and Slater, 2005):

- Feeling of being there, i.e., a sense of consciousness
- Feeling of having visited places (displayed in VR), instead of having seen images (*place illusion*)
- Feeling of doing there, i.e., being able to control the environment (*plausibility illusion*)
- The virtual environment dominates over the real environment, i.e., the participant "forgets" that they are in a VR lab but feel somewhere else, e.g., at a historically important place.

The first aspect is often referred to as *spatial presence*. Spatial presence is assessed in appropriate questionnaires, e.g., Igroup presence questionnaire (IPQ) (Schubert et al., 2001), along with other aspects of *presence*. Spatial presence includes the feeling of being surrounded by the virtual environment.

A high level of presence means that the user has the illusion to be at another place (Slater et al., 2010). This is a surprising state: Although the user knows that they are in a lab wearing VR headsets, they believe to a strong extent to be somewhere else. Many VR applications in medicine require high levels of presence: Only if surgeons perceive patient data, the OR, and the virtual representations of their colleagues as real and meaningful, they will fully engage and practice surgery, e.g., handling of complications. Similarly, only if a patient perceives fear of heights or other fears, a treatment application may help the patient to overcome this anxiety. The extent to which the place illusion works depends on display characteristics and presentation quality, whereas the extent to which the plausibility illusion works depends on the actual content of a virtual environment and to the interactivity provided. In this regard, Slater (2009) defines *valid actions*:

- Valid navigation actions comprise a set of movements that are tracked and lead to an update of the visualization, e.g., head tracking, walking, or moving a driving wheel.
- Valid effectual actions comprise interactions that change the environment, e.g., grasping objects, touching, feeling, and placing objects.

The role of display characteristics

The degree to which participants feel presence is strongly influenced by characteristics of immersions, including display characteristics, visual realism, haptics, sound, virtual body representation, and body engagement (Sanchez-Vives and Slater, 2005). Essential display characteristics to trigger (physical) immersion include:

- a very wide field of view
- a high spatial resolution
- a high color resolution

Moreover, a very low latency and a high frame rate are essential. That means powerful computer systems and efficient algorithms are required to update a complex (realistic) virtual environment presented in high spatial resolution. "Low latency" means that body movements or other interactions lead to a fast feedback without any noticeable delay. Thus a high and constant frame rate without sacrificing visual detail is required. The polygon count for the geometric model may be limited in the modeling process, where several modeling tools enable a *polygon budget*, meaning that the geometry is simplified as soon as this budget is reached. A precise understanding of the human visual system allows to simplify some calculations without generating noticeable artifacts. To give a few examples for this strategy: The level of detail to represent an object may be adjusted to its distance to the camera, billboards may be used to replace explicit and complex geometry with a texture and objects outside the current view frustum may be removed (Gaitatzes et al., 2001). A convincing implementation of these strategies, however, may be challenging. For example, frequent switches of the (discrete) level of detail, and thus the visual quality may be annoying. Ideally, such changes are carried out infrequently and seamlessly to get unnoticed. As a further strategy to achieve good trade-offs between visual quality and low latency, small positional changes of the user may be ignored, i.e., rendering is only activated after a significant movement. Hänel et al. (2016) discuss these and other strategies to adapt the visual quality.

Realism

A question of intense debate in VR research is how realistic a virtual environment should be depicted. Various levels of abstractions could be applied to simplify, e.g., a factory or a car design in VR. These abstractions relate to the geometry and to the illumination. The hypothesis that only a high degree of visual realism enables a high level of immersion is not convincingly and generally proven (Sanchez-Vives and Slater, 2005). Thus in a medical training environment, for example, the necessary level of detail needs to be investigated. A virtual body representation (an *avatar*) probably improves immersion, even if the body is represented in a crude manner, e.g., as a mannequin. Instead of aiming at a high degree of realism, it is often more appropriate to aim at plausibility, which basically means that users consider the virtual environment as believable, i.e., the trust in the environment is not disturbed.

The integration of audio and haptic feedback also improves immersion, whereas voices and other sounds from the real environment break it. Even noise generated in the VR application and perceived over the earphone is better than voices from the real environment. Spatialized audio is particularly beneficial. Also if participants need to be careful not to stumble across the cables of the VR headset, they feel disturbed in their virtual world.

Naturally, some users are more "willing" to believe they are in a virtual environment. For example, persons that can be easily hypnotized perceive strong levels of presence (Slater and Wilbur, 1997). Presence can also be assessed by studying whether users behave in VR as in reality. As an example: Do surgeons behave in a training system like in the OR? Biofeedback may be used to measure physiological reactions, e.g., heart rate and pulse, which could reveal the patient state in anxiety treatment.

Presence evaluation

Presence is assessed with standardized questionnaires, e.g., the questionnaire introduced by Witmer and Singer (1998). We mention a few early results of the presence-related research. A higher degree of realism and more interactivity increased the presence in a driving simulator (Welch et al., 1996). Stereopsis and wider field of view are also beneficial for presence (Hendrix and Barfield, 1996). A realistic simulation of friction, but not of elasticity, increased the presence in a bowling game scenario (Uno and Slater, 1997).

Co-presence

is the sense of being with other persons in a virtual environment (Durlach and Slater, 2000), i.e., the awareness for other participants and their intents. It is essential for collaborative VR, e.g., in a training system that involves surgeons, nurses, and anesthetists. Co-presence requires that other participants are visually represented and behave plausibly. When a high level of co-presence is achieved, a participant responds to actions of another participant, represented by their avatar, as they would respond in the real world. This means, when another avatar in VR looks at my avatar, approaches my avatar, smiles at my avatar, or looks aggressive towards my avatar, the same emotional reactions are triggered as in reality. Measurable changes of heart rate, pulse, and skin temperature reveal such changes in the emotional state. Many investigations showed that the response depends on the attitude of other avatars (facial expressions). Thus the behavior of other avatars is understood as caused by one's own behavior.

We have already mentioned that rich sensory feedback, e.g., spatial audio and at least limited tactile feedback (haptics) are essential for immersion. As an example for the role of haptics, Sanchez-Vives and Slater (2005) enabled persons who do not see each other to feel forces by holding a wire with a ring together. Based on the elasticity of the wire, a person felt the influence of others.

Summary

Presence and immersion are related, but slightly different terms that characterize to what extent users experience the illusion of being in a virtual world. Immersion is the more technical term, whereas presence is a subjective impression of the participants. Thus a virtual environment can be assessed regarding their immersion based on display characteristics. Presence, in contrast, is assessed with questionnaires and the perceived presence of different users may strongly differ. A high level of immersion is a prerequisite for presence, but cannot guarantee that all users perceive this state.

12.3 VR sickness

Whereas deep immersion is the promise of VR, VR sickness is the downside; it is a medical condition that may be severe, and thus limits the acceptance of VR. VR sickness is related, but slightly different than motion sickness, a condition that may arise when being in a car or bus as a consequence of conflicting perceptual cues. In particular when reading or focusing on points inside a car, the body perceives motion, whereas the visual system does not notify it. As a consequence, headache, vomiting, and other symptoms may arise. In a similar manner, certain locomotion techniques in VR may trigger similar symptoms. However, VR has some unique medical risks (Dörner et al., 2019). Like any long-term use of electronic displays, eye strain and headaches may result.

Influence factors

The likelihood that participants experience VR sickness depends on a number of attributes of the participants. Dörner et al. (2019) mention that women are more likely affected than men, and that persons with more experience in gaming and VR are less likely to be affected. Some persons that experienced VR sickness in their early encounters with VR later could use similar applications without problems. Thus a certain learning may take place on the user's side to avoid VR sickness.

More important than the influence of personal attributes is the influence of hard- and software characteristics. Can we create VR solutions where the likelihood for VR sickness is strongly reduced? Are there certain interactions where the risk for VR sickness is particularly high? These questions are particularly relevant for medical treatment. VR has a high potential for treating various anxieties, pain, and even neurodegenerative diseases. The patients, however, are particularly vulnerable. For ethical reasons, the risk they are exposed to should be really low.

VR sickness is more likely to occur when the refresh rate of the display is low. Insufficient performance in rendering leads to a delay that also increases the risk for VR sickness. Dörner et al. (2019) recommend to ensure latency values below 20 ms, whereas delays above 40 ms are clearly too long. Thus partially the same attributes that contribute to high immersion help to reduce or avoid VR sickness. When the user is rotated, in particular when the rotation is about more than one axis, the risk for VR sickness is considerable. To prevent or at least reduce VR sickness, Dörner et al. (2019) mention that chewing gum and sufficient drinking are considered beneficial, strategies that are also beneficial against motion sickness. A VR study or the actual use of VR should be designed such that it can be interrupted. This is also beneficial to reduce or avoid VR sickness. The reasons that actually cause VR sickness and the mechanisms that are involved are subject to current research.

Evaluation

Since VR sickness is an essential aspect, standardized questionnaires were developed to assess the occurrence and amount of this problem, i.e., participants of an evaluation should be asked to fill them. A widely used questionnaire for VR sickness was introduced by Ames et al. (2005). This questionnaire is used to asses eight general side-effects, such as fatigue, headache and nausea, and five visual effects, such as tired eyes, eyestrain, and blurred vision on a seven-point Likert scale.

12.4 VR hardware

In this section we discuss hardware for VR systems with focus on VR headsets and controllers. Before discussing the actual hardware, we explain stereo rendering since stereo perception is a key aspect of VR and the immersion that it may provide.

12.4.1 Stereo rendering

We interpret the sensations recorded at the retina as a 3D scene. This interpretation is based on a multitude of experiences and specific depth and shape cues. Depth is inferred from Wanger et al. (1992):

- partial occlusion (an object that appears interrupted must be behind another one)
- perspective foreshortening
- shadows
- shading effects (reflection, refraction)
- depth attenuation (distant objects appear darker in low saturated colors)
- texture gradients

These effects can be simulated in 3D renderings, and thus be incorporated in VR-based systems. However, even when realized efficiently, they may increase the computational effort and may hamper having a sufficient performance for enabling fast updates. Thus in practice only simple (local) illumination models are employed.

All these depth cues can be perceived with one eye (monoscopic depth cues). Stereo rendering adds another depth cue based on the slightly different images that the two eyes perceive. This effect naturally depends on the distance of our eyes to the currently focused objects. If these objects are far away, the viewing rays from our two eyes to them are basically parallel, and thus the images are almost equal. For objects, however, that are only a few meters in front of our eyes, the viewing rays differ considerably, leading to a strong stereo perception.

Horopter and panum

Some terms are essential to characterize stereo vision. The *horopter* is an elliptical section that comprises all points that can be seen theoretically by both eyes (Dörner et al., 2019). The *panum* is an extended region, where the convergence is enabled based on adaptation processes. The smallest extent of the panum occurs at the fixation point within the horopter. As a consequence of this observation, it may be beneficial to rescale a virtual world to enable stereo perception (Dörner et al., 2019).

Interpupil distance

Stereo rendering aims at providing this crucial depth cue in virtual environments. A pair of images is rendered from slightly different perspectives intended to be perceived by the two eyes. An essential aspect is the actual distance of the two eyes, the *interpupil distance* (IPD). It has an average value of 63 mm, but varies between 52 and 78 mm in a population of some 4000 adults in young or middle age (Dodgson, 2004). There are systematic gender differences (the IPD of male subjects is about 2 mm larger than the IPD of female subjects), and black subjects have a 4 mm larger IPD compared to white subjects (Dodgson, 2004). The interindividual differences in the IPD are large enough to justify facilities to adapt stereo displays of VR headsets. It is not easy to determine the IPD of an individual. Ideally, this is done by a professional optometrist, but there are also tutorials on the web that show how to do this yourself with a mirror and a ruler. Without an adaptation to the IPD, eye strain and blurry images may result when the deviation between the systems' adjustment and the actual IPD of the user is more than about 3 mm. Modern VR headsets are adaptable and provide support to define one's own IPD. As an example, the widespread OCULUS QUEST provides three IPD settings: 58, 63, and 68 mm.

Stereo blindness

We described the stereopsis, the perception of stereo in healthy persons. There are also deficiencies or even a stereo blindness among some persons. It is essential to ask for such problems in a user study to correctly interpret the results. Chopin et al. (2019) report that the prevalence of stereo blindness among persons younger than 60 years is about 7%, and it is likely higher for elderly people, a group of people who is more likely to seek medical treatment.

12.4.2 Principles of VR headsets

Users may experience a VR system either in a room where the image content is projected on the walls or by wearing VR headsets with a display directly in front of the eyes. In both cases, the users' position and orientation need to be tracked to display the virtual content correctly. This is achieved by wearing headsets to which retroreflective markers are attached. Various tracking methods, e.g., infrared tracking, are employed to compute the user's position and orientation. At least four markers must be identified to solve the underlying equation systems. When more markers are detected, a more robust solution can be expected. The creation of a room where back projectors display the content on the ceiling and sidewalls is the far more expensive solution. The room has to be specifically designed and built for this purpose, and the maintenance is also expensive. These CAVEs (cave automatic virtual environment) (Cruz-Neira et al., 1993) are employed in large companies for design reviews, but they are hardly affordable for private users. More recently, also cylinder-shaped or half-spherical spaces were constructed (*dome projections*), primarily for virtual environments representing our universe with stars and planets. Since CAVE-based systems and dome projections are currently not widely used in medicine, we focus on VR headsets.

The basic optical principle of VR headsets is shown in Fig. 12.1. Without correction, the images perceived via VR headsets would be distorted by the lenses, e.g., parallel lines do not appear parallel. Thus the images need to be corrected. Fig. 12.2 compares images with and without correction.

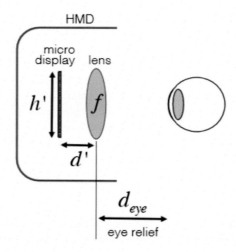

FIGURE 12.1

Principle of VR headsets (Courtesy of Gordon Wetzstein, Stanford University).

12.4.3 VR headsets

The following discussion of VR headsets relates to hardware systems that evolve rapidly. Thus the reader may notice that there are more powerful and modern devices available than the authors could consider at the time of writing. While some technical details will soon get outdated, this subsection should provide an overview using criteria that are likely more long-lived than specific versions of VR headsets. VR headsets experienced a considerable development in recent years, leading to lighter, more convenient headsets with larger fields of views. Device development also aims at reducing motion blur and noticeable boundaries of individual pixels.

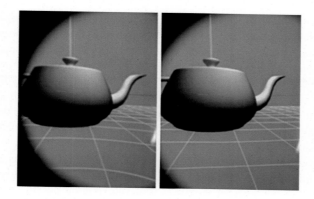

FIGURE 12.2

Without correction, the image would be perceived in distorted manner (left). The distortion can be reliably corrected (right) (Courtesy of Gordon Wetzstein, Stanford University).

An important distinction is between cable-based and wireless VR headsets. Typically, VR headsets are connected via a cable to a (powerful) desktop PC, which includes a recent graphics card, where the whole rendering process is carried out. This solution enable a high rendering performance, and thus high-quality graphics without significant latency. However, cables represent a significant usability problem. Users have to be aware of them, they have to avoid stumbling across them, and this limits *presence*, the feeling of being somewhere else. A recent alternative are wireless VR headsets, where this usability problem is completely avoided. However, this requires that the rendering is carried out within the VR glasses. Therefore these systems are also referred to as all-in-one-VR systems. An example is the METAQUEST from REALITYLABS. Currently, this solution typically does not provide the same performance as desktop PCs with modern graphics card. Thus the selection of a cable-based or wireless VR headset is a trade-off between performance and usability.

We employ the term VR headsets instead of the more classic term HMD (head-mounted display). A HMD is associated with the impression of a heavy military-looking helmet from the early days of VR, where military training was the major use case. In the following, we describe selected VR headsets, focusing on widely used and leading devices. The information is based on the English Wikipedia sites related to the specific VR headsets and considers the following criteria (see (Grimm et al., 2013; LaViola Jr. et al., 2017)):

- weight and comfort (ergonomics)
- adaptability to the interpupil distance and head size of the users
- resolution
- field of view
- availability of earphones for audio feedback

Whereas obviously a heavy VR headset is unfortunate, it is also a question how the weight is distributed, i.e., whether there is increased pressure on the frontal part of the skull or not. Some aspects of visual perception are relevant for our discussion of VR headsets (Traquair, 1949). The horizontal field of view of humans is about 210°. The vertical field of view is about 150°. The spatial resolution within this field of view is very irregular. In the *fovea*—a small part of the human retina with an increased density of light-sensitive cells—we perceive colors and fine geometric details. In the surrounding *parafovea* the visual acuity is already considerably reduced, and in the periphery it is an order of magnitude lower than in the fovea.

Some modern VR headsets provide integrated eye tracking. This can be used together with *foveatic rendering* techniques, which spend more effort to render details perceived in the fovea (Albert et al., 2017). With this strategy, the computing headsets may be efficiently used. Relevant details are rendered accurately, but most of the rendering is simplified making a fast update of the virtual environment possible.

HTC Vive

The HTC VIVE was released in April 2016. Two base stations are employed that regularly sweep the room with IR light pulses to allow the tracking of VR headsets and handheld controllers. The HTC VIVE provides a refresh rate of 90 Hz, a spatial resolution of 1080 × 1200 pixels per eye, and a horizontal field of view of 110°. It is equipped with sensors and two wireless 6 DOF controllers for bimanual 3D input. Objects can be translated and rotated by moving the controllers. By moving both controllers relative to each other, objects are scaled. The controllers are typically integrated in the user's view. A trigger button for mode switching and a circular touchpad for processing 2D input are also provided (see Fig. 12.3). The controllers may also provide haptic feedback (steady and unsteady vibrations), e.g., when the controller touches an object. The programmer has control over the duration and amount of vibration, and may even specify in detail how the vibration is increasing and decreasing over time, e.g., there may be two peaks, the second being one second after the first with a linear increase and decrease.

The HTC VIVE has a turning knob and grip buttons to adjust it to the actual interpupil distance. The controllers and the VR headsets are tracked based on infrared signals. The weight of a controller is 309 g, which is a lot for long-term use (for comparison: a badminton racket has a weight of 80 g). With 470 g, the headset has a similar weight as that of the OCULUS RIFT. In Fig. 12.4, we see a VIVE controller used in a cultural heritage application.

The setup requires two base stations that enable tracking in a room. The LIGHT-HOUSE tracking system is employed, currently in version LIGHTHOUSE 2.0. The base stations emit infrared light and synchronize each other, which requires that they "see" each other or are connected via a cable. They are often mounted to the ceiling. The base stations may be arbitrarily distributed; no cable connection to a computer required. The tracking area, where the user can move around, of the current version is about 6 m × 6 m.

FIGURE 12.3

A HTC VIVE with its two controllers that are tracked for 6 DOF input. Buttons and a touch-pad provide further interaction capabilities.

FIGURE 12.4

A HTC VIVE is used to explore a model of a virtual reconstruction as part of a public presentation (Courtesy of Patrick Saalfeld, University of Magdeburg).

Later versions include the HTC VIVE PRO (2018) and the HTC VIVE PRO EYE. They provide a higher spatial resolution (1440 × 1600 pixels) and an increased tracking space. The HTC VIVE PRO EYE integrates eye tracking. The STEAMVR API is used to develop VR applications with the HTC VIVE. It can be integrated with UNITY and UNREAL ENGINE. More recently (2020), the HTC VIVE COSMOS was introduced, which provides a superior spatial resolution (2880 × 1700 pixels).

The HTC VIVE is a good VR headset, even a couple of years after its introduction. However, its usability, in particular for elderly users is not ideal. In addition to the weight and problems related to the cables, the smooth surface of the buttons was considered as a problem, since they are hard to recognize (Coldham and Cook, 2017). The problem of the cables is resolved with the latest HTC VIVE COSMOS ELITE, where wireless connections are used instead.

Oculus Rift

The first commercial version of the OCULUS RIFT was released in March 2016 (https://en.wikipedia.org/wiki/Oculus_Rift). With a refresh rate of 90 Hz, a relatively large horizontal field of view of 110°, and a spatial resolution of 1080 × 1200 per eye; it was a reasonable basis for ambitious VR projects. The OCULUS RIFT can be adjusted for IPDs between 58 and 72 mm. It provides integrated headphones, and thus enables the perception of 3D audio. In December 2016, OCULUS TOUCH controllers were released and enabled a wide range of applications where haptic feedback is essential. The OCULUS QUEST is available since March 2019 (https://en.wikipedia.org/wiki/Oculus_Quest). The OCULUS QUEST is a standalone system and does not require a separate PC as does the classic OCULUS RIFT. Moreover, the OCULUS QUEST has an integrated inside-out tracking, and thus does not need external tracking or cables.

The display resolution was improved considerably to 1440 × 1600 pixels per eye. The refresh rate is relatively low; 72 Hz. It is more powerful but exhibits a higher weight of 570 g, which may lead to problems when using it for longer times. Stereo speakers are integrated. The successor, the OCULUS QUEST 2 is lighter (503 g) and has a refresh rate of up to 120 Hz (see https://en.wikipedia.org/wiki/Oculus_Quest_2 for more details on the technical specification).

Playstation VR

The PLAYSTATION VR (from Sony Interactive Entertainment) is another widely used VR headset aiming primarily at gaming applications. It is available since October 2016, provides a spatial resolution of 960 × 1080 pixels, a horizontal field of view of 100°, and supports refresh rates of 90 and 120 Hz. Its weight is 600 g. Spatial audio is available. With these characteristics, it is slightly less attractive for medical applications.

Valve index

is a VR headset created by VALVE and available since 2019. It also employs the LIGHTHOUSE tracking. The headset has 1440 × 1600 pixels and can be operated with different refresh rates up to 144 Hz. The specified horizontal field of view is 130°. With 810 g, it is a rather heavy VR headset. Fig. 12.5 shows the headset along with the controllers.

The VALVE INDEX controllers are considered as significant improvement compared to previous VR controllers. They provide finger tracking for every finger. Based on its special design, the controllers can be released without falling down. Two but-

FIGURE 12.5

The Valve Index VR headset along with its controllers that can be fixed to the hands, and thus released when not needed.

tons labeled *A* and *B* are provided; *A* invokes a menu and *B* starts a selection. Adjustments for different hand sizes are available, and in general the VALVE INDEX controllers are convenient for long-term use. In essence, the VALVE INDEX is a powerful VR headset. However, it is also more expensive than the previously described VR headsets; it is also quite heavy.

Varjo

Finally, we briefly want to introduce high-end VR headsets that provide a better immersion, but at a higher price since the construction is more elaborate (https://varjo.com/). The VARJO headsets, available since early 2019, provide a dual monitor construction that employs the fact that we only perceive high spatial detail in the fovea. As a consequence, one small display (0.7" inch) supports foveated vision in highest resolution (1.920 × 1.080 pixel, 60 pixels per degree viewing angle). Thus the spatial resolution in the foveatic region is an order of magnitude higher than in the previously presented VR headsets. A second and larger display (3.5" inch) is provided for contextual rendering in lower resolution (1.440 × 1.600 pixel).

These VR headsets are based on a very precise eye tracking to detect the regions on which the viewer focuses. This integrated focus-context display can be combined with *foveated rendering*, as software component to account for the properties of the human visual system (Albert et al., 2017). An essential challenge is to provide a smooth blend between the detailed view and the context view. According to customers, this is achieved when the user looks at a certain point for a while. However, in the case of fast movements, some artifacts are hard to avoid.

The interpupil distance is adaptable in a range of 61 to 73 mm, which is appropriate for most users. The weight of the headset is 487 g. The LIGHTHOUSE tracking system is employed. The professional version VARJO 2 also provides integrated hand tracking.

12.4.4 Hardware for semi-immersive VR

The term VR is widely used and not restricted to immersive settings. Many systems, also those intended for medical treatment, are described as *non-immersive*, which means that interactive 3D graphics is provided in a desktop setting with conventional input devices, such as mouse, keyboard, or joystick (Rizzo and Koenig, 2017). We do not focus on such systems. Somewhere in between these non-immersive and fully immersive VR systems, are those that are referred to as *semi-immersive*. Semi-immersive systems have some elements of immersive systems, such as stereo perception or head tracking, but not all. Very large displays, offering a field of view that is far beyond that of a desktop monitor, are also termed as semi-immersive. In this subsection, however, we focus on stereoscopic and autostereoscopic monitors and related input technology, since these have been tested for medical applications.

Autostereoscopic monitors

Stereo rendering can be provided by a display that renders a pair of images for the left and right eye and projects it to the user's eye. Parallax barriers or lenticular lenses are employed to ensure that each eye only perceives the image rendered for that eye. With such autostereoscopic devices, the stereo depth cues are provided in a narrow *sweet spot*, i.e., the user should stay in this fixed region. A certain amount of *cross talk*, where content generated for one eye is perceived by the other, leading, e.g., to double edges, may not be completely avoided. This effect may be perceived as inconvenient. The spatial resolution is reduced in the horizontal direction by a factor of two.

Autostereoscopic monitors were also evaluated with respect to medical applications, e.g., as display for minimally-invasive surgery. However, the advantage over monoscopic monitors were not so strong that these autostereoscopic monitors experienced widespread use in medicine (Wilhelm et al., 2014). Currently, stereoscopic monitors, where users wear glasses, are more widely used, e.g., in anatomy education and laparoscopy surgery.

Stereoscopic monitors

Stereoscopic monitors require the user to wear glasses to get a stereo impression of the virtual world. Often polarized light is used to switch between images for the left and right eye. Circular polarization leads to better visual quality than linear polarization. Wearing glasses is a disadvantage in many situations, such as in the OR. On the other hand, the stereo quality is often better and the user is not restricted to a small region. For educational applications, it may be acceptable to wear shutter glasses.

As a specific example for this type of device, we describe the zSpace that was used at the University of Magdeburg for a couple of medical projects, including planning ear surgery, patient and anatomy education (see Fig. 12.6). Head tracking is enabled by reflective markers attached to the glasses that can be tracked with infrared tracking. A pen is used for 6 DOF input. It contains buttons to trigger commands. For educational applications, it is beneficial to be able to select objects, e.g., a complex muscle and create a ghost copy that may be rotated, scaled, and displayed in an isolated manner without occlusion. The zSpace is a stereoscopic display with a diagonal of 24 inches and a full HD resolution (1920 × 1080 pixels). The high refresh rate of 120 Hz (60 Hz per eye) contributes to a pleasant experience. The current version zSpace 300 has a PC integrated into the display. Thus an additional PC is no longer necessary. A second person (*follower*) may use the same zSpace but is not tracked. This mode enables, e.g., student-teacher applications.

FIGURE 12.6

Use of the zSpace for placement of an implant in the middle ear (Courtesy of Patrick Saalfeld, University of Magdeburg).

Further display types

Another type of semi-immersive displays are large display walls often composed of many screens. These display walls provide a larger field of view, and thus a stronger immersion than a desktop. This is useful for supporting group discussions. We do not discuss this display type here, because it is rarely used in medical applications.

12.5 Avatar design

Avatars are digital representations of the user in the virtual environment. They follow movements of the user in real-time and may collide with the parts of the virtual environment or other avatars in collaborative VR. The simplest avatars only represent the users' head. More advanced avatars also represent the users' hands, whereas the most advanced avatars represent the full body. Depending on the sophistication, this requires more or less complex tracking of the users' movements. If only the head is visually represented, it is sufficient that the user's head position and orientation are tracked in real-time. It is considerably more challenging to provide precise hand tracking, and even more difficult to track also movements of the arms and legs to update the position and orientation of the corresponding parts of an avatar.

The default mode is typically to show for each user a VR headset and two VR controllers representing the position of these devices attached to the users' body. Thus every user would have the same avatar. It is slightly better if each avatar has a unique label, e.g., its role or name, and a unique feature, such as a distinct color (see Fig. 12.7). Although it is quite unnatural to represent a body by three disconnected components, this type of avatar is rather frequently used.

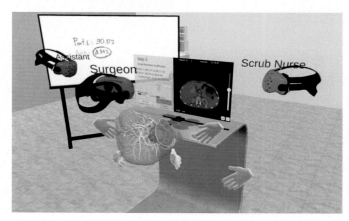

FIGURE 12.7

Three users cooperating in a medical training scenario, where they discuss a virtual resection. They are represented by VR glasses and hands. The distinct colors and labels enable a discrimination and an awareness for the other users (From: (Chheang et al., 2021), Reprinted from Computers & Graphics, Vol. 99, "A collaborative virtual reality environment for liver surgery planning," Page 241, ©Elsevier 2021).

Avatars may be associated with an identity (digital alter ego) and represent one or several aspects of the user. The level of identification differs based on user characteristics (Bartle, 2004). Avatars can be created with character modeling toolkits, such as the Autodesk Character Generator (https://charactergenerator.autodesk.com/). With such tools, polygonal meshes are created for individual body parts and hierarchical skeletal structure, which is useful to adapt the avatars' pose to movements of the user.

12.5.1 Virtual body illusion

The design of avatars is based on an understanding of *body ownership* and a *sense of embodiment* (Lopez et al., 2008; Kilteni et al., 2012). Humans feel that they have a physical body that they can control (*sense of agency*) and localize in space (*sense of localization*). Moreover, humans feel *inside* this body. There are exceptions, where the sense of embodiment is (mostly temporarily) destroyed, e.g., as a consequence of neurological diseases or the use of dependence-causing substances or in near-death experiences. In such situations people report to perceive a room as tilted or even as upside-down. Parts of their own body are not perceived or parts of other bodies are perceived as their own. People may even feel outside of their body or mislocate parts of their visual field (Lopez et al., 2008).

Avatar design aims at the illusion that the user considers an avatar (temporarily) as their body (*virtual body illusion*). The virtual body illusion contributes to the immersion that users experience in VR. There are many choices how an avatar may be designed. For example they may

- range from very abstract to highly realistic
- range from pure hand models to full bodies with faces, lip movements, and clothes
- exhibit a simple or quite complex behavior

An essential body transfer illusion related to avatars is the *rubber hand illusion* (Botvinick and Cohen, 1998). It can be observed in the following situation: A rubber hand with the same size as the human hand is placed near the real hand of the user. The sight to the real hand is blocked (see Fig. 12.8). The rubber hand and the real hand are stimulated tactilely in the same way (corresponding positions and intensity). When users should locate their hand, they typically locate the rubber hand. Thus subjects consider the rubber hand as their own and respond strongly to aggressive movements to the rubber hand. The design of avatars affects body perception, body ownership, and status.

12.5.2 Uncanny valley effect

When the realism of an artificial figure, e.g., in a movie is increased, users tend to find it more attractive, enjoyable, and believable up to a certain point (Mori, 1970; Mori et al., 2012). Beyond that degree of realism, attractiveness is strongly reduced, probably because users perceive the remaining differences strongly. Realism includes both visual appearance and behavior, e.g., biomechanics of human joint. Only with very high realism the attractiveness increases again: Mathur and Reichling (2016) provide many empirical measurements related to the perceived character of robots, depending on their degree of realism (see Fig. 12.9).

Many experiments related to avatar design in VR basically confirm the *uncanny valley effect*. The existence and severity of this effect seems to be user-dependent, i.e., younger users are less affected. Adding cartoonish features to avatars perceived in the valley may be beneficial. In essence, the uncanny valley effect is considered as a heterogeneous effect with multiple overlapping causes. For more discussion, see the Wikipedia article https://en.wikipedia.org/wiki/Uncanny_valley; associated herewith are many references.

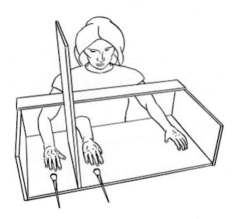

FIGURE 12.8

Principle of rubber hand experiments: The rubber hand is sized and oriented like the real hand that is occluded for the test person. Tactile stimulation of the rubber hand increasingly leads to acceptance of it as the hand of the test person (From: (de Haan et al., 2017), Reprinted from Acta psychologica, Vol. 179, "No consistent cooling of the real hand in the rubber hand illusion," Page 70, ©Elsevier 2017).

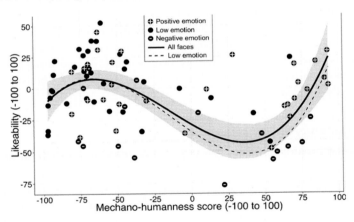

FIGURE 12.9

Trendlines summarize individual measurements related to users' assessment. Positive emotions occur primarily for low and high values of a measure for *humanness*, i.e., how strongly an avatar resembles a human. In the middle range, the valley, few emotions are triggered. (From: (Mathur and Reichling, 2016). This image is licensed under the Creative Commons Attribution-Share Alike 4.0 International license).

12.5.3 Customization

Users may strongly differ in their preference for a certain type of avatar, e.g., gender and specific look. Thus virtual worlds often provide a set of default avatars and editing functions for customization. Long-term users almost always customize their avatars also to be considered as more advanced (Neustaedter and Fedorovskaya, 2009). Essential attributes of avatars are (Latoschik et al., 2017):

- sex
- age
- skin color
- ethnicity
- figure (slim, thick)
- posture

Neustaedter and Fedorovskaya (2009) give examples of customized avatars used in SECOND LIFE. In a survey article, Liaw et al. (2018) mention that SECOND LIFE is most frequently used for multi-user virtual environments in healthcare.

Latoschik et al. (2017) described how 360° cameras may be used to create photorealistic avatars, including their movements and gestures. The acquisition process is shown in Fig. 12.10. In Fig. 12.11, we see such photorealistic avatars along with a highly abstract gender-neutral avatar.

FIGURE 12.10

Highly realistic personalized avatars acquired with motion suits and photogrammetric setup. Special setup for full body motion capturing and face capturing (From: (Latoschik et al., 2017)).

A special variant of customization that is quite useful for collaborative VR is to adapt the arm and leg length of an avatar to the size of a person, i.e., a basic variant of an avatar is *personalized* with respect to the users size. This can be easily achieved by asking the user to perform a few gestures, such as moving the arms extremely upwards and downwards while holding a VR controller. The difference in the position of the controllers enables the computation of the arm length. The impact of such personalized avatars is discussed by Steed et al. (2016).

FIGURE 12.11

Left: Gender-neutral wooden avatar. **Middle and Right:** Male and female avatars from photogrammetric scans, i.e., scans that extract 3D information from a collection of photographs (From: (Latoschik et al., 2017)).

12.5.4 Evaluation

How users actually perceive avatars,for example, whether avatars lead to an improved presence, whether users trust them, are questions that cannot be reliably predicted based on certain design decisions. Thus avatar design needs careful evaluation. The influence of co-presence in collaborative VR is a major criterion for such evaluations. Is a reduced representation of avatars, e.g., using only hands, sufficient for the awareness of other users? These and related questions are essential to provide an appropriate level of realism with respect to avatar appearance and behavior.

Ideally, users can compare different avatar designs, which makes it more likely that they make specific comments about what they like or dislike about the appearance or behavior of avatars. The results are probably not homogeneous for a target user group. A sufficient number and a representative selection of participants, e.g., in terms of gender, age, previous experiences with VR or games is essential. Customization options also need evaluation. On the one hand, customization options that are rarely used can probably be removed to simplify the use of the remaining features. On the other hand, an evaluation may reveal a lack of flexibility. Even some guidance may be useful, such as providing a customization workflow with a predefined sequence of customization steps.

12.6 Basic interaction techniques

Direct manipulation is a major interaction style for VR applications. It is based on a geometric representation of an application that may be directly controlled (Shneiderman, 1997). Object placement, for example, may be carried out by drag-and-drop, where a selected object is moved in direct-manipulative manner. Thus a geometric model of an implant or a surgical instrument can be placed intuitively. Though there are other interaction styles in VR, such as gesture input, we consider primarily direct-manipulative user interfaces.

There are four basic tasks in conventional graphical user interfaces that are typically considered also in VR (LaViola Jr. et al., 2017; Dörner et al., 2019). Objects need to be *selected* often as a first step. Selected objects may be *manipulated*, e.g., geometrically transformed. Users need to *navigate* the virtual world, and often they need to adjust parameters or other settings, tasks that are summarized as *system control*. In this section, we provide an introduction to the first three basic tasks: selection, manipulation, and system control. We postpone a discussion of navigation to the following Section 12.7. Before discussing the major tasks in VR, we briefly introduce the notion of *metaphors*.

12.6.1 The role of metaphors

Many interactions in VR are based on *metaphors* from the real world: Objects are *touched*, *grabbed* with a *virtual hand*, or *used* and we navigate in the virtual world, e.g., by *walking*, or *flying* or *leaning* forward and backward. Metaphors are basic components of thought and rely on our familiarity with a *source domain* to apply this knowledge in a new *target domain*. A metaphor may be *overarching*, such as *traveling* or *auxiliary*, such as adding signposts, maps, or other hints to support the overarching travel metaphor.

Using an appropriate metaphor, is a core decision in the design of VR systems. It involves the comparison of different candidate metaphors with respect to their familiarity and suitability. The successful use of metaphors in VR implies the use of an appropriate name (*linguistic metaphor*), the visual representation, and the behavior. The analogy between a real-world phenomenon or activity and its realization in an interactive system is never perfect. Not all properties of the real world are preserved in interactive systems, such as VR. And, on the other hand, additional properties or features may be added, the "magic" (see Fig. 12.12). The *Magic Lens*, for example, not only provides a movable tool to magnify the underlying content. The presented information may be changes as well, for example, more detail is added in the magnified region (Bier et al., 1993).

Thus metaphors may focus on the design on the one hand, and may support learning and efficient use of a VR-based system, on the other hand. For a discussion of the metaphor-based design of interactive system, we refer to (Neale and Carroll, 1997). The use of metaphors for VR is discussed by Stanney (1995).

12.6.2 Selection of objects

The selection task may range from an easy to a quite challenging task. In a static virtual world with a few objects rather far away from each other, it is easy to select an intended object, for example, with a simple straight selection ray from the controller in the pointing direction. The ray needs to be displayed with a prominent color to

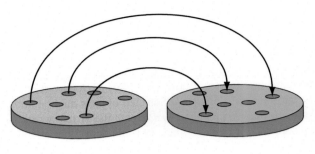

Source domain   Target domain

FIGURE 12.12

Metaphors help to translate the familiarity of a source domain to an unfamiliar target domain. The holes in the source domain represent the possible actions. Arrows denote *matches*, where there is an analogue in the target domain. Not all actions have a correspondence to the target domain, where also actions are possible, which are not associated to the metaphor.

provide feedback about the current selection direction. The selection becomes more difficult, the more of the following conditions are fulfilled:

- Objects in the virtual environment change their position.
- Objects are rendered semi-transparently, making several objects visible along a selection ray.
- Potential target objects are small or partially hidden.
- Objects are in a high density, e.g., articles placed in a supermarket.

Ray-based selection

This family of selection techniques gets particularly difficult in the above-mentioned cases, because of jittering that affects the hand, and thus the controller. In a similar way, like pointing on a small region on a slide with a laser pointer suffers from the reduced accuracy, ray-based selection gets a challenge. Subtle presses to the trigger button preview the selection ray, while applying more force performs the selection (see Fig. 12.13). This selection method may be combined with a *flashlight metaphor*, i.e., the controller acts like a spotlight and dynamically lightens parts of a geometric model according to the current controller position and orientation. This is useful to inspect objects with a complex shape, e.g., cultural artifacts (Saalfeld et al., 2021) or medical surfaces.

In a case where the ray is close to just one object, snapping may be enabled to conveniently select that object. Advanced variants of ray-based selection include the definition of curved selection rays based on two-handed interaction (Steinicke et al., 2006), refined selections in case of ambiguities where the set of candidate objects is progressively reduced (Kopper et al., 2011), and the definition of a sticky

FIGURE 12.13

For a virtual reconstruction project in a cathedral, the geometry of many broken bits was acquired with a 3D scanner as a basis for a virtual jigsaw puzzle. Before docking broken bits together, they are selected with selection rays triggered with a VR controller (Courtesy of Patrick Saalfeld, University of Magdeburg).

cursor that improves dynamic object selection, e.g., in the case of molecular dynamics simulations with a high density of moving atoms (De Haan et al., 2005).

Grabbing

While ray-based selection may be performed at a distance, *grabbing* is an alternative, where the controller directly touches an object to select it. This can be more time-consuming, because the user now has to reach the intended object, perhaps involving walking, but it reduces strongly ambiguity. An improvement over a naive implementation of grabbing is the HOMER technique (hand-centered object manipulation extending raycasting) (Bowman and Hodges, 1997). The translation is scaled by a factor that is defined by the distance from the user's hand to their torso. Thus objects may be brought quickly close to the user. In the case of difficult selection tasks, grabbing could be more appropriate. As a general strategy, it is often recommended to provide both ray-based selection and grabbing. Argelaguet and Andujar (2013) give a survey on 3D selection techniques for virtual environments.

In VR-based treatment, e.g., in motor rehabilitation of patients with a brain damage, grasping may be trained since it is part of many daily activities, such as buying food. It involves reaching an object, grabbing and transporting it, and training tasks involve objects of different size and form factor (Levin et al., 2015). An essential question in such situations bears on the *validity* of the movements, i.e., how similar grasping in VR is compared to the real world.

12.6.3 **Manipulation**

Object manipulation in medicine may involve the translation of a virtual biopsy needle or an adaptation of an implant that may consist of different parts that are tilted against each other. In virtual environments, direct manipulative techniques dominate, e.g., instead of using indirect commands and parameters, we want to directly initiate a change on the currently selected object. The manipulation of objects involves rigid geometric transformations, i.e., rotation and translation of objects, non-rigid transformations, such as scaling and stretching as well as free-form deformation. Such manipulations are often carried out with 3D widgets. A 3D widget, which has a 3D geometry, is included in the virtual environment when it is needed and provides *handles* to control one particular degree of freedom, e.g., movement in one direction. Whereas in a desktop context, the mouse cursor would be used to select the handles, in VR it is more likely the hand model that corresponds to the movements of a controller. In VR, it is possible to totally avoid 3D widgets. The user just grabs an object and moves the VR controller, thus controlling the movement of the selected object. This style of manipulation was introduced by Mine et al. (1997). An overview of manipulation techniques for VR and desktop applications is provided by Jankowski and Hachet (2015).

Human activities are characterized by a coordination between a *dominant hand*, which is more powerful and enables precise movements and a *non-dominant hand*, which is used for supporting tasks (Guiard, 1987). Object manipulation, e.g., rotation, is usually carried out with the *dominant hand*, which is the right hand for most users, but not for all. Thus VR applications should enable to adjust the dominant hand.

Direct manipulation is, in general, an intuitive interaction style. However, it is not precise. If an implant, for example, needs to be precisely attached to a certain anatomical structure, some guidance is essential. Constraints may be enabled, e.g., a biopsy needle cannot be moved through skeletal structures. Such constraints make object manipulation more efficient. Free-form deformation, e.g., to virtually resect parts of an organ as part of a surgical training process is particularly difficult. Free-form deformation and other geometric modeling tasks in a CAD system are often realized based on a B-spline grid or Bezier surfaces. However, modeling with such tools is indirect: Users translate control points of the underlying grids to modify the object shape. The direct use of deformation widgets is more intuitive. Geometric modeling in VR is discussed by Deisinger et al. (2000). It is also useful to look in the computer-aided design area, where modeling in VR is discussed as well (Bourdot et al., 2010).

12.6.4 **System control**

Virtual environments typically involve many settings and require to initiate commands, such as loading a medical data set in a medical application. In desktop systems, toolbars or pull-down menus are provided to select options and adjust parameters. Similar facilities are needed in VR (LaViola Jr. et al., 2017). In VR, however, it is challenging to ensure that these options are visible and recognizable for the current user. Thus to display these options at fixed positions is often not recommended, the system control options may be occluded or just too small to be recognized. As an alternative, slightly related to a pop-up menu, the options may be displayed at a position close to the current position of a controller (relative to the hand). With this option, the menu appears relative to one hand of the user. The second hand may be employed to trigger a selection, e.g., based on shooting a ray (see Fig. 12.14). Other placement options are possible, e.g., relative to a dynamic object.

FIGURE 12.14

A VR application enables to explore medical flow data. System control is provided with a menu attached to the user's right hand. The controller attached to the left hand is employed to select an entry (Courtesy of Benjamin Behrendt, University of Magdeburg).

System control involves the adjustment of numerical values (slider functionality, see Fig. 12.15) and the selection of options (radio button and check box functionality) in addition to the selection of menu entries. The selection of an appropriate font and font size and the placement such that text appears without or with low distortion are essential aspects for the usability of system control options in immersive VR.

A problem with the discussed variants of system control is that they may appear artificial and somehow reduce the perceived presence. Therefore more natural interaction styles for system control are investigated, such as gesture and speech input. With these interaction styles, no occlusion problems occur and also legibility of fonts is no longer an issue. However, the user has to learn which terms the system expects and can understand in the case of speech input. Moreover, a noise-free environment is required, a requirement that is not fulfilled, for example, in an OR. Gesture input may be more promising if gestures familiar from smartphones can be used. Typically, however, these gestures are not sufficient to control a complex virtual environment. Further gestures have to be learned and ambiguities in their interpretation may easily arise. Moreover, a precise hand tracking would be required. Therefore many VR systems still use some kind of 3D menus.

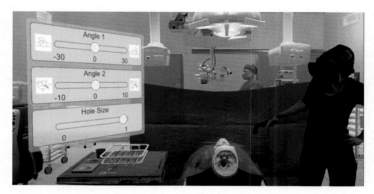

FIGURE 12.15

For a VR training system in neurosurgery some settings need to be adjusted. A hole is drilled in the skull based on specifying the diameter and two angles. With the VR controller, the corresponding sliders may be adjusted (Courtesy of Sylvia Saalfeld, University of Magdeburg).

In the shown examples, these interaction techniques in VR are realized by means of UNITY and UNREAL ENGINE and the virtual reality toolkit (VRTK).

12.6.5 Programming VR

Programming in VR has many aspects, e.g., related to the construction of a virtual environment, the mapping of user input to different parts of a virtual environment, and the invocation of appropriate methods to adapt the environment. Here, we briefly explain one essential concept, namely the processing of user input.

User input is mapped to *events*, and VR programming involves assigning functions to be invoked when an event is triggered. Examples for events include when the user starts or stops grabbing an object. Events have arguments that are essential for further processing, e.g., the time when the event occurred, the position of a VR controller, or the objects that were involved in a collection.

Objects that may trigger events, for example, a light switch, are called *interactables*. In medical applications, a virtual scalpel or a clipping plane may be an interactable. An interactable—a base class in Unity—has a rigid body, i.e., a mechanical object with a mass and potentially gravity enabled, a *collider*, i.e., a method to detect collisions, and *equipment logic*. When an event occurs, an *event handler* triggers an appropriate method. This mechanism is extensible to a wide range of objects and realizes a loose coupling between interactables and the methods that define the behavior. The communication is realized in an asynchronous manner, i.e., only when something actually happens, events are processed. This is way more effective than a synchronous communication, where regularly all possible sources of events are checked.

12.7 **Locomotion techniques**

Navigation in a virtual world has two essential components:

- a cognitive component, also referred to as wayfinding
- a motor component, also referred to as travel

Wayfinding

When a user aims to reach a certain position, e.g., a room in a game, an essential building in a city model, or a part of the human body, *wayfinding* describes the problem-solving activity involved in finding a viable path to the target (LaViola Jr. et al., 2017). During the exploration of a (virtual) environment, users build a mental map based on *landmarks*, that is, points, linear elements, or areas that are somehow unique and important. In a city model, cathedrals, crossings, rivers, or lakes may be such landmarks. In a digital patient model, organ boundaries and branchings of vascular structures are examples for landmarks. Users acquire *procedure knowledge* how to reach point *A* from point *B*. Map displays with the current position indicated and arrows are useful navigation aids. In VR, the placement of such navigation aids needs to be carefully considered to ensure visibility and legibility. A lot of research was carried out to understand wayfinding in reality, and as a consequence, to design virtual worlds where users can orient themselves. Thorndyke and Hayes-Roth (1982) provide an excellent discussion of human navigation.

Travel

The second component of navigation is the actual realization of the planned trajectory, often referred to as *travel* (LaViola Jr. et al., 2017). Traveling is a motor activity, involving muscles to control movements of a pedestrian or a car driver. In a conventional computer game, the cursor keys or the keys "WASD" are often used for traveling. In what follow, we describe techniques for maneuvering in VR and use the term *locomotion techniques*.

Locomotion techniques

When the virtual environment is larger than the tracking space of VR headsets and controllers, locomotion is required. Locomotion is not an end in itself: users should move in a position where they can perform a more important task, e.g., gather information in educational settings or study variants of a design in an architectural walkthrough. A locomotion technique (Bowman and Hodges, 1999; Bozgeyikli et al., 2016)

- needs to be easy to understand
- should be seamlessly integrated in the exploration of the virtual world
- needs to be precise
- affects presence and likelihood of VR sickness
- affects motion and distance perception, i.e., users may systematically over- or underestimate speed or distance traveled

The first two properties, being actually requirements, can be summarized as *minimization of the cognitive load* related to navigation (Bowman and Hodges, 1999). When navigation is a secondary task, it is essential that the user has sufficient cognitive resources available for the primary task. As an example, without collision detection, users may unintentionally move through a wall, get confused, and considerable mental effort is involved in returning to a meaningful path. Therefore collision detection and avoidance is useful to reduce necessary attention to stay on the path. Navigation in virtual endoscopy, where the camera moves inside the colon or the bronchial tree is a medical example (John et al., 2020). From a user experience perspective, it is also essential that locomotion avoids fatigue over time, which may occur, for example, if the user has to stand for a long time or has to wear a device in their hands. Finally, some locomotion techniques are known to involve a considerable risk for causing VR sickness. The combination of certain elements of the virtual world and a locomotion technique may be particularly risky in this regard, e.g., a fast movement along a strongly curved path.

Classification of locomotion techniques

According to Boletsis (2017), locomotion techniques can be classified at a high level in:

- *natural* techniques
- *artificial* techniques

Natural (sometimes also called physical) techniques simulate to a certain extent a locomotion technique from the real world, such as walking, cycling, or steering a vehicle. Artificial techniques do not have an orientation in the real world. Thus they are not immediately intuitive, however they can be designed such that some of the requirements specified above are fulfilled. A classification of artificial locomotion relates to *discrete* and *continuous* techniques (Boletsis, 2017). Discrete locomotion relates to sudden large movements triggered by a certain command. In contrast, continuous locomotion means that the viewing position and orientation change smoothly. Natural techniques are continuous (Boletsis, 2017). Obviously, discrete locomotion bears the risk of orientation problems for the users who find themselves at a radically new position.

The third criterion to classify locomotion techniques relates to the size of the virtual environment, which may be *limited* or *open*. We start our discussion with a simple artificial locomotion technique (teleportation) and go on with further artificial techniques before describing natural techniques, such as walking. We also briefly discuss strategies to compare and evaluate locomotion techniques.

Finally, we mention a classification of navigation tasks that is essential to assess the suitability of locomotion techniques (Bowman et al., 2004):

- *Exploration*. Users may want to get familiar with a virtual environment without a specific goal.
- *Search*. Users want to reach a particular target, e.g., in a digital patient model, a position where they can see specific anatomical or pathological structures.

- *Following a trajectory.* Users want to follow a particular path, e.g., a street or a river. In medicine, virtual endoscopy is the major application where users follow a path inside elongated structures, such as the colon or the bronchial tree.

12.7.1 Teleportation

Teleportation is a science fiction-inspired technique. It is also often referred to as *jumping* or the jumper metaphor. Teleportation is not completely unfamiliar to most users, since it is related to a cut in conventional movies. With teleportation the user selects a position (in a map or by pointing in the virtual environment) and is immediately moved to that position. The selection is carried out with a ray-based technique, i.e., the selection ray is clearly shown. Teleportation is a discrete, artificial locomotion technique. In movie making, there are guidelines for the use of cuts, e.g., the orientation of the camera should not change too strongly. Similar guidelines may be useful for teleportation in VR.

An essential advantage of teleportation is its low risk of inducing VR sickness. This, however, is achieved at the expense of orientation problems. The visual impression and sense of balance do not match. As a remedy, instead of a sudden jump, the movement may be animated (*fading*) to improve the orientation transforming teleportation to a continuous locomotion technique. Animation is typically realized along a straight line from the current position to the selected target. However, in the case of obstacles or predefined paths in a virtual environment, this behavior needs to be adapted. It would be unfortunate if teleportation brings the user to a point that is very close to a large object, e.g., a wall or the skull in a model of brain structures. In these cases, it is an alternative to define regions where teleportation is disabled and move the user to an allowed nearby position instead. Many VR systems provide teleportation, which is also a matter of convenience, since major game engines provide this locomotion technique. Fading with a constant duration leads to high speed when the target is far. Thus an adaptation of speed to the distance is often desirable. When fading leads to fast movements, it may be useful to combine it with motion blur to reduce the risk of VR sickness.

An alternative to a movement along a straight line is to bring the user to the target on an arc, i.e., the user rises first, reaches a maximum height, and then slowly reaches the ground close to the target, a kind of navigation that resembles flying. This arc may be initially shown to prepare the user to this (automatic) movement. Though this flying-inspired fading mechanism is quite natural, it may increase cyber sickness. Thus careful testing and adaptation of the speed and the height of the arc may be necessary. In Fig. 12.16, an example is shown where the arc is quite low.

A special variant, Point & Teleportation (Bozgeyikli et al., 2016) works as follows: The user determines the target, then triggers teleportation, e.g., with a button at the VR controller, and finally, the actual movement to the target is carried out. With this variant, the orientation of the camera is not changed. An earlier variant of this technique was introduced by Mackinlay et al. (1990). They animated the movement to the target and changed the speed logarithmically, e.g., the initial parts of the route are realized faster before slowly approaching the target.

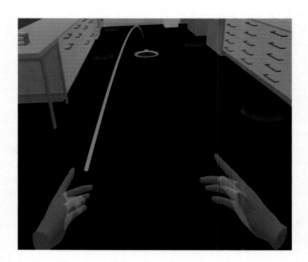

FIGURE 12.16

The user selected a target in a virtual chemistry lab. They will be moved along the displayed arc that has a low height (Courtesy of Vikram Apilla, University of Magdeburg).

Bozgeyikli et al. (2016) discuss how to avoid unintended teleportation, which would be annoying. They suggest to use the release event of a trigger button and wait for a short period, e.g., two seconds, while displaying the selection ray and highlighting the target before the movement actually starts. This allows the user to anticipate the changing viewing position. When a fading mode is enabled, they recommend to keep the orientation constant to avoid VR sickness.

Disorientation problems are severe when the target is selected from a list and users can hardly predict the movement that will be caused. Consequently, these problems are less severe when the target is pointed at, and thus, the changing viewing position can be anticipated. After teleportation, users may wonder how to get back, e.g., if they are too close to a wall.

With respect to navigation tasks, teleportation supports *search tasks*. It is not appropriate to *explore* an environment since the sudden change of the viewpoint does not help the user in creating a comprehensive mental map. When we discuss medical treatment, e.g., anxiety treatment, it is essential to be able to gradually approach to a stimulus that may provoke anxiety. In such applications, teleportation is not appropriate.

12.7.2 Further artificial techniques

In addition to teleportation, there are other *artificial* locomotion techniques that may be considered when designing a VR system (Boletsis, 2017; Ferracani et al., 2016):

FIGURE 12.17

Lean-based control is a continuous and artificial technique performed in a sitting context. The chair is equipped with special sensors to capture the motion. Applications include gaming and driving simulation (Courtesy of Steffi Beckhaus).

- Hand-based control (*pointing*) may be realized with an AR flystick, a game controller, or a VR controller. All these devices define a direction. The advantage of hand-based control is its flexibility and the precise control that is possible with the hand. However, one hand is required for controlling the direction. In the real world, hands are not occupied for navigation, we just walk in the desired direction.
- *Gaze-based control* is employed for direction control. Thus the hands are free and the navigation is simple. A disadvantage is that the user may not look around while standing at one position. At least, this requires a mode switch. Moreover, the locomotion via gaze-based control requires a starting command.
- *Lean-based control.* This locomotion technique requires the user to be in a sitting position. It is related to skiing or skateboarding, where leaning is also applied to control motion. A tracker is attached to the torso and controls the movement by leaning to a certain direction with a certain extent (Beckhaus et al., 2007) (see Fig. 12.17). Sitting is comfortable, and thus no fatigue will arise.
- *Gesture-based techniques* employ body gestures to control position and orientation. Body gestures include arm, hand, and finger movements, which are tracked or analyzed by means of a depth camera, e.g., INTEL REALSENSE.
- *World-in-miniature (WIM)-based techniques* are based on a strongly downscaled copy of the virtual environment in the user's hand (Stoakley et al., 1995). Whereas the initial concept suffers from scalability issues, Wingrave et al. (2006) provided a more feasible WIM. The user may move an avatar on the world in miniature. This movement is synchronized to the actual virtual environment, where the user's position is updated accordingly. Obviously, this technique enables fast large-scale

movements, but does not enable fine-grained control (Cherni et al., 2020; Pivovar et al., 2022).

Hand-based control is a discrete type of locomotion, whereas lean-based and gaze-based control are continuous. Gesture-based locomotion is discrete; the user moves a certain step size or rotates by a certain angle. Depending on the amount of the movement, orientation problems may be more or less severe.

12.7.3 Natural locomotion techniques

Natural locomotion techniques are more or less intuitive and exploit known movements (Usoh et al., 1999). The most natural locomotion technique is walking. Other techniques, such as steering a vehicle, are learned in life. The major natural locomotion techniques include:

- *Walking*: a 1:1 mapping of the users' position to the VE, most natural technique, but restricted to the tracking space, i.e., backward walking may be required.
- *Walking in place (WiP)*: users move while remaining stationary. This natural locomotion technique requires additional hardware or gesture recognition. Thus it is not fully "natural." Often sensors are attached to the legs and lifting them reveals the steps that are counted, leading to a corresponding displacement in the virtual world.
- *Redirected walking* is based on slight adjustments (reorientation and repositioning) of the user's movement, e.g., during saccadic movements.

Natural techniques typically require standing, and thus may cause fatigue over time. They are useful for *exploring* the virtual environment, a navigation task where teleportation is not beneficial (Jankowski and Hachet, 2015). Even walking may be refined to provide a more convenient sensation. Lécuyer et al. (2006) performed slight oscillar camera motion and a compensation motion changing orientation of the camera. An oscillation around the vertical axis was preferred by the users. We mention this as just one example for a realization of walking. WiP is actually a gesture-based technique; the participants perform a marching gesture. Frequency determines speed, and the head direction determines the direction of movement. Whereas WiP is typically realized based on sensors of the feet, also *arm swinging* may be employed to detect steps. Controllers in the hands may be employed to track the hand movement. It is also possible to use only arm swinging for WiP, i.e., the user's legs do not move. This variant is easier to realize, since only the VR controllers are needed. Arm swinging can also be carried out in a sitting position, and thus reduce fatigue. Another advantage of arm swinging (only) is that the user does not leave their position. Even when the user tries to walk in place (with the legs), they may slightly move, and over time reach the end of the tracking space or reach obstacles. On the other hand, a walking variant without moving legs is less intuitive.

In larger environments, it is desirable to adjust the walking speed, i.e., fast speed to cover large distances should be provided, and a lower speed for fine-grained locomotion. This can be achieved by not just counting the steps but also assessing the height of the feet. Ke and Zhu (2021) suggested to classify the height of the feet in three classes: with *low feet* mapped to normal walking speed, *moderately elevated feet* mapped to three times faster speed, and *highly elevated* feet to ten times faster speed.

The virtual interaction space is unlimited with walking in place, even if the physical interaction space is small. Re-directed walking increases the virtual interaction space compared to the physical interaction space, whereas classical walking only enables virtual interaction spaces that have the same space as the physical interaction space. In medical treatment, e.g., to treat fear of heights or fear of flying, we may have very large virtual environments, i.e., large virtual interaction spaces. Walking would not be appropriate for such applications. Nabiyouni and Bowman (2016) discuss many possible variants of walking-based locomotion.

Collision avoidance

Walking and redirected walking may lead to collisions with static or dynamic obstacles, e.g., another participant. Thus users need to be aware of obstacles in the real world. Redirected walking may be intentionally designed to avoid obstacles (Sun et al., 2018). Redirected walking was introduced by Razzaque et al. (2002). The gain that is added to the users' motion should be small enough to be in an unnoticeable range for users. Many experiments have been carried out to establish detection thresholds of redirected walking. An essential paper in this direction determined, e.g., a curvature radius of 22 m for straight movement; +/-20% when rotating, e.g., a rotation may be exaggerated to some extent without being noticed (Steinicke et al., 2009). Despite redirected walking, users may still reach the boundary of the tracking area. Various techniques have been designed to motivate the user to walk back towards the center of the tracking space.

12.7.4 Hardware for locomotion techniques

Whereas some locomotion techniques require no or very small hardware components, some techniques require considerable additional hardware (Boletsis, 2017). Special hardware typically leads to significantly increased costs and often also to a limited field of application. However, there are situations, also in medicine, where the increased cost may be justified, e.g., because a certain treatment of a rather frequent disorder benefits strongly. Locomotion hardware often serves to navigate in large-scale virtual environments, where even redirected walking may not be sufficient.

Boletsis (2017) mention the following devices:

- *Treadmills* (uni- or omnidirectional). These devices use a conveyor belt driven by a motor that leads the user to move at a certain speed (Darken et al., 1997). As a locomotion technique, it enables an unlimited space.
- *Balance boards.* Like treadmills, balance boards require good coordination skills. The WII BALANCE BOARD was a popular device in this group and was used for a variety of physical activities.

- *Stationary bicycles.* Since riding a bicycle is familiar to many persons, this is a natural locomotion technique.
- *Foot pedals.* This relatively cheap locomotion hardware provides a kind of speed control that is natural, at least for all car drivers. Similarly, also cross trainers are employed.
- *Virtusphere.* This device enables also unlimited walking-based movement in a human size hamster ball. It was used, e.g., for treating soldiers with post-traumatic disorder (Medina et al., 2008).

Treadmills and balance boards were used in VR systems to treat patients with a history of falling. Thus they may help to improve coordination skills, e.g., after a stroke. Before using such locomotion hardware, safety issues need to be carefully considered. Can patients hurt themselves using such devices? How can the severity of blessings be reduced? Do they likely trigger VR sickness? These are some of the questions that need to be discussed.

12.7.5 Evaluation of locomotion techniques

We have seen that there are a couple of locomotion techniques. Therefore it is essential in the design of VR systems to prototype several of them and to compare them in user studies with the target audience. The locomotion techniques should be embedded in a virtual world that resembles the final system, e.g., in an OR. The comparison should be realized based on specific navigation tasks and tasks that include additional activities, since locomotion is a secondary task only. Examples for navigation tasks include the following:

- Move from a position A to another position B and back.
- Move from A to B and avoid any obstacles.
- Move from A to B and grab a set of objects O. Bring them back to A.

Based on such tasks, the *travel time* and *collision avoidance* can be measured. This gives objective data. In addition, it is useful to ask the participants for the preference of a certain technique and to assess the naturalness. Since locomotion techniques may invoke VR sickness, it is essential to observe participants accordingly and ask them for any inconvenience. To interpret the answers, the participants need to be asked for their VR and video game experience. There are known gender differences in the perceived usability of VR solutions. Therefore the biological sex needs to be inquired as well.

To give an example for an evaluation of locomotion techniques, Ferracani et al. (2016) compared walking-in-place and three gesture-based locomotion techniques. Task completion time and obstacle avoidance were measured. A tap gesture leads to similarly good results than WiP. With the two other gestures (push and swing), participants were less effective.

12.8 **Haptics**

Humans have different communication channels to perceive information. The information from different channels may be complement or redundant and is integrated in a rich *multimodal* representation of the world around us. In a similar way, multimodality is essential in VR. Therefore in the next two sections we discuss the integration of touch and audio perception, the two most important channels in addition to the visual channel. Haptics refers to the interaction between a tactile stimulus provided by one's environment, and a "combination of cutaneous and kinesthetic sensors in tendons, joints and muscles" (Pinzon et al., 2016). Humans have a high number of sensors to perceive haptic properties. Different types of *mechanoreceptors* in the skin differ in their accuracy and in their temporal resolution, i.e., whether they perceive low- or high-frequency vibrations (Riener and Harders, 2012). It is essential for VR systems to provide at least some aspects of the haptic interaction (Srinivasan and Basdogan, 1997).

The perception and understanding of objects is based on an *integration* of visual and haptic cues that depends on the information available for these sensory channels. Previous experience also strongly influences this understanding. Although our perception is visually dominated, haptic cues add to an understanding and make it faster. Pinzon et al. (2016) add that haptic cues are particularly important when visual information is limited or may be distorted, e.g., in minimally invasive surgery, where visual information is provided by cameras only and subject to fisheye distortions.

Most real-world-inspired tasks involve more than just walking and exploring a virtual environment, but instead to interact with parts of the environment, typically involving the hands. The development of haptic devices, which provide touch sensations, is strongly driven by applications in geometric modeling and engineering. Two types of haptics are distinguished:

- *Passive haptics* employs "static physical replica that match the virtual environment" (Cheng et al., 2017). Hinckley et al. (1994) did pioneering work in this area by providing a static prop of the human skull and a physical plane to control neurosurgical resections. However, with the need for a static shape, passive haptics is not very flexible, and thus use cases remain quite limited.
- *Active haptics* "dynamically match the location of virtual shapes through active components," such as robotic arms and data gloves (Cheng et al., 2017). Active haptics is a dynamic research area and strongly driven by robotics applications.

In what follow, we focus on active haptics. Tactile feedback may intuitively convey information about the roughness of a surface and about the elasticity of an object. In medicine, haptics is essential in all operating disciplines where a physician employs surgical instruments to cut, deform, and palpate. Haptic feedback may convey the properties of different anatomical and pathological structures. With haptic feedback, activities, such as grasping, holding, and releasing objects, get a touch component, which adds to the perceived realism, even if it does not feel like a perfect simulation of human touch. Haptic feedback is also used to enhance medical image segmentation, in particular in the case of spatially complex anatomical structures, where the immersion provided by VR may be beneficial in the context of complex spatial relations (Harders et al., 2002).

Haptic feedback requires haptic rendering, i.e., in the case of collisions with soft objects, their geometry needs to be updated efficiently. Our tactile sense has a high temporal resolution. Thus there is agreement that a frame rate of at least 300 frames per second (fps) is required for haptic rendering compared to only about 90 fps for graphics rendering. Thus typically there are two coupled but separate rendering loops for updating haptic feedback and for the visual display. More simplifications and stronger abstractions from geometric detail are employed for haptic rendering. Even with modern computing hardware, latency remains a problem when users perform fast movements with their hands.

In what follow, we discuss devices for haptic feedback. According to LaViola Jr. et al. (2017) we discriminate

- *Body-referenced devices* connected to the body, e.g., to hand or wrist
- *Ground-referenced devices* attached to a support surface, wall, or ceiling

Description examples for these two categories follow.

12.8.1 Ground-referenced devices

Ground-referenced devices are heavy and need to create a counter force. Thus they need a support surface. Therefore in a VR setting, they are typically used by a user sitting at a table. For users who walk around, a wearable solution is needed.

The Phantom family of devices from 3D SYSTEMS (formerly SENSABLE TECHNOLOGIES) is an example of ground-referenced haptic feedback devices. These devices provide a stylus that may be dragged and rotated (see the degrees of freedom emphasized in Fig. 12.18). Haptic feedback is provided at the finger tips. The device controls a virtual representation with a haptic interface point (HIP). The HIP is evaluated in terms of possible collisions. In the case of a collision, feedback forces are computed, yielding a force vector representing a direction and the amount of force. For elastic objects, e.g., soft tissues in the human body, the (deformable) surface needs to be adapted. The force computation is based on material constants, primarily the stiffness. The force vectors are transferred to the force feedback device to generate an appropriate response.

Such devices are useful for understanding object and material properties and are used, e.g., in virtual assembly, surgical simulation, and geographic navigation. The different Phantom devices differ in the maximum force that can be generated. It is in the range of 3 N to 7 N, which is low compared to the forces a human being can generate (up to 100 N). The spatial resolution is quite high and amounts to 0.01 mm (Pan et al., 2020). In Chapter 13, we will see applications and refinements of these devices in surgery training.

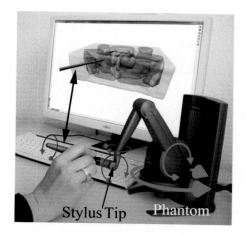

Stylus Tip   Phantom

FIGURE 12.18

Surgery simulation with tactile feedback. Stiffness values are associated with anatomical structures, leading to the experience that only soft tissue structures can be penetrated. Exploration of the surrounding of the spine to simulate minimally invasive spine surgery with a general device (Courtesy of Kerstin Kellermann, University of Magdeburg).

12.8.2 Body-referenced devices

Meanwhile, a large variety of wearable devices with haptic feedback exists, including a large collection of haptic suits. Wearable devices allow users to walk around, but since they have to be carried, they should be lightweight. Most commercially available body-referenced devices, however, are data gloves, which we now describe. A major requirement for data gloves is precise finger tracking. Moreover, data gloves should be convenient to wear and should not restrict finger movement. A practical question for long-term use is also how to clean them. As an example for modern data gloves providing wearable haptic feedback on the wrist, we describe the MANUS VR gloves (see Fig. 12.19). A VIVE tracker is attached to a bracelet connected to the wrist. The finger tips are free, which enables precise interactions with the fingers. The weight of 240 g (with trackers) is acceptable.

Most data gloves are expensive. Their cost exceeds that of VR headsets. For some medical applications and target user groups, such as students seeking solutions for anatomy education, they are still too expensive. For other medical applications, such as surgery training in specialized centers, they are already affordable.

This was a short introduction to haptics. For a more comprehensive discussion we recommend Riener and Harders (2012), Chapter 4. This book chapter explains the underlying psychophysics and the mechanisms behind the devices.

FIGURE 12.19

A user wearing MANUS VR data gloves with trackers for localization. Haptic feedback is provided for all fingers (Courtesy of Moritz Drittel, University of Magdeburg).

12.9 Audio feedback

Immersion in VR benefits from a plausible representation of information in different sensory channels, including the audio information. Also in medicine, there are various examples how auditory information may improve the experience and provide useful additional information compared to the sole visual display. Data that characterizes the current situation in navigated surgery can be mapped to properties of sound—a process called *sonification*—and delivered to the user, e.g., via head phones. The properties used in sonification include frequency, intensity, and timbre (Black et al., 2017a).

Imagine a VR-based training system in surgery that involves anesthesiologists, nurses, and surgeons. In anesthesiology, the vital status of the patient is monitored and acoustic signals convey abnormalities. Surgeons or interventionalists may get acoustic feedback about the current position of their devices in relation to structures at risk, e.g., the facial nerve. These signals act as warnings. Other sounds that occur in a real operating room are simulated as well, e.g., sounds related to the use of surgical instruments or of a person leaving the room and closing the door. Finally, it would be an advantage if the persons joining a virtual environment, e.g., from different remote positions, can speak to each other and the sound is perceived correctly and spatially localized as it corresponds to the position of the avatars.

The integration of such *spatialized audio* is challenging. Various physical effects have to be taken into account, e.g., diffraction of sound at low frequencies, scattering at high frequencies, acoustic absorption, and specular reflections (Lentz et al., 2007). Sound field modeling is typically performed to simulate these effects.

However, it is currently not possible to faithfully simulate all these effects at high accuracy. In fact, the computational effort would even exceed the effort needed to provide a photorealistic (visual) rendering. Therefore similar to the graphics component of VR, simplifications and approximations are carried out based on perceptual considerations. Thus instead of aiming at a realistic audio rendering, developers aim at a *plausible* realization of sound. Even this can only be achieved with very efficient algorithms: Computing sound rays in a virtual environment leads to many computations of intersections with the room geometry (Lentz et al., 2007). Efficient data structures, such as KD trees, are required to restrict such computations.

Existing implementations are typically based on computer networks, where one computer performs the whole sound rendering, whereas other computers perform graphics rendering and haptics (Lentz et al., 2007). Stereospeakers or headphones finally deliver the computed sound.

Sound rendering is performed by various software toolkits and plugins, e.g., UNITY provides a powerful audio system, where developers can define *audio sources* emitting sound waves and *audio listeners* to perceive this sound.

Medical applications

Black et al. (2017a) provide a survey of auditory displays in image-guided interventions. A straightforward use of auditory displays is to issue warning signals in case of a close proximity between a needle tip or another instrument to a vital structure. Numerous papers demonstrate that the awareness for critical anatomical structures arises. Beyond that, some groups provide more comprehensive guidance using audio (Black et al., 2017b; Hansen et al., 2013).

Black et al. (2017b) used audio to support needle placement tasks, e.g., for biopsies and tumor ablation. They evaluated the use of sound in comparison to a purely visual display in terms of task completion times and subjective workload. These are essential criteria to assess the usefulness of a sound integration.

12.10 **Applications**

VR has many applications, and thus quite different target users and tasks. As an example, there are many use cases in education and training (Bricken, 1991). Despite our focus on VR in medicine, it is interesting to briefly mention other areas as well. This may lead to new ideas for medicine, i.e., it may be treated as a creativity technique.

Virtual design

The most important industrial application of VR is support for the design process. This includes the visual design, e.g., of automotives, where many variants can be explored in VR, instead of creating expensive physical mock-ups. Moreover, functional aspects can be studied in VR, e.g., the reachability of all instruments from the drivers' seat or the maintainability from the perspective of mechanics. A relation to medicine is the design of medical instruments, e.g., vascular implants or hearing implants, which may be virtually operated within the target anatomy to understand whether their use is feasible in practice.

City models and urban planning

3D city models and their exploration in VR may serve different purposes, e.g., to attract and inform tourists. Whereas a tourist would just explore the city as it is, experts involved in urban planning may interact with the city model to support the decision-making process. The improved imagination may lead to better decisions of the experts. Interested citizens may also be involved early in the planning process. In a planning use case, what-if questions may be answered, e.g., what happens if we add further trees to an area with respect to shadowing houses or changing the impression of walking in that area.

Cultural heritage

VR is ideal to enable users to experience important old buildings, such as monasteries and castles, which may be too far away to be visited or even destroyed. Such virtual reconstruction projects may also support the involved scientists, e.g., by providing alternative reconstructions to be discussed. Since not all details about medieval architecture are preserved, virtual reconstruction often involves a lot of debate.

Medical applications

VR systems have been designed and deployed for many purposes in medicine. Beyond the training and rehabilitation applications that we will discuss in the following chapters, VR has been used for some diagnostic applications, e.g., virtual colonoscopy, where radiologists search for pathologic changes of the colon wall, e.g., polyps. The immersion of a VR system is beneficial to deeply assess the complex anatomy of the colon. Recently, a VR system was presented that supports diagnostic reading of CT and MRI data by providing a constant illumination situation (Sousa et al., 2017). This research was motivated by the potentially disturbing effect of different lighting situations in conventional screen-based diagnosis. With their system, users have a table display to provide gestures and control the visualization that appears on top of the table. VR has also been employed for therapy planning as early as in the year 2000 for neurosurgery (Kockro et al., 2000). However, the considerable effort to segment all target structures for the individual patient still hampers widespread use.

Similar to VR-based factory planning in industry, VR-based planning was also carried out in hospital settings, e.g., to design, discuss, and refine future OR, which are required to reflect the enormous technical developments in recent years. VR-based architectural design of ORs was already mentioned by Satava (1995). This enables an in-depth discussion of different spatial configurations with all stakeholders, e.g., they can walk in these OR designs, move elements, and assess consequences. Thus expensive mistakes when realizing an OR often can be avoided. VR is also used in medical research, for example, to study vascular structures and related blood flow.

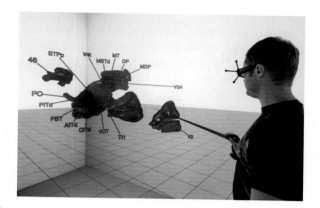

FIGURE 12.20

Labeling and interacting with geometric models representing brain components in VR. Labels are abbreviations typically used in neuroscience (Courtesy of Sebastian Pick, RWTH Aachen).

Also neuroscience research benefits from VR systems (Beck et al., 2010). Fig. 12.20 gives an example of brain structures and their associated labels in VR. An honest discussion of the current state of VR in medicine, however, needs to mention that most physicians do not embrace radically new technology. Thus, so far many VR-based developments remained in a research stage and were not translated to clinical practice. The fact that VR-based research and development is often not consequently focused on addressing real needs of a target user group is another reason that hampers a wider use of VR in practice so far.

12.11 Concluding remarks

We introduced virtual reality, explained why it has gained momentum in recent years, and why it has potential for medical applications. VR may be motivating and engaging. It is based on illusions that are deliberately created to *immerse* users surrounded by a virtual environment. A number of hardware and software aspects have to be considered when designing virtual environments. We discussed VR headsets, VR controllers, and haptic input devices on the hardware side and selection, object manipulation, avatar design, locomotion, and system control in VR. In the design of a VR system, even more questions have to be considered. The following questions are examples: How to design and scale a room, in which VR-based training is embedded? Which physical processes should be simulated, e.g., gravity and friction? A room may be quite sparsely decorated, for everything that is not needed may distract and may aggravate performance problems. A ground floor, however, is highly recommended to provide orientation (Buchholz et al., 2005).

These developments were primarily aimed at persons with an interest in 3D applications, often persons with a gaming background and an interest in technology. Therefore users of VR-based systems tend to be younger and male. Though the target user group for anatomy education, for example, may be similar to the intended audience for VR (except the higher portion of females among students of medicine), patients may differ strongly. They are often much older and less inclined to use advanced technology. Already the typical VR controllers with a number of buttons and other interaction facilities may be difficult to use for them (Coldham and Cook, 2017). Also psychological obstacles and technology acceptance need to be considered. In the interview described by Coldham and Cook, the majority of elderly persons considers VR a "frivolous undertaking that had little benefit" and is intended for young persons in a gaming context. Thus further developments are needed to design appropriate VR systems for elderly and disabled persons.

Ethical considerations

The growing trend to use VR requires to consider also its potential adverse effects. When VR is used for a long time, the illusions on which VR is based may have consequences for the attitudes and behaviors of the users. This may include desirable effects, e.g., when VR is used to treat chronic or acute pain or anxieties. But, of course, there is a risk for undesirable effects as well. As an example, in a training of disabled persons for street crossing, a realistic accident, where the user as a pedestrian in the first person perspective experiences a crash with a car can trigger very strong emotions of fear.

Careful investigation of such effects, including long-term investigations, as well as appropriate counter measures are needed. The use of VR for patient treatment requires official admission of such a system, where strong regulation is in place. Thus investigations are necessary to ensure patient safety which is a major aspect of the legal admission of technology for medical treatment.

Recommended reading

In this chapter, we could only provide a basic introduction to VR. For a deeper understanding, we recommend the following books and essential articles:

Grigore Burdea and Philippe Coiffet. *Virtual Reality Technology*, John Wiley and Sons, 2003.

Joseph J. LaViola, Ernst Kruijff, Ryan P. McMahan, Doug Bowman, Ivan P. Poupyrev. *3D User Interfaces: Theory and Practice*, Addison-Wesley Professional, 2017.

William R. Sherman and Alan B. Craig. *Understanding Virtual Reality: Interface, Application, and Design*, Morgan Kaufmann, 2018.

Mel Slater and Sylvia Wilbur. "A framework for immersive virtual environments (FIVE): Speculations on the role of presence in virtual environments," *Presence Teleoperators and Virtual Environments*, Vol. 6 (6): 603–616, 1997.

Mel Slater. "Place illusion and plausibility can lead to realistic behaviour in immersive virtual environments," *Philosophical Transactions of the Royal Society B: Biological Sciences*, Vol. 364(1535), 3549–3557, 2009.

Virtual Reality for medical education

13.1 Introduction

Educational applications of VR are particularly promising. The high *immersion* that results from using modern VR headsets and the ability to *naturally interact* with an environment enables a high motivation, which is a key component for successful learning. The complex anatomy of the human body with many small, elongated, intertwined structures, such as nerves and vascular structures, is hard to fully understand with desktop-based visualizations. Being able to explore, e.g., the skull, the lung, or the colon from inside may provide a deeper understanding. Moreover, being completely surrounded by VR automatically reduces distraction from the real world, which may contribute to improved learning of spatial relations (Tüzün and Özdinç, 2016). Beyond experiencing the human anatomy, physicians may better learn all kinds of surgical or radiological interventions. Being able to practice such interventions in a risk-free virtual environment is of paramount importance to yield high safety standards in clinical practice. Recently, also nurse education became a focus of VR-based developments. The focus of these developments is to train the actual handling of the patient in a hospital ward and to learn empathy (Elliman et al., 2016; Saab et al., 2021).

However, it is not straightforward to leverage the potential of VR in medical applications. Creating sufficiently detailed and realistic geometric models of the patient anatomy is already a challenge, as we discussed in Chapter 7. These models need to be enriched with textures and biomechanical properties. Substantial surgical knowledge is required to develop relevant scenarios, including rare but potentially important anatomical variants, the handling of instruments, and the reaction to complications. All kinds of learning require informative feedback. Thus VR-based training systems have to assess the performance of trainees as a basis for feedback. Validation studies are carried out to assess whether the content is correct, whether the tasks supported are realistic and finally whether training effects achieved in a VR setting translate to the real world, e.g., the operating room (OR).

Organization

We discussed most basics on VR in the previous chapter. In Section 13.2, we want to add one aspect that is particularly important for training, namely the collaborative activity in a virtual environment. The core of this chapter consists of anatomy education (Section 13.3) and surgery training (Section 13.4).

13.2 Collaborative Virtual Reality

Though early VR systems focused on an individual participant, increasingly use cases are explored where the collaboration in VR is crucial. A teacher and a student or a small group of students may meet in VR and explore, e.g., a historic site, the model of a cell, or a technical device.

Collaboration is relevant in medical education and training in different ways. A teacher may supervise a resident or a student or even a group of students to provide feedback or intervene. Collaborative competence is essential for many activities in clinical medicine and needs to be trained. Liaw et al. (2018) mention preparedness of hospital staff for disasters, but also normal working situations, where efficient teamwork contributes to patient safety. In a surgical intervention, the operating surgeon collaborates with at least one assistant and a nurse as well as with anesthesiologists. Clinical practice may require interdisciplinary cooperation and communication related to the treatment of a challenging case. As an example, a patient may arrive with multiple severe injuries (*polytrauma patient*). These patients are treated in the shock room by a team of specialists that has to collaborate effectively under severe time pressure.

Collaborative VR may enable training scenarios that comprise these types of collaboration. Fig. 13.1 shows an example of two collaborating users who jointly remove a gallbladder in a surgery simulator. To effectively act together, users need to be aware of each other, they need to communicate, and they need a shared understanding of the current situation. VR provides adequate support for such situations.

FIGURE 13.1

Two users with interactive 3D visualizations and force feedback devices that remove a gallbladder. One user (on the left) attaches anatomical structures, whereas the other cuts and carves the tissue and applies clips to vascular structures (From: (Diaz et al., 2014)).

Collaborative systems come in two flavors: *collocated collaborative VR systems* enable that different users inspect a virtual environment at the same physical place, whereas *remote collaborative VR systems* allow distantly located students and teachers to learn together in a "shared reality" (Brown, 2000). In collocated collaborative VR, a group of users is in a shared VR room seeing and being aware of each other.

As an example, Fairén González et al. (2017) introduced a VR system for anatomy education that was run on a Powerwall and in a CAVE. More frequently, collocated collaborative VR is realized by several users wearing VR headsets. Our discussion that follow is restricted to collocated collaborative VR.

We already introduced the term *co-presence*, the awareness for other users (recall Section 12.2). To achieve co-presence, every user should be represented by an avatar (recall Section 12.5). Thus any user can assess where other users are located, how close they are, and which movements they are currently performing. The avatars should be unique, and each should represent a particular user. Like in the real world, another person may occlude essential information, in particular in an operating room, where a variety of displays may be present. Therefore a rather sparse representation of the users may be beneficial, e.g., only a fraction of the human body. Collaboration may be *symmetric*, meaning that the users are on equal footing, or *asymmetric*, where one user has a superior position and others assist (Elvezio et al., 2018). In surgery, for example, an asymmetric collaboration occurs with the experienced operating physician as superior user.

Communication

Collaboration involves communication that is largely based on sound transmission. Thus a high-quality and low latency audio transmission is essential to enable users to communicate, e.g., in medical team training, such as the training of patient handover in a clear and unambiguous manner; a scenario for VR-based training is mentioned by Huber et al. (2018). Existing voice transmission systems often can be easily integrated in game engines. As an example, PHOTON VOICE integrates with UNITY.

Network architecture and performance

We have already discussed the importance of a high performance of VR systems to enable an efficient interaction in virtual environments and to reduce or avoid VR sickness (Section 12.2). In particular, low latency is essential. As an example, Elvezio et al. (2018) found that for the joint manipulation of objects the latency should be constantly kept around or below 10 ms.

For collaborative VR, additional challenges arise. Users are connected via a network with limited bandwidth, with certain delays, the length of which may vary, and a certain amount of packet loss. Despite these problems, it must be ensured that after manipulations in the virtual environment, *all* users perceive a fast update of the virtual environment. The virtual environment must have a *consistent state* for all users (Qin et al., 2010). Otherwise, an instrument or an organ may be on one computer screen several millimeters away from its position on another display (recall Fig. 13.1).

Major aspects of the performance are (Diaz et al., 2014):

- packet loss
- delay
- jitter (the standard deviation of delay)

Diaz et al. (2014) reported that errors and task completion time in surgery simulation increase strongly already when the delay is about 0.2 s or when the jitter is about 0.3 s. An *error* in surgery simulation means that a risk structure, such as a nerve, was damaged. Obviously, the errors made in surgical simulation should be only influenced by the skills of the user and not by the power of the network.

Client-server vs. peer-to-peer networks

Game engines, such as UNITY and UNREAL ENGINE, provide dedicated support for multi-user games, which can also be employed for collaborative training, e.g., the MLAPI (mid-level networking library), MIRROR NETWORKING, and PHOTON. Collaborative VR systems are typically realized as client-server systems (Elvezio et al., 2018; Chheang et al., 2019), where the first user's computer acts as a server to which others connect. With a client-server architecture, all clients share a *consistent state* of the virtual environment. This is in contrast to a peer-to-peer network, where all necessary calculations are performed on all computers in a different speed. The disadvantage of a pure client-server solution is that the server may become a bottleneck that has to handle too much computation load. Taking a surgery simulator as an example, users employ surgical instruments to handle human tissue. Collisions need to be detected, and resulting deformations and cuts need to be computed. Visualizations need to be updated, and haptic feedback needs to be computed. Therefore architectures are also used, where the server controls all computations, but delegates part of them to other computers in the network, see Diaz et al. (2014) for an example.

Even carefully chosen network architectures do not guarantee a sufficiently high performance. Various approximations and simplifications are typically necessary to enable fast computations and to avoid that too much data needs to be transmitted over networks. We discuss such strategies in Section 13.4. For readers interested in network architectures and communication protocols for collaborative surgery, the work of Qin et al. (2010) is highly recommended.

13.3 VR for anatomy education

We discussed anatomy education and in particular interactive 3D visualizations as a teaching mode in Chapter 7. Anatomy is a comprehensive subject, involving the bony skeleton, muscles, nerves, tendons, muscles, and ligaments in all areas of the human body where certain regions, such as head and neck, heart and the brain (neuroanatomy) are particularly challenging due to a high density of anatomical structures. Anatomy education is not an end in itself; in addition to all operating disciplines in medicine, it is an essential prerequisite for diagnostic and interventional radiology.

Here, we add immersive solutions that may provide an even better imagination of complex spatial relations, as they occur, for example, in the inner ear with its very small structures around the cochlea. Also the complex branching pattern of vascular structures and the related depth relations may be conveyed better with VR-based solutions (Hombeck et al., 2022a). We discuss VR-based systems intended for individual users, such as VR variants of the 3D puzzle and collaborative approaches, where a teacher observes and directs a student in VR. In principle, the same interaction techniques are required in VR as in desktop settings. Students should be able to:

- rotate, zoom, and translate an anatomical model
- clip and cut in a model
- inquire names of anatomical structures or further information

In immersive VR, these interactions are performed, e.g., with the VR controllers. Objects may be selected by means of picking rays or by directly touching them with a controller. Clipping planes or other objects may be added based on a menu selection and can then be manipulated. Further techniques need to be provided for navigation, e.g., the student may walk inside an anatomical structure, getting to know it from an egocentric perspective. Thus locomotion techniques (recall Section 12.7) are relevant. An essential requirement for basically all VR-based systems is *anatomical completeness*, i.e., in the target region, bones, muscles, tendons, ligaments, vessels, and nerves should be available.

We structure our discussion of VR for anatomy education based on special techniques that were employed (VR-based puzzles, collaborative VR) and based on the anatomical subfield that is supported (hand anatomy and heart anatomy). Neither the subfields, nor the techniques are comprehensive; they are selected primarily based on the availability of documented prototypes and systems.

13.3.1 VR-based 3D puzzles

3D jigsaw puzzles, as a game-inspired metaphor, may be useful for anatomy education. In VR, this idea is even more compelling, as the investigation and placement of single puzzle pieces—representing anatomical structures—can be realized more naturally. A 3D puzzle to help students learn the human anatomy was presented by Messier et al. (2016). The system was intended to be used in different modes, starting with a free exploration mode, where users get familiar with the system and the anatomical models (the skeletal anatomy of the skull and the thorax). In a *quiz mode*, the users actually use the puzzle in a guided manner.

As a further VR system based on the puzzling metaphor Seo et al. (2017) presented ANATOMY BUILDER VR, a system to learn skeletal canine anatomy. With this system, the student is able to take pieces out of a digital bone box containing 3D bone models, based on scans of real bones. After that, the student can inspect the model and place it in an "anti-gravity" field, where it is suspended in place. Positioning a bone near a connection on an already positioned bone triggers the appearance of a yellow line. If the user releases the controller button, the joints snap together (see Fig. 13.2). This is repeated until the skeleton is assembled to the user's satisfaction.

The most recent VR-based puzzle was presented by Pohlandt et al. (2019). In their system, the student can choose between several anatomical structures and scale them freely from their original size to large scales. Beside assembling a puzzle, the

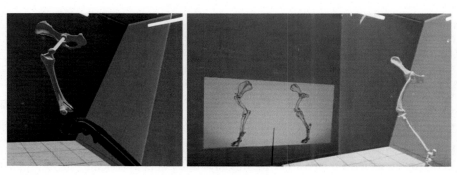

FIGURE 13.2

ANATOMY BUILDER VR allows to snap bones together (left) until a skeleton is assembled. As guidance, a reference image is shown (right) (From: (Seo et al., 2017), Reprinted by permission from Proceedings of Applied Human Factors and Ergonomics, Springer, ©2017).

VR puzzle allows the disassembly in a specific order, which mimics the dissection course. The combination of assembly (puzzling) and disassembly should enable a deep understanding of the spatial relations.

The interaction is carried out with HTC VIVE controllers (see Fig. 13.3). Students may select objects with ray-based interaction and grabbing. As visual feedback, an outline for the selected object is added and its color is slightly adapted. For anatomy education, it is useful to further add the object name. POHLANDTS' VR puzzle supports different stages of learning by allowing the user to enable/disable several guiding features. Snapping is enabled when the distance between two selected objects is below a threshold, and also the orientation only slightly deviates from the correct one. For example, slight guidance is offered by coloring the model from red to green that shows the user if the object is oriented and positioned correctly. Another guidance is called "ghost copy," which is inspired by a real-world jigsaw puzzle, where the user usually has a picture of the finished puzzle at hand. If the user takes two pieces, the goal position and orientation of the second piece is shown on the first piece. The user can then just match the piece they are holding with the copy they are seeing.

13.3.2 Collaborative anatomy education

Computer-based anatomy training is typically designed as an individual activity. However, individual learning has potential disadvantages. Users may follow unproductive paths in a learning environment and may skip essential issues just by not being aware of the actually important aspects. Thus in a VR system, it may be useful if a *teacher* supports one (or more) students, supervising them, highlighting essential information, and providing feedback with respect to the student's exploration strategy. As a step in this direction, SCHMEIER and SAALFELD developed a one-on-one

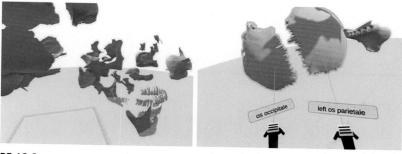

FIGURE 13.3

The VR Puzzle is embedded in a room, only equipped with a large round ground floor. Pieces are initially distributed. When users select two objects with their controllers, they can start docking them (From: (Pohlandt et al., 2019)).

tutoring system (Saalfeld et al., 2020b). According to advice from their medical partners, they focused on the human skull base. An *asymmetric* hardware setup is used, i.e., not all users have the same input and output modalities. Though a high level of immersion is beneficial for students, the teacher may benefit from a good overview of what one or several students are currently experiencing.

In the system by SCHMEIER and SAALFELD the teacher uses a ZSPACE (recall Section 12.4.4) to be able to see the surroundings and easily input text via a keyboard. The student uses a HTC VIVE and explores a scaled-up skull from inside (Fig. 13.4). To guide the student, the teacher may set landmarks and sketch 3D annotations in front of the student (see Fig. 13.5). The teacher may even reposition the student to direct their attention. This is achieved by grabbing the student's avatar. The latter, of course, is highly invasive and should be announced or even initiated by the student, who is somehow lost in a complex 3D model. Additionally, the student's first person view is shared with the teacher.

If a VR headset is used, special care must be taken for the representation of the students and teachers in the virtual environment. Avatars can be used to mimic movement, interactions, and viewing directions of the users. A teacher can benefit from knowing the location of all students. However, it can be distracting for students if they know where fellow students are.

13.3.3 Hand anatomy

Several VR-based systems have been deliberately designed to support hand anatomy education. The hand is responsible for fine-grained control of many activities. It is composed of 129 anatomical structures, such as joints, muscles, and tendons, which need to be coordinated well to perform, e.g., grasping movements (Netter, 2014). Fig. 13.6 illustrates the different layers of anatomical structures.

A conventional (desktop-based) training system requires a sufficiently realistic biomechanic model to study the interaction between the different anatomical struc-

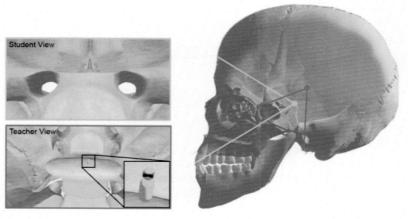

FIGURE 13.4

Initial position, orientation, and view of student and teacher within the virtual environment. The two holes, *foramina*, are interesting details, since nerves and other structures pass there. The teacher view contains an avatar of the student (shown enlarged) (From: (Saalfeld et al., 2020b), ©2020 The Author(s) Eurographics Proceedings ©The Eurographics Association).

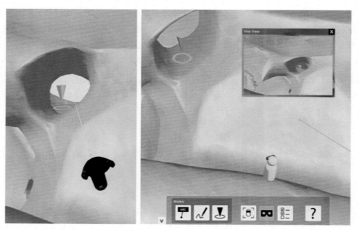

FIGURE 13.5

Left: The student's view on a landmark. **Right:** The corresponding view on the teacher system. The student's avatar can be seen, looking right at the landmark. The teacher can see the student's view with an extra window at the top right (From: (Saalfeld et al., 2020b), ©2020 The Author(s) Eurographics Proceedings ©The Eurographics Association).

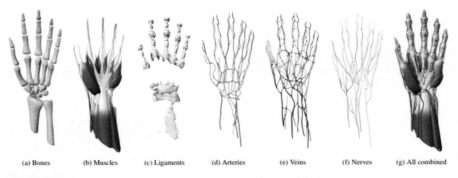

(a) Bones   (b) Muscles   (c) Ligaments   (d) Arteries   (e) Veins   (f) Nerves   (g) All combined

FIGURE 13.6

Anatomical structures representing all relevant layers of the human hand anatomy
(From: (Saalfeld et al., 2020a), ©2020 The Author(s) Eurographics Proceedings ©The
Eurographics Association).

tures. A real-time interaction with such a model is quite challenging. An alternative
for VR-based training is to track the movements of hands and fingers of the user
and to transfer them to a virtual hand that mirrors the physical hand posture. Besides displaying the biomechanics, such systems employ the sense of embodiment
(recall Section 12.5.1). The underlying motivation was well expressed by Lindgren
and Johnson-Glenberg (2013): "body activity can be an important catalyst for generating learning, and new technologies are being developed that use natural human
physicality and gesture as input." Jariyapong et al. (2016), for example, encouraged
students to draw bones and joints on their fingers (*body painting*).

In the following, we describe a VR-based hand anatomy system developed at
the University of Magdeburg (Saalfeld et al., 2020a). Based on a multi-layer hand
model from a commercial vendor (CDEROLIN), see https://sketchfab.com/cderolin/
collections/hand-anatomy; it involves all anatomical structures. Students may move
their hands and see corresponding movements of the hand model. To enable low
latency, the combined geometric model was reduced from around 800 K polygons
to around 200 K polygons. In Fig. 13.6, the already reduced structures are displayed.

Animating and tracking virtual hands

To create movements of the hand model, skeletal animation is used (Baran and
Popović, 2007). This requires the 3D model to be *rigged*, i.e., an invisible skeletal structure is created for them. The natural skeleton of the human hand served as
orientation. After rigging, the anatomical 3D structures are connected to the rig, a process referred to as *skinning*. Rigging and skinning are known techniques in character
modeling. For continuous tracking of the users' hands, the built-in hand tracking capabilities of the OCULUS QUEST are employed. Thus the virtual hands always have

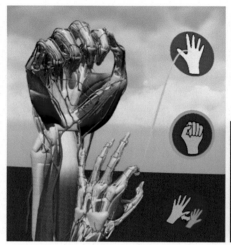

FIGURE 13.7

Left: An enlarged hand is shown in front of the user's hand, which can be set to three states via ray-based interaction: (1) open hand, (2) closed hand, and (3) mirroring the user's hand. To change the mode, the user has to point in the button direction and pinch their index finger and thumb. **Right:** By pressing buttons with the virtual hand, anatomical layers can be shown or hidden (From: (Saalfeld et al., 2020a), ©2020 The Author(s) Eurographics Proceedings ©The Eurographics Association).

the same orientation as the real hands (Fig. 13.7), which provides a feeling of *body ownership*.

User interface and evaluation

With a menu, students can control which layers from the anatomy are actually displayed. In a pilot study, this type of learning was appreciated (Saalfeld et al., 2020a). Evaluation relates to general and physical presence, usability, and the appropriateness of the geometric model. The major interaction, the movement of the fingers to control a corresponding virtual model, is basically limited to the hand. A conceivable extension is to track the feet and use foot movements to control the display of the foot anatomy.

13.3.4 Liver anatomy

Anatomy is an essential prerequisite for surgery; *surgical anatomy* is at the interface between both fields and comprises variants of the anatomy relevant for surgical decisions and intraoperative management. As an example, we describe a system for (surgical) liver anatomy that enables the exploration of a variety of organ models. These models are all derived from real patient data.

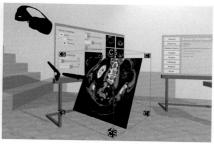

FIGURE 13.8

A liver shelf for liver anatomy training, equipped with 19 liver models representing major variants of the liver anatomy. On the right, the information board is shown with 2D slice-based visualizations and possibilities to adjust them (©2021 IEEE, Reprinted with permission from: (Schott et al., 2021)).

The liver is supplied by two vascular structures: the portal vein and the hepatic artery. The liver is drained by the hepatic vein. Moreover, the bile ducts are essential for the surgical strategy. Thus young surgeons should be aware of the variability, in particular of (topologically) different variants of blood supply and venous drainage. There may be trifurcations instead of the more typical bifurcations, there may be an accessory hepatic vein, and also the hepatic arteries exhibit a large variety. A correct assessment of the patient-specific variant is essential in planning the access to a pathology, typically a benign or malignant tumor.

Liver shelf

To convey this variability, the *liver shelf* was designed. It is inspired by a real shelf with liver models at the University Hospital in Mainz. This way, a shelf is used as metaphor to arrange different variants of the organ anatomy in a familiar way (see Fig. 13.8). All liver models are rendered semi-transparently to reveal the internal structures. The shelf is placed in a lecture room with little decoration to avoid distraction and unnecessary geometric detail to cope with the real-time requirements.

Users may select an organ model by grabbing it. They may zoom it by moving their controllers away from each other, an interaction that is inspired by the familiar pinch gesture on smartphones. The system is designed as a collaborative system, i.e., different students may meet in this room. Different modes of collaboration are possible, e.g., one student may observe what another one is doing and explaining. Ideally, they would later change their roles so that every student also has an active role (Schott et al., 2021).

Information board

In addition to the liver shelf as core component of a virtual anatomy system, an information board is provided where (anonymized) information related to the patient and its diagnosis is available. To avoid the presentation of too many textual components at once, the information is categorized and only selected categories are displayed. Ray-based interaction triggered with the VR controllers enables to adjust the visible information.

Discussion

In its current version, the liver shelf represents major variants of the anatomy and tumor location, arranged in four rows. Within certain limits, the liver shelf can be extended by adjusting the length of the shelf or adding rows. Also, an additional shelf may be created, e.g., to present livers from different parts of the world. This is motivated by the fact that the anatomy of Asian livers differs considerably from that of European livers. The idea can also be translated to other organs, such as the kidney, the pancreas, or the lung. The actual realization of the liver shelf from Schott et al. (2021) even supports diagnosis and surgery planning, since the cases contain pathologies that require surgical treatment. It is probably useful to present both 2D slice-based visualizations and 3D models. However, the student is not supported in the direct integration of this information. The system can also be used without VR equipment in a *spectator mode*. In this mode, users cannot manipulate the scene, but can observe what others are doing. This spectator mode can be used by a teacher to supervise students, resembling the system described in Section 13.3.2, where the teacher monitored a student without being immersed in VR.

13.3.5 **Heart anatomy**

As a first step to convey the heart anatomy, a static heart model with labeled structures may be employed in VR (see Fig. 13.9). The anatomy of the heart exhibits a strong variability, where, in particular, a number of congenital heart defects are clinically relevant. An immersive 3D visualization may help to understand the nature of such defects.

A major specialty of the heart is its strongly dynamic character. The beating heart undergoes severe geometric changes representing the elasticity of the involved structures. A VR-based system enables to observe this dynamics where individual structures are colored and textured such that they are recognizable (Falah et al., 2014). Falah et al. (2014) further emphasize that it is essential to select individual structures, to change their size, and control their visibility. More specific for the heart anatomy, different *layers* of information are provided and may be explored. The conductive system of the heart is presented. It comprises nodes and fibers that conduct electric impulses, and thus trigger the contraction of the heart muscle (Falah et al., 2014). The system also involves a quiz mode with multiple choice questions that may guide the exploration. It is primarily intended for semi-immersive settings, e.g., for stereoscopic displays. In Fig. 13.10, the system is shown in different modes of operation.

13.3.6 **Creating a comprehensive VR learning environment**

So far, we discussed individual solutions for some aspects or parts of anatomy education. It would be desirable to embed such individual solutions in a more comprehen-

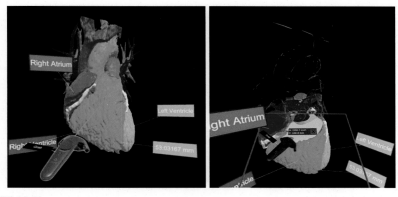

FIGURE 13.9

The heart anatomy is explored with a HTC VIVE controller. Objects may be selected, clipping planes may be inserted, translated, or tilted. Labeling and measurement results provide associated symbolic information. Appropriate placement and legibility of textual information in VR is challenging (Courtesy of Patrick Saalfeld, University of Magdeburg).

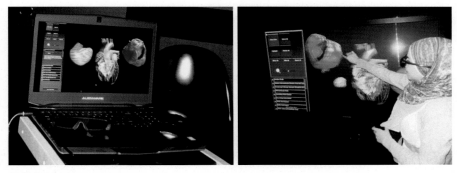

FIGURE 13.10

A VR heart anatomy system for semi-immersive use on a laptop with stereo glasses (left) or on a large display wall (right) (From: (Falah et al., 2014), Reprinted by permission from Proceedings of Science and Information Conference, Springer, ©2014).

sive environment, where access to all parts is possible. One could imagine embedding any individual solution in a *room* and providing a large foyer, where appropriately labeled rooms can be accessed. Richardson et al. (2011) provided a *virtual laboratory* with a number of *stations*. The stations are numbered suggesting that the students visit them in a certain sequence. The specific solution introduced by Richardson et al. (2011) was based on SECOND LIFE, a multi-user platform that was quite popular at that time. Among others, the extensive capabilities to create avatars turned out to be useful. The learning environment was intended to be used collaboratively by student groups (see Fig. 13.11). Compared to a real setting in a classroom, the students are a

FIGURE 13.11

Collaborative anatomy learning in well-defined stations. The virtual environment was created within SECOND LIFE (From: (Richardson et al., 2011), ©John Wiley & Sons Inc., 2011).

bit more anonymous in this environment. It turned out that this pseudoanonymity was beneficial for engaging them to ask questions and respond to questions from others.

13.3.7 Evaluation

Evaluations of VR-based anatomy training systems comprise questions and measurements related to the usability, presence, VR sickness, and cognitive load. The major criterion, however, is the *knowledge gain* of the user (the difference between pre-test and post-test results, recall Chapter 7). Often, evaluations are carried out as comparisons, where VR-based training is compared with other computer-based or more conventional types of training. There are standardized tasks and questionnaires to assess *stereoacuity* (the ability to assess stereoscopic cues) (Kurul et al., 2020). As a consequence, Kurul et al. (2020) distribute students in an evaluation such that the VR group and control group have very similar stereoacuity levels.

In the following, we briefly comment on three evaluations that were part of papers describing a new system and two papers, where the comparison of training methods was the sole purpose of the paper, i.e., no new VR designs are introduced. We can only focus on some key statements; a solid evaluation has to consider many aspects starting from recruiting test persons, to experiment design and statistical analysis, which cannot be discussed here. We start with two evaluations related to VR-based puzzle systems.

Example evaluations

Messier et al. (2016) employed different strategies to assess the effect of VR-based learning (recall Section 13.3.1). They measured the cognitive load according to the NASA-TLX questionnaire. The performance of the students was assessed in terms of completion time and a score that also considers the number of unnecessary moves. Their system was assessed in a comparative study, where three display paradigms (2D monitor, stereo monitor and OCULUS RIFT) and two input devices (space mouse and standard keyboard) were tested.

Seo et al. (2017) compared their system (recall Section 13.3.1) against a real bone box containing real thoracic limb bones and digital pelvic limb bones. Participants enjoyed using VR considerably more than the bone box. Additionally, they stated that they were able to manipulate bones and put them together with ease in VR. For the identification of bones, the VR environment did not show benefits compared to the bone box.

Weyhe et al. (2018) compared immersive VR with traditional forms of learning with participants from high school instead of medical students. This has the advantage that the previous anatomy knowledge is more homogeneous. They analyzed the usability of their immersive anatomy atlas (see Fig. 13.12) with ten questions. The knowledge test in both groups consisted—as usual—of some multiple choice questions and a sketching task. It is challenging to objectively analyze the results of the students sketching activities. Despite these problems, sketching is a reasonable task to test (spatial) anatomy knowledge.

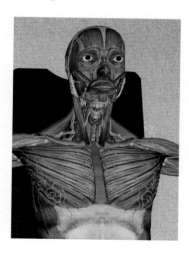

FIGURE 13.12

A detailed anatomical model as basis for an immersive anatomy atlas (From: (Weyhe et al., 2018)).

Maresky et al. (2019) performed a comparative study with 42 students, focused on the anatomy of the heart. The study was performed with first-year undergraduate medical students, who did not participate in any cardiac anatomy lecture. First, they completed a pre-intervention quiz containing conventional cardiac anatomy questions and visual-spatial questions. After that, the students were randomly split into two groups: a VR group and a control group, consisting of students who continued their study normally. Then, the students completed a post-intervention quiz. The students in the VR group scored 21% higher in conventional cardiac anatomy questions and 26% higher in visual-spatial questions, i.e., question concerning spatial relations.

Another comparative study regarding the learning and retention of neuroanatomy was performed by Ekstrand et al. (2018). They compared a VR system to traditional paper-based methods (books with appropriate figures). Both groups had only twelve minutes to deal with some neuroanatomical structures. In their study with 64 first- and second-year medical students, again, a pre-test and post-test were performed. Additionally, a test was administered about one week later to assess the retention. Long-term effects of VR-based anatomy education were not studied so far, which is often mentioned as a limitation of current evaluations.

13.3.8 Summary

VR typically enables an even better understanding of complex and dynamic anatomical structures compared to 3D (desktop) visualizations. Whether or not VR is beneficial depends on specific tasks, anatomical regional regions, and specific visualization techniques (Hombeck et al., 2022b). The navigation within anatomical structures, such as the brain or skull, enables memorable experiences and a deep understanding of the involved anatomical structures. The engaging and motivating character that was confirmed in a wide range of user studies is beneficial for anatomy education.

Entire geometric models or individual structures may be scaled strongly to enable this deep understanding. Beyond navigation, selection of individual structures and manipulation of their appearance and visibility are essential. Also, VR-based virtual anatomy teaching strongly benefits from tasks that structure and focus the student's exploration. The docking tasks as part of a puzzle-based VR system represent one example that fits well to the 3D nature of anatomical structures.

Birbara et al. (2020) mention a number of problems that are frequently noticed by users of VR anatomy teaching systems. Users sometimes consider navigation as challenging and miss tactile feedback. Indeed, to learn how anatomical structures feel in terms of roughness, texture, and elasticity would be beneficial as preparation for surgery training. Individual systems for anatomy education may be integrated in a larger system consisting of room or stations (recall (Richardson et al., 2011)).

13.4 VR for surgery training

Surgery is still a major type of medical treatment for a wide variety of severe diseases, e.g., vascular diseases, cancer, diseases of the heart valves, and severe musculoskeletal diseases. Surgery involves high risks based on the anesthesia that is required and the trauma related to a surgery, e.g., nerves or muscles may be damaged. As a consequence, surgical training is essential. It should be standardized and ensure a high quality of preparation before a surgeon performs a surgery. The increased importance of surgical training is also due to increased expectations in patient safety.

Surgical training involves patient selection, i.e., the crucial decision regarding which patients are eligible for surgery, the preparation, the actual surgery, and post-operative care. Moreover, surgeons need to be familiar with the principles and practice of post-operative care (Varras et al., 2020). Finally, team training is essential, i.e., a surgeon should be aware of the possibilities of the whole team to solve problems and should be able to communicate clearly and efficiently in surgery (Diaz et al., 2014). Computer-assisted and VR-based surgical training has been a research and development project since about 2000. An early example of a long-term development leading to a commercial surgery training system was the VOXEL-MAN TempoSurg for training surgery on the temporal bone, in particular for practicing drilling of the temporal bone (Leuwer et al., 2007). High-fidelity visual displays and tactile feedback turned out to be essential for this kind of surgical training.

Mentoring

Traditionally, *mentoring* plays an essential role in surgery training, i.e., resident surgeons learn by repeated participation in surgery, where they observe the operating surgeon and assist them. Also the term *apprenticeship* is frequently used to characterize this type of training. This traditional training, including the role model of an experienced surgeon, has clear benefits, but also obvious shortcomings.

The resident surgeon is dependent on the cases that are actually operated in their clinic. Some types of surgery are carried out less frequently than in the past, often because there are alternatives, such as (radiological) interventions, which are more convenient for the patient. Thus resident surgeons may have severe problems to "observe" enough cases. Resident surgeons also depend on the surgical competence of the operating surgeon and on their willingness and ability to explain. Moreover, practical limitations occur: operating rooms may be crowded, surgical fields may be rather small and partially occluded for the resident surgeon, e.g., by the hands of the operating surgeon (Pulijala et al., 2018).

Surgery often occurs under time pressure. Therefore the operating surgeon cannot provide lengthy and detailed explanations. Finally, during difficult parts of surgery, the surgeon is fully concentrated on surgery and cannot simultaneously explain it in a didactically useful manner adapted to the previous knowledge of the current mentee.

VR-based training cannot replace mentoring, but can add to surgical training and help to reduce the shortcomings of mentoring. Mentoring remains essential, since a teacher not only explains technical and procedural skills, but also passion and an attitude towards this challenging work.

Pilot training as role model

Many recent developments in surgery training are strongly inspired by aviation and flight trainers. Similar to a pilot learning to operate an airplane using a realistic visual representation of a cockpit, a surgeon should be able to train a special operation as often as necessary to become proficient. Like pilot simulators incorporating many different airports, a variety of weather conditions, and the simulation of technical problems, a surgery simulator includes anatomical variants, variants of the pathologies to be removed, and the handling of complications. The experience gained in surgical training should be transferable to the OR and lead to an improved outcome there.

Ideally, potential surgeons can initially be tested whether or not they have the necessary capabilities to become good surgeons. Later, surgeons can be certified based on their performance when using a surgical simulator. Whereas computer support and VR systems for individual surgery training has been a research focus since more than two decades (Satava, 1995), only recently communication and teamwork as essential aspects are also considered for computer-assisted training (Varras et al., 2020).

Classification of surgical knowledge and training

According to Varras et al. (2020), surgeons benefit from:

- observation and imitation
- practice with skill repetitions
- structured training
- informative feedback
- adaptation for developing cognitive and psychomotor surgical skills

Phases of surgical training

VR-based training may support all the aspects mentioned above.

Varras et al. (2020) discriminate phases of surgical training, which are quite generic and applicable to many other professional activities:

- cognitive phase
- association phase
- autonomous phase

In the section that follows, 13.4.1, we describe learning in the cognitive phase, where users get familiar with surgical strategies and surgical decisions. The association phase involves deliberate practice, i.e., the residents try to perform increasingly more parts of an intervention and repeat the basic steps, such as suturing and knot tying, again and again to perform the underlying movements more goal-directed and more efficiently.

Finally, in the autonomous phase residents perform whole surgical procedures themselves and still gain further knowledge by dealing with different patients, different pathologies, and by handling complications. For the association and autonomous phase, the actual handling of instruments needs to be trained (see Section 13.4.2). Varras et al. (2020) emphasize that "non-technical aspects, such as communication, teamwork and leadership play a substantial role in surgical success."

Part-task training and procedure simulators

According to Chan et al. (2013), a useful distinction of VR-based surgical training systems relates to

- part-task training
- procedure simulators

As the name suggests, a *part-task training* relates to one essential part of surgery, which can be trained independently. Chan et al. (2013) mention as an example catheter placement for ventriculostomy, i.e., a surgery where drainage of the cerebral ventricles is carried out. With such training systems, a particularly challenging part of a surgery is trained repeatedly in isolation from previous (preparatory) steps and following parts of the procedure. These training systems more often employ customized hardware, and they enable a more rigorous validation.

A *procedure simulator*, on the other hand, is comprehensive and enables a training of the sequence of the individual parts. It supports a training of *cognitive aspects*. Users are allowed to freely select the steps they are training, leading to a large variety of simulations.

13.4.1 Cognitive phase

Resident surgeons have to become familiar with the surgical anatomy, i.e., they need an in-depth understanding of the anatomical structures in the relevant area. This includes vascular structures, muscles, and nerves. Nerves often represent a particular challenge, since they are so small that they are not visible in preoperative medical image data. Thus surgeons need to know where to expect them relative to other larger structures to avoid damage to the nerves (Smit et al., 2016a).

Moreover, surgeons need to be aware of variations of anatomical structures in terms of shape, branching patterns, and appearance. They further need to be familiar with all instruments to be used in surgery and during the steps of surgery, including complications and appropriate responses. Also, they must know the information that is essential for surgical decision-making, e.g., with respect to

- the extent of surgery
- an appropriate access to the pathology
- the selection of appropriate instruments or implants

If an implant needs to be chosen, surgeons should know how to select an implant that fits well in the patient anatomy and that is also functionally a good fit, e.g., a hip implant, where the load on the remaining bones is similar to the preoperative situation (Dick et al., 2009). Moreover, it involves practical skills, handling the instruments appropriately to perform surgical tasks safely and efficiently.

Training cognitive issues

A careful selection of surgical workflows and scenarios, which may include major complications, may be trained based on 3D models of the patient anatomy. For each surgery, a representative number of cases may be selected to expose the residents to all major variants of the anatomy, in particular those that have a strong influence on surgical strategies. There are surgical training systems that primarily support the cognitive skills, i.e., based on the presentation of actual cases, surgeons should train their decisions and receive feedback based on expert opinions. In Fig. 13.13, we show an immersive system for training cognitive issues in liver surgery.

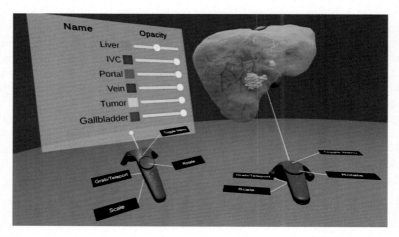

FIGURE 13.13

For training in the cognitive phase, a liver model with a tumor is shown for discussing operability of the patient. The menu enables the adjustment of the visibility of the intrahepatic structures (Courtesy of Patrick Saalfeld, University of Magdeburg).

13.4.2 Core components and tasks of VR-based surgical training

In what follow, we describe core components of surgical training that support the *association phase* and the *autonomous phase* of surgical training (recall (Varras et al., 2020)). Training in these phases is performed after the cognitive stage and involves primarily a training of psychomotor skills, such as the eye-hand coordination and the actual handling of instruments. In addition to realistic models of the patient anatomy, 3D models of the surgical instruments and implants need to be provided. Interaction facilities should enable surgeons to use the surgical tools to interact with human tissue, to deform and cut it. The VR-based system must be quite powerful to detect collisions between instruments and human tissue, to deform human tissue based on a sufficiently realistic mechanical model. Ideally, the systems also provide haptic feedback. Thus surgical training systems have a number of core components (Chan et al., 2013) that we discuss in the following:

- anatomical modeling
- realistic textures

- physics simulation
- haptics

These core components are illustrated in Fig. 13.14.

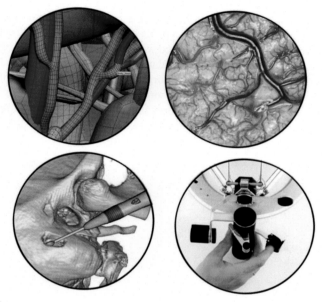

FIGURE 13.14

From top left to bottom right: **Anatomical models** are extracted from medical image data. **Realistic textures** enhance the visual realism. Bump mapping leads to highly realistic rendering. **Physics simulations** are carried out to enable a plausible handling of instruments. **Haptic devices** are integrated to provide force feedback dependent on the stiffness of the currently manipulated structure (From: (Chan et al., 2013), Reprinted with permission by Wolters Kluwer Health Inc., Neurosurgery Journal, Volume 72).

Anatomical modeling

in the context of a surgery, simulator is basically the same as it is for virtual anatomy systems. It comprises geometric modeling based on medical imaging data or photographic data and modeling of the visual appearance, e.g., by employing intraoperative photos for texturing the geometric models. The major extension of anatomical modeling for surgery simulators is the enrichment with tissue properties, such as elasticity and stiffness. Typically, known values from the literature are employed for this purpose. However, even such properties can be derived in a data-driven manner, e.g., by using MR elastography. Anatomical modeling serves to generate a variety of surgical scenes, which may represent different steps in surgery or different cases to convey anatomical or pathological variants.

Realistic textures

strongly contribute to the perceived quality of a surgical training system. Glossiness, shininess, transparency, smoothness, or patterns, such as elongated stripes along some muscles, may increase the realism of a surgical simulator (Sutherland et al., 2019). Intraoperatively acquired photos of organs and other anatomical structures may be employed, but also a procedural texture model is possible. A photo needs to be appropriately mapped to a curved surface, a process that involves some distortion. For a smooth appearance, textures may be filtered with spline-based functions. Bump maps perturb surface normals, and thus can simulate the effect of bumps more realistically than conventional 2D textures. In several organs, such as the nose and the colon, it is essential to convey the wetness of some structures. Also the display of surgical instruments benefits from appropriate textures that emphasize their metallic character (Qian et al., 2015). In Fig. 13.15, we compare two variants of the visualization of the nasal cavity as part of a training system for endoscopic surgery.

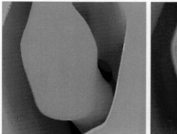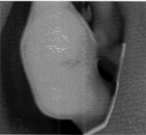

FIGURE 13.15

Comparison of a flat anatomy model of a polyp in the nasal cavity compared with a model textured to provide the impression of a wet structure as part of a training system for endoscopic surgery in the nasal cavities (©2008 IEEE, Reprinted with permission from: (Krüger et al., 2008)).

Physics simulation

is essential to represent the interaction between surgical instruments and human tissue in a *plausible manner*. In addition to the geometry of instruments and implants, also their behavior needs to be modeled, e.g., how parts of them may be moved relative to each other. As an example, a BONEBRIDGE is an implant for the treatment of deafness. Fig. 13.16 shows a model of this implant.

The simulation of the complex behavior of soft tissues is a trade-off between accuracy and performance. If accuracy would be the only aspect to consider, the biomechanics of human tissue would be simulated with the *finite element method* (FEM) (Bro-Nielsen and Cotin, 1996) and with a very fine decomposition of the geometric models in small volumetric elements (prisms, tetrahedra). The FEM was originally used in engineering and is based on principles of continuum mechanics, describing deformations using laws of physics, such as energy conservation. The un-

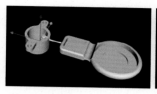 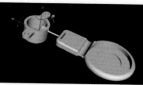 

FIGURE 13.16

A BONEBRIDGE is inserted in the inner ear to enable sound propagation in deaf patients. The arrows indicate the options to move and rotate parts of the implant to achieve an ideal fit (From: (Scherbinsky et al., 2015), Reprinted by permission from Proceedings of CURAC, Springer, ©2015).

derlying differential equations are numerically solved and the accuracy is directly related to the element sizes, i.e., the resolution of the model. Thus precise visual and haptic information could be generated.

However, for complex geometric models, as they are used in surgery, such solutions are not real-time capable, i.e., the accurate response to the users' input can only be generated after several seconds of computation. Instead, *mass-spring models* (Mollemans et al., 2003) are frequently used to provide a fast approximation of the instrument-tissue interaction. Mass-spring models are inherently one-dimensional, and thus represent a coarse approximation of volumetric tissue. The forces acting on the masses extend or reduce the lengths of the springs that connect them, a process that follows Hooke's law, where a stiffness value k defines how strongly a mass responds on a force.

A trade-off that was employed frequently in recent times is *position-based dynamics* (PBD) (Müller et al., 2007). It is based on laws of physics, just as FEM. The acceleration of vertices is not considered. Instead, only velocity and position changes are computed and vertices are updated accordingly. Pan et al. (2020) employ PBD for laparoscopy training. Soft tissue deformation can be realized with SOFAUNITY, a UNITY extension based on the long-term development of the SOFA framework that includes haptics, collision detection and soft tissue deformation in a scene-graph structure (Faure et al., 2012). Another widespread toolkit for soft tissue deformation is NVIDIA FLEX, which is based on particle simulation.

Collision detection

is part of the physics simulation component, see Lombardo et al. (1999) for a notable early paper. When a collision between a (rigid) instrument and a (mostly deformable) organ model is detected, the affected area needs to be defined as well as the penetration depth and the angle between the instrument direction and the surface normal of the affected area. This information is needed to compute appropriate force feedback. Also collision detection is computationally intensive. Therefore acceleration strategies using hardware and software are essential. The use of graphics hardware support for collision detection was already described by Lombardo et al. (1999). Software support comprises the use of *bounding volumes* with simple shapes, such as bounding spheres or bounding cylinders. The test whether the bounding volumes overlap is very fast, and if they do not overlap, the expensive test, whether an instrument collides with a complex organ model, can be avoided. For surgery simulation, collisions between deformable objects are particularly important. The survey article from Teschner et al. (2005) is an excellent overview of such approaches. As essential component of 3D interaction, different variants of collision detection are available, e.g., in UNITY.

Fluid simulation

In addition to the deformation of soft tissue, fluids need to be simulated for many surgical procedures. Parts of the human body are filled with blood and water and, moreover, water is often added in a surgical procedure. Thus to add effects related to fluids, such as bleedings, fluid simulations are performed. Again, precise solutions are based on physical laws, such as energy conservation, and involve finite element simulations. However, faster solutions are often sufficient, e.g., particle simulations (Müller et al., 2004). Such particle simulations and other physical simulation techniques are also readily available, for example NVIDIA FLEX provides them (https://developer.nvidia.com/flex). In a previous book (Preim and Botha, 2013), Chapter 21, these methods were explained in more detail.

Electrocautery simulation

Besides soft tissue modeling (Pan et al., 2020), it is essential to simulate thermal effects, e.g., when fat is burned to expose an anatomical structure. As a consequence of such a simulation, visual effects can be created that convey the vaporization of burned tissue. This process involves the conversion of electric energy to temperature changes, heat conduction, and diffusion. Physically, this process is described by the bio-heat transfer equation, a 2nd-order differential equation. Pan et al. (2020) discuss how to simplify this equation and to solve this simplified variant numerically in an efficient manner for training laparoscopic surgery.

Haptics

Haptic devices are often incorporated in VR training systems to provide touch sensations similar to a real surgery (recall Fig. 13.14). Haptic devices typically provide six degrees of freedom (DOF), which enables translational and rotational movements (recall Section 12.8). Sometimes, the end effector, i.e., the tip of the device provides further DOFs, as they are required to simulate grasping and cutting (Chan et al., 2013).

We explained that haptic rendering requires fast update rates (recall Section 12.8). In practice, this requires to decouple a *haptic rendering loop* from a *visual rendering loop*. The requirements for geometric accuracy are slightly lower for haptic rendering. As a consequence, a simplified geometric model is often used for haptic rendering (see Fig. 13.17).

For surgery simulation, *ground-referenced devices* are typically used and the end-effectors are often adapted to resemble actual surgical devices. As an example,

Pan et al. (2020) provide an L-shaped hook and a grasper, as they are used in laparoscopic surgery, associated with a PHANTOM OMNI device. Various toolkits support the programming of haptic devices. A popular example is OPENHAPTICS. The comprehensive survey article from Coles et al. (2010) provides many details on haptics in surgery simulation.

FIGURE 13.17

A geometric model of a liver with a tumor textured according to intraoperative images is used for visualization. A derived tetrahedra model serves for soft tissue computation. The simplified model consisting of bounding spheres serves for collision detection, and thus in the haptic feedback loop (Courtesy of Simon Adler, University of Magdeburg).

After the discussion of core components, we discuss tasks for VR-based surgical training.

Tasks in surgical training

VR-based surgical training systems aim at supporting some highly specialized tasks, but also a number of general tasks that are relevant for a wide variety of surgical procedures. The tasks discussed for anatomy training, e.g., transformation of geometric models, require further exploration by means of clipping and cutting for surgery training as well.

Additional tasks in surgery training include:

- manipulation, e.g., grasping and suturing
- measurements
- virtual resection

Measurements, in particular distance and angle measurements, are essential for surgical decisions. Thus trainees should be able to place points in the 3D models of a patient to inquire their distance, e.g., to assess the safety of removing a pathology in the vicinity of an essential risk structure. The involved risk strongly depends on the (minimum) distance between these structures. In maxillo-facial and orthopedic surgery, *angles* may be essential, e.g., angles between bones to assess a fracture. In catheter-based interventions, it may be useful to add a *ruler* to the catheter to convey the depth of the instrument tip (Lemole Jr. et al., 2007). Reitinger et al. (2006) did pioneering work on VR-based liver surgery planning, integrating various 3D measurement facilities.

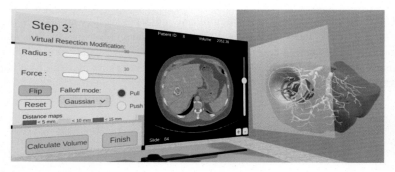

FIGURE 13.18

Resection planning in VR. The resection boundary is visible in 2D slices and a 3D surface model (Courtesy of Vuthea Chheang, University of Magdeburg).

Virtual resection, e.g., the possibility to try different variants of a resection, is an essential component of surgical training. For virtual resection, residents need an interaction facility to specify an arbitrarily-shaped resection volume. This interaction facility should be natural and efficient. As an example, specifying a resection by drawing on an organ surface is both efficient and similar to the actual surgery (see Fig. 13.18). A plane is fitted to the drawing on the organ surface and may be flexibly adapted, e.g., to save parts of a vascular tree.

The effects on the 3D organ model are also shown on the underlying slices of the CT data set. This resection method, originally developed for desktop planning (Konrad-Verse et al., 2004), was adapted to be steered with VR controllers (Chheang et al., 2021). The process can be carried out by two or three collaborating users, e.g., one pointing to a problem in the current resection plane (see Fig. 13.19). Trainees are enabled to operate geometric models of surgical devices, to interact with the human tissue, feel the resistance of different tissue types, cut in a similar way as they would do it in surgery, and can assess, e.g., the size and shape of an organ after resection.

13.4.3 Modeling the operating room

To further increase the realism of the surgical training, the trainee and the patient model should be embedded in a virtual operating room (OR). With an appropriate OR model, the virtual patient may lay on an operating table, the user initially is in a position to perceive the patient from a perspective that is similar to the surgeon's view. Embedding surgical training in an OR may enable a stronger impression of *presence* (recall Section 12.2), which is essential for motivation and engagement. Moreover, it is desirable not only to provide a realistic geometric model of the OR, but also a realistic representation of distracting acoustic factors, such as the typical noise in an OR, door movements, the ringing of pagers and telephones, and the (case-related) communication. Self-management with respect to such distractions is an essential aspect (Li et al., 2020).

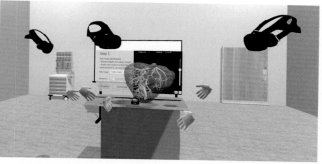

FIGURE 13.19

The training process (exploration of the anatomy and virtual resection) may be carried out by several surgeons in a collaborative manner (Courtesy of Vuthea Chheang, University of Magdeburg).

A model of an OR may be created

- from scratch with a geometric modeling software
- from using and eventually adapting a model from a commercial vendor, or
- from using a 360° camera

The first variant involves a very large modeling effort when a realistic model with a high level of detail is aimed at. The second variant is more feasible, since such models are available at reasonable costs, e.g., from the UNITY asset store. With such models all objects of the OR can be individually selected, highlighted, and translated. Thus it is possible to refine them, e.g., to resemble a certain target OR, which the trainer and trainee are familiar with. Huber et al. (2018) adapted the positions of the trocars, sterile equipment, and the team members' positions to increase the comfort for the VR-based training and increase the realism compared to the specific setting in their hospital.

Spherical video sequences by means of a 360° camera can faithfully represent a specific OR and involve rather low acquisition costs. The process involves acquiring and post-processing the videos, which takes some time, because the amount of data to be handled is quite large. There are two variants of these videos used in surgical training: monoscopic and stereoscopic 360° videos (Sutherland et al., 2019). The enhanced depth perception realized with stereoscopic videos is typically beneficial for training. Three hundred and sixty degrees (360°) videos may also capture distractions, such as noise and beeping telephones (Li et al., 2020).

A virtual OR created by means of a 360° camera capturing a real OR provides a high level of immersion, however, the environment is not interactive, i.e., a foot pedal or a light switch have no associated behavior (Sutherland et al., 2019). In contrast, an OR that is explicitly modeled may provide a high level of interaction, typically at the expense of reduced geometric detail. This reduced geometric model, however, can also be an advantage, because it allows to focus the geometric model on aspects that are actually essential for training, i.e., the developers can deliberately omit elements that are solely distracting. In Fig. 13.20, we see a comparison of a true situation in an OR with an appropriate geometric model, which was employed for training (in anesthesia).

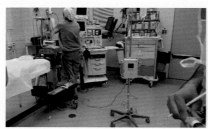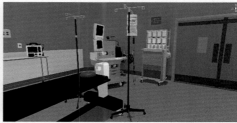

FIGURE 13.20

Comparison of a really crowded operating room and a geometric model focused on the components that are essential for surgical training (From: (Shewaga et al., 2018), ©ACM, reprinted with permission).

Huber et al. (2018) realized different scenarios: a first introductory scenario, where just the OR is acquired, and further scenarios that involve a simulated patient as well as all team members, who simulate an actual surgery by mimicking the necessary communication. Thus not only the geometric model is faithful, but also the movements of the staff members and the sound.

However, this is achieved at the expense of reduced flexibility. For example, it might be difficult to remove some details that are not needed, but require computational effort in the rendering process, or may distract the learner. Huber et al. (2018) examined both approaches: an adapted commercial model (see Fig. 13.21) and an environment created with a 360° camera (see Fig. 13.22).

13.4.4 Training for minimally-invasive surgery

Though computer-assisted training is potentially useful for basically all kinds of surgical interventions, it is particularly important for minimally-invasive surgery, such as endoscopic or laparoscopic surgery. As an example, cholecystectomy, the surgery where the gallbladder is removed, is a frequent minimally invasive surgery. Minimally invasive surgery is better tolerated by patients due to the reduced trauma. In the case of patients with a strongly reduced health state, this may be the only viable strategy. However, for surgeons, these procedures are more challenging compared to open surgery. The learning period for surgeons is longer. Another essential aspect is *patient safety*. There is considerable pressure to reduce staff-related complications, such as injuries, related to minimally invasive and robot-assisted surgery.

The increased difficulty is due to the fact that surgeons do not directly touch human tissue. Instead, they operate long thin instruments, inserted through small holes, to cut tissue, to suture, and to perform other surgical maneuvers, such as separating

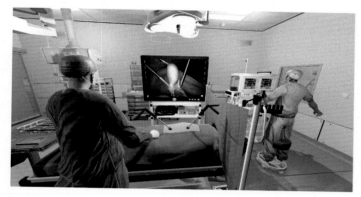

FIGURE 13.21

An artificial model of the OR provides maximum flexibility. It is used here for training minimally-invasive surgery (Courtesy of Tobias Huber, University Medicine, Mainz).

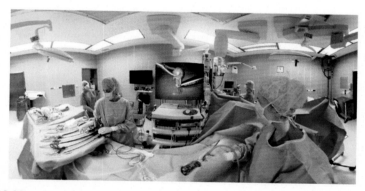

FIGURE 13.22

A model of the OR generated by means of a 360° camera. The realism is improved, but the interaction with the OR components is strongly limited (Courtesy of Tobias Huber, University Medicine, Mainz).

the liver from the gallbladder in cholecystectomy. Due to the restricted space, there is a higher risk of damaging structures (Qian et al., 2015). Surgeons have to constantly observe the position of their instruments in relation to anatomical landmarks and the pathology on a monitor, which is placed above the patient (recall Fig. 13.21).

A further complicating factor is the *fulcrum* effect which means that the movement of the hand to the left leads to a movement of the instrument to the right and vice versa. Thus handling laparoscopic instruments is not intuitive at all. The high cognitive load involved in this eye-hand coordination motivated also attempts to use augmented reality to display relevant anatomical structures extracted from preoperative medical image data on top of the patient. However, these solutions are technically demanding and still not widely available in clinical practice. Therefore the hand-eye coordination still should be trained in VR.

Learning by observation does not work in these settings. "The trainee is not able to observe the surgeons' hands, the instruments and operative results of manipulation simultaneously as it happens in open surgery" (Varras et al., 2020).

Minimally invasive surgery is typically performed by two collaborating physicians: the operating surgeon and the camera assistant who adjusts the camera to provide a good view to the operating field. A clear and smooth communication between these two is essential.

Training of laparoscopic surgery

Laparoscopic surgery, or short laparoscopy, is performed in the abdomen or pelvis. Small incisions in the body are used to insert a small camera and long instruments (up to 39 cm). Among the early and widely used systems is the LAPMENTOR from SIM-BIONIX released in 2003. The first version already enabled the complete simulation of laparoscopic cholecystectomy in VR (see Fig. 13.23). Other commercial systems include LAPSIM SURGICAL SCIENCE SIMULATOR and LAP VR CAE HEALTH-CARE INTERVENTIONAL SIMULATOR. Qian et al. (2015) introduced a number of techniques to improve the realism of laparoscopic surgery training. They described a flexible and efficient method for soft tissue deformation based on position-based dynamics. Moreover, new methods for efficient cutting were introduced.

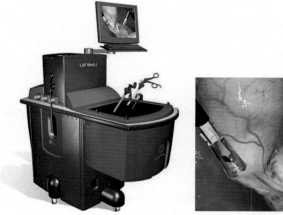
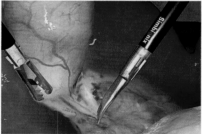

FIGURE 13.23

The LAPMENTOR provides a realistic environment for training laparoscopy, including replica of the instruments. On the display (right), the intraoperative situation is displayed in a high degree of realism (From: (Ayodeji et al., 2007). This paper is licensed under the Creative Commons Attribution-Share Alike 4.0 International license).

Until recently, the use of VR for surgical training was strongly limited, since VR-based surgical trainers did not provide a sufficiently realistic environment with a broad range of tasks to accomplish. Moreover, only team training raises the awareness of all team members for the surgical situation, an essential aspect in the development of transferable skills (Huber et al., 2018). Currently, there are promising developments in the direction of more powerful VR systems and their integration with other modes of surgical training.

Laparoscopic liver surgery

Liver surgery comprises the removal of benign and malignant tumors as well as liver transplantation. Liver surgery is challenging due to the complex vascular supply (recall our discussion of liver anatomy, Section 13.3.4) and the particular high risk of severe bleeding. Since the liver is the largest internal organ, deep-seated pathologies may be difficult to localize and remove. Thus though minimally invasive surgery began in the 1980s, laparoscopic liver surgery is a recent development.

The University Hospital in Mainz (Germany) and the University of Magdeburg perform long-term research in using VR for surgery education with a focus on liver surgery. Huber et al. (2018) combined the laparoscopy simulator LapSim (Surgical Science, Goeteborg, Sweden) with VR headsets to provide an immersive training experience (see Fig. 13.24). The SimBall devices, a kind of surgical joystick, of the LapSim simulator provide a haptic sensation that resembles the sensation of the real devices. Only with these devices the users interact with the virtual environment.

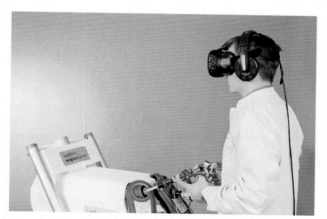

FIGURE 13.24

A surgeon operating the LapSim simulator in an immersive environment (Courtesy of Tobias Huber, University Medicine, Mainz).

The system was realized with Unity. The sound from the LapSim was integrated with an audio source object. In an evaluation, the VR-based training was carried out by 16 surgeons. They performed a cholecystectomy, where their performance was measured. Moreover, they were asked about ergonomics and VR sickness. Two female surgeons who were known to suffer from motion sickness indeed experienced slight VR sickness. The weight of the VR headsets (HTC Vive) was considered a problem for longer use and the spatial resolution was considered sufficient but not brilliant (Huber et al., 2018).

In a follow-up project, the COLLAVRLAP system was developed (Chheang et al., 2019), where the collaborative activities between the operating surgeon and the camera assistant may be trained. The system has an exploration mode, where the users make themselves familiar with the 3D patient model, using the VR controllers for interaction (see Fig. 13.25) and a surgery mode, where they employ the SIMBALL devices that correspond to the actual surgery devices (see Fig. 13.26).

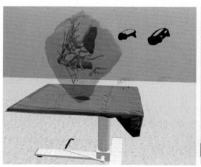

FIGURE 13.25

Left: Two users—represented by their VR headsets—explore the liver anatomy in the exploration mode in a sparse OR. **Right:** Users remove liver tissue with their controllers. A controller-attached menu enables mode switching (©2019 IEEE, Reprinted with permission from: (Chheang et al., 2019)).

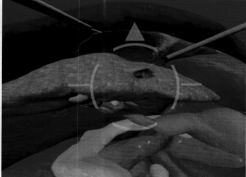

FIGURE 13.26

Left: In surgery mode, the surgeons operate with the SIMBALL devices. **Right:** Cutting, clipping, and camera movement are simulated (©2019 IEEE, Reprinted with permission from: (Chheang et al., 2019)).

13.4.5 **Training in robotic surgery**

We already discussed the special training demands related to minimally invasive surgery. Robotic surgery is an even more recent development and a further example of a radical change in surgery that requires extensive training, even for experienced surgeons (actually for them, considerable re-learning is required, which is particularly demanding). In robotic surgery, surgeons no longer directly move surgical instruments. Instead, they operate a Master/Slave robot, where the robot arm (the Slave) is controlled by the surgeon's movement on the robot console (the Master).

The movements of the surgeon are filtered, in particular to remove jitter, and may be scaled down by an order of magnitude, enabling surgery with strongly improved accuracy. As a consequence, the blood loss may be reduced, smaller incisions may be used, and faster patient recovery is possible. Robotic surgery is performed by a single surgeon. Thus the *mentoring approach* of learning is not possible.

Numerous surgical procedures were considered with respect to the potential benefit for robotic surgery. In particular in urology (removal of a tumor in the prostate), and in cardiac surgery (coronary artery bypass surgery, aortic valve repair), surgical robots are frequently used. The advantages described above, however, are not automatically achieved, but require a surgeon specifically trained for robotic surgery. There are many reports and discussions about complications after robot-assisted surgery (Cooper et al., 2015), including an increased number of nerve and tissue damages, further highlighting the importance of training. For training robotic surgery, the same options exist like for minimally-invasive surgery. These include operating animals (which involves severe ethical problems), cadavers, or artificial objects designed to resemble human anatomy.

The most prominent surgical robot is the DAVINCI system (from INTUITIVE SURGERY). Before a medical device is allowed to be used in clinical routine in the US, the Food and Drug Administration (FDA) needs to formally approve it. The DAVINCI system got FDA approval in 2001, which means that the system was allowed to be used in clinical routine. Shortly thereafter, the DV TRAINER (Mimics Technology) was released that provides VR-based training for the DAVINCI system (see Fig. 13.27). This training system involves standardized tasks, which are repeatedly performed. This kind of training can also be used to assess and certify surgeons in an objective manner (Perrenot et al., 2012). The DV TRAINER provides two-handed input and different simulation modes, such as camera movement, robot arm movement, manipulation, and suturing (Kenney et al., 2009). Moreover, the system involves a realistic replication of the interface of a surgical robot system, which is very similar to the realistic cockpit simulation in pilot training (Chan et al., 2013).

A more recent system for training the use of the DAVINCI system was provided by Christensen et al. (2018). They emphasized that a high degree of realism is required for successful training. This realism includes a faithful geometric model of the surgical robot and a complete and believable simulation of its behavior (including all joints and a plausible kinematics).

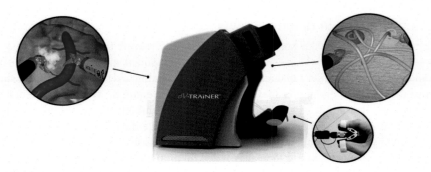

FIGURE 13.27

The DV TRAINER provides different scenarios, where surgeons can train the skills required to successfully use the DAVINCI robot (From: (Chan et al., 2013), Reprinted with permission by Wolters Kluwer Health Inc., Neurosurgery Journal, Volume 72).

13.4.6 Neurosurgery training

Neurosurgery treatment is an essential option to treat patients with tumors in the brain or in the spine, to treat neurovascular diseases, such as cerebral aneurysms and arterio-venous malformations, and to treat selected cases of epilepsy. Compared to surgery in the abdominal area, the requirements for precision are very high. Therefore operating microscopes are frequently used to magnify the target region. Stereoscopic digital microscopes are increasingly used to provide a very realistic impression of the surgical site (Bernardo, 2017). The relevant surgical anatomy includes vascular structures, key functional areas, nerves and skeletal structures, such as the mastoid bone.

Another specialty in neurosurgery is that the relevant information comes from a variety of different sources and needs to be integrated. The relevant data include CT and MRI data, CT or MR angiography data (to display the vascular structures), functional MRI data (to display functional brain regions, such as the visual cortex) and diffusion tensor data (to extract essential white matter structures). Information from these sources need to be fused either mentally in the surgeons' brain or algorithmically based on appropriate registration methods. For a VR solution, the relevant information is either modeled freely or extracted from clinical data. Pioneering work in the area of VR-based neurosurgery training was accomplished by Kockro et al. (2000).

Neurosurgery also experienced a considerable transformation with an increasing amount of minimally invasive surgery (Bernardo, 2017). An example for a minimally invasive neurosurgical procedure is ventriculostomy, which we discuss in the following.

Ventriculostomy training

A ventriculostomy is a surgical procedure, where a hole is drilled in the skull and a catheter is moved in the cerebral ventricles to drain them and reduce intracranial pressure. There are four connected cerebral ventricles filled with cerebrospinal fluid. On its way to the ventricles, the catheter penetrates the skull, the dura mater, and the brain. A ventriculostomy is primarily carried out for patients with a hydrocephalus, a condition characterized by an excess of cerebrospinal fluid. Ventriculostomy is a frequent surgical procedure, often the first that a resident in neurosurgery learns (Lemole Jr. et al., 2007). The neurosurgeon has to define an appropriate access path (entry point, trajectory, and depth of insertion), minimizing the risk for vital structures (John et al., 2016). Moreover, certain rules need to be followed to reduce the risk of infections, which represent a major complication.

Pioneering work on training ventriculostomy was carried out by Phillips and John (2000). They introduced a web-based system to enable a surgeon to define a trajectory and to guide them through the procedure. The system was assessed as useful, but since it was operated with mouse and keyboard, it was not highly immersive.

Lemole Jr. et al. (2007) presented an immersive system for the core part of ventriculostomy training (the authors classify it as part-task training). Their system provides bi-manual haptic feedback, hand and head tracking. The user wears glasses for perceiving stereo image data. The glasses are tracked by means of associated sensors. Similarly, the controllers are equipped with sensors to enable electromagnetic tracking. The patient model, consisting of surface representations of the skull, brain and other relevant neuroanatomical structures is enhanced with the following haptic properties: stiffness, viscosity, and friction. The viscosity effect is essential to simulate the process of passing gelatinous parenchyma. The system monitors the catheter movement and adapts the catheters' color in the case where its position and orientation is risky (see Fig. 13.28). The system involves a quite complex setup with a stereo display and half-silvered mirrors that enable operation in a sitting mode, which is convenient for longer usage. This setup also supports an augmented reality mode, where the user perceives the head model together with their hands. As limitations, the authors discuss that sidewall collisions are not detected and that the haptics stylus does not support all aspects of haptic feedback, e.g., torque is not perceived (Lemole Jr. et al., 2007).

Several research groups and companies dealt with ventriculostomy training. As an example for a more recent system, John et al. (2016) presented VCATH, a semi-immersive system using the zSPACE (recall Fig. 12.6) for presentation of the neuroanatomical structures and the associated stylus for practicing the procedure in a realistic manner.

13.4.7 Training in maxillofacial surgery

As final surgical discipline, we briefly discuss maxillofacial surgery, i.e., surgery related to the face and the oral cavity. This surgical discipline is also strongly influenced by technical developments and the demand for computer support is substantial. Maxillofacial surgery is carried out to treat pathologies and injuries in the mouth and face. It is an area where substantial computer support is used to analyze the relevant patient anatomy and support surgical decision-making. VR-based training was developed and evaluated by Pulijala et al. (2018). They provide training for one particular

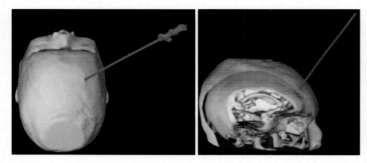

FIGURE 13.28

A catheter penetrates the skull as part of ventriculostomy training. **Left:** The green color indicates that the current trajectory is correct. **Right:** More brain structures are visible. The red color indicates an unfortunate trajectory (From: (Lemole Jr. et al., 2007), Reprinted with permission by Wolters Kluwer Health Inc., Neurosurgery Journal, Volume 61).

surgery, the LeFort I, maxillary osteotomy. An osteotomy is a kind of surgery where bones are cut and re-shaped.

The immersive VR system employs the OCULUS RIFT and an attached LEAP MOTION for gesture recognition (see Fig. 13.29). The system has two components: First 360° videos from actual surgeries are provided. Thus the resident can watch these videos, showing bone cuts and mobilization immersively in VR (Pulijala et al., 2018). Moreover, surface models from patient data are available and can be manipulated in VR with instruments that resemble the surgical instruments.

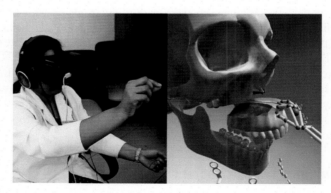

FIGURE 13.29

A trainee employs the OCULUS RIFT with an attached LEAP MOTION to train a maxillofacial osteotomy in VR (From: (Pulijala et al., 2018), Reprinted from Journal of Oral and Maxillofacial Surgery, Vol. 76, "Effectiveness of Immersive Virtual Reality in Surgical Training—A Randomized Control Trial," Page 273, ©Elsevier 2018).

13.4.8 Surgical team training

We already discussed that surgery is a team effort and a comprehensive training approach prepares residents for successful team work. Collaboration relates to the teamwork among nurses, anesthesiologists, and surgeons in the OR, but also to patient handover, where the current situation with sufficient background information and recommended treatments needs to be clearly communicated. Another collaboration scenario relates to the operating surgeon and their camera assistant. Whereas the previously mentioned collaboration scenarios relate to medical experts from one field, there is also interprofessional collaboration that may benefit from VR training, such as the collaboration between anesthesiologists and surgeons during surgery. Anesthesiologists monitor vital signs, in particular the systolic and diastolic arterial blood pressure, the pulse (beats per minute), the electrocardiogram, and a value that indicates whether sufficient muscle relaxation occurs. These values are shown on an anesthesiology monitor.

Different situations may arise in a surgical procedure, where the anesthesiologist and the surgeon need to communicate. As an example, during minimally invasive surgery, an *undetected bleeding* may occur. If the surgeon does not notice the bleeding, the anesthesiologist should notice it by a strong decrease in arterial blood pressure and an increase in the patients' pulse. Another scenario relates to *insufficient muscle relaxation*. The surgeon may observe that the patient's muscles start to contract, which would increase the risk for harming the patient.

The conventional training of such collaborative settings is based on a lab, where an appropriate monitor, a patient table, and a mannequin are available. This type of training is quite limited in its flexibility, which gave rise to the development of a VR-based system (Chheang et al., 2020). The developed VR environment integrates an anesthesiology simulation software (LEARDAL learning application). Thus an anesthesiology monitor is available that presents the usual values to monitor a narcosis and the anesthesiologist may also administer, e.g., a dose of muscle relaxant (see Fig. 13.30). The working place of the anesthesiologist is integrated in a model of the OR (see Fig. 13.31). The users of the virtual environment can communicate via voice chat. The two scenarios briefly described above, namely *undetected bleeding* and *insufficient muscle relaxation*, were trained with the system.

In the first scenario, the anesthesiologist must inform the surgeon, who has to place a clip to stop the bleeding, whereas in the second scenario the surgeon has to inform the anesthesiologist who has to add more muscle relaxant. The vital signs change accordingly so that the users see whether they solved the problem. Fig. 13.32 shows the interprofessional team, again involving also a camera assistant. The users are here only represented by the VR glasses and the VR controllers that move according to the users head and hand position and orientation. Discussions with the physicians revealed that more comprehensive and more realistic avatars are desirable. However, a full body avatar would occupy more space in the virtual environment, and thus aggravate occlusion problems.

The usefulness of such a system needs to be evaluated with respect to the quality of the collaboration. There are special questionnaires to assess whether users were

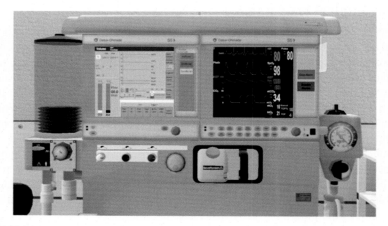

FIGURE 13.30

The LEARDAL learning application for anesthesiology integrated in a team training system. It provides a realistic environment of the anesthesiologists' workplace (From: (Chheang et al., 2020). This paper is licensed under the Creative Commons Attribution-Share Alike 4.0 International license). The user may interactively change every parameter in a real OR.

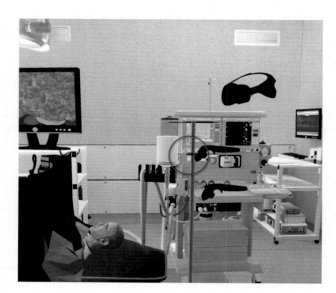

FIGURE 13.31

The OR with integrated anesthesiology monitor provides a realistic environment for inter-professional team training (From: (Chheang et al., 2020). This paper is licensed under the Creative Commons Attribution-Share Alike 4.0 International license).

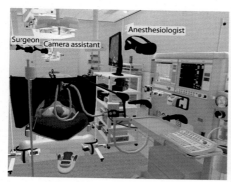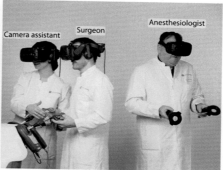

FIGURE 13.32

Two surgeons and an anesthesiologist collaborate in VR to train their interprofessional communication handling intraoperative complications (From: (Chheang et al., 2020). This paper is licensed under the Creative Commons Attribution-Share Alike 4.0 International license).

aware of each other and developed a shared understanding of the problem. Chheang et al. (2020) discuss such an evaluation and mention as limitation that more flexibility with respect to the setup would be desirable.

13.4.9 Integrated surgical training

Ideally, medical training is performed in an integrated manner. One may envision a *teaching hospital* as a metaphor, where different training facilities are arranged in different *rooms* and within each room different *stations* are prepared to perform a specific type of training. Students meet in a lobby—represented by their avatars—and form teams that carry out training in a collaborative manner. This vision and first steps to realize it was recently introduced by Chheang et al. (2022). The teaching hospital is still small; it consists of a lobby and two rooms with training facilities (see Fig. 13.33). In the surgical planning room, students can explore organ models and perform a virtual resection (see Figs. 13.34 and 13.35). In Fig. 13.35, we see photorealistic avatars of the users showing primarily their head. This type of avatar representation was motivated by earlier discussions with physicians (recall Section 13.4.8) who complained about the mere representation of users based on just the VR headsets and VR controllers. Since the avatars only represent the head, no severe occlusion problems arise.

Of course, this concept can be extended strongly in various directions, e.g., to design a more complete surgical training course or to integrate training of team meetings, such as tumor board discussions.

FIGURE 13.33

A small prototype of an integrated training environment with a lobby (1), a surgical planning room (2), and a room where laparoscopic surgery training can be performed (©IEEE 2022, Reprinted with permission from: (Chheang et al., 2022)).

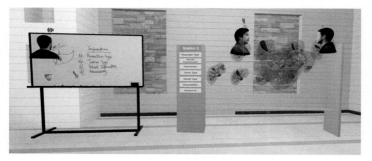

FIGURE 13.34

The surgical planning room has four stations. At station 1, users can explore geometric models of a liver arranged in a shelf. The models can be flexibly sorted according to criteria such as location of tumors and type of intended resection (©IEEE 2022, Reprinted with permission from: (Chheang et al., 2022)).

13.4.10 Discussion

A wide variety of VR-based surgical training systems is meanwhile available, including a considerable number of commercial products (John et al., 2016). Surgical training gained momentum with the widespread use of minimally invasive surgery methods, where the demand for comprehensive training became obvious. Robotic surgery triggered a further increase in surgery training, and it may be expected that further radical changes in operation technology similarly fuel the need for appropriate training methods. Like in any kind of training, feedback is essential in surgery training. Training sessions may be analyzed with respect to

- the time to complete tasks

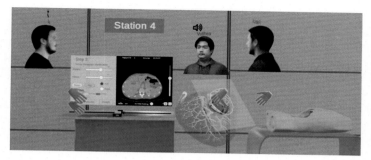

FIGURE 13.35

At station 4, the actual planning is performed where a virtual resection can be carried out (©IEEE 2022, Reprinted with permission from: (Chheang et al., 2022)).

- the efficiency and smoothness of movements
- blood loss
- the occurrence of errors or dangerous situations, where an instrument came very close to a vital structure

Recording and monitoring such values over different training sessions may provide a feeling of making actual progress.

Fusion of training and planning

In practice, the separation between *surgical training* and *surgical planning* often gets fuzzy. As Chan et al. (2013) discuss, some surgical training systems were extended to provide the possibility to integrate patient-specific data. With appropriate image analysis techniques (segmentation, registration, surface reconstruction), 3D models may be generated based on patient-specific data, and thus the training may be performed with a model of the patient that is intended to be operated soon. Such a training prepares for the actual surgery of that patient. On the other hand, a surgical planning system that already incorporates all the functions for creating 3D patient models from medical image data may be enhanced with training functionality.

Assessment of surgeons

VR-based training may also be designed such that the performance of residents is analyzed to provide appropriate feedback, stimulate self-reflection, and thus contribute to improved learning. We have not discussed the use of surgical simulators as an objective means for the *assessment* of surgeons, but it was an essential goal since the early days of the development of surgical simulators. Many authors discuss a certification and re-certification process of surgeons based on simulator performance.

Validation

Whether the high fidelity of a VR-based surgical simulator is beneficial compared to the lower fidelity of a web-based or tablet-based system is not always clear. A number of studies found that VR-based training had no significant benefit (John et al., 2016). This issue requires further research and in particular long-term evaluations. In the limited time frame of a user study, surgeons may not be sufficiently familiar with VR headsets or polarized glasses and stereo displays to fully exploit their potential. Study results for one surgical procedure may not easily translate to others where either the spatial relations or the complexity of the surgical procedure differ strongly.

For the sake of brevity, we have not carefully discussed the validation of surgical simulators, which is, of course, essential for using them in clinical practice. Validation includes (McDougall, 2007):

- *content validity*: the assessment whether the content is appropriate for teaching
- *face validity*: an analysis of the realism of the simulator
- *prediction validity*: an assessment whether the performance in the simulator predicts performance in practice
- *construct validity*: an analysis of the correlation between the performance with a simulator and in surgical practice

Content and face validity are assessed by surgical experts, e.g., in interviews or questionnaires. Prediction and construct validity are based on measurements, such as blood loss, occurrence, and severity of complications and efficiency. With a high construct validity, the strong performance of a surgeon experienced in a particular type of surgery leads to a strong performance with the simulator. For a VR-based system, it also needs to be ensured that VR sickness does not frequently occur. Any locomotion in the virtual scene not related to movements in real life bears a risk of inducing VR sickness, because the information perceived by the inner ear is conflicted with the information perceived by the eyes (Sutherland et al., 2019). As a consequence, validation requires a considerable investment in time and budget in such projects.

In addition to measuring the residents' performance, also their self-confidence is essential. Low self-confidence was found to be related to mishaps during surgery. Pulijala et al. (2018) analyzed self-confidence of surgeons before and after using VR-based training. In their study with 91 residents, an improved self-confidence after training was observed. Factual knowledge questions, related to surgical steps and handling of critical situations, were used to assess whether a higher self-confidence is justified and not an instance of overestimation of one's abilities. Liaw et al. (2018) mention that also *attitudes* should be assessed, i.e., the influence of surgical training on attitudes, e.g., related to patient safety measures. They emphasize, however, also that self-reported measures are not perfectly reliable.

13.5 Concluding remarks

We discussed the potential and actual use cases of VR for medical training. VR applications were designed for anatomy education, the training for interventions and minimally-invasive surgical procedures, as well as for training open surgery. Collaborative VR enables medical team training, e.g., the treatment of patients after a polytrauma in the shock room and the collaboration between radiologists and surgeons. Moreover, collaborative solutions are required to enable that an experienced physician can supervise the training of a younger physician or student.

Whereas some VR-based training systems, in particular for surgery training, are commercially available and legally admitted products, many of the described developments are rather recent and not widely applied beyond research settings. Therefore, evaluation plays a crucial role to understand how VR can be effectively used for medical education and training.

Our focus was on summarizing scientific research on virtual reality for medical education based on available books and publications. Meanwhile, there is also a large set of commercial systems to train students, nurses, and physicians in virtual reality. With search terms such as "Virtual reality surgery training" or "Virtual reality nurse training" you easily find vendors of such systems and videos that showcase their use.

Interdisciplinary character

The development of VR-based medical training systems is a strongly interdisciplinary team effort. In addition to different computer science fields, such as computer graphics and human-computer interaction, physics, mathematics, engineering, and illustration capabilities are needed. The simulation of instrument-tissue interaction and the resulting tissue deformations is particularly demanding. A key question in medical training systems is the required degree of realism with respect to the learning and training goals. Careful abstractions and simplifications are required to make system development feasible and to achieve a sufficient performance.

Value of VR-based medical training

The research results so far do not consistently support the hypothesis of the superiority of immersive VR over desktop solutions. Huettl et al. (2021) could demonstrate that the recall of anatomical structures was better with VR compared to using a 3D PDF document. However, a recent study from Hattab et al. (2021) could not demonstrate an advantage of immersive VR with respect to accuracy in target selection, spatial recall, and confidence of users. The study was based on up-to-date technology and employed examples from liver anatomy and surgery, thus it is highly relevant. Further research is clearly needed. As an example, the specific types of anatomical structures may influence the effectiveness of VR. Whereas skeletal structures, such as the spine, have a salient structure, organs, such as the liver and kidney, do not have such reference cues.

Integration with other learning modalities

Though VR may partially replace other, more conventional types of training, it will not be used as a sole training modality. Strategies to integrate VR-based training in a curriculum are essential. Our focus in this chapter was on the use of immersive VR for medical training. There are other use cases of interactive 3D visualizations for medical training, such as desktop-based interactive 3D visualizations and augmented reality solutions, where the display of real-life images and virtual content is combined. A related field is also 3D printing, where anatomical and pathological structures are physically realized, enabling tangible interaction, which is also beneficial to improve an understanding of complex shapes and their spatial relations. 3D printing may be an alternative to virtual reality as a presentation modality for surgical planning (Huettl et al., 2021).

VR-based training and learning theories

We have not discussed learning theories here, because only few publications of medical training systems explicitly link decisions to learning theories, such as constructivism or behaviorism. Liaw et al. (2018) mention (a few) collaborative training systems that are linked to these and other learning theories. Clearly, such a theoretical foundation can be very useful for designing future medical training systems.

Further research

As a thought for future research: Students and residents differ in their abilities and preferences, e.g., in their spatial ability and in their learning style. Current VR-based systems are quite generic and hardly adaptable to such differences. One may imagine that systems even themselves recognize the students' learning style and adapt themselves. Computer games are successful when they are engaging. Game-based strategies may be valuable for VR-based medical training as well. This may also include competition about trainees. There are already first VR-based training systems designed as serious games (Elliman et al., 2016). Whereas gamification plays a role in medical education, it is even more important in medical treatment (Section 14.2).

As a further thought on potential future developments, anatomy education may benefit from detailed 3D visualizations and from verbal descriptions of spatial relations. Thus a careful integration of textual explanations on demand or initiated by the system may guide learners. Also in surgery education, the integration of textual information may be beneficial. This, however, involves many decisions, such as when to place a text, where to place it, and how to connect it to the related parts of the virtual environment.

Recommended reading

The following papers are particularly useful to get an in-depth understanding of VR-based medical training. They are also chosen to make you familiar with different application areas, such as dentistry, neurosurgery, and liver surgery:

A. Alaraj, M.G. Lemole, J.H. Finkle, R. Yudkowsky, A. Wallace, C. Luciano, P.P. Banerjee, S.H. Rizzi, and F.T. Charbel (2011). "Virtual reality training in neurosurgery: review of current status and future applications," *Surgical Neurology International*, 2.

C. Basdogan, M. Sedef, M. Harders, S. Wesarg (2007). "VR-based simulators for training in minimally invasive surgery," *IEEE Comput. Graphics Appl.*, Vol. 27(2): 54–66.

T. Huber, M. Paschold, C. Hansen, T. Wunderling, H. Lang, W. Kneist (2017). "New dimensions in surgical training: immersive virtual reality laparoscopic simulation exhilarates surgical staff," *Surgical Endoscopy*, Vol. 31(11): 4472–4477.

P. Pohlenz, A. Groebe, A. Petersik, N. Von Sternberg, B. Pflesser, A. Pommert, K.H. Hoehne, U. Tiede, I. Springer, and M. Heiland (2010). "Virtual dental surgery as a new educational tool in dental school," *Journal of Cranio-Maxillofacial Surgery*, Vol. 38(8): 560–564.

M. Varras, N. Nikiteas, V.K. Varra, F.N. Varra, E. Georgiou, and C. Loukas (2020). "Role of laparoscopic simulators in the development and assessment of laparoscopic surgical skills in laparoscopic surgery and gynecology," *World Academy of Sciences Journal*, Vol. 2(2): 65–76.

Virtual Reality in treatment and rehabilitation

14

14.1 Introduction

In addition to its role in medical education, virtual reality (VR) has also a great potential in medical treatment. VR was extensively used to treat a wide range of anxieties, to treat patients with post-traumatic stress disorder, and to treat acute and chronic pain. Sutherland et al. (2019) summarize the potential of VR for such disorders as follows: "Because VR simulates reality, it can increase access to psychological therapies wherein patients can repeatedly experience problematic situations and be taught, via evidence-based psychological treatments, how to overcome encountered difficulties."

The rehabilitation of patients who suffered from an ischemic stroke also may benefit from VR-based treatment. This includes *motor rehabilitation*, where patients are trained in activities, such as coordinated movements, and *cognitive rehabilitation*, where patients get training in problem-solving and decision-making, such as planning a holiday or preparing a meal. Furthermore, other cognitive impairments, such as attention deficits or early stages of a dementia, give rise to VR-based training of memory, attention, and visual skills.

VR may also be useful to distract patients from actual medical treatment that may be perceived as uncomfortable and threatening. As an example, cancer patients who have to undergo chemotherapy may benefit from distraction with a convenient VR experience, such as the exploration of an attractive landscape (Chirico et al., 2020). To refer to such clinically useful applications of VR, the term *clinical virtual reality* is established (Rizzo and Koenig, 2017).

The solutions naturally are quite specific for the medical problem that should be tackled. However, there are common strategies, which we will highlight in this chapter. The basic strategy for all treatments related to anxieties is to expose the patients to the fear-inducing situation in a realistic and believable manner (*exposition therapy*). Exposition ranges from situations that only induce a moderate amount of anxiety to those where it is severe. This level of exposure should be gradually increased giving patients the safety that they can get along in situations that are more and more difficult (*graduate exposure therapy*). In a similar way, VR-based rehabilitation also follows a graded approach, where patients are exposed to real-life situations, such as moving in a city district or shopping. VR-based treatment has two major tasks:

- a reliable *assessment* of the state of the patient (pre- and post-treatment)
- an improvement of the patients' abilities

The treatment of pain and facilitating relief from the burden of some medical treatments follows a general principle, namely that patients benefit from being *distracted*. If a patient is deeply immersed in an attractive VR experience, there are less cognitive and mental resources left to perceive pain. The specific design and development of VR-based treatment is based on such general considerations and involves many details. Among others, the VR experience needs to be *adaptable* to fit individual patients, and a therapist must be able to *supervise* and guide the patient.

Finally, *evaluation* is again of utmost importance. VR-based treatments require a series of sessions, and the question arises whether a patient makes progress. Thus an objective measurement of the patients' performance is required, and it should be presented appropriately to the therapist and to the patient.

Most training systems for cognitive and motor rehabilitation aim at improvements in *activities of daily living* (ADL), such as crossing a street, use of public transportation, and shopping. Our focus is on the strategies for the evaluation of such training systems, on the criteria and tasks that are employed, and not on the actual results. One essential term in such evaluations is *ecological validity*, a term that we discussed already with respect to surgical training (recall Section 13.4.10). Again, it relates to the correlation between progress in a VR-based training and progress in the related real-world activities. The great potential of VR-based treatment is an improved *ecological validity* compared to many training methods in conventional neuropsychiatric treatment.

Already Rizzo and Kim (2005) discussed strength, weaknesses, opportunities, and threats related to VR in therapy. Although technical developments changed the picture slightly, e.g., cost-effectiveness is easier to achieve, the major statements are still valid and give an essential orientation. Major strengths of VR-based treatment include

- self-guided exploration and independent practice
- safe testing and training environment
- gaming elements to enhance motivation
- full control over the environment

In contrast, major weaknesses include

- interface challenges, e.g., interaction methods that are hard to understand
- wires as potential obstacles
- side-effects, such as VR sickness

Among the opportunities, Rizzo and Kim mention

- real-time analysis of the patient behavior and intelligence for adapting further treatment
- gaming industry developments

- widespread appeal to the public
- telerehabilitation

As threats they consider primarily:

- ethical challenges
- lawsuit potential
- the perception that the VR-based treatment may eliminate the need for a physician

Organization

We start this chapter with a discussion of gaming elements and their use for VR-based medical treatment (Section 14.2). Then, we present strategies to reduce pain with immersive VR (Section 14.3). We consider both acute pain (where VR serves to distract the patient) and chronic pain, where the distracting effect of VR needs to be combined with goal-directed training of beneficial movement patterns. In Section 14.4, we explain strategies for VR-based exposition therapy to treat anxieties. We discuss rehabilitation and the use of VR in this process in Section 14.5.

14.2 Potential of gamification

Before we go into detail about pain reduction, selected anxieties, rehabilitation tasks, and related VR-based treatment strategies, we briefly discuss the use of game-inspired strategies. There is increasing consensus that positive aspects of gaming (we do not deny that there are also negative aspects) may be employed for applications beyond entertainment. Thus the term *serious games* arose (Deterding et al., 2011). Medical treatment is among these serious applications, and there are important examples indicating that *gamification* may be beneficial for treatment. Essential aspects of gamification are (Nah et al., 2014):

- Use of a *scoring system*, e.g., users get points for their achievements as incentive
- Use of a *level system*, e.g., users can be promoted to a higher level as a further incentive
- *High score lists* enable to compare with other users leading to a potentially fruitful competition
- Users may get *awards* for certain achievements, e.g., for having used a system for a certain number of consecutive days
- A frequently used awarding strategy is to change the appearance of an avatar to a more noble appearance

As an example for gaming in medical treatment, Kato et al. (2008) designed a game for young cancer patients, where they control a nanobot that shoots cancer cells and helps to overcome side-effects of cancer treatment. The game aimed to improve the adherence to cancer treatment based on improved knowledge about the disease (Granic et al., 2014).

VR-based gaming strategies have been successfully applied to promote health education and self-management of chronic diseases as well as rehabilitation and other types of medical treatment (Trost et al., 2015). Successful games are obviously quite successful in attracting users, motivating them, providing fun, and supporting persistence. These aspects are essential for anxiety treatment, pain relief, and rehabilitation as well. Thus any computer support, including VR-based systems, may benefit from game-inspired strategies. Gamers experience failure often more frequently than success, but these failures are typically not perceived as frustrating, but instead further motivate users. "Game designers are wizards of engagement. They have mastered the art of pulling people of all ages into virtual environments, having them work towards meaningful goals, persevere in the face of multiple failures and celebrate the rare moments of triumph (Granic et al., 2014)." With these attributes, game designers may strongly contribute to VR-based medical treatment based on VR systems.

What exactly is gamification? Molina et al. (2014) consider a system a game if it fulfills several of the following criteria:

- It is highly interactive
- it has entertaining capabilities
- there are rules
- there are opponents
- there are incentives, such as collecting points or coins
- there are rewards

Games are based on immediate feedback and are designed to provide a sweet spot providing appropriate challenges but avoiding frustration. Feedback should be a positive reinforcement; negative feedback in clinical VR is rarely desirable (Stamm et al., 2020). Given the large differences in peoples' abilities, this requires dynamic adjustment of difficulty levels. This is particularly important to maintain long-term engagement, which is so important in anxiety treatment and rehabilitation as well. Further motivational elements may be different levels to which the user can be promoted, and leagues where users compete with each other. These strategies are often used for inspiration also in medical treatment scenarios.

An essential aspect of game design is *player agency*. Player agency means that users have control over their avatars, that they act with them, and these actions have clearly perceivable consequences. Player agency is strongly related to the engagement of participants in a virtual environment.

A special kind of games are combinations of game elements with exercises (so-called *exergames*). Exergames became popular with the Microsoft Kinect, the Nintendo Wii Mote, and the Nintendo Wii Balance Board, around 2010. These devices contain various sensors to track motions of users, such as accelerometers, gyroscopes, pressure, and optical sensors (Van Diest et al., 2013). The Wii Mote, for example, contains an accelerometer and two gyroscopes in the hand-held wireless controllers. Fusing these sensor signals enables a high accuracy in measures of direction, speed, and acceleration (Van Diest et al., 2013). Thus it can be evaluated, e.g., whether a ball was hit with a virtual racket. Instead of a hand-held controller, the MICROSOFT KINECT employs depth cameras and gesture recognition software to compute the position of body parts. More recently, VR headsets, such as the HTC VIVE COSMOS ELITE, provide good tracking of movements for improving the player's experience in exergames. Exergames are essential for motor rehabilitation and for treating patients with chronic pain.

14.3 VR-based pain management

Many persons suffer from severe acute or chronic pain. VR-based systems with their immersion may effectively *distract* patients from their pain, which is beneficial for the patient and the treating physician, e.g., in treatments that involve pain, such as dental treatments. Immersion in VR is important in this context, since the patient thus is isolated from the treating physicians or nurses.

Indovina et al. (2018) describe pain perception and mention various psychological factors that may increase or reduce pain signals, and thus modify whether and how pain is actually perceived. Emotional and cognitive factors play an essential role. Distraction employs these mechanisms and is used to improve the patients' emotional state and focus them on a pleasant activity. This way, the attention paid to pain is effectively reduced. Indovina et al. (2018) also describe various studies that helped to develop an understanding of the effects of VR on pain perception. Initial studies involved healthy volunteers, where pain was artificially induced, e.g., with mechanical or thermal stimuli. According to such studies, the pain intensity was reduced with VR, the threshold when pain was recognized, and thus the pain tolerance were increased. However, the development of clinical VR systems poses additional challenges. Patients, especially if they are disabled by severe pain, require particularly usable systems. Also, aspects of patient safety need to be carefully considered.

High levels of presence (recall Section 12.2) are correlated with better pain reduction. Therefore distraction is particularly successful if high-quality VR headsets are employed, if different sensory channels are incorporated, e.g., sound and haptics are relevant as well, and if the virtual environments provide engaging interaction facilities. In what follow, we discuss selected examples of such systems and discuss their specific design (Trost et al., 2015).

14.3.1 Acute pain

Acute pain may result from accidents, burnings, and injuries. Also medical procedures, such as surgery, interventions, and dental procedures may involve acute and intense pain. The wounds need to be regularly cleaned to avoid infections. As a consequence, bandages need to be removed, which is often perceived as particularly painful. In the treatment of severe burnings, for example, the healing process may take many weeks or even months. Often, pain-reducing drugs (*analgesia*) are given to help patients to cope with intense pain levels. Unfortunately, the effect of these drugs reduces over time, and thus more drugs are necessary to achieve the same effect. Given the side-effects of long-term use of drugs, including the risk of getting addicted to them, alternatives are urgently needed. There are a number of groups that designed, developed, and assessed VR systems for supporting patients with acute pain, focusing on a range of medical procedures. Gold et al. (2006), for example, developed a system for pediatric patients to distract them from painful venipuncture, which is required to administer a contrast agent.

The idea to *distract* patients, especially during wound treatment, is compelling and much older than the rise of VR. Relaxing music or the presentation of a film showing nice landscapes aim at requiring attention, calming patients, and thus limiting fear and pain perception. Studies showed that this may indeed have a positive effect, but they also show that this effect is limited. When a film is presented to distract a patient, nurses often have to frequently remind patients to look at the film instead of at their wound (Gold et al., 2006). When the pain level exceeds a certain level, patients need to focus on it. VR-based solutions enable better coping with more intense pain levels probably because of the stronger immersion. The physician removing the bandage is just not visible. Instead of a deep overview of such systems, we focus on the treatment of one particularly intense pain, namely burning wound-related pain.

Distracting from burn-related pain

The treatment of severely burn-injured patients is a challenging problem in medicine. Often children, adolescents, or younger adults are affected. For the sake of brevity, we cannot explain the whole treatment process here and refer the interested reader to Hoffman et al. (2011). Pioneering work in the VR-based distraction from acute pain was carried out by the pain specialist, Hunter Hoffman, and the VR pioneer David Patterson. Fig. 14.1 illustrates how the patient is distracted during the painful treatment being surrounded and engaged in a VR experience.

They already started in 1996 to develop SNOWWORLD, a VR system for burn patients. The key idea is to present a winter landscape, which is perceived as an opposite to (hot) burning wounds. Patients have the illusion of flying through an icy canyon, which consists of a frigid river and a waterfall and snowflakes (see Fig. 14.2). In this icy virtual environment, patients are first greeted by penguins, and then have the task to throw snowballs at snowmen, igloos, and robots, which seems to shift their attention effectively away from their pain. In the survey article on VR-related pain reduction from Indovina et al. (2018), 14 studies are mentioned that employ SNOWWORLD.

MOBIUSFLOE is the successor of SNOWWORLD and contains more elements from game design (Gromala et al., 2016). Whereas in SNOWWORLD the patient could be passive without any consequences, in the design of MOBIUSFLOE *player agency* is emphasized (recall Section 14.2).

Users have projectiles available to defend themselves and throw them at otters, for example. They receive *health points* that indicate their status. The locomotion (recall Section 12.7) is completely automated, i.e., the user is moved through the environment and does not need to care for navigation. MOBIUSFLOE is also more adaptive:

FIGURE 14.1

A special fiberoptic helmet is used to allow a burn patient to use VR pain distraction during wound care while sitting in a tub of water. (With this helmet, only light, but no electricity reaches the patient). Helmet designed by Hoffman, Magula, and Seibel. (Photo and copyright Hunter Hoffman, www.vrpain.com).

FIGURE 14.2

SNOWWORLD for patients with burning wounds. Users move through an icy canyon and throw snowballs in an immersive VR setup (Reprinted by permission of Oxford University Press from: (Hoffman et al., 2011), page 185).

it considers that the patients may be physically or mentally severely constrained. Relevant physical constraints include the location of the burning, e.g., burnings at a hand or even the head influence the possible VR interaction. Relevant mental constraints involve a sedated state, e.g., as a consequence of drugs. The amount of information that is perceived as pleasant differs, depending on this mental state with a risk of overwhelming the patient instead of distracting them.

14.3.2 Chronic pain

A considerable portion of the population suffers from chronic pain that severely influences the patients' well-being, their emotional state, and their ability to take part in many activities. Thus patients suffering from intense chronic pain are disabled to a certain extent. Among those who have to finish their working life early, chronic pain, especially chronic back pain, is a leading cause. Also chronic shoulder pain and chronic pain affecting the knees or hips are frequent problems. Chronic shoulder pain involves a limited range of motion, i.e., the upper arm movements are severely restricted. A variety of treatment options exist, including physiotherapy, physical therapy, drug treatment, and in severe cases also surgery.

None of these treatments is guaranteed to reduce the pain in a sustainable manner. With chronic pain, patients anticipate movements that are particularly painful and avoid them. In general, they tend to reduce physical activity. This strategy may not be beneficial in the long-term, because certain muscles may degenerate, further limiting the potential of the patient. Moreover, the lack of movement is a significant risk factor for many diseases.

The potential of immersive VR to distract the patient can also be exploited for chronic pain treatment. However, distraction is not sufficient for treating chronic pain. In contrast to acute pain, patients should be supported in active physical engagement instead of passively bearing painful treatment (Trost et al., 2015). VR-based training may support training sessions where patients try to avoid unfavorable movement patterns. In these situations, VR may distract the patient from the focus on pain and help to establish more fortunate movement patterns and encourage more physical activity (Indovina et al., 2018).

In their summary article, Trost et al. (2015) mention (only) ten VR applications for treating patients with chronic pain, four of which involve immersive VR. VR-based treatment is combined with other treatment options, such as cognitive behavior treatment, hypnosis, and physical therapy. Thus the treatment of chronic pain is *multimodal*. A similarity to VR-based treatment of acute pain is that "goal-oriented interaction is associated with greater pain reduction" (Trost et al., 2015).

Treatment of chronic back pain

As an example, we discuss the use of immersive VR for the treatment of chronic back pain. This description is based on Stamm et al. (2020), who provide an in-depth task and user analysis, and on Trost et al. (2015), who describe the conventional treatment of chronic back pain as a starting point to integrate VR-based treatment.

Chronic back pain is often treated with a therapy, called *graduated exposure*. Patients tend to overpredict pain and harm, and thus to avoid certain postures and physical exercises. In the exposure therapy, patients are gradually confronted with activities involved in their fear. Patients should learn to tolerate a certain amount of backpain in valuable activities. Unfortunately, this treatment—if realized in a conventional manner—leads to high dropout rates, i.e., patients do not finish the treatment. The major motivation of VR-based treatment is to increase the compliance of patients. According to Trost et al. (2015), the adaptive behavior of VR-based treatment, the real-time feedback, and the monitoring of the patients' performance are particularly beneficial for treating chronic back pain. Skeletal tracking based on devices, such as the MICROSOFT KINECT, is employed to assess the patients' movements. VR-based training may bring individuals' attention to hidden avoidance strategies.

As an example, for a specific VR environment, we briefly describe the system introduced by Stamm et al. (2020). They provide a game-based system, where the patient stands on a platform in a lake and has to collect coins that appear for a short period of time (see Fig. 14.3). The coins appear at positions that can be reached by the patient. These positions need to be adapted to the current patient, e.g., their size. The system measures the posture of the back and provides feedback such that the nice environment turns gray if the posture is unfortunate. Treatment is limited to 30 minutes, which is also justified by the fact that VR headsets should not be worn longer (without a break) (Stamm et al., 2020). The system is intended to be used in a supervised manner, where a physiotherapist can assist and stop the game, e.g., when movements are not executed properly or patients experience high levels of fear.

FIGURE 14.3

The user is engaged in a VR-based game standing on a platform in a lake and trying to select coins that shortly appear. The necessary movements of the patients are carefully considered to improve posture control (From: (Stamm et al., 2020). This paper is licensed under the Creative Commons Attribution-Share Alike 4.0 International license).

14.3.3 Evaluation

Just as other VR-based treatments, which will be discussed later, the effects of the use of VR need to be carefully assessed. This assessment should be as objective as possible. There are standardized scales for how patients can report their perceived level of pain, such as the FACES pain scale (Wong and Baker, 2001). This scale includes six cartoonish faces that differ in their expression from happy to very sad, a scale that was developed for children, but is also used for adults. Various refinements of this scale also received wide adoption (Hicks et al., 2001). Such scales allow to compute a pain reduction after a distraction strategy. They also allow to compare the effects due to different distraction strategies, such as video, music, and immersive VR. Wound care often involves a large amount of sessions, e.g., 20 to 40. Therefore it is essential that VR distraction is effective for a larger series of treatments and not only for the very first sessions, where curiosity is at a peak level (Indovina et al., 2018). Some evaluation studies examine this effect, e.g., Hoffman et al. (2001b), who analyzed VR for distracting from burning wound treatment.

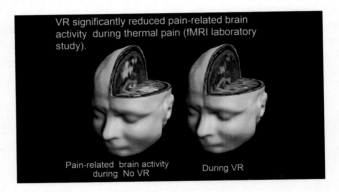

FIGURE 14.4

During fMRI brain scans, people report large reductions in pain during VR. Their brains reflect these large reductions in pain based on measured brain activity when they play SNOWWORLD. Not only does VR reduce patients' pain, it is also reduces the amount of pain processed by the brain (Image by Todd Richards and Aric Bills, UW, copyright Hunter Hoffman, University of Washington, Seattle, www.vrpain.com).

Evaluations address patients, and in the case of children also their parents. Moreover, physicians and nurses involved in the treatment, should be considered as well. Despite the focus on as-objective-as-possible data, also the satisfaction of the stakeholders is essential and should be analyzed, as done, e.g., by Gold et al. (2006). Hoffman et al. (2006) did a deep evaluation. Based on special VR headsets, which can be used inside an MRI scanner, they performed functional MRI measurements before, during, and after using a VR system (see Fig. 14.4). They could show that patients interacting with their SNOWWORLD exhibit significantly less activities in certain brain regions known to be responsible for the processing of pain perception.

In addition to standardized self-reported data, also physiologic data, such as pulse rate, should be analyzed to assess the state of patients. Evaluations with patients are more challenging to interpret compared to studies with healthy volunteers. As an example, patients usually need some pain-reducing drugs. In these cases, the dosage of drugs is a confounder for assessing the effect of VR distraction (when studying the influence of a variable x on another variable y, a confounder is a variable, which also has a relevant influence on y). In the case of intense pain, it is hardly possible to avoid the use of drugs.

Patients with chronic pain are often in a worse state compared to those with acute pain. They are often older and may be strongly disabled. Evaluations of VR-based treatment need to consider this and should ensure that participants are eligible for this kind of training. Patients with strong cognitive limits or severe balance problems cannot participate in an exercise-oriented training (Stamm et al., 2020).

Evaluations may also consider side effects of VR treatment and cost justification. The use of VR requires an appropriate setup; the devices need to be cleaned, the patients need to be trained, leading to an additional investment. On the other hand, VR distraction for medical treatments may calm patients and improve their collaboration. This is particularly relevant if children are involved. VR distraction may also reduce the time of treatment (Indovina et al., 2018).

14.4 VR exposure therapy for treatment of anxieties

Various psychological dysfunctions may severely restrict the life of patients, including post-traumatic stress disorder, eating disorders, addiction to drugs or alcohol, and anxieties. Due to a high prevalence, anxieties are a relevant problem in the general population. A medically relevant anxiety goes far beyond the normal anxiety that is necessary to make us careful and reduce risks for serious accidents. Medically relevant anxieties reduce people's abilities to perform certain activities, they may be overwhelming, and thus lead patients to avoid situations completely that would trigger their strong anxiety. There are general anxiety disorders and many specific anxiety disorders, such as fear of heights (acrophobia), fear of confined spaces (claustrophobia), fear of spiders, fear of flying, and fear of speaking publicly.

Exposure therapy

The conventional exposure therapy (ET) is either based on *imagination* or based on an actual confrontation with the fear-inducing stimuli. Imaginal ET means that patients are asked to imagine situations where they exhibit fear. This variant of ET is challenging for the therapist who needs considerable experience, and for the patient who needs to have very good imagination capabilities. The alternative, the *in vivo exposure therapy*, is usually more effective. However, it is limited to experiences that can be easily trained, e.g., fear of flying can hardly be treated this way.

VR exposure therapy

The situations that the patient experiences or should imagine in an exposure therapy get more and more severe, i.e., the exposure is gradually increasing. VR exposure therapy (VRET) is based on the same strategy with the strong advantage that the environment can be fully controlled such that the therapist exactly knows which stimuli the patient experiences. Moreover, the therapist can observe how the patient reacts in realistic situations. This is useful for an assessment of the patients' state. Conventional ET and VRET aim at creating new neutral memory structures that "overrule" old anxiety-provoking ones (Krijn et al., 2004b).

VR-based treatment benefits from a precise control over a wide variety of stimuli. For anxiety treatment, this is particularly helpful. As an example, a treatment of fear of flying benefits from precise control over flight and weather conditions. As a general strategy for VR-based anxiety treatment, but also for the later discussed rehabilitation systems, it is necessary to consider their influence on the relation between therapists and patients. "In any intervention that activates cognitive, behavioral and emotional processes for a clinical purpose, clinician review is an essential component" (Rizzo and Koenig, 2017). Consequently, such systems should have a "pause" button for review of the session with the therapist, as well as facilities to store and replay the session. For anxiety treatment, it is helpful if the therapist can intervene with coaching and coping strategies when the patient shows a strong reaction to a fear-inducing situation in VR (Rizzo and Koenig, 2017). We discussed similar thoughts for VR-based pain treatment (recall Section 14.3.2).

We consider two examples of anxiety treatment: treatment of the fear of heights and the fear of speaking publicly. All VR-based treatments of anxiety benefit from rather high levels of presence (recall Section 12.2). Further requirements are that the virtual environments trigger emotional responses, and that the experience in VR treatment can be generalized to the corresponding real-world situations (Krijn et al., 2004b). During system use, patients are often asked to rate their *subjective unit of discomfort* (SUD), often at a scale from 1 to 10. When they got used to a situation, indicated by a low SUD, they may enter a new stage of therapy, e.g., a flight with turbulences or a rough landing in the case of fear of flying. This *gradual* exposure may be realized in a game-inspired manner, i.e., the patient reaches a new level after succeeding at a lower level. Successful treatment requires time: in the review by Krijn et al. (2004b), most reported systems were used in five to ten sessions lasting about 40 to 120 minutes each.

14.4.1 Acrophobia

Acrophobia, the fear of height, is an anxiety that affects about 5% of the population at least to some extent (Krijn et al., 2004b). VRET of acrophobia is realized by a large variety of systems. Krijn et al. (2004b) considered it already the anxiety for which most systems have been developed for and many more followed in the meantime. The first controlled study was performed by Rothbaum et al. (1995) and involved twelve students exposed to VRET and a control group. Their virtual world consists of footbridges, outdoor balconies, and a glass elevator. Later systems employed similar elements to induce different degrees of fear of height. Wagner et al. (2020) present a system where primarily various bridges are employed (see Fig. 14.5). Bridges differ by

- the availability of railings and the narrowness of the bridge
- the perceived stability, for example by using a rope bridge
- their length
- their appearance, i.e., translucent bridges are challenging

On the journey that the participants are asked to follow, each bridge increases the perceived threat of falling down, and thus the exposure to height. Wagner et al. (2020) provide a careful discussion of *customization options*, i.e., how the therapist can adapt the training to the individual patient. Customization relates, e.g., to the height of bridges, towers, and railings. Moreover, gaming elements are included, i.e., patients collect treasures on the way and are deliberately motivated to continue.

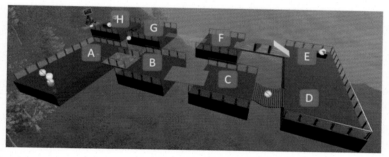

FIGURE 14.5

VR-based training for acrophobia with different types of bridges. The letters indicate positions where participants are asked to report their anxiety level (From: (Wagner et al., 2020), ©2020 The Author(s) Eurographics Proceedings ©The Eurographics Association).

The visualization of fear-inducing elements and the movement along them is the core of VRET for acrophobia, but should be added by multimodal feedback. A typical sound of wind in an outdoor scene may increase the perceived realism and add to the challenge of heights when the sound is more intense. Also holding a railing benefits from providing tactile feedback.

14.4.2 Fear of speaking publicly

The fear of speaking publicly is often considered the most frequent anxiety. According to Krijn et al. (2004b), about 70% of the population is affected at least to some extent by this fear. Affected persons are afraid that their speech is not well-received leading to laughter or a bored audience. Usually, the fear gets strongly reduced with increasing practice, but for a relevant portion of the population it remains a problem, often leading these persons to avoid such situations, potentially reducing possible professional success.

Like the treatment of acrophobia and basically all other graduated exposure therapies, training is based on easy, more difficult, and challenging tasks. Giving a short talk about a familiar topic in front of a small audience that appears to receive your talk well is a relatively easy task. Consequently, the difficulty increases with

- the length of the talk
- the size of the audience
- primarily the behavior of the audience.

If the majority of the audience is obviously distracted, it is challenging for the speaker to remain good-humored and focused.

A further component of such a training is to answer questions from the audience. Therefore a sufficiently realistic appearance and behavior of the audience needs to be realized. Typically, the virtual humans used to train fear of speaking are cartoonish and easy to recognize as non-realistic. Nevertheless, they trigger emotional reactions very similar to those that could be expected in a realistic situation. Different layouts of rooms and different lighting conditions add to a flexible training.

A popular VRET for fear of speaking publicly was designed by Pertaub et al. (2002). They demonstrate that an audience consisting of eight virtual humans can induce fear. Neutral, positive, and negative audiences were provided.

Due to the large market, there are a number of commercially available solutions for reducing fear of speaking publicly, such as

- VIRTUAL ORATOR (https://virtualorator.com/)
- VIRTUAL SPEECH (https://virtualspeech.com)

The VIRTUAL ORATOR, for example, provides a large set of speaking tasks and contexts intended to be used with the OCULUS RIFT or HTC VIVE (see Fig. 14.6). Though most VRET treatments are guided and supervised by a therapist, VR-based training for speaking publicly may also be used as a self-help tool. (See Table 14.1.)

FIGURE 14.6

VR-based training with the VIRTUAL ORATOR to overcome fear of speaking publicly. Training includes various settings, smaller and larger audiences, as well as audiences that are positive, neutral, or negative (Courtesy of VirtualOrator).

Table 14.1 Major scenarios and tasks for VR-based anxiety treatment.

Phobia	Major aspects	Complications
Fear of flying	Take offs, flying, landing	Turbulences, rough landings
Fear of heights	Bridges, elevators, towers	Hanging bridges, sparse staircases
Fear of speaking publicly	Seminar or lecture room, audience	Parts of the audience do not listen, play with smartphones, or even make noise

14.4.3 Evaluation

Since VR-based training is only successful if it triggers emotional responses similar to the corresponding real-world situation, measuring immersion and presence is an integral part of the evaluation of these systems. Evaluations of VRET serve to answer the following questions:

- What is the influence of VRET on the specific anxiety that is treated?
- What is the influence of VRET on the general anxiety level of the patient?
- How does VRET compare to other treatment options in terms of the achieved effect and the necessary effort?
- How sustainable is the effect of VRET on general and specific anxiety levels?

On a more detailed level, it is also essential to compare different variants of VRET with each other in terms of their efficiency. Only carefully designed virtual worlds are a basis for effective treatment. Therefore it is crucial to understand which specific design decisions are actually beneficial. Unfortunately, the last question is the least commonly studied one. As an exception, Krijn et al. (2004a) compared VRET for acrophobia in a CAVE, a large surround screen variant of immersive VR, and VR provided by VR headsets. Although the CAVE induced higher levels of presence, the overall treatment effect was similar for VR headsets that were not so advanced as they are today.

To study the influence of VR, standardized questionnaires are frequently used, where the patient answers questions and reports symptoms. Self-reported symptoms are not perfectly reliable, but most patients can rather consistently assess whether symptoms are more or less severe, providing a reasonable reproducibility. Thus *pretests* are performed initially and at least one final test (*posttest*) is performed at the end of treatment. The major criterion for the success of a VRET is the difference between the pre- and posttest results: A successful treatment strongly reduces the anxiety level for a large majority of the patients. This may remind you of the evaluation of VR-based training systems, where the *knowledge gain* is assessed similarly as the difference between a post- and pretest (recall Section 13.3.7).

Intermediate tests after every session and tests a few months after the end of the treatment are important to better characterize the impact. General questionnaires for this purpose include the *anxiety sensitivity index (ASI)* and the *rating of fear questionnaire (RFQ)* (Krijn et al., 2004b).

In addition, there are specific questionnaires, e.g., the *attitude towards height questionnaire (ATHQ)*. This attitude is relevant, because fear of something is likely correlated to considering something as particularly risky. Or in other words, when the risk of something is overestimated, fear may easily arise. Also for the fear of speaking publicly, standardized questionnaires, such as the *personal report of confidence as a public speaker (PRCS)*, are available (Krijn et al., 2004b).

14.5 VR for rehabilitation

Brain damage may occur after accidents or as consequence of bleedings in cerebral arteries, e.g., when an aneurysm ruptures. Moreover, patients with neurodegenerative diseases, such as Parkinson, may benefit from cognitive rehabilitation. Most patients with brain damage, however, are survivors of a stroke, where parts of the brain get ischemic as a consequence of missing blood supply. A stroke potentially causes a number of problems related to cognitive and motor function, including attention, memory deficits and paralysis. As an example, a considerable portion of post-stroke patients suffers from unilateral spatial neglect (USN), a condition where patients are not aware of objects and persons in one half of their surrounding. USN may relate to unawareness of visual information or noises from the affected region. Patients may also be unaware of the corresponding half of their own body. Actually, a damage in the left brain region leads to severe problems in detecting objects and sound in the right half of the surrounding and vice versa.

In addition to cognitive deficits, neurologic diseases and traumatic brain injuries may lead to problems, such as reduced balance, gait disorders, and difficulties to reach and grasp objects. These problems are due to impaired motor control and may affect the lower and upper extremities. Motor rehabilitation is a structured process, where exercises are carried out to reduce problems of motor control. Cognitive problems and problems of the motor system may reinforce each other, e.g., balance problems are more severe in case of cognitive problems. On the other hand, physical exercises also lead to improved cognition (Thornton et al., 2005).

Cognitive and motor rehabilitation should start early after brain damage and should be continued for a long time. Compared to anxiety treatment, where about ten sessions may already lead to substantial improvements, rehabilitation typically takes longer, rather several months than several weeks. As a consequence, it is more challenging to keep a high motivation and to *adhere* to treatment. The great potential of VR to motivate participants and to engage them is particularly relevant for rehabilitation. Therefore many VR-based systems involve game-like elements. Since adherence to therapy is so important, most evaluations are carried out on a longer scale, and the influence of VR on motivation, enjoyment, and adherence is systematically evaluated (Rose et al., 2018). Standen and Brown (2005) discriminate three groups of treatment for rehabilitation:

1. improving skills for independent living, i.e., skills related to activities of daily living
2. enhancing cognitive performance
3. improving social skills

According to Schultheis and Rizzo (2001) there are two approaches, namely the *restorative* approach, aiming at restoring memory and attention with repetitive tasks, and the *functional* approach, where activities of daily living (ADL) are directly trained.

In a similar vein, Schultheis and Rizzo (2001) consider two approaches for cognitive rehabilitation: the *functional rehabilitation* corresponds to type 1 treatment and the *restorative rehabilitation* corresponds to type 2 treatment, e.g., specific training of memory functions or attention deficits with repetitive tasks. While all treatment types are important, we focus on type 1 (functional rehabilitation), because the largest part of VR-based treatments was developed for improving skills related to ADLs. Probably, the benefit of VR compared to conventional treatment is also larger for these treatments.

Before we discuss cognitive and motor rehabilitation in more detail, we provide a definition:

Definition 14.1. "**Rehabilitation** is a problem-solving and educational process aimed at reducing the disability and handicap experienced by someone ... within the limitations imposed by the available resources and by the underlying disease" (Wade, 1992).

The goals of treatment can differ widely, depending on the capabilities and ongoing diseases of a patient. As a consequence, rehabilitation needs to be carefully adapted to an individual and their current state.

14.5.1 VR for cognitive rehabilitation

Since brain damage often results in reduced motor, sensory, and cognitive abilities, patients have difficulties to perceive and process information correctly, to solve problems and to plan and execute a plan. Moreover, they may be severely limited in tasks that require *multitasking*, which just exceeds their cognitive capabilities. As a consequence, patients with brain damage may be severely limited in their abilities to participate in many activities and to live independently. Cognitive rehabilitation is based on the observation that the brain—even in elderly patients—is able to adapt and to re-structure. This ability is referred to as *plasticity*. As a consequence of this plasticity, the functional consequences of a brain damage are not necessarily permanent and can be reduced with appropriate rehabilitation (Rose et al., 2005). In the following, we consider VR-based treatment related to the following ADLs:

- preparing a meal
- planning and conducting a shopping tour at a supermarket

- walking in an urban area without getting into risky situations, in particular when crossing streets

Each of these activities requires a spectrum of cognitive abilities, such as information processing, decision-making, problem-solving, spatial orientation, and wayfinding (Rand et al., 2009). For assessing the patients' state and improving it during treatment, sufficiently realistic environments and tasks are essential, similar to the requirements for VR-based training related to anxieties. VR was successfully used to enhance a number of conventional neuropsychiatric tests, e.g., spatial ability tests that benefit from realistic 3D environments as a basis for spatial orientation and navigation tasks (Rose et al., 2005).

Food preparation

Several desktop- and VR-based systems were developed to provide a training for meal preparation. The tasks supported a range of activities: from using a coffee machine to more complex cooking tasks. Pioneering work in this area was carried out by Christiansen et al. (1998). Their virtual world comprises a kitchen, and the preparation of a soup was decomposed in 30 steps that the patients performed in VR. The kitchen model (see Fig. 14.7) was enriched with textual labels, such as "trash can" to support orientation. The training of food preparation benefits from auditory and visual cues, which were provided. Even at that time, the 30 patients were reported to adapt well to the VR headsets, which were less comfortable and less powerful in the 1990s. Christiansen et al. (1998) and others who followed with similar developments emphasize that such systems enable a valid assessment of cognitive abilities, i.e., the food preparation skills are strongly correlated to results from memory and attention tests. Food preparation also benefits from appropriate audio feedback, such as the typical noise of a coffee machine.

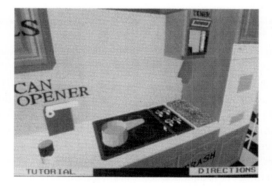

FIGURE 14.7

A simple 3D kitchen model as part of the virtual environment for training meal preparation (From: (Christiansen et al., 1998)).

Virtual shopping

Another essential set of ADL is to go shopping, find a supermarket, get a shopping cart, select a number of articles, and pay for them. This activity can also be trained well in immersive VR (Mondellini et al., 2018). Shopping involves a number of cognitive and motor functions: searching and identifying articles, orientation and navigation in the supermarket, and grasping articles. Shopping can be done efficiently in terms of the money spent and in terms of the length of the visit in a supermarket. These are further criteria to assess the patients' performance and to give patients appropriate feedback. The difficulty of a virtual shopping task also depends on *distracting factors*. For example, if many other persons are in the store, the patient may perceive difficulties to find some items that are currently hidden. Though most virtual shopping applications focus on a supermarket, one could also envision other stores, such as bookstores (Rand et al., 2009).

Similar to food preparation, the ability to go shopping is a good indicator for the state of the patient. Though the system developed by Mondellini et al. (2018) (see Fig. 14.8) aims at patients with mild cognitive impairment, it would also be useful for patients after a stroke. A long-term project on virtual shopping as part of cognitive rehabilitation is described by Rand et al. (2009). They designed, developed, and refined VMALL, a virtual mall with a number of shops, where the user first has to find the appropriate store. Products need to be selected, which involves movements of the upper extremities. VMALL contains other clients and salespersons, i.e., you may ask a salesperson a question related to the location of products but not other clients. An essential aspect is that VMALL considers cognitive and motor elements, i.e., the patients perform actual movements. They follow recommendations to train cognitive and motor aspects simultaneously, which has an advantage for learning and memorizing.

Various problems may occur and are detected and analyzed, e.g., patients take a very long time or spend too much money, or when patients enter a store twice, because they have not selected all desired products in their first visit.

Street crossing

A VR-based training of street crossing is relevant for a quite diverse set of users ranging from healthy children to diseased children and patients after brain damage. We focus again on the latter group.

Compared to food preparation and shopping, street crossing is a rather simple task. In terms of decision-making, the patient needs to carry out only a few decisions, namely, where and when to cross the street. However, these decisions involve to judge the distance and speed of different vehicles. Thus it may be difficult depending on the amount of traffic. When the cars are faster or when two lanes in every direction need to be considered, this increases the difficulty as well. A noisy environment with many people distracts the patient and increases the mental effort. Since safe street crossing is so important for an independent living, there were many efforts to train it in VR, often aiming at post-stroke patients suffering from unilateral spatial neglect (USN). It is important to note that USN patients have a normal field of view; their deficit is

FIGURE 14.8

The shelves of a virtual supermarket and the cash area. The patients use VR controllers to select articles and pay them (©2018 IEEE, Reprinted with permission from: (Mondellini et al., 2018)).

caused by an attention problem (Rose et al., 2005). In the affected part, the objects are not carefully scanned. Therefore training needs to improve this awareness.

Kim et al. (2007a) provided a training system with a moderately complex virtual world, including a crosswalk, where the patient waits while vehicles approach from both sides and at different speeds. The patient tries to detect the vehicles and presses a mouse button when they perceive a vehicle. As expected, the reaction time for USN patients is lower than that of a healthy control group when the vehicle approaches from the contralateral side.

Wagner et al. (2019) designed and realized a VR-based assessment and training, where a variety of distractors are present (see Fig. 14.9). Also typical sounds occurring in a busy city are added to further increase the realism. The humans integrated in the street scene, however, merely decorate the scene and do not exhibit a sophisticated behavior. Nevertheless, they have an important function as distractors.

Again, cars approach from both sides with random gaps and at two different speed levels. Training is intended to be done at different degrees of difficulty, where the speed of the approaching cars is increased and the gap size decreased. When patients press a button at the VR controller because they consider street crossing as safe, an

FIGURE 14.9

A street scene with trees, buildings, and humans designed for assessing street crossing capabilities. When it is considered safe, the (semi-transparent) avatar is crossing the street (Courtesy of Sebastian Wagner, University of Magdeburg).

avatar starts crossing the street at a normal walking speed. Street crossing is considered safe, when the avatar left at least 1.5 seconds before a car arrives.

The actual task of the user is to put a letter in a letter box. The street crossing is embedded in this task. After careful testing with healthy volunteers, the system was refined by adding further distractors, e.g., sounds of wind and dogs, and evaluated with nine neglect patients and nine stroke patients without USN. They could successfully use the system, which employs the HTC VIVE (Wagner et al., 2021). No major VR sickness problems occurred and the patients also accepted this type of training.

A major limitation is that only the cognitive component of street crossing is assessed and trained, i.e., the decision when to cross the street. The actual movement is not carried out by the patient. One may imagine that the incorporation of the movement, considering the actual walking speed of the patient, would improve the experience. A situation where you have to hurry up because you notice that a vehicle approaches faster than you initially expected certainly may have a considerable learning effect. Another limitation relates to the horizontal field of view of the HTC VIVE: for a street crossing task where humans heavily relate on peripheral vision, a field of view of 110° is not ideal, street crossing would benefit from 180° vision. (See Table 14.2.)

14.5.2 Evaluation

VR systems for cognitive rehabilitation are evaluated with respect to their usability, e.g., various questions relate to the efficient use of these systems. Patients with cognitive impairments need to focus on the tasks and have little additional resources available to operate a challenging user interface. Patients should be comfortable and trust the VR systems. Often pilot studies with healthy persons are carried out to identify problems before doing first tests with patients (recall (Wagner et al., 2021)).

Table 14.2 Major activities of daily living and tasks for VR-based cognitive rehabilitation.

ADL	Major aspects	Complications
Prepare a meal	Select necessary food, prepare food (cleaning, cutting), add spices	
Shopping	Select all objects from a given list in a supermarket, Pay selected objects	Consider a budget
Street crossing	Vehicles approaching on one or two lanes, simulation of sound	Many distractors, higher speed, different vehicle categories, e.g., higher cars, motor bikes

Evaluations with patients require a careful preparation: Patients need to be instructed properly, they need to get familiar with the VR system, which may require help, e.g., when patients wearing glasses use VR headsets. Before any performance can be measured, all setup problems need to be overcome.

Assessment of performance, ecological validity, and self-esteem

High levels of usability are a prerequisite for the usefulness of such systems. VR systems for cognitive rehabilitation are assessed with respect to their ecological validity, i.e., healthy persons should yield higher scores than patients. Moreover, patients who should be better when performing the related task in the real world should also be better in the VR system. Thus tests are carried out to check whether the requirements related to the ecological validity are fulfilled.

Ideally, VR-based training not only improves the performance of the patients, but also their self-confidence. As a consequence, evaluations should also comprise questions related to the patients' self-esteem, e.g., whether patients plan to execute the trained activities in the real world with the help of others or even alone.

Selection of participants

An essential aspect of evaluations is the selection of participants. Ideally, there is a sufficiently large number of participants eligible for a statistic evaluation of the results (at least 20). The participants should be representative with respect to age, gender, and health conditions. Publications thus report in detail about the inclusion and exclusion criteria. Often, for a scientific analysis of the results, it is useful to exclude patients with comorbidities, such as depression or mild dementia (Rand et al., 2009). On the other hand, rigid criteria lead to a study that is only valid for a rather small subset of the actual patients. Stroke patients, for example, often exhibit comorbidities. Finally, it is essential to understand which experience the participants had with VR in the past; this experience may influence the performance considerably, and thus may be a bias factor that may "distort" results, i.e., the performance of patients may be overestimated if the test group has considerable VR experience. Currently, it is untypical that patients with cognitive impairments have substantial VR experience.

Number and duration of sessions

Finally, the number and duration of sessions with a VR-based training system needs to be considered. Just as a drug treatment, a VR-based treatment needs to be delivered in the right *dose* to be defined by the therapist, depending on the initial state and progress of the patient. Also VR-based training is a long-term process, like conventional cognitive rehabilitation. As an example, the evaluation of the shopping environment VMALL comprised ten sessions (lasting about 45 minutes each) and was considered as probably not sufficient for a sustainable effect, i.e., to transfer the gained skills to the real world (Rand et al., 2009).

14.5.3 **VR for motor rehabilitation**

Motor rehabilitation is relevant for a large variety of patients, ranging from athletes, who suffer, e.g., from a knee injury, to patients with neurologic diseases, and patients who survived an accident with traumatic brain injury. We focus again on the treatment of neurologic diseases with a user group that is often elderly and partially disabled, such as survivors of an ischemic stroke, where a paralysis of the lower or upper limb needs to be overcome. Moreover, patients suffering from neurodegenerative diseases, such as Parkinson and multiple sclerosis, may be severely affected by *gait disorders*.

Also *lateral stability* is often affected, making weight-bearing tasks, such as carrying laundry in the basement, challenging or impossible. Though such chronic diseases cannot be cured, structured training of motor abilities may help to maintain or slightly improve a certain level. It is essential not only to improve the balance, but also increase the trust of patients in their balance leading them to take part in various activities. VR-based training may improve gait and balance, as well as global motor function. Such improvements have a similar importance for the quality of life, such as improvements due to cognitive rehabilitation.

Tasks and activities for motor rehabilitation

Activities to be trained include reaching and grasping, normal walking, catching a ball, and climbing staircases. A structured review of research prototypes and products indicates the clinical relevance of VR-based motor rehabilitation: Dockx et al. (2016) summarize eight high-quality studies on the use of VR for motor training, discussing their evidence and recommendations for clinical practice in treating Parkinson patients.

Input devices for training motor rehabilitation

In contrast to the previously described use cases of VR, physical activities and movements are here key elements of VR, which has consequences for the selection of hardware components and the design of training environments and tasks. The use of VR for motor rehabilitation includes body tracking. Though early systems based on body suits were quite expensive, commercial developments, such as the NINTENDO WII and MICROSOFT KINECT, around 2010 were beneficial and frequently used. Specialized systems admitted as medical products for motor rehabilitation include CAREN https://www.motekmedical.com/, where arms and trunk positions are tracked with electromagnetic sensors on the fingers to provide feedback on movement precision and speed. The use of gaming elements, in particular exergames (recall Section 14.2), is relevant for motor rehabilitation.

Lower and upper limb training

To classify training systems for motor rehabilitations, it is useful to discriminate systems that are used to train the *upper limbs*, i.e., the arms, elbows, shoulders, and hands and those that are intended for *lower limb training*, i.e., the legs and feet. The majority of such systems was designed for upper limb training (Molina et al., 2014). The systems for lower limb training often involve exergames and a display on a screen; they are referred to as VR-based training systems, but are not fully immersive as the VR systems that we described in other sections of this chapter. Following this classification, we describe VR-based systems for motor rehabilitation.

Upper limb training

An efficient use of the upper limbs is a prerequisite for many ADLs. We already discussed the virtual shopping task as a cognitive task with a focus on the search for and recognition of objects. However, shopping also involves grasping actions, e.g., it requires a certain dexterity. Grasping involves the following stages (Levin et al., 2015):

- reaching an object
- grabbing it
- transporting it

Reaching involves a good estimation of the distance to the target object, whereas grabbing requires an appropriate aperture of the hand and an appropriate pressure.

VR-based treatment for motor rehabilitation is more challenging than for cognitive rehabilitation or anxiety treatment, since the patients' movements need to be tracked and analyzed. Despite these problems, motor rehabilitation was already tackled in the late 1990s, pioneered by Holden et al. (1999). They provide a *virtual teacher* that shows movements the patient should follow as closely as possible to train reach-and-grasp tasks. These movements can be configured by a therapist and be designed such that they match the patients' impairment. The movements are intended to represent different levels of difficulty, i.e., again a *graded* therapy. This learning-by-imitation style was adopted by a number of later VR-based systems.

Rehabilitation again starts with a precise assessment of the patients' state, which can be realized in VR. Patients solve relevant tasks, typically with a data glove (recall Section 12.8.2), and based on the glove's sensors the reaching movement and the grabbing process can be analyzed. There are standardized scales to assess arm function and dexterity. For assessing the arm function, in particular for stroke patients, the *Wolf motor function test* is widely used (Wolf et al., 2001). For assessing dexterity of different clinical populations, the *box and blocks* test is a standard approach (Kontson et al., 2017). In this simple test, it is measured how many small cubes the patient can move from one side of the box to the other within a minute.

Subramanian et al. (2013) present VR-based training using the CAREN system. For reaching, six target positions were chosen based on a fix position of the patient to represent all relevant movement patterns. Joint angles, elbow extension, and shoulder flexion are computed to provide appropriate feedback. A supermarket scene was provided, where patients had to grab articles from the shelf.

Lower limb training

Lower limb training aims at *posture control*, a term defined by Van Diest et al. (2013) as "the ability to maintain, achieve or restore a state of balance during any posture or activity." The ability to walk with a reasonable speed, without risk of falling (also on uneven surfaces), in the case of obstacles and distractors, e.g., in a shopping mall is essential for many ADLs. Healthy humans easily change direction, step sidewards, or move over low obstacles. These abilities are hampered in many post-stroke patients and patients with neurodegenerative diseases. Conventional training includes the use of a treadmill, where an appropriate speed is adjusted and a therapist provides feedback aiming at improving coordination (Mirelman et al., 2010).

VR may contribute to lower limb training with appropriate tasks, increasing motivation and engagement. Again, it is beneficial that VR (or more general: computer support) can be adapted to the current user and their current state in a fine-grained manner. Thus the user may be confronted with navigation tasks that differ in their complexity, e.g., obstacles that need to be avoided.

Evaluation

Essential questions guiding evaluations relate to the health status of the patient before and immediately after treatment. To assess a sustainable effect, an assessment three months after treatment is also recommended (Subramanian et al., 2013). The health status is assessed clinically and kinematically, based on specific measurements related to movement speed, accuracy, and range of motion.

Moreover, actual activities of the patients and the motivation for performing activities are analyzed with standardized scales (Subramanian et al., 2013). The *Berg balance scale* is frequently used to evaluate the effect of exergames on balance and mobility (Van Diest et al., 2013). As an example for evaluating the confidence of patients in their balance, the *activities-specific balance confidence score* (ABC) is widely used in assessing motor rehabilitation. It is a self-report consisting of 16 questions related to perceived risks of falling in different situations (Thornton et al., 2005).

Another essential evaluation criterion is related to falls: Mirelman et al. (2010) asked patients to fill a diary with falls for six months after training. In addition to actual falls, also the fear of falling may be analyzed in a standardized manner. Directly related to everyday activities is the *community balance and mobility scale* (Thornton et al., 2005).

Also, testimonials may add to an evaluation, as shown by Thornton et al. (2005), where patients report about activities they are now able to perform without a cane or without being accompanied. These testimonials also indicate that the mobility goals of patients may widely differ and, of course, the success of an intervention primarily depends on whether patients achieve their individual goals.

VR-based training is considered as an alternative to classical physical exercises. Thus an essential evaluation goal is to compare the effectiveness of both. In a study dedicated to this purpose, Subramanian et al. (2013) compared training in VR and physical training, where the VR-based training was as similar as possible to the physical training. In particular, the duration and intensity of the training were the same (72 trials were performed on 12 days; each session lasted 45 minutes). Major differences were gaming elements for motivation and richer feedback in VR-based treatment. VR-based treatment leads to slightly better results. If other advantages of VR-based treatment, in particular its adaptivity would be exploited, probably the differences would increase.

Mirelman et al. (2010) compared training on a treadmill (alone) with a training combining screen-based 3D navigation and treadmill. The computer system was employed to give the user various navigation tasks, starting with infrequent obstacles always on one side to more frequent obstacles that may occur at both sides. The study indicates that the computer support enhanced the patients' abilities with respect to the risk of falls and other mobility-related criteria.

The use of VR for motor rehabilitation is also assessed with respect to ecological validity, i.e., do patients benefit in real life from movement patterns they learned in VR. For reaching movements, for example, it was shown that there are only slight differences between healthy persons in VR and in the real world. Also for post-stroke patients with semi-paresis, the movements were found to be very similar.

14.6 Concluding remarks

This chapter serves as an introduction to clinical VR and the outcomes resulting from its use. Clinical VR systems are useful for assessing the state of patients and for medical treatment with a focus on treating anxieties, post-traumatic stress disorder, pain management, and rehabilitation. Across all treatments, we saw that VR-based training provides different *levels of difficulty*. The possibility of a fine-grained control of the task difficulty is a major strength of VR-based treatment: the training should be in the narrow range of an appropriate challenge; not too easy to be perceived as boring, but also not too difficult for the patient to cope.

Many studies indicate the importance of rich interaction in VR, regarding interaction as major advantage over screen-based instructions. Avatars, at least virtual hands that follow the users' movements, are essential to provide natural interaction opportunities. We saw a couple of examples where gamification was employed in VR treatment. The goal-directed character and the motivation of games are beneficial for distraction, but also for motivation of patients in the treatment of chronic pain and in motor rehabilitation.

In addition to the direct impact on clinical treatment, the precisely controlled virtual environment enables research in rehabilitation. The development of clinical VR requires not only solid technical skills, but also a deep engagement in the relevant pathological processes, in current treatment strategies, and in the situation of typical patients and therapists. The design of VR-based rehabilitation also requires a deep understanding of learning processes, the crucial role of errors and feedback, and the importance of motivational elements. Moreover, *user experience*-related factors are crucial for the acceptance of clinical VR. As an example, closing a treatment session with a positive experience is beneficial, since users tend to remember the last experience particularly well (Kahneman, 2000).

The identification of essential requirements and constraints to be considered for the use of VR-based treatment is a challenge that requires to carry out an in-depth task analysis with all stakeholders, such as patients, psychotherapists, and physiotherapists (Stamm et al., 2020). As a consequence of this broad range of skills required for developing clinical VR, interdisciplinary teams need to be established.

Clinical VR is also motivated by a shortage of therapists, e.g., for the large and growing number of stroke survivors. Rehabilitation is a long-term process requiring many therapy sessions. However, clinical VR cannot replace therapists. Instead, a careful combination of guidance by a therapist and VR-based training is necessary. Whereas *blended learning* combines computer-based training with other forms of training, *blended therapy* solutions should be developed. This means that the use of VR-based treatment can be interrupted, that the treatment can be recorded, annotated, and replayed to point the patient to special situations.

The use of VR headsets that contribute to high levels of immersion is beneficial for training situations that are perceived as realistic. In addition to a few commercially available systems admitted for clinical use, there are many research prototypes dedicated to special types of treatment. Before such research prototypes can be clinically used on a routine basis, more long-term evaluations are necessary. Many studies compare one VR setting with a desktop system or a classic treatment without any computer support to determine whether VR is superior to other treatment strategies. Such studies are important, but too high-level to derive specific recommendations for VR design.

Telerehabilitation

Though clinical VR in some areas is in an advanced state, the use of VR-based treatment at home still is in its infancy. To extend VR-based rehabilitation such that patients employ them at home would be very useful due to the growing number of patients. However, it requires that often elderly and disabled patients get along with the VR technology at home, which is still a major hurdle (Rizzo and Koenig, 2017).

Outlook

Despite the large body of previous research there is still considerable demand for further research and development. It is necessary to better understand, which specific design decisions regarding avatars, locomotion, appearance of the virtual world, and interactive manipulation are actually beneficial, or in contrast adversial. This type of research would enable to develop guidelines with specific recommendations for the design of VR-based treatment, e.g., recommended locomotion techniques for acrophobia treatment. Guidelines are also required with respect to the use of motivational strategies and game-based elements.

Ethical considerations

In Chapter 12, we discussed some general ethical issues related to VR. Here, we need to add that elderly patients, patients with severe disabilities, such as paralysis, require solutions where patient safety is a key aspect. As an example, falling over the cable of a VR headset would have more severe consequences for an elderly person compared to a student. As a consequence, VR-based training, where the user remains seated may be more appropriate. Moreover, "a range of preparatory exercises to acclimatize older users towards a stress-free VR adoption" is recommended (Coldham and Cook, 2017). A summary of ethical concerns related to the use of clinical VR and recommendations how to reduce the related risks is discussed by Madary and Metzinger (2016).

Recommended reading

The following articles summarize many developments in the use of VR for the treatment of anxiety, pain, and for rehabilitation:

Paola Indovina, Daniela Barone, Luigi Gallo, Andrea Chirico, Giuseppe De Pietro, and Antonio Giordano. "Virtual reality as a distraction intervention to relieve pain and distress during medical procedures," *The Clinical Journal of Pain*, 34(9): 858–877, 2018.

Merel Krijn, Paul M.G. Emmelkamp, Ragnar P. Olafsson, and Roeline Biemond. "Virtual reality exposure therapy of anxiety disorders: A review," *Clinical Psychology Review*, 24(3): 259–281, 2004.

Albert Rizzo and Sebastian Koenig "Is clinical virtual reality ready for primetime?," *Neuropsychology*, Vol. 31(8), 877, 2017.

References

Abellán, Pascual, Tost, Dani, Grau, Sergi, Puig, Anna, 2013. Regions-based illustrative visualization of multimodal datasets. Computerized Medical Imaging and Graphics 37 (4), 263–271.

Agatson, A.S., Janowitz, W.R., Hildner, F., Zusner, N.R., Viamonte, M.J., Detrano, R., 1990. Quantification of coronary artery calcium using ultrafast computed tomography. Journal of the American College of Cardiology 15 (4), 827–832.

Agrawal, Rakesh, Srikant, Ramakrishnan, 1994. Fast algorithms for mining association rules. In: Proc. of Very Large Data Bases, VLDB, vol. 1215, pp. 487–499.

Aguerre, Cedric, Desbarats, Pascal, Dilharreguy, B., Moonen, Chrit T.W., 2003. 3D animation of cerebral activity using both spatial and temporal fMRI information. In: Proc. of 3-D Digital Imaging and Modeling, pp. 103–109.

Ahlberg, Christopher, Shneiderman, Ben, 1994. Visual information seeking using the filmfinder. In: Proc. of ACM Conference Companion on Human Factors in Computing Systems, pp. 433–434.

Ahrens, James, Geveci, Berk, Law, Charles, 2005. ParaView: an end-user tool for large data visualization. In: The Visualization Handbook, pp. 717–731.

Aigner, Wolfgang, Miksch, Silvia, 2006. CareVis: integrated visualization of computerized protocols and temporal patient data. Artificial Intelligence in Medicine 37 (3), 203–218.

Aigner, Wolfgang, Miksch, Silvia, Müller, Wolfgang, Schumann, Heidrun, Tominski, Christian, 2007. Visualizing time-oriented data: a systematic view. Computers & Graphics 31 (3), 401–409.

Aigner, Wolfgang, Miksch, Silvia, Schumann, Heidrun, Tominski, Christian, 2011. Visualization of Time-Oriented Data. Springer Science & Business Media.

Akiba, Hiroshi, Wang, Chaoli, Ma, Kwan-Liu, 2010. AniViz: a template-based animation tool for volume visualization. IEEE CG&A 30 (5), 61–71.

Alakuijala, J., Laitinen, J., Helminen, H., 1997. Beam's light view: visualization of radiotherapy treatment planning fields on anatomic surfaces. In: Proc. of IEEE Engineering in Medicine and Biology Society, vol. 3, pp. 970–973. https://doi.org/10.1109/IEMBS.1997.756505.

Albert, Rachel, Patney, Anjul, Luebke, David, Kim, Joohwan, 2017. Latency requirements for foveated rendering in virtual reality. ACM Transactions on Applied Perception (TAP) 14 (4), 1–13.

Albrecht, Irene, Haber, Jörg, Seidel, Hans-Peter, 2003. Construction and animation of anatomically based human hand models. In: Proc. of ACM SIGGRAPH, pp. 98–109.

Alemzadeh, Shiva, Hielscher, Tommy, Niemann, Uli, et al., 2017a. Subpopulation discovery and validation in epidemiological data. In: Proc. of EuroVis Workshop on Visual Analytics (EuroVA), pp. 43–47.

Alemzadeh, Shiva, Niemann, Uli, Ittermann, Till, et al., 2017b. Visual analytics of missing data in epidemiological cohort studies. In: Proc. of Eurographics Workshop on Visual Computing for Biology and Medicine (VCBM), pp. 43–52.

Alexander, Amy L., Wickens, Christopher D., 2005. Flightpath tracking, change detection and visual scanning in an integrated hazard display. In: Proc. of the Human Factors and Ergonomics Society Ann. Meeting, vol. 49, pp. 68–72.

Ali, M.A., Ahsan, Z., Amin, M., Latif, S., Ayyaz, A., Ayyaz, M.N., 2016. ID-Viewer: a visual analytics architecture for infectious diseases surveillance and response management in Pakistan. Public Health 134 (Supplement C), 72–85.

Allen, James F., 1983. Maintaining knowledge about temporal intervals. Communications of the ACM 26 (11), 832–843.

Allen, James F., Ferguson, George, 1994. Actions and events in interval temporal logic. Journal of Logic and Computation 4 (5), 531–579.

Ames, Shelly L., Wolffsohn, James S., Mcbrien, Neville A., 2005. The development of a symptom questionnaire for assessing virtual reality viewing using a head-mounted display. Optometry and Vision Science 82 (3), 168–176.

Amini, Fereshteh, Riche, Nathalie Henry, Lee, Bongshin, Monroy-Hernandez, Andres, Irani, Pourang, 2016. Authoring data-driven videos with dataclips. IEEE Transactions on Visualization and Computer Graphics 23 (1), 501–510.

Andersson, Magnus, Lantz, Jonas, Ebbers, Tino, Karlsson, Matts, 2015. Quantitative assessment of turbulence and flow eccentricity in an aortic coarctation: impact of virtual interventions. Cardiovascular Engineering and Technology 6 (3), 281–293. https://doi.org/10.1007/s13239-015-0218-x.

Andrienko, Natalia, Andrienko, Gennady, 2006. Exploratory Analysis of Spatial and Temporal Data: a Systematic Approach. Springer Science & Business Media.

Ang, Kathleen D., Samavati, Faramarz F., Sabokrohiyeh, Samin, Garcia, Julio, Elbaz, Mohammed S., 2019. Physicalizing cardiac blood flow data via 3D printing. Computers & Graphics 85, 42–54.

Angelelli, Paolo, Hauser, Helwig, 2011. Straightening tubular flow for side-by-side visualization. IEEE Transactions on Visualization and Computer Graphics 17 (12), 2063–2070.

Angelelli, Paolo, Oeltze, Steffen, Haasz, Judit, et al., 2014. Interactive visual analysis of heterogeneous cohort-study data. IEEE CG&A 34 (5), 70–82.

Ankerst, Mihael, Berchtold, Stefan, Keim, Daniel A., 1998. Similarity clustering of dimensions for an enhanced visualization of multidimensional data. In: Proc. of IEEE Symposium on Information Visualization, pp. 52–60.

Ankerst, Mihael, Breunig, Markus M., Kriegel, Hans-Peter, Sander, Jörg, 1999. OPTICS: ordering points to identify the clustering structure. SIGMOD Record 28 (2), 49–60.

Antiga, Luca, Ene-Iordache, Bogdan, Remuzzi, Andrea, 2003. Computational geometry for patient-specific reconstruction and meshing of blood vessels from MR and CT angiography. IEEE Transactions on Medical Imaging 22 (5), 674–684.

Apilla, Vikram, Behrendt, Benjamin, Lawonn, Kai, Preim, Bernhard, Meuschke, Monique, 2021. Automatic animations to analyze blood flow data. In: Proc. of Eurographics Workshop on Visual Computing for Biology and Medicine (VCBM), pp. 101–105.

Argelaguet, Ferran, Andujar, Carlos, 2013. A survey of 3D object selection techniques for virtual environments. Computers & Graphics 37 (3), 121–136.

Artero, Almir Olivette, 2004. Uncovering clusters in crowded parallel coordinates visualizations. In: Proc. of the IEEE Symposium on Information Visualization. IEEE Computer Society, pp. 81–88.

Aselmaa, Anet, van Herk, Marcel, Laprie, Anne, et al., 2017. Using a contextualized sensemaking model for interaction design: a case study of tumor contouring. Journal of Biomedical Informatics 65, 145–158. https://doi.org/10.1016/j.jbi.2016.12.001.

Aselmaa, Anit, Goossens, R.H., Laprie, Anne, et al., 2013. Workflow analysis report. Technical report. Delft University of Technology.

Assent, Ira, Krieger, Ralph, Müller, Emmanuel, Seidl, Thomas, 2007. VISA: visual subspace clustering analysis. ACM SIGKDD Explorations Newsletter 9 (2), 5–12.

Ayodeji, I.D., Schijven, M., Jakimowicz, J., Greve, J.W., 2007. Face validation of the Simbionix LAP Mentor virtual reality training module and its applicability in the surgical curriculum. Surgical Endoscopy 21 (9), 1641–1649.

Azer, Samy A., Azer, Sarah, 2016. 3D anatomy models and impact on learning: a review of the quality of the literature. Health Professions Education 2 (2), 80–98.

Azkue, Jon-Jatsu, 2013. A digital tool for three-dimensional visualization and annotation in anatomy and embryology learning. European Journal of Anatomy 17 (3), 146–154.

Bade, Ragnar, Schlechtweg, Stefan, Miksch, Silvia, 2004. Connecting time-oriented data and information to a coherent interactive visualization. In: Proc. of ACM SIGCHI Conference on Human Factors in Computing Systems (CHI), pp. 105–112.

Bade, Ragnar, Haase, Jens, Preim, Bernhard, 2006. Comparison of fundamental mesh smoothing algorithms for medical surface models. In: Proc. of Simulation and Visualization, pp. 289–304.

Baer, Alexandra, Gasteiger, Rocco, Cunningham, Douglas, Preim, Bernhard, 2011. Perceptual evaluation of ghosted view techniques for the exploration of vascular structures and embedded flow. Computer Graphics Forum 30 (3), 811–820.

Bair, Alethea, House, Donald, 2007. Grid with a view: optimal texturing for perception of layered surface shape. IEEE Transactions on Visualization and Computer Graphics 13 (6), 1656–1663.

Bamberg, Fabian, Kauczor, Hans-Ulrich, Weckbach, Sabine, et al., 2015. Whole-body MR imaging in the German national cohort: rationale, design, and technical background. Radiology 277 (1), 206–220.

Bannach, Andreas, Bernard, Jürgen, Jung, Florian, Kohlhammer, Jörn, May, Thorsten, Scheckenbach, Kathrin, Wesarg, Stefan, 2017. Visual analytics for radiomics: combining medical imaging with patient data for clinical research. In: Proc. of IEEE Workshop on Visual Analytics in Healthcare (VAHC), pp. 84–91.

Baran, Ilya, Popović, Jovan, 2007. Automatic rigging and animation of 3D characters. ACM Transactions on Graphics 26 (3), 72–es.

Barentsz, Jelle O., Richenberg, Jonathan, Clements, Richard, Choyke, Peter, Verma, Sadhna, Villeirs, Geert, Rouviere, Olivier, Logager, Vibeke, Fütterer, Jurgen J., 2012. ESUR prostate MR guidelines 2012. European Radiology 22 (4), 746–757.

Bartle, Richard A., 2004. Designing Virtual Worlds. New Riders.

Bartram, Lyn, Ware, Colin, Calvert, Tom, 2001. Moving icons: detection and distraction. In: Proc. of INTERACT, vol. 1, pp. 157–165.

Bartz, Dirk, 2005. Virtual endoscopy in research and clinical practice. Computer Graphics Forum 24 (1), 111–126.

Basole, Rahul C., Park, Hyunwoo, Gupta, Mayank, Braunstein, Mark L., Chau, Duen Horng, Thompson, Michael, 2015. A visual analytics approach to understanding care process variation and conformance. In: Proc. of IEEE Workshop on Visual Analytics in Healthcare, pp. 1–8.

Bates, Alister J., Doorly, Denis J., Cetto, Raul, Calmet, Hadrien, Gambaruto, A.M., Tolley, N.S., Houzeaux, Guillaume, Schroter, R.C., 2015. Dynamics of airflow in a short inhalation. Journal of the Royal Society Interface 12 (102), 20140880.

Bauer, Armelle, Paclet, Florent, Cahouet, Violaine, Dicko, Ali Hamadi, Palombi, Olivier, Faure, Francois, Troccaz, Jocelyne, 2014. Interactive visualization of muscle activity during limb movements: towards enhanced anatomy learning. In: Proc. of Eurographics Workshop on Visual Computing for Biology and Medicine (VCBM). Eurographics Association, pp. 191–198.

Baur, Charles, Guzzoni, Didier, Georg, Olivier, 1998. VIRGY: a virtual reality and force feedback-based endoscopic surgery simulator. In: Proc. of Medicine Meets Virtual Reality, pp. 110–116.

Beale, Linda L., Abellan, Jose Juan, Hodgson, Susan S., Jarup, Lars L., 2008. Methodologic issues and approaches to spatial epidemiology. Environmental Health Perspectives 116 (8), 1105–1110.

Beck, Lydia, Wolter, Marc, Mungard, Nan F., Vohn, Rene, Staedtgen, Mario, Kuhlen, Torsten, Sturm, Walter, 2010. Evaluation of spatial processing in virtual reality using functional magnetic resonance imaging (fMRI). Cyberpsychology, Behavior, and Social Networking 13 (2), 211–215.

Becker, Richard A., Cleveland, William S., 1987. Brushing scatterplots. Technometrics 29 (2), 127–142.

Beckhaus, Steffi, Blom, Kristopher J., Haringer, Matthias, 2007. ChairIO–the chair-based interface. In: Concepts and Technologies for Pervasive Games: a Reader for Pervasive Gaming Research, vol. 1, pp. 231–264.

Behr, J., Eschler, P., Jung, Y., Zöllner, M., 2009. X3DOM: a DOM-based HTML5/X3D integration model. In: Proc. of Web 3D Conference, Web3D, pp. 127–135.

Behr, Johannes, Alexa, Marc, 2001. Volume visualization in VRML. In: Proc. of Web 3D Conference, pp. 23–27. https://doi.org/10.1145/363361.363370.

Behrendt, Benjamin, Köhler, Benjamin, Preim, Uta, Preim, Bernhard, 2016. Enhancing visibility of blood flow in volume rendered cardiac 4DPC-MRI data. In: Proc. of Workshop Bildverarbeitung für die Medizin, pp. 188–193.

Behrendt, Benjamin, Berg, Philipp, Preim, Bernhard, Saalfeld, Sylvia, 2017. Combining pseudo chroma depth enhancement and parameter mapping for vascular surface models. In: Proc. of Eurographics Workshop on Visual Computing for Biology and Medicine (VCBM), pp. 159–168.

Behrendt, Benjamin, Berg, Philipp, Beuing, Oliver, Preim, Bernhard, Saalfeld, Sylvia, 2018a. Explorative blood flow visualization using dynamic line filtering based on surface features. Computer Graphics Forum 37 (3), 183–194.

Behrendt, Benjamin, Ebel, Sebastian, Gutberlet, Matthias, Preim, Bernhard, 2018b. A framework for visual comparison of 4D PC-MRI aortic blood flow data. In: Proc. of Eurographics Workshop on Visual Computing for Biology and Medicine (VCBM), pp. 117–121. https://doi.org/10.2312/vcbm.20181236.

Bekos, Michael A., Niedermann, Benjamin, Nöllenburg, Martin, 2019. External labeling techniques: a taxonomy and survey. Computer Graphics Forum 38 (3), 833–860.

Benichou, Fabien, Elber, Gershon, 1999. Output sensitive extraction of silhouettes from polygonal geometry. In: Proc. IEEE Pacific Conference on Computer Graphics and Applications, pp. 60–69. https://doi.org/10.1109/PCCGA.1999.803349.

Bentzen, Søren M., 2008. Dose painting and theragnostic imaging: towards the prescription, planning and delivery of biologically targeted dose distributions in external beam radiation oncology. In: Radiation Oncology Advances. Springer, pp. 40–61.

Bernard, Jürgen, Sessler, David, May, Thorsten, Schlomm, Thorsten, Pehrke, Dirk, Kohlhammer, Jörn, 2015. A visual-interactive system for prostate cancer cohort analysis. IEEE CG&A 35 (3), 44–55.

Bernard, Jürgen, Sessler, David, Kohlhammer, Joern, Ruddle, Roy A., 2018. Using dashboard networks to visualize multiple patient histories: a design study on post-operative prostate cancer. IEEE Transactions on Visualization and Computer Graphics 25 (3), 1615–1628.

Bernardo, Antonio, 2017. Virtual reality and simulation in neurosurgical training. World Neurosurgery 106, 1015–1029.

Berney, Sandra, Bétrancourt, Mireille, Molinari, Gaëlle, Hoyek, Nady, 2015. How spatial abilities and dynamic visualizations interplay when learning functional anatomy with 3D anatomical models. Anatomical Sciences Education 8 (5), 452–462.

Bernhard, Matthias, Waldner, Manuela, Plank, Paskal, Soltészová, Veronika, Viola, Ivan, 2016. The accuracy of gauge-figure tasks in monoscopic and stereo displays. IEEE CG&A 36 (4), 56–66.

Bernold, Georg, Matkovic, Kresimir, Gröller, Eduard, Raidou, Renata, 2019. preha: establishing precision rehabilitation with visual analytics. In: Proc. of Eurographics Workshop on Visual Computing for Biology and Medicine (VCBM), pp. 79–89.

Berthelsen, Anne Kiil, 2007. What's new in target volume definition for radiologists in ICRU Report 71? How can the ICRU volume definitions be integrated in clinical practice? Cancer Imaging 7 (1), 104–116. https://doi.org/10.1102/1470-7330.2007.0013.

Bertin, Jacques, 1966. Sémiologie graphique: Diagrammes, réseaux, cartographie. Mouton.

Beyer, Johanna, Hadwiger, Markus, Wolfsberger, Stefan, Bühler, Katja, 2007. High-quality multimodal volume rendering for preoperative planning of neurosurgical interventions. IEEE Transactions on Visualization and Computer Graphics 13 (6), 1696–1703.

Beyer, Johanna, Hadwiger, Markus, Pfister, Hanspeter, 2015. State-of-the-art in GPU-based large-scale volume visualization. Computer Graphics Forum 34 (8), 13–37.

Bhavnani, Suresh K., Drake, Justin, Divekar, Rohit, 2014. The role of visual analytics in asthma phenotyping and biomarker discovery. In: Heterogeneity in Asthma. Springer, pp. 289–305.

Bichlmeier, Christoph, Heining, Sandro Michael, Feuerstein, Marco, Navab, Nassir, 2009. The virtual mirror: a new interaction paradigm for augmented reality environments. IEEE Transactions on Medical Imaging 28 (9), 1498–1510.

Bieh-Zimmert, Oliver, Koschtial, Claudia, Felden, Carsten, 2013. Representing multidimensional cancer registry data. In: Proc. of Knowledge Management and Knowledge Technologies. ACM, p. 35.

Bier, Eric A., Stone, Maureen C., Pier, Ken, Buxton, William, DeRose, Tony D., 1993. Toolglass and magic lenses: the see-through interface. In: Proc. of ACM SIGGRAPH, pp. 73–80.

Birbara, Nicolette S., Sammut, Claude, Pather, Nalini, 2020. Virtual reality in anatomy: a pilot study evaluating different delivery modalities. Anatomical Sciences Education 13 (4), 445–457.

Birkeland, Åsmund, Viola, Ivan, 2009. View-dependent peel-away visualization for volumetric data. In: Proc. of Spring Conference on Computer Graphics, pp. 121–128.

Birkeland, Åsmund, Bruckner, Stefan, Brambilla, Andrea, Viola, Ivan, 2012. Illustrative membrane clipping. Computer Graphics Forum 31 (3pt1), 905–914.

Birkfellner, Wolfgang (Ed.), 2014. Applied Medical Image Processing. Taylor & Francis Inc.

Birr, Steven, Mönch, Jeanette, Preim, Uta, Preim, Bernhard, 2013. The Web3D LiverAnatomyExplorer. IEEE CG&A 33, 48–58.

Black, David, Hansen, Christian, Nabavi, Arya, Kikinis, Ron, Hahn, Horst, 2017a. A survey of auditory display in image-guided interventions. International Journal of Computer Assisted Radiology and Surgery 12 (10), 1665–1676.

Black, David, Hettig, Julian, Luz, Maria, Hansen, Christian, Kikinis, Ron, Hahn, Horst, 2017b. Auditory feedback to support image-guided medical needle placement. International Journal of Computer Assisted Radiology and Surgery 12 (9), 1655–1663.

Bock, Jelena, 2012. Development and Testing of New Strategies for Pre-Processing and Analysis of 4D Flow-Sensitive MRI Data. Radiologische Klinik-Medizin Physik, Universitätsklinikum Freiburg.

Boejen, Annette, Grau, Cai, 2011. Virtual reality in radiation therapy training. Surgical Oncology 20 (3), 185–188. https://doi.org/10.1016/j.suronc.2010.07.004.

Boletsis, Costas, 2017. The new era of virtual reality locomotion: a systematic literature review of techniques and a proposed typology. Multimodal Technologies and Interaction 1 (4), 24.

Bonaventura, Xavier, Feixas, Miquel, Sbert, Mateu, Chuang, Lewis, Wallraven, Christian, 2018. A survey of viewpoint selection methods for polygonal models. Entropy 20 (5), 370.

Bonekamp, David, Jacobs, Michael A., El-Khouli, Riham, Stoianovici, Dan, Macura, Katarzyna J., 2011. Advancements in MR imaging of the prostate: from diagnosis to interventions. Radiographics 31 (3), 677–703.

Born, Silvia, Markl, Michael, Gutberlet, Matthias, Scheuermann, Gerik, 2013a. Illustrative visualization of cardiac and aortic blood flow from 4D MRI data. In: Proc. of IEEE Pacific Visualization, pp. 129–136.

Born, Silvia, Pfeifle, Matthias, Markl, Michael, Gutberlet, Matthias, Scheuermann, Gerik, 2013b. Visual analysis of cardiac 4D MRI blood flow using line predicates. IEEE Transactions on Visualization and Computer Graphics 19 (6), 900–912.

Boskamp, Tobias, Rinck, Daniel, Link, Florian, Kümmerlen, Bernd, Stamm, Georg, Mildenberger, Peter, 2004. New vessel analysis tool for morphometric quantification and visualization of vessels in CT and MR imaging data sets. Radiographics 24 (1), 287–297.

Botvinick, Matthew, Cohen, Jonathan, 1998. Rubber hands 'feel' touch that eyes see. Nature 391 (6669), 756.

Bourdot, Patrick, Convard, Thomas, Picon, Flavien, Ammi, Mehdi, Touraine, Damien, Vézien, J.-M., 2010. VR–CAD integration: multimodal immersive interaction and advanced haptic paradigms for implicit edition of CAD models. Computer Aided Design 42 (5), 445–461.

Bowman, Doug, Kruijff, Ernst, LaViola Jr., Joseph J., Poupyrev, Ivan P., 2004. 3D User Interfaces: Theory and Practice, CourseSmart eTextbook. Addison-Wesley.

Bowman, Doug A., Hodges, Larry F., 1997. An evaluation of techniques for grabbing and manipulating remote objects in immersive virtual environments. In: Proc. of Symposium on Interactive 3D Graphics, pp. 35–38.

Bowman, Doug A., Hodges, Larry F., 1999. Formalizing the design, evaluation, and application of interaction techniques for immersive virtual environments. Journal of Visual Languages and Computing 10 (1), 37–53.

Bozgeyikli, Evren, Raij, Andrew, Katkoori, Srinivas, Dubey, Rajiv, 2016. Point & teleport locomotion technique for virtual reality. In: Proc. of Computer-Human Interaction in Play, pp. 205–216.

Bramon, Roger, Boada, Imma, Bardera, Anton, Rodriguez, Joaquim, Feixas, Miquel, Puig, Josep, Sbert, Mateu, 2012. Multimodal data fusion based on mutual information. IEEE Transactions on Visualization and Computer Graphics 18 (9), 1574–1587.

Brecheisen, Ralph, Bartroli, Anna Vilanova, Platel, Bram, ter Haar Romeny, Bart M., 2008. Flexible GPU-based multi-volume ray-casting. In: Proc. of VMV, pp. 303–312.

Brehmer, Matthew, Munzner, Tamara, 2013. A multi-level typology of abstract visualization tasks. IEEE Transactions on Visualization and Computer Graphics 19 (12), 2376–2385.

Brenton, H., Hernandez, J., Bello, F., Strutton, P., Purkayastha, S., Firth, T., Darzi, A., 2007. Using multimedia and Web3D to enhance anatomy teaching. Computers and Education 49 (1), 32–53.

Bricken, Meredith, 1991. Virtual reality learning environments: potentials and challenges. ACM SIGGRAPH Computer Graphics 25 (3), 178–184.

Brinkley, James F., Rosse, Cornelius, 1997. The Digital Anatomist distributed framework and its applications to knowledge based medical imaging. Journal of the American Medical Informatics Association 4 (3), 165–183.

Bro-Nielsen, Morten, Cotin, Stephane, 1996. Real-time volumetric deformable models for surgery simulation using finite elements and condensation. Computer Graphics Forum 15 (3), 57–66.

Broos, Arjan J.M., de Hoon, Niels H.L.C., de Koning, Patrick J.H., Geest, Rob J., Vilanova, Anna, Jalba, Andrei C., 2016. A framework for fast initial exploration of PC-MRI cardiac flow. In: Eurographics Workshop on Visual Computing for Biology and Medicine.

Brosz, John, Samavati, Faramarz, Sousa, Mario Costa, 2004. Silhouette rendering based on stability measurement. In: Proc. SCCG. ACM, pp. 157–167. https://doi.org/10.1145/1037210.1037235.

Brown, Judith R., 2000. Enabling educational collaboration-a new shared reality. Computers & Graphics 24 (2), 289–292.

Bruckner, Stefan, Gröller, Eduard, 2005. VolumeShop: an interactive system for direct volume illustration. In: Proc. of IEEE Visualization, pp. 671–678. https://doi.org/10.1109/VISUAL.2005.1532856.

Bruckner, Stefan, Gröller, Eduard, Mueller, Klaus, Preim, Bernhard, Silver, Deborah, 2010. Illustrative focus+context approaches in interactive volume visualization. In: Scientific Visualization: Advanced Concepts, pp. 136–162.

Bryan, Chris, Wu, Xue, Mniszewski, Susan, Ma, Kwan-Liu, 2015. Integrating predictive analytics into a spatiotemporal epidemic simulation. In: Proc. of IEEE Visual Analytics Science and Technology, pp. 17–24.

Bryant, P.J., 1994. A brief history and review of accelerators. CERN European Organization for Nuclear Research - Reports CERN, pp. 1–16.

Buchholz, Henrik, Bohnet, Johannes, Dollner, Jurgen, 2005. Smart and physically-based navigation in 3D geovirtual environments. In: Proc. of IEEE Conference on Information Visualisation, pp. 629–635.

Buck, Andreas K., Nekolla, Stephan, Ziegler, Sibylle, Beer, Ambros, Krause, Bernd J., Herrmann, Ken, et al., 2008. SPECT/CT. Journal of Nuclear Medicine 49 (8), 1305–1319.

Bui, M.D., 1997. New concepts in nasal evaluation. Advances in Oto-Rhino-Laryngology 51, 77–80.

Bullitt, Elizabeth, Aylward, Stephen R., Bernard Jr., Estrada J., Gerig, Guido, 2001. Computer-assisted visualization of arteriovenous malformations on the home personal computer. Neurosurgery 48 (3), 576–582.

Buonocore, Michael H., 1998. Visualizing blood flow patterns using streamlines, arrows, and particle paths. Magnetic Resonance in Medicine 40 (2), 210–226.

Burmester, E., Leineweber, T., Hacker, S., Tiede, U., Hütteroth, T.H., Höhne, K.H., 2004. EUS Meets Voxel-Man: three-dimensional anatomic animation of linear-array endoscopic ultrasound images. Endoscopy 36 (8), 726–730.

Burns, Michael, Klawe, Janek, Rusinkiewicz, Szymon, Finkelstein, Adam, DeCarlo, Doug, 2005. Line drawings from volume data. ACM Transactions on Graphics 24 (3), 512–518. https://doi.org/10.1145/1073204.1073222.

Burns, Michael, Haidacher, Martin, Wein, Wolfgang, Viola, Ivan, Gröller, Eduard, 2007. Feature emphasis and contextual cutaways for multimodal medical visualization. In: Proc. of EuroVis, pp. 275–282.

Byrne, Greg, Cebral, Juan R., 2013. Vortex dynamics in cerebral aneurysms. arXiv e-prints. arXiv:1309.7875.

Byrne, Greg, Mut, Fernando, Cebral, Juan R., 2014. Quantifying the large-scale hemodynamics of intracranial aneurysms. American Journal of Neuroradiology 35 (2), 333–338. https://doi.org/10.3174/ajnr.A3678.

Caballero, Humberto S. Garcia, Corvó, Alberto, van Meulen, Fokke, Fonseca, Pedro, Overeem, Sebastiaan, van Wijk, Jarke J., Westenberg, Michel A., 2021. PerSleep: a visual analytics approach for performance assessment of sleep staging models. In: Proc. of Eurographics Workshop on Visual Computing for Biology and Medicine (VCBM), pp. 123–133.

Cabral, Brian, Leedom, Leith Casey, 1993. Imaging vector fields using line integral convolution. In: Proc. of ACM SIGGRAPH, pp. 263–270. https://doi.org/10.1145/166117.166151.

Cai, Wenli, Sakas, Georgios, 1999. Data intermixing and multi-volume rendering. Computer Graphics Forum 18 (3), 359–368.

Cai, Wenli, Walter, Stefan, Karangelis, Grigorios, Sakas, Georgios, 2000. Collaborative virtual simulation environment for radiotherapy treatment planning. Computer Graphics Forum 19 (3), 379–390. https://doi.org/10.1111/1467-8659.00430.

Çakmak, Hüseyin K., Kühnapfel, Uwe, 2000. Animation and simulation techniques for VR-training systems in endoscopic surgery. In: Proc. of Computer Animation and Simulation, pp. 173–185.

Cardona, Luis, Saito, Suguru, 2015. Hybrid-space localized stylization method for view-dependent lines extracted from 3D models. In: Proc. NPAR. Eurographics Association, pp. 79–89. https://doi.org/10.2312/exp.20151181.

Carnecky, Robert, Fuchs, Raphael, Mehl, Stephanie, Jang, Yun, Peikert, Ronald, 2012. Smart transparency for illustrative visualization of complex flow surfaces. IEEE Transactions on Visualization and Computer Graphics 19 (5), 838–851.

Carroll, Lauren N., Au, Alan P., Detwiler, Landon Todd, Fu, Tsung Chieh, Painterd, Ian S., Abernethy, Neil F., 2014. Visualization and analytics tools for infectious disease epidemiology: a systematic review. Journal of Biomedical Informatics 51 (Supplement C), 287–298.

Casares-Magaz, Oscar, Raidou, Renata G., Rorvik, Jarle, Vilanova, Anna, Muren, Ludvig P., 2018. Uncertainty evaluation of image-based tumour control probability models in radiotherapy of prostate cancer using a visual analytic tool. Physics and Imaging in Radiation Oncology 5.

Castronovo, Denise A., Chui, Kenneth K.H., Naumova, Elena N., 2009. Dynamic maps: a visual-analytic methodology for exploring spatio-temporal disease patterns. Environmental Health 8 (1), 61–69.

Catalano, Onofrio A., Rosen, Bruce R., Sahani, Dushyant V., Hahn, Peter F., Guimaraes, Alexander R., Vangel, Mark G., Nicolai, Emanuele, Soricelli, Andrea, Salvatore, Marco, 2013. Clinical impact of PET/MR imaging in patients with cancer undergoing same-day PET/CT: initial experience in 134 patients - a hypothesis-generating exploratory study. Radiology 269 (3), 857–869.

Catmull, Edwin, 1972. A system for computer generated movies. In: Proc. of the ACM Annual Conference, pp. 422–431.

Cebral, Juan R., Mut, Fernando, Weir, Jane, Putman, Christopher, 2011a. Quantitative characterization of the hemodynamic environment in ruptured and unruptured brain aneurysms. American Journal of Neuroradiology 32 (1), 145–151.

Cebral, Juan R., Mut, Fernando, Weir, Jane, Putman, Christopher M., 2011b. Association of hemodynamic characteristics and cerebral aneurysm rupture. American Journal of Neuroradiology 32 (2), 264–270.

Cebral, Juan R., Vazquez, Mariano, Sforza, Daniel M., Houzeaux, Guillaume, et al., 2015. Analysis of hemodynamics and wall mechanics at sites of cerebral aneurysm rupture. Journal of Neurointerventional Surgery 7 (7), 530–536.

Cebral, Juan R., Chung, BongJae, Mut, Fernando, van Nijnatten, Fred, Ruijters, Danny, 2016. Comparison of cerebral aneurysm flow fields obtained from CFD and DSA. In: Summer Biomechanics, Bioengineering and Biotransport Conference.

Ceneda, Davide, Gschwandtner, Theresia, May, Thorsten, Miksch, Silvia, Schulz, Hans-Jörg, Streit, Marc, Tominski, Christian, 2017. Characterizing guidance in visual analytics. IEEE Transactions on Visualization and Computer Graphics 23 (1), 111–120.

Chan, Sonny, Conti, François, Salisbury, Kenneth, Blevins, Nikolas H., 2013. Virtual reality simulation in neurosurgery: technologies and evolution. Neurosurgery 72 (suppl_1), A154–A164.

Chao, Edmund Y.S., Lynch, J.D., Vanderploeg, M.J., 1993. Simulation and animation of musculoskeletal joint system. Journal of Biomechanical Engineering 115 (4B), 562–568.

Chavan, Satishkumar S., Talbar, Sanjay N., 2014. Multimodality image fusion in frequency domain for radiation therapy. In: International Conference on Medical Imaging, m-Health and Emerging Communication Systems, pp. 174–178. https://doi.org/10.1109/MedCom.2014.7005998.

Chazard, Emmanuel, Ficheur, Grégoire, Bernonville, Stéphanie, Luyckx, Michel, Beuscart, Régis, 2011. Data mining to generate adverse drug events detection rules. IEEE Transactions on Information Technology in Biomedicine 15 (6), 823–830.

Chen, Dongliang, Zhang, Yue, Liu, Huimin, Xu, Pin, 2015. Real-time artistic silhouettes rendering for 3D models. In: Proc. Computational Intelligence and Design, vol. 1. IEEE Computer Society, pp. 494–498. https://doi.org/10.1109/ISCID.2015.201.

Chen, Jin, Roth, Robert E., Naito, Adam T., Lengerich, Eugene J., MacEachren, Alan M., 2008. Geovisual analytics to enhance spatial scan statistic interpretation: an analysis of us cervical cancer mortality. International Journal of Health Geographics 7 (1), 57.

Chen, Long, Day, Thomas W., Tang, Wen, John, Nigel W., 2017. Recent developments and future challenges in medical mixed reality. In: Proc. of IEEE International Symposium on Mixed and Augmented Reality (ISMAR), pp. 123–135.

Cheng, Lung-Pan, Ofek, Eyal, Holz, Christian, Benko, Hrvoje, Wilson, Andrew D., 2017. Sparse haptic proxy: touch feedback in virtual environments using a general passive prop. In: Proc. of ACM SIGCHI Conference on Human Factors in Computing Systems (CHI), pp. 3718–3728.

Cherni, Heni, Métayer, Natacha, Souliman, Nicolas, 2020. Literature review of locomotion techniques in virtual reality. International Journal of Virtual Reality.

Cheung, M. Rex, Krishnan, Karthik, 2009. Interactive deformation registration of endorectal prostate MRI using ITK thin plate splines. Academic Radiology 16 (3), 351–357. https://doi.org/10.1016/j.acra.2008.09.011.

Chheang, Vuthea, Saalfeld, Patrick, Huber, Tobias, et al., 2019. Collaborative virtual reality for laparoscopic liver surgery training. In: Proc. of IEEE Conference on Artificial Intelligence and Virtual Reality, pp. 1–8. https://doi.org/10.1109/AIVR46125.2019.00011.

Chheang, Vuthea, Fischer, Virve, Buggenhagen, Holger, et al., 2020. Toward interprofessional team training for surgeons and anesthesiologists using virtual reality. International Journal of Computer Assisted Radiology and Surgery 15 (12), 2109–2118.

Chheang, Vuthea, Saalfeld, Patrick, Joeres, Fabian, et al., 2021. A collaborative virtual reality environment for liver surgery planning. Computers & Graphics 99, 234–246.

Chheang, Vuthea, Schott, Danny, Saalfeld, Patrick, et al., 2022. Towards virtual teaching hospitals for advanced surgical training. In: Proc. of IEEE Virtual Reality and 3D User Interfaces Abstracts and Workshops, pp. 410–414.

Chirico, Andrea, Maiorano, Patrizia, Indovina, Paola, et al., 2020. Virtual reality and music therapy as distraction interventions to alleviate anxiety and improve mood states in breast cancer patients during chemotherapy. Journal of Cellular Physiology 235 (6), 5353–5362.

Chittaro, Luca, Ranon, Roberto, 2007. Web3D technologies in learning, education and training: motivations, issues, opportunities. Computers and Education 49 (1), 3–18.

Chiu, Peter, Miller, D. Craig, 2016. Evolution of surgical therapy for Stanford acute type a aortic dissection. Annals of Cardiothoracic Surgery 5 (4), 275.

Chopin, Adrien, Bavelier, Daphne, Levi, Dennis Michael, 2019. The prevalence and diagnosis of 'stereoblindness' in adults less than 60 years of age: a best evidence synthesis. Ophthalmic & Physiological Optics 39 (2), 66–85.

Choyke, Peter L., Dwyer, Andrew J., Knopp, Michael V., 2003. Functional tumor imaging with dynamic contrast-enhanced magnetic resonance imaging. Journal of Magnetic Resonance Imaging 17 (5), 509–520.

Christensen, Nicklas H., Hjermitslev, Oliver G., Stjernholm, Niclas H., et al., 2018. Feasibility of team training in virtual reality for robot-assisted minimally invasive surgery. In: Proc. of the ACM Virtual Reality International Conference-Laval Virtual, pp. 1–4.

Christiansen, Charles, Abreu, Beatriz, Ottenbacher, Kenneth, Huffman, Kenneth, Masel, Brent, Culpepper, Robert, 1998. Task performance in virtual environments used for cognitive rehabilitation after traumatic brain injury. Archives of Physical Medicine and Rehabilitation 79 (8), 888–892.

Chu, Alan, Chan, Wing-Yin, Guo, Jixiang, Pang, Wai-Man, Heng, Pheng-Ann, 2008. Perception-aware depth cueing for illustrative vascular visualization. In: Proc. of International Conference on BioMedical Engineering and Informatics, pp. 341–346.

Chu, James Ch., Gong, Xing, Cai, Yang, et al., 2009. Application of holographic display in radiotherapy treatment planning II: a multi-institutional study. Journal of Applied Clinical Medical Physics 10 (3), 2902.

Chui, Kenneth K.H., Wenger, Julia B., Cohen, Steven A., Naumova, Elena N., 2011. Visual analytics for epidemiologists: understanding the interactions between age, time, and disease with multi-panel graphs. PLoS ONE 6 (2).

Chung, Seung-Kyu, Kim, Sung Kyun, 2008. Digital particle image velocimetry studies of nasal airflow. Respiratory Physiology & Neurobiology 163 (1–3), 111–120. https://doi.org/10.1016/j.resp.2008.07.023.

Cockburn, Andy, Karlson, Amy, Bederson, Benjamin B., 2009. A review of overview+detail, zooming, and focus+context interfaces. ACM Computing Surveys 41 (1), 1–31.

Coldham, George, Cook, David M., 2017. VR usability from elderly cohorts: preparatory challenges in overcoming technology rejection. In: Proc. of National Information Technology Conference (NITC). IEEE, pp. 131–135.

Cole, Forrester, Sanik, Kevin, DeCarlo, Doug, Finkelstein, Adam, Funkhouser, Thomas, Rusinkiewicz, Szymon, Singh, Manish, 2009. How well do line drawings depict shape? ACM Transactions on Graphics 28 (3), 28:1–28:9. https://doi.org/10.1145/1531326.1531334.

Coles, Timothy R., Meglan, Dwight, John, Nigel W., 2010. The role of haptics in medical training simulators: a survey of the state of the art. IEEE Transactions on Haptics 4 (1), 51–66.

Cook, D.A., Dupras, D.M., 2004. A practical guide to developing effective web-based learning. Journal of General Internal Medicine 19 (6), 698–707.

Cooper, Michol A., Ibrahim, Andrew, Lyu, Heather, Makary, Martin A., 2015. Underreporting of robotic surgery complications. Journal for Healthcare Quality 37 (2), 133–138.

Coppin, Peter, Harvey, John, Valen-Sendstad, Kristian, Steinman, Dolores, Steinman, David A., 2014. Illustration-inspired visualization of blood flow dynamics. In: Proc. of Int. Conf. on Info Vis., pp. 333–335.

Corl, Frank M., Garland, Melissa R., Fishmann, Elliot K., 2000. Role of computer technology in medical illustration. American Journal of Roentgenology 175, 1519–1524.

Corvó, Alberto, Westenberg, Michel A., van Driel, Marc A., van Wijk , Jarke J., 2016. PATHONE: from one thousand patients to one cell. In: Eurographics Workshop on Visual Computing for Biology and Medicine. https://doi.org/10.2312/vcbm.20161278.

Corvó, Alberto, van Driel, Marc A., Westenberg, Michel A., 2017. PathoVA: a visual analytics tool for pathology diagnosis and reporting. In: Proc. of IEEE Workshop on Visual Analytics in Healthcare (VAHC), pp. 77–83.

Corvó, Alberto, Caballero, Humberto Simon Garcia, Westenberg, Michel A., 2019a. SurviVIS: visual analytics for interactive survival analysis. In: Proc. of EuroVAA@ EuroVis, pp. 73–77.

Corvó, Alberto, Westenberg, Michel A., Wimberger-Friedl, Reinhold, Fromme, Stephan, Peeters, Michel M.R., van Driel, Marc A., van Wijk, Jarke J., 2019b. Visual analytics in digital pathology: challenges and opportunities. In: Proc. of Eurographics Workshop on Visual Computing for Biology and Medicine (VCBM), pp. 129–143.

Cosentino, Francesco, John, Nigel W., Vaarkamp, Jaap, 2017. RAD-AR: RADiotherapy - augmented reality. In: International Conference on Cyberworlds, pp. 226–228. https://doi.org/10.1109/CW.2017.56.

Cox, Michael A.A., Cox, Trevor F., 2008. Multidimensional scaling. In: Handbook of Data Visualization. Springer, pp. 315–347.

Cruz-Neira, Carolina, 1993. Virtual reality overview. In: Proc. of SIGGRAPH Course Notes, vol. 93.

Cruz-Neira, Carolina, Sandin, Daniel J., DeFanti, Thomas A., 1993. Surround-screen projection-based virtual reality: the design and implementation of the cave. In: Proc. of ACM SIGGRAPH, pp. 135–142.

Cutting, C., Oliker, A., Haring, J., Dayan, J., Smith, D., 2002. Use of three-dimensional computer graphic animation to illustrate cleft lip and palate surgery. Computer Aided Surgery 7 (6), 326–331.

Cypko, Mario A., Wojdziak, Jan, Stoehr, Matthaeus, Kirchner, Bettina, Preim, Bernhard, Dietz, Andreas, Lemke, Heinz U., Oeltze-Jafra, Steffen, 2017. Visual verification of cancer staging for therapy decision support. Computer Graphics Forum 36 (3), 109–120.

Darken, Rudolph P., Cockayne, William R., Carmein, David, 1997. The omni-directional treadmill: a locomotion device for virtual worlds. In: Proc. of ACM Symposium on User Interface Software and Technology, pp. 213–221.

Davies, Michelle, deSilva, C.J., 2000. An animated model of the knee joint. In: Proc. of Advances in Medical Signal and Information Processing, pp. 117–122.

Davies, Peter F., 1995. Flow-mediated endothelial mechanotransduction. Physiological Reviews 75 (3), 519–560.

Dayan, Joseph H., Oliker, Aaron, Sharony, Ram, Baumann, F. Gregory, Galloway, Aubrey, Colvin, Stephen B., Miller, D. Craig, Grossi, Eugene A., 2004. Computer-generated three-dimensional animation of the mitral valve. Journal of Thoracic and Cardiovascular Surgery 127 (3), 763–769.

de Geus, Klaus, Watt, Alan, 1996. Three-dimensional stylization of structures of interest from computed tomography images applied to radiotherapy planning. International Journal of Radiation Oncology, Biology, Physics 35 (1), 151–159.

de Haan, Alyanne M., Van Stralen, Haike E., Smit, Miranda, Keizer, Anouk, Van der Stigchel, Stefan, Dijkerman, H. Chris, 2017. No consistent cooling of the real hand in the rubber hand illusion. Acta Psychologica 179, 68–77.

De Haan, Gerwin, Koutek, Michal, Post, Frits H., 2005. IntenSelect: using dynamic object rating for assisting 3D object selection. In: IPT/EGVE, pp. 201–209.

de Hoon, Niels H.L.C., van Pelt, Roy, Jalba, Andrei, Vilanova, Anna, 2014. 4D MRI flow coupled to physics-based fluid simulation for blood-flow visualization. Computer Graphics Forum 33 (3), 121–130.

DeCarlo, Doug, Finkelstein, Adam, Rusinkiewicz, Szymon, Santella, Anthony, 2003. Suggestive contours for conveying shape. ACM Transactions on Graphics 22 (3), 848–855.

DeChello, Laurie M., Sheehan, T. Joseph, 2007. Spatial analysis of colorectal cancer incidence and proportion of late-stage in Massachusetts residents: 1995–1998. International Journal of Health Geographics 6 (1), 20.

Deisinger, Joachim, Blach, Roland, Wesche, Gerold, Breining, Ralf, Simon, Andreas, 2000. Towards immersive modeling challenges and recommendations: a workshop analyzing the needs of designers. In: Proc. of Virtual Environments, pp. 145–156.

Deng, Yangdong, Ni, Yufei, Li, Zonghui, Mu, Shuai, Zhang, Wenjun, 2017. Toward real-time ray tracing: a survey on hardware acceleration and microarchitecture techniques. ACM Computing Surveys (CSUR) 50 (4), 1–41.

Deterding, Sebastian, Sicart, Miguel, Nacke, Lennart, O'Hara, Kenton, Dixon, Dan, 2011. Gamification. Using game-design elements in non-gaming contexts. In: Proc. of CHI'11 Extended Abstracts on Human Factors in Computing Systems, pp. 2425–2428.

Dev, Parvati, 1999. Tutorial: imaging and visualization in medical education. IEEE CG&A 19 (3), 21–31.

Devalia, J.L., Bayram, H., Rusznak, C., Calderon, M., Sapsford, R.J., Abdelaziz, M.A., Wang, J., Davies, R.J., 1997. Mechanisms of pollution-induced airway disease: in vitro studies in the upper and lower airways. Allergy 52, 45–51.

Díaz, Carlos, Robles, Leopoldo Altamirano, 2004. Fast noncontinuous path phase-unwrapping algorithm based on gradients and mask. In: Iberoamerican Congress on Pattern Recognition. Springer, pp. 116–123.

Diaz, Christian, Trefftz, Helmuth, Quintero, Lucia, Acosta, Diego A., Srivastava, Sakti, 2014. Collaborative networked virtual surgical simulators (CNVSS) implementing hybrid client–server architecture: factors affecting collaborative performance. Presence: Teleoperators & Virtual Environments 23 (4), 393–409.

DiBiase, David, MacEachren, Alan M., Krygier, John B., Reeves, Catherine, 1992. Animation and the role of map design in scientific visualization. Cartography and Geographic Information Systems 19 (4), 201–214.

DiBiase, David, Reeves, Catherine, Krygier, J., MacEachren, A.M., von Weiss, M., Sloan, J., Detweiller, M., 1994. Multivariate display of geographic data: applications in Earth system science. In: Visualization in Modern Cartography, pp. 287–312.

Dick, Christian, Georgii, Joachim, Burgkart, Rainer, Westermann, Rüdiger, 2009. Stress tensor field visualization for implant planning in orthopedics. IEEE Transactions on Visualization and Computer Graphics 15 (6), 1399–1406.

DiLullo, Camille, Coughlin, Patrick, D'Angelo, Marina, McGuinness, Michael, Bandle, Jesse, Slotkin, Eric M., Shainker, Scott A., Wenger, Christopher, Berray, Scott J., 2006. Anatomy in a new curriculum: facilitating the learning of gross anatomy using web access streaming dissection videos. Journal of Visual Communication in Medicine 29 (3), 99–108.

Dinka, David, Nyce, James M., Timpka, Toomas, 2009. Situated cognition in clinical visualization: the role of transparency in GammaKnife neurosurgery planning. Artificial Intelligence in Medicine 46 (2), 111–118. https://doi.org/10.1016/j.artmed.2008.11.003.

do Carmo, Manfredo P., 1976. Differential Geometry of Curves and Surfaces. Prentice-Hall, Englewood Cliffs, NJ.

do Carmo, Manfredo P., 1992. Riemannian Geometry. Birkhäuser, Boston, MA.

Dockx, Kim, Bekkers, Esther M.J., Van den Bergh, Veerle, Ginis, Pieter, Rochester, Lynn, Hausdorff, Jeffrey M., Mirelman, Anat, Nieuwboer, Alice, 2016. Virtual reality for rehabilitation in Parkinson's disease. Cochrane Database of Systematic Reviews 12.

Dodgson, Neil A., 2004. Variation and extrema of human interpupillary distance. In: Proc. of Stereoscopic Displays and Virtual Reality Systems XI, vol. 5291. International Society for Optics and Photonics, pp. 36–46.

Doll, Richard, Hill, A. Bradford, 1956. Lung cancer and other causes of death in relation to smoking. British Medical Journal 2 (5001), 1071–1081.

Donnan, Geoffrey A., Fisher, Marc, Macleod, Malcom, Davis, Stephen M., 2008. Stroke. The Lancet 371 (9624), 1612–1623.

Dooley, Debra, Cohen, Michael F., 1990. Automatic illustration of 3D geometric models: lines. ACM SIGGRAPH Computer Graphics 24 (2), 77–82. https://doi.org/10.1145/91394.91422.

Doorly, D.J., Taylor, D.J., Gambaruto, A.M., Schroter, R.C., Tolley, N., 2008. Nasal architecture: form and flow. Philosophical Transactions of the Royal Society of London, Series A 366, 3225–3246.

Dörner, Ralf, Broll, Wolfgang, Grimm, Paul, Jung, Bernhard, 2019. Virtual und Augmented Reality: Grundlagen und Methoden der Virtuellen und Augmentierten Realität. Springer.

Drake, R.L., 2008. Gray's Atlas of Anatomy. Gray's Anatomy Series. Churchill Livingstone/Elsevier.

Drebin, Robert A., Carpenter, Loren, Hanrahan, Pat, 1988. Volume rendering. ACM SIGGRAPH Computer Graphics 22 (4), 65–74.

Drucker, Steven M., Zeltzer, David, 1994. Intelligent camera control in a virtual environment. In: Proc. of Graphics Interface, pp. 190–199.

Drzymala, R.E., Mohan, R., Brewster, L., Chu, J., Goitein, M., Harms, W., Urie, M., 1991. Dose-volume histograms. International Journal of Radiation Oncology, Biology, Physics 21 (1), 71–78. https://doi.org/10.1016/0360-3016(91)90168-4.

Du, Yi, Ma, Cuixia, Wu, Chao, Xu, Xiaowei, Guo, Yike, Zhou, Yuanchun, Li, Jianhui, 2016. A visual analytics approach for station-based air quality data. Sensors 17 (1), 30.

Dunne, Cody, Muller, Michael, Perra, Nicola, Martino, Mauro, 2015. VoroGraph: visualization tools for epidemic analysis. In: Proc. of ACM Conference Extended Abstracts on Human Factors in Computing Systems, pp. 255–258.

Durlach, Nat, Slater, Mel, 2000. Presence in shared virtual environments and virtual togetherness. Presence: Teleoperators & Virtual Environments 9 (2), 214–217.

Dyverfeldt, Petter, Bissell, Malenka, Barker, Alex J., Bolger, Ann F., Carlhäll, Carl-Johan, Ebbers, Tino, et al., 2015. 4D flow cardiovascular magnetic resonance consensus statement. Journal of Cardiovascular Magnetic Resonance 17 (1), 1.

Ebel, Sebastian, Dufke, Josefin, Köhler, Benjamin, Preim, Bernhard, Behrendt, Benjamin, Riekena, Boris, et al., 2020. Automated quantitative extraction and analysis of 4D flow patterns in the ascending aorta: an intraindividual comparison at 1.5 T and 3 T. Scientific Reports 10 (1), 2949.

Ebel, Sebastian, Kühn, Alexander, Aggarwal, Abhinav, Köhler, Benjamin, Behrendt, Benjamin, Gohmann, Robin, Riekena, Boris, Lücke, Christian, Ziegert, Juliane, Vogtmann, Charlotte, et al., 2022. Quantitative normal values of helical flow, flow jets and wall shear stress of healthy volunteers in the ascending aorta. European Radiology, 1–11.

Ehrhardt, Jan, Werner, Rene, Richberg, Alexander Schmidt, Schulz, Benny, Handels, Heinz, 2008. Generation of a mean motion model of the lung using 4D-CT image data. In: Eurographics Workshop on Visual Computing for Biomedicine, pp. 69–76. https://doi.org/10.2312/VCBM/VCBM08/069-076.

Ekstrand, Chelsea, Jamal, Ali, Nguyen, Ron, Kudryk, Annalise, Mann, Jennifer, Mendez, Ivar, 2018. Immersive and interactive virtual reality to improve learning and retention of neuroanatomy in medical students: a randomized controlled study. CMAJ Open 6 (1), E103.

El Naqa, I., Bradley, J.D., Deasy, J.O., 2008. Nonlinear kernel-based approaches for predicting normal tissue toxicities. In: International Conference on Machine Learning and Applications, pp. 539–544. https://doi.org/10.1109/ICMLA.2008.126.

Elber, Gershon, 1999. Interactive line art rendering of freeform surfaces. Computer Graphics Forum 18 (3), 1–12. https://doi.org/10.1111/1467-8659.00322.

Elber, Gershon, Cohen, Elaine, 2006. Probabilistic silhouette based importance toward line-art non-photorealistic rendering. The Visual Computer 22 (9–11), 793–804. https://doi.org/10.1007/s00371-006-0065-8.

Elliman, James, Loizou, Michael, Loizides, Fernando, 2016. Virtual reality simulation training for student nurse education. In: Proc. of Games and Virtual Worlds for Serious Applications (VS-Games), pp. 1–2.

Elliott, Paul, Wartenberg, Daniel, 2004. Spatial epidemiology: current approaches and future challenges. Environmental Health Perspectives 112 (9), 998.

Ellis, Geoffrey, Dix, Alan, 2006. Enabling automatic clutter reduction in parallel coordinate plots. IEEE Transactions on Visualization and Computer Graphics 12 (5), 717–724.

Elvezio, Carmine, Ling, Frank, Liu, Jen-Shuo, Feiner, Steven, 2018. Collaborative virtual reality for low-latency interaction. In: Proc. of ACM Symposium on User Interface Software and Technology Adjunct Proceedings, pp. 179–181.

Englund, Rickard, Ropinski, Timo, Hotz, Ingrid, 2016. Coherence maps for blood flow exploration. In: Eurographics Workshop on Visual Computing for Biology and Medicine, pp. 79–88.

Estai, Mohamed, Bunt, Stuart, 2016. Best teaching practices in anatomy education: a critical review. Annals of Anatomy-Anatomischer Anzeiger 208, 151–157.

Ester, Martin, Kriegel, Hans-Peter, Sander, Jörg, Xu, Xiaowei, et al., 1996. A density-based algorithm for discovering clusters in large spatial databases with noise. In: Proc. of KDD, vol. 96, pp. 226–231.

Eubank, Stephen, 2002. Scalable, efficient epidemiological simulation. In: Proc. of the ACM Symposium on Applied Computing, pp. 139–145.

Eulzer, Pepe, Meuschke, Monique, Klingner, Carsten, Lawonn, Kai, 2021a. Visualizing carotid blood flow simulations for stroke prevention. Computer Graphics Forum 40 (3), 435–446.

Eulzer, Pepe, Richter, Kevin, Meuschke, Monique, Hundertmark, Anna, Lawonn, Kai, 2021b. Automatic cutting and flattening of carotid artery geometries. In: Proc. of Eurographics Workshop on Visual Computing for Biology and Medicine (VCBM), pp. 79–89.

Eulzer, Pepe, Meuschke, Monique, Mistelbauer, Gabriel, Lawonn, Kai, 2022. Vessel maps: a survey of map-like visualizations of the cardiovascular system. Computer Graphics Forum 41 (3), 645–673.

Evans, Philip M., 2008. Anatomical imaging for radiotherapy. Physics in Medicine and Biology 53 (12), R151–R191. https://doi.org/10.1088/0031-9155/53/12/R01.

Fabrikant, Sara Irina, Goldsberry, Kirk, 2005. Thematic relevance and perceptual salience of dynamic geovisualization displays. In: Proc. ICA/ACI Int. Cartographic Conf., pp. 6–11.

Fairén González, Marta, Farrés, Mariona, Moyes Ardiaca, Jordi, Insa, Esther, 2017. Virtual reality to teach anatomy. In: Proc. of Eurographics: Education Papers, pp. 51–58.

Fairfield, Adam J., Plasencia, Jonathan, Jang, Yun, Theodore, Nicholas, Crawford, Neil R., Frakes, David H., Maciejewski, Ross, 2014. Volume curtaining: a focus+context effect for multimodal volume visualization. In: Proc. of SPIE Medical Imaging, pp. 903527–903527.

Falah, Jannat, Charissis, Vassilis, Khan, Soheeb, Chan, Warren, Alfalah, Salsabeel F.M., Harrison, David K., 2014. Development and evaluation of virtual reality medical training system for anatomy education. In: Proc. of Science and Information Conference. Springer, pp. 369–383.

Faure, François, Duriez, Christian, Delingette, Hervé, Allard, Jérémie, Gilles, Benjamin, Marchesseau, Stéphanie, et al., 2012. SOFA: A multi-model framework for interactive physical simulation. In: Soft Tissue Biomechanical Modeling for Computer Assisted Surgery. Springer, pp. 283–321.

Federico, Paolo, Unger, Jürgen, Amor-Amorós, Albert, Sacchi, Lucia, Klimov, Denis, Miksch, Silvia, 2015. Gnaeus: utilizing clinical guidelines for knowledge-assisted visualisation of EHR cohorts. In: Proc. of EuroVA@ EuroVis, pp. 79–83.

Feliciani, Giacomo, Potters, Wouter V., van Ooij, Pim, Schneiders, Joppe J., Nederveen, Aart J., van Bavel, Ed, Majoie, Charles B., Marquering, Henk A., 2015. Multiscale 3-D + T intracranial aneurysmal flow vortex detection. IEEE Transactions on Biomedical Engineering 62 (5), 1355–1362.

Fellner, Franz A., 2016. Introducing cinematic rendering: a novel technique for post-processing medical imaging data. Journal of Biomedical Science and Engineering 10 (8), 170–175. https://doi.org/10.4236/jbise.2016.93013.

Fellner, Franz A., Engel, Klaus, Kremer, Christoph, 2017. Virtual anatomy: the dissecting theatre of the future—implementation of cinematic rendering in a large 8 K high-resolution projection environment. Journal of Biomedical Science and Engineering 10 (8), 367–375.

Ferlay, Jacques, Colombet, Murielle, Soerjomataram, Isabelle, Parkin, Donald M., Piñeros, Marion, Znaor, Ariana, Bray, Freddie, 2021. Cancer statistics for the year 2020: an overview. International Journal of Cancer 149 (4), 778–789.

Fernandez, Hector, Macho, Juan M., Blasco, Jordi, Roman, Luis San, Mailaender, Werner, Serra, Luis, Larrabide, Ignacio, 2015. Computation of the change in length of a braided device when deployed in realistic vessel models. International Journal of Computer Assisted Radiology and Surgery 10 (10), 1659–1665.

Ferracani, Andrea, Pezzatini, Daniele, Bianchini, Jacopo, Biscini, Gianmarco, Del Bimbo, Alberto, 2016. Locomotion by natural gestures for immersive virtual environments. In: Proc. of Workshop on Multimedia Alternate Realities, pp. 21–24.

Ferre, Maria, Puig, Anna, Tost, Dani, 2004. A framework for fusion methods and rendering techniques of multimodal volume data. Computer Animation and Virtual Worlds 15 (2), 63–77.

Few, Stephen, 2006. Information Dashboard Design. O'Reilly, Sebastopol, CA.

Firth, Joseph, Stubbs, Brendon, Teasdale, Scott B., Ward, Philip B., Veronese, Nicola, Shivappa, Nitin, Hebert, James R., Berk, Michael, Yung, Alison R., Sarris, Jerome, 2018. Diet as a hot topic in psychiatry: a population-scale study of nutritional intake and inflammatory potential in severe mental illness. World Psychiatry 17 (3), 365–367.

Fisher, Peter F., 1993. Visualizing uncertainty in soil maps by animation. Cartographica: The International Journal for Geographic Information and Geovisualization 30 (2–3), 20–27.

Fisk, Gary, 2008. Using animation in forensic pathology and science education. Laboratory Medicine 39 (10), 587–592.

Fletcher, R.H., Fletcher, S.W., 2011. Clinical Epidemiology. Lippincott Williams and Wilkins, Philadelphia.

Floricel, Carla, Nipu, Nafiul, Biggs, Mikayla, Wentzel, Andrew, Canahuate, Guadalupe, Van Dijk, Lisanne, Mohamed, Abdallah, Fuller, C. David, Marai, G. Elisabeta, 2021. THALIS: human-machine analysis of longitudinal symptoms in cancer therapy. IEEE Transactions on Visualization and Computer Graphics 28 (1), 151–161.

Folkman, Judah, 2002. Role of angiogenesis in tumor growth and metastasis. Seminars in Oncology 29 (6), 15–18.

Fonseca, Telma Cristina Ferreira, Campos, Tarcisio Passos Ribeiro, 2016. SOFT-RT: software for IMRT simulations based on MCNPx code. Applied Radiation and Isotopes 117, 111–117. https://doi.org/10.1016/j.apradiso.2015.12.061.

Friman, Ola, Hennemuth, Anja, Harloff, Andreas, Bock, Jelena, Markl, Michael, Peitgen, Heinz-Otto, 2010a. Probabilistic 4D blood flow mapping. In: Medical Image Computing and Computer-Assisted Intervention, pp. 416–423.

Friman, Ola, Hindennach, Milo, Kühnel, Caroline, Peitgen, Heinz-Otto, 2010b. Multiple hypothesis template tracking of small 3D vessel structures. Medical Image Analysis 14 (2), 160–171.

Frydrychowicz, A., Harloff, A., Jung, B., Zaitsev, M., Weigang, E., Bley, T.A., Langer, M., Hennig, J., Markl, M., 2007. Time-resolved, 3-dimensional magnetic resonance flow analysis at 3 T: visualization of normal and pathological aortic vascular hemodynamics. Computer Assisted Tomography 31 (9), 9–15.

Fua, Ying-Huey, Ward, Matthew O., Rundensteiner, Elke A., 1999. Hierarchical parallel coordinates for exploration of large datasets. In: Proc. of IEEE Visualization, pp. 43–50.

Furmanová, Katarína, Großmann, Nicolas, Muren, L.P., Casares-Magaz, Oscar, Moiseenko, V., Einck, John P., Gröller, Eduard, Raidou, R., 2020. VAPOR: visual analytics for the exploration of pelvic organ variability in radiotherapy. In: Special Section on VCBM 2019. Computers & Graphics 91, 25–38. https://doi.org/10.1016/j.cag.2020.07.001.

Furmanová, Katarína, Muren, Ludvig P., Casares-Magaz, Oscar, Moiseenko, Vitali, Einck, John P., Pilskog, Sara, Raidou, Renata G., 2021. PREVIS: predictive visual analytics of anatomical variability for radiotherapy decision support. Computers & Graphics 97, 126–138.

Furnas, George W., 1986. Generalized fisheye views. ACM SIGCHI Bulletin 17 (4), 16–23.

Gaitatzes, Athanasios, Christopoulos, Dimitrios, Roussou, Maria, 2001. Reviving the past: cultural heritage meets virtual reality. In: Proc. of Virtual Reality, Archeology, and Cultural Heritage, pp. 103–110.

Galande, Ashwini, Patil, Rahul, 2013. The art of medical image fusion: a survey. In: Proc. of Advances in Computing, Communications and Informatics (ICACCI), pp. 400–405.

Gambarini, G., Danesi, U., Foroni, R., Mauri, M., Pirola, L., Birattari, C., 2000. Prompt imaging of absorbed dose in tissue-equivalent gel-phantoms and new toolkit for 3D data visualization. In: IEEE Nuclear Science Symposium (NSS/MIC), vol. 3, pp. 19/52–19/55, https://doi.org/10.1109/NSSMIC.2000.949283.

Gambaruto, A.M., João, A.J., 2012. Flow structures in cerebral aneurysms. Computers & Fluids 65, 56–65.

Garcia, G.J.M., Bailie, N., Martins, D.A., Kimbell, J.S., 2007. Atrophic rhinitis: a CFD study of air conditioning in the nasal cavity. Journal of Applied Physiology 103, 1082.

Garcia Caballero, Humberto S., Westenberg, Michel A., Gebre, Binyam, van Wijk, Jarke J., 2019. V-awake: a visual analytics approach for correcting sleep predictions from deep learning models. Computer Graphics Forum 38 (3), 1–12.

Garg, Amit, Norman, Geoffrey R., Spero, Lawrence, Maheshwari, Puroo, 1999. Do virtual computer models hinder anatomy learning? Academic Medicine 74, S87–S89.

Garg, Amit X., Norman, Geoff, Sperotable, Lawrence, 2001. How medical students learn spatial anatomy. The Lancet 357 (9253), 363–364.

Gasteiger, Rocco, 2014. Visual Exploration of Cardiovascular Hemodynamics. PhD thesis. University of Magdeburg.

Gasteiger, Rocco, Tietjen, Christian, Baer, Alexandra, Preim, Bernhard, 2008. Curvature- and model-based surface hatching of anatomical structures derived from clinical volume datasets. In: Proc. SmartGraphics, pp. 255–262. https://doi.org/10.1007/978-3-540-85412-8_25.

Gasteiger, Rocco, Neugebauer, Mathias, Kubisch, Christoph, Preim, Bernhard, 2010. Adapted surface visualization of cerebral aneurysms with embedded blood flow information. In: Proc. of Eurographics Workshop on Visual Computing for Biology and Medicine (VCBM), pp. 25–32.

Gasteiger, Rocco, Neugebauer, Mathias, Beuing, Oliver, Preim, Bernhard, 2011. The FLOWLENS: a focus-and-context visualization approach for exploration of blood flow in cerebral aneurysms. IEEE Transactions on Visualization and Computer Graphics 17 (12), 2183–2192.

Gasteiger, Rocco, Lehmann, Dirk J., van Pelt, Roy, Janiga, Gábor, Beuing, Oliver, Vilanova, Anna, Theisel, Holger, Preim, B., 2012. Automatic detection and visualization of qualitative hemodynamic characteristics in cerebral aneurysms. IEEE Transactions on Visualization and Computer Graphics 18 (12), 2178–2187.

GBD 2016 Stroke Collaborators, 2019. Global, regional, and national burden of stroke, 1990–2016: a systematic analysis for the global burden of disease study 2016. The Lancet Neurology 18 (5), 439–458.

Gerbaulet, Alain, Potter, Richard, Mazeron, Jean-Jacques, Meertens, Harm, Van Limbergen, Erik, 2002. The GEC ESTRO Handbook of Brachytherapy. European Society for Therapeutic Radiology and Oncology, Leuven, Belgium.

Gerl, Moritz, Isenberg, Tobias, 2013. Interactive example-based hatching. Computers & Graphics 37 (1–2), 65–80. https://doi.org/10.1016/j.cag.2012.11.003.

German National Cohort (GNC) Consortium, 2014. The German National Cohort: aims, study design and organization. European Journal of Epidemiology 29 (5), 371–382.

Gesteland, Per Hans, Livnat, Yarden, Galli, Nathan, Samore, Matthew H., Gundlapalli, Adi V., 2012. The EpiCanvas infectious disease weather map: an interactive visual exploration of temporal and spatial correlations. Journal of the American Medical Informatics Association 19 (6), 954–959.

Ghosh, Sanjib K., 2015. Evolution of illustrations in anatomy: a study from the classical period in Europe to modern times. Anatomical Sciences Education 8 (2), 175–188.

Gibson, James J., 1950a. The perception of visual surfaces. The American Journal of Psychology 63 (3), 367–384.

Gibson, James J., 1950b. The Perception of the Visual World. Houghton Mifflin, Boston.

Gibson, Sarah F.F., 1998. Constrained elastic surface nets: generating smooth surfaces from binary segmented data. In: Proc. of Medical Image Computing and Computer-Assisted Intervention (MICCAI), pp. 888–898.

Gillmann, Christina, Smit, Noeska N., Gröller, Eduard, Preim, Bernhard, Vilanova, Anna, Wischgoll, Thomas, 2021. Ten open challenges in medical visualization. IEEE CG&A 41 (5), 7–15. https://doi.org/10.1109/MCG.2021.3094858.

Glaßer, S., Saalfeld, P., Berg, P., Merten, N., Preim, B., 2016a. How to evaluate medical visualizations on the example of 3D aneurysm surfaces. In: Proc. of Eurographics Workshop on Visual Computing for Biology and Medicine (VCBM), pp. 153–162.

Glaßer, Sylvia, Oeltze, Steffen, Hennemuth, Anja, Kubisch, Christoph, Mahnken, Andreas, Wilhelmsen, Skadi, Preim, Bernhard, 2010. Automatic transfer function specification for visual emphasis of coronary artery plaque. Computer Graphics Forum 29 (1), 191–201.

Glaßer, Sylvia, Lawonn, Kai, Hoffmann, Thomas, Skalej, Martin, Preim, Bernhard, 2014. Combined visualization of wall thickness and wall shear stress for the evaluation of aneurysms. IEEE Transactions on Visualization and Computer Graphics 20 (12), 2506–2515.

Glaßer, Sylvia, Hirsch, Jan, Berg, Philipp, Saalfeld, Patrick, Beuing, Oliver, Janiga, Gabor, Preim, Bernhard, 2016b. Evaluation of time-dependent wall shear stress visualizations for cerebral aneurysms. In: Bildverarbeitung für die Medizin, pp. 236–241.

Gold, J.I., Kim, S.H., Kant, A.J., Joseph, M.H., Rizzo, A.S., 2006. Effectiveness of virtual reality for pediatric pain distraction during IV placement. Cyberpsychology & Behavior 9 (2), 207–212.

Goldsberry, Kirk, Battersby, Sarah, 2009. Issues of change detection in animated choropleth maps. Cartographica: The International Journal for Geographic Information and Geovisualization 44 (3), 201–215.

Golland, P., Kikinis, R., Umans, C., Halle, M., Shenton, M.E., Richolt, J.A., 1998. Anatomy-Browser: a framework for integration of medical information. In: Proc. of Medical Image Computing and Computer-Assisted Intervention (MICCAI), pp. 720–731.

Gonna, John, 2000. The global infectious disease threat and its implications for the United States. Technical report. National Intelligence Council, Washington, DC.

Gooch, Bruce, Sloan, Peter-Pike J., Gooch, Amy, Shirley, Peter, Riesenfeld, Richard, 1999. Interactive technical illustration. In: ACM Symposium on Interactive 3D Graphics. ACM, pp. 31–38. https://doi.org/10.1145/300523.300526.

Gorelick, Philip B., 2019. The global burden of stroke: persistent and disabling. The Lancet Neurology 18 (5), 417–418.

Gotz, David, Wang, Fei, Perer, Adam, 2014. A methodology for interactive mining and visual analysis of clinical event patterns using electronic health record data. Journal of Biomedical Informatics 48, 148–159.

Götzelmann, Timo, Ali, Kamran, Hartmann, Knut, Strothotte, Thomas, 2005. Adaptive labeling for illustrations. In: Proc. Pacific Graphics.

Götzelmann, Timo, Hartmann, Knut, Strothotte, Thomas, 2007. Annotation of animated 3D objects. In: Proc. of Simulation und Visualisierung, pp. 209–222.

Goubergrits, Leonid, Thamsen, Bente, Berthe, André, Poethke, Jens, Kertzscher, Ulrich, Affeld, Klaus, Petz, Christoph, Hege, H.-C., Hoch, Heinrich, Spuler, Andreas, 2010. In vitro study of near-wall flow in a cerebral aneurysm model with and without coils. American Journal of Neuroradiology 31 (8), 1521–1528.

Goubergrits, Leonid, Schaller, Jens, Kertzscher, Ulrich, van den Bruck, Nils, Pöthkow, Kai, Petz, Christian, Hege, Hans-Christian, Spuler, Andreas, 2012. Statistical wall shear stress maps of ruptured and unruptured middle cerebral artery aneurysms. Journal of the Royal Society Interface 9 (69), 677–688.

Goubergrits, Leonid, Riesenkampff, Eugenie, Yevtushenko, Pavlo, Schaller, Jens, Kertzscher, Ulrich, Hennemuth, Anja, Berger, Felix, Schubert, Stephan, Kuehne, Titus, 2015. MRI-based computational fluid dynamics for diagnosis and treatment prediction: clinical validation study in patients with coarctation of aorta. Journal of Magnetic Resonance Imaging 41 (4), 909–916.

Grabli, Stéphane, Turquin, Emmanuel, Durand, Frédo, Sillion, François X., 2004. Programmable style for NPR line drawing. In: Proc. EGSR. Eurographics Association, pp. 33–44. https://doi.org/10.2312/EGWR/EGSR04/033-044.

Granic, Isabela, Lobel, Adam, Engels, Rutger C.M.E., 2014. The benefits of playing video games. The American Psychologist 69 (1), 66.

Gregory, Richard L., 2015. Eye and Brain: The Psychology of Seeing, vol. 38. Princeton University Press.

Griethe, Henning, Schumann, Heidrun, 2006. Visualizing uncertainty for improved decision making. In: Proc. of Simulation and Visualization.

Grimm, Paul, Herold, Rigo, Reiners, Dirk, Cruz-Neira, Carolina, 2013. VR-Ausgabegeräte. In: Virtual und Augmented Reality (VR/AR). Springer, pp. 127–156.

Gromala, D., Tong, X., Shaw, C., Amin, A., Ulas, S., Ramsay, G., 2016. Mobius floe: an immersive virtual reality game for pain distraction. Electronic Imaging 4, 1–5.

Grossmann, Nicolas, Casares-Magaz, Oscar, Muren, Ludvig Paul, Moiseenko, Vitali, Einck, John P., Gröller, Eduard, Raidou, Renata Georgia, 2019. Pelvis runner: visualizing pelvic organ variability in a cohort of radiotherapy patients. In: Proc. of Eurographics Workshop on Visual Computing for Biology and Medicine (VCBM), pp. 69–78. https://doi.org/10.2312/vcbm.20191233.

Gschwandtner, Theresia, Aigner, Wolfgang, Kaiser, Katharina, Miksch, Silvia, Seyfang, Andreas, 2011. CareCruiser: exploring and visualizing plans, events, and effects interactively. In: Proc. PacificVis, pp. 43–50.

Gschwandtner, Theresia, Aigner, Wolfgang, Miksch, Silvia, Gärtner, Johannes, Kriglstein, Simone, Pohl, Margit, Suchy, Nikolaus, 2014. TimeCleanser: a visual analytics approach for data cleansing of time-oriented data. In: Proc. of Knowledge Management and Data-Driven Business, pp. 18:1–18:8.

Guerra, Carlos A., Hay, Simon I., Lucioparedes, Lorena S., Gikandi, Priscilla W., Tatem, Andrew J., Noor, Abdisalan M., Snow, Robert W., 2007. Assembling a global database of malaria parasite prevalence for the malaria atlas project. Malaria Journal 6 (1), 17.

Guiard, Yves, 1987. Asymmetric division of labor in human skilled bimanual action: the kinematic chain as a model. Journal of Motor Behavior 19 (4), 486–517.

Günther, Tobias, Rössl, Christian, Theisel, Holger, 2013. Opacity optimization for 3D line fields. ACM Transactions on Graphics 32 (4), 120.

Guo, D., 2007. Visual analytics of spatial interaction patterns for pandemic decision support. International Journal of Geographical Information Science 21 (8), 859–877.

Gupta, Shruti, Ramesh, Karthik P., Blasch, Erik P., 2008. Mutual information metric evaluation for PET/MRI image fusion. In: Proc. of Aerospace and Electronics Conference, pp. 305–311.

Habbal, O.A., Harris, P.F., 1995. Teaching of human anatomy: a role for computer animation. The Journal of Audiovisual Media in Medicine 18 (2), 69–73.

Hacker, S., Handels, H., 2009. A framework for representation and visualization of 3D shape variability of organs in an interactive anatomical atlas. Methods of Information in Medicine 48 (3), 272–281.

Hahn, Horst K., Preim, Bernhard, Selle, Dirk, Peitgen, H.-O., 2001. Visualization and interaction techniques for the exploration of vascular structures. In: Visualization, pp. 395–402.

Hahsler, Michael, 2017. arulesViz: interactive visualization of association rules with R. The R Journal 9 (2), 163.

Haidacher, Martin, Bruckner, Stefan, Kanitsar, Armin, Gröller, Eduard, 2008. Information-based transfer functions for multimodal visualization. In: Proc. of Eurographics Workshop on Visual Computing for Biology and Medicine (VCBM), pp. 101–108.

Hajagos, Balázs, Szécsi, László, Csébfalvi, Balázs, 2012. Fast silhouette and crease edge synthesis with geometry shaders. In: Proc. SCCG. ACM, pp. 71–76. https://doi.org/10.1145/2448531.2448540.

Hall, Eric J., Wuu, Cheng-Shie, 2003. Radiation-induced second cancers: the impact of 3D-CRT and IMRT. International Journal of Radiation Oncology, Biology, Physics 56 (1), 83–88. https://doi.org/10.1016/S0360-3016(03)00073-7.

Halle, Michael, Demeusy, Valentin, Kikinis, Ron, 2017. The open anatomy browser: a collaborative web-based viewer for interoperable anatomy atlases. Frontiers in Neuroinformatics 11.

Halliday, Alison, Harrison, Michael, Hayter, Elizabeth, Kong, Xiangling, Mansfield, Averil, Marro, Joanna, Pan, Hongchao, Peto, Richard, Potter, John, Rahimi, Kazem, et al., 2010. 10-year stroke prevention after successful carotid endarterectomy for asymptomatic stenosis (ACST-1): a multicentre randomised trial. The Lancet 376 (9746), 1074–1084.

Halm, Ethan A., Tuhrim, Stanley, Wang, Jason J., Rockman, Caron, Riles, Thomas S., Chassin, Mark R., 2009. Risk factors for perioperative death and stroke after carotid endarterectomy: results of the New York carotid artery surgery study. Stroke 40 (1), 221–229.

Hamdan, Iyas, Bert, Julien, Rest, Catherine Cheze Le, Tasu, Jean Pierre, Boussion, Nicolas, Valeri, Antoine, Dardenne, Guillaume, Visvikis, Dimitris, 2017. Fully automatic deformable registration of pretreatment MRI/CT for image-guided prostate radiotherapy planning. Medical Physics 44 (12), 6447–6455. https://doi.org/10.1002/mp.12629.

Hänel, Claudia, Weyers, Benjamin, Hentschel, Bernd, Kuhlen, Torsten W., 2016. Visual quality adjustment for volume rendering in a head-tracked virtual environment. IEEE Transactions on Visualization and Computer Graphics 22 (4), 1472–1481.

Hansen, Christian, Black, David, Lange, Christoph, Rieber, Fabian, Lamadé, Wolfram, Donati, Marcello, Oldhafer, Karl J., Hahn, Horst K., 2013. Auditory support for resection guidance in navigated liver surgery. The International Journal of Medical Robotics and Computer Assisted Surgery 9 (1), 36–43.

Harders, Matthias, Wildermuth, Simon, Székely, Gábor, 2002. New paradigms for interactive 3D volume segmentation. Computer Animation and Virtual Worlds 13 (1), 85–95. https://doi.org/10.1002/vis.277.

Harrower, Mark, 2003. Tips for designing effective animated maps. Cartographic Perspectives 44, 63–65.

Harrower, Mark, 2007. The cognitive limits of animated maps. Cartographica: The International Journal for Geographic Information and Geovisualization 42 (4), 349–357.

Harrower, Mark, Brewer, Cynthia A., 2003. Colorbrewer.org: an online tool for selecting colour schemes for maps. The Cartographic Journal 40 (1), 27–37.

Hartmann, Knut, Ali, Kamran, Strothotte, Thomas, 2004. Floating labels: applying dynamic potential fields for label layout. In: Proc. Smart Graphics, pp. 101–113.

Hartmann, Knut, Götzelmann, Timo, Ali, Kamran, Strothotte, Thomas, 2005. Metrics for functional and aesthetic label layouts. In: Proc. Smart Graphics, pp. 115–126.

Hastreiter, Peter, Ertl, Thomas, 1998. Integrated registration and visualization of medical image data. In: Proc. of Computer Graphics International, pp. 78–85.

Hattab, Georges, Hatzipanayioti, Adamantini, Klimova, Anna, Pfeiffer, Micha, Klausing, Peter, Breucha, Michael, et al., 2021. Investigating the utility of VR for spatial understanding in surgical planning: evaluation of head-mounted to desktop display. Scientific Reports 11 (1), 1–11.

Hauser, Helwig, Ledermann, Florian, Doleisch, Helmut, 2002. Angular brushing of extended parallel coordinates. In: Proc. of IEEE Symposium on Information Visualization, pp. 127–130.

Heeringa, Jan, van der Kuip, Deirdre A.M., Hofman, Albert, et al., 2006. Prevalence, incidence and lifetime risk of atrial fibrillation: the Rotterdam study. European Heart Journal 27 (8), 949–953.

Hege, Hans-Christian, Stalling, Detlev, Seebass, Martin, Zockler, Malte, 1997. A generalized marching cubes algorithm based on non-binary. Technical Report SC-97-05. Zuse-Institute, Berlin.

Heinrich, Julian, Weiskopf, Daniel, 2013. State of the art of parallel coordinates. In: Proc. of Eurographics (State of the Art Reports), pp. 95–116.

Hendrix, Claudia, Barfield, Woodrow, 1996. Presence within virtual environments as a function of visual display parameters. Presence: Teleoperators & Virtual Environments 5 (3), 274–289.

Hennemuth, Anja, 2012. Computer-Assisted Diagnosis and Therapy Planning in Coronary Artery Disease Based on Cardiac CT and MRI. PhD thesis. Universität Bremen.

Hennemuth, Anja, Seeger, Achim, Friman, Ola, Miller, Stephan, Klumpp, Bernhard, Oeltze, Steffen, Peitgen, Heinz-Otto, 2008. A comprehensive approach to the analysis of contrast enhanced cardiac MR images. IEEE Transactions on Medical Imaging 27 (11), 1592–1610.

Hennemuth, Anja, Friman, Ola, Schumann, Christian, Bock, Jelena, Drexl, Johann, Huellebrand, Markus, Markl, Michael, Peitgen, Heinz-Otto, 2011. Fast interactive exploration of 4D MRI flow data. In: Proc. of SPIE Medical Imaging, vol. 7964, pp. 79640E–79640E–11.

Hermann, M., 2002. Dreidimensionale Computeranimation–neues Medium zur Unterstützung des Aufklärungsgesprächs vor Operationen Akzeptanz und Bewertung der Patienten anhand einer prospektiv randomisierten Studie–Bild versus Text. Der Chirurg 73 (5), 500–507.

Hertzmann, Aaron, 1999. Introduction to 3D non-photorealistic rendering: silhouettes and outlines. In: SIGGRAPH Course Notes. ACM.

Hertzmann, Aaron, Zorin, Denis, 2000. Illustrating smooth surfaces. In: Proc. of ACM SIGGRAPH, pp. 517–526. https://doi.org/10.1145/344779.345074.

Hicks, C.L., von Baeyer, C.L., Spafford, P.A., van Korlaar, I., 2001. The Faces Pain Scale Revised: toward a common metric in pediatric pain measurement. Pain 93 (2), 173–183.

Hielscher, Tommy, Niemann, Uli, Preim, Bernhard, Völzke, Henry, Ittermann, Till, Spiliopoulou, Myra, 2018. A framework for expert-driven subpopulation discovery and evaluation using subspace clustering for epidemiological data. Expert Systems with Applications 113, 147–160.

Higuera, Fernando Vega, Naraghi, Ramin, Nimsky, Christopher, Fahlbusch, Rudolf, Greiner, Günther, Hastreiter, Peter, 2003a. Standardized 3D documentation for neurosurgery. Computer Aided Surgery 8 (6), 274–282.

Higuera, Fernando Vega, Sauber, Natascha, Tomandl, Bernd, Nimsky, Christopher, Greiner, Günther, Hastreiter, Peter, 2003b. Enhanced 3D-visualization of intracranial aneurysms involving the skull base. In: Proc. of Medical Image Computing and Computer-Assisted Intervention (MICCAI), pp. 256–263.

Higuera, Fernando Vega, Sauber, Natascha, Tomandl, Bernd, Nimsky, Christopher, Greiner, Guenther, Hastreiter, Peter, 2004. Automatic adjustment of bidimensional transfer functions for direct volume visualization of intracranial aneurysms. In: Proc. of SPIE Medical Imaging, pp. 275–284.

Hildebrandt, Thomas, Goubergrits, Leonid, Heppt, Werner, Bessler, Stefan, Zachow, Stefan, 2013a. Evaluation of the intranasal flow field through computational fluid dynamics (CFD). Journal of Facial and Plastic Surgery 29 (2), 93–98. https://doi.org/10.1055/s-0033-1341591.

Hildebrandt, Thomas, Heppt, Werner Johannes, Kertzscher, Ulrich, Goubergrits, Leonid, 2013b. The concept of rhinorespiratory homeostasis - a new approach to nasal breathing. Facial Plastic Surgery 29 (2), 85–92.

Hinckley, Ken, Pausch, Randy, Goble, John C., Kassell, Neal F., 1994. Passive real-world interface props for neurosurgical visualization. In: Proc. of ACM SIGCHI Conference on Human Factors in Computing Systems (CHI), pp. 452–458.

Hintze, Jerry L., Nelson, Ray D., 1998. Violin plots: a box plot-density trace synergism. The American Statistician 52 (2), 181–184.

Hochman, Jordan B., Unger, Bertram, Kraut, Jay, Pisa, Justyn, Hombach-Klonisch, Sabine, 2014. Gesture-controlled interactive three dimensional anatomy: a novel teaching tool in head and neck surgery. Journal of Otolaryngology-Head & Neck Surgery 43 (1), 38.

Hoffman, Helene, Murray, Margaret, Curlee, Robert, Fritchle, Alicia, 2001a. Anatomic VisualizeR: teaching and learning anatomy with virtual reality. In: Information Technologies in Medicine: Medical Simulation and Education, vol. I. John Wiley & Sons, Inc., pp. 205–218.

Hoffman, Hunter G., Patterson, David R., Carrougher, Gretchen J., Sharar, Sam R., 2001b. Effectiveness of virtual reality-based pain control with multiple treatments. The Clinical Journal of Pain 17 (3), 229–235.

Hoffman, Hunter G., Richards, Todd L., Bills, Aric R., Van Oostrom, Trevor, Magula, Jeff, Seibel, Eric J., Sharar, Sam R., 2006. Using fMRI to study the neural correlates of virtual reality analgesia. CNS Spectrums 11 (1), 45–51.

Hoffman, Hunter G., Chambers, Gloria T., Meyer III, Walter J., Arceneaux, Lisa L., Russell, William J., Seibel, Eric J., et al., 2011. Virtual reality as an adjunctive non-pharmacologic analgesic for acute burn pain during medical procedures. Annals of Behavioral Medicine 41 (2), 183–191.

Höhne, Karl Heinz, Bernstein, Ralph, 1986. Shading 3D-images from CT using gray-level gradients. IEEE Transactions on Medical Imaging 5 (1), 45–47.

Höhne, Karl-Heinz, Bomans, Michael, Tiede, Ulf, Riemer, Martin, 1988. Display of multiple 3D-objects using the generalized voxel-model. In: Proc. of Medical Imaging II. International Society for Optics and Photonics, pp. 850–854.

Höhne, Karl Heinz, Bomans, M., Riemer, Matthias, Schubert, Rainer, Tiede, Ulf, Lierse, Werner, 1992a. A 3D anatomical atlas based on a volume model. IEEE CG&A 12, 72–78.

Höhne, Karl Heinz, Pommert, Andreas, Riemer, Martin, Schiemann, Thomas, Schubert, Rainer, Tiede, Ulf, Lierse, Werner, 1992b. Anatomical atlases based on volume visualization. In: Proc. of IEEE Visualization, pp. 115–123. https://doi.org/10.1109/VISUAL.1992.235218.

Höhne, Karl Heinz, Pflesser, Bernhard, Pommert, Andreas, Riemer, Martin, Schiemann, Thomas, Schubert, Rainer, Tiede, Ulf, 1995. A new representation of knowledge concerning human anatomy and function. Nature Medicine 1 (6), 506–511.

Höhne, Karl Heinz, Pflesser, Bernhard, Pommert, Andreas, Priesmeyer, Kay, Riemer, Martin, Schiemann, Thomas, Schubert, Rainer, Tiede, Ulf, Frederking, Hans, Gehrmann, Sebastian, et al., 2000. VOXEL-MAN 3D-Navigator: Inner Organs: Regional, Systemic and Radiological Anatomy. Springer.

Holden, Maureen, Todorov, Emanuel, Callahan, Janet, Bizzi, Emilio, 1999. Virtual environment training improves motor performance in two patients with stroke: case report. Neurology Report 23 (2), 57–67.

Holten, Danny, 2006. Hierarchical edge bundles: visualization of adjacency relations in hierarchical data. IEEE Transactions on Visualization and Computer Graphics 12 (5), 741–748. https://doi.org/10.1109/TVCG.2006.147.

Holten, Danny, Van Wijk, Jarke J., 2009. Force-directed edge bundling for graph visualization. Computer Graphics Forum 28 (3), 983–990.

Hombeck, Jan, Meuschke, Monique, Lieb, Simon, et al., 2022a. Distance visualizations for vascular structures in desktop and VR: overview and implementation. In: Proc. of Eurographics Workshop on Visual Computing for Biology and Medicine (VCBM).

Hombeck, Jan, Meuschke, Monique, Zyla, Lennert, et al., 2022b. Evaluating perceptional tasks for medicine: a comparative user study between a virtual reality and a desktop application. In: Proc. of IEEE Conference on Virtual Reality and 3D User Interfaces, pp. 514–523.

Honaker, James, King, Gary, Blackwell, Matthew, et al., 2011. Amelia II: a program for missing data. Journal of Statistical Software 45 (7), 1–47.

Hong, Helen, Bae, Juhee, Kye, Heewon, Shin, YeongGil, 2005. Efficient multimodality volume fusion using graphics hardware. In: Computational Science. In: Lecture Notes in Computer Science, vol. 3516. Springer, pp. 842–845.

Hong, Lichan, Muraki, Shigeru, Kaufman, Arie E., Bartz, Dirk, He, Taosong, 1997. Virtual voyage: interactive navigation in the human colon. In: Proc. of ACM SIGGRAPH, pp. 27–34.

Hope, M.D., Hope, T.A., Meadows, A.K., Ordovas, K.G., Urbania, T.H., Alley, M.T., Higgins, C.B., 2010. Bicuspid aortic valve: four-dimensional MR evaluation of ascending aortic systolic flow patterns. Radiology 255 (1), 53–61.

Hope, M.D., Wrenn, J., Sigovan, M., Foster, E., Tseng, E.E., Saloner, D., 2012. Imaging biomarkers of aortic disease - increased growth rates with eccentric systolic flow. Journal of the American College of Cardiology 60, 356–357.

Hope, T.A., Markl, M., Wigström, L., Alley, M.T., Miller, D., Herfkens, R., 2007. Comparison of flow patterns in ascending aortic aneurysms and volunteers using four-dimensional magnetic resonance velocity mapping. Journal of Magnetic Resonance Imaging 26 (6), 1471–1479.

Hosmer, David W., Lemeshow, Stanley, 1980. Goodness of fit tests for the multiple logistic regression model. Communications in Statistics. Theory and Methods 9 (10), 1043–1069.

Hotelling, Harold, 1933. Analysis of a complex of statistical variables into principal components. Journal of Educational Psychology 24 (6), 417.

Howard, David, MacEachren, Alan M., 1996. Interface design for geographic visualization: tools for representing reliability. Cartography and Geographic Information Systems 23 (2), 59–77.

Hoyek, Nadi, Collet, Christian, Di Rienzo, Franck, De Almeida, Mikael, Guillot, Aymeric, 2014. Effectiveness of three-dimensional digital animation in teaching human anatomy in an authentic classroom context. Anatomical Sciences Education 7 (6), 430–437.

Hricak, Hedvig, Choyke, Peter L., Eberhardt, Steven C., Leibel, Steven A., Scardino, Peter T., 2007. Imaging prostate cancer: a multidisciplinary perspective. Radiology 243 (1), 28–53.

Hripcsak, George, Duke, Jon D., Shah, Nigam H., Reich, Christian G., Huser, Vojtech, Schuemie, Martijn J., et al., 2015. Observational Health Data Sciences and Informatics (OHDSI): opportunities for observational researchers. Studies in Health Technology and Informatics 216, 574–578.

Hripcsak, George, Ryan, Patrick B., Duke, Jon D., Shah, Nigam H., Park, Rae Woong, Huser, Vojtech, et al., 2016. Characterizing treatment pathways at scale using the OHDSI network. Proceedings of the National Academy of Sciences 113 (27), 7329–7336.

Hrovat, Goran, Stiglic, Gregor, Kokol, Peter, Ojsteršek, Milan, 2014. Contrasting temporal trend discovery for large healthcare databases. Computer Methods and Programs in Biomedicine 113 (1), 251–257.

Hsu, Wei-Hsien, Zhang, Yubo, Ma, Kwan-Liu, 2013. A multi-criteria approach to camera motion design for volume data animation. IEEE Transactions on Visualization and Computer Graphics 19 (12), 2792–2801.

Huang, Xuan, Wu, Lei, Ye, Yinsong, 2019. A review on dimensionality reduction techniques. International Journal of Pattern Recognition and Artificial Intelligence 33 (10), 1950017.

Huber, Tobias, Wunderling, Tom, Paschold, Markus, Lang, Hauke, Kneist, Werner, Hansen, Christian, 2018. Highly immersive virtual reality laparoscopy simulation: development and future aspects. International Journal of Computer Assisted Radiology and Surgery 13 (2), 281–290. https://doi.org/10.1007/s11548-017-1686-2.

Huettl, Florentine, Saalfeld, Patrick, Hansen, Christian, Preim, Bernhard, Poplawski, Alicia, Kneist, Werner, Lang, Hauke, Huber, Tobias, 2021. Virtual reality and 3D printing improve preoperative visualization of 3D liver reconstructions: results from a preclinical comparison of presentation modalities and users preference. Annals of Translational Medicine 9 (13).

Hund, Michael, Färber, Ines, Behrisch, Michael, Tatu, Andrada, Schreck, Tobias, Keim, Daniel A., Seidl, Thomas, 2016. Visual quality assessment of subspace clusterings. In: Proc. of Workshop on Interactive Data Exploration and Analytics, pp. 53–62.

Ikram, M. Arfan, Brusselle, Guy G.O., Murad, Sarwa Darwish, et al., 2017. The Rotterdam Study: 2018 update on objectives, design and main results. European Journal of Epidemiology 32 (9), 807–850.

Indovina, Paola, Barone, Daniela, Gallo, Luigi, Chirico, Andrea, De Pietro, Giuseppe, Giordano, Antonio, 2018. Virtual reality as a distraction intervention to relieve pain and distress during medical procedures. The Clinical Journal of Pain 34 (9), 858–877.

Inselberg, Alfred, Dimsdale, Bernard, 1990. Parallel coordinates: a tool for visualizing multi-dimensional geometry. In: Proc. of IEEE Visualization, pp. 361–378.

Interrante, Victoria, Fuchs, Henry, Pizer, Stephen, 1995. Enhancing transparent skin surfaces with ridge and valley lines. In: Proc. of IEEE Visualization, pp. 52–59.

Interrante, Victoria, Fuchs, Henry, Pizer, Stephen, 1996. Illustrating transparent surfaces with curvature-directed strokes. In: Proc. of IEEE Visualization, pp. 211–218, 487, https://doi.org/10.1109/VISUAL.1996.568110.

Interrante, Victoria, Fuchs, Henry, Pizer, Stephen, 1997. Conveying the 3D shape of smoothly curving transparent surfaces via texture. IEEE Transactions on Visualization and Computer Graphics 3 (2), 98–117. https://doi.org/10.1109/2945.597794.

Iqbal, Usman, Hsu, Chun-Kung, Nguyen, Phung Anh (Alex), Clinciu, Daniel Livius, Lu, Richard, Syed-Abdul, Shabbir, Yang, Hsuan-Chia, Wang, Yao-Chin, Huang, Chu-Ya, Huang, Chih-Wei, Chang, Yo-Cheng, Hsu, Min-Huei, Jian, Wen-Shan, Li, Yu-Chuan (Jack), 2016. Cancer-disease associations: a visualization and animation through medical big data. Computer Methods and Programs in Biomedicine 127 (Supplement C), 44–51.

Irani, Jasmine, Pise, Nitin, Phatak, Madhura, 2016. Clustering techniques and the similarity measures used in clustering: a survey. International Journal of Computer Applications 134 (7), 9–14.

Isenberg, Tobias, Brennecke, Angela, 2006. G-strokes: a concept for simplifying line stylization. Computers & Graphics 30 (5), 754–766. https://doi.org/10.1016/j.cag.2006.07.006.

Isenberg, Tobias, Halper, Nick, Strothotte, Thomas, 2002. Stylizing silhouettes at interactive rates: from silhouette edges to silhouette strokes. Computer Graphics Forum 21 (3), 249–258. https://doi.org/10.1111/1467-8659.00584.

Isenberg, Tobias, Freudenberg, Bert, Halper, Nicolas, Schlechtweg, Stefan, Strothotte, Thomas, 2003. A developer's guide to silhouette algorithms for polygonal models. IEEE CG&A 23 (4), 28–37. https://doi.org/10.1109/MCG.2003.1210862.

Iserhardt-Bauer, Sabine, Hastreiter, Peter, Tomandl, Bernd, Köstner, N., Schempershofe, M., Nissen, U., Ertl, Thomas, 2002. Standardized analysis of intracranial aneurysms using digital video sequences. In: Proc. of Medical Image Computing and Computer-Assisted Intervention (MICCAI), pp. 411–418.

Jaffar, Akram Abood, 2012. YouTube: an emerging tool in anatomy education. Anatomical Sciences Education 5 (3), 158–164.

Jaffray, D.A., Yan, D., Wong, J.W., 1999. Managing geometric uncertainty in conformal intensity-modulated radiation therapy. Seminars in Radiation Oncology 9 (1), 4–19. https://doi.org/10.1016/s1053-4296(99)80051-4.

James, Alex Pappachen, Dasarathy, Belur V., 2014. Medical image fusion: a survey of the state of the art. Information Fusion 19, 4–19.

Jang, Seong Soon, Huh, Gil Ja, Park, Suk Young, Yang, Po Song, Cho, EunYoun, 2015. Usefulness of target delineation based on the two extreme phases of a four-dimensional computed tomography scan in stereotactic body radiation therapy for lung cancer: SBRT planning using 2 extreme phases. Thoracic Cancer 6 (3), 239–246. https://doi.org/10.1111/1759-7714.12170.

Jang, Susan, Vitale, Jonathan M., Jyung, Robert W., Black, John B., 2017. Direct manipulation is better than passive viewing for learning anatomy in a three-dimensional virtual reality environment. Computers and Education 106, 150–165. https://doi.org/10.1016/j.compedu.2016.12.009.

Jankowski, Jacek, Hachet, Martin, 2015. Advances in interaction with 3D environments. Computer Graphics Forum 34 (1), 152–190.

Janović, Nataša, Ćоćić, Aleksandar, Stamenić, Mirjana, Janović, Aleksa, Djurić, Marija, 2020. Side asymmetry in nasal resistance correlate with nasal obstruction severity in patients with septal deformities: computational fluid dynamics study. Clinical Otolaryngology 45 (5), 718–724.

Jariyapong, Pitchanee, Punsawad, Chuchard, Bunratsami, Suchirat, Kongthong, Paranyu, 2016. Body painting to promote self-active learning of hand anatomy for preclinical medical students. Medical Education Online 21 (1), 30833.

Jastrow, H., Hollinderbäumer, A., 2004. On the use and value of new media and how medical students assess their effectiveness in learning anatomy. Anatomical Record. Part B 280B (1), 20–29.

Jeong, Dong Hyun, Ziemkiewicz, Caroline, Fisher, Brian, Ribarsky, William, Chang, Remco, 2009. iPCA: an interactive system for PCA-based visual analytics. Computer Graphics Forum 28 (3), 767–774.

Jerald, Jason, 2015. The VR Book: Human-Centered Design for Virtual Reality. Morgan & Claypool.

Jerrett, Michael, Gale, Sara, Kontgis, Caitlin, 2010. Spatial modeling in environmental and public health research. International Journal of Environmental Research and Public Health 7 (16), 1302–1329.

Jessup, Jared, Krueger, Robert, Warchol, Simon, Hoffer, John, Muhlich, Jeremy, Ritch, Cecily C., Gaglia, Giorgio, Coy, Shannon, Chen, Yu-An, Lin, Jia-Ren, et al., 2021. Scope2Screen: focus+context techniques for pathology tumor assessment in multivariate image data. IEEE Transactions on Visualization and Computer Graphics 28 (1), 259–269.

Jiang, Kai, Yu, Xin, 2014. Quantification of regional myocardial wall motion by cardiovascular magnetic resonance. Quantitative Imaging in Medicine and Surgery 4 (5), 345.

Jilin, Liu, Affeld, Klaus, Engelhorn, Michael W., Schartl, Michael, 1987. Animated 3D-model of the human heart based on echocardiograms. In: Proc. of Aachener Symposium für Signaltheorie, pp. 155–158.

Johansson, Jimmy, Forsell, Camilla, 2016. Evaluation of parallel coordinates: overview, categorization and guidelines for future research. IEEE Transactions on Visualization and Computer Graphics 22 (1), 579–588. https://doi.org/10.1109/TVCG.2015.2466992.

Johansson, Jimmy, Ljung, Patric, Jern, Mikael, Cooper, Matthew, 2005. Revealing structure within clustered parallel coordinates displays. In: Proc. of IEEE Information Visualization, pp. 125–132.

Johansson, Sara, Johansson, Jimmy, 2009. Interactive dimensionality reduction through user-defined combinations of quality metrics. IEEE Transactions on Visualization and Computer Graphics 15 (6), 993–1000.

John, Nigel W., Phillips, Nicholas I., Cenydd, Llyr ap, Pop, Serban R., Coope, David, Kamaly-Asl, Ian, de Souza, Christopher, Watt, Simon J., 2016. The use of stereoscopy in a neuro-surgery training virtual environment. Presence: Teleoperators & Virtual Environments 24 (4), 289–298.

John, Nigel W., Day, Thomas W., Wardle, Terrence, 2020. An endoscope interface for immersive virtual reality. In: Proc. of Eurographics Workshop on Visual Computing for Biology and Medicine (VCBM). Eurographics Association.

John, Ulrich, Hensel, Elke, Lüdemann, Jan, et al., 2001. Study of Health in Pomerania (SHIP): a health examination survey in an east German region: objectives and design. Sozial- und Präventivmedizin 46 (3), 186–194.

Johnson, Matilda O., Cohly, Hari H.P., Isokpehi, Raphael D., Awofolu, Omotayo R., 2010. The case for visual analytics of arsenic concentrations in foods. International Journal of Environmental Research and Public Health 7 (5), 1970–1983.

Jolesz, Ferenc A., Lorensen, William E., Shinmoto, Hiroshi, Atsumi, Hideki, Nakajima, Shin, Kavanaugh, Peter, et al., 1997. Interactive virtual endoscopy. American Journal of Roentgenology 169 (5), 1229–1235.

Jönsson, Daniel, Bergström, Albin, Forsell, Camilla, Simon, Rozalyn, Engström, Maria, Walter, Susanna, Ynnerman, Anders, Hotz, Ingrid, 2020. VisualNeuro: a hypothesis formation and reasoning application for multi-variate brain cohort study data. Computer Graphics Forum 39 (6), 392–407.

Joshi, A., Qian, X., Dione, D.P., Bulsara, K.R., Breuer, C.K., Sinusas, A.J., Papademetris, X., 2008. Effective visualization of complex vascular structures using a non-parametric vessel detection method. IEEE Transactions on Visualization and Computer Graphics 14 (6), 1603–1610.

Joshi, Ashish, Amadi, Chioma, Katz, Benjamin, Kulkarni, Sarah, Nash, Denis, 2017. A human-centered platform for HIV infection reduction in New York: development and usage analysis of the ending the epidemic (ETE) dashboard. JMIR Public Health and Surveillance 3 (4), e95.

Joshi, Krishna Chaitanya, Larrabide, Ignacio, Saied, Ahmed, Elsaid, Nada, Fernandez, Hector, Lopes, Demetrius K., 2018. Software-based simulation for preprocedural assessment of braided stent sizing: a validation study. Journal of Neurosurgery 131 (5), 1423–1429.

Juanes, J.A., Prats, A., Lagándara, M.L., Riesco, J.M., 2003. Application of the visible human project in the field of anatomy: a review. European Journal of Anatomy 7 (3), 147–160.

Judd, Tilke, Durand, Frédo, Adelson, Edward, 2007. Apparent ridges for line drawing. ACM Transactions on Graphics 26 (3), 19:1–19:8.

Jung, Yvonne, Behr, Johannes, 2008. Extending H-Anim and X3D for advanced animation control. In: Proc. of the ACM Symposium on 3D Web Technology, pp. 57–65.

Kahn, Kenneth M., 1979. Creation of computer animation from story descriptions. PhD thesis. Massachusetts Institute of Technology.

Kahneman, Daniel, 2000. Evaluation by moments: past and future. In: Choices, Values, and Frames, pp. 693–708.

Kailing, Karin, Kriegel, Hans-Peter, Kroeger, Peer, Wanka, Stefanie, 2003. Ranking interesting subspaces for clustering high dimensional data. In: Proc. of European Conference on Principles of Data Mining and Knowledge Discovery, pp. 241–252.

Kajiya, James T., 1986. The rendering equation. In: Proc. of ACM SIGGRAPH, pp. 143–150.

Kalnins, Robert D., Davidson, Philip L., Markosian, Lee, Finkelstein, Adam, 2003. Coherent stylized silhouettes. ACM Transactions on Graphics 22 (3), 856–861. https://doi.org/10.1145/882262.882355.

Kampstra, Peter, 2008. Beanplot: a boxplot alternative for visual comparison of distributions. Journal of Statistical Software 28, 1–9.

Kandil, Heba, Soliman, Ahmed, Fraiwan, Luay, Shalaby, Ahmed, Mahmoud, Ali, ElTanboly, Ahmed, et al., 2018. A novel MRA framework based on integrated global and local analysis for accurate segmentation of the cerebral vascular system. In: Proc. of IEEE International Symposium on Biomedical Imaging, pp. 1365–1368.

Kanzler, Mathias, Ferstl, Florian, Westermann, Rüdiger, 2016. Line density control in screen-space via balanced line hierarchies. Computer Graphics 61, 29–39.

Karangelis, Grigorios, Zamboglou, Nikolaos, Baltas, Dimos, Sakas, Georgios, 2001. EX-OMIO: a 3D simulator for external beam radiotherapy. In: Volume Graphics, pp. 355–367. https://doi.org/10.2312/VG/VG01/355-367.

Karp, Peter, Feiner, Steven, 1993. Automated presentation planning of animation using task decomposition with heuristic reasoning. In: Proc. of Graphics Interface, pp. 118–125.

Karsch, Kevin, Hart, John C., 2011. Snaxels on a plane. In: Proc. NPAR. ACM, pp. 35–42. https://doi.org/10.1145/2024676.2024683.

Kato, Pamela M., Cole, Steve W., Bradlyn, Andrew S., Pollock, Brad H., 2008. A video game improves behavioral outcomes in adolescents and young adults with cancer: a randomized trial. Pediatrics 122 (2), e305–e317.

Ke, Pingchuan, Zhu, Kening, 2021. Larger step faster speed: investigating gesture-based locomotion in place with different walking speed in virtual reality. In: Proc. of IEEE Virtual Reality.

Keim, Daniel, Andrienko, Gennady, Fekete, Jean-Daniel, Görg, Carsten, Kohlhammer, Jörn, Melançon, Guy, 2008a. Visual analytics: definition, process, and challenges. In: Information Visualization. Springer, pp. 154–175.

Keim, Daniel A., Müller, Wolfgang, Schumann, Heidrun, 2002. Visual data mining. In: Proc. of Eurographics - State of the Art Reports.

Keim, Daniel A., Mansmann, Florian, Schneidewind, Jim, Thomas, Jörnand, Ziegler, Hartmut, 2008b. Visual Analytics: Scope and Challenges. Springer, pp. 76–90. https://doi.org/10.1007/978-3-540-71080-6_6.

Kelc, R., 2012. Zygote body: a new interactive 3-dimensional didactical tool for teaching anatomy. WebmedCentral ANATOMY 3 (1).

Kenney, Patrick A., Wszolek, Matthew F., Gould, Justin J., Libertino, John A., Moinzadeh, Alireza, 2009. Face, content, and construct validity of dV-trainer, a novel virtual reality simulator for robotic surgery. Urology 73 (6), 1288–1292.

Kerst, Donald W., 1941. The acceleration of electrons by magnetic induction. Physical Review 60 (1), 47.

Kersten-Oertel, Marta, Chen, Sean Jy-Shyang, Collins, D. Louis, 2014. An evaluation of depth enhancing perceptual cues for vascular volume visualization in neurosurgery. IEEE Transactions on Visualization and Computer Graphics 20 (3), 391–403.

Khalil, M.K., Paas, F., Johnson, T.E., Payer, A.F., 2005. Design of interactive and dynamical anatomical visualizations: the implication of cognitive load theory. Anatomical Record. Part B, New Anatomist 286 (1), 15–20.

Khamene, Ali, Zikic, Darko, Diallo, Mamadou, Boettger, Thomas, Rietzel, Eike, 2009. A novel intensity similarity metric with soft spatial constraint for a deformable image registration problem in radiation therapy. In: Proc. of Medical Image Computing and Computer-Assisted Intervention (MICCAI), pp. 828–836. https://doi.org/10.1007/978-3-642-04268-3_102.

Kheradvar, Arash, Rickers, Carsten, Morisawa, Daisuke, Kim, Minji, Hong, Geu-Ru, Pedrizzetti, Gianni, 2019. Diagnostic and prognostic significance of cardiovascular vortex formation. Journal of Cardiology 74 (5), 403–411.

Kiefer, Gundolf, Lehmann, Helko, Weese, Jürgen, 2006. Fast maximum intensity projections of large medical data sets by exploiting hierarchical memory architectures. IEEE Transactions on Information Technology in Biomedicine 10 (2), 385–394.

Kikinis, R., Shenton, M.E., Iosifescu, D.V., McCarley, R.W., Saiviroonporn, P., Hokama, H.H., et al., 1996. A digital brain atlas for surgical planning, model driven segmentation and teaching. IEEE Transactions on Visualization and Computer Graphics 2 (3), 232–241.

Kilteni, Konstantina, Groten, Raphaela, Slater, Mel, 2012. The sense of embodiment in virtual reality. Presence: Teleoperators & Virtual Environments 21 (4), 373–387.

Kim, Dong-Joon, Kim, Bohyoung, Lee, Jeongjin, Shin, Juneseuk, Kim, Kyoung Won, Shin, Yeong-Gil, 2016. High-quality slab-based intermixing method for fusion rendering of multiple medical objects. Computer Methods and Programs in Biomedicine 123, 27–42.

Kim, Jaehun, Kim, Kwanguk, Kim, Deog Young, Chang, Won Hyek, Park, Chang-Il, Ohn, Suk Hoon, et al., 2007a. Virtual environment training system for rehabilitation of stroke patients with unilateral neglect: crossing the virtual street. Cyberpsychology & Behavior 10 (1), 7–15.

Kim, Jinman, Cai, Weidong, Eberl, Stefan, Feng, Dagan, 2007b. Real-time volume rendering visualization of dual-modality PET/CT images with interactive fuzzy thresholding segmentation. IEEE Transactions on Information Technology in Biomedicine 11 (2), 161–169.

Kim, Jinman, Eberl, Stefan, Feng, David Dagan, 2007c. Visualizing dual-modality rendered volumes using a dual-lookup table transfer function. Computing in Science & Engineering 9 (1), 20–25.

Kim, Yongjin, Yu, Jingyi, Yu, Xuan, Lee, Seungyong, 2008. Line-art illustration of dynamic and specular surfaces. ACM Transactions on Graphics 27 (5), 156:1–156:10. https://doi.org/10.1145/1409060.1409109.

Kimura, A., Yamashita, T., Akagi, T., Sasaki, T., Tatsumi, Y., Hasegawa, K., Tanaka, S., 2010. DICOM-RT extension support of visualization tool for radiotherapy simulation. In: IEEE Nuclear Science Symposium (NSS/MIC), pp. 1856–1859. https://doi.org/10.1109/NSSMIC.2010.5874096.

Kleinau, Anna, Stupak, Evgenia, Moerth, Eric, Garrison, Laura A., Mittenentzwei, Sarah, Smit, Noeska N., Lawonn, Kai, Bruckner, Stefan, Gutberlet, Matthias, Preim, Bernhard, Meuschke, Monique, 2022. Is there a tornado in Alex's blood flow? A case study for narrative medical visualization. In: Proc. of Eurographics Workshop on Visual Computing for Biology and Medicine (VCBM).

Kleinstreuer, Clement, 2016. Biofluid Dynamics: Principles and Selected Applications. CRC Press.

Klemm, Paul, Lawonn, Kai, Rak, Marko, Preim, Bernhard, Toennies, Klaus, Hegenscheid, Katrin, Völzke, Henry, Oeltze, Steffen, 2013. Visualization and analysis of lumbar spine canal variability in cohort study data. In: Proc. of Vision, Modeling, and Visualization, pp. 121–128.

Klemm, Paul, Oeltze-Jafra, Steffen, Lawonn, Kai, Hegenscheid, Katrin, Völzke, Henry, Preim, Bernhard, 2014. Interactive visual analysis of image-centric cohort study data. IEEE Transactions on Visualization and Computer Graphics 20 (12), 1673–1682.

Klemm, Paul, Lawonn, Kai, Glaßer, Sylvia, Niemann, Uli, Hegenscheid, Katrin, Völzke, Henry, Preim, Bernhard, 2016. 3D regression heat map analysis of population study data. IEEE Transactions on Visualization and Computer Graphics 22 (1), 81–90.

Kockro, Ralf A., Serra, Luis, Tseng-Tsai, Yeo, Chan, Chumpon, Yih-Yian, Sitoh, Gim-Guan, Chua, Lee, Eugene, Hoe, Lee Yen, Hern, Ng, Nowinski, Wieslaw L., 2000. Planning and simulation of neurosurgery in a virtual reality environment. Neurosurgery 46 (1), 118–137.

Koenderink, Jan J., Van Doorn, Andrea J., Kappers, Astrid ML, 1992. Surface perception in pictures. Perception & Psychophysics 52 (5), 487–496.

Köhler, Benjamin, Gasteiger, Rocco, Preim, Uta, Theisel, Holger, Gutberlet, Matthias, Preim, Bernhard, 2013. Semi-automatic vortex extraction in 4D PC-MRI cardiac blood flow data using line predicates. IEEE Transactions on Visualization and Computer Graphics 19 (12), 2773–2782.

Köhler, Benjamin, Meuschke, Monique, Preim, Uta, Fischbach, Katharina, Gutberlet, Matthias, Preim, Bernhard, 2015. Two-dimensional plot visualization of aortic vortex flow in cardiac 4D PC-MRI data. In: Bildverarbeitung für die Medizin, pp. 257–261.

Köhler, Benjamin, Preim, Uta, Grothoff, Matthias, Gutberlet, Matthias, Fischbach, Katharina, Preim, Bernhard, 2016a. Robust cardiac function assessment in 4D PC-MRI data of the aorta and pulmonary artery. Computer Graphics Forum 35 (1), 32–43.

Köhler, Benjamin, Preim, Uta, Grothoff, Matthias, Gutberlet, Matthias, Fischbach, Katharina, Preim, Bernhard, 2016b. Motion-aware stroke volume quantification in 4D PC-MRI data of the human aorta. International Journal of Computer Assisted Radiology and Surgery 11 (2), 169–179. https://doi.org/10.1007/s11548-015-1256-4.

Köhler, Benjamin, Preim, Uta, Grothoff, Matthias, Gutberlet, Matthias, Preim, Bernhard, 2016c. Adaptive animations of vortex flow extracted from cardiac 4D PC-MRI data. In: Proc. of Workshop Bildverarbeitung für die Medizin, pp. 194–199.

Köhler, Benjamin, Born, Silvia, van Pelt, Roy, Hennemuth, Anja, Preim, Uta, Preim, Bernhard, 2017. A survey of cardiac 4D PC-MRI data processing. Computer Graphics Forum 36 (5), 5–35.

Köhler, Benjamin, Grothoff, Matthias, Gutberlet, Matthias, Preim, Bernhard, 2018. Visual and quantitative analysis of great arteries' blood flow jets in cardiac 4D PC-MRI data. Computer Graphics Forum 37 (3), 195–204.

Köhler, Benjamin, Grothoff, Matthias, Gutberlet, Matthias, Bloodline, Bernhard Preim, 2019. A system for the guided analysis of cardiac 4D PC-MRI data. Computers & Graphics 82, 32–43.

Kolomenkin, Michael, Shimshoni, Ilan, Tal, Ayellet, 2008. Demarcating curves for shape illustration. ACM Transactions on Graphics 27 (5), 157:1–157:9. https://doi.org/10.1145/1409060.1409110.

Kong, V., Wenz, J., Craig, T., Milosevic, M., 2013. Image-guided adaptive radiotherapy – delivering personalized radiation medicine to improve treatment quality and patients' outcome. Journal of Medical Imaging and Radiation Sciences 44 (1), 55–56. https://doi.org/10.1016/j.jmir.2012.12.039.

Konrad-Verse, Olaf, Littmann, Arne, Preim, Bernhard, 2004. Virtual resection with a deformable cutting plane. In: Proc. of Simulation and Visualization, pp. 203–214.

Kontson, Kimberly, Marcus, Ian, Myklebust, Barbara, Civillico, Eugene, 2017. Targeted box and blocks test: normative data and comparison to standard tests. PLoS ONE 12 (5), e0177965.

Kopper, Regis, Bacim, Felipe, Bowman, Doug A., 2011. Rapid and accurate 3D selection by progressive refinement. In: Proc. of IEEE Symposium on 3D User Interfaces (3DUI), pp. 67–74.

Kosslyn, Stephen M., Thompson, William L., Wraga, Mary, Alpert, Nathaniel M., 2001. Imagining rotation by endogenous versus exogenous forces: distinct neural mechanisms. NeuroReport 12 (11), 2519–2525.

Kraak, Menno-Jan, Edsall, Rob, MacEachren, Alan M., 1997. Cartographic animation and legends for temporal maps: exploration and or interaction. In: Proc. of Cartographic Conference, vol. 1, pp. 253–261.

Kraima, A.C., Smit, N.N., Jansma, D., Wallner, C., Bleys, R., van de Velde, C.J.H., et al., 2013. Toward a highly-detailed 3D pelvic model: approaching an ultra-specific level for surgical simulation and anatomical education. Clinical Anatomy 26 (3), 333–338.

Krause, Josua, Perer, Adam, Stavropoulos, Harry, 2015. Supporting iterative cohort construction with visual temporal queries. IEEE Transactions on Visualization and Computer Graphics 22 (1), 91–100.

Kreiser, Julian, Meuschke, Monique, Mistelbauer, Gabriel, Preim, Bernhard, Ropinski, Timo, 2018. A survey of flattening-based medical visualization techniques. Computer Graphics Forum 37 (3), 597–624.

Kretschmer, Jan, Godenschwager, Christian, Preim, Bernhard, Stamminger, Marc, 2013. Interactive patient-specific vascular modeling with sweep surfaces. IEEE Transactions on Visualization and Computer Graphics 19 (12), 2828–2837.

Kriegel, Hans-Peter, Kröger, Peer, Zimek, Arthur, 2009. Clustering high-dimensional data: a survey on subspace clustering, pattern-based clustering, and correlation clustering. ACM Transactions on Knowledge Discovery from Data 3 (1), 1–58.

Krijn, Merel, Emmelkamp, Paul M.G., Biemond, Roeline, de Wilde de Ligny, Claudius, Schuemie, Martijn J., van der Mast, Charles A.P.G., 2004a. Treatment of acrophobia in virtual reality: the role of immersion and presence. Behaviour Research and Therapy 42 (2), 229–239.

Krijn, Merel, Emmelkamp, Paul M.G., Olafsson, Ragnar P., Biemond, Roeline, 2004b. Virtual reality exposure therapy of anxiety disorders: a review. Clinical Psychology Review 24 (3), 259–281.

Krings, Timo, Mandell, Daniel M., Kiehl, Tim-Rasmus, Geibprasert, Sasikhan, Tymianski, Michael, Alvarez, Hortensia, terBrugge, Karel G., Hans, Franz-Josef, 2011. Intracranial aneurysms: from vessel wall pathology to therapeutic approach. Nature Reviews Neurology 7 (10), 547–559.

Kroes, Thomas, Post, Frits H., Botha, Charl, 2012. Exposure render: an interactive photo-realistic volume rendering framework. PLoS ONE 7 (7), e38586.

Krueger, Robert, Beyer, Johanna, Jang, Won-Dong, Kim, Nam Wook, Sokolov, Artem, Sorger, Peter K., Pfister, Hanspeter, 2019. Facetto: combining unsupervised and supervised learning for hierarchical phenotype analysis in multi-channel image data. IEEE Transactions on Visualization and Computer Graphics 26 (1), 227–237.

Krüger, Arno, Kubisch, Christoph, Strauß, Gero, Preim, Bernhard, 2008. Sinus endoscopy - application of advanced GPU volume rendering for virtual endoscopy. IEEE Transactions on Visualization and Computer Graphics 14 (6), 1491–1498.

Kuhn, Alexander, Lehmann, Dirk J., Gasteiger, Rocco, Neugebauer, Mathias, Preim, Bernhard, Theisel, Holger, 2011. A clustering-based visualization technique to emphasize meaningful regions of vector fields. In: Vision, Modeling and Visualization, pp. 191–198.

Kühnel, Wolfgang, 2006. Differential Geometry: Curves - Surfaces - Manifolds. Student mathematical library. American Mathematical Society. https://doi.org/10.1007/978-3-658-00615-0.

Kurul, Ramazan, Oeguen, Muhammed Nur, Neriman Narin, Ayse, Avci, Sebnem, Yaz-gan, Beyza, 2020. An alternative method for anatomy training: immersive virtual reality. Anatomical Sciences Education 13 (5), 648–656.

Kwon, Bum Chul, Anand, Vibha, Severson, Kristen A., Ghosh, Soumya, Sun, Zhaonan, Frohnert, Brigitte I., Lundgren, Markus, Ng, Kenney, 2020. DPVis: visual analytics with hidden Markov models for disease progression pathways. IEEE Transactions on Visualization and Computer Graphics 27 (9), 3685–3700.

Kwon, Yunmi, Yang, Heekyung, Min, Kyungha, 2012. Pencil rendering on 3D meshes using convolution. Computers & Graphics 36 (8), 930–944. https://doi.org/10.1016/j.cag.2012.08.002.

Lake, Adam, Marshall, Carl, Harris, Mark, Blackstein, Marc, 2000. Stylized rendering techniques for scalable real-time 3D animation. In: Proc. NPAR. ACM, pp. 13–20. https://doi.org/10.1145/340916.340918.

Lam, Heidi, Bertini, Enrico, Isenberg, Petra, Plaisant, Catherine, Carpendale, Sheelagh, 2011. Empirical studies in information visualization: seven scenarios. IEEE Transactions on Visualization and Computer Graphics 18 (9), 1520–1536.

Lamecker, Hans, Seebaß, Martin, Lange, Thomas, Hege, Hans-Christian, Deuflhard, Peter, 2004. Visualization of the variability of 3D statistical shape models by animation. Studies in Health Technology and Informatics, 190–196.

Lamecker, Hans, Mansi, Tommaso, Relan, Jatin, Billet, Florence, Sermesant, Maxime, Ayache, Nicholas, Delingette, Hervé, 2009. Adaptive tetrahedral meshing for personalized cardiac simulations. In: Proc. of MICCAI Workshop on Cardiovascular Interventional Imaging and Biophysical Modelling, pp. 149–158.

Lange, Devin, Polanco, Eddie, Judson-Torres, Robert, Zangle, Thomas, Lex, Alexander, 2021. Loon: using exemplars to visualize large-scale microscopy data. IEEE Transactions on Visualization and Computer Graphics 28 (1), 248–258.

Lantz, Jonas, Dyverfeldt, Petter, Ebbers, Tino, 2014. Improving blood flow simulations by incorporating measured subject-specific wall motion. Cardiovascular Engineering and Technology 5 (3), 261–269. https://doi.org/10.1007/s13239-014-0187-5.

Larrabide, I., Aguilar, M.L., Morales, H.G., Geers, A.J., Kulcsár, Z., Rüfenacht, D., Frangi, A.F., 2012. Intra-aneurysmal pressure and flow changes induced by flow diverters: relation to aneurysm size and shape. American Journal of Neuroradiology 34 (4), 816–822.

Lasseter, John, 1987. Principles of traditional animation applied to 3D computer animation. In: Proc. of ACM SIGGRAPH, pp. 35–44.

Läthen, Gunnar, Lindholm, Stefan, Lenz, Reiner, Persson, Anders, Borga, Magnus, 2012. Automatic tuning of spatially varying transfer functions for blood vessel visualization. IEEE Transactions on Visualization and Computer Graphics 5, 2345–2352.

Latoschik, Marc Erich, Roth, Daniel, Gall, Dominik, Achenbach, Jascha, Waltemate, Thomas, Botsch, Mario, 2017. The effect of avatar realism in immersive social virtual realities. In: Proc. of ACM Symposium on Virtual Reality Software and Technology, pp. 1–10.

Latzitis, N., Sundmacher, L., Busse, R., 2010. Regional differences in life expectancy in Germany at county levels and their possible determinants. Gesundheitswesen (Bundesverband der Arzte des Offentlichen Gesundheitsdienstes (Germany)) 73 (4), 217–228.

LaViola Jr., Joseph J., Kruijff, Ernst, McMahan, Ryan P., Bowman, Doug, Poupyrev, Ivan P., 2017. 3D User Interfaces: Theory and Practice. Addison-Wesley Professional.

Lawonn, Kai, 2014. Illustrative Visualization of Medical Data Sets. PhD thesis. University of Magdeburg, Germany.

Lawonn, Kai, Preim, Bernhard, 2016. Feature lines for illustrating medical surface models: mathematical background and survey. In: Linsen, Lars, Hamann, Bernd, Hege, Hans-Christian (Eds.), Visualization in Medicine in Life Sciences III. Springer, Berlin/Heidelberg, pp. 93–132. https://doi.org/10.1007/978-3-319-24523-2_5.

Lawonn, Kai, Gasteiger, Rocco, Preim, Bernhard, 2013a. Adaptive surface visualization of vessels with embedded blood flow based on the suggestive contour measure. In: Proc. of Vision, Modeling, and Visualization, pp. 113–120.

Lawonn, Kai, Gasteiger, Rocco, Preim, Bernhard, 2013b. Qualitative evaluation of feature lines on anatomical surfaces. In: Proc. of Workshop Bildverarbeitung für die Medizin. Springer, Berlin/Heidelberg, pp. 187–192. https://doi.org/10.1007/978-3-642-36480-8_34.

Lawonn, Kai, Mönch, Tobias, Preim, Bernhard, 2013c. Streamlines for illustrative real-time rendering. Computer Graphics Forum 32 (3), 321–330. https://doi.org/10.1111/cgf.12119.

Lawonn, Kai, Baer, Alexandra, Saalfeld, Patrick, Preim, Bernhard, 2014a. Comparative evaluation of feature line techniques for shape depiction. In: Proc. of Vision, Modeling, and Visualization, pp. 31–38. https://doi.org/10.2312/vmv.20141273.

Lawonn, Kai, Gasteiger, Rocco, Preim, Bernhard, 2014b. Adaptive surface visualization of vessels with animated blood flow. Computer Graphics Forum 33 (8), 16–27.

Lawonn, Kai, Krone, Michael, Ertl, Thomas, Preim, Bernhard, 2014c. Line integral convolution for real-time illustration of molecular surface shape and salient regions. Computer Graphics Forum 33 (3), 181–190. https://doi.org/10.1111/cgf.12374.

Lawonn, Kai, Saalfeld, Patrick, Preim, Bernhard, 2014d. Illustrative visualization of endoscopic views. In: Bildverarbeitung für die Medizin (BVM), pp. 276–281.

Lawonn, Kai, Luz, Maria, Preim, Bernhard, Hansen, Christian, 2015a. Illustrative visualization of vascular models for static 2D representations. In: Proc. of Medical Image Computing and Computer-Assisted Intervention (MICCAI), pp. 399–406. https://doi.org/10.1007/978-3-319-24571-3_48.

Lawonn, Kai, Smit, Noeska N., Preim, Bernhard, Vilanova, Anna, 2015b. Illustrative multi-volume rendering for PET/CT scans. In: Proc. of Eurographics Workshop on Visual Computing for Biology and Medicine (VCBM), pp. 103–112.

Lawonn, Kai, Glaßer, Sylvia, Vilanova, Anna, Preim, Bernhard, Isenberg, Tobias, 2016. Occlusion-free blood flow animation with wall thickness visualization. IEEE Transactions on Visualization and Computer Graphics 22 (1), 728–737.

Lawonn, Kai, Luz, Maria, Hansen, Christian, 2017. Improving spatial perception of vascular models using supporting anchors and illustrative visualization. Computers & Graphics 63, 37–49. https://doi.org/10.1016/j.cag.2017.02.002.

Lawonn, Kai, Smit, Noeska N., Bühler, Katja, Preim, Bernhard, 2018a. A survey on multimodal medical data visualization. Computer Graphics Forum 37 (1), 413–438.

Lawonn, Kai, Viola, Ivan, Preim, Bernhard, Isenberg, Tobias, 2018b. A survey of surface-based illustrative rendering for visualization. Computer Graphics Forum 37 (6), 205–234.

Lawonn, Kai, Meuschke, Monique, Wickenhöfer, Ralph, Preim, Bernhard, Hildebrandt, Klaus, 2019. A geometric optimization approach for the detection and segmentation of multiple aneurysms. Computer Graphics Forum 38 (3), 413–425.

Lécuyer, Anatole, Burkhardt, J.-M., Henaff, J.-M., Donikian, Stéphane, 2006. Camera motions improve the sensation of walking in virtual environments. In: Proc. of IEEE Virtual Reality Conference, pp. 11–18.

Lee, Hyunjun, Kwon, Sungtae, Lee, Seungyong, 2006. Real-time pencil rendering. In: Proc. NPAR. ACM, pp. 37–45. https://doi.org/10.1145/1124728.1124735.

Lee, J.S., Jani, A.B., Pelizzari, C.A., Haraf, D.J., Vokes, E.E., Weichselbaum, R.R., Chen, G.T., 1999. Volumetric visualization of head and neck CT data for treatment planning. International Journal of Radiation Oncology, Biology, Physics 44 (3), 693–703.

Lee, Percy, Kupelian, Patrick, Czernin, Johannes, Ghosh, Partha, 2012. Current concepts in F18 FDG PET/CT-based radiation therapy planning for lung cancer. Frontiers in Oncology 2. https://doi.org/10.3389/fonc.2012.00071.

Lee, Tong-Yee, Lin, Chao-Hung, 2000. Interactive animation of 4D medical imaging. In: Proc. of IEEE EMBS Int. Conf. on Information Technology Applications in Biomedicine, pp. 232–237.

Leibel, Steven A., Fuks, Zvi, Zelefsky, Michael J., Wolden, Suzanne L., Rosenzweig, Kenneth E., Alektiar, Kaled M., Hunt, Margie A., Yorke, Ellen D., Hong, Linda X., Amols, Howard I., et al., 2002. Intensity-modulated radiotherapy. The Cancer Journal 8 (2), 164–176.

Lemole Jr., G. Michael, Banerjee, P. Pat, Luciano, Cristian, Neckrysh, Sergey, Charbel, Fady T., 2007. Virtual reality in neurosurgical education: part-task ventriculostomy simulation with dynamic visual and haptic feedback. Neurosurgery 61 (1), 142–149.

Lengyel, Zoltán, Umenhoffer, Tamás, Szécsi, László, 2013. Screen space features for real-time hatching synthesis. In: Képfeldolgozók és Alakfelismerők Társaságának, pp. 82–94.

Lengyel, Zoltán, Umenhoffer, Tamás, Szécsi, László, 2014. Realtime, coherent screen space hatching. In: Proc. Hungarian Computer Graphics and Geometry Conference, pp. 131–137.

Lentz, Tobias, Schröder, Dirk, Vorländer, Michael, Assenmacher, Ingo, 2007. Virtual reality system with integrated sound field simulation and reproduction. EURASIP Journal on Advances in Signal Processing 2007, 1–19.

Leuwer, Rudolf, Petersik, Andreas, Pflesser, Bernhard, Pommert, Andreas, Tolsdorff, Boris, Höhne, Karl Heinz, Tiede, Ulf, 2007. VOXEL-MAN TempoSurg: a virtual reality temporal bone surgery simulator. Journal of Japan Society for Head and Neck Surgery 17 (3), 203–207.

Levin, Daniel T., Momen, Nausheen, Drivdahl IV, Sarah B., Simons, Daniel J., 2000. Change blindness blindness: the metacognitive error of overestimating change-detection ability. Visual Cognition 7 (1–3), 397–412.

Levin, Mindy F., Magdalon, Eliane C., Michaelsen, Stella M., Quevedo, Antonio A.F., 2015. Quality of grasping and the role of haptics in a 3-D immersive virtual reality environment in individuals with stroke. IEEE Transactions on Neural Systems and Rehabilitation Engineering 23 (6), 1047–1055.

Levoy, Marc, 1988. Display of surfaces from volume data. IEEE CG&A 8 (3), 29–37.

Lewis, T.L., Burnett, B., Tunstall, R.G., Abrahams, P.H., 2014. Complementing anatomy education using three-dimensional anatomy mobile software applications on tablet computers. Clinical Anatomy 27 (3), 313–320.

Li, Guang, Xie, Huchen, Ning, Holly, Capala, Jacek, Arora, Barbara C., Coleman, C. Norman, Camphausen, Kevin, Miller, Robert W., 2005. A novel 3D volumetric voxel registration technique for volume-view-guided image registration of multiple imaging modalities. International Journal of Radiation Oncology, Biology, Physics 63 (1), 261–273. https://doi.org/10.1016/j.ijrobp.2005.05.008.

Li, Jia, Huang, Shanqing, Li, Gui, Cao, Ruifen, Pei, Xi, Zheng, Huaqing, Song, Gang, Wu, Yican, 2010. Reconstruction and visualization of 3D surface model from serial-sectioned contour points. In: International Congress on Image and Signal Processing, vol. 5, pp. 2396–2400. https://doi.org/10.1109/CISP.2010.5646297.

Li, Meng, Ganni, Sandeep, Ponten, Jeroen, Albayrak, Armagan, Rutkowski, Anne-F., Jakimowicz, Jack, 2020. Analysing usability and presence of a virtual reality operating room

(VOR) simulator during laparoscopic surgery training. In: Proc. of IEEE Conference on Virtual Reality and 3D User Interfaces, pp. 566–572.

Liaw, Sok Ying, Carpio, Guiller Augustin C., Lau, Ying, Tan, Seng Chee, Lim, Wee Shiong, Goh, Poh Sun, 2018. Multiuser virtual worlds in healthcare education: a systematic review. Nurse Education Today 65, 136–149.

Lichtenberg, Nils, Lawonn, Kai, 2019. Parameterization, feature extraction and binary encoding for the visualization of tree-like structures. Computer Graphics Forum 39 (1), 497–510.

Lichtenberg, Nils, Smit, Noeska, Hansen, Christian, Lawonn, Kai, 2016. Sline: seamless line illustration for interactive biomedical visualization. In: Proc. of Eurographics Workshop on Visual Computing for Biology and Medicine (VCBM), pp. 133–142. https://doi.org/10.2312/vcbm.20161281.

Lichtenberg, Nils, Hansen, Christian, Lawonn, Kai, 2017. Concentric circle glyphs for enhanced depth-judgment in vascular models. In: Proc. of Eurographics Workshop on Visual Computing for Biology and Medicine (VCBM), pp. 178–188.

Lichtenberg, Nils, Smit, Noeska, Hansen, Christian, Lawonn, Kai, 2018. Real-time field aligned stripe patterns. Computers & Graphics 74, 137–149. https://doi.org/10.1016/j.cag.2018.04.008.

Lim, M.W., Burt, G., Rutter, S.V., 2004. Use of three-dimensional animation for regional anaesthesia teaching: application to interscalene brachial plexus blockade. British Journal of Anaesthesia 94 (3), 372–377.

Lim, Stephen S., Vos, Theo, Flaxman, Abraham D., Danaei, Goodarz, Shibuya, Kenji, Adair-Rohani, Heather, et al., 2012. A comparative risk assessment of burden of disease and injury attributable to 67 risk factors and risk factor clusters in 21 regions, 1990–2010: a systematic analysis for the Global Burden of Disease Study 2010. The Lancet 380 (9859), 2224–2260.

Lindemann, Florian, Ropinski, Timo, 2011. About the influence of illumination models on image comprehension in direct volume rendering. IEEE Transactions on Visualization and Computer Graphics 17 (12), 1922–1931.

Lindemann, Joerg, Keck, Tilman, Wiesmiller, Kerstin, Sander, Bjoern, Brambs, Hans-Juergen, Rettinger, Gerhard, Pless, Daniela, 2006. Nasal air temperature and airflow during respiration in numerical simulation based on multislice computed tomography scan. American Journal of Rhinology 20, 219–223.

Lindgren, Robb, Johnson-Glenberg, Mina, 2013. Emboldened by embodiment: six precepts for research on embodied learning and mixed reality. Educational Researcher 42 (8), 445–452.

Lindley, Sarah J., Handley, John F., McEvoy, Darryn, Peet, Elizabeth, Theuray, Nicolas, 2007. The role of spatial risk assessment in the context of planning for adaptation in UK urban areas. Built Environment 33 (1), 46–69.

Liu, Yanmei, Xue, Dingyu, Xu, Xinhe, Li, Yibo, Cui, Jianguo, 2006. Computer simulation of radiotherapy dose distribution in tissue. In: World Congress on Intelligent Control and Automation, vol. 2, pp. 6142–6145. https://doi.org/10.1109/WCICA.2006.1714262.

Liu, Yu, Zhang, Chao, Li, Chang, Cheng, Juan, Zhang, Yadong, Xu, Huiqin, Song, Tao, Zhao, Liang, Chen, Xun, 2020. A practical PET/CT data visualization method with dual-threshold PET colorization and image fusion. Computers in Biology and Medicine 126, 104050.

Livnat, Yarden, Rhyne, Theresa-Marie, Samore, Matthew H., 2012. Epinome: a visual-analytics workbench for epidemiology data. IEEE CG&A 32 (2), 89–95.

Ljung, Patric, Winskog, Calle, Persson, Anders, Lundstrom, Claes, Ynnerman, Anders, 2006. Full body virtual autopsies using a state-of-the-art volume rendering pipeline. IEEE Transactions on Visualization and Computer Graphics 12 (5), 869–876.

Ljung, Patric, Krüger, Jens, Groller, Eduard, Hadwiger, Markus, Hansen, Charles D., Ynnerman, Anders, 2016. State of the art in transfer functions for direct volume rendering. Computer Graphics Forum 35 (3), 669–691.

Löhner, Rainald, 1996. Progress in grid generation via the advancing front technique. Engineering With Computers 12 (3–4), 186–210.

Lombardo, Jean-Christophe, Cani, Marie-Paule, Neyret, Fabrice, 1999. Real-time collision detection for virtual surgery. In: Proc. of Computer Animation. IEEE, pp. 82–90.

Lopez, Christopher, Halje, Pär, Blanke, Olaf, 2008. Body ownership and embodiment: vestibular and multisensory mechanisms. Neurophysiologie Clinique/Clinical Neurophysiology 38 (3), 149–161.

Lorensen, William, Jolesz, Ferenc, Kikinis, Ron, 1995. The exploration of cross-sectional data with a virtual endoscope. In: Interactive Technology and the New Medical Paradigm for Health Care, pp. 221–230.

Lorensen, William E., Cline, Harvey E., 1987. Marching cubes: a high resolution 3D surface construction algorithm. ACM SIGGRAPH Computer Graphics 21 (4), 163–169.

Lorenz, Ramona, Bock, Jelena, Snyder, Jeff, Korvink, Jan G., Jung, Bernd A., Markl, Michael, 2014. Influence of eddy current, Maxwell and gradient field corrections on 3D flow visualization of 3D CINE PC-MRI data. Magnetic Resonance in Medicine 72 (1), 33–40.

Lou, Liming, Wang, Lu, Meng, Xiangxu, 2015. Stylized strokes for coherent line drawings. Computational Visual Media 1 (1), 79–89. https://doi.org/10.1007/s41095-015-0009-1.

Lu, J., Pan, Z., Lin, H., Zhang, M., Shi, J., 2005. Virtual learning environment for medical education based on VRML and VTK. Computers & Graphics 29 (2), 283–288.

Lundervold, Alexander Selvikvåg, Lundervold, Arvid, 2018. An overview of deep learning in medical imaging focusing on MRI. Zeitschrift für Medizinische Physik. https://doi.org/10.1016/j.zemedi.2018.11.002.

Lundström, Claes, Ljung, Patric, Persson, Anders, Ynnerman, Anders, 2007. Uncertainty visualization in medical volume rendering using probabilistic animation. IEEE Transactions on Visualization and Computer Graphics 13 (6), 1648–1655.

Luz, Saturnino, Masoodian, Masood, 2014. Readability of a background map layer under a semi-transparent foreground layer. In: Proc. of ACM Conference on Advanced Visual Interfaces, pp. 161–168.

Lysaker, Marius, Lundervold, Arvid, Tai, Xue-Cheng, 2003. Noise removal using fourth-order partial differential equation with applications to medical magnetic resonance images in space and time. IEEE Transactions on Image Processing 12 (12), 1579–1590.

Ma, Kwan-Liu, Liao, Isaac, Frazier, Jennifer, Hauser, Helwig, Kostis, Helen-Nicole, 2012. Scientific storytelling using visualization. IEEE CG&A 32 (1), 12–19.

Ma, Minhua, Zheng, Huiru, Lallie, Harjinder, 2010. Virtual reality and 3D animation in forensic visualization. Journal of Forensic Sciences 55 (5), 1227–1231.

Maass, Stefan, Döllner, Jürgen, 2008. Seamless integration of labels into interactive virtual 3D environments using parameterized hulls. In: Proc. of Eurographics Workshop on Computational Aesthetics, pp. 33–40.

Mabray, Marc C., Barajas, Ramon F., Cha, Soonmee, 2015. Modern brain tumor imaging. Brain Tumor Research and Treatment 3 (1), 8–23.

MacEachren, Alan M., Boscoe, Francis P., Haug, Daniel, Pickle, Linda W., 1998. Geographic visualization: designing manipulable maps for exploring temporally varying georeferenced statistics. In: Proc. of IEEE Symposium on Information Visualization, pp. 87–94.

MacEachren, Alan M., Gahegan, Mark, Pike, William, Brewer, Isaac, Cai, Guoray, Lengerich, Eugene, Hardisty, Frank, 2004. Geovisualization for knowledge construction and decision support. IEEE CG&A 24 (1), 13–17.

MacEachren, Alan M., Robinson, Anthony, Hopper, Susan, Gardner, Steven, Murray, Robert, Gahegan, Mark, Hetzler, Elisabeth, 2005. Visualizing geospatial information uncertainty: what we know and what we need to know. Cartography and Geographic Information Science 32 (3), 139–160.

MacEachren, Alan M., Roth, Robert E., O'Brien, James, Li, Bonan, Swingley, Derek, Gahegan, Mark, 2012. Visual semiotics & uncertainty visualization: an empirical study. IEEE Transactions on Visualization and Computer Graphics 18 (12), 2496–2505.

Maciejewski, R., Tyner, B., Jang, Y., Zheng, C., Nehme, R.V., Ebert, D.S., Cleveland, W.S., Ouzzani, M., Grannis, S.J., Glickman, L.T., 2007. LAHVA: linked animal-human health visual analytics. In: Proc. of IEEE Visual Analytics Science and Technology, pp. 27–34.

Maciejewski, Ross, Rudolph, Stephen, Hafen, Ryan, Abusalah, Ahmad M., Yakout, Mohamed, Ouzzani, Mourad, Cleveland, William S., Grannis, Shaun J., Wade, Michael, Ebert, David S., 2008. Understanding syndromic hotspots - a visual analytics approach. In: Proc. of IEEE Visual Analytics Science and Technology, pp. 35–42.

Maciejewski, Ross, Hafen, Ryan, Rudolph, Stephen, Tebbetts, George, Cleveland, William S., Grannis, Shaun J., Ebert, David S., 2009. Generating synthetic syndromic-surveillance data for evaluating visual-analytics techniques. IEEE CG&A 29 (3), 18–28.

Maciejewski, Ross, Livengood, Philip, Rudolph, Stephen, Collins, Timothy F., Ebert, David S., Brigantic, Robert T., et al., 2011. A pandemic influenza modeling and visualization tool. Journal of Visual Languages and Computing 22 (4), 268–278.

Mackinlay, Jock D., Card, Stuart K., Robertson, George G., 1990. Rapid controlled movement through a virtual 3D workspace. In: Proc. of ACM SIGGRAPH, pp. 171–176.

Madary, Michael, Metzinger, Thomas K., 2016. Real virtuality: a code of ethical conduct. Recommendations for good scientific practice and the consumers of VR-technology. Frontiers in Robotics and AI 3 (3).

Mahadevia, R., Barker, A.J., Schnell, S., Entezari, P., Kansal, P., Fedak, P.W.M., Malaisrie, S.C., McCarthy, P., Collins, J., Carr, J., Markl, M., 2015. Bicuspid aortic cusp fusion morphology alters aortic 3D outflow patterns, wall shear stress and expression of aortopathy. Circulation 129 (6), 673–682.

Mahmud, Waqas, Hyder, Omar, Butt, Jamaal, Aftab, Arsalan, 2011. Dissection videos do not improve anatomy examination scores. Anatomical Sciences Education 4 (1), 16–21.

Manssour, Isabel H., Furuie, Sergio S., Olabarriaga, Silvia D., Freitas, C.M.D.S., 2002. Visualizing inner structures in multimodal volume data. In: Proc. of Computer Graphics and Image Processing, pp. 51–58.

Marathe, Madhav, Vullikanti, Anil Kumar S., 2013. Computational epidemiology. Communications of the ACM 56 (7), 88–96.

Maresky, H.S., Oikonomou, A., Ali, I., Ditkofsky, N., Pakkal, M., Ballyk, B., 2019. Virtual reality and cardiac anatomy: exploring immersive three-dimensional cardiac imaging, a pilot study in undergraduate medical anatomy education. Clinical Anatomy 32 (2), 238–243.

Mariani, Giuliano, Bruselli, Laura, Kuwert, Torsten, Kim, Edmund E., Flotats, Albert, Israel, Ora, Dondi, Maurizio, Watanabe, Naoyuki, 2010. A review on the clinical uses of SPECT/CT. European Journal of Nuclear Medicine and Molecular Imaging 37 (10), 1959–1985.

Markl, M., Brendecke, S., Simon, J., Frydrychowicz, A., Harloff, A., 2010. Coregistration of wall shear stress and plaque distribution within the thoracic aorta of acute stroke patients. In: Proc. of the International Society for Magnetic Resonance in Medicine, vol. 18, p. 63.

Markl, M., Frydrychowicz, A., Kozerke, S., Hope, M., Wieben, O., 2012. 4D flow MRI. Journal of Magnetic Resonance Imaging 36 (5), 1015–1036.

Markosian, Lee, Kowalski, Michael A., Goldstein, Daniel, Trychin, Samuel J., Hughes, John F., Bourdev, Lubomir D., 1997. Real-time nonphotorealistic rendering. In: Proc. of ACM SIGGRAPH. ACM, pp. 415–420. https://doi.org/10.1145/258734.258894.

Marks, Lawrence B., Yorke, Ellen D., Jackson, Andrew, Ten Haken, Randall K., Constine, Louis S., Eisbruch, Avraham, Bentzen, Søren M., Nam, Jiho, Deasy, Joseph O., 2010. Use of normal tissue complication probability models in the clinic. International Journal of Radiation Oncology, Biology, Physics 76 (3), S10–S19.

Marks, Stefan, White, David, Singh, Manpreet, 2017. Getting up your nose: a virtual reality education tool for nasal cavity anatomy. In: Proc. of SIGGRAPH Asia Symposium on Education, pp. 1–7.

Martin, N.A., Khanna, R., Doberstein, C., Bentson, J., 2000. Therapeutic embolization of arteriovenous malformations: the case for and against. Clinical Neurosurgery 46, 295–318.

Martinez, Ramon, Ordunez, Pedro, Soliz, Patricia N., Ballesteros, Michael F., 2016. Data visualisation in surveillance for injury prevention and control: conceptual bases and case studies. Injury Prevention 22 (Suppl 1), i27–i33.

Masoodian, Masood, Luz, Saturnino, Kavenga, David, 2016. Nu-view: a visualization system for collaborative co-located analysis of geospatial disease data. In: Proc. of the Australasian Computer Science Week Multiconference. ACM, p. 48.

Mathur, Maya B., Reichling, David B., 2016. Navigating a social world with robot partners: a quantitative cartography of the uncanny valley. Cognition 146, 22–32.

Matkovic, Kresimir, Freiler, Wolfgang, Gracanin, Denis, Hauser, Helwig, 2008. ComVis: a coordinated multiple views system for prototyping new visualization technology. In: Proc. of Information Visualisation. IEEE Computer Society, pp. 215–220.

McDougall, Elspeth M., 2007. Validation of surgical simulators. Journal of Endourology 21 (3), 244–247.

McGhee, John, 2010. 3-D visualization and animation technologies in anatomical imaging. Journal of Anatomy 216 (2), 264–270.

McInnes, Leland, Healy, John, Melville, James, 2018. UMAP: uniform manifold approximation and projection for dimension reduction. arXiv preprint. arXiv:1802.03426.

McKenzie, Alan, van Herk, Marcel, Mijnheer, Ben, 2002. Margins for geometric uncertainty around organs at risk in radiotherapy. Radiotherapy and Oncology 62 (3), 299–307.

Medeiros, Jonatas, Sousa, Mario, Velho, Luiz, Freitas, Carla Maria Dal Sasso, 2009. Perspective contouring in illustrative visualization. In: Proc. Computer Graphics and Image Processing. IEEE Computer Society, Los Alamitos, pp. 48–55. https://doi.org/10.1109/SIBGRAPI.2009.49.

Medina, Eliana, Fruland, Ruth, Weghorst, Suzanne, 2008. Virtusphere: walking in a human size VR "hamster ball". In: Proc. of the Human Factors and Ergonomics Society Annual Meeting, vol. 52, pp. 2102–2106.

Menter, F.R., 1994. Two-equation eddy-viscosity turbulence models for engineering applications. AIAA Journal 32 (8), 269–289.

Merten, Nico, Glaßer, Sylvia, Lassen-Schmidt, Bianca, Großer, Oliver Stephan, Ricke, Jens, Amthauer, Holger, Preim, Bernhard, 2016. Illustrative PET/CT visualisation of SIRT-treated lung metastases. In: Proc. of Eurographics Workshop on Visual Computing for Biology and Medicine (VCBM), pp. 99–103. https://doi.org/10.2312/vcbm.20161276.

Messier, Erik, Wilcox, Jascha, Dawson-Elli, Alexander, Diaz, Gabriel, Linte, Cristian A., 2016. An interactive 3D virtual anatomy puzzle for learning and simulation-initial demonstration and evaluation. In: Proc. of Medicine Meets Virtual Reality, pp. 233–240.

Meuschke, Monique, Köhler, Benjamin, Preim, Uta, Preim, Bernhard, Lawonn, Kai, 2016a. Semi-automatic vortex flow classification in 4D PC-MRI data of the aorta. Computer Graphics Forum 35 (3), 351–360.

Meuschke, Monique, Lawonn, Kai, Köhler, Benjamin, Preim, Uta, Preim, Bernhard, 2016b. Clustering of aortic vortex flow in cardiac 4D PC-MRI data. In: Proc. of Workshop Bildverarbeitung für die Medizin, pp. 182–187.

Meuschke, Monique, Engelke, Wito, Beuing, Oliver, Preim, Bernhard, Lawonn, Kai, 2017a. Automatic viewpoint selection for exploration of time-dependent cerebral aneurysm data. In: Proc. of Workshop Bildverarbeitung für die Medizin, pp. 352–357.

Meuschke, Monique, Voß, Samuel, Beuing, Oliver, Preim, Bernhard, Lawonn, Kai, 2017b. Combined visualization of vessel deformation and hemodynamics in cerebral aneurysms. IEEE Transactions on Visualization and Computer Graphics 23 (1), 761–770. https://doi.org/10.1109/TVCG.2016.2598795.

Meuschke, Monique, Voß, Samuel, Beuing, Oliver, Preim, Bernhard, Lawonn, Kai, 2017c. Glyph-based comparative stress tensor visualization in cerebral aneurysms. Computer Graphics Forum 36 (3), 99–108. https://doi.org/10.1111/cgf.13171.

Meuschke, Monique, Günther, Tobias, Berg, Philipp, Wickenhöfer, Ralph, Preim, Bernhard, Lawonn, Kai, 2018a. Visual analysis of aneurysm data using statistical graphics. IEEE Transactions on Visualization and Computer Graphics 25 (1), 997–1007.

Meuschke, Monique, Günther, Tobias, Wickenhöfer, Ralph, Gross, Markus H., Preim, Bernhard, Lawonn, Kai, 2018b. Management of cerebral aneurysm descriptors based on an automatic ostium extraction. IEEE CG&A 38 (3), 58–72. https://doi.org/10.1109/MCG.2018.032421654.

Meuschke, Monique, Voß, Samuel, Preim, Bernhard, Lawonn, Kai, 2018c. Exploration of blood flow patterns in cerebral aneurysms during the cardiac cycle. Computers & Graphics 72, 12–25.

Meuschke, Monique, Oeltze-Jafra, Steffen, Beuing, Oliver, Preim, Bernhard, Lawonn, Kai, 2019a. Classification of blood flow patterns in cerebral aneurysms. IEEE Transactions on Visualization and Computer Graphics 25 (7), 2404–2418.

Meuschke, Monique, Smit, Noeska N., Lichtenberg, Nils, Preim, Bernhard, Lawonn, Kai, 2019b. EvalViz–surface visualization evaluation wizard for depth and shape perception tasks. Computers & Graphics 82, 250–263.

Meuschke, Monique, Preim, Bernhard, Lawonn, Kai, 2021a. Aneulysis - a system for the visual analysis of aneurysm data. Computers & Graphics 98, 197–209.

Meuschke, Monique, Voß, Samuel, Gaidzik, Franziska, Preim, Bernhard, Lawonn, Kai, 2021b. Skyscraper visualization of multiple time-dependent scalar fields on surfaces. Computers & Graphics 99, 22–42. https://doi.org/10.1016/j.cag.2021.05.005.

Meuschke, Monique, Garrison, Laura A., Smit, Noeska N., Bach, Benjamin, Mittenentzwei, Sarah, Weiß, Veronika, Bruckner, Stefan, Lawonn, Kai, Preim, Bernhard, 2022a. Narrative medical visualization to communicate disease data. Computers & Graphics 107, 144–157.

Meuschke, Monique, Niemann, Uli, Behrendt, Benjamin, Gutberlet, Matthias, Preim, Bernhard, Lawonn, Kai, 2022b. GUCCI-guided cardiac cohort investigation of blood flow data. IEEE Transactions on Visualization and Computer Graphics.

Meuschke, Monique, Voß, Samuel, Eulzer, Pepe, Janiga, Gabor, Arens, Christoph, Wickenhøfer, Ralph, Preim, Bernhard, Lawonn, Kai, 2022c. COMFIS - comparative visualization of simulated medical flow data. In: Proc. of Eurographics Workshop on Visual Computing for Biology and Medicine (VCBM).

Miksch, Silvia, Aigner, Wolfgang, 2014. A matter of time: applying a data–users–tasks design triangle to visual analytics of time-oriented data. Computers & Graphics 38, 286–290.

Miksch, Silvia, Shahar, Yuval, Johnson, Peter, 1997. ASBRU: a task-specific, intention-based, and time-oriented language for representing skeletal plans. In: Proc. of the Workshop on Knowledge Engineering: Methods & Languages (KEML), pp. 9–19.

Min, Kyungha, 2013. Drawing features of 3D meshes in pencil-drawing style. Software Engineering and Its Applications 7 (6), 359–366. https://doi.org/10.14257/ijseia.2013.7.6.30.

Min, Kyungha, 2015. Feature-guided convolution for salient rendering of 3D meshes. Engineering Systems Modelling and Simulation 7 (1), 1–5. https://doi.org/10.1504/IJESMS.2015.066122.

Mine, Mark R., Brooks Jr., Frederick P., Sequin, Carlo H., 1997. Moving objects in space: exploiting proprioception in virtual-environment interaction. In: Proc. of ACM SIGGRAPH, pp. 19–26.

Minsky, Marvin, 1980. Telepresence. Omni, 45–52.

Mirelman, Anat, Maidan, Inbal, Herman, Talia, Deutsch, Judith E., Giladi, Nir, Hausdorff, Jeffrey M., 2010. Virtual reality for gait training: can it induce motor learning to enhance complex walking and reduce fall risk in patients with Parkinson's disease? Journals of Gerontology: Series A 66A (2), 234–240.

Mistelbauer, Gabriel, Schmidt, Johanna, Sailer, Anna-Margaretha, Bäumler, Kathrin, Walters, Shannon, Fleischmann, Dominik, 2016. Aortic dissection maps: comprehensive visualization of aortic dissections for risk assessment. In: Proc. of Eurographics Workshop on Visual Computing for Biology and Medicine (VCBM), pp. 143–152.

Mistelbauer, Gabriel, Rössl, Christian, Bäumler, Kathrin, Preim, Bernhard, Fleischmann, Dominik, 2021. Implicit modeling of patient-specific aortic dissections with elliptic Fourier descriptors. Computer Graphics Forum 40 (3), 423–434.

Mitchell, Jason L., Brennan, Chris, Card, Drew, 2002. Real-time image-space outlining for non-photorealistic rendering. In: Proc. of ACM SIGGRAPH, pp. 239–239, https://doi.org/10.1145/1242073.1242252.

Mittelstädt, Sebastian, Hao, Ming C., Dayal, Umeshwar, Hsu, Meichun, Terdiman, Joseph, Keim, Daniel A., 2014. Advanced visual analytics interfaces for adverse drug event detection. In: Proc. of ACM Conference on Advanced Visual Interfaces, pp. 237–244.

Mittenentzwei, Sarah, Beuing, Oliver, Neyazi, Belal, Sandalcioglu, I. Erol, Larsen, Naomi, Preim, Bernhard, Saalfeld, Sylvia, 2021. Definition and extraction of 2D shape indices of intracranial aneurysm necks for rupture risk assessment. International Journal of Computer Assisted Radiology and Surgery 16 (11), 1977–1984.

Molina, Karina Iglesia, Ricci, Natalia Aquaroni, de Moraes, Suzana Albuquerque, Perracini, Monica Rodrigues, 2014. Virtual reality using games for improving physical functioning in older adults: a systematic review. Journal of NeuroEngineering and Rehabilitation 11 (1), 1–20.

Mollemans, Wouter, Schutyser, Filip, Van Cleynenbreugel, Johan, Suetens, Paul, 2003. Tetrahedral mass spring model for fast soft tissue deformation. In: Proc. of International Symposium on Surgery Simulation and Soft Tissue Modeling, pp. 145–154.

Mönch, Tobias, Adler, Simon, Preim, Bernhard, 2010. Staircase-aware smoothing of medical surface meshes. In: Proc. of Eurographics Workshop on Visual Computing for Biology and Medicine (VCBM), pp. 83–90.

Mondellini, Marta, Arlati, Sara, Pizzagalli, Simone, Greci, Luca, Sacco, Marco, Ferrigno, Giancarlo, 2018. Assessment of the usability of an immersive virtual supermarket for the cognitive rehabilitation of elderly patients: a pilot study on young adults. In: Proc. of IEEE Serious Games and Applications for Health (SeGAH), pp. 1–8.

Monmonier, Mark, 2006. Cartography: uncertainty, interventions, and dynamic display. Progress in Human Geography 30 (3), 373–381.

Monmonier, Mark, Gluck, Myke, 1994. Focus groups for design improvement in dynamic cartography. Cartography and Geographic Information Systems 21 (1), 37–47.

Monroe, Megan, Lan, Rongjian, del Olmo, Juan Morales, Shneiderman, Ben, Plaisant, Catherine, Millstein, Jeff, 2013a. The challenges of specifying intervals and absences in temporal queries: a graphical language approach. In: Proc. of ACM SIGCHI Conference on Human Factors in Computing Systems (CHI), pp. 2349–2358.

Monroe, Megan, Lan, Rongjian, Lee, Hanseung, Plaisant, Catherine, Shneiderman, Ben, 2013b. Temporal event sequence simplification. IEEE Transactions on Visualization and Computer Graphics 19 (12), 2227–2236.

Moore, C.J., Graham, P.A., MacKay, R.I., Sharrock, P.J., 1997. Multi-modal surface/outline projection and simulation of target/critical tissue movement. In: Proc. IEEE Conference on Information Visualization, pp. 10–17. https://doi.org/10.1109/IV.1997.626463.

Moreno, Roxana, Mayer, Richard E., 1999. Cognitive principles of multimedia learning: the role of modality and contiguity. Journal of Educational Psychology 91 (2), 358.

Mori, Masahiro, 1970. Bukimi no tani [the uncanny valley]. Energy 7, 33–35.

Mori, Masahiro, MacDorman, Karl F., Kageki, Norri, 2012. The uncanny valley [from the field]. IEEE Robotics & Automation Magazine 19 (2), 98–100.

Mörth, Eric, Wagner-Larsen, Kari, Hodneland, Erlend, Krakstad, Camilla, Haldorsen, Ingfrid S., Bruckner, Stefan, Smit, Noeska N., 2020. RadEx: integrated visual exploration of multi-parametric studies for radiomic tumor profiling. Computer Graphics Forum 39 (7), 611–622.

Mroz, L., Hauser, H., Gröller, E., 2000. Interactive high-quality maximum intensity projection. Computer Graphics Forum, 341–350.

Mueller, Klaus, Papenhausen, Eric, 2021. Using demographic pattern analysis to predict COVID-19 fatalities on the US county level. Digital Government: Research and Practice 2 (1), 12, pp. 1–11.

Mühlbacher, Thomas, Piringer, Harald, 2013. A partition-based framework for building and validating regression models. IEEE Transactions on Visualization and Computer Graphics 19 (12), 1962–1971.

Mühler, Konrad, Preim, Bernhard, 2009. Automatic textual annotation for surgical planning. In: Proc. of Vision, Modeling, and Visualization, pp. 277–284.

Mühler, Konrad, Preim, Bernhard, 2010. Reusable visualizations and animations for surgery planning. Computer Graphics Forum 29 (3), 1103–1112.

Mühler, Konrad, Bade, Ragnar, Preim, Bernhard, 2006. Adaptive script based animations for intervention planning. In: Proc. of Medical Image Computing and Computer-Assisted Intervention (MICCAI), pp. 478–485.

Mühler, Konrad, Neugebauer, Mathias, Tietjen, Christian, Preim, Bernhard, 2007. Viewpoint selection for intervention planning. In: Proc. of EuroVis, pp. 267–274.

Mühler, Konrad, Tietjen, Christian, Ritter, Felix, Preim, Bernhard, 2010. The medical exploration toolkit: an efficient support for visual computing in surgical planning and training. IEEE Transactions on Visualization and Computer Graphics 16 (1), 133–146.

Müller, Juliane, Stoehr, Matthaeus, Oeser, Alexander, Gaebel, Jan, Streit, Marc, Dietz, Andreas, Oeltze-Jafra, Steffen, 2020. A visual approach to explainable computerized clinical decision support. Computers & Graphics 91, 1–11.

Müller, Matthias, Schirm, Simon, Teschner, Matthias, 2004. Interactive blood simulation for virtual surgery based on smoothed particle hydrodynamics. Technology and Health Care 12 (1), 25–31.

Müller, Matthias, Heidelberger, Bruno, Hennix, Marcus, Ratcliff, John, 2007. Position based dynamics. Journal of Visual Communication and Image Representation 18 (2), 109–118.

Müller, Meinard, 2007. Dynamic time warping. In: Information Retrieval for Music and Motion, pp. 69–84.

Müller-Stich, Beat P., Löb, Nicole, Wald, Diana, Bruckner, Thomas, Meinzer, Hans-Peter, Kadmon, Martina, Büchler, Markus W., Fischer, Lars, 2013. Regular three-dimensional presentations improve in the identification of surgical liver anatomy–a randomized study. BMC Medical Education 13 (1), 1–8.

Munzner, Tamara, 2014. Visualization Analysis and Design. CRC Press.

Nabiyouni, Mahdi, Bowman, Doug A., 2016. A taxonomy for designing walking-based locomotion techniques for virtual reality. In: Proc. of ACM Companion on Interactive Surfaces and Spaces, pp. 115–121.

Nah, Fiona Fui-Hoon, Zeng, Qing, Telaprolu, Venkata Rajasekhar, Ayyappa, Abhishek Padmanabhuni, Eschenbrenner, Brenda, 2014. Gamification of education: a review of literature. In: Proc. of International Conference on HCI in Business, pp. 401–409.

Neale, Dennis C., Carroll, John M., 1997. The role of metaphors in user interface design. In: Handbook of Human-Computer Interaction. Elsevier, pp. 441–462.

Netter, Frank H., 2014. Atlas of Human Anatomy. Professional Edition E-Book: including NetterReference.com access with full downloadable image bank. Elsevier Health Sciences.

Neugebauer, Mathias, Gasteiger, Rocco, Beuing, Oliver, Diehl, Volker, Skalej, Martin, Preim, Bernhard, 2009a. Map displays for the analysis of scalar data on cerebral aneurysm surfaces. Computer Graphics Forum 28 (3), 895–902.

Neugebauer, Mathias, Gasteiger, Rocoo, Diehl, Volker, Beuing, Oliver, Preim, Bernhard, 2009b. Automatic generation of context visualizations for cerebral aneurysms from MRA datasets. International Journal of Computer Assisted Radiology and Surgery (CARS) 4 (Supplement 1), 112–121.

Neugebauer, Mathias, Janiga, Gabor, Beuing, Oliver, Skalej, Martin, Preim, Bernhard, 2011. Anatomy-guided multi-level exploration of blood flow in cerebral aneurysms. Computer Graphics Forum 30 (3), 1041–1050.

Neugebauer, Mathias, Lawonn, Kai, Beuing, Oliver, Berg, Philipp, Janiga, Gábor, Preim, Bernhard, 2013. AmniVis–a system for qualitative exploration of near-wall hemodynamics in cerebral aneurysms. Computer Graphics Forum 32 (3pt3), 251–260.

Neustaedter, Carman, Fedorovskaya, Elena Alexandrovna, 2009. Avatar appearances and representation of self: learning from Second Life®. In: Proc. of AAAI Fall Symposium Series.

Newe, Axel, Becker, Linda, Schenk, Andrea, 2014. Application and evaluation of interactive 3D PDF for presenting and sharing planning results for liver surgery in clinical routine. PLoS ONE 9 (12), e115697.

Nguyen, Ngan, Nelson, Andrew J., Wilson, Timothy D., 2012. Computer visualizations: factors that influence spatial anatomy comprehension. Anatomical Sciences Education 5 (2), 98–108.

Nguyen, Tan Khoa, Ohlsson, Henrik, Eklund, Anders, Hernell, Frida, Ljung, Patric, Forsell, Camilla, Andersson, Mats, Knutsson, Hans, Ynnerman, Anders, 2010. Concurrent volume visualization of real-time fMRI. In: Proc. of IEEE/EG International Symposium on Volume Graphics, pp. 53–60.

Nicholson, Daren T., Chalk, Colin, Funnell, W. Robert J., Daniel, Sam J., 2006. Can virtual reality improve anatomy education? A randomised controlled study of a computer-generated three-dimensional anatomical ear model. Medical Education 40 (11), 1081–1087.

Niemann, Uli, Spiliopoulou, Myra, Völzke, Henry, Kühn, Jens-Peter, 2014a. Interactive medical miner: interactively exploring subpopulations in epidemiological datasets. In: Proc. of European Conference on Machine Learning and Knowledge Discovery in Databases, pp. 460–463.

Niemann, Uli, Spiliopoulou, Myra, Völzke, Henry, Kühn, Jens-Peter, 2014b. Subpopulation discovery in epidemiological data with subspace clustering. Foundations of Computing and Decision Sciences 39 (4), 271–300.

Njeh, C.F., 2008. Tumor delineation: the weakest link in the search for accuracy in radiotherapy. Journal of Medical Physics 33 (4), 136.

Nordsborg, Rikke Baastrup, Meliker, Jaymie R., Ersbøll, Annette Kjær, Jacquez, Geoffrey M., Poulsen, Aslak Harbo, Raaschou-Nielsen, Ole, 2014. Space-time clusters of breast cancer using residential histories: a Danish case–control study. BMC Cancer 14 (1), 255.

Northrup, J.D., Markosian, Lee, 2000. Artistic silhouettes: a hybrid approach. In: Proc. NPAR. ACM, pp. 31–37. https://doi.org/10.1145/340916.340920.

Novotny, Matej, Hauser, Helwig, 2006. Outlier-preserving Focus+Context visualization in parallel coordinates. IEEE Transactions on Visualization and Computer Graphics 12 (5), 893–900.

Nunes, Miguel, Laruelo, Andrea, Ken, SoleaKhena, Laprie, Anne, Bühler, Katja, 2014. A survey on visualizing magnetic resonance spectroscopy data. In: Eurographics Workshop on Visual Computing for Biology and Medicine. ISBN 978-3-905674-62-0, pp. 21–30. https://doi.org/10.2312/vcbm.20141180.

Oeltze, Steffen, Preim, Bernhard, 2005. Visualization of vascular structures: method, validation and evaluation. IEEE Transactions on Medical Imaging 25 (4), 540–549.

Oeltze, Steffen, Lehmann, Dirk J., Kuhn, Alexander, Janiga, Gábor, Theisel, Holger, Preim, Bernhard, 2014. Blood flow clustering and applications in virtual stenting of intracranial aneurysms. IEEE Transactions on Visualization and Computer Graphics 20 (5), 686–701.

Oeltze-Jafra, Steffen, Preim, Bernhard, 2014. Survey of labeling techniques in medical visualizations. In: Proc. of Eurographics Workshop on Visual Computing for Biology and Medicine (VCBM), pp. 199–208. https://doi.org/10.2312/vcbm.20141192.

Oeltze-Jafra, Steffen, Cebral, Juan R., Janiga, Gábor, Preim, Bernhard, 2016. Cluster analysis of vortical flow in simulations of cerebral aneurysm hemodynamics. IEEE Transactions on Visualization and Computer Graphics 22 (1), 757–766.

Oeltze-Jafra, Steffen, Meuschke, Monique, Neugebauer, Mathias, Saalfeld, Sylvia, Lawonn, Kai, Janiga, Gabor, Hege, Hans-Christian, Zachow, Stefan, Preim, Bernhard, 2019. Generation and visual exploration of medical flow data: survey, research trends and future challenges. Computer Graphics Forum 38 (1), 87–125.

Ogao, Patrick J., Kraak, M.-J., 2002. Defining visualization operations for temporal cartographic animation design. International Journal of Applied Earth Observation and Geoinformation 4 (1), 23–31.

Oh, Seungjong, Jaffray, David, Cho, Young-Bin, 2014. A novel method to quantify and compare anatomical shape: application in cervix cancer radiotherapy. Physics in Medicine and Biology 59 (11), 2687–2704. https://doi.org/10.1088/0031-9155/59/11/2687.

Ohtake, Yutaka, Belyaev, Alexander, Seidel, Hans-Peter, 2004. Ridge-valley lines on meshes via implicit surface fitting. ACM Transactions on Graphics 23 (3), 609–612. https://doi.org/10.1145/1015706.1015768.

Okemow, Stefanie Joelle, 2020. Storyboarding in medical animation. Biomedical Visualisation, 131–143.

Ola, O., Sedig, K., 2014. The challenge of big data in public health: an opportunity for visual analytics. Online Journal of Public Health Informatics 5 (3), 223.

Olabarriaga, S.D., Smeulders, A.W.M., 2001. Interaction in the segmentation of medical images: a survey. Medical Image Analysis 5 (2), 127–142. https://doi.org/10.1016/s1361-8415(00)00041-4.

Olson, James Stuart, 1989. The History of Cancer: An Annotated Bibliography, 3rd ed. Greenwood.

Orban de Xivry, Jonathan, Janssens, Guillaume, Bosmans, Geert, De Craene, Mathieu, Dekker, André, Buijsen, Jeroen, van Baardwijk, Angela, De Ruysscher, Dirk, Macq, Benoit, Lambin, Philippe, 2007. Tumour delineation and cumulative dose computation in radiotherapy based on deformable registration of respiratory correlated CT images of lung cancer patients. Radiotherapy and Oncology 85 (2), 232–238. https://doi.org/10.1016/j.radonc.2007.08.012.

Ostendorf, Kai, Mastrodicasa, Domenico, Bäumler, Kathrin, Codari, Marina, Turner, Valery, Willemink, Martin J., Fleischmann, Dominik, Preim, Bernhard, Mistelbauer, Gabriel, 2021. Shading style assessment for vessel wall and lumen visualization. In: Proc. of Eurographics Workshop on Visual Computing for Biology and Medicine (VCBM). https://doi.org/10.2312/vcbm.20211350.

O'Shea, James P., Banks, Martin, Agrawala, Maneesh, 2008. The assumed light direction for perceiving shape from shading. In: Proc. of the Symposium on Applied Perception in Graphics and Visualization, pp. 135–142.

Pahr, Daniel, Wu, Hsiang-Yun, Raidou, Renata Georgia, 2021. Vologram: an educational holographic sculpture for volumetric medical data physicalization. In: Proc. of Eurographics Workshop on Visual Computing for Biology and Medicine (VCBM). https://doi.org/10.2312/vcbm.20211341.

Pallanch, J.F., McCaffrey, T.V., Kern, E.B., 1985. Normal nasal resistance. Arch Otolaryngology-Head and Neck Surgery 93 (6), 778–785.

Pan, Junjun, Zhang, Leiyu, Yu, Peng, Shen, Yang, Wang, Haipeng, Hao, Haimin, Qin, Hong, 2020. Real-time VR simulation of laparoscopic cholecystectomy based on parallel position-based dynamics in GPU. In: Proc. of IEEE Conference on Virtual Reality and 3D User Interfaces, pp. 548–556.

Parent, Rick, 2012. Computer Animation: Algorithms and Techniques. Newnes.

Park, J.S., Chung, M.S., Hwang, S.B., Shin, B.S., Park, H.S., 2006. Visible Korean Human: its techniques and applications. Clinical Anatomy 19 (3), 216–224.

Patel, Daniel, Muren, Ludvig Paul, Mehus, Anfinn, Kvinnsland, Yngve, Ulvang, Dag Magne, Villanger, Kåre P., 2007. A virtual reality solution for evaluation of radiotherapy plans. Radiotherapy and Oncology 82 (2), 218–221. https://doi.org/10.1016/j.radonc.2006.11.024.

Pavone, P., Marsili, L., Catalano, C., Petroni, G.A., Aytan, E., Cardone, G.P., Passariello, R., 1992. Carotid arteries: evaluation with low-field-strength MR angiography. Radiology 184 (2), 401–404.

Pearce, Neil, 2012. Classification of epidemiological study designs. International Journal of Epidemiology 41 (2), 393–397.

Peden, D.B., 1997. Mechanisms of pollution-induced airway disease: in vivo studies. Allergy 52, 37–44.

Pelengaris, Stella, Khan, Michael, 2013. The Molecular Biology of Cancer: A Bridge from Bench to Bedside. John Wiley & Sons.

Peng, Wei, Ward, Matthew O., Rundensteiner, Elke A., 2004. Clutter reduction in multi-dimensional data visualization using dimension reordering. In: Proc. of IEEE Symposium on Information Visualization, pp. 89–96.

Perlin, Ken, Fox, David, 1993. Pad: an alternative approach to the computer interface. In: Proc. of ACM SIGGRAPH, pp. 57–64.

Perrenot, Cyril, Perez, Manuela, Tran, Nguyen, Jehl, Jean-Philippe, Felblinger, Jacques, Bresler, Laurent, Hubert, Jacques, 2012. The virtual reality simulator dV-Trainer® is a valid assessment tool for robotic surgical skills. Surgical Endoscopy 26 (9), 2587–2593.

Pertaub, David-Paul, Slater, Mel, Barker, Chris, 2002. An experiment on public speaking anxiety in response to three different types of virtual audience. Presence: Teleoperators & Virtual Environments 11 (1), 68–78.

Petersik, Andreas, Pflesser, Bernhard, Tiede, Ulf, Höhne, Karl Heinz, Leuwer, Rudolf, 2002. Haptic volume interaction with anatomic models at sub-voxel resolution. In: Proc. of Symposium on Haptic Interfaces for Virtual Environment and Teleoperator Systems. IEEE, pp. 66–72.

Petersson, Helge, Sinkvist, David, Wang, Chunliang, Smedby, Örjan, 2009. Web-based interactive 3D visualization as a tool for improved anatomy learning. Anatomical Sciences Education 2 (2), 61–68.

Petz, Christoph, Pöthkow, Kai, Hege, Hans-Christian, 2012. Probabilistic local features in uncertain vector fields with spatial correlation. Computer Graphics Forum 31 (3), 1045–1054.

Pflesser, Bernhard, Tiede, Ulf, Höhne, Karl Heinz, 1998. Specification, modeling and visualization of arbitrarily shaped cut surfaces in the volume model. In: Proc. of Medical Image Computing and Computer-Assisted Intervention (MICCAI), pp. 853–860. https://doi.org/10.1007/BFb0056273.

Phillips, A.W., Smith, S., Straus, C., 2013. The role of radiology in preclinical anatomy: a critical review of the past, present, and future. Academic Radiology 20 (3), 297–304.

Phillips, Nicholas I., John, Nigel W., 2000. Web-based surgical simulation for ventricular catheterization. Neurosurgery 46 (4), 933–937.

Pihuit, Adeline, Cani, Marie-Paule, Palombi, Olivier, 2010. Sketch-based modeling of vascular systems: a first step towards interactive teaching of anatomy. In: Proc. of Sketch-Based Interfaces and Modeling. Eurographics, pp. 151–158.

Pinter, Csaba, Lasso, Andras, Wang, An, Jaffray, David, Fichtinger, Gabor, 2012. SlicerRT: radiation therapy research toolkit for 3D Slicer. Medical Physics 39 (10), 6332–6338. https://doi.org/10.1118/1.4754659.

Pinzon, David, Byrns, Simon, Zheng, Bin, 2016. Prevailing trends in haptic feedback simulation for minimally invasive surgery. Surgical Innovation 23 (4), 415–421.

Pitt, Ian, Preim, Bernhard, Schlechtweg, Stefan, 1999. An evaluation of interaction techniques for the exploration of 3D-illustrations. In: Proc. of Software-Ergonomie, pp. 275–286.

Pivovar, Jarod, DeGuzman, Jasmine, Rosenberg, Evan Suma, 2022. Virtual reality on a SWIM: scalable world in miniature. In: Proc. of IEEE Conference on Virtual Reality and 3D User Interfaces Abstracts and Workshops, pp. 912–913.

Plaisant, Catherine, Milash, Brett, Rose, Anne, Widoff, Seth, Shneiderman, Ben, 1996. LifeLines: visualizing personal histories. In: Proc. of ACM SIGCHI Conference on Human Factors in Computing Systems (CHI), pp. 221–227.

Plaisant, Catherine, Mushlin, Richard, Snyder, Aaron, Li, Jia, Heller, Dan, Shneiderman, Ben, 2003. Lifelines: using visualization to enhance navigation and analysis of patient records. In: The Craft of Information Visualization. Elsevier, pp. 308–312.

Pohlandt, Daniel, Preim, Bernhard, Saalfeld, Patrick, 2019. Supporting anatomy education with a 3D puzzle in a VR environment - results from a pilot study. In: Proc. of Mensch und Computer, pp. 91–102.

Pommert, A., Höhne, K.H., Pflesser, B., Richter, E., Riemer, M., Schiemann, T., Schubert, R., Schumacher, U., Tiede, U., 2001. Creating a high-resolution spatial/symbolic model of the inner organs based on the visible human. Medical Image Analysis 5 (3), 221–228.

Pommert, Andreas, Höhne, Karl Heinz, Burmester, Eike, Gehrmann, Sebastian, Leuwer, Rudolf, Petersik, Andreas, Tiede, Ulf, 2006. Computer-based anatomy: a prerequisite for computer-assisted radiology and surgery. Academic Radiology 13 (1), 104–112.

Pop, Mihai, Duncan, Christian, Barequet, Gill, Goodrich, Michael, Huang, Wenjing, Kumar, Subodh, 2001. Efficient perspective-accurate silhouette computation and applications. In: Proc. Computational Geometry. ACM, pp. 60–68. https://doi.org/10.1145/378583.378618.

Pöthkow, Kai, Hege, Hans-Christian, 2013. Nonparametric models for uncertainty visualization. Computer Graphics Forum 32 (3), 131–140.

Praun, Emil, Finkelstein, Adam, Hoppe, Hugues, 2000. Lapped textures. In: Proc. of ACM SIGGRAPH, pp. 465–470. https://doi.org/10.1145/344779.344987.

Praun, Emil, Hoppe, Hugues, Webb, Matthew, Finkelstein, Adam, 2001. Real-time hatching. In: Proc. of ACM SIGGRAPH, pp. 581–586. https://doi.org/10.1145/383259.383328.

Preim, Bernhard, Bartz, Dirk, 2007. Visualization in Medicine: Theory, Algorithms, and Applications. Elsevier.

Preim, Bernhard, Botha, Charl P., 2013. Visual Computing for Medicine: Theory, Algorithms, and Applications. Elsevier.

Preim, Bernhard, Lawonn, Kai, 2020. A survey of visual analytics for public health. Computer Graphics Forum 39 (1), 543–580.

Preim, Bernhard, Meuschke, Monique, 2020. A survey of medical animations. Computer Graphics 90, 145–168. https://doi.org/10.1016/j.cag.2020.06.003.

Preim, Bernhard, Raab, Andreas, 1998. Annotation von topographisch komplizierten 3D-Modellen. In: Proc. of Simulation and Visualization, pp. 128–140.

Preim, Bernhard, Saalfeld, Patrick, 2018. A survey of virtual human anatomy education systems. Computers & Graphics 71, 132–153. https://doi.org/10.1016/j.cag.2018.01.005.

Preim, Bernhard, Ritter, Alf, Forsey, Dave R., Bartram, Lyn, Pohle, Thilo, Strothotte, Thomas, 1995. Consistency of rendered images and their textual labels. In: Proc. of CompuGraphics, pp. 201–210.

Preim, Bernhard, Ritter, Alf, Strothotte, Thomas, 1996. Illustrating anatomic models: a semi-interactive approach. In: Proc. Visualization in Biomedical Computing. In: Lecture Notes in Computer Science, vol. number 1131. Springer, pp. 23–32.

Preim, Bernhard, Raab, Andreas, Strothotte, Thomas, 1997. Coherent zooming of illustrations with 3D-graphics and text. In: Proc. Graphics Interface, pp. 105–113.

Preim, Bernhard, Michel, Rainer, Hartmann, Knut, Strothotte, Thomas, 1998. Figure captions in visual interfaces. In: Proc. of Advanced Visual Interfaces, pp. 235–246.

Preim, Bernhard, Cordes, Jeanette, Heinrichs, Thomas, Krause, Dieter, Jachau, Katja, 2005. Quantitative Bildanalyse und Visualisierung für die Analyse von post-mortem Datensätzen. In: Proc. of BVM, pp. 6–10.

Preim, Bernhard, Oeltze, Steffen, Mlejnek, Matej, Groller, Eduard, Hennemuth, Anja, Behrens, Sarah, 2009. Survey of the visual exploration and analysis of perfusion data. IEEE Transactions on Visualization and Computer Graphics 15 (2), 205–220.

Preim, Bernhard, Baer, Alexandra, Cunningham, Douglas, Isenberg, Tobias, Ropinski, Timo, 2016. A survey of perceptually motivated 3D visualization of medical image data. Computer Graphics Forum 22 (5), 501–525. https://doi.org/10.1111/cgf.12927.

Pulijala, Yeshwanth, Ma, Minhua, Pears, Matthew, Peebles, David, Ayoub, Ashraf, 2018. Effectiveness of immersive virtual reality in surgical training a randomized control trial. Journal of Oral and Maxillofacial Surgery 76 (5), 1065–1072.

Putora, Paul Martin, Peters, Samuel, Bovet, Marc, 2015. Informatics in radiation oncology. In: Machine Learning in Radiation Oncology. Springer International Publishing, pp. 57–70. https://doi.org/10.1007/978-3-319-18305-3_5.

Qian, Kun, Bai, Junxuan, Yang, Xiaosong, Pan, Junjun, Zhang, Jianjun, 2015. Virtual reality based laparoscopic surgery simulation. In: Proc. of ACM Symposium on Virtual Reality Software and Technology, pp. 69–78.

Qin, Jing, Choi, Kup-Sze, Pang, Wai-Man, Yi, Zhang, Heng, Pheng-Ann, 2010. Collaborative virtual surgery: techniques, applications and challenges. International Journal of Virtual Reality 9 (3), 1–7.

Qu, Huamin, Chan, Wing-Yi, Xu, Anbang, Chung, Kai-Lun, Lau, Kai-Hon, Guo, Ping, 2007. Visual analysis of the air pollution problem in Hong Kong. IEEE Transactions on Visualization and Computer Graphics 13 (6), 1408–1415.

Qualter, J., Triola, M.M., Weiner, M.J., Hopkins, M.A., Kirov, M., Nachbar, M.S., 2004. The virtual surgery patient: development of a digital, three-dimensional model of human anatomy designed for surgical education. In: Proc. of IEEE Symposium on Computer-Based Medical Systems, pp. 34–38.

Qualter, J., Sculli, F., Oliker, A., Napier, Z., Lee, S., Garcia, J., Frenkel, S., Harnik, V., Triola, M., 2012. The BioDigital human: a web-based 3D platform for medical visualization and education. Studies in Health Technology and Informatics 173, 359–361.

Radeva, Nadezhda, Levy, Lucien, Hahn, James, 2014. Generalized temporal focus + context framework for improved medical data exploration. Journal of Digital Imaging 27 (2), 207–219.

Raghupathi, Wullianallur, Raghupathi, Viju, 2018. An empirical study of chronic diseases in the United States: a visual analytics approach to public health. International Journal of Environmental Research and Public Health 15 (3), 431.

Raidou, Renata G., Marcelis, Freek J.J., Breeuwer, Marcel, Gröller, Eduard, Vilanova, Anna, van de Wetering, Huub M.M., 2016a. Visual analytics for the exploration and assessment of segmentation errors. In: Proc. of Eurographics Workshop on Visual Computing for Biology and Medicine (VCBM), pp. 193–202.

Raidou, Renata G., Breeuwer, Marcel, Vilanova, Anna, 2017. Visual analytics for digital radiotherapy: towards a comprehensible pipeline. In: Eurographics - Dirk Bartz Prize, pp. 1–4. https://doi.org/10.2312/egm.20171042.

Raidou, R.G., Casares-Magaz, O., Muren, L.P., van der Heide, U.A., Rørvik, J., Breeuwer, M., Vilanova, A., 2016b. Visual analysis of tumor control models for prediction of radiotherapy response. Computer Graphics Forum 35 (3), 231–240. https://doi.org/10.1111/cgf.12899.

Raidou, R.G., Casares-Magaz, O., Amirkhanov, A., Moiseenko, V., Muren, L.P., Einck, J.P., Vilanova, A., Gröller, M.E., 2018. Bladder runner: visual analytics for the exploration of RT-induced bladder toxicity in a cohort study. Computer Graphics Forum 37 (3), 205–216. https://doi.org/10.1111/cgf.13413.

Rand, Debbie, Weiss, Patrice L. Tamar, Katz, Noomi, 2009. Training multitasking in a virtual supermarket: a novel intervention after stroke. The American Journal of Occupational Therapy 63 (5), 535–542.

Rao, Ramana, Card, Stuart K., 1994. The table lens: merging graphical and symbolic representations in an interactive focus+context visualization for tabular information. In: Proc. of ACM SIGCHI Conference on Human Factors in Computing Systems (CHI), pp. 318–322.

Raskar, Ramesh, 2001. Hardware support for non-photorealistic rendering. In: Proc. Workshop on Graphics Hardware. ACM, pp. 41–47. https://doi.org/10.1145/383507.383525.

Raskar, Ramesh, Cohen, Michael, 1999. Image precision silhouette edges. In: ACM Symposium on Interactive 3D Graphics, pp. 135–140. https://doi.org/10.1145/300523.300539.

Razzaque, Sharif, Swapp, David, Slater, Mel, Whitton, Mary C., Steed, Anthony, 2002. Redirected walking in place. In: Proc. of EGVE, vol. 2, pp. 123–130.

Reiter, Oliver, Breeuwer, Marcel, Gröller, Eduard, Raidou, Renata Georgia, 2018. Comparative visual analysis of pelvic organ segmentations. In: EuroVis - Short Papers, pp. 37–41. https://doi.org/10.2312/eurovisshort.20181075.

Reitinger, Bernhard, Bornik, Alexander, Beichel, Reinhard, Schmalstieg, Dieter, 2006. Liver surgery planning using virtual reality. IEEE CG&A 26 (6), 36–47.

Revere, Debra, Turner, Anne M., Madhavan, Ann, Rambo, Neil, Bugni, Paul F., Kimball, AnnMarie, Fuller, Sherrilynne S., 2007. Understanding the information needs of public health practitioners: a literature review to inform design of an interactive digital knowledge management system. Journal of Biomedical Informatics 40 (4), 410–421.

Richardson, April, Hazzard, Matthew, Challman, Sandra D., Morgenstein, Aaron M., Brueckner, Jennifer K., 2011. A "second life" for gross anatomy: applications for multiuser virtual environments in teaching the anatomical sciences. Anatomical Sciences Education 4 (1), 39–43.

Rieder, Christian, Ritter, Felix, Raspe, Matthias, Peitgen, Heinz-Otto, 2008. Interactive visualization of multimodal volume data for neurosurgical tumor treatment. Computer Graphics Forum 27 (3), 1055–1062.

Riener, Robert, Harders, Matthias, 2012. Virtual Reality in Medicine. Springer.

Rietzel, Eike, Chen, George T.Y., Choi, Noah C., Willet, Christopher G., 2005. Four-dimensional image-based treatment planning: target volume segmentation and dose calculation in the presence of respiratory motion. International Journal of Radiation Oncology, Biology, Physics 61 (5), 1535–1550. https://doi.org/10.1016/j.ijrobp.2004.11.037.

Rind, Alexander, Aigner, Wolfgang, Wagner, Markus, Miksch, Silvia, Lammarsch, Tim, 2016. Task cube: a three-dimensional conceptual space of user tasks in visualization design and evaluation. Information Visualization 15 (4), 288–300.

Rind, Alexander, Slijepčević, Djordje, Zeppelzauer, Matthias, Unglaube, Fabian, Kranzl, Andreas, Horsak, Brian, 2022. Trustworthy visual analytics in clinical gait analysis: a case study for patients with cerebral palsy. arXiv preprint. arXiv:2208.05232.

Ritter, Felix, Preim, Bernhard, Deussen, Oliver, Strothotte, Thomas, 2000. Using a 3D puzzle as a metaphor for learning spatial relations. In: Proc. of Graphics Interface, pp. 171–178.

Ritter, Felix, Berendt, Bettina, Fischer, Berit, Richter, Robert, Preim, Bernhard, 2002. Virtual 3D jigsaw puzzles: studying the effect of exploring spatial relations with implicit guidance. In: Proc. of Mensch & Computer, pp. 363–372.

Ritter, Felix, Hansen, Christian, Dicken, Volker, Konrad-Verse, Olaf, Preim, Bernhard, Peitgen, Heinz-Otto, 2006. Real-time illustration of vascular structures. IEEE Transactions on Visualization and Computer Graphics 12 (5), 877–884. https://doi.org/10.1109/TVCG.2006.172.

Rizzo, Albert, Kim, Gerard Jounghyun, 2005. A SWOT analysis of the field of virtual reality rehabilitation and therapy. Presence: Teleoperators & Virtual Environments 14 (2), 119–146.

Rizzo, Albert A., Koenig, S.T., 2017. Is clinical virtual reality ready for primetime? Neuropsychology 31 (8), 877–899. https://doi.org/10.1109/MC.2014.199.

Roberts, Jonathan C., 2007. State of the art: coordinated & multiple views in exploratory visualization. In: Proc. of Coordinated and Multiple Views in Exploratory Visualization, pp. 61–71.

Robinson, A.C., MacEachren, A.M., Roth, R.E., 2011. Designing a web-based learning portal for geographic visualization and analysis in public health. Health Informatics Journal 17 (3), 191–208.

Rocha, Allan, Alim, Usman, Silva, Julio Daniel, Sousa, Mario Costa, 2017. Decal-maps: real-time layering of decals on surfaces for multivariate visualization. IEEE Transactions on Visualization and Computer Graphics 23 (1), 821–830.

Ropinski, Timo, Steinicke, Frank, Hinrichs, Klaus, 2006. Visually supporting depth perception in angiography imaging. In: Smart Graphics, vol. 4073, pp. 93–104.

Ropinski, Timo, Praßni, Jörg-Stefan, Roters, Jan, Hinrichs, Klaus H., 2007. Internal labels as shape cues for medical illustration. In: Proc. of Vision, Modeling, and Visualization, pp. 203–212.

Ropinski, Timo, Oeltze, Steffen, Preim, Bernhard, 2011. Survey of glyph-based visualization techniques for spatial multivariate medical data. Computers & Graphics 35 (2), 392–401.

Rose, F. David, Brooks, Barbara M., Rizzo, Albert A., 2005. Virtual reality in brain damage rehabilitation. Cyberpsychology & Behavior 8 (3), 241–262.

Rose, Tyler, Nam, Chang S., Chen, Karen B., 2018. Immersion of virtual reality for rehabilitation-review. Applied Ergonomics 69, 153–161.

Rosen, George, 2015. A History of Public Health. JHU Press.

Rosse, Cornelius, Mejino, José L.V., 2008. The Foundational Model of Anatomy Ontology. Springer, London, pp. 59–117. https://doi.org/10.1007/978-1-84628-885-2_4.

Rosse, Cornelius, Shapiro, L.G., Brinkley, James F., 1998. The digital anatomist foundational model: principles for defining and structuring its concept domain. In: Proc. of American Medical Informatics Association Fall Symposium, pp. 820–824.

Rosset, Antoine, Spadola, Luca, Pysher, Lance, Ratib, Osman, 2006. Navigating the fifth dimension: innovative interface for multidimensional multimodality image navigation. Radiographics 26 (1), 299–308.

Rossignac, Jarek R., van Emmerik, Maarten, 1992. Hidden contours on a frame-buffer. In: Proc. EGGH. Eurographics Association, pp. 188–203. https://doi.org/10.2312/EGGH/EGGH92/188-203.

Rössl, Christian, Kobbelt, Leif, 2000. Line-art rendering of 3D-models. In: Proc. Pacific Graphics. IEEE Computer Society, pp. 87–96. https://doi.org/10.1109/PCCGA.2000.883890.

Rössl, Christian, Kobbelt, Leif, Seidel, Hans-Peter, 2000. Line art rendering of triangulated surfaces using discrete lines of curvature. In: Proc. WSCG, pp. 168–175. https://dspace5.zcu.cz/handle/11025/15452.

Rößler, Friedemann, Tejada, Eduardo, Fangmeier, Thomas, Ertl, Thomas, Knauff, Markus, 2006. GPU-based multi-volume rendering for the visualization of functional brain images. In: Proc. of SimVis, pp. 305–318.

Rößler, Friedemann, Wolff, Torsten, Iserhardt-Bauer, Sabine, Tomandl, Bernd, Hastreiter, Peter, Ertl, Thomas, 2007. Distributed video generation on a GPU-cluster for the web-based analysis of medical image data. In: Proc. of SPIE Medical Imaging: Visualization and Image-Guided Procedures, vol. 6509, p. 650903.

Rossling, Ivo, Dornheim, Jana, Dornheim, Lars, Boehm, Andreas, Preim, Bernhard, 2011. The tumor therapy manager - design, refinement and clinical use of a software product for ENT surgery planning and documentation. In: Proc. of Information Processing in Computer-Assisted Interventions, pp. 1–12.

Rothbaum, Barbara Olasov, Hodges, Larry F., Kooper, Rob, Opdyke, Dan, Williford, James S., North, Max, 1995. Virtual reality graded exposure in the treatment of acrophobia: a case report. Behavior Therapy 26 (3), 547–554.

Ruiz, Jorge G., Cook, David A., Levinson, Anthony J., 2009. Computer animations in medical education: a critical literature review. Medical Education 43 (9), 838–846.

Rustagi, Pramod, 1989. Silhouette line display from shaded models. IRIS Universe 1989 (9), 42–44.

Saab, Mohamad M., Hegarty, Josephine, Murphy, David, Landers, Margaret, 2021. Incorporating virtual reality in nurse education: a qualitative study of nursing students' perspectives. Nurse Education Today 105, 105045.

Saalfeld, Patrick, Baer, Alexandra, Preim, Uta, Preim, Bernhard, Lawonn, Kai, 2015. Sketching 2D vessels and vascular diseases with integrated blood flow. In: International Conference on Computer Graphics Theory and Applications, pp. 379–390.

Saalfeld, Patrick, Stojnic, Aleksandar, Preim, Bernhard, Oeltze-Jafra, Steffen, 2016. Semi-immersive 3D sketching of vascular structures for medical education. In: Proc. of Eurographics Workshop on Visual Computing for Biology and Medicine (VCBM), pp. 123–132.

Saalfeld, Patrick, Glaßer, Sylvia, Beuing, Oliver, Preim, Bernhard, 2017. The FAUST framework: free-form annotations on unfolding vascular structures for treatment planning. Computers & Graphics 65, 12–21.

Saalfeld, Patrick, Albrecht, Aylin, D'Hanis, Wolfgang, Rothkötter, Hermann-Josef, Preim, Bernhard, 2020a. Learning hand anatomy with sense of embodiment. In: Proc. of Eurographics Workshop on Visual Computing for Biology and Medicine (VCBM), pp. 43–47.

Saalfeld, Patrick, Schmeier, Anna, D'Hanis, Wolfgang, Rothkötter, Hermann-Josef, Preim, Bernhard, 2020b. Student and teacher meet in a shared virtual reality: a one-on-one tutoring system for anatomy education. In: Proc. of Eurographics Workshop on Visual Computing for Biology and Medicine (VCBM), pp. 55–59.

Saalfeld, Patrick, Böttcher, Claudia, Klink, Fabian, Preim, Bernhard, 2021. VR system for the restoration of broken cultural artifacts on the example of a funerary monument. In: Proc. of IEEE Virtual Reality and 3D User Interfaces, pp. 739–748.

Sailer, Anna M., Van Kuijk, Sander M.J., Nelemans, Patricia J., Chin, Anne S., Kino, Aya, Huininga, Mark, Schmidt, Johanna, Mistelbauer, Gabriel, Bäumler, Kathrin, Chiu, Peter, et al., 2017. Computed tomography imaging features in acute uncomplicated Stanford type-B aortic dissection predict late adverse events. Circulation: Cardiovascular Imaging 10 (4), e005709.

Saito, Takafumi, Takahashi, Tokiichiro, 1990. Comprehensible rendering of 3-D shapes. ACM SIGGRAPH Computer Graphics 24 (4), 197–206. https://doi.org/10.1145/97880.97901.

Sakas, Georgios, Grimm, Marcus, Savopoulos, Alexandros, 1995. Optimized maximum intensity projection (MIP). In: Proc. of EG Workshop on Rendering Techniques, pp. 51–63.

Sakchaicharoenkul, Thanakorn, 2006. MCFI-based animation tweening algorithm for 2D parametric motion flow/optical flow. Machine Graphics & Vision International Journal 15 (1), 29–49.

Salzbrunn, Tobias, Scheuermann, Gerik, 2006. Streamline predicates. IEEE Transactions on Visualization and Computer Graphics 12 (6), 1601–1612.

Salzbrunn, Tobias, Garth, Christoph, Scheuermann, Gerik, Meyer, Jörg, 2008. Pathline predicates and unsteady flow structures. The Visual Computer 24 (12), 1039–1051.

Sanchez-Vives, Maria V., Slater, Mel, 2005. From presence to consciousness through virtual reality. Nature Reviews. Neuroscience 6 (4), 332–339.

Santhanam, Anand P., Willoughby, Twyla, Shah, Amish, Meeks, Sanford, Rolland, Jannick P., Kupelian, Patrick, 2008. Real-time simulation of 4D lung tumor radiotherapy using a breathing model. In: Proc. of Medical Image Computing and Computer-Assisted Intervention (MICCAI), pp. 710–717. https://doi.org/10.1007/978-3-540-85990-1_85.

Saraiya, Purvi, North, Chris, Duca, Karen, 2005. An insight-based methodology for evaluating bioinformatics visualizations. IEEE Transactions on Visualization and Computer Graphics 11 (4), 443–456.

Satava, Richard M., 1993. Virtual reality surgical simulator. Surgical Endoscopy 7 (3), 203–205.

Satava, Richard M., 1995. Medical applications of virtual reality. Journal of Medical Systems 19 (3), 275–280.

Sato, Yoshinobu, Shiraga, Nobuyuki, Nakajima, Shin, Tamura, Shinichi, Kikinis, Ron, 1998. Local maximum intensity projection (LMIP): a new rendering method for vascular visualization. Journal of Computer Assisted Tomography 22 (6), 912–917.

Saxena, Amit, Prasad, Mukesh, Gupta, Akshansh, Bharill, Neha, Patel, Om Prakash, Tiwari, Aruna, Er, Meng Joo, Ding, Weiping, Lin, Chin-Teng, 2017. A review of clustering techniques and developments. Neurocomputing 267, 664–681.

Scheid-Rehder, Alexander, Lawonn, Kai, Meuschke, Monique, 2019. Robustness evaluation of CFD simulations to mesh deformation. In: Proc. of Eurographics Workshop on Visual Computing for Biology and Medicine (VCBM).

Scherbinsky, Mandy, Lexow, G. Jakob, Rau, Th.S., Preim, Bernhard, Majdani, Omid, 2015. Computerunterstützte Planung von Bonebridge Operationen. In: Proc. of Bildverarbeitung für die Medizin, pp. 179–184.

Schiemann, Thomas, Tiede, Ulf, Höhne, Karl Heinz, 1997. Segmentation of the visible human for high quality volume based visualization. Medical Image Analysis 1, 263–271.

Schiemann, Thomas, Freudenberg, Jan, Pflesser, Bernhard, Pommert, Andreas, Priesmeyer, Kay, Riemer, Martin, Schubert, Rainer, Tiede, Ulf, Höhne, Karl Heinz, 2000. Exploring the Visible Human using the VOXEL-MAN framework. Computerized Medical Imaging and Graphics 24 (3), 127–132.

Schinagl, D.A.X., Kaanders, J.H.A.M., Oyen, W.J.G., 2006. From anatomical to biological target volumes: the role of PET in radiation treatment planning. Cancer Imaging 6, S107–S116. https://doi.org/10.1102/1470-7330.2006.9017.

Schindler, Marwin, Wu, Hsiang-Yun, Raidou, Renata, 2020. The anatomical edutainer. In: IEEE VIS Short Papers 2020, pp. 1–5.

Schindler, Marwin, Korpitsch, Thorsten, Raidou, Renata, Wu, Hsiang-Yun, 2022. Nested papercrafts for anatomical and biological edutainment. Computer Graphics Forum 41, 1–13.

Schlachter, M., Fechter, T., Nestle, U., Bühler, K., 2014. Visualization of 4D-PET/CT, target volumes and dose distribution: applications in radiotherapy planning. In: Proc. of MICCAI Workshop on Image-Guided Adaptive Radiation Therapy.

Schlachter, Matthias, Fechter, Tobias, Jurisic, Miro, Schimek-Jasch, Tanja, Oehlke, Oliver, Adebahr, Sonja, Birkfellner, Wolfgang, Nestle, Ursula, Buhler, Katja, 2016. Visualization of deformable image registration quality using local image dissimilarity. IEEE Transactions on Medical Imaging 35 (10), 2319–2328. https://doi.org/10.1109/TMI.2016.2560942.

Schlachter, Matthias, Fechter, Tobias, Adebahr, Sonja, Schimek-Jasch, Tanja, Nestle, Ursula, Bühler, Katja, 2017. Visualization of 4D multimodal imaging data and its applications in radiotherapy planning. Journal of Applied Clinical Medical Physics 18 (6), 183–193. https://doi.org/10.1002/acm2.12209.

Schlachter, Matthias, Raidou, Renata G., Muren, Ludvig P., Preim, Bernhard, Putora, Paul Martin, Bühler, Katja, 2019. State-of-the-art report: visual computing in radiation therapy planning. Computer Graphics Forum 38 (3), 753–779.

Schlaefer, Alexander, Viulet, Tiberiu, Muacevic, Alexander, Fürweger, Christoph, 2013. Multicriteria optimization of the spatial dose distribution. Medical Physics 40 (12), 121720. https://doi.org/10.1118/1.4828840.

Schott, Danny, Saalfeld, Patrick, Schmidt, Gerd, Joeres, Fabian, Boedecker, Christian, Huettl, Florentine, Lang, Hauke, Huber, Tobias, Preim, Bernhard, Hansen, Christian, 2021. A VR/AR environment for multi-user liver anatomy education. In: Proc. of IEEE Virtual Reality.

Schubert, Nicole, Scholl, Ingrid, 2011. Comparing GPU-based multi-volume ray casting techniques. Computer Science-Research and Development 26 (1–2), 39–50.

Schubert, Rainer, Höhne, Karl Heinz, Pommert, Andreas, Riemer, Martin, Schiemann, Thomas, Tiede, Ulf, 1993. Spatial knowledge representation for visualization of human anatomy and function. In: Proc. of Information Processing in Medical Imaging. In: Lecture Notes in Computer Science, vol. 687. Springer, pp. 168–181.

Schubert, Thomas, Friedmann, Frank, Regenbrecht, Holger, 2001. The experience of presence: factor analytic insights. Presence: Teleoperators & Virtual Environments 10 (3), 266–281.

Schultheis, M.T., Rizzo, Albert A., 2001. The application of virtual reality technology in rehabilitation. Cochrane Database of Systematic Reviews 46 (3), 296.

Schulz, Hans-Jorg, 2011. Treevis.net: a tree visualization reference. IEEE CG&A 31 (6), 11–15.

Schulz, Hans-Jörg, Nocke, Thomas, Heitzler, Magnus, Schumann, Heidrun, 2013. A design space of visualization tasks. IEEE Transactions on Visualization and Computer Graphics 19 (12), 2366–2375.

Schumann, Christian, Hennemuth, Anja, 2015. Three-dimensional visualization of relative pressure in vascular structures. In: CURAC, pp. 337–342.

Schumann, Christian, Neugebauer, Matthias, Bade, Ragnar, Preim, Bernhard, Peitgen, Heinz-Otto, 2007. Model-free surface visualization of vascular trees. In: Proc. of EuroVis, pp. 283–290.

Schwenke, Michael, Hennemuth, Anja, Fischer, Bernd, Friman, Ola, 2011. Blood flow computation in phase-contrast MRI by minimal paths in anisotropic media. In: Medical Image Computing and Computer-Assisted Intervention, pp. 436–443.

Segel, Edward, Heer, Jeffrey, 2010. Narrative visualization: telling stories with data. IEEE Transactions on Visualization and Computer Graphics 16 (6), 1139–1148.

Seo, Jinsil Hwaryoung, Smith, Brian Michael, Cook, Margaret, Malone, Erica, Pine, Michelle, Leal, Steven, Bai, Zhikun, Suh, Jinkyo, 2017. Anatomy builder VR: applying a constructive learning method in the virtual reality canine skeletal system. In: Proc. of Applied Human Factors and Ergonomics, pp. 245–252.

Seo, Jinwook, Shneiderman, Ben, 2005. A rank-by-feature framework for interactive exploration of multidimensional data. Information Visualization 4 (2), 96–113.

Sereno, Mickäel Francisco, Köhler, Benjamin, Preim, Bernhard, 2018. Comparison of divergence-free filters for cardiac 4D PC-MRI data. In: Proc. of Workshop Bildverarbeitung für die Medizin, pp. 139–144.

Sforza, Daniel M., Putman, Christopher M., Cebral, Juan Raul, 2009. Hemodynamics of cerebral aneurysms. Annual Review of Fluid Mechanics 41, 91–107.

Sherman, William R., Craig, Alan B., 2018. Understanding Virtual Reality: Interface, Application, and Design. Morgan Kaufmann.

Shewaga, Robert, Uribe-Quevedo, Alvaro, Kapralos, Bill, Lee, Kenneth, Alam, Fahad, 2018. A serious game for anesthesia-based crisis resource management training. Computers in Entertainment (CIE) 16 (2), 1–16.

Shneiderman, Ben, 1996. The eyes have it: a task by data type taxonomy for information visualizations. In: Proc. of IEEE Symposium on Visual Languages, pp. 336–343. https://doi.org/10.1109/VL.1996.545307.

Shneiderman, Ben, 1997. Direct manipulation for comprehensible, predictable and controllable user interfaces. In: Proc. of International Conference on Intelligent User Interfaces. ACM, pp. 33–39. https://doi.org/10.1145/238218.238281.

Shneiderman, Ben, 2003. The eyes have it: a task by data type taxonomy for information visualizations. In: The Craft of Information Visualization. Elsevier, pp. 364–371.

Shneiderman, Ben, Plaisant, Catherine, 2019. Interactive visual event analytics: opportunities and challenges. IEEE Computer 52 (1), 27–35.

Shojima, Masaaki, Oshima, Marie, Takagi, Kiyoshi, Torii, Ryo, Hayakawa, Motoharu, Katada, Kazuhiro, Morita, Akio, Kirino, Takaaki, 2004. Magnitude and role of wall shear stress on cerebral aneurysm computational fluid dynamic study of 20 middle cerebral artery aneurysms. Stroke 35 (11), 2500–2505.

Siirtola, Harri, 2000. Direct manipulation of parallel coordinates. In: Proc. of IEEE Information Visualization, pp. 373–378.

Sikachev, Peter, Rautek, Peter, Bruckner, Stefan, Gröller, Eduard, 2010. Dynamic focus+context for volume rendering. In: Proc. of Vision, Modeling, and Visualization, pp. 331–338.

Simons, Daniel J., Levin, Daniel T., 1997. Change blindness. Trends in Cognitive Sciences 1 (7), 261–267.

Sims, Jennifer N., Isokpehi, Raphael D., Cooper, Gabrielle A., Bass, Michael P., Brown, Shyretha D., St John, Alison L., Gulig, Paul A., Cohly, Hari H.P., 2011. Visual analytics of surveillance data on foodborne vibriosis, United States, 1973–2010. Environmental Health Insights 5, 71.

Singh, Mayank, Schaefer, Scott, 2010. Suggestive hatching. In: Proc. CAe. Eurographics Association, pp. 25–32. https://doi.org/10.2312/COMPAESTH/COMPAESTH10/025-032.

Slater, James M., 2012. From X-rays to ion beams: a short history of radiation therapy. In: Ion Beam Therapy – Fundamentals, Technology, Clinical Applications. Springer, pp. 3–16.

Slater, Mel, 2009. Place illusion and plausibility can lead to realistic behaviour in immersive virtual environments. Philosophical Transactions of the Royal Society of London. Series B, Biological Sciences 364 (1535), 3549–3557.

Slater, Mel, Wilbur, Sylvia, 1997. A framework for immersive virtual environments (FIVE): speculations on the role of presence in virtual environments. Presence: Teleoperators & Virtual Environments 6 (6), 603–616.

Slater, Mel, Spanlang, Bernhard, Sanchez-Vives, Maria V., Blanke, Olaf, 2010. First person experience of body transfer in virtual reality. PLoS ONE 5 (5), e10564.

Smit, N.N., Kraima, A.C., Jansma, D., de Ruiter, M.C., Botha, C.P., 2012. A unified representation for the model-based visualization of heterogeneous anatomy data. In: Proc. of EuroVis-Short Papers, pp. 85–89.

Smit, Noeska, Bruckner, Stefan, 2019. Towards advanced interactive visualization for virtual atlases. In: Biomedical Visualisation. Springer, pp. 85–96. https://doi.org/10.1007/978-3-030-19385-0_6.

Smit, Noeska N., 2016. The Virtual Surgical Pelvis: Anatomy Visualization for Education and Surgical Planning. PhD thesis.

Smit, Noeska Natasja, Hofstede, Cees-Willem, Kraima, Anne C., Jansma, Daniel, Deruiter, Marco C., Eisemann, Elmar, Vilanova, Anna, 2016a. The online anatomical human: web-based anatomy education. In: Proc. of Eurographics 2016 - Education Papers, pp. 37–40.

Smit, Noeska Natasja, Kraima, Anne C., Jansma, Daniel, Deruiter, Marco C., Eisemann, Elmar, Vilanova, Anna, 2016b. VarVis: visualizing anatomical variation in branching structures. In: EuroVis 2016 - Short Papers.

Smith, Lindsay I., 2002. A tutorial on principal components analysis.

Šoltészová, Veronika, Patel, Daniel, Viola, Ivan, 2011. Chromatic shadows for improved perception. In: Proc. of Non-Photorealistic Animation and Rendering, vol. 2011, pp. 105–116.

Somarakis, Antonios, Ijsselsteijn, Marieke E., Luk, Sietse J., Kenkhuis, Boyd, de Miranda, Noel F.C.C., Lelieveldt, Boudewijn P.F., Höllt, Thomas, 2021. Visual cohort comparison for spatial single-cell omics-data. IEEE Transactions on Visualization and Computer Graphics 27 (2), 733–743. https://doi.org/10.1109/TVCG.2020.3030336.

Song, William, Schaly, Bryan, Bauman, Glenn, Battista, Jerry, Van Dyk, Jake, 2005. Image-guided adaptive radiation therapy (IGART): radiobiological and dose escalation considerations for localized carcinoma of the prostate: IGART: radiobiological and dose escalation considerations. Medical Physics 32 (7Part1), 2193–2203. https://doi.org/10.1118/1.1935775.

Sousa, Maurício, Mendes, Daniel, Paulo, Soraia, Matela, Nuno, Jorge, Joaquim A., Lopes, Daniel Simões, 2017. VRRRRoom: virtual reality for radiologists in the reading room. In: Proc. of ACM SIGCHI Conference on Human Factors in Computing Systems (CHI), pp. 4057–4062.

Sprengel, Ulrike, Saalfeld, Patrick, Mittenentzwei, Sarah, Drittel, Moritz, Neyazi, Belal, Berg, Philipp, Preim, Bernhard, Saalfeld, Sylvia, 2021. Interactive visualization of cerebral blood flow for arteriovenous malformation embolisation. In: Proc. of Workshop Bildverarbeitung für die Medizin, pp. 36–41.

Srinivasan, Mandayam A., Basdogan, Cagatay, 1997. Haptics in virtual environments: taxonomy, research status, and challenges. Computers & Graphics 21 (4), 393–404.

Stalling, Detlev, Westerhoff, Malte, Hege, Hans-Christian, 2005. Amira: a highly interactive system for visual data analysis. In: The Visualization Handbook, pp. 749–767 (chap. 38).

Stamm, Oskar, Dahms, Rebecca, Müller-Werdan, Ursula, 2020. Virtual reality in pain therapy: a requirements analysis for older adults with chronic back pain. Journal of NeuroEngineering and Rehabilitation 17 (1), 1–12.

Standen, Penny J., Brown, David J., 2005. Virtual reality in the rehabilitation of people with intellectual disabilities. Cyberpsychology & Behavior 8 (3), 272–282.

Stanney, Kay, 1995. Realizing the full potential of virtual reality: human factors issues that could stand in the way. In: Proc. of Virtual Reality Annual International Symposium'95. IEEE, pp. 28–34.

Steed, Anthony, Pan, Ye, Zisch, Fiona, Steptoe, William, 2016. The impact of a self-avatar on cognitive load in immersive virtual reality. In: Proc. of IEEE Virtual Reality, pp. 67–76.

Steenblik, Richard A., 1987. The chromostereoscopic process: a novel single image stereoscopic process. In: Proc. of SPIE, vol. 0761, pp. 27–34.

Steenwijk, Martin D., Milles, Julien, van Buchem, M.A., Reiber, Johan H.C., Botha, Charl P., 2010. Integrated visual analysis for heterogeneous datasets in cohort studies. In: Proc. of IEEE Workshop on Visual Analytics in Healthcare.

Steinicke, Frank, Ropinski, Timo, Hinrichs, Klaus, 2006. Object selection in virtual environments using an improved virtual pointer metaphor. In: Proc. of Computer Vision and Graphics 2004, pp. 320–326. https://doi.org/10.1007/1-4020-4179-9_46.

Steinicke, Frank, Bruder, Gerd, Jerald, Jason, Frenz, Harald, Lappe, Markus, 2009. Estimation of detection thresholds for redirected walking techniques. IEEE Transactions on Visualization and Computer Graphics 16 (1), 17–27.

Sterne, Jonathan A.C., White, Ian R., Carlin, John B., Spratt, Michael, Royston, Patrick, Kenward, Michael G., Wood, Angela M., Carpenter, James R., 2009. Multiple imputation for missing data in epidemiological and clinical research: potential and pitfalls. British Medical Journal 338, b2393.

Sterzik, Anna, Lichtenberg, Nils, Krone, Michael, Cunningham, Douglas, Lawonn, Kai, 2022. Perceptual evaluation of common line variables for displaying uncertainty on molecular surfaces. In: Proc. of Eurographics Workshop on Visual Computing for Biology and Medicine (VCBM).

Stevens, Kent, 1983. Slant-tilt: the visual encoding of surface orientation. Biological Cybernetics 46, 183–195.

Stoakley, Richard, Conway, Matthew J., Pausch, Randy, 1995. Virtual reality on a WIM: interactive worlds in miniature. In: Proc. of ACM SIGCHI Conference on Human Factors in Computing Systems (CHI), pp. 265–272.

Stollfuß, Sven, 2017. Animierte Anatomie. In: In Bewegung setzen... Springer, pp. 149–168.

Stoppel, Sergej, Bruckner, Stefan, 2017. Vol2velle: printable interactive volume visualization. IEEE Transactions on Visualization and Computer Graphics 23 (1), 861–870.

Stoppel, Sergej, Bruckner, Stefan, 2018. Smart surrogate widgets for direct volume manipulation. In: Proc. PacificVis, pp. 36–45.

Strauss, Gero, Limpert, E., Fischer, Milos, Hofer, Matthias, Kubisch, Christoph, Krüger, Arno, Dietz, Andreas, 2009. Virtuelle Echtzeit-Endoskopie der Nase und Nasennebenhöhlen. HNO 57 (8), 789–796.

Stritzel, Oliver, Raidou, Renata Georgia, 2022. Predicting, Analyzing and Communicating Outcomes of COVID-19 Hospitalizations with Medical Images and Clinical Data. The Eurographics Association. ISBN 978-3-03868-177-9.

Stroom, Joep C., Heijmen, Ben J.M., 2002. Geometrical uncertainties, radiotherapy planning margins, and the ICRU-62 report. Radiotherapy and Oncology 64 (1), 75–83.

Strothotte, Thomas, Preim, Bernhard, Raab, Andreas, Schumann, Jutta, Forsey, Dave R., 1994. How to render frames and influence people. Computer Graphics Forum 13 (3), 455–466. https://doi.org/10.1111/1467-8659.1330455.

Stull, A.T., Hegarty, M., Mayer, R.E., 2009. Getting a handle on learning anatomy with interactive three-dimensional graphics. Journal of Educational Psychology 101 (4), 803–816.

Su, T.S., Sung, W.H., Jiang, C.F., Sun, S.P., Wu, C.J., 2005. The development of a VR-based treatment planning system for oncology. In: Proc. of IEEE Engineering in Medicine and Biology, pp. 6104–6107. https://doi.org/10.1109/IEMBS.2005.1615886.

Suarez, Jordane, Belhadj, Farès, Boyer, Vincent, 2017. Real-time 3D rendering with hatching. The Visual Computer 33 (10), 1319–1334. https://doi.org/10.1007/s00371-016-1222-3.

Subramanian, Sandeep K., Lourenço, Christiane B., Chilingaryan, Gevorg, Sveistrup, Heidi, Levin, Mindy F., 2013. Arm motor recovery using a virtual reality intervention in chronic stroke: randomized control trial. Neurorehabilitation and Neural Repair 27 (1), 13–23.

Suhling, Michael, Arigovindan, Muthuvel, Jansen, Christian, Hunziker, Patrick, Unser, Michael A., 2003. Myocardial motion analysis and visualization from echocardiograms. In: Proc. of SPIE Medical Imaging: Image Processing, vol. 5032, pp. 306–314.

Sun, Qi, Patney, Anjul, Wei, Li-Yi, Shapira, Omer, Lu, Jingwan, Asente, Paul, Zhu, Suwen, McGuire, Morgan, Luebke, David, Kaufman, Arie, 2018. Towards virtual reality infinite walking: dynamic saccadic redirection. ACM Transactions on Graphics (TOG) 37 (4), 1–13.

Sunden, Erik, Kottravel, Sathish, Ropinski, Timo, 2015. Multimodal volume illumination. Computers & Graphics 50, 47–60.

Sutherland, Justin, Belec, Jason, Sheikh, Adnan, Chepelev, Leonid, Althobaity, Waleed, Chow, Benjamin J.W., Mitsouras, Dimitrios, Christensen, Andy, Rybicki, Frank J., La Russa, Daniel J., 2019. Applying modern virtual and augmented reality technologies to medical images and models. Journal of Digital Imaging 32 (1), 38–53.

Sweet, Graeme, Ware, Colin, 2004. View direction, surface orientation and texture orientation for perception of surface shape. In: Proc. Graphics Interface, pp. 97–106. https://doi.org/10.20380/GI2004.13.

Sweller, John, 2004. Instructional design consequences of an analogy between evolution by natural selection and human cognitive architecture. Instructional Science 32 (1–2), 9–31.

Szécsi, László, Szirányi, Marcell, Kacsó, Ágota, 2016. Tonal art maps with image space strokes. In: Eurographics Posters. https://doi.org/10.2312/egp.20161046.

Tan, Desney S., Robertson, George G., Czerwinski, Mary, 2001. Exploring 3D navigation: combining speed-coupled flying with orbiting. In: Proc. of ACM SIGCHI Conference on Human Factors in Computing Systems (CHI), pp. 418–425.

Tan, Jie, Han, Demin, Wang, Jie, Liu, Ting, Wang, Tong, Zang, Hongrui, Li, Yunchuan, Wang, Xiangdong, 2012. Numerical simulation of normal nasal cavity airflow in Chinese adult: a computational flow dynamics model. European Archives of Oto-Rhino-Laryngology 269 (3), 881–889.

Tanderup, Kari, Olsen, Dag Rune, Grau, Cai, 2006. Dose painting: art or science? Radiotherapy and Oncology 79 (3), 245–248.

Tanoue, Tetsuya, Tateshima, S., Villablanca, J.P., Viñuela, F., Tanishita, K., 2011. Wall shear stress distribution inside growing cerebral aneurysm. American Journal of Neuroradiology 32 (9), 1732–1737.

Tatu, Andrada, Zhang, Leishi, Bertini, Enrico, Schreck, Tobias, Keim, Daniel, Bremm, Sebastian, Von Landesberger, Tatiana, 2012. ClustNails: visual analysis of subspace clusters. Tsinghua Science and Technology 17 (4), 419–428.

Termeer, Maurice, Bescós, Javier Oliván, Breeuwer, Marcel, Vilanova, Anna, Gerritsen, Frans, Gröller, M. Eduard, 2007. CoViCAD: comprehensive visualization of coronary artery disease. IEEE Transactions on Visualization and Computer Graphics 13 (6), 1632–1639.

Teschner, Matthias, Kimmerle, Stefan, Heidelberger, Bruno, Zachmann, Gabriel, Raghupathi, Laks, Fuhrmann, Arnulph, Cani, M.-P., Faure, François, Magnenat-Thalmann, Nadia, Strasser, Wolfgang, Volino, Pascal, 2005. Collision detection for deformable objects. Computer Graphics Forum 24 (1), 61–81.

Thali, Michael J., Braun, Marcel, Buck, Ursula, Aghayev, Emin, Jackowski, Christian, Vock, Peter, Sonnenschein, Martin, Dirnhofer, Richard, 2005. VIRTOPSY: scientific documentation, reconstruction and animation in forensic: individual and real 3D data based geometric approach including optical body/object surface and radiological CT/MRI scanning. Journal of Forensic Sciences 50 (2), 428–442. https://doi.org/10.1520/JFS2004290.

Thariat, Juliette, Hannoun-Levi, Jean-Michel, Myint, Arthur Sun, Vuong, Te, Gérard, Jean-Pierre, 2013. Past, present, and future of radiotherapy for the benefit of patients. Nature Reviews. Clinical Oncology 10 (1), 52–60.

Theisel, Holger, 2000. Higher order parallel coordinates. In: Proc. of Vision, Modeling, and Visualization, pp. 415–420.

Thew, S., Sutcliffe, A., Procter, R., de Bruijn, O., McNaught, J., Venters, C.C., Buchan, I., 2009. Requirements engineering for E-science: experiences in epidemiology. IEEE Software 26 (1), 80–87.

Thomas, James J., Cook, Kristin A., 2005. Illuminating the Path: The Agenda for Visual Analytics. National Visualization and Analytics Center.

Thomas, James J., Cook, Kristin A., 2006. A visual analytics agenda. IEEE CG&A 26 (1), 10–13.

Thompson, Paul M., Toga, Arthur W., 1997. Detection, visualization and animation of abnormal anatomic structure with a deformable probabilistic brain atlas based on random vector field transformations. Medical Image Analysis 1 (4), 271–294.

Thorndyke, Perry W., Hayes-Roth, Barbara, 1982. Differences in spatial knowledge acquired from maps and navigation. Cognitive Psychology 14 (4), 560–589. https://doi.org/10.1016/0010-0285(82)90019-6.

Thornton, M., Marshall, S., McComas, J., Finestone, H., McCormick, A., Sveistrup, H., 2005. Benefits of activity and virtual reality based balance exercise programmes for adults with traumatic brain injury: perceptions of participants and their caregivers. Brain Injury 19 (12), 989–1000.

Tiede, Ulf, Schiemann, Thomas, Höhne, Karl Heinz, 1998. High quality rendering of attributed volume data. In: Proc. of IEEE Visualization, pp. 255–262. https://doi.org/10.1109/VISUAL.1998.745311.

Tietjen, Christian, Isenberg, Tobias, Preim, Bernhard, 2005. Combining silhouettes, surface, and volume rendering for surgery education and planning. In: Proc. of EuroVis, pp. 303–310. https://doi.org/10.2312/VisSym/EuroVis05/303-310.

Tietjen, Christian, Meyer, Björn, Schlechtweg, Stefan, Preim, Bernhard, Hertel, Ilka, Strauss, Gero, 2006. Enhancing slice-based visualizations of medical volume data. In: Proc. of EuroVis, pp. 123–130.

Tong, Chao, Roberts, Richard, Laramee, Robert S., Berridge, Damon, Thayer, Daniel, 2017. Cartographic treemaps for visualization of public healthcare data. In: Proc. of Computer Graphics and Visual Computing (CGVC).

Tönnies, Klaus D., Gloger, Oliver, Rak, Marko, Winkler, Charlotte, Klemm, Paul, Preim, Bernhard, Völzke, Henry, 2015. Image analysis in epidemiological applications. it - Information Technology 57 (1), 22–29.

Townsend, D.W., Carney, J.P., Yap, J.T., Hall, N.C., 2004. PET/CT today and tomorrow. Journal of Nuclear Medicine 45 (1), 4S–14S.

Traquair, Harry Moss, 1949. An Introduction to Clinical Perimetry. Mosby.

Trofimov, Alexei, Unkelbach, Jan, DeLaney, Thomas F., Bortfeld, Thomas, 2012. Visualization of a variety of possible dosimetric outcomes in radiation therapy using dose-volume histogram bands. Practical Radiation Oncology 2 (3), 164–171. https://doi.org/10.1016/j.prro.2011.08.001.

Trost, Zina, Zielke, Marjorie, Guck, Adam, Nowlin, Liza, Zakhidov, Djanhangir, France, Christopher R., Keefe, Francis, 2015. The promise and challenge of virtual gaming technologies for chronic pain: the case of graded exposure for low back pain. Pain Management 5 (3), 197–206.

Turkbey, Baris, Thomasson, David, Pang, Yuxi, Bernardo, Marcelino, Choyke, Peter L., 2010. The role of dynamic contrast-enhanced MRI in cancer diagnosis and treatment. Diagnostic and Interventional Radiology 16 (3), 186–192.

Tüzün, Hakan, Özdinç, Fatih, 2016. The effects of 3D multi-user virtual environments on freshmen university students' conceptual and spatial learning and presence in departmental orientation. Computers and Education 94, 228–240.

Tversky, Barbara, Morrison, Julie Bauer, Betrancourt, Mireille, 2002. Animation: can it facilitate? International Journal of Human-Computer Studies 57 (4), 247–262.

Uno, S., Slater, Mel, 1997. The sensitivity of presence to collision response. In: Proc. of IEEE International Symposium on Virtual Reality, pp. 95–103.

Unwin, Antony, Hofmann, Heike, Bernt, Klaus, 2001. The twokey plot for multiple association rules control. In: Proc. of European Conference on Principles of Data Mining and Knowledge Discovery, pp. 472–483.

Usoh, Martin, Arthur, Kevin, Whitton, Mary C., Bastos, Rui, Steed, Anthony, Slater, Mel, Brooks Jr., Frederick P., 1999. Walking > walking-in-place > flying, in virtual environments. In: Proc. of ACM SIGGRAPH, pp. 359–364.

Van der Maaten, Laurens, Hinton, Geoffrey, 2008. Visualizing data using t-SNE. Journal of Machine Learning Research 9 (11).

Van Diest, Mike, Lamoth, Claudine J.C., Stegenga, Jan, Verkerke, Gijsbertus J., Postema, Klaas, 2013. Exergaming for balance training of elderly: state of the art and future developments. Journal of NeuroEngineering and Rehabilitation 10 (1), 1–12.

van Herk, Marcel, 2004. Errors and margins in radiotherapy. Seminars in Radiation Oncology 14 (1), 52–64. https://doi.org/10.1053/j.semradonc.2003.10.003.

van Pelt, Roy, Bescos, Javier Olivan, Breeuwer, Marcel, Clough, Rachel E., Groller, M. Eduard, ter Haar Romenij, Bart, Vilanova, Anna, 2010. Exploration of 4D MRI blood flow using stylistic visualization. IEEE Transactions on Visualization and Computer Graphics 16 (6), 1339–1347.

van Pelt, Roy, Besc'os, Javier Oliv'an, Breeuwer, Marcel, Clough, R.E., Gröller, Eduard, ter Haar Romeny, Bart, Vilanova, Anna, 2011. Interactive virtual probing of 4D MRI blood-flow. IEEE Transactions on Visualization and Computer Graphics 17 (12), 2153–2162.

van Pelt, Roy, Jacobs, S.S.A.M., ter Haar Romeny, Bart M., Vilanova, Anna, 2012. Visualization of 4D blood-flow fields by spatiotemporal hierarchical clustering. Computer Graphics Forum 31 (3pt2), 1065–1074.

van Pelt, Roy, Fuster, Andrea, Claassen, Geert, Vilanova, Anna, 2014a. Characterization of blood-flow patterns from phase-contrast MRI velocity fields. In: EuroVis - Short Papers.

van Pelt, Roy, Gasteiger, Rocco, Lawonn, Kai, Meuschke, Monique, Preim, Bernhard, 2014b. Comparative blood flow visualization for cerebral aneurysm treatment assessment. Computer Graphics Forum 33 (3), 131–140.

Van Wijk, Jarke J., Van de Wetering, Huub, 1999. Cushion treemaps: visualization of hierarchical information. In: Proc. of IEEE Symposium on Information Visualization, pp. 73–78.

Vandenberg, Steven G., Kuse, Allan R., 1978. Mental rotations, a group test of three-dimensional spatial visualization. Perceptual and Motor Skills 47 (2), 599–604.

Vandenbossche, Vicky, Van de Velde, Joris, Avet, Stind, Willaert, Wouter, Soltvedt, Stian, Smit, Noeska, Audenaert, Emmanuel, 2022. Digital body preservation: technique and applications. Anatomical Sciences Education 15 (4), 731–744. https://doi.org/10.1002/ase.2199.

Varras, Michail, Nikiteas, Nikolaos, Varra, Viktoria Konstantina, Varra, Fani Niki, Georgiou, Evangelos, Loukas, Constantinos, 2020. Role of laparoscopic simulators in the development and assessment of laparoscopic surgical skills in laparoscopic surgery and gynecology (review). World Academy of Sciences Journal, 65–76. https://doi.org/10.3892/wasj.2020.41.

Vázquez, Pere-Pau, Feixas, Miquel, Sbert, Mateu, Heidrich, Wolfgang, 2001. Viewpoint selection using viewpoint entropy. In: Proc. of Vision, Modeling, and Visualization, vol. 1, pp. 273–280.

Vázquez, Pere-Pau, Götzelmann, Timo, Hartmann, Knut, Nürnberger, Andreas, 2008. An interactive 3D framework for anatomical education. International Journal of Computer Assisted Radiology and Surgery 3 (6), 511–524. https://doi.org/10.1007/s11548-008-0251-4.

Veiga, Catarina, Lourenço, Ana Mónica, Mouinuddin, Syed, van Herk, Marcel, Modat, Marc, Ourselin, Sébastien, Royle, Gary, McClelland, Jamie R., 2015. Toward adaptive radiotherapy for head and neck patients: uncertainties in dose warping due to the choice of deformable registration algorithm: dose warping uncertainties due to registration algorithm. Medical Physics 42 (2), 760–769. https://doi.org/10.1118/1.4905050.

Venkatesh, Viswanath, Morris, Michael G., Davis, Gordon B., Davis, Fred D., 2003. User acceptance of information technology: toward a unified view. MIS Quarterly, 425–478.

Vernon, Tim, Peckham, Daniel, 2002. The benefits of 3D modelling and animation in medical teaching. Journal of Audiovisual Media in Medicine 25 (4), 142–148.

Vidal, Franck Patrick, Garnier, Manuel, Freud, Nicolas, Létang, Jean-Michel, John, Nigel W., 2009. Simulation of X-ray attenuation on the GPU. In: Proc. of EG UK Theory and Practice of Computer Graphics, pp. 25–32. https://doi.org/10.2312/LocalChapterEvents/TPCG/TPCG09/025-032.

Viega, John, Conway, Matthew J., Williams, George, Pausch, Randy, 1996. 3D magic lenses. In: Proc. UIST, pp. 51–58.

Villa, C., Olsen, K.B., Hansen, S.H., 2017. Virtual animation of victim-specific 3D models obtained from CT scans for forensic reconstructions: living and dead subjects. Forensic Science International 278, e27–e33.

Viola, Ivan, Gröller, Eduard, 2005. Smart visibility in visualization. In: Proc. of Computational Aesthetics in Graphics, Visualization and Imaging, pp. 209–216.

Viola, Ivan, Kanitsar, Armin, Gröller, Eduard, 2004. Importance-driven volume rendering. In: Proc. of IEEE Visualization, pp. 139–146.

Viola, Ivan, Feixas, Miquel, Sbert, Mateu, Gröller, Eduard, 2006. Importance-driven focus of attention. IEEE Transactions on Visualization and Computer Graphics 12 (5), 933–940.

Völzke, Henry, Alte, Dietrich, Schmidt, Carsten Oliver, et al., 2011. Cohort profile: the study of health in pomerania. International Journal of Epidemiology 40 (2), 294–307.

Wade, Derick T., 1992. Measurement in neurological rehabilitation. Current Opinion in Neurology 5 (5), 682–686.

Wagner, Markus, Slijepcevic, Djordje, Horsak, Brian, Rind, Alexander, Zeppelzauer, Matthias, Aigner, Wolfgang, 2018. KAVAGait: knowledge-assisted visual analytics for clinical gait analysis. IEEE Transactions on Visualization and Computer Graphics 25 (3), 1528–1542.

Wagner, Sebastian, Joeres, Fabian, Gabele, Mareike, Hansen, Christian, Preim, Bernhard, Saalfeld, Patrick, 2019. Difficulty factors for VR cognitive rehabilitation training - crossing a virtual road. Computer Graphics 83, 11–22. https://doi.org/10.1016/j.cag.2019.06.009.

Wagner, Sebastian, Illner, Kay, Weber, Matthias, Preim, Bernhard, Saalfeld, Patrick, 2020. VR acrophobia treatment–development of customizable acrophobia inducing scenarios. In: Proc. of Eurographics Workshop on Visual Computing for Biology and Medicine (VCBM).

Wagner, Sebastian, Belger, Julia, Joeres, Fabian, Thöne-Otto, Angelika, Hansen, Christian, Preim, Bernhard, Saalfeld, Patrick, 2021. iVRoad: immersive virtual road crossing as an assessment tool for unilateral spatial neglect. Computer Graphics 99, 70–82.

Wallis, Jerold W., Miller, Tom R., Lerner, Charles A., Kleerup, Eric C., 1989. Three-dimensional display in nuclear medicine. IEEE Transactions on Medical Imaging 8 (4), 297–330.

Wang, C., Lee, T., Fang, C., 2009a. A volume visualization system with augmented reality interaction for evaluation of radiotherapy plans. In: International Conference on Innovative Computing, Information and Control, pp. 433–436. https://doi.org/10.1109/ICICIC.2009.62.

Wang, Chang-Yu, Lee, Tsair-Fwu, Fang, Chun-Hsiung, 2009b. A multimodality image registration framework for synchronous visualization of radiotherapy plans with longitudinal imaging studies. In: Proc. of the International Conference on Ubiquitous Information Management and Communication, ICUIMC '09. ACM, pp. 411–415. https://doi.org/10.1145/1516241.1516313.

Wang, Huamin, Hecht, Florian, Ramamoorthi, Ravi, O'Brien, James F., 2010. Example-based wrinkle synthesis for clothing animation. ACM Transactions on Graphics 29 (4), 107.

Wang, Yu-Shuen, Lee, Tong-Yee, 2008. Example-driven animation synthesis. The Visual Computer 24 (7–9), 765–773.

Wang Baldonado, Michelle Q., Woodruff, Allison, Kuchinsky, Allan, 2000. Guidelines for using multiple views in information visualization. In: Proc. of ACM Conference on Advanced Visual Interfaces, pp. 110–119.

Wanger, Leonard R., Ferwerda, James A., Greenberg, Donald P., 1992. Perceiving spatial relationships in computer-generated images. IEEE CG&A 12 (3), 44–58.

Ward, James W., Phillips, R., Boejen, Annette, Grau, Cai, Jois, Deepak, Beavis, Andy W., 2011. A virtual environment for radiotherapy training and education - VERT. In: Eurographics - Dirk Bartz Prize, pp. 5–8. https://doi.org/10.2312/EG2011/med/005-008.

Ware, Colin, Arthur, Kevin, Booth, Kellogg S., 1993. Fish tank virtual reality. In: Proc. of ACM SIGCHI Conference on Human Factors in Computing Systems (CHI), pp. 37–42.

Warrick, Philip A., Funnell, W. Robert J., 1998. A VRML-based anatomical visualization tool for medical education. IEEE Transactions on Information Technology in Biomedicine 2 (2), 55–61.

Washington, C.M., Leaver, D.T., 2015. Principles and Practice of Radiation Therapy. Elsevier - Health Sciences Division.

Watadani, Takeyuki, Sakai, Fumikazu, Johkoh, Takeshi, Noma, Satoshi, Akira, Masanori, Fujimoto, Kiminori, Bankier, Alexander A., Lee, Kyung Soo, Müller, Nestor L., Song, Jae-Woo, et al., 2013. Interobserver variability in the ct assessment of honeycombing in the lungs. Radiology 266 (3), 936–944.

Wattenberg, Martin, Viégas, Fernanda, Johnson, Ian, 2016. How to use t-SNE effectively. Distill 1 (10), e2.

Webb, Matthew, Praun, Emil, Finkelstein, Adam, Hoppe, Hugues, 2002. Fine tone control in hardware hatching. In: Proc. NPAR. ACM, pp. 53–59. https://doi.org/10.1145/508530.508540.

Webb, Steve, 2001. Intensity-Modulated Radiation Therapy. CRC Press, Taylor & Francis.

Webb, Steve, Nahum, A.E., 1993. A model for calculating tumour control probability in radiotherapy including the effects of inhomogeneous distributions of dose and clonogenic cell density. Physics in Medicine and Biology 38 (6), 653.

Weiler, Florian, Rieder, Christian, David, C.A., Wald, Christoph, Hahn, Horst K., 2011. AVM-explorer: multi-volume visualization of vascular structures for planning of cerebral AVM surgery. In: Bühler, K., Vilanova, A. (Eds.), Proc. of Eurographics 2011 - Dirk Bartz Prize. Eurographics Association, pp. 9–12.

Weiler, Florian, Rieder, Christian, David, C.A., Wald, C., Hahn, Horst K., 2012. On the value of multi-volume visualization for preoperative planning of cerebral AVM surgery. In: Proc. of Eurographics Workshop on Visual Computing for Biology and Medicine (VCBM). Eurographics Association, pp. 49–56.

Weiskopf, Daniel, Engel, Klaus, Ertl, Thomas, 2002. Volume clipping via per-fragment operations in texture-based volume visualization. In: Proc. of IEEE Visualization, pp. 93–100.

Welch, Robert B., Blackmon, Theodore T., Liu, Andrew, Mellers, Barbara A., Stark, Lawrence W., 1996. The effects of pictorial realism, delay of visual feedback, and observer interactivity on the subjective sense of presence. Presence: Teleoperators & Virtual Environments 5 (3), 263–273.

Wemple, C.A., Wessol, D.E., Nigg, D.W., Cogliati, J.J., Milvich, M.L., Frederickson, C., Perkins, M., Harkin, G.J., 2004. MINERVA-a multi-modal radiation treatment planning system. Applied Radiation and Isotopes 61 (5), 745–752. https://doi.org/10.1016/j.apradiso.2004.05.049.

Wentzel, A., Hanula, Peter, Luciani, Timothy, Elgohari, Baher, Elhalawani, Hesham, Canahuate, Guadalupe, Vock, D., Fuller, Clifton D., Marai, G. Elisabeta, 2019. Cohort-based T-SSIM visual computing for radiation therapy prediction and exploration. IEEE Transactions on Visualization and Computer Graphics 26 (1), 949–959.

Wermer, M., van der Schaaf, I., Algra, A., Rinkel, G.J., 2007. Risk of rupture of unruptured intracranial aneurysms in relation to patient and aneurysm characteristics: an updated meta-analysis. Stroke 38 (4), 1404–1410.

Weyhe, Dirk, Uslar, Verena, Weyhe, Felix, Kaluschke, Maximilian, Zachmann, Gabriel, 2018. Immersive anatomy atlas—empirical study investigating the usability of a virtual reality environment as a learning tool for anatomy. Frontiers in Surgery 5, 73.

Wigström, Lars, Ebbers, Tino, Fyrenius, Anna, Karlsson, Matts, Engvall, Jan, Wranne, Bengt, Bolger, Ann F., 1999. Particle trace visualization of intracardiac flow using time-resolved 3D phase contrast MRI. Magnetic Resonance in Medicine 41 (4), 793–799.

Wilhelm, Dirk, Reiser, Silvano, Kohn, Nils, Witte, Michael, Leiner, Ulrich, Mühlbach, Lothar, Ruschin, Detlef, Reiner, Wolfgang, Feussner, Hubertus, 2014. Comprehensive evaluation of latest 2D/3D monitors and comparison to a custom-built 3D mirror-based display in laparoscopic surgery. In: Proc. of SPIE: Stereoscopic Displays and Applications XXV, vol. 9011, p. 90110H.

Willard, Christer-Daniel, Kjaestad, Erik, Stimec, Bojan V., Edwin, Bjorn, Ignjatovic, Dejan, 2019. Preoperative anatomical road mapping reduces variability of operating time, estimated blood loss, and lymph node yield in right colectomy with extended D3 mesenterectomy for cancer. International Journal of Colorectal Disease 34 (1), 151–160.

Wilson, Brett, Lum, Eric B., Ma, Kwan-Liu, 2002. Interactive multi-volume visualization. In: Computational Science. Springer, New York, pp. 102–110.

Wingrave, Chadwick A., Haciahmetoglu, Yonca, Bowman, Doug A., 2006. Overcoming world in miniature limitations by a scaled and scrolling WIM. In: Proc. of IEEE 3D User Interfaces, pp. 11–16.

Winslow, Charles-Edward Amory, 1920. The untilled field of public health. Science 51, 23–33.

Witmer, Bob G., Singer, Michael J., 1998. Measuring presence in virtual environments: a presence questionnaire. Presence 7 (3), 225–240.

Wolf, Steven L., Catlin, Pamela A., Ellis, Michael, Archer, Audrey Link, Morgan, Bryn, Piacentino, Aimee, 2001. Assessing wolf motor function test as outcome measure for research in patients after stroke. Stroke 32 (7), 1635–1639.

Wolthaus, J.W.H., Sonke, J.-J., Van Herk, M., Damen, E.M.F., 2008. Reconstruction of a time-averaged midposition CT scan for radiotherapy planning of lung cancer patients using deformable registration. Medical Physics 35 (9), 3998–4011.

Wong, Donna L., Baker, Connie M., 2001. Smiling face as anchor for pain intensity scales. Pain 89 (2), 295–297.

Wong, Kelvin K.L., Kelso, Richard M., Worthley, Stephen G., Sanders, Prashanthan, Mazumdar, Jagannath, Abbott, Derek, 2009. Cardiac flow analysis applied to phase contrast magnetic resonance imaging of the heart. Annals of Biomedical Engineering 37 (8), 1495–1515. https://doi.org/10.1007/s10439-009-9709-y.

Woodring, Jonathan, Shen, Han-Wei, 2007. Incorporating highlighting animations into static visualizations. In: Proc. of Visualization and Data Analysis, vol. 6495, p. 649503.

Wright, Pauliina, Redpath, Anthony Thomas, Høyer, Morten, Grau, Cai, Muren, Ludvig Paul, 2008. The normal tissue sparing potential of adaptive strategies in radiotherapy of bladder cancer. Acta Oncologica 47 (7), 1382–1389. https://doi.org/10.1080/02841860802266763.

Wu, Hui-Yin, Palù, Francesca, Ranon, Roberto, Christie, Marc, 2018. Thinking like a director: film editing patterns for virtual cinematographic storytelling. ACM Transactions on Multimedia Computing Communications and Applications 14 (4), 81:1–81:22.

Wu, Yingcai, Xu, Anbang, Chan, Ming-Yuen, Qu, Huamin, Guo, Ping, 2007. Palette-style volume visualization. In: Proc. of Volume Graphics, pp. 33–40.

Wundram, Maximilian, Falk, Volkmar, Eulert-Grehn, Jaime-Jürgen, Herbst, Hermann, Thurau, Jana, Leidel, Bernd A., Göncz, Eva, Bauer, Wolfgang, Habazettl, Helmut, Kurz, Stephan D., 2020. Incidence of acute type a aortic dissection in emergency departments. Scientific Reports 10 (1), 1–6.

Xi, Jinxiang, Si, Xiuhua, Zhou, Yue, Kim, JongWon, Berlinski, Ariel, 2014. Growth of nasal-laryngeal airways in children and their implications in breathing and inhaled aerosol dynamics. Respiratory Care 59 (2), 263–273. https://doi.org/10.4187/respcare.02568.

Xia, Jiazhi, Jiang, Guang, Zhang, YuHong, Li, Rui, Chen, Wei, 2017. Visual subspace clustering based on dimension relevance. Journal of Visual Languages and Computing 41, 79–88.

Xie, Xuexiang, He, Ying, Tian, Feng, Seah, Hock-Soon, Gu, Xianfeng, Qin, Hong, 2007. An effective illustrative visualization framework based on photic extremum lines (PELs). IEEE Transactions on Visualization and Computer Graphics 13, 1328–1335. https://doi.org/10.1109/TVCG.2007.70538.

Yammine, K., Violato, C., 2015. A meta-analysis of the educational effectiveness of three-dimensional visualization technologies in teaching anatomy. Anatomical Sciences Education 8 (6), 525–538.

Yang, Deshan, Brame, Scott, El Naqa, Issam, Aditya, Apte, Wu, Yu, Goddu, S. Murty, Mutic, Sasa, Deasy, Joseph O., Low, Daniel A., 2011. Technical note: DIRART–a software suite for deformable image registration and adaptive radiotherapy research. Medical Physics 38 (1), 67–77. https://doi.org/10.1118/1.3521468.

Ynnerman, Anders, Rydell, Thomas, Persson, Anders, Ernvik, Aron, Forsell, Camilla, Ljung, Patric, Lundström, Claes, 2015. Multi-touch table system for medical visualization. In: Eurographics 2015 - Dirk Bartz Prize, pp. 9–12. https://doi.org/10.2312/egm.20151030.

Zachow, Stefan, Steinmann, Alexander, Hildebrandt, Thomas, Weber, Rainer, Heppt, Werner, 2006. CFD simulation of nasal airflow: towards treatment planning for functional rhinosurgery. International Journal of Computer Assisted Radiology and Surgery 1 (7), 165–167.

Zachow, Stefan, Muigg, Philipp, Hildebrandt, Thomas, Doleisch, Helmut, Hege, Hans-Christian, 2009. Visual exploration of nasal airflow. IEEE Transactions on Visualization and Computer Graphics 15 (6), 1407–1414.

Zakkar, Moutasem, Sedig, Kamran, 2017. Interactive visualization of public health indicators to support policymaking: an exploratory study. Online Journal of Public Health Informatics 9 (2).

Zander, Johannes, Isenberg, Tobias, Schlechtweg, Stefan, Strothotte, Thomas, 2004. High quality hatching. Computer Graphics Forum 23 (3), 421–430. https://doi.org/10.1111/j.1467-8659.2004.00773.x.

Zeltzer, David, 1991. Task-level graphical simulation: abstraction, representation, and control. In: Making Them Move. Morgan Kaufmann Publishers Inc., San Francisco, CA, USA, pp. 3–33.

Zettl, Herbert, 2013. Sight, Sound, Motion: Applied Media Aesthetics. Cengage Learning.

Zhang, Jingxiong, Goodchild, Michael F., 2002. Uncertainty in Geographical Information. CRC Press.

Zhang, Long, He, Ying, Xia, Jiazhi, Xie, Xuexiang, Chen, Wei, 2011. Real-time shape illustration using Laplacian lines. IEEE Transactions on Visualization and Computer Graphics 17 (7), 993–1006. https://doi.org/10.1109/TVCG.2010.118.

Zhang, S.-X., Heng, P.-A., Liu, Z.-J., 2006. Chinese visible human project. Clinical Anatomy 19 (3), 204–215.

Zhang, Zhiyuan, Gotz, David, Perer, Adam, 2015. Iterative cohort analysis and exploration. Information Visualization 14 (4), 289–307.

Zhao, Lingxiao, Botha, Charl P., Bescos, Javier, Truyen, Roel, Vos, Frans, Post, Frits H., 2006. Lines of curvature for polyp detection in virtual colonoscopy. IEEE Transactions on Visualization and Computer Graphics 12 (5), 885–892.

Zhou, Hong, Cui, Weiwei, Qu, Huamin, Wu, Yingcai, Yuan, Xiaoru, Zhuo, Wei, 2009. Splatting the lines in parallel coordinates. Computer Graphics Forum 28, 759–766.

Zhou, Zhiguang, Ye, Zhifei, Liu, Yanan, Liu, Fang, Tao, Yubo, Su, Weihua, 2017. Visual analytics for spatial clusters of air-quality data. IEEE CG&A 37 (5), 98–105.

Zikanov, Oleg, 2019. Essential Computational Fluid Dynamics. Wiley. ISBN 9781119474623.

Zilske, Michael, Lamecker, Hans, Zachow, Stefan, 2008. Adaptive remeshing of non-manifold surfaces. In: Proc. of Eurographics - Short Papers. https://doi.org/10.2312/egs.20081013.

Zindy, E., Moore, C., Burton, D., Lalor, M., 2000. Morphological definition of anatomic shapes using minimal datasets. In: IEEE Conference on Information Visualization, pp. 366–370. https://doi.org/10.1109/IV.2000.859783.

Zitova, Barbara, Flusser, Jan, 2003. Image registration methods: a survey. Image and Vision Computing 21 (11), 977–1000.

Zwicker, Matthias, Jarosz, Wojciech, Lehtinen, Jaakko, Moon, Bochang, Ramamoorthi, Ravi, Rousselle, Fabrice, Sen, Pradeep, Soler, Cyril, Yoon, S.-E., 2015. Recent advances in adaptive sampling and reconstruction for Monte Carlo rendering. Computer Graphics Forum 34 (2), 667–681.

Index